Certificate Stage

Module D

Managerial Finance

ACCA Textbook

7776/J98

British Library Cataloguing-in-Publication Data

A catalogue record for this book is available from the British Library.

Published by AT Foulks Lynch Ltd
Number 4
The Griffin Centre
Staines Road
Feltham
Middlesex
TW14 0HS

ISBN 0 7483 3777 6

© AT Foulks Lynch Ltd, 1998
Printed in Great Britain by Ashford Colour Press.
Acknowledgements

We are grateful to the Association of Chartered Certified Accountants, the Chartered Institute of Management Accountants and the Institute of Chartered Accountants in England and Wales for permission to reproduce past examination questions. The answers have been prepared by AT Foulks Lynch Ltd.

CONTENTS

PREFACE

This Textbook is the ACCA's official text for paper 8, Managerial Fiance, and is part of the ACCA's official series produced for students taking the ACCA examinations.

It has been produced with direct guidance from the examiner specifically for paper 8, and covers the syllabus and teaching guide in great detail giving appropriate weighting to the various topics.

This Textbook is, however, very different from a reference book or a more traditional style textbook. It is targeted very closely on the examinations and is written in a way that will help you assimilate the information easily and give you plenty of practice at the various techniques involved.

Particular attention has been paid to producing an interactive text that will maintain your interest with a series of carefully designed features.

- **Introduction with learning objectives**. We put the chapter into context and set out clearly the learning objectives that will be achieved by the reader.

- **Definitions**. The text clearly defines key words or concepts. The purpose of including these definitions is **not** that you should learn them - rote learning is not required and is positively harmful. The definitions are included to focus your attention on the point being covered.

- **Brick-building style**. We build up techniques slowly, with simpler ideas leading to exam standard questions. This is a key feature and it is the natural way to learn.

- **Activities**. The text involves you in the learning process with a series of activities designed to arrest your attention and make you concentrate and respond.

- **Conclusions**. Where helpful, the text includes conclusions that summarise important points as you read through the chapter rather than leaving the conclusion to the chapter end. The purpose of this is to summarise concisely the key material that has just been covered so that you can constantly monitor your understanding of the material as you read it.

- **Self test questions**. At the end of each chapter there is a series of self test questions. The purpose of these is to help you revise some of the key elements of the chapter. The answer to each is a paragraph reference, encouraging you to go back and re-read and revise that point.

- **End of chapter questions**. At the end of each chapter we include examination style questions. These will give you a very good idea of the sort of thing the examiner will ask and will test your understanding of what has been covered.

Complementary Revision Series and Lynchpins

Revision Series

The ACCA Revision Series contains all the relevant new syllabus exam questions from June 1994 to December 1997 with the examiner's own official answers, all updated in January 1998.

What better way to revise for your exams than to read and study the examiner's own answers!

Lynchpins

The ACCA Lynchpins, pocket-sized revision aids which can be used throughout your course, contain revision notes of all main syllabus topics plus numerous examples and diagrams. They provide invaluable focus and assistance in keeping key topics in the front of your mind.

FORMAT OF THE EXAMINATION

The examination has the following format:

	Marks
Section A: Compulsory mini - case study	40
Section B: 1 (out of 2) questions on financial management	20
Section C: 2 (out of 3) questions on management accounting	40
	100

Time allowed: 3 hours

The management accounting content will account for approximately 40% of the marks and the financial management content for the remainder. Section A will be primarily financial management but may draw upon some management accounting concepts to a limited degree. Section B contains financial management questions only and Section C contains only management accounting questions.

A present value table and an annuity table (shown later in this introduction) will be provided in the exam as required. Formulae will be provided in the exam where relevant.

SYLLABUS

Certificate stage - Module D Paper 8: MANAGERIAL FINANCE

Introduction

Paper 8 examines two related subjects, Management Accounting (weighting of 40%) and Financial Management (weighting of 60%).

The paper builds on the overview of cost accounting from paper 3 and covers

- the application of the management accounting techniques used in planning, control and decision making and the interpretation of information available from their use

- the preparation, organisation, summarisation and presentation of management information/reports.

The paper introduces financial management areas, including

- the understanding of current practical methods used in making financial management decisions and the influence of the environment on such decisions

- the appreciation of the workings of the financial system, the evaluation of alternative sources of finance and the assessment of investment possibilities

- the communication of the consequences of financial management decisions to accountants and non-accountants.

Chapter reference

Management Accounting

(1)   **COST AND MANAGEMENT ACCOUNTING METHODS**   1 - 6

     (a)   Determining and allocating/apportioning costs of activities and outputs through the use of appropriate concepts, methods and techniques

         (i)   absorption, marginal and opportunity cost approaches to the accumulation of costs for specific orders (job, batch, contract) or operations (process, service)

         (ii)   activity based costing; use of cost drivers and activities.

     (b)   Consideration and application of information required in relation to

         (i)   costing of products and services
         (ii)   preparing plans
         (iii)   monitoring/controlling performance
         (iv)   decision making.

(2)   **INFORMATION FOR PLANNING AND CONTROL**   7 - 15

       (a)   Budgeting and budgetary control

               (i)   identify objectives of budgetary planning and control systems (including an introduction to behavioural influences)

               (ii)   identify/evaluate budgetary systems such as fixed and flexible, zero based and incremental, periodic and continuous

               (iii)   developing/implementing budgeting systems: functional/subsidiary and master budgets (including cash budgeting)

               (iv)   monitoring and controlling performance; calculation of variances; determination of cause of variances

               (v)   quantitative aids in budgeting; least squares regression; scatter diagram with correlation; forecasting with regression; introduction to time series and seasonality to analyse time related data.

       (b)   Standard costing

               (i)   uses and limitations of standard costing

               (ii)   determination of standards

               (iii)   identification and calculation of variances; sales variances (including quantity and mix), cost variances (including mix and yield); absorption and marginal approaches

               (iv)   identify significance and inter-relationship of variances

               (v)   relevance to business performance measurement and control.

       (c)   Cost allocation/apportionment/absorption

               (i)   absorption and marginal costing; impact on profit reporting; relevance in planning and control

               (ii)   activity based costing; use in costing of products and services; use as a planning and control device.

(3)   **THE COSTING/PRICING OF PRODUCTS AND SERVICES**   1 - 5

       (a)   Consideration and application of information requirements in relation to

               (i)   job costs
               (ii)   process costs
               (iii)   service industries
               (iv)   internal services.

Financial management

(4)   **FINANCIAL OBJECTIVES**   20, 21

        (a)   The nature, purpose and scope of financial management.

        (b)   The relationship between financial management, management accounting and financial accounting.   1

        (c)   The relationship of financial objectives to organisational strategy and ethos and to other organisational objectives. The constraints/conflicts which different objectives may put upon each other.

        (d)   The nature, scope and form (long term and short term) of financial objectives of different types of organisation, including not-for-profit organisations.

        (e)   The roles, responsibilities and relationships of key personnel involved in and with organisations (shareholders, lenders, managers, employees, customers, suppliers, government).

(5)   **FINANCIAL MANAGEMENT FRAMEWORK**   16 - 19

        (a)   The commercial and financial environment in which organisations operate (the nature and function of the money and capital markets including banks and other financial intermediaries, the Stock Exchange, the Unlisted Securities Market and Over the Counter markets).

        (b)   The economic environment in which organisations operate

                (i)   application of macro-economic theory as a basis for understanding the key economic variables affecting the business environment

                (ii)   fiscal policy, its nature, effectiveness of fiscal policy

                (iii)   money and interest rates, the role of money in the economy, the supply and demand for money

                (iv)   monetary policy, attitudes to monetary policy, problems of monetary policy

                (v)   supply-side policies, supply side problems, policies to improve supply side

                (vi)   policies towards monopolies and oligopolies, privatisation and deregulation

                (vii)   green policies; implications for management of the economy and the firm

(viii)   the significance of corporate securities (share capital, debt and preference shares) to commercial organisations and the markets in which they operate, and the influence of markets on organisations

(ix)   the Efficient Markets Hypothesis and its relevance to decision making and to financial management practice.

(6)   MANAGEMENT OF WORKING CAPITAL   22, 23

(a)   The nature and scope of working capital management.

(b)   The importance of effective working capital management to corporate survival.

(c)   Cash: selection of appropriate cash balances, managing cash surpluses and deficits. The nature and functions of the short term money market.

(d)   The management of debtors (including those overseas) involving credit evaluation, terms of credit, cash discounts, debt collection techniques, credit management monitoring and evaluation, factoring and invoice discounting.

(e)   Creditors: advantages and disadvantages of alternative methods of paying suppliers (including those overseas), the dangers of trading on credit.

(f)   Stock: alternative stock management systems and models including Total Quality Management (TQM), Just in Time (JIT), Economic Order Quantity (EOQ), etc.

(7)   SOURCES OF FINANCE   24 - 26

(a)   Sources and relative costs (including issue costs but not calculations of the cost of capital) of various types of finance and their suitability to different circumstances and organisations (both large and small companies, listed and unlisted) including

(i)   the nature and importance of internally generated funds

(ii)   capital markets (types of share capital, new issues, rights issues, loan capital, convertibles, warrants)

(iii)   the effect of dividend policy on financing needs

(iv)   bank finance (the various forms of short, medium and long term finance that are available, including leasing)

(v)   trade credit

(vi)   government sources: grants, regional and national aid schemes, tax incentives etc

(vii)   venture capital and financial sources particularly suited to the small company

(viii) international money and capital markets, including an introduction to international banking, and the finance of foreign trade.

(b) Determining requirements for finance (how much, for how long, for what purpose) in relation to a client's operational and strategic objectives. The importance of the choice of capital structure to an organisation.

(c) Calculating financial gearing and other key financial ratios and analysing their significance to the organisation.

(d) Determining appropriate sources of finance by identifying and evaluating appropriate sources, taking into account such factors as

(i) cost of finance including its servicing
(ii) timing of cash payments
(iii) effect on gearing and other ratios
(iv) effect on the company's existing investors.

(8) CAPITAL EXPENDITURE AND INVESTMENT   27 - 32

(a) Identifying potential investment opportunities.

(b) Appraising capital investments (domestic) for commercial and non commercial organisations through the use of appropriate methods and techniques

(i) return on capital employed and payback

(ii) discounting based methods, including the importance of the cost of capital to investment appraisal (but not the calculation of cost of capital)

(iii) internal rate of return

(iv) net present value

(v) capital rationing (single and multi-period)

(vi) lease or buy decisions

including the effects of taxation and inflation on investment decisions, the handling of risk and uncertainty, eg through the use of probabilities, sensitivity analysis and simulations.

THE OFFICIAL ACCA TEACHING GUIDE

Paper 8 - Managerial Finance

		Syllabus Reference	Chapter Reference
Session 1	***Management Accounting - Cost Accumulation***		1

- discuss the role of the management accounting function in meeting the needs of management
- outline the nature and scope of management accounting
- explain why the management accountant can be described as a 'gatekeeper' and 'information manager' — 1 a (i), 4b
- describe the relationship between management accounting, financial management and financial accounting
- evaluate the absorption and marginal cost approaches to the accumulation of costs for specific orders, jobs, batches, contracts or operations

		Syllabus Reference	Chapter Reference
Session 2	***A Critical Review of Product Costing***		2, 3, 4

- compute costs using an opportunity cost accumulation approach — 1a(i),1b(i) 3a(i), (ii)
- make a critical evaluation of the absorption, marginal and opportunity approaches to cost accumulation
- discuss the costing/pricing and information requirements of job and process costs

		Syllabus Reference	Chapter Reference
Session 3	***Internal Services & Service Industry: Activity Based Costing***		5

- discuss the costing/pricing and information requirements of internal services and service industries — 1a(ii) 3a(iii),(iv)
- outline the differences between activity based costing and traditional absorption costing systems
- prepare product cost computations using activity based costing
- evaluate the validity of the cost drivers which are used

		Syllabus Reference	Chapter Reference
Session 4	***Absorption v Marginal Revisited: An Introduction to Cost Control***		6

- illustrate and explain the impact on profit reporting of using absorption costing and marginal costing — 1b(ii), (iii) 2c(i)
- consider the information requirements for the planning process associated with:
  - cost control, including feedback
  - monitoring and controlling performance
- highlight the advantages of predetermined systems of cost control over historic costing systems
- assess the suitability of cost control techniques across a range of organisations

	Syllabus reference	Chapter reference

Present value table

Present value of £1 ie, $\dfrac{1}{(1+r)^n}$

where   r   =   discount rate

           n   =   number of periods until payment

Discount rates (r)

Periods (n)	1%	2%	3%	4%	5%	6%	7%	8%	9%	10%	
1	0.990	0.980	0.971	0.962	0.952	0.943	0.935	0.926	0.917	0.909	1
2	0.980	0.961	0.943	0.925	0.907	0.890	0.873	0.857	0.842	0.826	2
3	0.971	0.942	0.915	0.889	0.864	0.840	0.816	0.794	0.772	0.751	3
4	0.961	0.924	0.888	0.855	0.823	0.792	0.763	0.735	0.708	0.683	4
5	0.951	0.906	0.863	0.822	0.784	0.747	0.713	0.681	0.650	0.621	5
6	0.942	0.888	0.837	0.790	0.746	0.705	0.666	0.630	0.596	0.564	6
7	0.933	0.871	0.813	0.760	0.711	0.665	0.623	0.583	0.547	0.513	7
8	0.923	0.853	0.789	0.731	0.677	0.627	0.582	0.540	0.502	0.467	8
9	0.914	0.837	0.766	0.703	0.645	0.592	0.544	0.500	0.460	0.424	9
10	0.905	0.820	0.744	0.676	0.614	0.558	0.508	0.463	0.422	0.386	10
11	0.896	0.804	0.722	0.650	0.585	0.527	0.475	0.429	0.388	0.350	11
12	0.887	0.788	0.701	0.625	0.557	0.497	0.444	0.397	0.356	0.319	12
13	0.879	0.773	0.681	0.601	0.530	0.469	0.415	0.368	0.326	0.290	13
14	0.870	0.758	0.661	0.577	0.505	0.442	0.388	0.340	0.299	0.263	14
15	0.861	0.743	0.642	0.555	0.481	0.417	0.362	0.315	0.275	0.239	15

	11%	12%	13%	14%	15%	16%	17%	18%	19%	20%	
1	0.901	0.893	0.885	0.877	0.870	0.862	0.855	0.847	0.840	0.833	1
2	0.812	0.797	0.783	0.769	0.756	0.743	0.731	0.718	0.706	0.694	2
3	0.731	0.712	0.693	0.675	0.658	0.641	0.624	0.609	0.593	0.579	3
4	0.659	0.636	0.613	0.592	0.572	0.552	0.534	0.516	0.499	0.482	4
5	0.593	0.567	0.543	0.519	0.497	0.476	0.456	0.437	0.419	0.402	5
6	0.535	0.507	0.480	0.456	0.432	0.410	0.390	0.370	0.352	0.335	6
7	0.482	0.452	0.425	0.400	0.376	0.354	0.333	0.314	0.296	0.279	7
8	0.434	0.404	0.376	0.351	0.327	0.305	0.285	0.266	0.249	0.233	8
9	0.391	0.361	0.333	0.308	0.284	0.263	0.243	0.225	0.209	0.194	9
10	0.352	0.322	0.295	0.270	0.247	0.227	0.208	0.191	0.176	0.162	10
11	0.317	0.287	0.261	0.237	0.215	0.195	0.178	0.162	0.148	0.135	11
12	0.286	0.257	0.231	0.208	0.187	0.168	0.152	0.137	0.124	0.112	12
13	0.258	0.229	0.204	0.182	0.163	0.145	0.130	0.116	0.104	0.093	13
14	0.232	0.205	0.181	0.160	0.141	0.125	0.111	0.099	0.088	0.078	14
15	0.209	0.183	0.160	0.140	0.123	0.108	0.095	0.084	0.074	0.065	15

Annuity Table

Present value of an annuity of 1 ie, $\dfrac{1-(1+r)^{-n}}{r}$

where   r   =   discount rate
          n   =   number of periods

Discount rates (r)

Periods (n)	1%	2%	3%	4%	5%	6%	7%	8%	9%	10%	
1	0.990	0.980	0.971	0.962	0.952	0.943	0.935	0.926	0.917	0.909	1
2	1.970	1.942	1.913	1.886	1.859	1.833	1.808	1.783	1.759	1.736	2
3	2.941	2.884	2.829	2.775	2.723	2.673	2.624	2.577	2.531	2.487	3
4	3.902	3.808	3.717	3.630	3.546	3.465	3.387	3.312	3.240	3.170	4
5	4.853	4.713	4.580	4.452	4.329	4.212	4.100	3.993	3.890	3.791	5
6	5.795	5.601	5.417	5.242	5.076	4.917	4.767	4.623	4.486	4.355	6
7	6.728	6.472	6.230	6.002	5.786	5.582	5.389	5.206	5.033	4.868	7
8	7.652	7.325	7.020	6.733	6.463	6.210	5.971	5.747	5.535	5.335	8
9	8.566	8.162	7.786	7.435	7.108	6.802	6.515	6.247	5.995	5.759	9
10	9.471	8.983	8.530	8.111	7.722	7.360	7.024	6.710	6.418	6.145	10
11	10.37	9.787	9.253	8.760	8.306	7.887	7.499	7.139	6.805	6.495	11
12	11.26	10.58	9.954	9.385	8.863	8.384	7.943	7.536	7.161	6.814	12
13	12.13	11.35	10.63	9.986	9.394	8.853	8.358	7.904	7.487	7.103	13
14	13.00	12.11	11.30	10.56	9.899	9.295	8.745	8.244	7.786	7.367	14
15	13.87	12.85	11.94	11.12	10.38	9.712	9.108	8.559	8.061	7.606	15

	11%	12%	13%	14%	15%	16%	17%	18%	19%	20%	
1	0.901	0.893	0.885	0.877	0.870	0.862	0.855	0.847	0.840	0.833	1
2	1.713	1.690	1.668	1.647	1.626	1.605	1.585	1.566	1.547	1.528	2
3	2.444	2.402	2.361	2.322	2.283	2.246	2.210	2.174	2.140	2.106	3
4	3.102	3.037	2.974	2.914	2.855	2.798	2.743	2.690	2.639	2.589	4
5	3.696	3.605	3.517	3.433	3.352	3.274	3.199	3.127	3.058	2.991	5
6	4.231	4.111	3.998	3.889	3.784	3.685	3.589	3.498	3.410	3.326	6
7	4.712	4.564	4.423	4.288	4.160	4.039	3.922	3.812	3.706	3.605	7
8	5.146	4.968	4.799	4.639	4.487	4.344	4.207	4.078	3.954	3.837	8
9	5.537	5.328	5.132	4.946	4.772	4.607	4.451	4.303	4.163	4.031	9
10	5.889	5.650	5.426	5.216	5.019	4.833	4.659	4.494	4.339	4.192	10
11	6.207	5.938	5.687	5.453	5.234	5.029	4.836	4.656	4.486	4.327	11
12	6.492	6.194	5.918	5.660	5.421	5.197	4.988	4.793	4.611	4.439	12
13	6.750	6.424	6.122	5.842	5.583	5.342	5.118	4.910	4.715	4.533	13
14	6.982	6.628	6.302	6.002	5.724	5.468	5.229	5.008	4.802	4.611	14
15	7.191	6.811	6.462	6.142	5.847	5.575	5.324	5.092	4.876	4.675	15

1 MANAGEMENT ACCOUNTING - COST ACCUMULATION

INTRODUCTION & LEARNING OBJECTIVES

When you have studied this chapter you should be able to do the following:

- Distinguish between management accounting, cost accounting, financial accounting and financial management
- Explain the role of management accounting and the management accountant.

1 ACCOUNTING

1.1 Financial, cost and management accounting

The financial accounts record transactions between the business and its customers, suppliers, employees and owners eg, shareholders. The managers of the business must account for the way in which funds entrusted to them have been used and, therefore, records of assets and liabilities are required, as well as a statement of any increase in the total wealth of the business. This is done by presenting a balance sheet, profit and loss account, and cash flow statement at least once every year. The law requires that accounts of certain businesses shall be presented in a specific way and particular details of transactions may be required by the Inspector of Taxes.

However, in performing their job, managers will need to know a great deal about the detailed working of the business. This knowledge must embrace production methods and the cost of processes, products etc. It is not the function of financial accounting to provide such detail and therefore the managers require additional accounting information geared to their own needs.

Cost accounting involves the application of a comprehensive set of principles, methods and techniques to the determination and appropriate analysis of costs to suit the various parts of the organisation structure within a business.

Management accounting is a wider concept involving professional knowledge and skill in the preparation and particularly the presentation of information to all levels of management in the organisation structure. The source of such information is the financial and cost accounts. The information is intended to assist management in its policy and decision-making, planning and control activities.

The particular concern of this text is with the cost accounting branch of management accounting.

1.2 Management accounting

Definition An integral part of management concerned with identifying, presenting and interpreting information used for:

- formulation of strategy;
- planning and controlling the activities;

- decision taking;
- optimising the use of resources;
- disclosure to shareholders and others external to the entity;
- disclosure to employees;
- safeguarding assets.

The above involves participation in management to ensure that there is effective:

- formulation of plans to meet objectives (strategic planning);

- formulation of short term operations plans (budgeting/profit planning);

- acquisition and use of finance (financial management) and recording of actual transactions (financial accounting and cost accounting);

- communication of financial and operating information;

- corrective action to bring plans and results into line (financial control);

- reviewing and reporting on systems and operations (internal audit, management audit).

1.3   Cost accounting

Definition   The establishment of budgets, standard costs and actual costs of operations, processes, activities or products and the analysis of variances, profitability or social use of funds.   The use of the term costing is not recommended except with a qualifying adjective eg, standard costing.

1.4   Profit statements

It may be helpful at this stage to examine a simple trading and profit and loss account to consider the work of the cost accountant:

XYZ Company
Trading and profit and loss account for the year ended . . .

		£	£
Sales			200,000
Cost of sales:	Materials consumed	80,000	
	Wages	40,000	
	Production expenses	15,000	135,000
Gross profit			65,000
Marketing expenses		15,000	
General administrative expenses		10,000	
Financing costs		4,000	
			29,000
Net profit before tax			36,000

The above statement may be adequate to provide outsiders with a superficial picture of the trading results of the business, but managers would need much more detail to answer questions such as:

(a)   What are our major products and which ones are most profitable?

(b)   How much has our stock of raw materials increased?

(c)   How does our labour cost per unit compare with last period?

(d)   Are our personnel department expenses more than we expected?

The cost accountant will aim to maintain a system which will provide the answers to those (and many other) questions on a regular and **ad-hoc** basis. In addition, the cost accounts will contain detailed information concerning stocks of raw materials, work-in-progress and finished goods as a basis for the valuation necessary to prepare final accounts.

1.5   Activity

(a)   Distinguish between financial accounting, cost accounting and management accounting.

(b)   What is the work of the cost accountant likely to include in a typical manufacturing situation?

1.6   Activity solution

(a)   In modern business, the three functions of financial, cost and management accounting merge together in many ways. It will be very difficult clearly to define the three terms. However, a generalised definition could be:

(i)   **Financial accounting**

The recording of the financial transactions of a firm and their summary in periodic financial statements for the use of persons outside the organisation who wish to analyse and interpret the firm's financial position.

(ii)   **Cost accounting**

Involves a careful evaluation of the resources used within the business. The techniques employed are designed to provide monetary information about the performance of a business and possibly the direction which future operations should take.

(iii)   **Management accounting**

(1)   has accounting as its essential foundation;

(2)   is essentially concerned with offering advice to management based upon information collected;

(3)   may include involvement in:

-     decision-making;
-     planning (budgetary);
-     controlling the business.

(b)   The cost accountant's work may include the following:

(i)   The application of accounting principles and costing principles, methods and techniques in the ascertainment of costs.

(ii)   The analysis of savings and excesses as compared with previous experience or with standards.

(iii)   Operating costing systems to provide the following information:

(1)   Details of product profitability.
(2)   Stock valuation records (raw materials, work-in-progress, finished goods).
(3)   Labour cost records.
(4)   Overhead control records.
(5)   Bases for evaluation of selling prices.

2   RESPONSIBILITY ACCOUNTING

2.1   Introduction

In a typical organisation, lower levels of management report on an area of the business to more senior managers. Each manager is in charge of a 'responsibility centre'.

Definition   A responsibility centre is a segment of an organisation whose manager is accountable for a specified set of activities.

Definition   Responsibility accounting is a system where the plans or budgets for each responsibility centre are compared with the actual level achieved, and explanations are sought for any discrepancies.

Management will need information concerning

-     cost units
-     cost centres
-     profit centres
-     investment centres.

2.2   Cost units

Definition   A cost unit is a unit of product or service in relation to which costs are ascertained.

The ascertainment of the cost per cost unit is important for a variety of reasons:

(a)   making decisions about pricing, acceptance of orders, and so on
(b)   measuring changes in costs and relative levels of efficiency
(c)   inventory valuation for financial reporting
(d)   planning future costs (budgeting and standard costs).

2.3   Cost centres

Definition   A cost centre is a production or service location, function, activity or item of equipment whose costs may be attributed to cost units.

ie, it is a part of a business for which costs can be identified and then allocated to cost units. It might be a whole department (eg, packaging) or just a sub-division (eg, a few machines).

2.4   Profit centre

Definition   A profit centre is a production or service location, function, activity or item of equipment whose costs and revenues can be ascertained.

ie, a profit centre is similar to a cost centre but it also earns revenue and thus profits which can be identified separately.

2.5   Investment centre

Definition   An investment centre is a production or service location, function, activity or item of equipment for which costs, revenues and investment can be ascertained.

ie, an investment centre is similar to a profit centre but the investment can be identified separately as well as costs and revenues.

2.6   Activity

Suggest suitable cost units, cost centres, profit centres and investment centres for the following sectors

(a)   Hotel and catering
(b)   Professional services (accountants, architects)
(c)   Manufacturing.

2.7   Activity solution

	(a)	(b)	(c)
Cost units	Room, Meal	Chargeable hour	Widget
Cost centres	Housekeeping, Reception, Kitchen, Administration	Library, Word-processing, Maintenance, Administration	Assembly, Machining, Maintenance, Administration
Revenue centres	Room, Meal	Audit, Accountancy, Taxation	Shops and Showrooms
Investment centres	Hotels	Area offices	Factories Shops and Showrooms

3   CLASSIFICATION OF COSTS

3.1   Introduction

Costs may be classified using a number of different criteria. Classification is the logical grouping of similar items and the purpose of classifying costs is so that meaningful cost accounting reports may be prepared based upon such costs.

The classification criterion chosen will depend on both the purpose of the classification and the type of organisation. Some classifications (eg, by element) greatly assist the collection of costs. Different classifications are dealt with below:

(a)   **Elements of cost**

The initial classification of costs is according to the **elements** upon which expenditure is incurred:

- Materials;
- Labour;
- Expenses.

Within the cost elements, costs can be further classified according to the **nature** of expenditure. This is the usual analysis in a financial accounting system eg, raw materials, consumable stores, wages, salaries, rent, rates, depreciation.

(b)   **Direct and indirect costs**

> [Definition]   **Direct costs** are costs which are incurred for, and can be conveniently identified with, a particular cost unit. The aggregate of direct materials, direct wages and direct expenses is known as **prime cost**.

> [Definition]   **Indirect costs** are costs which cannot be associated with a particular unit of output. The total of indirect materials, indirect wages and indirect expenses represents **overheads**.

To ascertain the total cost of a cost unit, indirect costs are allotted to cost centres and cost centre costs are shared over (absorbed by) cost units. The subject of allotment and absorption of overhead costs is explained later.

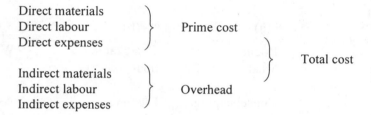

(c)   **Functional analysis of cost**

(i)   **Overhead classification**

Overheads are usually categorised into the principal activity groups:

- manufacturing;
- administration;
- selling;
- distribution; and
- research.

(ii)   **Prime cost classification**

Prime costs are usually regarded as being solely related to manufacturing, and so are not classified.

(d)   **Normal and abnormal**

An important feature of management reporting is that it should emphasise the areas of the business which require management attention and possible action.

The classification of costs between normal costs and abnormal costs recognises that some costs are expected to be incurred as part of the business' activities whereas others are not expected either to be incurred or to be of the value which is actually incurred.

Normal costs are those which are expected; the abnormal costs, being unusual, are those to which management's attention should be drawn. You will learn later in this text that this cost classification is used especially in process costing techniques.

(e)   **Controllable and non-controllable**

The need to emphasise abnormal costs to management has been explained above. The purpose of this is to encourage management action. The distinction between controllable and non-controllable costs is dependent on the person to whom any report is directed. The classification emphasises the costs which can be affected by the actions of a particular manager.

(f)   **Relevant and irrelevant**

In the context of decision-making management needs information to assist them in making the correct choice between alternatives. For these purposes and to ensure that valuable management time is not wasted only those costs affected by the management's decision are important. These are classified as relevant costs.

To be relevant a cost must be future and incremental (ie, changed by the project)

For example:

- money already spent on market research is irrelevant when deciding whether to go ahead with a project or not. It is money already spent and is not changed by the decision being made now.

- fixed costs not changed by the decision are irrelevant. Thus the rent paid on a factory is ignored when deciding whether to make product A or B.

(g)   **Notional costs and real costs**

A notional cost is a cost which will not result in an outflow of cash either now or in the future. This compares to other 'real' costs which will cause cash outflows. Notional costs are sometimes used when comparing performances of two or more operating units.

The above classifications may be used independently or they may be combined. For example, a material which is used by a production department and which is readily identifiable with the product to which it relates may be classified as

- material;
- production; and
- direct.

Since all direct costs must by definition be production costs, the material described above would usually be classified as **direct materials**.

3.2   Activity

Classify the following cost:

Wages of an employee who supervises the machine operators within a production process which makes engines.

3.3   Activity solution

Production overhead (indirect wages).

3.4   Manufacturing and service industries

Whereas manufacturing industries are concerned with converting raw materials into a product which they sell, service industries do not have a manufactured output. Instead, their output consists of services to a customer. Nevertheless, in the process of providing such services, they may use considerable quantities of consumable materials.

Since there is no manufacturing element, service industries cannot have factory, prime or manufacturing overhead costs.

3.5   Components of total cost

The following diagram summarises components of total cost in a typical manufacturing organisation:

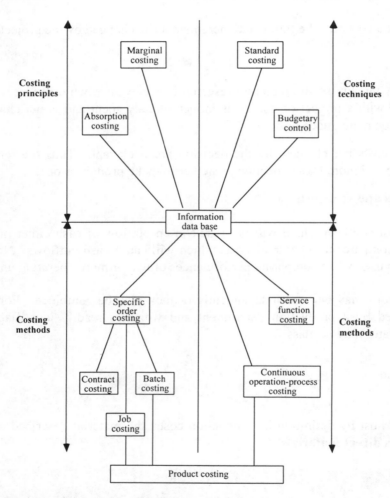

4   THE ROLES OF THE MANAGEMENT ACCOUNTANT

4.1   Introduction

Management accountants are important members of a management team; their broad base of knowledge and experience in business matters will greatly assist with the decisions to be made. There are two terms which are often used to describe the role of the management accountant: gate-keeper; and information manager.

4.2   The gate-keeper

The management accountant is often viewed as the keeper of the gate through which all transactions and information flow.

Management accountants have been trained to ensure that transactions must be properly authorised and payments not made until it is confirmed that the goods/services have been provided and that the price charged is that agreed. Consequently other managers may see the management accountant as the person who approves the transaction, though in non-financial decisions this is unlikely; the management accountant is merely responsible for ensuring that approval has been received.

The management accountant is likely, however, to control the flow of information within an organisation.

It is the management accountant who decides

(a)   which information concerning costs and revenues is collected

(b)   the basis on which calculations and valuations are made

(c)   how information is presented and with what frequency

(d)   who receives the information.

4.3   The information manager

Accounting information is part of the overall information system of the organisation. Since management accounting uses numeric and other quantitative data in its reports and analysis, the management accountant is often seen as the focal point for such information.

Other managers will ask the management accountant to provide data in respect of certain decisions. These may be historical using data already available, or they may involve the prediction of future outcomes. In either case they make use of the quantitative data which is assessed via the management accounting system.

5   MANAGEMENT ACCOUNTING AND FINANCIAL MANAGEMENT

5.1   Introduction

Definition   Financial management covers all the functions concerned in attempting to ensure that financial resources are obtained and used in the most effective way to secure attainment of the objectives of the organisation.

Management accounting has been described earlier as being the part of the accounting function which provides information to managers.

5.2   The similarities and differences between management accounting and financial management

Management accounting and financial management are both concerned with the use of resources to achieve a given target. Therefore much of the information used and reported is common to both of them.

The main difference is that management accounting usually operates within a 12-month time horizon, it is either reporting results compared with an annual target (budget) or providing information for short-term decision-making. In contrast financial management is more concerned with long-term objectives.

6   CHAPTER SUMMARY

This chapter has introduced the principles of management accounting, cost accounting, financial accounting and financial management. Subsequent chapters will consider the management accounting and financial management aspects in more detail.

7   SELF TEST QUESTIONS

7.1   What is management accounting? (1.2)

7.2   What is cost accounting? (1.3)

7.3   Describe the inadequacies of trading and profit and loss accounts as a source of management information. (1.4)

7.4   What is a cost unit? (2.2)

7.5   What is a cost centre? (2.3)

7.6   List the possible classifications of total cost. (3.1)

8   EXAMINATION TYPE QUESTION

8.1   Definitions

(a)   Define the terms 'cost centre' and 'cost unit'.   **(4 marks)**

(b)   Distinguish between direct and indirect costs and discuss the factors which should influence whether a particular cost is treated as direct or indirect in relation to a cost unit.   **(7 marks)**
                                                                                      (Total: 11 marks)

9   ANSWER TO EXAMINATION TYPE QUESTION

9.1   Definitions

(a)   A cost centre is a production or service location, function, activity or item of equipment whose costs may be attributed to cost units.

         A cost unit is a unit of product or service in relation to which costs are ascertained.

(b)   Direct costs are all costs which are physically traceable to the finished good in an economically feasible manner (CT Horngren). All other costs are indirect.

         There are several factors which will affect whether a cost is direct or whether it is treated as being indirect. For example, as the definition suggests, certain costs may be traceable to finished goods but it may not be economically worthwhile to do so.

         If the cost unit is very large eg, contract costing, then the majority of costs, including depreciation of plant and machinery and foreman's salary will be direct costs for a particular contract. For 'small' cost units where for example, cost units are processed on a machine, the depreciation of the machine is not traceable to individual cost units. If would, therefore, be treated as production overhead and included in unit cost via the overhead absorption rate.

         Another cost which may be direct or indirect is overtime premium. It may be possible to, for example, trace which jobs are carried out during overtime hours, and charge the premium to those jobs. However, if overtime is worked to increase the overall volume of production it would not be equitable to charge the premium to certain units. The premium would therefore be treated as a production overhead unless the overtime is worked at the specific request of a customer in which case it would be treated as direct.

         Hence, whether costs are direct or indirect depends on the individual circumstances.

2 REVIEW OF PRODUCT COSTING

INTRODUCTION & LEARNING OBJECTIVES

When you have studied this chapter you should be able to do the following:

- Account for overhead costs using absorption costing.
- Deal appropriately with the costs of production service departments.
- Explain the differences between marginal and absorption costing.
- Compute opportunity costs.
- Discuss the use of opportunity costs in a cost accumulation system.

1 OVERHEADS

1.1 Objectives

Overheads may be classified into direct and indirect, according to whether or not they are directly related to the production process. In many businesses overheads represent a large element of cost; they also present the biggest problems in terms of accounting treatment, as will become apparent.

The objectives of accounting for overheads are:

(a)   to identify costs in relation to output products and services;
(b)   to identify costs in relation to activities and divisions of the organisation;
(c)   to control overhead costs.

The procedures described in the rest of this section are largely concerned with objective (a) above; their relationship to objectives (b) and (c) are discussed subsequently. The steps involved are directed at establishing an **overhead absorption rate**. This rate is used to relate overheads to cost units.

Whilst such an overhead absorption rate may be a blanket rate for the whole enterprise, normally departmental absorption rates will be established for application to cost units passing through all the production cost centres.

1.2 Production overhead

Overhead represents indirect materials, indirect wages and indirect expenses attributable to production and the service activities associated with production. Marketing, general administration, research and development costs which are not associated with production are not usually treated as overheads for this purpose; consequently, the term 'overhead' may be assumed to mean **production overhead**.

Indirect production costs are incurred in three main ways:

(a) **Production activities** - costs arising in production departments such as fuel, protective clothing, depreciation and supervision.

(b) **Service activities** - the cost of operating non-producing departments or sections within the factory eg, materials handling, production control, canteen.

(c) **Establishment costs** - general production overhead such as factory rent/rates, heating and lighting and production management salaries.

It is important to note that analysis of overhead may be used for two purposes:

(a) To facilitate allotment to cost units.
(b) To relate costs to responsibility as an aid to control.

The following section attempts to explain the principle of absorption costing in general. Detailed procedures, however, may be different depending on the costing method used.

2 COST ALLOTMENT PROCEDURES

2.1 Illustration of overhead allotment

The ABC Washing Machine Co produces a standard washing machine in three production departments (Machining, Assembling and Finishing) and two service departments (Materials handling and Production control).

Costs for last year, when 2,000 machines were produced, were as follows:

Materials:
Machine shop	£240,000
Assembly	£160,000
Finishing	£40,000
Materials handling	£4,000

Wages:
Machining	10,000 hours at £3.72
Assembly	5,000 hours at £2.88
Finishing	3,000 hours at £3.60
Materials handling	£8,000
Production control	£11,200

Other costs:
Machine shop	£41,920
Assembly	£12,960
Finishing	£7,920
Materials handling	£8,000
Production control	£2,400

It is estimated that the benefit derived from the service departments is as follows:

Materials handling:
Machine shop	60%
Assembly	30%
Finishing	10%

Production control:
Machine shop	40%
Assembly	30%
Finishing	20%
Materials handling	10%

You are required:

(a)   to prepare a statement showing the overhead allotted to each of the production departments;

(b)   to calculate the unit cost of a washing machine.

2.2   Solution

(a)   Overhead allotment

Materials and wages incurred by the production departments may be assumed to be direct costs and therefore excluded from the overhead distribution.

	Total	Machining	Assembly	Finishing	Production control	Materials handling
	£	£	£	£	£	£
Indirect materials	4,000	-	-	-	-	4,000
Indirect wages	19,200	-	-	-	11,200	8,000
Other	73,200	41,920	12,960	7,920	2,400	8,000
	96,400	41,920	12,960	7,920	13,600	20,000
Production control	-	5,440	4,080	2,720	(13,600)	1,360
Materials handling	-	12,816	6,408	2,136	-	(21,360)
	96,400	60,176	23,448	12,776	-	-

Service department costs have been apportioned to production departments using the percentage benefit shown in the question.

(b)   Unit cost

	Machining	Assembly	Finishing	Total
	£	£	£	£
Direct materials	240,000	160,000	40,000	440,000
Direct wages	37,200	14,400	10,800	62,400
Production overheads	60,176	23,448	12,776	96,400
	337,376	197,848	63,576	598,800
Units produced				2,000
Cost per unit				£299.40

2.3   Measuring activity

The overhead absorption rate is the fraction:

$$\frac{\text{Cost centre overhead in £}}{\text{Cost centre volume in units}}$$

and in the ABC illustration the number of washing machines used was the measure of volume. This was acceptable because the question stated that a standard machine was produced. As all the machines were of the same type it is fair that each one should bear the same share of the costs of operating the departments which produced them.

If, however, the ABC Washing Machine Co produced three types of machine (say regular, super and de-luxe), then the amount of work (and therefore the cost) would be different for each type. The difference in direct cost can be measured; more or less materials would be requisitioned and more or less labour hours would be spent. It would now be unreasonable to use units as the basis for absorbing overheads. It may take longer to produce a de-luxe machine than a regular model and, therefore, the de-luxe machine uses more of the production resources represented by overhead costs.

Thus, volume is usually expressed in terms of a **time** measure, viz:

(a)   direct labour hours; or

(b)   machine hours;

for the purposes of overhead absorption.

Overhead can be absorbed in cost units by means of:

(a)   Rate per unit.

(b)   Percentage of prime cost (direct labour, direct material and direct expenses).

(c)   Percentage of direct wages.

(d)   Direct labour hour rate.

(e)   Machine hour rate.

2.4   Example

Facts as in the ABC illustration. A separate absorption rate for each cost centre is to be calculated as follows:

(a)   Machining: machine hour rate (each machine is manned by four operatives).

(b)   Assembly: direct labour hour rate.

(c)   Finishing: percentage of direct wages.

Absorption rates

$$\text{Machining} = \frac{\text{Cost centre overhead}}{\text{Machine hours}} = \frac{£60,176}{10,000 \div 4} \qquad = \quad £24.07 \text{ per machine hour}$$

$$\text{Assembly} = \frac{\text{Cost centre overhead}}{\text{Direct labour hours}} = \frac{£23,448}{5,000} \qquad = \quad £4.69 \text{ per labour hour}$$

$$\text{Finishing} = \frac{\text{Cost centre overhead} \times 100}{\text{Direct wages}} = \frac{£12,776 \times 100}{£10,800} \qquad = \quad 118.3\% \text{ of direct wages}$$

The overhead absorbed by a particular washing machine could then be accumulated.

Assume that a regular machine takes 1 hour machining, 2 hours assembly and 1 hour finishing.

Overhead absorbed

		£
Machining	1 hour × £24.07	24.07
Assembly	2 hours × £4.69	9.38
Finishing	118.3% of (1 × £3.60)	4.25
		37.70

2.5   Predetermined absorption rates

The washing machine illustration implies that absorption rates were calculated after the event ie, when overhead and volume for the period had been ascertained. This is not so. Unit costs are a continuous requirement for management information and will invariably reflect overhead absorption on a predetermined basis, viz:

$$\text{Absorption rate} = \frac{\text{Budgeted overhead}}{\text{Budgeted volume}}$$

Generally, the rate is derived from the annual budget to avoid distortion caused by seasonal fluctuation and to provide a consistent basis for measuring variations.

Actual overhead and/or volume will rarely coincide exactly with budget and therefore a difference between overhead absorbed and overhead incurred will arise.

2.6   Example

In year 9 the budget for a machine shop shows:

Overhead	£60,000
Volume	12,000 machine hours

In January, year 9, the machine shop incurred £5,400 of overhead and 1,050 machine hours were worked.

Calculate the predetermined absorption rate and the overhead under- or over-absorbed in January.

$$\text{Absorption rate} = \frac{\text{Budgeted overhead}}{\text{Budgeted volume}} = \frac{£60,000}{12,000 \text{ machine hours}} = £5.00 \text{ per machine hour}$$

	£
Overhead incurred	5,400
Overhead absorbed (1,050 hours × £5.00)	5,250
Under absorbed overhead	150

The under absorption arises from a combination of two factors:

(a)   overhead costs were higher than budget ($\frac{£60,000}{12}$) for the month;

(b)   volume was greater than budget ($\frac{12,000 \text{ hours}}{12}$) for the month.

In practice a separate absorption rate may be calculated for fixed and variable overhead to enable the effect of cost and volume changes to be shown more clearly. Analysis of over/under absorbed overhead is perhaps covered more appropriately under **standard costing**.

Note that overhead absorbed (sometimes called **recovered**) represents:

$$\begin{array}{ccc} \text{Actual production} & & \text{Predetermined rate per unit} \\ \text{(machine hours in this instance)} & \times & \text{(machine hours)} \end{array}$$

3   PROBLEMS IN ABSORPTION COSTING

3.1   Problematic cost items

It will be difficult to arrive at an accurate method of allotting certain overhead costs to centres because of their general nature or because of the way they are incurred or merely because the amount does not warrant complicated calculation. The following are suggestions for dealing with problematic items:

(a)   **Remuneration of executive directors** - directors' remuneration may be apportioned between factory, administration and marketing according to the estimated proportion of total time devoted to each aspect.

(b)   **National insurance and pensions** - it may be convenient to treat employer's contributions for direct workers as overhead expenditure.

(c)   **Insurance of factory buildings and plant** - the precise nature of the insurance must be considered as a direct expense or as factory overhead.

(d)   **Research expenditure** - in some cases it may be considered appropriate to treat certain expenditure as a direct expense or as factory overhead. Research into new products or directed towards new discoveries would normally be excluded from costs.

(e)   **Estimating expenses and cost of drawing office** - where there are a large number of draughtsmen, they may be required to analyse their time and the jobs on which they have been engaged will be charged accordingly. Estimating expenses are normally treated as general expenses.

(f)   **Depreciation of buildings** - this item may be apportioned between functions on the basis of area of cubic capacity. Where there is a substantial difference in the value of certain sections of the whole building (eg, where the offices are located in a more costly structure) it may be necessary to apportion part of the total charge on the basis of value.

(g)   **Royalties** - these may be classified as direct production costs or as selling expenses according to whether the royalty is payable on units produced or units sold.

(h)   **Accident and employer's liability insurance** - premiums paid should be apportioned according to the total wages of each department. Where, however, there is greater risk of accident in some departments, it may be necessary to weight the charge.

3.2   Volume of activity

It is generally considered that the production budget will be the basis for activity volume used in calculating pre-determined overhead absorption rates, thereby ensuring that unit costs reflect a share of the resources used in manufacture which is based on careful evaluation of the circumstances which will apply at the time such costs are prepared. Other bases are:

(a)   **Average past output** - this basis would be simple to calculate but would be inaccurate when output fluctuates.

(b)   **Normal capacity** - this basis should result in consistency of stock values but may cause misleading conclusions to be drawn from cost information and hide the effect on costs of under-utilisation of capacity.

3.3   Example

Discuss the arguments for and against calculating an overhead absorption rate on the basis of 80,000 direct labour hours, which is the level of activity which is expected to operate next year, instead of a basis of 100,000 direct labour hours, which is the normal level of operations. (No calculations are required in this answer).

3.4   Suggested answer

By using the expected level of activity of 80,000 to calculate the overhead absorption rate, the company is more likely to recover all the production overhead and avoid a large under-recovery of fixed costs which will have to be written off. In consequence, product costs will reflect 'actual' incurred costs so that stock values can be said to be more realistic. If selling prices are based upon these costs, it will safeguard the profitability of the company.

The danger, however, of using the lower level of working is that by increasing the cost, and in consequence increasing selling prices, sales may further decline because prices become less competitive. Thus, in the following year the volume of business may be reduced to the equivalent of 60,000 direct labour hours, and the company would be tempted to increase overhead rates and selling prices yet again.

The recommended treatment is for 'normal costs' to be absorbed by 'normal volume'. It provides a reasonable basis for selling prices and gives a product cost which is more meaningful for management.

3.5   Idle time and idle facilities

A substantial proportion of total costs is incurred as a result of time eg, wages and salaries, rent, rates and depreciation. It is vital that the business gets the maximum benefit from the expenditure on costs, which means that employees must be provided with work, and machines, equipment and factory space must be fully utilised. The economic utilisation of resources involves two aspects: the provision of sufficient work for the resources to work on, and ensuring that resources are used efficiently ie, that the maximum output is obtained from a given input of resources.

The cost accountant is, therefore, concerned to measure the use of available time. To do this it is necessary to record when employees are idle and to report these facts, including the cost of idle time, to management. The cost accountant also needs to take into account normal idle time and normal under-utilisation of facilities, especially when setting cost rates for use in estimating. If it is unlikely that a machine will be engaged in productive work twenty-four hours in each day, it is misleading to assume full capacity in setting overhead rates.

3.6   Example

A factory contains a rework department consisting of two men to whom all completed reject units go for correction. If the volume of rejects becomes larger than they can handle, then one or more assemblers are transferred to assist the two rework men.

You are required to advise whether the cost of rework labour should be treated as direct or indirect wages.

3.7   Suggested answer

The decision as to whether rework labour is treated as a direct or as an indirect cost will largely depend upon whether rework is an infrequent occurrence or may be considered to be a normal production cost.

In the situation described, the existence of a rework department plus occasional assistance implies that rework is frequent and, therefore, it may be advantageous to treat the rework department as a service cost centre. In that way, rework labour plus associated costs can be collected to facilitate control and then charged to specific jobs by means of a predetermined hourly rate.

The above procedure will result in rework costs being treated as a direct expense to jobs and may be inequitable in that rework caused by inefficiency will be treated in the same way as rework arising from the requirements of a particular job. The alternative would be to allocate rework costs to jobs or to departmental overhead depending on the reason for rectification.

3.8   Appraisal of total absorption costing

Total absorption costing is useful in that it allows a total cost to be calculated which is useful for managerial decisions such as pricing. But it does have some problems.

(1)   Allocation, apportionment and absorption methods are arbitrary. For example it is common to split heating costs on the basis of floor area - but clearly that is not the only acceptable method. Also, it may be difficult to justify absorption on labour hours rather than machine hours. This problem is increased when service departments exist and a basis of re-apportionment of their costs must be agreed on. Often the selection of the basis used for allocation, apportionment and absorption owes more to the debating skills of the various managers at costing meetings than to the underlying production and selling and distribution realities.

(2)   It treats what are predominantly fixed costs as if they varied per unit. For example, rent or depreciation of the factory will be absorbed per labour hour, but, of course, it does not really change with the number of hours worked, or number of units of production produced.

(3)   Under or over absorption will almost certainly need adjusting for at the year end. Only if both expenditure and the activity level are exactly as budgeted will the 'correct' amount of overheads be absorbed into production. This is very unlikely.

Some, though not all of these problems are addressed by the activity based costing approach (ABC) covered in Chapter 5.

4   MARGINAL COSTING

4.1   Introduction

Marginal costing is a system of cost accounting which does not attribute fixed production overhead costs to cost units. Instead it treats such costs as costs of the period in which they are incurred.

4.2   Marginal costing and cost accumulation

Under marginal costing the direct costs and variable overhead costs will be attributed to the cost unit. Any fixed costs incurred will be deducted in total in the profit and loss account. As a result the cost attributed to the cost unit is lower than that of absorption costing and is not acceptable for external stock valuations as regulated by SSAP 9.

4.3   Marginal costing and management information

The emphasis of marginal costing on variable costs is considered by many people to be more relevant to managers on the basis that variable costs tend to be more controllable, at least in the short-term. Also since absorption costs per unit are dependent on the volume of activity their use can be misleading when making volume-related decisions.

5   OPPORTUNITY COSTS

5.1   Introduction

Definition   An opportunity cost is the value of a benefit sacrificed in favour of an alternative course of action

5.2   Cost accumulation and opportunity costs

If opportunity costs are to be used within a cost accumulation system, then each resource would be valued at its opportunity cost instead of its historic actual cost.

The clear advantage of using an opportunity cost approach is that managers are made aware of the real value of a resource. This should ensure that resources are used efficiently.

The disadvantage is the difficulty of identifying the relevant opportunity cost of each resource, and the costs associated with doing so. The following examples illustrate the information required to identify the opportunity costs.

5.3   Using opportunity costs

If there are scarcities of resources to be used on projects (eg, labour, materials, machines), then consideration must be given to revenues which could have been earned from alternative uses of the resources.

Example 1

The skilled labour which is needed on a new project might have to be withdrawn from normal production causing a loss in contribution. This is obviously relevant to the project appraisal. The cash flows of a single department or division cannot be looked at in isolation. It is always the effects on cash flows of the whole organisation which must be considered.

There are several ways of defining opportunity cost. For our purposes, the opportunity cost of a resource may be defined as: **the revenue forgone if a unit of resource is used on the project instead of in the best alternative way.**

Example 2

A new contract requires the use of 50 tons of metal ZX 81. This metal is used regularly on all the firm's projects. There are 100 tons of ZX 81 in stock at the moment, which were bought for £200 per ton. The current purchase price is £210 per ton, and the metal could be disposed of for net scrap proceeds of £150 per ton. With what cost should the new contract be charged for the ZX 81?

Solution

The use of the material in stock for the new contract means that more ZX 81 must be bought for normal workings. The cost to the organisation is therefore the money spent on purchase, no matter whether existing stock or new stock is used on the contract. Assuming that the additional purchases are made in the near future, the relevant cost to the organisation is current purchase price ie,

50 tons × £210   =   £10,500

Example 3

Suppose the organisation has no use for the ZX 81 in stock. What is the relevant cost of using it on the new contract?

Solution

Now the only alternative use for the material is to sell it for scrap. To use 50 tons on the contract is to give up the opportunity of selling it for

$$50 \times £150 \qquad = \quad \underline{£7,500}$$

The contract should therefore be charged with this amount.

Example 4

Suppose that there is no alternative use for the ZX 81 other than a scrap sale, but that there is only 25 tons in stock.

Solution

The relevant cost of 25 tons is £150 per ton. The organisation must then purchase a further 25 tons, and assuming this is in the near future, it will cost £210 per ton.

The contract must be charged with:

	£
25 tons @ £150	3,750
25 tons @ £210	5,250
	9,000

Example 5

A mining operation uses skilled labour costing £4 per hour, which generates a contribution, after deducting these labour costs, of £3 per hour.

A new project is now being considered which requires 5,000 hours of skilled labour. There is a shortage of the required labour. Any used on the new project must be transferred from normal working. What is the relevant cost of using the skilled labour on the project?

Solution

What contribution cash flow is lost if the labour is transferred from normal working?

	£
Contribution per hour lost from normal working	3
Add back: labour cost per hour which is not saved	4
Cash lost per labour hour as a result of the labour transfer	7

The contract should be charged with 5,000 × £7	£35,000

Example 6

Suppose the facts are as in Example 5, but there is a surplus of skilled labour already employed (and paid) by the business and sufficient to cope with the new project. The presently idle men are being paid full wages.

Solution

What contribution cash flow is lost if the labour is transferred to the project from doing nothing? Nothing.

The relevant cost is zero.

6   CHAPTER SUMMARY

In this chapter we have revised the techniques of absorption and marginal costing and compared them from the point of view of cost accumulation.

Opportunity costs were then introduced and their use as part of a cost accumulation system discussed.

7   SELF TEST QUESTIONS

7.1   List the objectives of accounting for overhead cost (1.1)

7.2   Explain clearly the differences between the techniques of allocation, apportionment and absorption. (2.2)

7.3   Why are pre-determined absorption rates used? (2.5)

7.4   Explain the causes of over/under absorption of overhead cost. (2.6)

7.5   What are the problems of absorption costing? (3)

7.6   Explain the use of marginal costing for cost accumulation. (4.2)

7.7   Explain the use of opportunity costs for cost accumulation. (5.2)

3 JOB AND CONTRACT COSTING

INTRODUCTION & LEARNING OBJECTIVES

When you have studied this chapter you should be able to do the following:

- Prepare records using job costing.
- Prepare records using batch costing.
- Prepare records using contract costing.
- Recognise when it is appropriate to use each of these costing methods.

1 APPLICATIONS OF SPECIFIC ORDER COSTING

1.1 Specific order costing

Definition **Specific order costing** is a collective term for **job, batch** and **contract costing.** The distinguishing features are:

(a) work is separated as opposed to a continuous flow;

(b) work can be identified with a particular customer's order or contract.

1.2 Introduction to job costing

This method of costing is adopted when the factory issues an order to produce one cost unit for a customer. Jobbing firms are engaged in 'one-off' products of a specialist nature such as tools, machines, replacement parts, etc. The firm may meet a demand for products which need to be of a much higher standard than mass-produced equivalents or where the quantity required is so small that the planning and setting up involved for other firms would not be worthwhile.

Jobbing firms normally operate with a variety of machines in order to be able to tackle the majority of operations that will be required in the product. They will handle a wide range of work and are often used as sub-contractors to larger firms which have to off-load work where they have not the resources required for particular products or operations. The jobbing firm, therefore, probably has only a small amount of work of a repetitive nature which means that production plans may be prepared for just a few weeks or months ahead, and have to be flexible to meet urgent orders.

1.3 Introduction to batch costing

Businesses which manufacture a variety of products eg, household electrical goods, to be held in stock prior to sale, will operate **batch costing.** Jobbing methods are still used and the costing system is practically the same as for job costing. The only difference is that instead of charging costs to each separate cost unit, they are charged to the one production order which covers a quantity of cost units. When the order is completed the unit cost is found by dividing the quantity into the total batch cost.

1.4   Introduction to contract costing

The difference between a contract and a job is one of size and time-span. Contract costing is used by businesses undertaking building or other constructional contracts which take months or years to complete. In many cases the work will be done on site and not in the contractor's own works. Each contract is treated as a separate cost unit since management will want to know the profit or loss on each. For major contracts it may be necessary to designate sub-units for each stage of work either to facilitate control or to enable the invoicing of progress claims and the calculation of profit to date.

1.5   Costing principles

Either marginal or absorption costing can be applied in job, batch, and contract costing. Again the decision is influenced by **SSAP 9**, which requires absorption costing for stock valuation purposes, and therefore encourages its application for all costing. The assumption made in the following sections is that absorption costing is to be applied. This is the more complex situation, in that it involves the use of pre-determined overhead rates, and the problems of over-or under-absorption. If marginal costing is applied, then only variable overheads are charged to the production units; other costs are expensed on a time basis.

2   JOB COSTING

2.1   Job cost sheet (or card)

The focal point of a job costing system is the cost sheet (or card). A separate sheet will be opened for each customer's order, on which will be recorded:

(a)   materials purchased specifically for the job (from GRNs or suppliers' invoices);
(b)   materials drawn from stock (from requisitions);
(c)   direct wages (from time sheet/job cards);
(d)   direct expenses (from invoices, etc).

When the job is finished, the cost sheet gives the total direct cost, and overhead can be calculated and entered using one of the accepted methods. If the job is unfinished at the end of an accounting period the total cost recorded to date on the cost sheets will give the work in progress figure. The job cost can be compared with the estimate to analyse the difference between actual and estimated cost. Where the product contains a number of components it is advisable to check that the costs of all the components have been recorded.

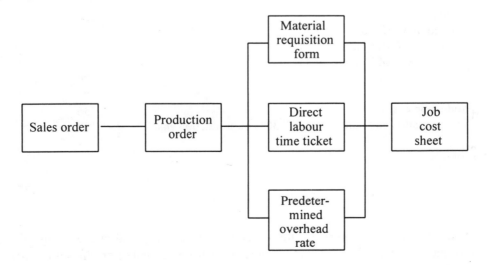

2.2   Example of a job cost

Jobbers Ltd undertakes jobbing engineering work. Among the requests for quotations received in December was one from A for a small machine to be manufactured according to the customer's drawings supplied. Jobbers Ltd prepared an estimate of the material and labour content based on the drawings, and amounts were added for overhead and profit. The estimate indicated a price of £600 and this price was quoted to, and accepted by, A.

The work on A's order was put in hand in January on the authority of Production Order No. 1001 signed by the works manager and was completed in that month. The abstract of stores requisitions issued in January showed the following against Production Order No. 1001:

Stores requisition	£
D57	48
D61	24
D70	26
Total	98

Two operatives paid at £2.20 per hour each had been employed in separate cost centres on Production Order No. 1001 during January and their time-sheets showed that each had worked for thirty hours on that order. The overhead rates for the cost centres in which the operatives are employed are in one centre £2.00 per direct labour hour and 100% on direct wages in the other. Administration and other overhead is recovered at the rate of 30% on production cost.

You are required to prepare a statement showing the cost and profitability of the order from A.

2.3   Solution

**Statement of cost and profitability - production order number 1001
machine for A per customer's drawing**

	£	£	£
Selling price per estimate			600
Costs:			
Direct materials, per stores abstract		98	
Direct wages, 60 hours @ £2.20		132	
Prime cost		230	
Production overhead:			
30 hours @ £2.00	60		
100% of 30 hours @ £2.20	66		
		126	
Production cost		356	
Administration and other overhead, 30% of production cost		107	
Total cost of sales			463
Net profit			137

Note: actual and estimated profit on the order would be compared and any significant difference reported to management. The estimate should have been compiled on the same lines as the actual cost in the above statement to assist in locating the particular costs which were not as estimated.

2.4   Effect of inaccurate overhead absorption rates

The above illustration shows that selling prices can reflect estimates and that the major uncertainty in estimating is calculation of an accurate figure for overhead recovery. Inaccurate estimating can seriously harm the business because:

(a)   if jobs are over-priced, customers will go elsewhere;

(b)   if jobs are under-priced, sales revenue will fail to cover costs and/or provide an adequate return.

2.5   Inaccurate estimate of volume

Predetermined overhead rates are based on a volume estimate. If actual volume is significantly higher or lower than expected, then estimates, and consequently selling prices, will be inaccurate.

2.6   Example

Company A's budget for the year is as follows:

	£
Prime costs	50,000
Overhead	30,000
	80,000
Profit (40% on cost)	32,000
Sales	112,000
Volume	3,000 labour hours

If volume is half budget ie, 1,500 hours, actual results would show:

	£
Prime costs (half budget)	25,000
Overhead absorbed	15,000 (1,500 hours × $\frac{£30,000}{3,000}$)
	40,000
Profit (40% on cost)	16,000
Sales	56,000

Actual overhead incurred would not fall to half the budget, however, because of the fixed element. It may fall to, perhaps, £24,000 but job costs would reflect overhead at the predetermined rate of £10 per hour, leaving £9,000 under-absorbed.

Actual profit would therefore be £(16,000 – 9,000) = £7,000.

2.7   Inaccurate absorption basis

Estimated costs should reflect overhead in relation to the way it is incurred, so that selling prices are competitive but profitable.

2.8   Example

Company B bases its estimates on the following formulae:

Total cost	=	Prime cost plus 40% for overhead
Selling price	=	Total cost plus 25% for profit

Estimates for two jobs show:

Item	Job X £	Job Y £
Direct materials	200	100
Direct wages @ £2 per hour	200	300
Prime cost	400	400
Overhead absorbed (40%)	160	160
Total cost	560	560
Profit (25%)	140	140
Selling price	700	700

Thus both jobs will be priced the same even though it would appear from the direct wages estimate that Job Y takes 50% more time to complete and therefore uses much more of the factory's resources.

Job X may be over-priced in relation to competitors whereas Job Y is under-priced and the business would lose its Job X customers and get more orders for Job Y.

Consider what would happen if 1,500 hours were available. The factory could produce 10 of Job Y compared to 15 of Job X.

2.9   Insufficient analysis by cost centre

A similar effect could arise if overhead rates do not recognise use of more or less expensive resources.

2.10   Example

Company C uses a 'blanket' overhead rate calculated as follows:

	Overhead cost £	Labour hours
Cost centre Y	40,000	4,000
Cost centre Z	80,000	4,000
	120,000	8,000

$$\text{Absorption rate} = \frac{£120,000}{8,000}$$

$$= £15 \text{ per labour hour}$$

Thus a job which takes one hour in Y will be charged the same amount for overhead as a job which takes an hour in Z even though the latter centre costs twice as much per hour to operate.

Once again, estimates would not reflect a realistic charge for the use of resources and over or under-pricing may result.

2.11 Cost control

When production is related to a specification or to customers' orders, the costing system will be interlocked with estimating so that the estimate can be used as a standard to locate excessive usage of materials and time.

Control will be assisted by:

(a)   **Detailed production orders**

These should be subject to serial number control. The production order is the authority to obtain or allocate specific resources in the form of materials, labour and machines.

(b)   **Excess material requisitions**

Additional requirements for material would be supplied only on presentation of a properly authorised document which would show the reason for additional need.

(c)   **Route cards**

Each production order can be supported by route cards which specify the sequence of operations and the estimated time for each operation or stage. Actual time would be recorded and causes of excess time noted where appropriate.

(d)   **Regular reports**

The above documents will form the basis of a report to show the incidence of excess usage together with an analysis of main causes. The aim would be to prevent recurrence, where possible by appropriate action, eg:

- amendment of existing methods of estimating usages;
- change of supplier;
- increased labour training;
- introduction of incentive payment to all grades of works labour;
- improved system of preventive plant maintenance.

2.12 Job profitability and pricing

Management of a jobbing firm would be very interested in comparing the profitability of different types of work to assist:

(a)   selection of the most profitable mix, possibly by rejection of some jobs, giving priority to others and by sub-contracting;

(b)   identification of work where prices could be shaded or where increases may be necessary.

One of the major obstacles to accurate job cost ascertainment is the calculation of a reasonable proportion of fixed overhead to be recovered. Accurate estimation of volumes and costs is difficult and the diversity of production methods in a jobbing business complicates any attempt to establish an equitable basis for apportionment and absorption of costs. It may be more realistic for price fixing purposes, therefore, to ignore indirect costs and to base selling prices on direct cost plus contribution; control of fixed costs will, of course, still be a vital area.

An inherent danger when prices are based on contribution is the tendency to under-price because 'any contribution is better than losing the order'. That approach may be justifiable in exceptional circumstances but in the long run selling prices must cover all costs and provide an acceptable return.

3   BATCH COSTING

3.1   Combined job and batch costing

Many businesses combine job costing with batch costing. This occurs where the business assembles a product to meet a customer's specification, but the assembly contains a number of components that can also be used in other assemblies. The components will be produced in batches and a batch cost sheet will record the costs. When the components are finished the order will be closed and the components will be transferred into a finished parts store at, say, the average cost of the batch. When the customer orders his particular assembly, a new order number will be raised and the required components drawn from store and charged against the assembly order.

3.2   Economic batch quantity

Where products are made in batches for stock to await sale or use in assemblies, the quantity to be produced in any one batch is a recurring and major problem, which involves consideration of:

(a)   Rate of consumption.

(b)   Storage costs and availability.

(c)   Time required to set up and take down production facilities.

(d)   Capacity available in terms of machines, labour and services in relation to requirements for other products.

The **Economic batch quantity** (EBQ) can be estimated by:

(a)   Tabulated analysis; calculating unit costs for a range of batch quantities to select the batch with the lowest unit cost.

(b)   Graphical analysis: plotting storage costs against production costs.

(c)   Formula:

$$EBQ = \sqrt{\frac{2CD}{H}}$$

where   D   =   annual demand
C   =   setting up/taking down costs
H   =   annual storage costs

Note that this is the same as the EOQ formula for stock holding. In fact the problem is identical.

3.3   Product line information

Batch costing is typically employed where a wide variety of products are held in stock. The cost accountant will be called upon for detailed information on product costs to satisfy the following needs:

(a)   **Production planning/control**

Scheduling to maintain stock levels and to meet demand fluctuations could be a major problem requiring continuous information on set up costs, machine utilisation and stock movements.

(b)   **Product profitability pricing**

Management are likely to require regular analyses of product costs and profits; maintenance or improvement of margins will be a recurring problem. The information will also assist in directing sales effort and formulating sales policy.

(c)   **Research**

Cost information, perhaps on an **ad hoc** basis, will be required in the development of new products or in improving operations.

3.4   Batch production

There are many organisations (eg, motor vehicle manufacturers) who operate a continuous production line or series of lines which individually perform tasks, the combined result of which is the finished product.

These organisations do not manufacture to the requirements of a specific customer however they may use a version of batch costing to place a cost value on their product.

The principles are as described above, namely that costs are collected for a batch and an average cost per unit calculated. The difference is in determining the batch. This is often done by reference to time, either an accounting period or some shorter timescale determined by the organisation.

4   CONTRACT COSTING

4.1   Contract ledger entries

In contract costing each contract is a separately identifiable **cost unit,** so that costs will be accumulated in a separate ledger account for **each** contract. The various elements of cost are dealt with as follows:

(a)   **Direct materials**

Materials charged to the contract may include both materials purchased specially and materials issued from the contractor's store. The appropriate costs are debited to the contract account. Control of materials at the site can be impaired by the difficulty of organising effective procedures for recording receipts and for returns from site to store of materials surplus to contract requirements.

(b)   **Direct wages**

Labour charges to the contract may include design and drawing office work (involving a time-booking procedure for salaried staff), manufacturing operations in the factory, and work on the site. All labour employed at the site of a contract will be direct. Time sheets may be necessary to disclose the time spent by workers at different sites. All such labour costs are debited to the contract account.

(c)   **Direct expenses**

Direct contract costs other than materials and labour are often very significant. The two major items falling within this category are **plant** and **sub-contracted work.**

•   **Plant**

Plant or equipment may be purchased specifically for a contract, in which case the contract account is debited with the cost. Alternatively, plant may be transferred from another contract, in which case it is the written down value that is debited to this contract and credited to the contract from which it has been moved. At the end of each financial period the depreciated value of any plant owned is shown as a credit entry in the contract account (ie, as a balance carried down on the account to the next period). The net effect of the bookkeeping entries is that depreciation on the plant is automatically debited to the contract. Plant may be hired for use on a particular contract. As the business does not own such plant, the only ledger entries are the hire charges which are debited to the contract account. It is also possible to charge the contract account with a notional hire charge for plant owned by the business, thus treating the plant hire department as a separate entity.

- **Sub-contracted work**

    In the case of a large contract or one involving specialist activities, the business may engage sub-contractors in certain aspects of the work. The cost of any sub-contracted work is a direct expense of a contract and is debited to the contract account.

(d)   **Indirect costs**

Many contractors do not attempt to apportion such costs to specific contracts as they are often negligible compared with direct costs. However, if such apportionment of indirect costs is carried out, the resultant amount is debited to the contract account.

4.2   Architects' certificates and retention monies

For each contract a price is agreed between the business and the client. This is known as the contract price. In the case of large contracts, where the work involved may spread over many months or even years, the contractor will expect interim payments from the client in respect of the contract price. Such payments will be related to the work done so far on the contract. The procedure involved is as follows:

(a)   **Architects' certificates**

As the work on a contract proceeds, the client's architects (or surveyors) will issue certificates indicating that so much of the contract price is now due to the contractor in respect of the work completed. In most cases at this stage the contractor will invoice the contractee with a progress payment.

(b)   **Retention monies**

The contractor normally receives only a proportion of the value shown on the architects' certificates while the contract is still in progress. The amounts held back by the client are known as retention monies. Such retention monies would only be paid over to the contractor some time after the completion of the contract when any faulty work has been rectified.

4.3   Attributable profit on uncompleted contracts

Where a contract extends over a long period **SSAP 9 (Stocks and long-term contracts)** allows the contractor to take credit for part of the profit **attributable** to the contract in each year's accounts. This percentage of completion method avoids the inconsistency of having a number of years with no profit from a particular contract and then suddenly making a profit in the year when it is completed. In deciding to what extent profit can be taken on uncompleted contracts the following matters are important considerations:

(a)   the successful outcome of the contract should be certain before any interim profit is taken;

(b)   any profit should only be taken in proportion to the work completed to date on the contract; and

(c)   any anticipated overall loss on the contract should be provided for as soon as it is recognised.

4.4   Calculation of interim profit

The calculation of the profit to be taken on an uncompleted contract involves five steps:

Step 1   Determine the total sales value of the contract (for a fixed price contract this will be the contract price). Call this (a)

Step 2   Compute the total expected costs to complete the contract. Call this (b); it consists of two elements:

(i)   the actual costs incurred to date on the contract; plus

(ii)   the estimated future costs necessary to complete the contract.

Step 3   The expected overall profit on the contract is given by (a) minus (b).

Step 4   The attributable profit to date on the contract should reflect the amount of work that has been completed so far. It is calculated as follows:

Attributable profit to date $=$

$$\frac{\text{Value of work certified to date}}{\text{Total sales value of contract}} \times \text{Expected overall profit}$$

It is important to realise that the attributable profit thus calculated is the **cumulative** figure to date.

Step 5   The profit to be taken **this year** (ie, debited to the contract account this year) is the cumulative attributable profit calculated at step 4 less the profit on the contract already recognised in previous years.

Unfortunately, some examination questions do not provide sufficient information to use this approach. If not told the estimated future costs, it is necessary to use the following procedure:

		£	£
Profit to date:			
Value of work certified			200,000
Less: Cost to date		80,000	
Less: Cost of work not yet certified		15,000	
			65,000
Profit to date			135,000

Sometimes this figure is reduced by an arbitrary amount (eg, one-third) to allow for the fact that the contract is incomplete and therefore the outcome is not certain.

The profit to be taken **this year** is the profit to date (reduced if necessary) less the profit on the contract already recognised in previous years.

Notes:

(1)   It is always necessary to calculate profit to ensure that losses are identified and provided for.

(2)   Attention must be paid to the cost of work not yet certified. This arises where some work has been done but not checked/certified by the architects. Hence the costs will be included in the ledger but the selling price of this work is excluded from the value of work certified. The idea is, therefore, to calculate only profit on work that has been certified.

4.5   Valuation of contracts in progress

Accurate valuation of work in progress, represented by uncompleted contracts, is vital for preparing realistic financial statements for a contracting business. The following suggestions may merit consideration:

(a)   **Contract analysis**

Divide the contract into identifiable sections to aid cost control and comparison of the cost of completed work with certified work. Allocation of codes to sections and sub sections of contracts will help to locate excess expenditure.

(b)   **Prefabricated units**

Where these are held in central store and issued to sites on request, standard costs may be established so that purchase or manufacture of prefabricated units is controlled centrally.

(c)   **Plant**

Where items of plant are transferred from one site to another, it may be beneficial to treat plant handling as a service department ie, by developing standard hire charges and by controlling plant utilisation against budget.

4.6   A worked example

Contract No. 412 commenced during 19X1 and has a fixed contract price of £200,000. The costs incurred during the year 19X1 for materials, wages and sub-contractors' charges totalled £90,000. Plant costing £20,000 was purchased during 19X1 specifically for Contract No. 412.

At the end of 19X1:

(a)   the plant was valued at £15,000;

(b)   unused materials on the site were valued at £19,000;

(c)   architects' certificates had been issued showing that the value of work completed was £100,000.

It is estimated that further costs totalling £74,000 would be incurred in order to complete the contract. The figure includes the appropriate cost of plant and sub-contractors in the future.

Retention money representing 20% of the certified value of the work completed has been held back by the client. The balance of the money due has been paid. The contractor credits the contract account with the full value of the architects' certificates as they are received.

You are required to prepare a calculation of the profit to be taken to the profit and loss account for 19X1.

4.7   Solution

Profit taken on contract for 19X1

		£
Actual costs incurred to date:		
	Materials, labour and sub-contractors' costs	90,000
	Less: Materials on site at end of 19X1	19,000
		71,000
	Add: Plant depreciation £(20,000 – 15,000)	5,000
	Contract costs incurred to end of 19X1	76,000
	Contract costs incurred to end of 19X1	76,000
	Add: Estimated future costs to complete the contract	74,000
	Total estimated contract costs	150,000
Contract profit:		
	Contract price (fixed)	200,000
	Less: Contract costs (as above)	150,000
	Contract profit (estimated)	50,000

$$\text{Profit taken in 19X1} = \frac{\text{Work certified}}{\text{Contract price}} \times \text{Estimated contract profit}$$

$$= \frac{£100,000}{£200,000} \times £50,000$$

$$= £25,000$$

Note: as contract number 412 commenced during 19X1, this cumulative attributable profit is recognised in 19X1. No profit had been taken on this contract in earlier years.

5   MANAGERIAL ACCOUNTING PROBLEMS ENCOUNTERED IN JOB AND CONTRACT COSTING

In job and contract costing the role of the management accountant is critical. They must decide:

(a)   the information requirements and method of capture. The time sheets, job cards etc must be designed and instructions for their completion issued. If the system is computerised, the files must be designed and created and instructions issued for data input.

(b)   methods for controlling costs. This becomes critical if jobs have been quoted for in advance. The management accountant must ensure that there is adequate information available to monitor costs to date, and estimated to completion, against pre-determined budgeted levels. Corrective action must be taken if costs differ by more than an agreed amount from their expected levels.

(c)   how overheads are to be allocated to each job, and how any subsequent adjustment for the under or over absorption of overheads is to be handled.

(d)   how profits are to be taken on long-term contracts. It is the management accountant who must provide the 'to date' and 'expected to completion' cost figures on which the profit allocation will be based.

6   CHAPTER SUMMARY

In this chapter we have explained the methods of job, batch and contract costing in detail with particular reference to the measurement of profit.

7   SELF TEST QUESTIONS

7.1   What is job costing? (1.2)

7.2   What is batch costing? (1.3)

7.3   What is contract costing? (1.4)

7.4   In the context of contract costing, explain the use of architects' certificates. (4.2)

7.5   In the context of contract costing, explain the meaning of 'attributable profit' on uncompleted contracts. (4.3)

7.6   List the steps required to calculate interim profits on uncompleted contracts. (4.4)

7.7   Why is it necessary to calculate interim profits on uncompleted contracts? (4.4)

8   EXAMINATION TYPE QUESTION

8.1   Jigantic plc

Jigantic plc is a building company engaged in the construction of hospitals and other major public buildings; most of the contracts undertaken extend over a three or four year period.

Shown below are the expenses incurred for the year ended 31 May 19X1, together with other operating details for three of the contracts in which the company is currently engaged:

	Contract A £'000	Contract B £'000	Contract C £'000
Contract price	4,000	10,200	12,000
Value of work certified by contractees' architects	2,350	7,500	11,000
Cash received from contractees	2,000	6,750	9,900
Costs incurred to 1 June 19X0	-	2,400	5,550
Cost incurred during the year:			
Materials	1,100	1,600	1,050
Labour	700	1,150	975
Other expenses, excluding depreciation	350	475	775
Plant and equipment:			
Written down value at 1 June 19X0	300	800	700
Written down value at 31 May 19X1	600	525	175
Purchases during the year	725	400	125
Cost of work not yet certified	75	-	800

The agreed retention rate is 10% of the value of work certified by the contractees' architects.

Contract C is nearing completion and the site manager estimates that costs of £425,000, in addition to those tabulated above, will be incurred in order to complete the contract. He also considers that the plant and equipment on site will be worthless by the time the contract is complete.

The nature of the work undertaken by Jigantic plc is such that it may be regarded as reasonable for the company to include in its annual accounts a prudent estimate for profit attributable to that part of the work on each contract certified as complete at the end of each accounting year.

Profit of £1,150,000 was taken on Contract C in the accounting periods up to and including 31 May 19X0. No profit had been taken on contract B as, at the 31 May 19X0, work on the project had only recently commenced.

The directors of Jigantic plc propose to incorporate into the company's profit and loss account for the year ended 31 May 19X1, the following amounts of profit/(loss) for each contract:

Contract A	Nil
Contract B	£720,000
Contract C	£2,400,000

Making whatever calculations you consider necessary, **you are required** to carefully explain whether you agree with the proposed profit/(loss) figures for the above contracts. If you consider any of the proposed amounts are inappropriate suggest, with supporting explanations and calculations a more suitable figure.   **(20 marks)**

9   ANSWER TO EXAMINATION TYPE QUESTION

9.1   Jigantic plc

Note: the key to dealing with the profit calculation is to try to calculate the attributable profit for each contract.

If there is insufficient information (ie, estimated costs to completion not given), then calculate profit to date based on value of work certified ie, profit should always be calculated so as to identify any losses - in this case on Contract A.

It is then necessary to consider whether the contracts are sufficiently far advanced for it to be **'prudent'** to recognise profit.

For Contract B the contract is, based on 'sale value', ($\frac{7,500}{10,200} \times 100\%$) approximately 75% completed.

It is therefore assumed reasonable to take profit.

It is also reasonable to take profit on Contract C as it is 'nearing completion'.

(i)   **Cost of contracts as at 31 May 19X1**

	Contract A £'000	Contract B £'000	Contract C £'000
Cost to 1 June 19X0		2,400	5,550
Costs incurred during the year:			
Materials	1,100	1,600	1,050
Labour	700	1,150	975
Other expenses	350	475	775
Depreciation (ii)	425	675	650
Total cost to 31 May 19X1	2,575	6,300	9,000

(ii)   **Depreciation of plant and equipment**

	Contract A £'000	Contract B £'000	Contract C £'000
Written down value, 1 June 19X0	300	800	700
Purchases	725	400	125
	1,025	1,200	825
Written down value, 31 May 19X1	600	525	175
Depreciation for the year	425	675	650

Contract A

	£'000	£'000
Value of work certified		2,350
Cost as at 31 May 19X1 (i)	2,575	
Less: Cost of work not yet certified	75	
		2,500
Loss to date		(150)

To include a 'nil' profit in the accounts would be inappropriate since clearly the contract has incurred a loss of £150,000 to date. In accordance with the prudence concept of **SSAP 2** and the requirements of **SSAP 9** relating to long-term contract work-in-progress, this loss should be incorporated into the year's accounts. Strictly speaking the loss expected to arise on the whole of the contract should be provided for but insufficient information has been given to do this (ie, estimated completion costs not given).

Contract B

	£'000
Value of work certified	7,500
Cost as at 31 May 19X1 (i)	6,300
Profit to date	1,200

The proposed profit figure of £720,000 is well below the profit which has been earned to date. However, because of the uncertainty surrounding long-term contracts, considerable caution should be exercised when allocating profits over the life of a contract. Hence a figure lower than £1.2m, presumably reduced in accordance with the accounting policy of the company, is acceptable.

Note: it would appear that the examiner used the following formula for estimating the amount of profit to incorporate into the profit and loss account:

$$\frac{2}{3} \times \frac{\text{Cash received}}{\text{Value of work certified}} \times \text{Profit to date} \ = \ \frac{2}{3} \times \frac{6,750}{7,500} \times 1,200 = 720$$

This formula is recognised in many textbooks but represents only one possible way of prudently reducing profits to take account of the uncertainty surrounding uncompleted contracts.

Contract C

	£'000	£'000
Contract price		12,000
Cost as at May 19X1 (i)	9,000	
Estimated completion costs (425 + 175)	600	
		9,600
Estimated total profit		2,400

The proposal to incorporate a profit of £2,400,000 in the profit and loss account for the year ended 31 May 19X1 is not allowable for three reasons:

(i)   an estimated profit of £1,150,000 for Contract C has already been included in previous years' accounts;

(ii)   some provision should be made for expenses which have not been anticipated but which may well arise, for example, the cost of rectification work; and

(iii)   part of the work is yet to be carried out. Profit should only prudently be taken on work completed by the end of the accounting period.

Hence the figure of £2,400,000 needs to be reduced in two respects: firstly to reflect the work done to date - by using the formula:

$$\text{Total profit} \times \frac{\text{Value of work certified}}{\text{Contract price}}$$

and secondly by the profit incorporated in previous years' profit and loss accounts.

	£'000
Profit on contract to date $2,400 \times \dfrac{11,000}{12,000}$	2,200
Less: Profit already taken	1,150
Profit applicable to this year's accounts	1,050

4 PROCESS COSTING

INTRODUCTION & LEARNING OBJECTIVES

When you have studied this chapter you should be able to do the following:

- Understand the circumstances in which process costing might be used.

- Explain the meaning of and differences between normal losses and abnormal losses/gains.

- Account for process costs involving losses.

- Explain and apply the equivalent units concept to opening and closing work in process.

- Explain and use both the FIFO and weighted average methods of dealing with opening work in process (including recognising which method to use when the information provided is limited).

- Distinguish between joint and by-products.

- Account for by-products.

- Account for joint products using different apportionment bases for common (pre-separation) costs.

- Critically appraise the use of common cost apportionments in the measurement of product profitability.

- Evaluate the decision whether to further process a product (or products) beyond the separation point.

1 PROCESS COSTING

1.1 Continuous production

In the previous chapter costs were directly allocated to a particular job or batch. When standardised goods or services result from a sequence of repetitive and continuous operations, it is useful to work out the cost of each operation. Then, because every unit produced may be assumed to have involved the same amount of work, costs for a period are charged to processes or operations, and unit costs are ascertained by dividing process costs by units produced. This is known as **process costing.**

1.2 Process costing

 Process costing applies when standardised goods are produced from a series of inter-connected operations eg,

    (a)   oil refining;
    (b)   breweries;
    (c)   canned food.

1.3 Special features of process costing

The basic physical feature of a processing system is that as products pass from the raw material input stage to becoming finished products they pass through a number of distinct stages or **processes** of manufacture. In such a situation it is not feasible to link the cost of specific inputs to specific units of output. For example, in the production of paint it would be impossible to isolate one unit of output (a litre can of paint) and determine precisely which inputs have finished up in that particular litre of paint. The nature of a processing business is such that inputs are being added continuously to the manufacturing process, losing their identity, and a continuous output of production is being achieved.

Ascertaining the cost of production involves:

(a)   determination of the costs (direct and indirect) associated with each process;

(b)   calculation of the average process unit cost by dividing the appropriate costs by the appropriate number of units of output;

(c)   valuation of the units of output transferred from one process to the next and any work in process by applying the unit costs;

(d)   the cost of output from the first process becomes the cost of input to the second process and so on until output from the final process has accumulated the cost of all processes.

This procedure is complicated by the following factors:

(a)   output units will not equal input units to the extent that losses are sustained during processing;

(b)   the existence of partially processed units ie, work in process, at the end of the period;

Each of these factors will be considered in this chapter.

1.4   Information requirements of process costing

When designing the cost accounting system for use in process costing the management accountant must ensure that the following information is recorded:

(a)   issues of direct materials and supplies to each process. This information will be recorded on stores requisitions and priced by referring to suppliers invoices or stock records.

(b)   payroll costs of each process. Clock cards or time sheets must be analysed and summarised by process, so that the labour costs incurred by each process can be identified.

(c)   overheads or indirect conversion costs for each process. This information will either come from suppliers invoices or will be applied to each process according to a predetermined absorption rate.

(d)   transfers of finished goods to the next process or to finished stock. Transfers of goods at the end of the process must be recorded in production reports.

(e)   details of work in progress and spoilt units. This information must also be included in production reports.

1.5   Normal loss

The nature of the processing operation is such that the input volume rarely equals the output volume; the difference, or loss, is analysed between that which is expected (and considered to be unavoidable) and any additional loss (or lack of loss) which actually occurs.

Definition   Normal loss is the amount of loss expected from the operation of a process. This expectation is based on past experience, and this loss is considered to be unavoidable.

The normal loss is usually expressed as a percentage of the input volume; in accounting for the normal loss the cost of its production is borne by the remaining forms of output.

1.6   Normal losses having a scrap sales value

When losses have a scrap value, two alternative accounting treatments exist:

(a)   credit the income from such sales to a miscellaneous income account, transferring the balance directly to the profit and loss account; or

(b)   reduce the cost of the process by the income anticipated from the normal loss.

Method (b) is the preferred method and should be used in examinations.

1.7   Activity

Calculate the cost per tonne from the following data:

Input 5,000 tonnes costing	£15,000
Labour cost	£6,000
Overhead cost	£10,000

Normal loss is 10% of input and has a scrap value of £4/tonne.

1.8   Activity solution

Normal loss = 500 tonnes and has a value of £2,000 (500 × £4)

Process costs   = £31,000 – £2,000 = £29,000

$$\text{Cost per tonne} = \frac{£29,000}{4,500} = £6.44$$

2   ABNORMAL LOSSES AND GAINS

2.1   Introduction

Often the operation of these processes results in the actual loss being different from that expected. The differences are referred to as abnormal losses and gains.

2.2   Abnormal losses

Definition   The extent to which the actual loss exceeds the normal loss is referred to as the abnormal loss. This loss is unexpected and considered to be avoidable consequently the cost of producing abnormal loss units is not treated in the same way as the cost of the normal loss.

The following example shows how to account for abnormal losses.

2.3   Example

The following data relates to one process during April:

Input materials 1,000 kg costing	£9,000
Labour cost	£18,000
Overhead cost	£13,500

A normal loss equal to 10% of input was expected.
Actual output was 850 kg.
Losses are sold as scrap for £9/kg.

2.4   Solution

The following steps can be carried out:

Step 1   The normal loss equals 10% of 1,000 kg = 100 kg.

Step 2   The expected output units equals the input less the normal loss
= 1,000 kg – 100 kg = 900 kg.

Step 3   The process costs equal £40,500 – (100 kg × £9) = £39,600.

Step 4   The cost per unit equals

$$\frac{£39,600}{900} = £44$$

This is used to value both output (good production) and the abnormal loss

Step 5

Process account

	Units	£		Units	£/Units	£
Material input	1,000	9,000	Normal loss	100	9	900
Labour		18,000	Abnormal loss			
			(W1)	50	44	2,200
Overhead		13,500	Output	850	44	37,400
	1,000	40,500		1,000		40,500

WORKINGS

(W1)   The abnormal loss units equals the difference between the actual and expected output. These are then valued at the cost calculated in step four.

Normal loss

	Units	£		Units	£
Process account	100	900	Cash/bank	150	1,350
Abnormal loss	50	450			
	150	1,350		150	1,350

Abnormal loss

	Units	£		Units	£
Process account	50	2,200	Normal loss	50	450
			Profit & Loss		1,750
	50	2,200		50	2,200

(W2)   The distinction between normal and abnormal losses is purely an accounting one, all of the loss may be sold as scrap for £9/kg. All of these proceeds are credited to the normal loss account and any balance on this account is transferred to the abnormal loss account.

Note that the transfer to profit and loss shown in the abnormal loss account is the net cost of producing the unexpected loss (after deducting its scrap value). This is used to control the costs of excess losses.

2.5   Losses having a disposal cost

Sometimes, instead of having a sale value losses have a disposal cost (this occurs particularly when toxic chemicals are processed). From an accounting viewpoint the treatment is the same as that shown above for losses having a sale value except that the value is negative.

The disposal cost of the normal loss must be entered in the process account either alongside the normal loss quantity as a negative value on the credit side or as a debit (ie, an extra cost). In either case the quantity MUST be entered on the credit side.

2.6   Actual loss is less than normal loss (abnormal gains)

Definition   The extent to which the actual loss is less than the normal loss is referred to as an abnormal gain.

The following example shows how to account for abnormal gains.

2.7   Example

The following data relates to one process during May:

Input materials 1,000 kg costing	£9,000
Labour cost	£18,000
Overhead cost	£13,500

A normal loss equal to 10% of input was expected.
Actual output was 920 kg.
Losses are sold as scrap for £9/kg.

2.8   Solution

The steps are the same as was shown earlier:

Step 1   The normal loss equals 10% of 1,000 kg = 100 kg.

Step 2   The expected output units equals the input less the normal loss
= 1,000 kg – 100 kg = 900 kg

Step 3   The process costs equal £40,500 – (100 kg × £9) = £39,600

Step 4   The cost per unit equals $\dfrac{£39,600}{900} = £44$

Step 5   **Process account**

	Units	£		Units	£/Units	£
Material input	1,000	9,000	Normal loss	100	9	900
Labour		18,000	Output	920	44	40,480
Overhead		13,500				
Abnormal gain	20	880				
	1,020	41,380		1,020		41,380

WORKINGS

(W1)   The abnormal gain units equals the difference between the actual and expected output. These are then valued at the cost per unit calculated. Note that these entries are made on the debit side of the process account, thus causing it to balance.

Normal loss

	Units	£		Units	£
Process account	100	900	Cash/bank	80(W2)	720
			Abnormal gain	20	180
	100	900		100	900

Abnormal gain

	Units	£		Units	£
Normal loss	20	180	Process account	20	880
Profit and loss (W3)		700			
	20	880		20	880

(W2)   This is the actual loss being sold at £9/kg.

(W3)   This represents the net benefit of producing less loss than expected (after deducting the lost income from the anticipated scrap sales).

3   PARTIALLY PROCESSED UNITS

3.1   Introduction

At the end of a period there may be some units which have been started but have not been completed. These are said to be closing work in process units.

Assuming at this stage that there is no opening work in process, the output for a period will consist of:

(a)   units of production that have been started and fully processed within the period;

(b)   units of production that have been started in the period but which are only part-processed at the end of the period; this closing work in process will be completed next period when further costs will be incurred in completing it.

3.2   Equivalent units

Costs in a process costing system are allocated to units of production on the basis of **equivalent units.** The idea behind this concept is that once processing has started on a unit of output, to the extent that it remains in an uncompleted state it can be expressed as a proportion of a completed unit. For example, if 100 units are exactly half-way through the production process in terms of the amount of cost they have absorbed, they are effectively equal to 50 complete units. Therefore, 100 units which are half-complete can be regarded as 50 equivalent units that are complete.

3.3   Example

A manufacturer starts processing on 1 March. In the month of March he starts work on 20,000 units of production. At the end of March there are 1,500 units still in process and it is estimated that each is two thirds complete. Costs for the period total £19,500.

Calculate the value of the completed units and the work in process at 31 March.

Step 1   Trace the physical flow of units so that units input to the production process are reconciled with units output or in process at the end of the period.

Step 2   Convert the physical units determined in Step 1 into equivalent units of production for each factor of production (ie, materials, labour, etc.)

Step 3   Calculate the total cost for each factor for the period.

Step 4   Divide the total costs by equivalent units to establish a cost per equivalent unit.

Step 5   Multiply equivalent units by the cost per equivalent unit to cost out finished production and work in process. Reconcile these values to the total costs for the period as calculated in Step 3.

Step 6   Write up the ledger accounts.

3.4   Solution

Step 1

Units started	20,000
Opening work in process	nil
Closing work in process	(1,500)
Units started and completed	18,500

Step 2

	Units	Proportion complete	Equivalent units
	(a)	(b)	(c)=(a)×(b)
Started and completed	18,500	1	18,500
Work in process	1,500	$\frac{2}{3}$	1,000
			19,500

Step 3

Costs of period	£19,500

Step 4

Cost per equivalent unit $= \dfrac{£19,500}{19,500} = £1$

Step 5

		Cost £
Cost of completed units	18,500 × £1	18,500
Cost of work in process	1,000 × £1	1,000
Total costs for period		19,500

The 1,500 physical units in process at the end of the period have a value (based on 1,000 equivalent units) of £1,000.

Step 6

Process account

	Units	£		Units	£
Opening work in process	-	-	Output	18,500	18,500
Units transferred in and costs	20,000	19,500	Closing work in process	1,500	1,000
	20,000	19,500		20,000	19,500

3.5 Extension of the equivalent units approach

In practice it is unlikely that all inputs to production will take place at the same time, as was suggested in the example above. For instance, materials are frequently added at the beginning of a process, whereas labour may be applied throughout the process. Thus, work in process may be **more complete** as regards one input or cost element than as regards another. Equivalent units must thus be calculated for each input and costs applied on that basis.

3.6 Example

As in the example above, except that:

(a)   all materials have been input to the process;
(b)   work in process is only one-third complete as regards labour;
(c)   costs for the period are:

	£
Materials	10,000
Labour	9,500
Total	19,500

3.7 Solution

Step 1

Units started	20,000
Opening work in process	nil
Closing work in process	(1,500)
Units started and completed	18,500

Step 2

	Units	Materials		Labour	
		Proportion complete	*Equivalent units*	*Proportion complete*	*Equivalent units*
Started and completed	18,500	1	18,500	1	18,500
Work in process	1,500	1	1,500	$\frac{1}{3}$	500
Total equivalent units			20,000		19,000

Step 3

Costs of period		£10,000	£9,500

Step 4

Cost per equivalent unit	$\dfrac{£10,000}{20,000} = 50\text{p}$	$\dfrac{£9,500}{19,000} = 50\text{p}$

Step 5

	Materials	Labour	Total £
Cost of completed units	18,500 × £0.50 = £9,250	18,500 × £0.50 = £9,250	18,500
Cost of work in process	1,500 × £0.50 = £750	500 × £0.50 = £250	1,000
Total costs for period			19,500

Step 6

Process account

	Units	£		Units	£
Opening work in process	-	-	Output	18,500	18,500
Units transferred in and materials	20,000	10,000	Closing work in process	1,500	1,000
Labour		9,500			
	20,000	19,500		20,000	19,500

4   OPENING WORK IN PROCESS

4.1   Introduction

In the previous examples it was assumed that there was no opening stock of work in process. In reality, of course, this is unlikely to be the case, and changes in levels of work in process during the period can give rise to problems. There are basically two methods of accounting for such changes, namely:

(a)   the weighted average (or averaging) method;

(b)   the FIFO method.

4.2   Weighted average (or averaging) method

Under this method the opening stock values are added to the current costs to provide an overall average cost per equivalent unit. No distinction is, therefore, made between units in process at the start of the period and those added during it and the costs associated with them.

4.3   Example

FL Manufacturing Co Ltd
Process information for month ended 31 December

Work in process, 1 December (15,000 units, two-fifths complete) £10,250 (work in process value made up of: materials £9,000 plus conversion costs £1,250).

Units started during December	30,000
Units completed during December	40,000
Work in process, 31 December	5,000 (half-completed)
Material cost added in month	£24,750
Conversion cost added in month	£20,000

Materials are wholly added at the start of the process. Conversion takes place evenly throughout the process.

Calculate the values of finished production for December and work in process at 31 December, using the weighted average method.

4.4   Solution

It is easiest to use the six step method, proceeding as follows:

FL Manufacturing Co Ltd
Production cost report for month ended 31 December

Step 1   physical flows

	Units	Units
Opening work in process	15,000	
Units started	30,000	
To be accounted for		45,000
Units completed	40,000	
Closing work in process	5,000	
Units accounted for		45,000

Step 2   equivalent units

	Units	Materials Proportion complete	Materials Equivalent Units	Conversion Proportion Complete	Conversion Equivalent Units
Completed	40,000	1	40,000	1	40,000
Closing work in process	5,000	1	5,000	½	2,500
Total equivalent units			45,000		42,500

Note: at this point the degree of completion of opening work in process is irrelevant under the weighted average method. It would, of course, have been used to value work at 30 November.

	Materials £	Conversion £	Total £
Step 3 costs to be accounted for			
Work in process at 1 December	9,000	1,250	10,250
Add: Costs incurred in December	24,750	20,000	44,750
	33,750	21,250	55,000

Step 4   costs per equivalent unit

$$\frac{£33,750}{45,000} = 75p \qquad \frac{£21,250}{42,500} = 50p$$

Step 5

			Total £
Cost of completed units	$40,000 \times 75p = £30,000$	$40,000 \times 50p = £20,000$	50,000
Cost of work in progress	$5,000 \times 75p = £3,750$	$2,500 \times 50p = £1,250$	5,000
Total costs (agreed with total per Step 3)			55,000

The important feature of this method is that the costs associated with opening work in process are added to the costs arising in the current period and then they all become part of an averaging procedure.

Step 6

Process account

	Units	£		Units	£/unit	£
Opening WIP	15,000	10,250	Output	40,000	1.25	50,000
Materials	30,000	24,750	Closing WIP	5,000	1	5,000
Conversion cost		20,000				
	45,000	55,000		45,000		55,000

Do not proceed until you have re-worked this example correctly without consulting the solution.

4.5   FIFO method

In contrast to the weighted average method, the FIFO method distinguishes between units completed in the period that were in opening work in process and those started **and** completed in the period.

4.6   Example

Process information as stated in example above, but we must identify opening WIP now completed separately from units started and completed in the period.

Calculate values of finished production and work in process using the FIFO method.

Step 1   **physical flows**

	Units
Opening work in process	15,000
Units started	30,000
To be accounted for	45,000
Units completed:	
opening work in process now complete	15,000
units started and completed in period	25,000
Closing work in process	5,000
Units accounted for	45,000

Note: the separate identification of units in opening work in process.

Step 2   **equivalent units**

	Units	Materials Proportion complete in period	Materials Equivalent units	Conversion Proportion complete	Conversion Equivalent units
Opening WIP now complete	15,000	-	-	$\frac{3}{5}$	9,000
Units started and completed in period	25,000	1	25,000	1	25,000
Closing work in process	5,000	1	5,000	½	2,500
Total equivalent units			30,000		36,500

Step 3   **costs to be accounted for**

	£	£	£
Work in process at 1 December			10,250
Costs added materials	24,750	conversion 20,000	44,750
			55,000

Step 4   **costs per equivalent unit**

$$\frac{£24,750}{30,000} = £0.825 \qquad \frac{£20,000}{36,500} = £0.548$$

Step 5   **cost of production**

	Cost	
	£	£
Opening work in process now completed		
Value at 1 December	10,250	
Add: Conversion, 9,000 × £0.548	4,930	
		15,180

Started and completed in period:

Materials, 25,000 × £0.825	20,625	
Conversion, 25,000 × £0.548	13,700	
		34,325

Total value of work completed   49,505

Value of closing work in process:

Materials, 5,000 × £0.825	4,125	
Conversion, 2,500 × £0.548	1,370	

Total value of work in process   5,495

Total costs for period (agreed with total per Step 3)   55,000

Step 6

Process account

	Units	£		Units	£/Unit	£
Opening WIP	15,000	10,250	Output	40,000	1.24	49,505
Materials	30,000	24,750	Closing			
Conversion cost		20,000	WIP	5,000	1.10	5,495
	45,000	55,000		45,000		55,000

Now re-work the above example without looking at the solution.

4.7 Choosing the valuation method - in practice

In practice the FIFO method is little used, for two main reasons:

(a) It is more complicated to operate.

(b) In process costing, it seems unrealistic to relate costs for the previous period to the current period of activities.

4.8 Choosing the valuation method - in examinations

In order to use the weighted average or FIFO methods to account for opening work in process different information is needed:

For weighted average:

An analysis of the opening work in process value into cost elements (ie, materials, labour)

For FIFO:

The degree of completion of the opening work in process for each cost element.

If all of the information is available so that either method may be used, the question will specify the required method.

5   LOSSES IN PROCESS - INTERACTION WITH WORK IN PROCESS

5.1   Introduction

The examples so far have considered the treatment of losses and work in process (equivalent units) in isolation. We shall now consider an example in which losses occur during the process, when the units are partially complete.

5.2   Example

Input to Process A was 1,000 units costing £4,500. Process costs for the month were £3,608.

780 units were transferred to Process B in the month and 100 units were in progress at the end of the month (conversion 50% complete). Normal loss is estimated as 10% of input and losses occur when the process is 60% complete, as regards conversion.

Calculate the costs attributable to completed units, abnormal loss units and closing work in process.

Step 1   Physical flow of units

		Units
Opening work in process		nil
Units started		1,000
		————
To be accounted for		1,000
		————
Units completed		780
Normal less (10% × 1,000)		100
Closing work in process		100
Abnormal loss (balance)		20
		————
		1,000
		————

Step 2   Equivalent units

	Units	*Materials*		*Conversion*	
		Proportion complete	*Equivalent units*	*Proportion complete*	*Equivalent units*
Completed units	780	1	780	1	780
Normal loss	100	1	100	60%	60
Closing work in process	100	1	100	50%	50
Abnormal loss	20	1	20	60%	12
			———		———
Total equivalent units			1,000		902
			———		———

Step 3   Costs of period

Materials	£4,500	Conversion	£3,608

Step 4   Cost per equivalent unit

Materials $\dfrac{£4,500}{1,000} = £4.50$ Conversion $\dfrac{£3,608}{902} = £4$

Step 5   Costs of production

Normal loss		£
Materials	100 × £4.50 =	450
Conversion	60 × £4 =	240
		£690

This is shared by the completed 780 units and the abnormally lost 20 units.

Completed units	$\frac{780}{800} \times 690 =$	£672.75
Abnormal loss	$\frac{20}{800} \times 690 =$	£17.25

		£
Completed units	(780 × 8.50) + 672.75 =	7,302.75
Abnormal loss		
Materials	(20 × £4.50) +	
Conversion	(12 × £4) + 17.25 =	155.25
Closing work in process		
Materials	(100 × £4.50) +	
Conversion	(50 × £4) =	650
		£8,108

Step 6

Process A

	Units	£		Units	£
Opening WIP	-	-	Completed	780	7,302.75
Materials	1,000	4,500	Normal loss	100	-
Conversion		3,608	Abnormal loss	20	155.25
			Closing WIP	100	650
	1,000	8,108		1,000	8,108

6   JOINT PRODUCTS AND BY PRODUCTS

6.1   Introduction

The nature of process costing is that the process often produces more than one product. These additional products may be described as either **joint** or **by-products**. The distinction is of great importance, and is a matter of drawing a dividing line. Essentially joint products are both main products whereas by-products are incidental to the main products. Costs incurred in processing prior to the separation of the products are known as common costs (or joint costs).

6.2   Joint products

Definition   Two or more products separated in the course of processing, each having a sufficiently high saleable value to merit recognition as a main product.

6.3   By-product

> [Definition]   Output of some value produced incidentally in manufacturing something else (main products).

These definitions still leave scope for subjective judgement, but they provide a basis for such judgement. The distinction is important because the accounting treatment of joint and by-products differs.

6.4   Relationship between processes, joint and by-products

The following diagram illustrates the relationships:

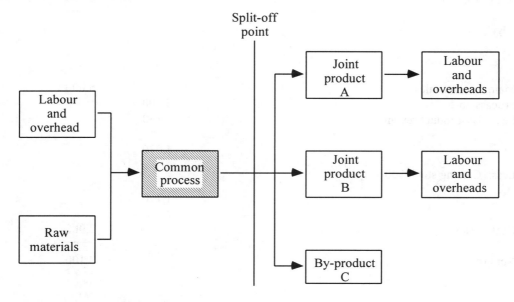

6.5   Accounting for by-products

Either of the following methods may be adopted:

(a)   the proceeds from the sale of the by-product may be treated as pure profit;

(b)   the proceeds from the sale, less any handling and selling expenses, may be applied in reducing the cost of the main products.

If a by-product needs further processing to improve its marketability, such cost will be deducted in arriving at net revenue, treated as in (a) or (b) above.

Note that recorded profits will be affected by the method adopted if stocks of the main product are maintained.

6.6   Example

Output from a process was 1,300 kilos of the main product and 100 kilos of a by-product. Sales of the main product were 1,000 kilos realising £6,000; sales of the by-product realised £160 but incurred £30 distribution cost. Process costs were £5,200.

Method (a)

		£	£
Main product sales			6,000
Process costs		5,200	
Less: Closing stock $\dfrac{300}{1,300} \times £5,200$		1,200	
			4,000
			2,000
Add: Net profit of by-product sales (£160 − 30)			130
Net profit			2,130

Method (b)

		£	£
Main product sales			6,000
Process costs		5,200	
Less: By-product revenue		130	
		5,070	
Less: Closing stock $300 \times \dfrac{£5,070}{1,300}$			
		1,170	
Cost of sales			3,900
Net profit			2,100

Under method (b), a portion of by-product revenue is deferred in the stock value of the main product.

6.7   Accounting for joint products

Joint products are, by definition, subject to individual accounting procedures. Common costs may require apportionment between products if only for joint valuation purposes.

The main bases for apportionment are:

(a)   **Physical measurement of joint products**

When the unit of measurement is different eg, litres and kilos, some method should be found of expressing them in a common unit. Some common costs are not incurred strictly equally for all joint products: such costs can be separated and apportioned by introducing weighting factors.

(b)   **Market value**

The effect is to make each product appear to be equally profitable. Where certain products are processed after the point of separation, further processing costs must be deducted from the market values before common costs are apportioned.

(c)   **Technical estimates of relative use of common resources**

Apportionment is, of necessity, an arbitrary calculation and product costs which include such an apportionment can be misleading if used as a basis for decision making.

6.8 Valuation of joint product stocks

In the following example common costs are apportioned on the following bases:

(a)   physical measurement;
(b)   market value at point of separation;
(c)   net realisable value/net relative sales value.

The methods will result in different stock valuations and, therefore, different recorded profits.

6.9 Example

	Kgs produced	Kgs sold	Selling price per kg	Common cost
Product A	100	80	£5	
				£750
Product B	200	150	£2	

(a)   Apportionment by physical measurement

$$\frac{\text{Common cost}}{\text{Kgs produced}} = \frac{£750}{300} = £2.50 \text{ per kg for A } + \text{ B}$$

Trading results:

	Product A		Product B		Total
		£		£	£
Sales	80 × £5.00	400	150 × £2.00	300	700
Cost of sales	80 × £2.50	200	150 × £2.50	375	575
Profit/(loss)		200		(75)	125
Value of closing stock	20 × £2.50	50	50 × £2.50	125	

The main point to emphasise about joint products is the production mix. In this case the production ratio is 100 : 200 which means that, in order to obtain 1 kg of A, it is necessary also to produce 2 kgs of B, at least in the short term. (In the longer term it may be possible through research and development work to change the mix.)

In attempting to assess the profitability of the common process it is necessary to assess the overall position as follows:

		£
Sale value of production A	100 × £5	500
Sale value of production B	200 × £2	400
		900
Common cost		750
Profit		150

This profit figure should be used to evaluate the profitability of the common process.

Referring back to the trading results, it is important to appreciate that the 'loss' on B has been created by the common cost apportionment, ie.

	£
Selling price	2.00
Share of common cost	2.50
Loss	0.50

A decision not to produce and sell B is not possible ie, if B were not produced, then neither could A be produced.

A further point to note is that stock of B could not be valued at £2.50 bearing in mind that stock should be valued at the lower of cost and net realisable value.

(b)   **Apportionment by market value at point of separation**

		Sales value of production £	Proportion	Common cost apportionment £	Per kg £
A	100 × £5	500	5/9	417	4.17
B	200 × £2	400	4/9	333	1.67
				750	

Trading results:

		£	£	£
Sales				700
Common cost			750	
Less: Closing stock:				
A	20 × £4.17	83		
B	50 × £1.67	83		
			166	
Cost of sales				584
Profit				116

Notes:

(1)   Apportionment is on the basis of proportionate sales value of production.

(2)   Further processing or marketing costs specifically attributable to one product would be deducted from selling price to arrive at an estimated market value at split-off point.

(3)   This approach provides a more realistic estimate of cost to use for valuing stock of B ie, £1.67.

(c)   **Apportionment by net realisable value**

This approach should be used in situations where the sale value at the split-off point is not known, either because the product is not saleable, or if the examiner does not tell you - or if specifically asked for by the examiner.

Further information needed:

	Further processing costs	*Selling price after further processing*
Product A	£280 + £2.00 per kg	£8.40
Product B	£160 + £1.40 per kg	£4.50

Apportionment of common costs:

Final sale value of production	*Allocatable further processing cost*	*Net realisable*	*Common cost apportionment*	*Per kg*

	£	£	value £		£ £
Product A	100 × £8.40 = 840	280 + 100 × £2.00 = 480	360	$\dfrac{360}{360+460} \times £750 = 329$	3.29
Product B	200 × £4.50 = 900	160 + 200 × £1.40 = 440	460	$\dfrac{460}{360+460} \times £750 = 421$	2.10

Trading results (for common process only):

	£	£	£
Sales			700
Common cost		750	
Less: Closing stock:			
A 20 × £3.29	66		
B 50 × £2.10	105		
		171	
Cost of sales			579
Profit			121

Note:

As we **know** sale value of B at the point of separation is £2, we can see that this method results in an unrealistic stock value of £2.10. Bear in mind that this approach should only be used where the sale value at the split-off point is not known - or if instructed to by the examiner.

7 CRITICAL EVALUATION OF PROCESS COSTING

Process costing and joint cost allocation give a valuation of good production, lost units (or by-products) and work in progress which accords with the requirements of SSAP 9, but is unlikely to be of much use in managerial decision making or cost control.

When making production decisions managers need relevant costs, ie, those additional costs which are incurred when a product is made, or are eliminated if the product is not made. Thus the allocation of joint costs (which will be incurred anyway) should be ignored when making production decisions; the only joint costs that can possibly be relevant are any variable joint costs. The decision maker must calculate opportunity costs, not costs which depend on how historical joint costs are arbitrarily shared out between various products.

Similarly, pricing decisions should not be influenced by the chosen allocation of joint costs. Such a process is clearly a nonsense if sales values have been used to allocate joint costs (ie, prices are used to calculate costs, then we try to use costs to calculate prices).

In cost control or responsibility accounting, the management accountant wants to compare the actual costs controllable in the current period with the budgeted controllable costs for the current period. Process costing can cause two problems.

(1) The arbitrary allocation of joint costs is outside the control of individual process or product managers and thus must be excluded from any appraisal reports.

(2) Where there is work in progress at the beginning or end of the period, calculations of cost per equivalent unit must be reviewed to ensure that costs and production from prior periods are excluded. Such costs and production are relevant to stock valuations and profit calculations but are irrelevant to cost control or appraisal reports.

8   CHAPTER SUMMARY

This chapter has explained two more methods of costing: output costing and process costing. Each of these is used in organisations whose operations are continuous and are only artificially stopped and re-started by the preparation of monthly cost accounts.

In dealing with process costing the problems of losses and work in process have been illustrated and their solution methods shown. Joint and by-products have been distinguished and the various apportionment methods illustrated and their limitations discussed.

9   SELF TEST QUESTIONS

9.1   What is process costing? (1.2, 1.3)

9.2   What is a normal loss? (1.5)

9.3   What is an abnormal loss? (2.2)

9.4   What is an abnormal gain? (2.6)

9.5   Explain the concept of equivalent units. (3.2)

9.6   What is a joint product? (6.2)

9.7   What is a by-product? (6.3)

10   EXAMINATION TYPE QUESTIONS

10.1   Armor plc

Armor plc operates a process which produces an industrial cleansing chemical, and shown below are the costs incurred by the process during month 7 together with other relevant operating data.

Direct materials transferred into process:	
10,000 kilos at £0.15 per kilo	£1,500
Conversion costs	£1,330
Output:	
Finished production	8,400 kilos
By-product	500 kilos
Toxic waste	800 kilos

The toxic waste is the same chemical as the finished product except that it has been polluted at the final operation. The cost of disposing of the toxic waste is £0.80 per kilo. The by-product is transferred to a subsidiary operation where it is packed at a cost of £0.25 per kilo. These costs are not included in the direct materials and conversion costs tabulated above.

The selling price of the by-product is £0.75 per kilo and the process is credited with the net realisable value of the by-product produced. During month 7, 30 kilos of the by-product were sold.

The normal output from the process per 1,000 kilos of direct material is:

Finished production	850 kilos
By-product	50 kilos
Toxic waste	60 kilos
Loss as a result of evaporation, caused by processing	40 kilos

You are required:

(a)   to prepare the following accounts recording month 7 transactions for the above process:

- Process account
- By-product account
- Normal toxic waste account
- Any relevant abnormal loss/gain accounts.   **(15 marks)**

(b)   to explain the reasons for your treatment of the toxic waste including an explanation of how the total cost of abnormal toxic waste has been calculated.   **(5 marks)**

(Total: 20 marks)

10.2   XY Ltd

XY Ltd operates a chemical process which jointly produces four products, A, B, C and D. Product B is sold without further processing, but additional work is necessary on the other three before they can be sold. Budgeted data for the year were as follows:

	Production	*Closing stock*	*Sales*
	lb	*lb*	*lb*
Production:			
Product A	150,000	10,000	140,000
Product B	110,000	15,000	95,000
Product C	60,000	5,000	55,000
Product D	180,000	Nil	180,000

There were no opening stocks of the four products. Closing stocks were ready for sale.

	Selling prices per lb	*Cost of additional work to make product saleable per lb*
	£	
Product A	0.70	0.10
Product B	0.60	-
Product C	0.60	0.20
Product D	1.35	0.35

	£
Production cost of the joint process	180,000
Other costs:	
Administration (fixed)	45,000
Selling:	
Fixed	35,000
Variable (£0.01 per lb sold)	4,700

An overseas customer has expressed interest in buying from existing production 50,000lb each in one year of any or all of Products A, C and D before they have been further processed by XY Ltd. He has offered to pay the following prices:

	Price per lb
	£
Product A	0.65
Product C	0.52
Product D	0.90

On such sales, variable selling costs would be only £0.006 per lb. Fixed administration and selling costs would remain as stated above.

The costs of the joint process are to be apportioned to individual products on the following bases:

(a)   weight of products produced;

(b)   sales value of products produced less the cost of additional work incurred to make products saleable.

You are required for each of the above bases to calculate for the year:

(a)   gross profit per product (ie, before deducting administration and selling overhead);
(b)   total gross profit;
(c)   total net profit.

You are also required:

(d)   to state which products you would recommend XY Ltd to sell to the overseas customer before further processing at the prices quoted in order to increase net profit;

(e)   to calculate the increase in the annual net profit of XY Ltd if your advice at (d) above was followed.

11   ANSWERS TO EXAMINATION TYPE QUESTIONS

11.1   Armor plc

Note: the approach is to prepare the process account in the usual way taking the relevant cost and output figures from the question, except for the toxic waste.

The way to deal with the losses is to put in the pre-determined figures first (based on input) ie,

Normal toxic waste: $10,000 \times \dfrac{60}{1,000} =$ 600

Hence, abnormal toxic waste (bal fig) 200

Total toxic waste 800

Normal loss from evaporation: $10,000 \times \dfrac{40}{1,000} =$ 400

The balancing figure in the quantity columns of the process account is the abnormal gain.

The next stage is to prepare the by-product account to find the net realisable value of the by-product; this value is then credited to the process account.

It is then possible to compute the cost per kilo, bearing in the mind that it is necessary to add the disposal cost of the normal waste to total cost. The cost per kilo figure can then be used to complete the value columns in the process account and then complete the entries in the waste/gain accounts.

(a)

Process account - Month 7

	kilos	£		kilos	£
Direct material	10,000	1,500	Finished production	8,400	3,024
Conversion costs		1,330	By-product	500	250
		———	Normal toxic waste	600	-
		2,830	Abnormal toxic waste	200	72
Waste disposal costs			Normal evaporation loss	400	-
(600 @ 0.8)		480			
Abnormal gain	100	36			
	10,100	3,346		10,100	3,346

By-product account

	kilos	£		kilos	£
Packing cost:			Sales	30	22.50
500 @ 0.25		125	Balance c/d	470	352.50
Process account					
(bal fig)	500	250			
	500	375		500	375.00

Normal toxic waste account

	kilos	£		kilos	£
Cash	600	480	Process account	600	480

Abnormal gain account

	kilos	£		kilos	£
Profit and loss account	100	36	Process account	100	36

Abnormal toxic waste account

	kilos	£		kilos	£
Process account	200	72	P&L a/c	200	232
Cash: 200 @ £0.8		160			
	200	232		200	232

WORKING

Calculation of cost per kilo

$$= \frac{\text{Total cost } + \text{ Disposal cost of normal toxic waste } - \text{ Net realisable value of by-product}}{\text{Input } - \text{ Normal toxic waste } - \text{ By-product } - \text{ Normal evaporation loss}}$$

$$= \frac{2,830 + 480 - 250}{10,000 - 600 - 500 - 400}$$

$$= \frac{3,060}{8,500}$$

$$= £0.36 \text{ per kilo}$$

(b)   The general principle behind treatment of the toxic waste is whether the waste is considered normal or abnormal.

Normal waste is waste which arises as a result of the nature of the process and is therefore regarded as unavoidable. The cost of this normal waste should therefore be incorporated into the cost of the product - the cleansing chemical. In this case the normal waste increases the normal cost in two ways:

(1)   yield is reduced: this causes a higher unit cost;
(2)   there is an additional cost of disposing of the waste.

The amount by which actual waste exceeds the normal or expected waste is termed 'abnormal' and is assumed to be controllable/avoidable. This waste should not have occurred and the cost is therefore excluded from the cost of output and written off to the profit and loss account. The cost comprises the normal output cost plus the additional disposal cost.

The management of Armor plc should investigate to ascertain the cause of this abnormal waste.

11.2   XY Ltd

(a)   )
(b)   )   Profit statement (see below)
(c)   )

(i)   **Joint costs apportioned on weight of products**

	Product A 000 lb	B 000 lb	C 000 lb	D 000 lb	Total 000 lb
Sales	140	95	55	180	470

	A £	B £	C £	D £	Total £
Sales	98,000	57,000	33,000	243,000	431,000
Less: cost of sales	64,400	34,200	30,800	127,800	257,200
Gross profit	33,600	22,800	2,200	115,200	173,800

Less: Administration costs		45,000
Less: Selling costs: Fixed		35,000
Variable		4,700
		84,700
Net profit		89,100

WORKINGS

$$\text{Joint cost per lb} = \frac{\text{Costs}}{\text{Weight produced}}$$

$$= \frac{£180,000}{500,000}$$

$$= 0.36$$

As closing stocks are **ready for sales**, cost of sales is valued at joint plus additional costs, ie:

Product	Joint £	Cost per lb additional £	Total	Sales 000 lb	Cost of sales £
A	0.36	0.10	0.46	140	64,400
B	0.36	-	0.36	95	34,200
C	0.36	0.20	0.56	55	30,800
D	0.36	0.35	0.71	180	127,800

(ii)   **Joint costs apportioned on net sales value of production**

	Product A £	B £	C £	D £	Total £
Sales	98,000	57,000	33,000	243,000	431,000
Less: Cost of sales	56,000	28,500	22,000	153,000	259,500
Gross profit	42,000	28,500	11,000	90,000	171,500
Less: Administration and selling costs:					84,700
Net profit					86,800

WORKINGS

	A	B	C	D	Total
	000 lb	*000 lb*	*000 lb*	*000 lb*	*000 lb*
Production	150	110	60	180	500
	£	£	£	£	£
Selling prices	0.70	0.60	0.60	1.35	
Sales value of production	105,000	66,000	36,000	243,000	450,000
Less: Additional costs	15,000	-	12,000	63,000	90,000
Net sales value of production	90,000	66,000	24,000	180,000	360,000
Apportioned joint cost (50%)	45,000	33,000	12,000	90,000	180,000
Additional costs	15,000	-	12,000	63,000	90,000
Production costs	60,000	33,000	24,000	153,000	270,000
Closing stock	$(\frac{10}{150})$4,000	$(\frac{15}{110})$4,500	$(\frac{5}{60})$2,000	-	10,500
Cost of sales	56,000	28,500	22,000	153,000	259,500

(d)   **Price comparison**

	Product		
	A	C	D
	£	£	£
Existing price per lb	0.70	0.60	1.35
Less: Additional costs per lb	0.10	0.20	0.35
Net revenue per lb	0.60	0.40	1.00
Overseas offer	0.65	0.52	0.90
Gain/(loss) per lb	0.05	0.12	(0.10)
Reduction in variable selling costs per lb	0.004	0.004	0.004
Net gain/(loss) per lb	0.054	0.124	(0.096)

Recommendation: sell Products A and B to the overseas customer.

(e)   **Increase in annual net profit**

	£
Additional revenue:	
Product A 50,000 lb @ £0.05	2,500
Product B 50,000 lb @ £0.12	6,000
	8,500
Add: Reduction in variable selling costs 100,000 lb @ £0.004	400
Net profit increase	8,900

Note: all other costs and revenue will be unaffected.

5 INTERNAL SERVICES AND SERVICE COSTING : ACTIVITY BASED COSTING

INTRODUCTION & LEARNING OBJECTIVES

When you have studied this chapter you should be able to do the following:

- Prepare records using service costing.

- Explain how costs per cost unit are used in service costing situations.

- Recognise when it is appropriate to use service costing.

- Appreciate the differences between activity based costing, (ABC) and traditional costing system.

- Prepare product cost computations using ABC.

- Evaluate the validity of the cost drivers used in ABC.

1 SERVICE COSTING

1.1 Service costing

Definition Service costing is the cost accounting method used in a business which provides a service, or in a service activity within any business to ascertain the cost of providing each unit of service.

Examples of organisations where services are being sold include:

- the utilities - electricity, gas, water and telephone
- the professions - accountancy, architects etc
- passenger and freight transport
- broadcasting
- hospitals
- theatres
- education.

Examples of types of service activities within businesses (most of which will not earn any external revenue) include:

- canteens
- training departments
- maintenance departments
- power generating departments
- cleaning departments
- welfare departments
- stores.

Management needs to ascertain the cost of providing each unit of service for both decision making and evaluation and control purposes. In decision making the cost per unit is important for pricing decisions if the service is being sold, and for deciding if it is better to provide the service 'in-house' or buy it in if the service is part of a business.

It is vital for evaluation and cost control purposes that management can compare (1) cost per unit in different locations or years, and (2) actual cost per unit with expected or budgeted cost per unit.

1.2   Selection of cost units

A major problem in service industries is the selection of a suitable cost unit. Management must decide how to measure the service being provided and what measures of performance are most appropriate to the control of costs. Some cost units used in different activities are:

Service	*Cost unit*
Electricity generation	Kilowatt hours
Canteens and restaurants	Meals served
Freight transport	Miles travelled: ton-miles
Hospitals	Patient-days
Passenger transport	Passenger-miles: seat-miles
Television	Hours of programmes
Education/training	Students taught

A service undertaking may use several different units to measure the various kinds of service provided eg, an hotel may use:

Service	*Cost unit*
Restaurant	Meals served
Hotel services	Guest-days
Function facilities	Hours

When appropriate cost units have been determined for a particular service, provision will need to be made for the collection of the appropriate statistical data. In a transport organisation this may involve the recording of mileages day-to-day for each vehicle in the fleet. For this each driver would be required to complete a log sheet. Fuel usage per vehicle and loads or weight carried may be appropriate for the business.

1.3   Calculation of cost per unit of service

Direct and indirect costs must be identified or assigned to each service department and described under suitable headings. This will be achieved by coding suppliers invoices and by applying predetermined absorption rates.

For a transport undertaking the main cost classification could be based on the following activities:

(a)   operating and running the fleet;
(b)   repairs and maintenance;
(c)   fixed charges;
(d)   administration.

Within each of these there would need to be a sub-classification of costs, each with its own code, so that under (c) fixed charges, there might appear the following breakdown:

(a)   road fund licences;
(b)   insurances;
(c)   depreciation;
(d)   vehicle testing fees; and
(e)   others.

In service costing it is often important to classify costs into their fixed and variable elements. Many service applications involve high fixed costs and the higher the number of cost units the lower the fixed costs per unit. The variable cost per unit will indicate to management the additional cost involved in the provision of one extra unit of service. In the context of a transport undertaking, fixed and variable costs are often referred to as standing and running costs respectively.

1.4   Cost sheets

At appropriate intervals (usually weekly or monthly) cost sheets will be prepared by the costing department to provide information to management about the appropriate service. A typical cost sheet for a service would incorporate the following for the current period and the cumulative year to date:

(a)   Cost information over the appropriate expense or activity headings totalled to give the total operating cost.

(b)   Information concerning the number of cost units produced.

(c)   Cost per unit calculations using the data in (a) and dividing by the data in (b). Different cost units may be used for different elements of costs and the same cost or group of costs may be related to different cost unit bases to provide additional control information to management. In the transport organisation, for example, the operating and running costs may be expressed in per mile and per day terms.

(d)   Analyses based on the physical cost units.

On a transport cost sheet, the following non-cost statistics may be shown:

- average miles covered per day;
- average miles per gallon of fuel.

2   EXAMPLE - BANKING

(a)   **Nature of the business**

Banking covers an enormously wide spectrum from multi-national universal banks at one end to the specialised institutions at the other.

The wider context is referred to only to the extent necessary to focus on one key area, that of domestic retail banking as represented by the British Clearing Banks.

The primary function of banking may be described as taking deposits and borrowing, lending, transmitting, exchanging and investing with the objectives of making profits out of the use of funds and the provision of services. Less obviously, the very heart and essence of the banking industry is the handling of information.

(b)   **Functional peculiarities, including funding**

'Banking', bankers have always claimed, 'is different'. But this must not be taken to imply that management techniques, developed in other industries have no application in banking, nor indeed that other industries can learn nothing from banking.

- Banks function by seeking to attract funds.

- Fund holding and funds transfer have historically been the main services provided, but many other services are now offered.

- The importance of the confidence factor.

- A final functional peculiarity is one that banks share with other organisations with similar economic characteristics of 'high volume, repetitive production of joint products, using large fixed investment and subject to uneven workflow'.

(c)   **Principal accounting problems**

From the accounting viewpoint banks differ from most other industrial organisations in that their business is entirely based on data and information.

Two further differences stem from the bank's product, financial value. The first is the need to maintain security - vital for instilling confidence. The second difference derives from the increasingly onerous reporting requirements of the regulatory authorities.

(d)   **Objectives of the accounting system**

- **Managerial**

  Information must be continuously available, certainly daily, and at all levels, to enable a mix of assets and liabilities to be managed.

- **Proprietorial and statutory**

  The format and content of financial statements of UK banks is determined by the Companies Acts, accounting standards and custom in the industry.

- **Regulation**

  The supervision of the Banking Sector by the Bank of England.

(e)   **Elements of cost**

Although the principles of costing are generally applicable, some understanding is necessary of cost characteristics, cost behaviour and the cost flow pattern fashioned by factors peculiar to banking.

- Variable work loads
- High fixed expenses
- Large fixed investment
- Production-line type of activities
- Joint products
- Predictability of activity
- Cost traceability
- Costing for marketing information.

3   ACTIVITY BASED APPROACHES TO COST ANALYSIS

3.1   Introduction

Definition   Activity Based Costing is the process of cost attribution to cost units on the basis of benefit received from indirect activities eg, ordering, setting up, assuring quality.

Bromwich & Bhimani give a somewhat wider definition using the term "Activity Based Accounting."

"Examination of activities across the entire chain of value adding organisational processes underlying causes (drivers) of cost and profit."

The wider definition introduces the important aspect that costs are incurred in selling and distributing a product and the costs of servicing customers are possibly now more important than production.

Another important definition is the cost driver:

Definition   A cost driver is an activity or factor which generates cost.

3.2   The origins of activity based costing

ABC first appeared in the 1950s when some US firms made attempts to accurately allocate their selling and distribution overheads. There was a plea in the literature in 1968 when Solomons (**Studies in Cost Analysis**) explored the need to obtain a reasonably accurate and objective indication of the differing factors driving overhead as a basis for more reliable variance computations. In the 1970s, when Zero-based budgeting came into vogue, some of the analysis was based upon activity. However, it was the work of Robin Cooper and R S Kaplan that eventually codified ABC into a coherent framework and disseminated it among academics, consultants and practitioners.

ABC is most appropriate where overhead is a relatively important cost element and there is a diversity of product lines and possibly markets. Essentially, it requires pooling the overhead spend and allocating it out over activities. Note the use of the term "allocate" indicating an objective cost driven charge rather than a subjective apportionment.

3.3   The mechanics of ABC

Three stages can be identified.

Step 1   The collection of overhead costs in the same way as traditional overhead control accounts would operate.

Step 2   The pooling of costs based upon the activities which have consumed resources rather than on the basis of production departments or centres. The activities selected are based upon four classes of transaction:-

- Logistical transactions - the moving and tracking of materials in and through the production process.

- Balancing transactions - matching resources with the demands of the production operation. This will include ensuring that resources are available when required.

- Quality transactions - ensuring output conforms with established specifications which will meet all market expectations.

- Change transactions - the need to respond to changes in customer demand, design changes, scheduling, supply and production methods.

Such transactions will frequently cross the traditional functional boundaries of an organisation.

Step 3   The various overhead transactions are then allocated to the products based upon a series of cost drivers which indicate how the product has made demands upon the various activities. The rates for charging out are based upon dividing the activity cost for a period by the cost driver volume. Thus the cost of the purchasing function will be divided by the number of purchase orders raised by each department.

3.4   Illustrative example

Oceanides has four departments who make use of the procurement function. The total cost of the function is £10,000,000 per annum. The four departments use the function in the following way:-

Department	No of orders	Cost allocation £
A	200,000	6,666,667

B	50,000	1,666,667
C	40,000	1,333,333
D	10,000	333,333
	300,000	10,000,000

Simply dividing the total cost by the cost driver we get:

$$\frac{£10,000,000}{300,000} = £33.33 \text{ per order}$$

3.5   Activity

Pelleas has the following indirect costs:

	£	No. of cost drivers
Quality control	90,000	450 inspections
Process set-up	135,000	450 set-ups
Purchasing	105,000	1,000 purchase orders
Customer order processing	120,000	2,000 customers
Occupancy costs	150,000	75,000 machine hours
	600,000	

Calculate the charge out rates for each of the activities.

3.6   Activity solution

Quality control	90,000	÷	450	=	£200 per inspection
Process set-up	135,000	÷	450	=	£300 per set-up
Purchasing	105,000	÷	1,000	=	£105 per order
Customer order processing	120,000	÷	2,000	=	£60 per customer
Occupancy costs	150,000	÷	75,000	=	£2 per machine hour

Note that occupancy cost has been allocated on traditional machine hours. The cost driver there is time, and as such, a conventional ABC method is not applicable. The student should remember that ABC will never cater 100% for all overheads.

3.7   Example

Pelleas, (the company in the above activity), makes a standard product called the Melisande.

The cost details are as follows:

Unit material cost	£0.50
Unit labour cost	£0.40
Total production for the coming year	1,000,000 units
Number of production runs	50
No. of purchase orders required	50
Number of customer orders	10
Unit machine time	3 minutes

The product run is inspected once at the end of each production run.

You are required to calculate the standard cost of a Melisande.

3.8   Solution

We need to draw up a grid for the overheads.

Function	Rate × Usage		£
Quality control	£200 × 50	=	10,000
Process set-up	£300 × 50	=	15,000
Purchasing	£105 × 50	=	5,250
Customer orders	£60 × 10	=	600
Occupancy	£2 × 50,000	=	100,000
			130,850

Dividing the total overhead cost by the number of units produced we get:

$$\frac{130,850}{1,000,000} = £0.1385 \text{ (say £0.14)}$$

Thus the standard unit cost for a Melisande is:

	£
Material	0.50
Labour	0.40
Overhead	0.14
	1.04

The typical examination question that has appeared thus far has required the student to compute overhead rates in the traditional manner and using the ABC method and compare the results over two or more products, one like the Melisande, (standard and with long runs), and others which are likely to be non-standard with short runs.

3.9   Selecting the cost drivers

In the main, the cost driver will be measured in terms of volume of transactions. However, ABC also tries to identify costs that are not contributing to the value of the product/service so the following questions are relevant:

- What services does this activity provide?
- Who receives the services?
- Why do you require so many people?
- What might cause you to require more/less staff?
- Why does over/idle time exist?

Three types of cost driver have emerged.

(a)   **Pure activity output volume** - where the basic transactions of the activity are identical in terms of their resource demands such as the purchasing of raw materials or a similar range of items.

(b)   **Activity/output volume/complexity** - where the basic transactions differ in terms of their resource demands as when purchases are made from different overseas suppliers.

(c)   **Situation** - where an underlying factor can be identified as driving the workload of an activity such as the number of suppliers when supplier vetting and liaison were vital components of the cost pool.

3.10   Examples of cost drivers

The following are examples of cost drivers.

Activity	Cost driver
Material procurement	No. of purchase orders
Material handling	No. of movements
Quality control	No. of inspections
Engineering services	No. of change orders
Maintenance	No. of break-downs
Line set-up	No. of set-ups

For the service sector the following taken from the field of Health Care may serve as an example. The cost drivers form the basis of costs charged to patients.

Activity	Cost driver
Patient movement	No. of in-patients
Booking appointments	No. of patients
Patient reception	No. of patients
X-ray:	
Equipment preparation	Time taken
Patient preparation	Time taken
Patient aftercare	Time taken
Film processing	No. of images
Film reporting	No. of images

From Kirton "ABC at Luton & Dunstable Hospital"

3.11   The merits of ABC

An improved more accurate product cost may enable a company to concentrate on a more profitable mix of products or customers. ABC has been effectively used in identifying customers who are unprofitable to service.

It is argued that traditional overhead apportionment leads to incorrect commitment of resources to products.

ABC extends the variable cost rationale to both short and long term costs by quantitatively addressing the cost behaviour patterns in terms of both short run volume changes as well as long term cost trends.

It helps identify value added and non-value added costs so that the non-value added items can be appraised effectively with a view to elimination. As such it forces managers and supervisors to consider the drivers that effect costs and what these drivers contribute to the final product.

Thus the managers will have a better understanding of the economics of production and the economics of the activities performed by the company.

3.12   A warning

Ahmed and Scapens (**Cost allocation: theory and practice 1991**) warned that ABC was unlikely to relate all overheads to specific activities. It also ignores the potential for conflict, especially where there are more than one potential cost driver.

More recently, the warning has been reiterated by emphasising that there is no such thing as a 100% accurate cost. At best, ABC will only improve the quality of cost information. The student should perhaps note Brimson's 1991 definition of product cost - "a summation of the cost of all traceable activities to design, procure material, manufacture and distribute a product."

Perhaps the key word in that definition is traceable, whether or not a cost can be traced objectively to the production/delivery of a good/service.

3.13 Activity based costing and traditional total absorption costing

As production processes become ever more complex and as overhead costs continually replace direct costs (for example as processes become less labour intensive, depreciation costs replace wages) the method used to allocate indirect costs to cost units becomes increasingly vital.

Which method gives the better treatment of overheads and thus provides the best information for decision making?

Generally, the arguments come down in favour of ABC because it treats each cost type separately, using a different cost driver each time. This is an improvement on traditional methods which tend to add all overheads together and then absorb on a single measure of activity, commonly labour hours. Although, under traditional methods, different absorption methods could be used for each type of cost there are only a limited number of bases available.

4   CHAPTER SUMMARY

This chapter has explained the method of costing appropriate to service departments and service industries and has explained the techniques and principles of activity based costing.

5   SELF-TEST QUESTIONS

5.1   Explain how cost units are identified in service industries. (1.3)

5.2   Why is it necessary to collect service costs? (1.4)

5.3   What is Activity Based Costing? (3.1)

5.4   Explain the mechanics of ABC. (3.3)

5.5   Explain how cost drivers are selected. (3.9)

6   EXAMINATION TYPE QUESTIONS

6.1   Hotel rooms

(a)   Describe the benefits which cost accounting provides for an organisation.

Note: You may refer to your own experience in answering this question.   **(7 marks)**

(b)   The following information is provided for a 30 day period for the Rooms Department of a hotel:

	Rooms with twin beds	Single rooms
Number of rooms in hotel	260	70
Number of rooms available to let	240	40
Average number of rooms occupied daily	200	30
Number of guests in period	6,450	
Average length of stay	2 days	
Total revenue in period	£774,000	
Number of employees	200	
Payroll costs for period	£100,000	
Items laundered in period	15,000	
Cost of cleaning supplies in period	£5,000	
Total cost of laundering	£22,500	
Listed daily rate for twin-bedded room	£110	
Listed daily rate for single room	£70	

The hotel calculates a number of statistics, including the following:

Room occupancy	Total number of rooms occupied as a percentage of rooms available to let.
Bed occupancy	Total number of beds occupied as a percentage of beds available.
Average guest rate	Total revenue divided by number of guests.
Revenue utilisation	Actual revenue as a percentage of maximum revenue from available rooms.
Average cost per occupied bed	Total cost divided by number of beds occupied.

You are required to

Prepare a table which contains the following statistics, calculated to one decimal place:

Room occupancy (%)
Bed occupancy (%)
Average guest rate (£)
Revenue utilisation (%)
Cost of cleaning supplies per occupied room per day (£)
Average cost per occupied bed per day (£)   **(12 marks)**

(c)   Explain what you understand by the following terms:

Cost unit
Cost centre   **(4 marks)**

(d)   Identify **one cost centre** which might exist in a hotel, excluding the Rooms Department. For the cost centre identified give an appropriate **cost unit**.   **(2 marks)**
                                                                             (Total: 25 marks)

6.2   ABC terms

(a)   In the context of activity based costing (ABC), it was stated in **Management Accounting - Evolution not Revolution** by Bromwich and Bhimani, that

"Cost drivers attempt to link costs to the scope of output rather than the scale of output thereby generating less arbitrary product costs for decision making."

You are required to explain the terms 'activity based costing' and 'cost drivers'.   **(8 marks)**

(b)   XYZ plc manufactures four products, namely A, B, C and D, using the same plant and processes.

The following information relates to a production period:

Product	Volume	Material cost per unit	Direct labour per unit	Machine time per unit	Labour cost per unit
A	500	£5	½ hour	¼ hour	£3
B	5,000	£5	½ hour	¼ hour	£3
C	600	£16	2 hours	1 hour	£12
D	7,000	£17	1½ hours	1½ hours	£9

Total production overhead recorded by the cost accounting system is analysed under the following headings:

Factory overhead applicable to machine-oriented activity is £37,424.

Set-up costs are £4,355.

The cost of ordering materials is £1,920.

Handling materials - £7,580.

Administration for spare parts - £8,600.

These overhead costs are absorbed by products on a machine hour rate of £4.80 per hour, giving an overhead cost per product of:

A = £1.20   B = £1.20   C = £4.80   D = £7.20

However, investigation into the production overhead activities for the period reveals the following totals:

Product	Number of set-ups	Number of material orders	Number of times material was handled	Number of spare parts
A	1	1	2	2
B	6	4	10	5
C	2	1	3	1
D	8	4	12	4

You are required:

(i)   to compute an overhead cost per product using activity based costing, tracing overheads to production units by means of cost drivers;   **(6 marks)**

(ii)   to comment briefly on the differences disclosed between overheads traced by the present system and those traced by activity based costing.   **(3 marks)**
                                                                                   (Total: 17 marks)

7   ANSWER TO EXAMINATION TYPE QUESTION

7.1   Hotel rooms

(Tutorial notes

(1)   Part (a) requires a general knowledge of cost accounting. Those students with practical experience will have little difficulty with this part of the question, but full-time students or those who do not work in a manufacturing environment will not find it easy to produce an answer worth seven marks.

(2)   Part (b) initially appears to be 'odd' and rather difficult. But read carefully the notes relating to the calculation of the statistics and this turns out to be an easy question.

(3)   Parts (c) and (d) are both basic cost accounting. Well-prepared students will not find these difficult.)

(a)   The cost accounting systems will take basic cost data and, by following the basic costing principles, using one or more of the costing techniques in accordance with one or more of the costing methods, will produce information which can be used by management for planning, controlling and decision-making. The establishment of budgets, standard costs and actual costs will aid in the management of the organisation.

A specific example would be the establishment of standard costs and the reporting of actuals against these standards, the resulting variances being used for the control of operations, processes and departments.

(b)   Room occupancy $= \dfrac{\text{Total number of rooms occupied}}{\text{Rooms available to be let}}$

$= \dfrac{200 + 30}{240 + 40}$

$= 82.1\%$

Bed occupancy $= \dfrac{\text{Total number of beds occupied}}{\text{Total number of beds available}}$

$= \dfrac{6{,}450 \text{ guests} \times 2 \text{ days per guest}}{((240 \times 2) + (40 \times 1)) \times 30 \text{ days}}$

$= \dfrac{12{,}900}{15{,}600}$

$= 82.7\%$

Average guest rate $= \dfrac{\text{Total revenue}}{\text{Number of guests}}$

$= \dfrac{\pounds774{,}000}{6{,}450}$

$= \pounds120$

Revenue utilisation $= \dfrac{\text{Actual revenue}}{\text{Maximum revenue from available rooms}}$

$= \dfrac{\pounds774{,}000}{((240 \times \pounds110) + (40 \times \pounds70)) \times 30 \text{ days}}$

$= \dfrac{\pounds774{,}000}{876{,}000}$

$= 88.4\%$

Cost of cleaning supplies
per occupied room per day $= \dfrac{\pounds5{,}000}{(200 + 30) \times 30 \text{ days}}$

$= \pounds0.7$

Average cost per occupied bed
per day $= \dfrac{\text{Total cost}}{\text{Number of beds occupied}}$

$= \dfrac{\pounds100{,}000 + \pounds5{,}000 + \pounds22{,}500}{6{,}450 \times 2}$

$= \pounds9.9$

(c)   **Cost unit**

A quantitative unit of product in relation to which costs are ascertained. They can be used to help build up the cost of a unit of output. In manufacturing firms the cost unit will often be the unit product, while for servicing firms (eg, road haulage) it will relate to the type of service eg, cost per tonne/mile.

Cost centre

This is a location, function or item of equipment in respect of which costs may be ascertained and related to cost units for control purposes. They often enable production costs to be related to cost units in a structured manner.

(d)   **Note**:   Students should try to consider all the separate activities that take place in a hotel and select one where they are carried out in a separately identifiable department or area.

Cost centre:	Kitchen	or	Restaurant
Cost unit:	Meals produced	or	Meals served

7.2   ABC terms

(a)   Activity based costing is a method of costing which is based on the principle that activities cause costs to be incurred not products. Costs are attributed to activities and the performance of those activities is then linked to products.

A cost driver is the factor which causes costs to be incurred (eg, placing an order, setting up a machine).

(b)   (i)   Cost per set-up $\dfrac{£4,355}{1+6+2+8} = \dfrac{£4,355}{17} = $ **£256**

Cost per order $\dfrac{£1,920}{1+4+1+4} = \dfrac{£1,920}{10} = $ **£192**

Cost per handling of materials $\dfrac{£7,580}{2+10+3+12} = \dfrac{£7,580}{27} = $ **£281**

Cost per spare part $\dfrac{£8,600}{2+5+1+4} = \dfrac{£8,600}{12} = $ **£717**

Cost per machine hour (No. of m/c hours = 125 + 1,250 + 600 + 10,500)

$= \dfrac{£37,424}{12,475} = $ **£3.00/hr**

Costs are then attributed to products using the cost driver rates calculated above, for example:

Product A requires one machine set-up, therefore 1 × £256 = £256;
Product B requires six machine set-ups, therefore 6 × £256 = £1,536;
and so on.

Product	A	B	C	D
	£	£	£	£
Activities:				
Set-ups	256	1,536	512	2,048
Orders	192	768	192	768
Handling	562	2,810	843	3,372
Spare parts	1,434	3,585	717	2,868
Machine time	375	3,750	1,800	31,500
	2,819	12,449	4,064	40,556
No. of units	500	5,000	600	7,000
Cost per unit	£5.64	£2.49	£6.77	£5.79

The costs are then totalled and divided by the number of units to give the cost per unit for each product.

(ii)   The activity based costing approach attributes more costs to products A, B and C and less to product D than the traditional method of accounting for overhead costs. The activity based costing method gives a more accurate cost by relating it to the resources used to manufacture each product, consequently these costs are more useful for decision making than those provided by the traditional method.

6 ABSORPTION V MARGINAL REVISITED : AN INTRODUCTION TO COST CONTROL

INTRODUCTION & LEARNING OBJECTIVES

When you have studied this chapter you should be able to do the following:

- Prepare reports under both absorption costing and marginal costing.
- Explain why the profit reported by these systems may be different.
- Explain the principles of cost control.

1 MARGINAL COSTING

1.1 Introduction

This section is concerned with the application of the marginal cost technique as a costing system which is an alternative to the absorption costing system described earlier.

Marginal costing is the term applied when the routine cost accounting system incorporates the marginal principle. Under absorption costing the unit cost includes an absorbed amount calculated from total overheads ie, fixed plus variable. Under marginal costing only variable costs are charged to cost units; fixed costs for a period are fully written off against contribution.

1.2 Marginal costing

 The accounting system in which variable costs are charged to cost units and fixed costs of the period are written off in full against the aggregate contribution of the period.

The fundamental difference between marginal and absorption costing is therefore one of timing; under marginal costing fixed production overheads are charged in the period incurred. Under absorption costing fixed production overheads are absorbed into units made and charged in the period of sale.

1.3 Example

Company A produces a single product with the following budget:

Selling price	£10
Direct materials	£3 per unit
Direct wages	£2 per unit
Variable overhead	£1 per unit
Fixed overhead	£10,000 per month.

The fixed overhead absorption rate is based on volume of 5,000 units per month. Show the operating statement for the month, when 4,800 units were produced and sold under:

(a) absorption costing;
(b) marginal costing.

Assume that costs were as budget.

1.4   Solution

(a)   **Absorption costing**

	£
Sales (4,800 units)	48,000
Cost of sales (4,800 × £8) (W1)	38,400
Operating margin	9,600
Under absorbed overhead (W2)	(400)
Operating profit	9,200

WORKINGS

(W1)   Unit cost represents materials (£3) + wages (£2) + variable overhead (£1) + fixed overhead absorbed $(\frac{£10,000}{5,000})$ = £8 per unit.

The actual activity level is not the same as the budgeted level and thus the predetermined absorption rate of $\frac{£10,000}{5,000 \text{ units}}$ ie, £2 per unit results in an under absorption of fixed overheads which must be adjusted for in the operating statement.

ie,

		£
(W2)	Fixed overhead incurred	10,000
	Fixed overhead absorbed	9,600 (4,800 × £2)
	Under absorption	400

An adjustment for under or over absorption of fixed overheads will be necessary if (i) the actual activity level is different to that budgeted, or (ii) actual expenditure on fixed overheads is different to that budgeted.

(b)   **Marginal costing**

	£
Sales	48,000
Variable cost of sales (4,800 × £6)	28,800
Contribution	19,200
Fixed costs	10,000
Operating profit	9,200

In the example operating profit is the same under both methods. That will not be so, however, when production is more or less than sales ie, stocks of finished goods are maintained.

Under marginal costing stocks of work in progress and finished products will be valued at variable costs only. Where production and sales levels are not in sympathy and stock levels are fluctuating, the net profit will be different from that disclosed by an absorption method of costing which values stocks of work in progress and finished products to include an amount of absorbed fixed production overheads.

1.5   Example

Use the same price and cost information as in the example at 1.3 but assume that production was 4,800 units and sales were 4,500 units. The company has no opening stocks. Show the operating statement for the month under

(a)   absorption costing
(b)   marginal costing, and
(c)   reconcile the difference in reported profit.

1.6   Solution

(a)   **Absorption costing**

	£	£
Sales (4,500 × £10)		45,000
Cost of sales		
opening stock	-	
production cost (4,800 × £8)	38,400	
closing stock (300 × £8)	(2,400)	
		(36,000)
Operating margin		9,000
Under absorbed overhead		(400)
Operating profit		8,600

(b)   **Marginal costing**

	£	£
Sales (4,500 × £10)		45,000
Cost of sales		
opening stock	-	
production cost (4,800 × £6)	28,800	
closing stock (300 × £6)	(1,800)	
		(27,000)
Contribution		18,000
Fixed costs		10,000
Operating profit		8,000

(c)   **Reconciliation of profit figures**

	£	£
Profit under marginal costing		8,000
Closing stock valuation under absorption costing (300 × £8)	2,400	
Closing stock valuation under marginal costing (300 × £6)	1,800	
Fixed costs absorbed into closing stock in absorption costing		600
Profit under absorption costing		£8,600

1.7   Advantages claimed for marginal costing

Preparation of routine operating statements using absorption costing is considered less informative because:

(a)   Profit per unit is a misleading figure: in the example the operating margin of £2 per unit arises because fixed overhead per unit is based on 5,000 units. If another basis were used, margin per unit would differ even though fixed overhead was the same amount in total.

(b)   Build-up or run-down of stocks of finished goods can distort comparison of period operating statements and obscure the effect of increasing or decreasing sales. Note that in the first example if production had been 6,000 units ie, 4,800 sold plus 1,200 held in stock, the absorption costing statement would show:

	£	£
Sales		48,000
Cost of sales:		
Production 6,000 × £8	48,000	
Closing stock 1,200 × £8	9,600	
		38,400
Operating margin		9,600
Over absorbed fixed overhead (6,000 × £2) – £10,000		2,000
Operating profit		11,600

A marginal costing statement would, however, still show a profit of £9,200 because production and closing stocks are valued at the variable cost of £6 per unit.

(c)   Comparison between products can be misleading because of the effect of arbitrary apportionment of fixed costs.

1.8   Defence of absorption costing

Absorption costing is widely used and the student should understand both principles. Defenders of the absorption principle point out that:

(a)   it is necessary to include fixed overhead in stock values for financial statements; routine cost accounting using absorption costing produces stock values which include a share of fixed overhead;

(b)   for small jobbing business, overhead allotment is the only practicable way of obtaining job costs for estimating and profit analysis;

(c)   analysis of under/over absorbed overhead is useful to identify inefficient utilisation of production resources.

2   BUDGETARY CONTROL

2.1   Introduction - Control system

Definition   'A control system is a communications network that monitors activities within the organisation and provides the basis for corrective action in the future' (Drury).

A budgetary control system is widely regarded as the most important financial control system in an organisation. This section is primarily concerned with factors that affect the effectiveness of the budget as a control system.

2.2   Classification of controls

There is a widely accepted three-way classification of controls into **organisational, informal group** and **individual**. The table below compares these classes:

Type	Objectives	Performance criteria	Feedback	Incentives	
				Rewards or reinforcements	Punishments or sanctions
Organisation	Profits, share of market: quality of service	Budgets, standard costs, past performance	Quantitative variances	Commendation, promotions, salary rises	Condemnation, dismissal, salary cuts
Informal group	Mutual commitment, group ideals	Group norms	Deviant behaviour	Peer approval, membership, leadership	Kidding, hostility, ostracism
Individual	Personal goals, aspirations	Expectations, interim targets	Reaching or missing targets	Self-satisfaction, elation	Disappointment, self-hatred

Though the main concern in management accounting is with organisational controls, all three categories are relevant in the management process.

2.3   Concept of budgetary control

The budgetary control cycle can be illustrated as follows:

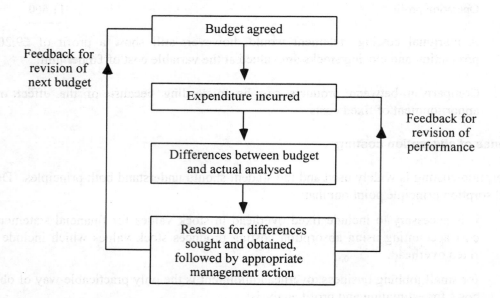

The various stages in the cycle will be discussed in turn.

2.4   Feedforward control

In order to have overall organisational control it is essential to have **feedforward** control as well as **feedback** control. Feedback control compares actual outputs with predetermined objectives, while in feedforward control predictions are made of what outputs are expected to be at some future time. In some ways all planning is a form of feedforward control. If the initial plans differ from what is desired at that time, control actions are implemented that will minimise these differences.

An important example of feedforward control is cash planning. This is especially important where an enterprise must work within predetermined overdraft limits. Failure to do so may result in the liquidation of the enterprise. Feedback control is not appropriate in these circumstances. The possibility of exceeding the overdraft limits must be appreciated in advance; it is of little use to know that the strict limits have been exceeded, which is how the information would be reported in a feedback control system. Stock control systems with minimum and maximum stores levels also require the use of feedforward control eg, system required to prevent 'stock-outs' of vital materials and components.

Feedforward controls give management warnings that they should not ignore.

2.5   Agreement of budget

The first stage is marked 'Budget agreed'. Budgets should not be imposed on those who have to work within them, but should be arrived at by a process of discussion between those who are to spend the money, their superiors and the finance department.

2.6   Analysis of variances

This is the stage marked 'Differences between budget and actual analysed'. This stage presents several problems: how often are the variances to be extracted (most businesses use monthly, weekly or even daily systems - a year is too long for control purposes) and how are they to be analysed? Variance analysis is described in detail later.

2.7   Use of variances

The aim of a budgetary control system is not to assign blame for past variances, which cannot be retrieved, but to use the knowledge gained from the explanation of those variances to:

(a)   take immediate action to improve current and future performance;
(b)   improve the plans for future periods.

The reporting of variances to appropriate managers within the organisation structure is a good example of the well-established concept of **management by exception.** This involves highlighting for the attention of management the deviations or exceptions from the plan, rather than inundating managers with a lot of information about actual results which are very much in line with the budgets. In this way the important items which require the attention of management are not camouflaged amongst the whole information package. This approach should reduce the delay and speed up the decision-making process.

2.8   Applicability of budgetary control

Budgetary control can be operated to a greater or lesser degree in most types of organisation. It may or may not be linked to a system of standard costing - a point that will be dealt with later. Budgeting is often discussed in the context of an industrial organisation where sales budgets usually dictate the levels of other budgets (ie, sales are the principal budget factor). However, non-trading organisations also operate budgetary control systems eg, local authorities budget their expenditure (and revenue) to fix the council tax for the year. It is then of great importance that expenditure levels are closely controlled, for it is difficult (and usually politically embarrassing) to attempt to impose supplementary charges at a later date in the same financial year. Budgetary control takes on a very important role in these circumstances.

2.9   Budget reporting

The feedback loop in the control system requires a formal reporting procedure. This link is vital in that the budget system may identify variances, and hence problems, but unless these are effectively communicated to management, that knowledge is ineffective. In the context of budget systems, feedback reports consist of comparisons of budget targets and actual financial achievements, with differences highlighted as variances.

General criteria may be laid down for such reports:

(a)   **Reports should be relevant to the information needs of their recipients.** This means that the report should contain all relevant information to the decisions to be made, and responsibilities exercised by the manager who receives the report. Generally, other information should be excluded although there is an argument for including background information on divisional/company performance.

(b)   **Reporting should be linked to responsibility.** This is discussed in more detail below.

(c)   **Reports should be timely.** One of the most frequent reporting problems is that reports are received after the decision for which they are required. In such cases managers must often rely on informal information sources outside the budget system. This may be less efficient, and also reduces the credibility of the budgetary control system in the eyes of that manager.

(d)   **Reports should be reliable.** The reports should be regarded as containing reliable information (though not necessarily exact to the penny). There may be a conflict between reliability and timeliness, and often an assessment must be made of what is an acceptable error rate and/or degree of approximation.

(e)   **Reports should be designed to communicate effectively.** Reports should be specifically designed to communicate effectively, often with managers who are not professional accountants. Reports should avoid jargon, be concise, but contain sufficient detail (often in supporting schedules). Maximum use should be made of graphical presentation.

(f)   **Reports should be cost-effective.** A report is only worthwhile if the benefits from its existence exceed the cost of producing it.

2.10   Control of non-manufacturing costs

Non-manufacturing costs present their own specific problems of budgetary control, in addition to those already discussed in the context of manufacturing costs. Such costs are unlikely to vary with the level of production activity, but they may represent a significant proportion of total costs. Therefore, specific budgetary control techniques must be developed to deal with such costs.

These costs would include research and development, administration and finance, marketing and distribution.

(a)   **Alternative activity measures**

Since the costs are not related to production activity, some alternative activity measure must be identified. Possible examples would be marketing costs per sales order and purchasing costs per delivery.

(b)   **Committed fixed costs**

> **Definition**   These are fixed costs incurred for a series of accounting periods because of some past decision. An example would be lease costs as a result of entering into a lease agreement. Because of their implications for future accounting periods such costs must be considered in the same way as a capital expenditure proposal.

(c)   **Discretionary fixed costs**

> **Definition**   These are costs which are fixed only in the sense that they are unaffected by the level of production; from a decisional point of view they are entirely within the discretion of management. Examples include advertising expenditure, research and development and training costs. In all of these cases there is no direct link between expenditure and revenues.

This makes the task of defining an appropriate level of expenditure extremely difficult. Various approaches are possible, but they all have failings:

(i)   Past expenditure - but this may perpetuate past mistakes.
(ii)   Other similar companies - but they may have it wrong.
(iii)   A percentage of sales - but the percentage selected must be arbitrary.

From the management control point of view, it is essential that such costs are controlled by fixed budgets that form ceilings on expenditure.

(d)   **Measuring effectiveness**

It follows from the above that controlling the effectiveness of non-manufacturing costs can be very difficult. However, this is not to suggest that it is impossible, and the cost accountant should actively seek measures of effectiveness. Examples would include percentage utilisation of training instructor's time, sales per marketing campaign, etc.

2.11   Control in non-profit organisations

The major problems of non-profit organisations are:

(a)   difficulty of quantifying objectives - eg, animal welfare may be a legitimate objective, but it is not easily amenable to quantification;

(b)   lack of outputs quantifiable in monetary terms - eg, if the output is improved health care in an Asian village, the gains may be real, but they are not monetary.

The largest examples of non-profit organisations are government bureaucracies, and effective budgetary control continues to create problems in these areas in spite of government's attempts to control expenditure.

2.12   Management audit

Management audits tend to have developed in the context of non-profit organisations, but can also be an effective management control in profit-orientated entities. Their objective is to improve management performance by identifying waste and inefficiencies, and recommending corrective action. In this sense management audits should be clearly distinguished from traditional financial audits. A management audit would concentrate on the following specific aspects:

(a)   nature and functioning of the entity's managerial systems and procedures;
(b)   economy and efficiency with which the entity's services are provided; and
(c)   the entity's effectiveness in achieving objectives.

Generally a management audit should consist of the following phases:

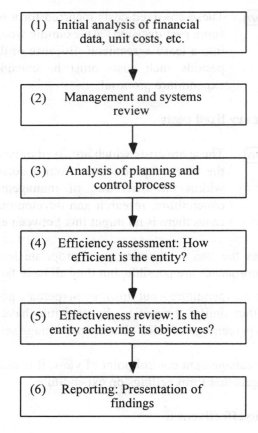

(1)   Initial analysis of financial data, unit costs, etc.

(2)   Management and systems review

(3)   Analysis of planning and control process

(4)   Efficiency assessment: How efficient is the entity?

(5)   Effectiveness review: Is the entity achieving its objectives?

(6)   Reporting: Presentation of findings

Management audits can be undertaken either by an internal team of specialists or by external consultants.

2.13   Responsibility accounting

Budgetary control and responsibility accounting are inseparable. An organisation chart must be drawn up in order to implement a budgetary control system. It may even be necessary to revise the existing organisation structure before designing the system. The aim is to ensure that each manager has a well-defined area of responsibility and the authority to make decisions within that area, and that no parts of the organisation remain as 'grey' areas where it is uncertain who is responsible for them. This area of responsibility may be simply a **cost centre** or it may be a **profit centre** (implying that the manager has control over sales revenues as well as costs) or an **investment centre** (implying that the manager is empowered to take decisions about capital investment for his department). Once senior management have set up such a structure, with the degree of delegation implied, some form of responsibility accounting system is needed. Each centre will have its own budget, and the manager will receive control information relevant to that budget centre. Costs (and possibly revenue, assets and liabilities) must be traced to the person primarily responsible for taking the related decisions, and identified with the appropriate department.

Some accountants would go as far as to advocate charging ie, actually debiting, departments with costs that arise strictly as a result of decisions made by the management of those departments. For example, if the marketing department insists on a special rush order which necessitates overtime working in production departments, then the marketing department and not the production departments should be charged with the overtime premiums incurred. However, there are practical problems with such an approach:

(a)   The rush order itself might actually be produced during normal time because, from a production scheduling angle, it might be more convenient to do it then (eg, because it would not involve a clean-down of the machines as it was compatible with some other orders currently in production) - normal orders thereby actually being produced during the period of 'overtime'.

(b)   Re-charging costs to other departments can become a common occurrence because managers see it as a way of passing on not only the costs but also the associated responsibility eg, if the rush order is produced inefficiently in overtime, should the costs of the inefficiency also be charged to the marketing department?

(c)   Re-charging on a large scale can cause a lot of extra administration and explanation to the recipient department at the reporting stage.

It is worth concluding with the comment that all the managers do work for the same organisation and, if the costs are shunted around, there is a nil effect on the overall profit of the organisation (except to the extent of any extra costs incurred in operating such a recharging system). Perhaps the effort expended on such a system could be more positively used to increase overall profit.

2.14   Controllable costs

Performance reports should concentrate only on **controllable costs.** Controllable costs are those costs controllable by a particular manager in a given time period. Over a long enough time-span most costs are controllable by someone in the organisation eg, factory rental may be fixed for a number of years but there may eventually come an opportunity to move to other premises. Such a cost, therefore, is controllable in the long term by a manager fairly high in the organisation structure. However, in the short term it is uncontrollable even by him, and certainly not by managers lower down in the organisation.

There is no clear-cut distinction between controllable and non-controllable costs for a given manager, who may in any case be exercising control jointly with another manager. The aim under a responsibility accounting system will be to assign and report on the cost to the person having **primary** responsibility. Most effective control is thereby achieved, since immediate action can be taken.

Some authorities would favour the alternative idea that reports should include all costs caused by a department, whether controllable or uncontrollable by the departmental manager. The idea here is that, even if he has no direct control, he might influence the manager who does have control. There is the danger of providing the manager with too much information and confusing him but, on the other hand, the uncontrollable element could be regarded as for 'information only', and in this way the manager obtains a fuller picture.

An illustration of the two different approaches is provided by raw materials. The production manager will have control over usage, but not over price, when buying is done by a separate department. For this reason the price and usage variances are separated and, under the first approach, the production manager would be told only about the usage variance, a separate report being made to the purchasing manager about the price variance. The alternative argument is that if the production manager is also told about the price variance, he may attempt to persuade the purchasing manager to try alternative sources of supply.

2.15   The problem of dual responsibility

A common problem is that the responsibility for a particular cost or item is shared between two (or more) managers. For example, the responsibility for payroll costs may be shared between the personnel and production departments; material costs between purchasing and production departments; and so on. The reporting system should be designed so that the responsibility for performance achievements (ie, better or worse than budget) is identified as that of a single manager.

The following guidelines may be applied:

(a)   If manager controls quantity **and** price - responsible for all expenditure variances.

(b)   If manager controls quantity but **not** price - only responsible for variances due to usage.

(c)   If manager controls price but **not** quantity - only responsible for variances due to input prices.

(d)   If manager controls **neither** quantity **nor** price - variances uncontrollable from the point of view of that manager.

2.16   Budgetary control and responsibility centres

The table below indicates how standard cost variances might be the responsibility of different responsibility centres:

Responsibility centre				*Product*			
	A	*B*	*C*	*D*	*E*	*F*	*G*
1	x	x		x			
2			x		x	x	
3				x	x		x
4		x	x			x	

Thus, for all the products except A, C and G more than one centre is responsible for their production. Therefore, it is not possible for products B, D, E and F to make one centre exclusively responsible for variances in relation to that product. Instead the system must ensure that each centre is made responsible for the variances within its control.

2.17   Guidelines for reporting

There are several specific problems in relation to reporting which must be identified and dealt with:

(a)   **Levels of reporting**

The problem is how far down the management structure should responsibility centres be identified for reporting purposes? On the one hand, lower reporting levels encourage delegation and identify responsibility closer to the production process. On the other hand, more responsibility centres increase the number of reports and hence the cost of their production. One solution may be to combine small responsibility centres into groups (eg, departments) for reporting purposes.

(b)   **Frequency of reports and information to be reported**

The frequency of reports should be linked to the purposes for which they are required. This may well mean a variety of reports being produced to different time-scales for different purposes eg, some control information will be required weekly, or even daily. However, comprehensive budget reports are only likely to be required monthly.

The related problem is the content of such reports. It has been suggested that in computerised information systems the problem is often too much, rather than too little information. Generally, as reporting proceeds up the management pyramid, the breadth of the report should increase, and the detail should decrease. The following series of reports illustrate this principle:

	Budget		Variance	
	Current month	*Year to date*	*Current month*	*Year to date*

Managing director

Factory A
Factory B
Administration costs
Selling costs
Distribution costs
R&D costs

Production director Factory A

Machining department
Casting department
Assembly department
Inspection and quality control
Factory manager's office

Head of machining department

Direct materials
Direct labour
Indirect labour
Power
Maintenance
Other

The above layout should only be regarded as illustrative, but it does indicate how detail increases as span decreases.

2.18   Limitations of using historic costs

The cost accountant must be careful when using analysis of historical costs as a basis for predicting future costs. This is true even if he is fully satisfied with the accuracy of the analysis. The reasons are:

(a)   It is difficult and costly to obtain sufficient data to be confident that a representative sample is used.

(b)   Prediction implies a continuing relationship of costs to volume. In practice, methods and efficiency change.

(c)   The relationship between costs and volume may be obscured by time-lags eg, recruiting trainee labour in anticipation of increased production.

(d)   Factors other than volume of production can influence costs eg, purchasing in small lots could increase handling and incidental material costs.

(e)   Prices of the input factors may change eg, due to inflation or technical change.

(f)   The analysis is based on the assumption that the cost/activity relationship is linear.

3   COST CONTROL AND DIFFERENT BUSINESSES

3.1   Introduction

Many different types of business exist, most of which use some form of cost control. The following paragraphs illustrate some of the different approaches to cost control which may be used.

3.2   Product based business

These businesses are those which produce a standard product range. Volumes of product may be estimated and their costs predicted with much accuracy. These target costs may then be compared with actual results.

3.3   Specific order businesses

These businesses use a range of skills to provide a product which are specific to the needs of individual customers.

In these businesses, measurement of output is often resource related eg, labour hours, machine hours. Other direct costs depend on the work obtained and as such will be passed on to the customer. In these businesses control is exercised by measuring capacity utilisation and efficiency.

4   CHAPTER SUMMARY

In this chapter, marginal costing and absorption costing were compared with particular reference to the effect on profits reported.

The second part of this chapter considered the principles of cost control.

5   SELF TEST QUESTIONS

5.1   Define 'Marginal Costing'. (1.2)

5.2   What are the advantages of marginal costing? (1.7)

5.3   What is feedforward control? (2.4)

5.4   What are committed fixed costs? (2.10)

5.5   What are discretionary fixed costs? (2.10)

6   EXAMINATION TYPE QUESTION

6.1   RH Ltd

RH Ltd makes and sells one product, the standard production cost of which is as follows for one unit:

		£
Direct labour	3 hours at £6 per hour	18
Direct materials	4 kilograms at £7 per kg	28
Production overhead	Variable	3
	Fixed	20
Standard production cost		69

Normal output is 16,000 units per annum and this figure is used for the fixed production overhead calculation.

Costs relating to selling, distribution and administration are

Variable	20 per cent of sales value
Fixed	£180,000 per annum.

The only variance is a fixed production overhead volume variance. There are no units in finished goods stock at 1 October 19X2. The fixed overhead expenditure is spread evenly throughout the year. The selling price per unit is £140.

For the two six-monthly periods detailed below, the number of units to be produced and sold are budgeted as:

	Six months ending *31 March 19X3*	*Six months ending* *30 September 19X3*
Production	8,500	7,000
Sales	7,000	8,000

You are required:

(a)   to prepare statements for management showing sales, costs and profits for **each** of the six-monthly periods, using

(i)   marginal costing,   **(6 marks)**

(ii)   absorption costing;   **(9 marks)**

(b)   to prepare an explanatory statement reconciling for **each** six-monthly period the profit using marginal costing with the profit using absorption costing;   **(4 marks)**

(c)   to state and explain **three** business situations where the use of marginal costing may be beneficial to management in making a decision.   **(6 marks)**

                                                                                                                   (Total: 25 marks)

7   ANSWER TO EXAMINATION TYPE QUESTION

7.1   RH Ltd

(a)   (i)   **Marginal costing statement**

	Six months ending *31 March 19X3*		*Six months ending* *30 September 19X3*	
	£'000	£'000	£'000	£'000
Sales		980		1,120
Variable cost of sales				
opening stock	-		73.5	
production cost				
8,500 units @ £49	416.5			
7,000 units @ £49			343	
	416.5		416.5	
less closing stock				
1,500 units @ £49	73.5			
500 units @ £49			24.5	
		343		392
		637		728
Variable selling costs		196		224
Contribution		441		504
Fixed costs				
production (W1)	160		160	
selling, etc	90		90	
		250		250
Profit		191		254

(ii)   **Absorption costing statement**

	Six months ending 31 March 19X3		Six months ending 30 September 19X3	
	£'000	£'000	£'000	£'000
Sales		980		1,120
Cost of sales				
opening stock	-		103.5	
production cost				
8,500 units @ £69	586.5			
7,000 units @ £69			483	
	586.5		586.5	
less closing stock				
1,500 units @ £69	103.5			
500 units @ £69			34.5	
		483		552
		497		568
(under)/over absorption (W2)		10		(20)
Gross profit		507		548
Selling, etc costs				
variable	196		224	
fixed	90		90	
		286		314
Profit		221		234

WORKINGS

(W1)   Fixed production overhead is £20 per unit and the normal level of activity is 16,000 units per annum. The budgeted overhead per annum is therefore 16,000 × 20 = £320,000. The budgeted overhead per six-month period is therefore £160,000. The question states that there are no variances apart from a volume variance, therefore, actual overheads are as expected in the budget.

(W2)   Under/over absorption is the difference between overheads incurred and overheads absorbed

1st 6 months

	£'000
Overhead incurred (W1)	160
Overhead absorbed	
8,500 units × £20/unit	170
Over absorption	10

2nd 6 months

	£'000
Overhead incurred (W1)	160
Overhead absorbed	
7,000 units × £20/unit	140
Under absorption	20

(b)   The difference in profit = fixed production OAR × change in stock

	1st 6 mths £'000	2nd 6 mths £'000
Marginal costing profit	191	254
Stock difference		
Increase 1,500 units × £20/unit	30	
Decrease 1,000 units × £20/unit		(20)
Absorption costing profit	221	234

(c)   Marginal costing is useful in the following business situations:

(1)   Shutdown decisions. Using absorption costing it may appear that a product is unprofitable and should be discontinued. The product will have been charged with a share of fixed costs, however, which will usually remain at the same level, regardless of whether the product is continued or not. In the short term at least the focus should be on contribution and if the product has a positive contribution it should be continued.

(2)   Limiting factor decisions. When there is a scarce resource, production should be organised so that those products which give the highest contribution per unit of scarce resource are given the highest priority. Fixed costs can and should be ignored as they will be the same irrespective of which products are made.

(3)   Make or buy decisions. When a company has the choice of making or buying a component/product it should choose the cheaper option. The focus should be on variable costs alone as again the fixed costs will not change whichever option is chosen.

7 BUDGET PREPARATION

INTRODUCTION & LEARNING OBJECTIVES

This chapter is concerned with identifying an organisation's objectives, quantifying them and communicating them through plans for the future.

Such plans can be divided into long-term and short-term; short-term plans are often referred to as budgets.

When you have studied this chapter you should be able to do the following:

- List the objectives which an organisation may pursue and explain conflicts between them.

- Explain the purposes of planning.

- Explain the workings of the budgeting process.

- Prepare budgets based on given data.

- Explain the problems and techniques of forecasting.

1 WHY PLAN FOR THE FUTURE?

1.1 Introduction

Given the increasing complexity of business and the ever-changing environment faced by firms (social, economic, technological and political) it is doubtful whether any firm can survive by simply continuing to do what it has always done in the past. If the firm wishes to earn satisfactory levels of profit in the future, it must plan its course of action.

1.2 Corporate planning

Definition   Corporate planning is essentially a long run activity which seeks to determine the direction in which the firm should be moving in the future.

A frequently asked question in formulating the corporate plan is 'Where do we see ourselves in ten years time'. To answer this successfully the firm must consider:

(a)   what it wants to achieve (its objectives);
(b)   how it intends to get there (its strategy);
(c)   what resources will be required (its operating plans);
(d)   how well it is doing in comparison to the plan (control).

These areas are discussed below.

1.3 Objectives

[Definition] Objectives are simply statements of what the firm wishes to achieve.

Traditionally it was assumed that all firms were only interested in the maximisation of profit (or the wealth of their shareholders). Nowadays it is recognised that for many firms profit is but one of the many objectives pursued. Examples include:

(a) maximisation of sales (whilst earning a 'reasonable' level of profit);
(b) growth (in sales, asset value, number of employees etc);
(c) survival;
(d) research and development leadership;
(e) quality of service;
(f) contented workforce;
(g) respect for the environment.

Many of these non-profit goals can in fact be categorised as:

(a) surrogates for profit (eg, quality of service);

(b) necessary constraints on profit (eg, quality of service);

(c) 'sub-optimal' objectives that benefit individual parties in the firm rather than the firm as a whole (eg, managers might try to maximise sales as this would bring them greater personal rewards than maximising profit).

A variety of objectives can therefore be suggested for the firm and it is up to the individual company to make its own decisions. For corporate planning purposes it is essential that the objectives chosen are quantified and have a timescale attached to them. A statement such as maximise profits and increase sales would be of little use in corporate planning terms. The following would be far more helpful:

(a) achieve a growth in EPS of 5% per annum over the coming ten year period;
(b) obtain a turnover of £x million within six years;
(c) launch at least two new products per year, etc.

Some objectives may be difficult to quantify (eg, contented workforce) but if no attempt is made there will be no yardstick against which to compare actual performance.

1.4 Importance of long-range planning for successful budgeting

No doubt some managers would argue that because long-range forecasting can never be completely accurate, it is pointless. However, a system of budgetary control introduced in isolation without any form of corporate or long-range planning is unlikely to yield its full potential benefit, and it is important to understand the reasons for this.

Firstly, a budget is not (or should not be) the same as a forecast. A forecast is a statement of what is expected to happen; a budget is a statement of what it is reasonable to believe can be made to happen. An organisation without a long-range plan probably starts with the sales forecast and perhaps tries to improve the expected results slightly by increasing the advertising budget. This modified sales forecast then becomes the budget on which the other budgets are based. However, this approach has several limitations, some of which are listed below:

(a) In the absence of specified long-term objectives, there are no criteria against which to evaluate possible courses of action. Managers do not know what they should be trying to achieve.

(b)   Performance evaluation can only be on a superficial 'better/worse than last year' basis: no one has assessed the **potential** of the business.

(c)   Many decisions eg, capital expenditure decisions or the decision to introduce a new product, can only be taken on a long-term basis. Long-term forecasts may be inaccurate, but they are better than no forecast at all. A company with no long-range forecasting would be in dire straits when, sooner or later, sales of its existing products decline.

(d)   There is a limit to the influence a company can exert over events in the short term (eg, by increased advertising). If it wishes to improve its position markedly, it must think long term.

(e)   Eventually some factor other than sales may become the limiting factor eg, shortage of materials or labour. If the company has not anticipated the situation, it may simply have to live with the problem. With adequate long-range planning it might be able to avoid or overcome it.

1.5   Overview of the planning process

The overall planning process is described in the following diagram:

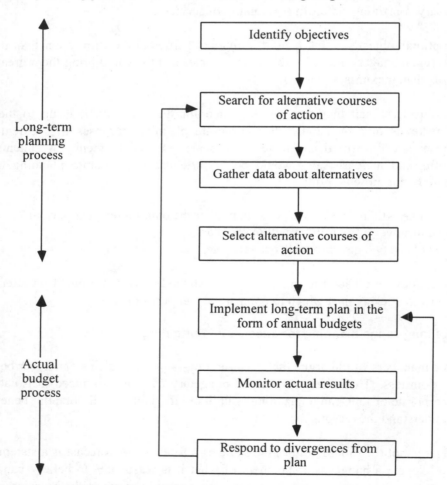

The seven stages are expanded below:

(a)   **Identify objectives**

This first stage requires the company to specify objectives towards which it is working. These objectives may be in terms of:

- economic targets;
- type of business;
- goods/services to be sold;
- markets to be served;
- market share;
- profit objectives; and
- required growth rates of sales, profits, assets.

(b)   **Search for possible courses of action**

A series of specific strategies should be developed dealing particularly with:

- developing new markets for existing products;
- developing new products for existing markets; and
- developing new products for new markets.

(c)   **Gathering data about alternatives and measuring pay-offs**

This is an information-gathering stage.

(d)   **Select course of action**

Having made decisions, long-term plans based on those decisions are created.

(e)   **Implementation of long-term plans**

This stage signals the move from long-term planning to annual budgeting. The budget provides the link between the strategic plans and their implementation in management decisions. The budget should be seen as an integral part of the long-term planning process.

(f)   **Monitor actual outcomes**

This is the particular role of the cost accountant, keeping detailed financial and other records of actual performance compared with budget targets (variance accounting).

(g)   **Respond to divergences from plan**

This is the control process in budgeting, responding to divergences from plan either through budget modifications or through identifying new courses of action.

2   THE NATURE OF BUDGETS

2.1   Introduction

In general, budgets are set for specific periods of time in the future, for example the budget for next year. Sometimes budgets are constructed for specific projects that are to be undertaken but again these can be analysed into the periods of time that the projects are expected to last. Thus, if a project is planned to last two years, the total budget for it can be split into that relating to the first year and that relating to the second year.

Budgets are plans expressed in financial and/or quantitative terms for either the whole of a business or for the various parts of a business for a specified period of time in the future. The budgets are prepared (**the planning activity**) within the framework of objectives (**targets or goals**) and policies that have been determined by senior management as part of its own planning activities.

2.2   The budgetary control process

Essentially the budgetary control process consists of two distinct elements:

(a)   **Planning**

This involves the setting of the various budgets for the appropriate future period. Management at the various levels in an organisation should be involved in the budgetary planning stage for its own area of responsibility. In many medium and large businesses this activity can take a considerable amount of time. There is a need to co-ordinate the budgets of the various parts of a business to ensure that they are all complementary and in line with overall company objectives and policies.

(b)   **Control**

Once the budgets have been set and agreed for the future period under review, the formal control element of budgetary control is ready to start.

This control involves the comparison of the plan in the form of the budget with the actual results achieved for the appropriate period. Any significant divergences between the budgeted and the actual results should be reported to the appropriate management so that the necessary action can be taken.

2.3   Benefits of budgetary control

(a)   **Planning** - budgetary control provides a formal framework for planning, which involves making sure that problems are anticipated and that steps are taken to avoid or reduce them.

(b)   **Co-ordination** - the system integrates budgets for the various sections of a business into a master budget for the whole business; individual managers will, therefore, recognise the overall objectives in forming their plans.

(c)   **Authorising and delegating** - approval of the master budget explicitly authorises the policy represented by the budget; by accepting their budgets, the responsibility for carrying out the policy is delegated to individual managers.

(d)   **Evaluating performance** - the budget represents a target against which the performance of managers can be assessed.

(e)   **Communicating and motivating** - preparing budgets involves communication between top management and lower levels on how to attain the objectives. Agreement motivates managers to achieve the targets set.

(f)   **Control** - continuous comparison of actual against plan indicates where control is needed.

2.4   Budget centres and budget periods

A **budget centre** is a clearly defined part of an organisation for the purposes of operating a budgetary control system. Each function within an organisation will be sub-divided into appropriate budget centres. In determining budget centres it is important to be able to define them in terms of management responsibility. The manager responsible for a budget centre (eg, the machining department within the production function) will be involved in the planning stage of setting the budget for his area of responsibility and he will be the recipient of control information in due course.

The **budget period** is the period of time for which a budget is prepared and over which the control aspect takes place. The length of such a period will depend on:

(a)   **The nature of the business** - in the ship-building or power supply industries budget periods of ten to twenty years may be appropriate; periods of less than one year may be appropriate for firms in the clothing and fashion industries.

(b)   **The part of the business being budgeted** - capital expenditure will usually be budgeted for longer periods ahead than the production output.

(c)   **The basis of control** - many businesses use a twelve month period as their basic budget period, but at the same time it is very common to find the annual budget broken down into quarterly or monthly sub-units. Such a breakdown is usually for control purposes because actual and budgeted results need to be monitored continuously. It is not practicable to wait until the end of a twelve month budget period before making control comparisons.

2.5   Introduction of a budgetary control system

Before a budgetary control system can be introduced, it is essential that:

(a)   key executives are committed to the proposed system;

(b)   the long-term objectives of the organisation have been defined (as previously discussed);

(c)   there is an adequate foundation of data on which to base forecasts and costs;

(d)   an organisation chart should be drawn up, clearly defining areas of authority and responsibility. The organisation can then be logically divided into budget centres, such that each manager has a budget for, and is given control information about, the area which he can control. This is the essence of **responsibility accounting**.

(e)   a budget committee should be set up and a budget manual produced;

(f)   the limiting factor is identified (see below).

2.6   Budget committee

A typical budget committee comprises the chief executive, the management accountant (acting as budget officer) and functional heads. The functions of the committee are to:

(a)   agree policy with regard to budgets;

(b)   co-ordinate budgets;

(c)   suggest amendments to budgets (eg, because there is inadequate profit);

(d)   approve budgets after amendment, as necessary;

(e)   examine comparisons of budgeted and actual results and recommend corrective action if this has not already been taken.

The budget officer is secretary to the committee and is responsible for seeing that the timetables are adhered to and for providing the necessary specialist assistance to the functional managers in drawing up their budgets and analysing results.

2.7   **Budget manual**

A budget manual is a document which sets out standing instructions governing the responsibilities of persons, and the procedures, forms and records relating to the preparation and use of budgets. It sets out the procedures to be observed in budgeting, the responsibilities of each person concerned, and the timetable to be observed.

2.8   **Continuous v periodic budgeting**

The effect of inflation on budgets can be very serious. In the past rapid inflation has led to widespread use of continuous rolling budgets. A budget is prepared for a year ahead (or whatever budget period has been chosen) and at the end of the first control period the budget for the remainder of the year is revised in the light of inflation to date or changed expectations concerning future inflation, in the light of which a budget is prepared for the first control period of the following year. This procedure is repeated after each control period, so that a budget for a year ahead is always available and budgets are as up-to-date as possible. This continual revision of budget figures leads to more up-to-date forecasts of future performance. Even though the days of hyper-inflation now seem to have gone, many firms still maintain a rolling budgeting system, regularly updating budgets for changes in the firm's circumstances.

While continuous budgets have a fixed planning horizon, periodic budgets have planning horizons which shorten as the period progresses. Periodic budgets are established for an accounting period, usually one year but can be as short as three months, and while the forecast for that year may change as the period progresses, the original periodic budget remains unchanged. This means that management will tend only to look to the end of the period for financial planning, while with continuous budgets they must always plan a full twelve months ahead. However, periodic budgets are used extensively in practice, mainly because they are less of an administrative burden. Continuous budgets may seem like a good idea, but periodic budgets are more practical.

3   **PREPARATION AND MONITORING PROCEDURES**

3.1   **How to budget - the seven steps**

Preparation of the budget involves seven steps. These are illustrated diagrammatically below:

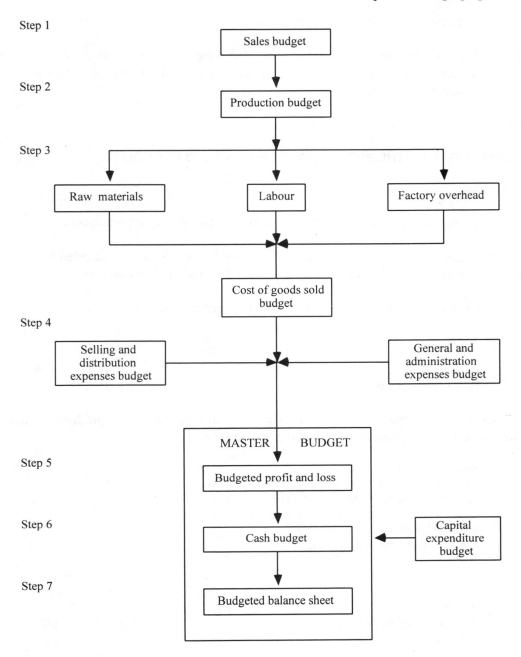

3.2 Principal budget factor

The sales budget is shown in the diagram because this is the pattern in most businesses, where it is the volume of the demand for the product which limits the scale of operation. It is possible, however, for there to be some other limiting factor eg, labour, material, cash or machinery. The limiting factor must be identified at the first stage of the budgeting process, since it will determine all the other budgets. In this context the limiting factor is referred to as the **principal budget factor.**

The determination and valuation of the principal budget factor is achieved using forecasting techniques. These are dealt with later in this text.

The budgeting process is, therefore, more fully described as follows:

(a)   Prepare:

- sales forecast;
- raw material availability forecast;
- cash availability forecast, etc.

(b)   Determine the principal budget factor.

(c)   Decide whether the limitations can be removed, and at what cost eg, by additional advertising expenditure, by intensive recruitment and training, etc. This is a matter for the budget committee.

(d)   Draw up budgets on the agreed basis.

4   PREPARATION OF THE BUDGETED PROFIT AND LOSS ACCOUNT

4.1   Illustration

The following data will be used to explain the technique of budget preparation

Hash Ltd makes two products - PS and TG. Sales for next year are budgeted at 5,000 units of PS and 1,000 units of TG. Planned selling prices are £65 and £100 respectively.

Hash Ltd has the following opening stock and required closing stock.

	PS units	TG units
Opening stock	100	50
Required closing stock	1,100	50

You are also given the following data about the materials required to produce PS and TG and the whittling and fettling processes involved in production.

	PS	TG
Finished products:		
Kg of raw material X, per unit of finished product	12	12
Kg of raw material Y, per unit of finished product	6	8
Direct labour hours per unit of finished product	8	12
Machine hours per unit - whittling	5	8
Machine hours per unit - fettling	3	4

	Raw material	
	X	Y
Direct materials:		
Desired closing stock in kg	6,000	1,000
Opening stock in kg	5,000	5,000

Standard rates and prices:

Direct labour	£2.20 per hour
Raw material X	£0.72 per kg
Raw material Y	£1.56 per kg

Production overheads:

Variable	£1.54 per labour hour
Fixed	£0.54 per labour hour
	£2.08 per labour hour

4.2   The sales budget

The sales budget represents the plan in terms of the quantity and value of sales, for sales management. In practice this is often the most difficult budget to calculate.

What is next year's sales budget?

The sales budget would be:

	Total	PS	TG
Sales units	6,000	5,000	1,000
Sales value	£425,000	£325,000	£100,000

In practice a business would market many more than two products. Moreover, the sales budget would probably be supported by subsidiary budgets to show analysis according to:

(a)   responsibility eg, Northern area, Western area, etc

(b)   type of customer eg, wholesale, retail, government, etc

4.3   The production budget

The production budget is usually expressed in quantity and represents the sales budget adjusted for opening/closing finished stocks and work in progress.

Production budget	PS units	TG units
Sales budget	5,000	1,000
Budgeted stock increase (1,100 – 100)/(50 – 50)	1,000	-
Production in units	6,000	1,000

The production budget needs to be translated into requirements for:

(a)   raw materials;

(b)   direct labour;

(c)   machine utilisation;

(d)   factory overheads;

(e)   closing stock levels.

4.4   The raw materials budget

(Remember that Hash Ltd is going to produce 6,000 units of PS and 1,000 units of TG.)

		X kg		Y kg
For production of PS	6,000 × 12 kg	72,000	6,000 × 6 kg	36,000
For production of TG	1,000 × 12 kg	12,000	1,000 × 8 kg	8,000
		84,000		44,000
Budgeted raw material stock increase/(decrease)	(6,000 – 5,000)	1,000	(1,000 – 5,000)	(4,000)
Raw materials required		85,000		40,000
		£		£
Budgeted value:				
X £0.72 per kg × 85,000		61,200		
Y £1.56 per kg × 40,000				62,400

4.5   The direct labour budget

		Hours		£
For PS	6,000 × 8 hrs	48,000		
For TG	1,000 × 12 hrs	12,000		
		60,000	@ £2.20	132,000

4.6   The machine utilisation budget

		whittling hours		*fettling hours*
For PS	6,000 × 5 hrs	30,000	6,000 × 3 hrs	18,000
For TG	1,000 × 8 hrs	8,000	1,000 × 4 hrs	4,000
		38,000		22,000
Total hours	=			60,000

4.7   Production overheads

		£
Variable costs	60,000 hours × £1.54	92,400
Fixed costs	60,000 hours × £0.54	32,400
		124,800

4.8   Opening and closing stocks

Remember that we are calculating the cost of sales. So far we have calculated the amounts of material, labour and overheads used in **production**. To arrive at the figures for cost of sales you have to remember that **production** is used not just for sales but also to increase/decrease stock levels - hence the need to adjust for the opening and closing stock position of both raw material and finished goods.

4.9   Closing stock of raw materials

		£
X	6,000 kg × £0.72	4,320
Y	1,000 kg × £1.56	1,560
		5,880

4.10   Closing stock of finished goods

		PS £		*TG* £
Standard cost of finished goods:				
Materials:				
X	12 kg × £0.72	8.64	12 kg × £0.72	8.64
Y	6 kg × £1.56	9.36	8 kg × £1.56	12.48
		18.00		21.12
Wages	8 hours × £2.20	17.60	12 hours × £2.20	26.40
Overhead	8 hours × £2.08	16.64	12 hours × £2.08	24.96
		52.24		72.48
Stock in units		1,100		50
Stock value		£57,464		£3,624

4.11   Activity

Calculate the values of the opening stocks of raw material and finished goods.

4.12   Activity solution

Raw material	X:	5,000 kg × £0.72	=	£3,600
Raw material	Y:	5,000 kg × £1.56	=	£7,800
Finished good	PS:	100 units × £52.24	=	£5,224
Finished good	TG:	50 units × £72.48	=	£3,624

4.13   Cost of sales budget

We can now bring all the above elements together.

	£	£
Opening stocks:		
Raw materials (3,600 + 7,800)	11,400	
Finished goods (5,224 + 3,624)	8,848	
		20,248
Raw materials (61,200 + 62,400)		123,600
Direct labour		132,000
Production overhead		124,800
		400,648
Less: Closing stocks:		
Raw materials	5,880	
Finished goods (57,464 + 3,624)	61,088	
		66,968
		333,680

4.14   Marketing and administration budget

Marketing and administration budgets will be a summary of the budget centres within those functions.

For the purposes of this example, the marketing/administration budget is assumed to be £45,000.

4.15   Budgeted profit and loss account

The budgeted profit and loss account is prepared by summarising the operating budgets.

Master budget - profit and loss account

	£	£
Sales		425,000
Cost of sales:		
Opening stocks	20,248	
Raw materials	123,600	
Direct labour	132,000	
Production overhead	124,800	
	400,648	
Closing stocks	66,968	
		333,680
Operating margin		91,320
Marketing/administration		45,000
Operating profit		46,320

Note: that the above budgets are presented to highlight planned requirements rather than for costing purposes. Most businesses will obviously be more complex than that illustrated and supporting analyses would be prepared as required eg,

Production units by month or weeks
Raw materials by supplier
Direct labour by grade

4.16   Cash budgets

Cash budgets are illustrated later.

4.17   Budgeted balance sheet

The total company plan will include a statement to show the financial situation at the end of the budget period. Subsidiary budgets will be prepared to analyse movements in fixed and working capital during the budget period based on the operating budgets and reflecting financial policy formulated by the budget committee.

4.18   Other budgets - capital expenditure

Obtaining finance for investment and selecting capital investment projects are aspects of long-term planning. The capital expenditure included in the master budget will essentially be an extract from the long-term capital budget.

The cash required to finance the capital expenditure will be incorporated in the cash budget (as illustrated later).

A capital expenditure budget is in many respects the most problematic budget to prepare in that the types of projects for which capital expenditure is to be incurred tend to have long time spans and uncertain outcomes.

The considerations involved in the capital expenditure budget are:

(1)   Predictions of outcomes of potential projects throughout their lifetime. This is often difficult because of the uncertainty surrounding factors in the future that are outside the control of the organisation such as the actions of competitors, climatic or economic conditions. Also, benefits may be difficult to quantify; for example the purchase of a new computer system may produce 'faster' and 'better' information.

(2)   How are capital projects to be chosen ie, what method of investment appraisal will be used to rank potential projects? Possibilities are net present value, payback, accounting return etc.

(3)   How are projects to be financed?

The choice of method will affect the cashflows and profits reflected in the capital expenditure budget.

(4)   The actual performance of the project must be continuously monitored, and management should investigate all deviations from the original estimates.

4.19   Other miscellaneous budgets

Depending on the requirements of management, additional budgets may be prepared for:

(a)   **Purchasing** - consolidates purchases of raw materials, supplies and services in raw materials/expense budgets, analysed to show when the goods are received (for control of supply) and also when they are paid for (for cash budget).

(b)   **Personnel (manpower)** - shows detailed requirements, month by month, for production and administration personnel.

(c)   **Stocks** - itemises quantity and value, month by month, of planned stock levels for raw materials, work in progress and finished goods.

(d)   **Debtors** - details time analysis of collections from sales suitably analysed by type of customer or type of product.

5   CASH BUDGETS

5.1   Objectives

(a)   Part of the budgeting process;

(b)   to anticipate cash shortages/surpluses and to provide information to assist management in short and medium-term cash planning and longer term financing for the organisation.

5.2   Method of preparation

(a)   Forecast sales;

(b)   forecast time-lag on converting debtors to cash, and hence forecast cash receipts from credit sales;

(c)   determine stock levels, and hence purchase requirements;

(d)   forecast time-lag on paying suppliers, and thus cash payments for purchases;

(e)   incorporate other cash payments and receipts, including such items as capital expenditure and tax payments;

(f)   collate all this cash flow information, so as to determine the net cash flows.

5.3   Layout

A tabular layout should be used, with:

(a)   columns for weeks, months or quarters (as appropriate);
(b)   rows for cash inflows and outflows.

5.4   Example

A wholesale company ends its financial year on 30 June. You have been requested, in early July 19X5, to assist in the preparation of a cash forecast. The following information is available regarding the company's operations:

(a)   Management believes that the 19X4/19X5 sales level and pattern are a reasonable estimate of 19X5/19X6 sales. Sales in 19X4/19X5 were as follows:

		£
19X4	July	360,000
	August	420,000
	September	600,000
	October	540,000
	November	480,000
	December	400,000

19X5	January	350,000
	February	550,000
	March	500,000
	April	400,000
	May	600,000
	June	800,000
Total		6,000,000

(b)   The accounts receivable at 30 June 19X5 total £380,000. Sales collections are generally made as follows:

During month of sale	60%
In first subsequent month	30%
In second subsequent month	9%
Uncollectable	1%

(c)   The purchase cost of goods averages 60% of selling price. The cost of the stock on hand at 30 June 19X5 is £840,000, of which £30,000 is obsolete. Arrangements have been made to sell the obsolete stock in July at half the normal selling price on a cash on delivery basis. The company wishes to maintain the stock, as of the first of each month, at a level of three months' sales as determined by the sales forecast for the next three months. All purchases are paid for on the tenth of the following month. Accounts payable for purchases at 30 June 19X5 total £370,000.

(d)   Payments in respect of fixed and variable expenses are forecast for the first three months of 19X5/19X6 as follows:

	£
July	160,620
August	118,800
September	158,400

(e)   It is anticipated that cash dividends of £40,000 will be paid each half year, on the fifteenth day of September and March.

(f)   During the year unusual advertising costs will be incurred that will require cash payments of £10,000 in August and £15,000 in September. The advertising costs are in addition to the expenses in item (d) above.

(g)   Equipment replacements are made at a rate which requires a cash outlay of £3,000 per month. The equipment has an average estimated life of six years.

(h)   A £60,000 payment for corporation tax is to be made on 15 September 19X5.

(i)   At 30 June 19X5 the company had a bank loan with an unpaid balance of £280,000. The entire balance is due on 30 September 19X5, together with accumulated interest from 1 July 19X5 at the rate of 12% pa.

(j)   The cash balance at 30 June 19X5 is £100,000.

You are required to prepare a cash forecast statement, by months, for the first three months of the 19X5/19X6 financial year. The statement should show the amount of cash on hand (or deficiency of cash) at the end of each month. All computations and supporting schedules should be presented in clear and concise form.

5.5   Solution

The solution can be best approached as in the following paragraphs.

5.6   Activity

Work out the cash received from sales.

5.7   Activity solution

	Sales	Cash received July	August	September
	£	£	£	£
May	600,000	54,000	-	-
June	800,000	240,000	72,000	-
July	360,000	216,000	108,000	32,400
August	420,000	-	252,000	126,000
September	600,000	-	-	360,000
		510,000	432,000	518,400

5.8   Obsolete stock

	£
Obsolete stock at cost	30,000
Normal sales price	
$\frac{100}{60} \times £30,000$	50,000
Realised ½ × £50,000	25,000

5.9   Payment to trade creditors

		£	£	£
(i)	10 July - Balance b/d			370,000
(ii)	10 August - sales in July		360,000	
	Cost of goods sold (60%)		216,000	
	Less: Opening stock	(840,000)		
	Less: Obsolete stock	30,000		
		(810,000)		
	Add: Closing stock 60%			
	(420,000 + 600,000 + 540,000)	936,000		
			126,000	
				342,000

(iii)	10 September - sales in August	420,000

Cost of goods sold (60%)		252,000
Less: Opening stock	(936,000)	
Add: Closing stock 60% (600,000 + 540,000 + 480,000)	972,000	
		36,000
		288,000

5.10   Cash budget

	July £	August £	September £
Receipts:			
Receipts from debtors	510,000	432,000	518,400
Obsolete stock	25,000	-	-
	535,000	432,000	518,400

	July £	August £	September £
Payments:			
Payments to creditors	370,000	342,000	288,000
Expenses	160,620	118,800	158,400
Dividends	-	-	40,000
Advertising	-	10,000	15,000
Capital expenditure	3,000	3,000	3,000
Corporation tax	-	-	60,000
Bank loan	-	-	288,400
	533,620	473,800	852,800
Net cash inflow/(outflow)	1,380	(41,800)	(334,400)
Balance	100,000	101,380	59,580
Balance/ (deficiency) at month end	101,380	59,580	(274,820)

6   CHAPTER SUMMARY

This chapter has considered the need for long term planning and conversion of these plans into short-term plans known as budgets.

7   SELF TEST QUESTIONS

7.1   List five organisational objectives. (1.3)

7.2   What is the difference between a budget and a forecast? (1.4)

7.3   List the seven stages of the planning process. (1.5)

7.4   What is a budget? (2.1)

7.5   What is a budget centre? (2.4)

7.6   Why is it important to identify the principal budget factor? (3.2)

8   EXAMINATION TYPE QUESTIONS

8.1   Cash budget

From the following statements, prepare a month-by-month cash budget for the six months to 31 December.

(a)   **Revenue budget (ie, trading and profit and loss account)**

Six months to 31 December (all revenue/costs accrue evenly over the six months)

	£'000	£'000
Sales (cash received one month in arrear)		1,200
Cost of sales:		
Paid one month in arrear	900	
Paid in month of purchase	144	
Depreciation	72	
	———	1,116
Budgeted profit		84

(b)   **Capital budget**

	£'000	£'000
Payments for new plant:		
July	12	
August	25	
September	13	
November	50	
	———	100
Increase in stocks, payable August		20
		120
Receipts:		
New issue of share capital (October)		30

(c)   **Balance sheet**

	Actual 1 July £'000
Assets side:	
Fixed assets	720
Stocks	100
Debtors	210
Cash	40
	1,070
Liabilities side:	
Capital and reserves	856
Taxation (payable December)	30
Creditors - trade	160
Dividends (payable August)	24
	1,070

8.2   S Ltd

S Ltd manufactures three products - A, C and E - in two production departments - F and G - each of which employs two grades of labour. The cost accountant is preparing the annual budgets for Year 2 and he has asked you as his assistant to prepare, using the data given below:

(a)   the production budget in units for Products A, C and E;

(b)   the direct wages budget for Departments F and G with the labour costs of Products A, C and E and totals shown separately.

Data	*Total*		*Product*	
		A	*C*	*E*
		£'000	£'000	£'000
Finished stocks:				
Budgeted stocks are:				
1 January, year 2		720	540	1,800
31 December, year 2		600	570	1,000
All stocks are valued at				
expected cost per unit		£24	£15	£20
Expected profit:				
Calculated as percentage of selling price		20%	25%	$16\frac{2}{3}\%$
	£'000	£'000	£'000	£'000
Budgeted sales:				
South	6,600	1,200	1,800	3,600
Midlands	5,100	1,500	1,200	2,400
North	6,380	1,500	800	4,080
	18,080	4,200	3,800	10,080
Normal loss in production		10%	20%	5%

Expected labour times per unit and expected rates per hour	*Rate* £	*Hours per unit*	*Hours per unit*	*Hours per unit*
Department F:				
Grade 1	1.80	1.00	1.50	0.50
Grade 2	1.60	1.25	1.00	0.75
Department G:				
Grade 1	2.00	1.50	0.50	0.50
Grade 2	1.80	1.00	0.75	1.25

9   ANSWERS TO EXAMINATION TYPE QUESTIONS

9.1   Cash budget

	Jul £'000	Aug £'000	Sep £'000	Oct £'000	Nov £'000	Dec £'000	Total £'000
Receipts:							
Sales	210	200	200	200	200	200	1,210
New issue of share capital	-	-	-	30	-	-	30
Payments:							
Expenses and purchases	160	150	150	150	150	150	900
Expenses and purchases	24	24	24	24	24	24	144
Plant	12	25	13	-	50	-	100
Stock	-	20	-	-	-	-	20
Tax	-	-	-	-	-	30	30
Dividends	-	24	-	-	-	-	24
	196	243	187	174	224	204	1,228
Surplus/(deficiency)	14	(43)	13	56	(24)	(4)	12
Opening balance	40	54	11	24	80	56	52
Closing balance	54	11	24	80	56	52	64

9.2   S Ltd

(a)   **Production budget**

	Product A 000 units	Product C 000 units	Product E 000 units
Sales	140	190	420
Stock increase/(decrease)	(5)	2	(40)
Production required	135	192	380
Add: Excess to cover normal loss	15	48	20
Production budget	150	240	400

Notes:

(1)   Sales units $= \dfrac{\text{Budgeted sales value}}{\text{Expected selling price}}$

(2)   Expected selling price = Expected unit cost plus expected profit ie,

Product A $£24 \times {}^{100}\!/_{80}$ =   £30

Product C $£15 \times {}^{100}\!/_{75}$ =   £20

Product E $£20 \times {}^{100}\!/_{83\frac{1}{3}}$ =   £24

(3)   Stock units $= \dfrac{\text{Budgeted stock values}}{\text{Expected unit costs}}$

(4)   Additional requirements to cover normal loss of production:

$$\text{Required production} \times \frac{\text{Loss percentage}}{\text{Normal production percentage}}$$

ie,   Product A $135 \times \frac{10}{90}$ =   15

Product C $192 \times \frac{20}{80}$ =   48

Product E $380 \times \frac{5}{95}$ =   20

(b)   **Direct wages budget**

	Product A 000		Product C 000		Product E 000		Total
	hours	*£'000*	*hours*	*£'000*	*hours*	*£'000*	*£'000*
Department F:							
Grade 1 (@ £1.80/hr)	150	270	360	648	200	360	1,278
Grade 2 (@ £1.60/hr)	187.5	180	240	384	300	480	1,044
		450		1,032		840	2,322
Department G:							
Grade 1 (@ £2.00/hr)	225	450	120	240	200	400	1,090
Grade 2 (@ £1.80/hr)	150	270	180	324	500	900	1,494
		720		564		1,300	2,584
Total budget		1,170		1,596		2,140	4,906

Note: hours budgeted represent production budget units at expected labour times.

8 FIXED AND FLEXIBLE BUDGETS

INTRODUCTION & LEARNING OBJECTIVES

When you have studied this chapter you should be able to do the following:

- Compute and evaluate fixed and flexible budgets
- Explain the reasons for variances occurring.
- Explain the behavioural aspects of budgeting.

---

1 FLEXIBLE BUDGETS

1.1 Introduction

Definition   A flexible budget is one which, by recognising the distinction between fixed and variable costs, is designed to change in response to changes in output.

The concept of responsibility accounting requires the use of flexible budgets for control purposes. Many of the costs under a manager's control are variable and will therefore change if the level of activity is different from that in the budget. It would be unreasonable to criticise a manager for incurring higher costs if these were a result of a higher than planned volume of activity. Conversely, if the level of activity is low, costs can be expected to fall and the original budget must be amended to reflect this.

A variance report based on a flexible budget therefore compares actual costs with the costs budgeted for the level of activity actually achieved. It does not explain any change in budgeted volume, which should be reported on separately.

1.2 Flexible budgeting

The key points to note are:

(a) A fixed budget is set at the beginning of the period, based on estimated production. This is the original budget.

(b) This is then **flexed** to correspond with the actual level of activity.

(c) The result is compared with actual costs, and differences (variances) are reported to the managers responsible.

1.3 Example

Bug Ltd manufactures one uniform product only, and activity levels in the assembly department vary widely from month to month. The following statement shows the departmental overhead budget based on an average level of activity of 20,000 units production per four-week period and the actual results for four weeks in October.

	Budget average for four-week period £	Actual for 1 to 28 October £
Indirect labour - variable	20,000	19,540
Consumables - variable	800	1,000
Other variable overheads	4,200	3,660
Depreciation - fixed	10,000	10,000
Other fixed overheads	5,000	5,000
	40,000	39,200
Production (units)	20,000	17,600

You are required:

(a)   to prepare a columnar flexible four-week budget at 16,000, 20,000 and 24,000 unit levels of production;

(b)   to prepare two performance reports based on production of 17,600 units by the department in October, comparing actual with:

(i)   average four-week budget; and
(ii)   flexible four-week budget for 17,600 units of production;

(c)   to state which comparison ((b) (i) or (b) (ii)) would be the more helpful in assessing the foreman's effectiveness and why; and

(d)   to sketch a graph of how the flexible budget total behaves over the 16,000 to 24,000 unit range of production.

1.4   Solution

(a)

Production level	16,000 units £	20,000 units £	24,000 units £
Variable costs:			
Indirect labour	16,000	20,000	24,000
Consumables	640	800	960
Other overheads	3,360	4,200	5,040
	20,000	25,000	30,000
Fixed costs:			
Depreciation	10,000	10,000	10,000
Other overheads	5,000	5,000	5,000
	35,000	40,000	45,000

(b)   (i)

	Average four-week budget £	Actual results £	Variances fav./(adv.) £
Indirect labour	20,000	19,540	460
Consumables	800	1,000	(200)
Other variable overheads	4,200	3,660	540
Depreciation	10,000	10,000	-
Other fixed overheads	5,000	5,000	-
	40,000	39,200	800

(ii)

	Flexed four-week budget	Actual results	Variances fav./(adv.)
Sales (units)	17,600	17,600	-
	£	£	£
Indirect labour	17,600	19,540	(1,940)
Consumables	704	1,000	(296)
Other variable overheads	3,696	3,660	36
Depreciation	10,000	10,000	-
Other fixed overheads	5,000	5,000	-
	37,000	39,200	(2,200)

(c)   The flexed budget provides more useful data for comparison because:

(i)   the fixed original budget makes no distinction between fixed and variable costs;

(ii)   hence no data is available concerning the appropriate level of costs at the actual production level;

(iii)   this would lead to the conclusion that the foreman had done well, when in fact costs had not fallen nearly as much as anticipated for the actual production;

(iv)   responsibility for the production shortfall is not known.

(d)   **Graph of costs in the production range 16,000 to 24,000 units**

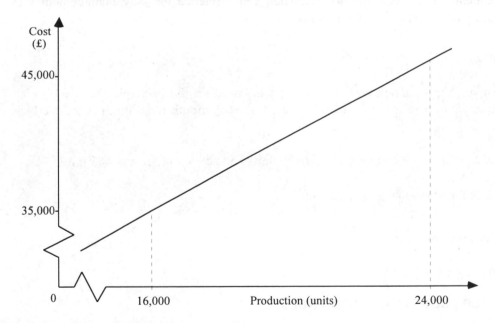

1.5   Flexible budgeting and management attitudes

The nature of cost behaviour patterns is not changed according to whether fixed or flexible budgets are used; what is changed is the way in which management view costs.

1.6   Example

The Alic Co Ltd has many small customers. Work measurement of the debtors' ledger shows that one clerk can handle 2,000 customer accounts. The company employs 30 clerks on the debtors' ledger at a salary of £3,600 each. The outlook for next year is of a decline in the number of customers from 59,900 to 56,300. However, management decides not to reduce the number of clerks.

Show the effect of this decision if debtors' ledger clerks' salaries are treated as:

(a)   variable expenses per customer per year;

(b)   fixed overhead.

1.7   Solution

			£
(a)	Allowed expense $56,300 \times \dfrac{£3,600}{2,000}$		101,340
	Actual expenditure $30 \times £3,600$		108,000
			6,660 A

		£
(b)	Allowed expense	108,000
	Actual expenditure	108,000
		Nil

Neither approach says whether the management decision was right. Approach (a), however, does give the cost of that decision.

Consequently the way costs are classified can influence the way management views costs, and ultimately the decisions that are made.

1.8   Activity

A company's production overhead budget is based on the principle that each unit of production incurs variable overhead cost of £5.40 and that each month fixed production overhead of £6,750 is incurred.

During June the budgeted output was 460 units and actual output was 455 units.

Calculate the allowed expense for June.

1.9   Activity solution

(455 units × £5.40) + £6,750 = £9,207

2   FLEXIBLE BUDGETS AND VARIANCES

2.1   Introduction

The use of flexible budgets enables costs to be predicted for a number of different activity levels. This should allow a meaningful comparison of actual results to be made but the mechanics of flexible budgeting simplify the circumstances which exist for the organisation.

2.2   Flexible budgeting and activity

Flexible budgets recognise fixed and variable costs in relation to a single measure of activity. In reality costs may be affected by more than one activity measure, and not all costs will be affected by the same activity measures.

2.3   Variances

Variances are calculated by comparing actual costs with the flexed budget (cost allowance) when using flexible budgets for cost control. This is appropriate provided the cost is flexed correctly using an appropriate measure of activity.

In contrast fixed budgets make no allowance for any differences between actual and budget activity. This assumes that costs are fixed and can result in a meaningless comparison.

2.4   Reasons for variances

There are a number of reasons why variances may occur:

(a)   invalid target
(b)   poor actual performance
(c)   random fluctuations.

A target may be invalid if it does not reflect an attainable standard. This may be caused because the standard is too ideal, or it may be out-of-date if there has been a change in internal or external circumstances.

Internal circumstances may change by a change in the manufacturing method or in the type of materials or labour used.

External circumstances may change due to the economic climate, which affects costs, revenues and demand from customers.

Poor actual performance may be due to controllable or non-controllable causes. Controllable causes may include labour inefficiency due to a lack of training. Non-controllable causes may include idle time caused by a breakdown in a supplier's machinery which delays delivery of materials.

Random fluctuations arise because standards are averages, set for a period of time (often one year). It is inevitable therefore that there will be fluctuations from one accounting period to the next. These may be caused by a failure to correctly recognise prepayments and accruals.

3   BEHAVIOURAL ASPECTS OF BUDGETING

3.1   Introduction

If budgetary control is to be successful, attention must be paid to behavioural aspects ie, the effect of the system on people in the organisation and *vice versa*. Poor performance and results are more often due to the method of implementation and subsequent operation of a system, with a failure to allow properly for the human side of the enterprise, than to the system itself. The management needs to be fully committed to the budgeting system, and through leadership and education lower levels of management in the organisation should be similarly committed and motivated.

Budgets are one important way of influencing the behaviour of managers within an organisation. There are very few, if any, decisions and actions that a manager in an organisation can take which do not have some financial effect and which will not subsequently be reflected in a comparison between budgeted and actual results. This all-embracing nature of budgets is probably the most important advantage that a budgetary system has over most other systems in a typical organisation.

3.2   Roles of budgets

As identified earlier, budgets can take on a number of different roles in any organisation and each has important behavioural implications. Each is now reexamined from a behavioural aspect:

(a)   **Authorisation**

Once a budget has been agreed, it is not interpreted by many managers merely as an authorisation to 'spend up to the budget' but rather as an authorisation to 'spend the budget', otherwise there is a real fear that the following year's budget will be cut. Therefore, there is a tendency in an underspend situation, when approaching the end of the financial year, to spend money when it is not really necessary to do so.

(b)   **Planning**

The budgeting system provides a formal, co-ordinated approach to short-term planning throughout the organisation. Each manager has a framework in which to plan for his own area of responsibility. Without budgeting it is difficult to imagine an alternative system, affecting all parts of an organisation, in which such planning could take place.

(c)   **Forecasting**

Short-term budgets covering the next one or two years may provide the basis for making forecasts beyond that period eg, in appraising a project with a five year life, data may be extracted from the budgets and used to make forecasts for another three years. The danger with this approach is that, if the budgets are incorrect, the extrapolations beyond the budget period are also likely to be wrong and the financial analysis of the project may be unsound. The budgets could be incorrect because 'slack' has been built into them. Budgetary slack is a common phenomenon in practice. It involves building 'padding' into a cost or expense budget to allow some leeway in actual performance; in a revenue budget it involves a deliberate understatement of budgeted sales or other revenue.

(d)   **Communicating and co-ordinating**

A budgeting system encourages good communications and co-ordination in an organisation. Information about objectives, strategies and policies has to be communicated down from top management and all the individual budgets in an organisation need to be co-ordinated in order to arrive at the master budget.

(e)   **Motivation**

Agreed budgets should motivate individual managers towards their achievement, which in turn should assist the organisation in attaining its longer-term objectives. Motivational effects and the concept of budget difficulty are dealt with later.

(f)   **Evaluation of performance**

A comparison between the predetermined budget and the actual results is the most common way in which an individual manager's performance is judged on a regular basis. The way this appraisal is made and how deviations are dealt with may influence how the individual manager behaves in the future. This role is also the subject of further discussion later.

The various roles identified for budgets may not all prevail at the same time, and some may assume greater importance than others. This will depend on each individual organisation and its operational environment. Some of the roles are indeed likely to conflict with others.

3.3   Problems associated with implementing budgetary control

(a)   There may be a general fear and misunderstanding about the purpose of budgetary control. It is often regarded as a penny-pinching exercise rather than recognised as a tool of management at all levels in an organisation structure. If this tends to be the attitude, a carefully planned campaign of education and understanding should be undertaken. Managers should be encouraged to discover what is in the budgetary control system for them.

(b) Employees may become united against management and devote their energies to finding excuses for not meeting targets. Targets that are realistic, and are seen by the employees as being realistic, are what is required. Good communications involving consultation and participation should help to minimise this problem.

(c) One of the key roles in any organisation is at the supervisor/foreman level where the continual interface between management and employees exists. The leadership and motivational function of a supervisor or foreman is very important if the work is to be done and targets are to be achieved.

(d) The breaking down of an organisation into many sub-areas of managerial responsibility can lead to sub-optimisation problems as far as the whole company is concerned ie, the optimisation of an individual manager's department or section at the expense of the organisation overall. Such dysfunctional behaviour should be minimised. It reflects a lack of goal congruence.

(e) If budgets are built up from the base of the organisation, with individual departmental budgets providing the input to the overall master budget, the tendency to incorporate slack into budgets needs to be carefully monitored.

(f) Some desirable projects could be lost because they were not foreseen and therefore not budgeted for. The system needs to be flexible enough to avoid this problem.

All of these problems really relate to criticisms of the manner in which budgetary control systems tend to be operated, rather than of budgetary control *per se*.

3.4 Motivating effect of budgets

Empirical evidence suggests that if a budget is set such that it does not contain a suitable element of targetry (ie, difficulty), then actual performance should be a little better than the budget but it will not be optimised. In other words, managers do not usually work to their full potential if they know that a lower level of performance will still meet the budget (and they are evaluated on the basis of a favourable result compared with the budget). On the other hand, if the budget is too difficult, because it is based on idealistic levels of performance, managers become discouraged at what they regard as an unattainable standard. The effect of such demotivation is that actual performance falls short of what might reasonably have been expected. The aim should be to agree a budget that falls between these two extremes and therefore incorporates just the right degree of difficulty which will lead to the optimal level of performance. At this level the budget should be challenging enough to motivate a manager to optimise on his performance without being too ambitious. The right level of difficulty is that element of targetry which is acceptable to that individual manager. This level of acceptability will differ from manager to manager, as each individual behaves and reacts in a different way in similar circumstances. This concept of budget difficulty can be demonstrated diagrammatically as follows:

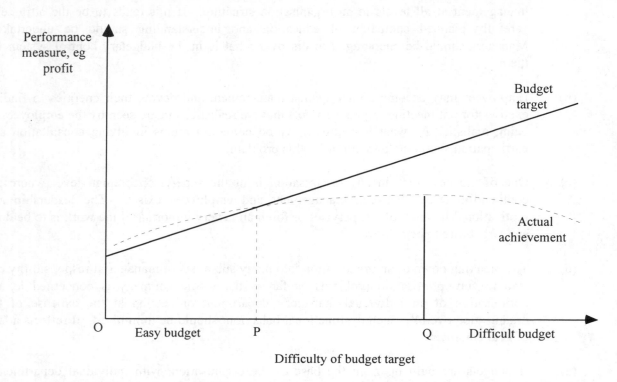

A budget set at the point where OP represents the degree of difficulty or targetry in it is referred to as an 'expectations budget' as budget and actual are likely to coincide. However, a relatively easy-to-achieve budget is likely to lead to a sub-optimal actual performance. In order to achieve a higher actual performance a more difficult budget needs to be set (an 'aspirations budget'). A budget set at the point where OQ represents the degree of difficulty or targetry in it should lead to optimal performance (highest point on the 'actual' performance curve). However, it should be noted that this would give rise to an adverse variance compared with budget. Senior management's interpretation of the reaction to such a variance needs to be carefully considered if the individual manager is not to react adversely in the future to not achieving the budgeted performance. It is in the overall company's best interest to optimise an individual manager's actual performance.

How the degree of difficulty, OQ, is determined is not at all easy in practice because it involves a knowledge of how each individual manager will react and behave. Attempts to quantify the degree of difficulty using work study assessments are a highly simplified approach to a very complex problem.

Furthermore, attempts to use the budget as a motivating tool in the manner described may in fact lead to the need for two budgets: one which is the summation of what all the individual managers have agreed to achieve (with the different degrees of budget difficulty incorporated into them); and a second which recognises that actual performance is likely to fall short of aspiration and is, therefore, a more realistic basis for planning purposes eg, placing capital expenditure contracts (budgets used for forecasting purposes).

3.5   Evaluation of managerial performance

In the previous section the motivating effect of budgets was considered, but it should be remembered that the budgets by themselves have a limited motivational effect. It is the reward structure that is linked to achieving the budget requirements, or lack of reward for non-achievement, which provides the real underlying motivational potential of budgets. The rewards need not be directly financial but could be in terms of future prospects of promotion.

A manager will need to regard the reward as being worthwhile if his behaviour is to be influenced so that he strives actively towards the achievement of the budget.

It has already been mentioned in an earlier section that it is a common practice to attempt to assess the performance of a manager by a comparison of budgeted and actual results for his area of responsibility in the organisation. The choice of which particular measures to use is important to ensure that the individual manager sees the attainment of his targets as worthwhile for himself and at the same time in the best interests of the organisation as a whole. In practice, conflicts can and often do arise between individual managers' personal objectives and those of the organisation as a whole.

The way in which the information in budget reports is used in the assessment of managerial performance has to be considered. Different degrees of emphasis on the results of budget versus actual comparisons can lead to different attitudes and feelings among managers. There is a need to achieve the correct balance between, on the one extreme, an over-emphasis on results leading to pressure and feelings of injustice from the system; and on the other, too little stress on results leading to a budget irrelevancy attitude and low morale.

AG Hopwood reported in 1973 on his research in this area. He studied the manufacturing division of a US steelworks involving a sample of more then two hundred managers with cost centre responsibility.   He identified the following three distinct styles of using budget/actual cost information in the evaluation of managerial performance.

(a)   **Budget constrained style**

Here the primary emphasis is on the evaluation of a manager's performance in terms of meeting the budget in the short term.

(b)   **Profit conscious style**

The performance of a manager is measured in terms of his ability to increase the overall effectiveness of his area of responsibility in the context of meeting the longer term objectives of the organisation. At cost centre levels of responsibility the reduction of long-run average costs could be seen as achieving this. Short-term budgetary information needs to be used with care and in a flexible way to achieve this purpose.

(c)   **Non-accounting style**

A manager's evaluation is not based on budgetary information. Accounting information plays a relatively unimportant role in such a style. Other, non-accounting performance indicators are as important as the budget information.

A brief summary of the major effects that these three styles had on managers now follows.

The *budget constrained* style resulted in a great involvement in costs and cost information and a high degree of job-related pressure and tension. The latter often led to the manipulation of data for inclusion in accounting reports. Relations with both colleagues and the manager's superior were poor.

The *profit conscious* style showed good relations with colleagues and superiors. There was still a high involvement with costs but less job-related pressure. Consequently, the manipulation of accounting data was reduced.

The *non-accounting* style showed very similar effects to the profit conscious style except for the much lower impact of costs and cost information on the manager. Hopwood found some evidence that better managerial performance was being achieved where a profit conscious or non-accounting style was in use. Poor performance was often associated with a budget constrained style.

Subsequent studies involving profit centre managers in the UK coal mining industry undertaken by

DT Otley (published 1978) did not always mirror Hopwood's earlier results. One particular area of difference was that the UK study showed a closer link between the budget constrained style and good performance.

The manager evaluated on a rather tight budget constrained basis tended to meet the budget more closely than if it was evaluated in a less rigid way.

The results of these studies by Hopwood and Otley can be reconciled in terms that each took place in a different organisational environment. The US study involved highly interdependent cost centres in a highly integrated production function; the UK study involved largely independent profit centres. Any generalisations about evaluation styles must take into account the contingent variables associated with differing organisational structures.

3.6   Participation in the setting of budgets

In some organisations budgets are set by higher levels of management and then communicated to the lower levels of management to whose areas of responsibility they relate. Thus, such budgets are seen by those lower-level managers as being imposed upon them by their superiors in the organisational hierarchy without their being allowed to participate in the budget-setting process and therefore without their being able directly to influence the budget figures. This approach to involvement in the budgetary system is consistent with Douglas McGregor's Theory X view of how people behave in organisations. The Theory X view is based on the assumptions that people in work environments are basically lazy and dislike work and any responsibility associated with it. They are motivated by money to meet their basic needs. Therefore, the Theory X style of management is authoritarian, based on direction and control down through the organisation and typified by a host of rules and regulations.

The other end of the spectrum is described by McGregor as Theory Y. This is a participative theory of management, assuming that people in a work environment do seek more responsibility and do not have to be so tightly controlled. Therefore, it is in organisations where a Theory Y style of management predominates that one is more likely to come across a fully participative approach to the setting of budgets.

The general argument is that the more individual managers are allowed to participate ie, to influence the budgets for which they are held responsible, the more likely it is that they will accept the targets in the budgets and strive actively towards the attainment of those targets. In this way actual performances should be increased by the motivational impact of budgets. An important point to recognise is the difference between *actual* and *perceived* participation. It is the extent to which an individual manager *perceives* that he has influenced the budget that is crucial in that manager's acceptance of it.

There are limitations on the extent of the effectiveness of participation in the budget-setting process. If budgets are used both in a motivational role and for the evaluation of managerial performance, then a serious conflict can arise. A manager through participation may be able to influence the very budget upon which he is subsequently evaluated. By lowering the standard in the budget he has biased the budget and he may then appear to attain a better actual performance in any comparison with it. There is evidence to show that this tends to occur where a manager is actively seeking progression up in an organisation. The effects of this sort of bias can be minimised by careful control, at the budget setting stage, over any changes in the budget from one year to the next which are not due to external factors.

Some people in organisations, by the very nature of the make-up of their personality, do not wish to participate in the wider aspects of their jobs. They prefer an authoritarian style of leadership and do not strive for independence. Participative approaches to budget-setting will be very limited in their effect in such circumstances.

Participation will be less effective in organisational situations where a manager or employee feels that he has little scope to influence the actual results for the budgeted area of responsibility. The lower down in the organisation structure the budget holder is, the more constrained is he by factors imposed from above. For example, objectives, strategies and policies, as well as the sales forecast and budget, limit the extent that a subordinate manager in the production function has for real participation in the setting of the budget for his area of responsibility.

3.7   Budget bias

Budget bias, or budget 'slack' as it is sometimes referred to, is the common process of building room for manoeuvre when setting a budget by overstating the level of budgeted expenditure or by understating the level of budgeted sales. The following are possible reasons for the creation of the bias:

(a)   It should lead to the most favourable result when actual is compared with budget. Such a result should lead to the optimisation of personal gain for the individual manager.

(b)   Where reward structures are based on comparisons of actual with budgeted results, bias can help to influence the outcome.

(c)   In an uncertain business environment it is a way of relieving some of the pressures of a tight situation. The bias will allow some leeway if things do not go according to plan. An example at the factory floor level of this is where workers deliberately do not show how quickly a job can be completed when they are being closely studied by work study (time-and-motion) personnel. The standard time that results will leave the workers with room to manoeuvre in the case of non-standard or different work or where through more general dissatisfaction they do not want to work flat out.

(d)   Some people may see the creation of bias in a budget as a way of 'legally' beating the system. Human behaviour generally in other fields tends to follow such an approach eg, the legal avoidance of tax is a way of getting round the (tax) system. Therefore, a manager may regard the creation of bias as a desirable personal objective and success in achieving it as motivational towards the best actual performance.

Budget bias can sometimes be in the opposite direction to that which has been described already. A manager in the marketing function may bias his budget in an optimistic way by overstating budgeted sales. This could be due to a desire to please senior management by showing an optimistic forecasted sales trend. Alternatively, a manager whose performance has been weak previously may wish to show a promising situation in order to gain approval by his superiors. The short-term approval will usually be at the risk of future disapproval if the optimistic result is not reflected in the actual results.

Finally there is the question 'Is budget bias or slack good or bad?' It depends how the budget is used. If the bias has the effect of motivating a manager to his best actual performance, there would appear to be a good reason for its existence. However, if budgets are used to make forecasts and consequent major decisions then, to the extent that the budgets are biased , there will be errors in the forecasts being made beyond the budget period. Erroneous decisions may then be made. If budgets are to be made in this way the bias needs to be removed from any budgets before the forecasts are made.

4   CHAPTER SUMMARY

This chapter has distinguished fixed and flexible budgets and then considered the behavioural aspects of budgeting.

5 SELF TEST QUESTIONS

5.1 What is a flexible budget? (1.1)

5.2 What is the problem of using flexible budgets? (2.2)

5.3 Why do variances arise? (2.4)

5.4 Identify the roles of budgets. (3.2)

5.5 How do managers use budgets? (3.5)

5.6 Why is participation by managers in the preparation of their budgets important? (3.6)

5.7 What is 'budget bias?' (3.7)

6 EXAMINATION TYPE QUESTION

6.1 Discussion

You are required to discuss separately each of the following statements.

(a) Most budgeting systems are bureaucratic and reinforce organisational inertia whereas what is required is continuous adaptation to deal with a volatile environment. **(5 marks)**

(b) The typical flexible budget is virtually useless as a control device because for convenience it is common practice for all the variable elements in the budget to be flexed according to the same activity indicator whereas in reality the elements vary according to different activity indicators. **(5 marks)**

(c) Participation by managers in setting budget levels is a laudable philosophy but it is naive to think that participative approaches are always more effective than authoritarian styles.
(10 marks)
(Total: 20 marks)

7 ANSWER TO EXAMINATION TYPE QUESTION

7.1 Discussion

(a) Many writers on motivational theory have suggested that the leadership style is likely to be reflected in the organisation structure, and hence on the budgetary system developed.

Hopwood pointed out that although the budgeting process appears to be technical and formal (and therefore may appear bureaucratic) it is really an informal bargaining process, whereby managers compete for organisational resources.

If the budgeting system is seen to be bureaucratic, the workforce may perceive it to be a pressure device by management to force employees to achieve higher performance ratings for no extra benefits. This could lead to a 'them' and 'us' solution.

However in the current economic climate, and in a rapidly changing situation, only those firms with efficient managers are likely to be successful. These managers will adopt systems that include both adaptive and dynamic elements that can not be regarded as bureaucratic.

(b) A flexible budget allowance is calculated on the basis of a single output based activity indicator eg, budgeted fixed overhead cost + (budgeted variable overhead cost per unit × the actual number of units produced). These variable costs tend to vary with input rather than output. Thus variable absorption rates based on input rather than output and variable overhead absorption rates based on input of machine/direct labour hours are used to estimate the flexible budget allowance.

However, for control purposes the budget is flexed on the basis of an output rather than an input indicator to ensure that input inefficiencies are not covered up. In this manner, the typical flexible budget can be of some value as a control device.

(c)   The application of contingency theory to management accounting tells us that there is no universal appropriate accounting system applicable to all organisations in all circumstances. It depends upon the circumstances. Therefore the circumstances will determine to what extent managerial participation in the budgeting process will lead to higher levels of motivation and thus lead to enhanced managerial performance. Certainly there are clear examples where real participation has shown benefits, but it may not be a universal truth.

9 FORECASTING AND REGRESSION

INTRODUCTION & LEARNING OBJECTIVES

When you have studied this chapter you should be able to do the following:

- Describe different intuitive forecasting methods for qualitative issues.
- Calculate a regression line using the method of least squares.
- Calculate and interpret the correlation coefficient r.
- Interpret the meaning of the coefficient of determination r^2.

---

1 FORECASTING METHODOLOGY

1.1 Introduction

Budgeting for future profit or cashflows requires us to forecast future costs and revenues, at varying levels of activity. How do we use past experience to make forecasts?

1.2 Designing a system

A system of forecasting must be designed, having regard to the following items:

(a) *Data.* Any forecast will take into consideration results which have been obtained in the past. No situation is static and the most up-to-date results are the most relevant to the forecasting model.

(b) *Models.* The forecaster must try to make a model which will fit the situation under review. He will need to plot graphs of past results to look for patterns, trends, seasonal fluctuations and other cycles which might appear from past results, which must be reflected in the model.

(c) *Forecasting.* The projections of the model must then be evaluated in the light of any outside factors or changed conditions.

(d) *Errors.* Any forecast is, at best, a close approximation of an actual result, and the forecaster will want to make allowances for errors. Statistical theory can be applied to errors in forecasting by assuming that errors came from a normal distribution with a mean of zero. This enables the forecaster to calculate the tolerances on the forecast.

1.3 The uses of cost forecasts

(a) **Budgeting**

Without being able to forecast costs, firms would be unable to implement any budgetary control system. All budgets are based on forecasted figures, even if these figures are based on intuition. Obviously, the more accurate the forecasts, the more accurate and useful will be the budgets and hence the control on costs.

(b)   **Setting of standards**

If an organisation uses standard costing as a control method, it needs to set the standards as accurately as possible taking into account the management philosophy of standard setting ie, low but obtainable, or high as an incentive. Such costs included in the standard will all be forecast figures.

2   COST PREDICTION

2.1   Introduction

There are five methods that can be used to predict future figures from the analysis of past data:

(a)   The engineering approach.
(b)   The account analysis approach.
(c)   Scatter diagrams.
(d)   The high-low method.
(e)   Regression analysis.

2.2   The engineering approach

This approach is based on building up a complete specification of all inputs (eg, materials, labour, overheads) required to produce given levels of output. This approach is therefore based on the technical specification, which is then costed out using expected input prices.

This approach works reasonably well in a single product or start-up situation – indeed in the latter it may be the only feasible approach. However, it is difficult to apply in a multi-product situation, especially where there are joint costs, or the exact output mix is not known.

2.3   The account analysis approach

Rather than using the technical information, this approach uses the information contained in the ledger accounts. These are analysed and categorised as either fixed or variable (or semi-fixed or semi-variable). Thus, for example, material purchase accounts would represent variable costs, office salaries a fixed cost. Since the ledger accounts are not designed for use in this way, some reorganisation and reclassification of accounts may be required.

Students should note that this is the approach implicit in many examination questions.

The problems with this approach are several:

(a)   Inspection does not always indicate the true nature of costs. For example, today factory wages would normally be a fixed cost, with only overtime and/or bonuses as the variable element.

(b)   Accounts are by their nature summaries, and often contain transactions of different categories.

(c)   It rests on historical information with the problems noted above.

2.4   Scatter diagrams

Information about two variables that are considered to be related in some way can be plotted on a scatter diagram. For example, the amount of rainfall and the crop yield per acre could be plotted against each other, or the level of advertising expenditure and sales revenue of a product.

It is important to decide which variable can be used to predict the other – ie, which is the *independent* and which the *dependent variable*. In many cases it is quite clear eg, the amount of rainfall obviously causes a particular crop yield, and not vice-versa. Here, rainfall is the independent variable and crop yield the dependent variable (ie, yield depends on the amount of rainfall). Some relationships have classic 'chicken and egg' characteristics; for example, advertising and sales revenue. Whether a given level of advertising causes a particular level of sales or whether a particular level of sales provokes a certain level of advertising is not quite so clear. In fact, advertising tends to *directly* affect sales levels whereas sales only have an indirect influence on decisions about advertising expenditure and therefore sales tends to be regarded as the dependent variable and advertising expenditure the independent variable.

The independent variable is marked along the horizontal (x) axis and the dependent variable along the vertical (y) axis.

Students are advised to think in terms of the x-axis being the cause, and the y-axis the effect.

One advantage of a scatter diagram is that it is possible to see quite easily if the points indicate that a relationship exists between the variables ie, to see if any correlation exists between them.

It is not possible to measure the degree of correlation from a scatter diagram. However, as will be seen later, there are methods of calculating a numerical value for this.

Examples of scatter diagrams

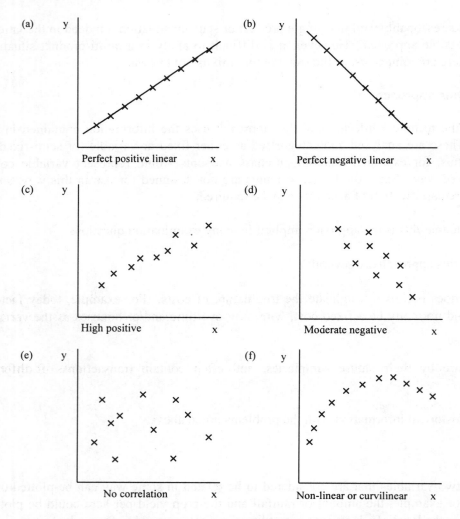

These six scatter diagrams illustrate some of the different types of correlation. Scatter graphs of non-linear correlation can assume many different types of curve.

If the points lie exactly on a straight line, then the correlation is said to be perfect linear correlation. In practice this rarely occurs and it is more usual for the points to be scattered in a band, the narrower the band the higher the degree of correlation.

Positive correlation exists where the values of the variables increase together. Negative correlation exists where one variable increases as the other decreases in value.

Thus, considering the six diagrams:

(a)   This is an example of perfect positive linear correlation since the points lie exactly on a straight line and as 'x' increases so 'y' increases.

(b)   This is an example of perfect negative linear correlation since the points again lie on a straight line, but as the x values increase so the y values decrease.

(c)   In this diagram, the points lie in a narrow band rather than on a straight line, but x and y still tend to increase together, therefore a high degree of positive correlation is evident.

(d)   This time the points lie in a much wider band and, as x increases, y tends to decrease, so this is an example of low negative correlation where, because of the wider spread of the points than those in (c), the correlation is only moderate.

(e)   When the points are scattered all over the diagram, as in this case, then little or no correlation exists between the two variables.

(f)   Here the points lie on an obvious curve. There is a relationship between x and y, but it is not a straight line relationship.

2.5   Line of best fit

To obtain a description of the relationship between two variables in the form of an equation in order to forecast values, it is necessary to fit a straight line through the points on the scatter diagram which best represents all of the plotted points. If we are looking at predicting costs from a knowledge of the activity level then remember we are looking for a straight line of the form $y = a + bx$.

The equation for any straight line is of the form:

$$y \quad = \quad a + bx$$

where x and y are the variables and a and b are constants for the particular line in question.

a is called the **intercept** on the y-axis and measures the point at which the line will cut the y-axis.

b is called the **gradient** of the line and measures its degree of slope.

a and b can take any value, including zero, and may be positive or negative.

In order to locate any particular line, it is therefore necessary to determine the values of a and b for that line.

Parameters of a straight line by inspection

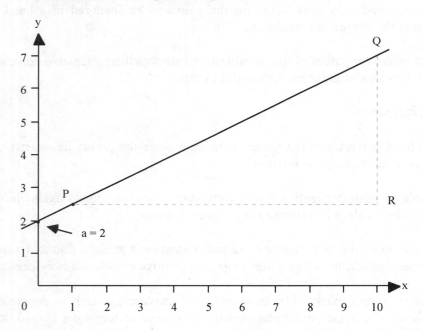

The diagram shows a line which has been fitted to a scatter graph by eye. The points of the scatter graph have been omitted for clarity. It is required to find the values of *a* and *b* for this line in the general equation $y = a + bx$.

Method

a is the intercept on the y-axis ie, the value of *y* at which the line cuts the y-axis. Hence $a = 2$.

To find the slope, *b*, take any two points (*P* and *Q*) on the line.

The further apart *P* and *Q* are, the more accurate will be the result.

Draw horizontal and vertical lines through *P* and *Q* to meet at *R*.

The length of PR **as measured on the x-scale**   =   9 units

The length of RQ **as measured on the y-axis**   =   4.5 units

The slope $= \dfrac{RQ}{PR} = \dfrac{4.5}{9} = 0.5$, hence $b = 0.5$

The equation is therefore:

$$y = 2 + 0.5x$$

Note: that for this method, no part of the x-scale can be omitted, otherwise the vertical axis is not the true y-axis and the intercept will not be correct.

An alternative method which can be used if part of the x-scale needs to be omitted is to read off from the graph the values of *x* and *y* at *P* and *Q*, substitute these values into the general equation and solve the resulting simultaneous equations for *a* and *b*.

$$y = a + bx$$
at P, $x = 1$, $y = 2.5$, hence:
$$2.5 = a + b \times 1$$

ie,   a + b   =   2.5   ....   (1)

at Q,   x = 10,   y = 7,   hence:

7   =   a + b × 10

ie,   a + 10b   =   7   ....   (2)

Subtract (1) from (2) to eliminate a:

a + 10b   =   7

a +   b   =   2.5
_____

9b   =   4.5

b   = $\dfrac{4.5}{9}$ =   0.5

Substitute in (1) to find a:

a + 0.5   =   2.5

a   =   2.5 – 0.5

∴   a   =   2.0

Hence   a = 2.0   and   b = 0.5   as before.

If we are trying to predict total cost from past data of costs and activity levels then in the general equation y = a + bx

y is total cost
a is fixed costs
b is variable cost per unit
x is the activity level ie, quantity produced.

How do we predict the values of a and b that 'best fit' the historical data?

One method is simply to fit a line 'by eye' which appears to suit all the points plotted. This method has the disadvantage that if there is a large amount of scatter no two people's lines will coincide and it is, therefore, only suitable where the amount of scatter is small, or where the degree of accuracy of the prediction is not critical. Better methods to identify the line are high low or least squares regression.

The method of least squares regression is the most mathematically correct method of fitting a straight line to a set of data. This is a very important topic and we shall look at it in detail later in the chapter.

2.6   High low (or range) method

This and the next method that follows are based on an analysis of historic information of costs at different activity levels. What we need to do is to separately identify the fixed and variable cost elements (ie, those that do not and do change with the activity level) so that each can be predicted for anticipated future activity levels.

Example

The data for the six months to 31 December 19X8 is as follows:

Month	Units	Inspection costs
		£
July	340	2,260
August	300	2,160
September	380	2,320
October	420	2,400
November	400	2,300
December	360	2,266

The variable cost is estimated by calculating the unit cost between the highest and lowest volumes.

Six months to 31/12/X8	Units produced	Inspection costs
		£
Highest month - October	420	2,400
Lowest month - August	300	2,160
Difference	120	240

The additional cost per unit between high and low is $\dfrac{£240}{120 \text{ units}}$ = £2 per unit

which is the estimated variable content of inspection costs.

Fixed inspection costs are, therefore:

$$£2,400 - (420 \times £2) = £1,560 \text{ per month}$$
$$\text{or} \quad £2,160 - (300 \times £2) = £1,560 \text{ per month.}$$

To predict costs in the future we could use

$$y = 1,560 + 2x$$

where y is total cost and x is the quantity produced.

The limitations of the high low method are:

(a)   Its reliance on historic data, assuming that (i) activity is the only factor affecting costs and (ii) historic costs reliably predict future costs.

(b)   The use of only two values, the highest and the lowest, means that the results may be distorted due to random variations in these values.

2.7 Activity

Use the high-low points method to calculate the fixed and variable elements of the following cost:

	Activity	£
January	400	1,050
February	600	1,700
March	550	1,600
April	800	2,100
May	750	2,000
June	900	2,300

2.8 Activity solution

		£
High (June)	900	2,300
Low (January)	(400)	(1,050)
	500	1,250

Variable cost = £1,250/500 = £2.50/unit

Fixed cost = £1,050 − (400 × £2.50) = £50.

Relationship to use for prediction y = 50 + 2.5x.

3 REGRESSION

3.1 Introduction

Least squares regression, like the high-low method, is used to predict a linear relationship between two variables. Unlike the high low method it uses **all** past data to calculate the line of best fit.

3.2 Least squares linear regression

It is possible to calculate two different regression lines for a set of data, depending on whether the horizontal deviations or the vertical deviations of the points from the line are considered. It is the sum of the **squares** of these deviations which is minimised; this overcomes problems that might arise because some deviations would be positive and some negative, depending on whether the point was above or below the line. It is not necessary to go into the theory of this method any more deeply at this level.

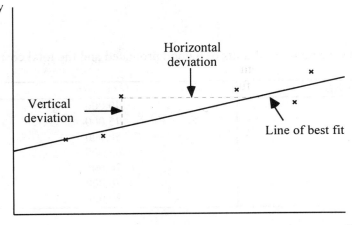

The regression line of y on x must be used when an estimate of y is required for a given value of x. This line minimises the sum of the squares of the vertical distances of the points from the line. The regression line of x on y must be used when an estimate of x is required for a known value of y. This line minimises the sum of the squares of the horizontal distances of the points from the line.

The scatter diagram has the following appearance when the regression lines are graphed:

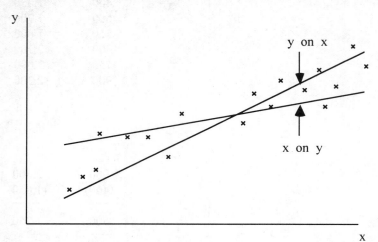

The two lines will intersect at the point $(\overline{x}, \overline{y})$ ie, the mean of the x-values and the mean of the y-values.

3.3   The regression line of y on x

Assuming that the equation of the regression line of y on x is:

$$y \quad = \quad a + bx,$$

as it will be if we are trying to predict cost (y) from activity level (x) it is necessary to calculate the values of a and b so that the equation can be completely determined.

The following formulae are used; a knowledge of their derivation is not necessary. They do not need to be memorised since they are supplied in the exams.

$$a \quad = \quad \overline{y} - b\overline{x} \quad = \quad \frac{\sum y}{n} - \frac{b\sum x}{n}$$

$$b \quad = \quad \frac{n\sum xy - \sum x\sum y}{n\sum x^2 - (\sum x)^2}$$

n is the number of pairs of x, y values ie, the number of points on the scatter graph.

The value of b must be calculated first as it is needed to calculate a.

3.4   Example

The following table shows the number of units of a good produced and the total costs incurred:

Units produced	Total costs
100	40,000
200	45,000
300	50,000
400	65,000
500	70,000
600	70,000
700	80,000

Calculate the regression line for y on x.

3.5   Solution

Notes on the calculation

(a)   A scatter diagram is always a useful aid in answering questions on correlation and regression. Even if it is not specifically requested, a sketch diagram can be included as part of a solution.

(b)   The calculation can be reduced to a series of steps:

Step 1   Tabulate the data and determine which is the dependent variable, y, and which the independent, x.

Step 2   Calculate Σx, Σy, Σx^2, Σxy; (leave room for a column for Σy^2 which may well be needed subsequently).

Step 3   Substitute in the formulae in order to find b and a in that order.

Step 4   Substitute a and b in the regression equation.

The calculation is set out as follows, where x is the activity level in units of **hundreds** and y is the cost in units of £1,000.

x	y	xy	x^2	
1	40	40	1	
2	45	90	4	
3	50	150	9	
4	65	260	16	
5	70	350	25	
6	70	420	36	
7	80	560	49	
28	420	1,870	140	$n = 7$

$$b = \frac{n\Sigma xy - \Sigma x \Sigma y}{n\Sigma x^2 - (\Sigma x)^2}$$

(Try to avoid rounding at this stage since, although $n\Sigma xy$ and $\Sigma x \Sigma y$ are large, their difference is much smaller.)

$$= \frac{(7 \times 1,870) - (28 \times 420)}{(7 \times 140) - (28 \times 28)}$$

$$= \frac{13,090 - 11,760}{980 - 784}$$

$$= \frac{1,330}{196}$$

$$= 6.79$$

$$a = \frac{\Sigma y}{n} - \frac{b\Sigma x}{n}$$

$$= \frac{420}{7} - 6.79 \times \frac{28}{7}$$

$$= 60 - 27.16$$

$$= \quad 32.84$$

$\therefore$ the regression line for y on x is:

$$y \quad = \quad 32.84 + 6.79x \qquad \text{(x in hundreds of units produced,}$$
$$\text{y in £1,000's)}$$

(Always specify what x and y are very carefully.)

This line would be used to estimate the total costs for a given level of output. If, say, 250 units were made we can predict the expected yield by using the regression line where $x = 2.5$:

$$y \quad = \quad 32.84 + 6.79 \times 2.5$$
$$= \quad 32.84 + 16.975$$
$$= \quad 49.815$$

ie, we predict total costs of £49,815 for production of 250 units.

3.6   Interpolation and extrapolation

As has been shown, regression lines can be used to calculate intermediate values of variables ie, values within the known range. This is known as **interpolation** and it is one of the main uses of regression lines.

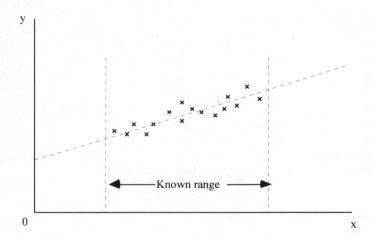

It is also possible to extend regression lines beyond the range of values used in their calculation. It is then possible to calculate values of the variables that are outside the limits of the original data, this is known as **extrapolation**.

The problem with extrapolation is that it assumes that the relationship already calculated is still valid. This may or may not be so.

For example, if output was increased outside the given range there might come a point where economies of scale reduce costs and total costs might actually fall.

The resultant diagram could be of this form:

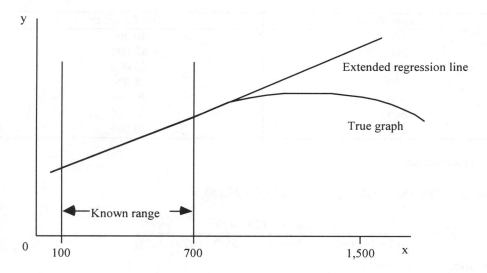

Therefore the cost of making 1,500 units as estimated from the regression line may be very different from that actually achieved in practice.

Generally speaking, extrapolation must be treated with caution, since once outside the range of known values other factors may influence the situation, and the relationship which has been approximated as linear over a limited range may not be linear outside that range. Nevertheless, extrapolation of a time series is a valuable and widely used technique for forecasting.

4   CORRELATION

4.1   Introduction

Through regression analysis it is possible to derive a linear relationship between two variables and hence estimate unknown values. However, this does not measure the **degree of correlation** between the variables ie, how strong the connection is between the two variables. It is possible to find a line of best fit through any assortment of data points; this doesn't mean that we are justified in using the equation of that line for prediction.

Earlier in the chapter we discussed **correlation** and how two variables can be plotted together on a scatter diagram and the correlation between the variables intuitively estimated by simply looking at the diagram. However a more scientific measure of the strength of the correlation is available by calculating the correlation coefficient.

4.2   Correlation coefficient

Pearson's correlation coefficient, also called the 'product moment correlation coefficient', r, is defined as:

$$r = \frac{n\sum xy - \sum x \sum y}{\sqrt{(n\sum x^2-(\sum x)^2)(n\sum y^2-(\sum y)^2)}}$$

where x and y represent pairs of data for two variables x and y, and n is the number of pairs of data used in the analysis.

This formula does not have to be memorised, since it is also supplied in the exam, but practice is needed at applying it to data and interpreting the result.

4.3   Example

Units produced	Total costs £
100	40,000
200	45,000
300	50,000
400	65,000
500	70,000
600	70,000
700	80,000

The totals required are:

$\Sigma x = 28$, $\Sigma y = 420$, $\Sigma xy = 1,870$, $\Sigma x^2 = 140$, $\Sigma y^2 = 26,550$, n = 7

$$\text{Thus} \quad r = \frac{(7 \times 1,870) - (28 \times 420)}{\sqrt{((7 \times 140) - (28 \times 28))((7 \times 26,550) - (420 \times 420))}}$$

$$= \frac{13,090 - 11,760}{\sqrt{(980 - 784)(185,850 - 176,400)}}$$

$$= \frac{1,330}{\sqrt{(196 \times 9,450)}}$$

$$= 0.98$$

4.4   Interpretation of coefficient of correlation

Having calculated the value of r, it is necessary to interpret this result.   Does $r = 0.98$ mean that there is high correlation, low correlation or no correlation?

the value of r varies between +1 and −1 where:

r =   +1   means perfect positive linear correlation;

r =   0   means no correlation; and

r =   − 1   means perfect negative linear correlation.

So in this case the value of 0.98 indicates a high degree of positive correlation between the variables.

In general, the closer that r is to +1 (or − 1) the higher the degree of correlation.   This will be confirmed by the scatter diagram where the points will lie in a narrow band for such values.

It must be realised that r only measures the amount of linear correlation ie, the tendency to a straight line relationship.   It is quite possible to have strong non-linear correlation and yet have a value of r close to zero.   This is one reason why it is important in practice to draw the scatter graph first.

The more data points the farther r may be from 1 and still indicate good correlation.   If there are few data points, as here, we would wish to see r very close to 1 (clearly if there were only 2 points they will lie exactly on the line of best fit).

4.5   Coefficient of determination

The coefficient of determination is the square of the coefficient of correlation, and so is denoted by r^2. The advantage of knowing the coefficient of determination is that it is a measure of how much of the variation in the dependent variable is 'explained' by the variation of the independent variable. The variation not accounted for by variations in the independent variable will be due to random fluctuations, or to other specific factors which have not been identified in considering the two-variable problem.

In the example on output and cpsts, r had a value of 0.98 and so $r^2 = 0.96$ and $100r^2 = 96\%$.

Thus, variations in the amount of fertiliser applied account for 96% of the variation in the yield obtained.

This is an important measure because of the effect of squaring 'r'. A correlation coefficient of 0.7 appears not too significantly different from one of 0.5. However r^2 is 49% in the former case and 25% in the latter. In other words, the correlation is almost twice as strong since 49% is almost twice the size of 25%.

4.6   Activity

If $r = 0.42$, how much of the variation in the dependent variable is explained by the variation of the independent variable?

4.7   Activity solution

If $r = 0.42$, then $r^2 = 0.1764$, so about 17.6% of the variation is explained by variations in the independent variable (poor correlation).

4.8   Spurious correlation

Students should be aware of the big danger involved in correlation analysis. Two variables, when compared, may show a high degree of correlation but they may still have no direct connection. Such correlation is termed **spurious** or **nonsense** correlation and unless two variables can reasonably be assumed to have some direct connection the correlation coefficient found will be meaningless, however high it may be.

The following are examples of variables between which there is high but spurious correlation:

(a)   Salaries of school teachers and consumption of alcohol.

(b)   Number of television licences and the number of admissions to mental hospitals.

Such examples clearly have no direct **causal** relationship. However, there may be some other variable which is a causal factor common to both of the original variables. For example, the general rise in living standards and real incomes is responsible both for the increase in teachers' salaries and for the increase in the consumption of alcohol.

5   THE USE OF CORRELATION AND REGRESSION IN FORECASTING

5.1   Introduction

So far we have looked at the technicalities of correlation and regression and how to interpret the results of such calculations. What we have not done is to make the link between these techniques and forecasting, bearing in mind forecasting is the part of the syllabus that this and the following chapter is all about.

Thus what we are establishing here is:

[Step 1]   Is there a causal relationship between two variables? (Correlation)

↓

If yes

↓

[Step 2]   Deduce the coefficient 'a' and 'b' in order to establish a line of best fit in the form
$y = a + bx$. (Regression)

↓

[Step 3]   Use the equation to forecast the value of an unknown variable given that the value of
the other variable can be ascertained for the period for which the forecast is to be made.
(Forecasting)

Example

If there is a correlation between the demand for sun roofs in a given year and the sales of new cars
in the previous year, then this year's car sales could be used to predict sun roof demand for next
year.

6   CHAPTER SUMMARY

This chapter has been concerned with forecasting; the three quantitative methods described were:

(a)   Scatter diagrams.
(b)   Regression analysis.
(c)   Correlation coefficients.

A number of formulae have been used; these must be well practised so that calculations can be
made quickly and accurately. We shall go on to look at more quantitative forecasting techniques in
the next chapter.

7   SELF TEST QUESTIONS

7.1   Name three methods of predicting costs. (2.1)

7.2   What is a scatter diagram? (2.4)

7.3   What is a 'line of best fit'? (2.5)

7.4   What is the equation of a straight line? (2.5)

7.5   What is the difference between interpolation and extrapolation? (3.6)

7.6   What values do r take if there is perfect positive linear correlation and perfect negative
linear correlation? (4.4)

7.7   What is the coefficient of determination and why is it important? (4.5)

7.8   What is spurious correlation? (4.8)

8   EXAMINATION TYPE QUESTION

8.1   D & E Ltd

D & E Ltd produces brakes for the motor industry. Its management accountant is investigating the
relationship between electricity costs and volume of production. The following data for the last ten
quarters has been derived, the cost figures having been adjusted (ie, deflated) to take into account
price changes.

Quarter	1	2	3	4	5	6	7	8	9	10
Production, X, ('000 units)	30	20	10	60	40	25	13	50	44	28
Electricity costs, Y, (£'000)	10	11	6	18	13	10	10	20	17	15

(Source: Internal company records of D & E Ltd.)

$$\sum X^2 = 12{,}614, \qquad \sum Y^2 = 1{,}864, \quad \sum XY = 4{,}728$$

You are required:

(a)   to draw a scatter diagram of the data on squared paper;   **(4 marks)**

(b)   to find the least squares regression line for electricity costs on production and explain this result;   **(8 marks)**

(c)   to predict the electricity costs of D & E Ltd for the next two quarters (time periods 11 and 12) in which production is planned to be 15,000 and 55,000 standard units respectively;   **(4 marks)**

(d)   to assess the likely reliability of these forecasts.   **(4 marks)**
(Total: 20 marks)

9   ANSWER TO EXAMINATION TYPE QUESTION

9.1   D & E Ltd

(a)   **Scatter graph of electricity cost against production**

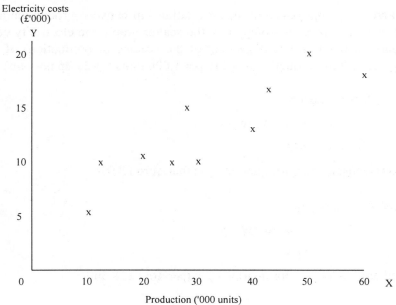

Notes:

(i)   Choose the scales so that the graph fits the graph paper.

(ii)   Do not attempt to draw a line through the scatter graph unless the question requires it.

(iii)   Label the axes and state the units.

(b)   The regression line of Y on X is $Y = a + bX$ where

$$b = \frac{n\sum XY - \sum X \sum Y}{n\sum X^2 - (\sum X)^2} \quad \text{and} \quad a = \frac{\sum Y - b\sum X}{n}$$

$$\sum X \quad = \quad 320$$

$$\sum Y \quad = \quad 130$$

$$n \quad = \quad 10$$

$$b \quad = \quad \frac{10 \times 4,728 - 320 \times 130}{10 \times 12,614 - (320)^2} \quad = \quad \frac{5,680}{23,740}$$

$$= \quad 0.239$$

$$a \quad = \quad \frac{130 - 0.239 \times 320}{10}$$

$$= \quad 5.34$$

The least squares regression line of electricity costs (Y) on production (X) is therefore

$$Y \quad = \quad 5.34 + 0.239X$$

where Y is in £'000 and X in '000 units.

Explanation

Assuming there is an approximately linear relationship between production and electricity costs, which is shown to be reasonable by the scatter graph, the electricity costs are made up of two parts, a fixed cost (independent of the volume of production) of £5,340 and a variable cost per unit of production of £239 per 1,000 units (or 23.9p per unit).

(c)   For quarter 11, X = 15, hence

$$Y \quad = \quad 5.34 + 0.239 \times 15$$

$$= \quad 8.93$$

The predicted electricity cost for quarter 11 is therefore £8,930.

For quarter 12, X = 55, hence

$$Y \quad = \quad 5.34 + 0.239 \times 55$$

$$= \quad 18.5$$

The predicted electricity cost for quarter 12 is therefore £18,500.

(d)   There are two main sources of error in the forecasts:

(i)   The assumed relationship between Y and X.

The scatter graph shows that there can be fairly wide variations in Y for a given X. Also the forecast assumes that the same conditions will prevail over the next two quarters as in the last ten quarters.

(ii)   The predicted production for quarters 11 and 12.

No indication is given as to how these planned production values were arrived at, so that it is not possible to assess how reliable they are. If they are based on extrapolation of a time series for production over the past ten quarters, they will be subject to the errors inherent in such extrapolations.

Provided conditions remain similar to the past ten quarters, it can be concluded that the forecasts would be fairly reliable but subject to some variation.

Note: methods for calculation of confidence limits for forecasts are available, but are outside the scope of this syllabus. At this level it is impossible to quantify the reliability, so that comments can only be in general terms, although a correlation coefficient would be worth calculating **if time allowed.**

10 FORECASTING AND TIME SERIES

INTRODUCTION & LEARNING OBJECTIVES

When you have studied this chapter you should be able to do the following:

- Explain the use of time series analysis.

- Distinguish between additive and multiplicative time series models.

- Identify and quantify cyclical variations in time series data.

1 TIME SERIES

1.1 Definition of terms

A time series is the name given to a set of observations taken at equal intervals of time eg, daily, weekly, monthly, etc. The observations can be plotted against time to give an overall picture of what is happening. **The horizontal axis is always the time axis** (ie, time is the independent variable).

Examples of time series are total annual exports, monthly unemployment figures, daily average temperatures, etc.

1.2 Example

The following data relates to the production (in tonnes) of floggels by the North West Engineering Co. These are the quarterly totals taken over four years from 19X2 to 19X5.

	1st Qtr	2nd Qtr	3rd Qtr	4th Qtr
19X2	91	90	94	93
19X3	98	99	97	95
19X4	107	102	106	110
19X5	123	131	128	130

This time series will now be graphed so that an overall picture can be gained of what is happening to the company's production figures.

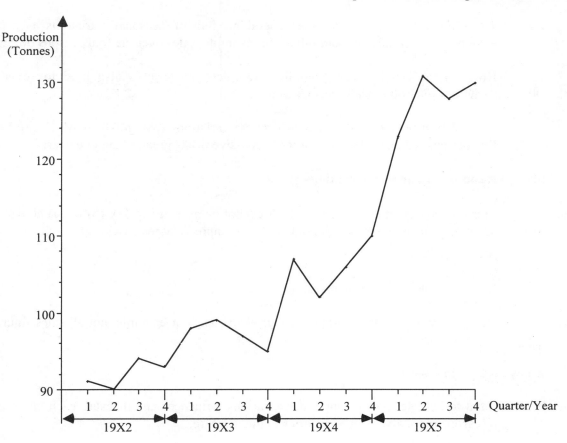

Note: that each point must be plotted at the **end** of the relevant quarter.

The graph shows clearly how the production of floggels has increased over the four-year time period. This is particularly true during the last year considered.

1.3   Variations in observations

A time series is influenced by a number of factors, the most important of these being:

(a)   **Long-term trends**

This is the way in which the graph of a time series appears to be moving over a long interval of time when the short-term fluctuations have been smoothed out. The rise or fall is due to factors which change slowly eg,

(i)   increase or decrease in population;
(ii)   technological improvements;
(iii)   competition from abroad.

(b)   **Cyclical variations**

This is the wave-like appearance of a time series graph when taken over a number of years. Generally, it is due to the influence of booms and slumps in industry. The period in time from one peak to the next is often approximately 5 to 7 years.

(c)   **Seasonal variations**

This is a regular rise and fall over specified intervals of time. The interval of time can be any length – hours, days, weeks etc, and the variations are of a periodic type with a fairly definite period, eg:

(i)   rises in the number of goods sold before Christmas and at sale times;
(ii)   rises in the demand for gas and electricity at certain times during the day;
(iii)   rises in the number of customers using a restaurant at lunch-time and dinner time.

These are referred to under the general heading of 'seasonal' variations as a common example is the steady rise and fall of, for example, sales over the four seasons of the year.

However, as can be seen from the examples, the term is also used to cover regular variations over other short periods of time.

They should not be confused with cyclical variations (paragraph b) which are long-term fluctuations with an interval between successive peaks greater than one year.

(d)   **Residual or random variations**

This covers any other variation which cannot be ascribed to (a), (b) or (c) above. This is taken as happening entirely at random due to unpredictable causes, eg:

(i)   strikes;
(ii)   fires;
(iii)   sudden changes in taxes.

Not all time series will contain all four elements. For example, not all sales figures show seasonal variations.

1.4   Analysis of a time series

It is essential to be able to disentangle these various influences and measure each one separately. The main reasons for analysing a time series in this way are:

(a)   To be able to predict future values of the variable ie, to make forecasts.

(b)   To attempt to control future events.

(c)   To 'seasonally adjust' or 'de-seasonalise' a set of data, that is to remove the seasonal effect. For example, seasonally adjusted unemployment values are more useful than actual unemployment values in studying the effects of the national economy and Government policies on unemployment.

2   ANALYSIS OF A TIME SERIES

2.1   Additive and multiplicative models

To analyse a time series, it is necessary to make an assumption about how the four components described combine to give the total effect. The simplest method is to assume that the components are added together ie, if:

A	=	Actual value for the period
T	=	Trend component
C	=	Cyclical component
S	=	Seasonal component
R	=	Residual component

then $A = T + C + S + R$.   This is called an **additive model**.

Another method is to assume the components are multiplied together, ie:

$$A = T \times C \times S \times R$$

This is called a **multiplicative model**.

The additive model is the simplest, and is satisfactory when the fluctuations about the trend are within a constant band width. If, as is more usual, the fluctuations about the trend increase as the trend increases, the multiplicative model is more appropriate. Illustrated diagrammatically:

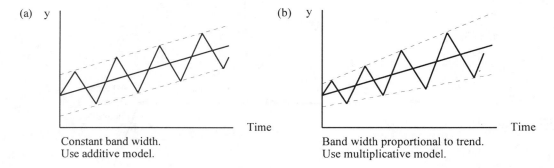

(a)   y   (b)   y

              Time   Time

Constant band width.   Band width proportional to trend.
Use additive model.   Use multiplicative model.

2.2   Trend

The trend can be obtained by using regression analysis to obtain the line of best fit through the points on the graph, taking x as the year numbers (1, 2, 3.... etc) and y as the vertical variable. It is not necessary for the trend to be a straight line, as non-linear regression can be used, but for this method it is necessary to assume an appropriate mathematical form for the trend, such as parabola, hyperbola, exponential, etc. If the trend does not conform to any of these, the method cannot be used.

An alternative, which requires no assumption to be made about the nature of the curve, is to smooth out the fluctuations by moving averages.

The simplest way to explain the method is by means of an example.

2.3   Estimation of trend by moving averages

Example

The following are the sales figures for Bloggs Brothers Engineering Ltd for the fourteen years from 19X1 to 19Y4.

Year	Sales (£'000)
19X1	491
19X2	519
19X3	407
19X4	452
19X5	607
19X6	681
19X7	764
19X8	696
19X9	751
19Y0	802
19Y1	970
19Y2	1,026
19Y3	903
19Y4	998

Using the method of moving averages the general trend of sales will be established.

2.4   Solution

[Step 1]   First, it is advisable to draw a graph of the time series so that an overall picture can be gained and the cyclical movements seen.

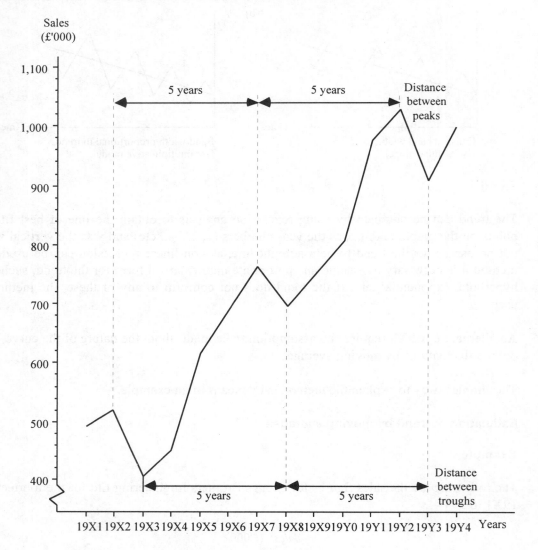

In order to calculate the trend figures it is necessary to establish the span of the cycle. From the graph it can easily be seen that the distance in time between successive peaks (and successive troughs) is 5 years; therefore a 5 point moving average must be calculated.

Step 2   A table of the following form is now drawn up:

Year	Sales (£'000)	5 yearly moving total	5 yearly moving average
19X1	491	-	-
19X2	519	-	-
19X3	407	2,476	495
19X4	452	2,666	533
19X5	607	2,911	582
19X6	681	3,200	640
19X7	764	3,499	700
19X8	696	3,694	739
19X9	751	3,983	797
19Y0	802	4,245	849
19Y1	970	4,452	890
19Y2	1,026	4,699	940
19Y3	903	-	-
19Y4	998	-	-

Notes on the calculation

(a)   As the name implies, the five yearly moving total is the sum of successive groups of 5 years' sales ie,

491 + 519 + 407 + 452 + 607   =   2,476

Then, advancing by one year:

519 + 407 + 452 + 607 + 681   =   2,666, etc.

802 + 970 + 1,026 + 903 + 998   =   4,699

(b)   These moving totals are simply divided by 5 to give the moving averages, ie,

2,476 ÷ 5   =   495

2,666 ÷ 5   =   533

4,699 ÷ 5   =   940

(c)   Averages are always plotted in the middle of the time period ie, 495 is the average of the figures for 19X1, 19X2, 19X3, 19X4 and 19X5 and so it is plotted at the end of 19X3, this being the mid-point of the time interval from the end of 19X1 to the end of 19X5. Similarly, 533 is plotted at the end of 19X4, and 940 is plotted at the end of 19Y2.

Step 3   The trend figures ie, the five yearly moving averages, can now be drawn onto the original graph alongside the raw data.

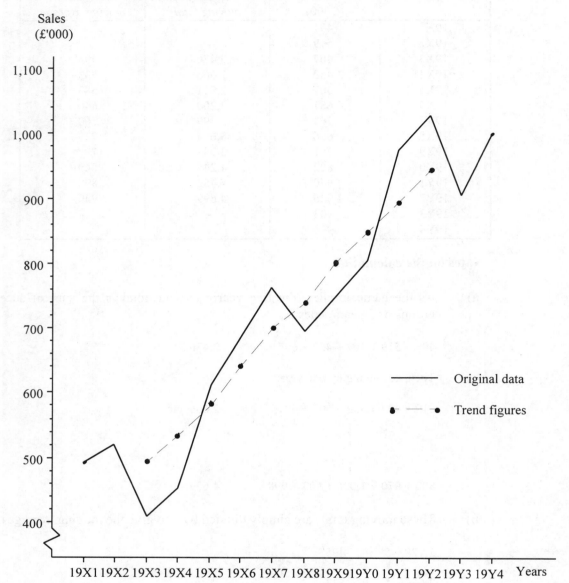

2.5   Cyclical variation

Having calculated the trend figures it is a simple matter to work out the cyclical variations.

For annual data, there cannot be a seasonal component. Hence, using the additive model,

$$A = T + C + R$$

Subtracting T from both sides,

$$A - T = C + R$$

So, by subtracting the trend values from the actual values, the combined cyclical and residual variation will be obtained.

If the multiplicative model is used, A must be divided by T,

$$A = T \times C \times R$$

$$\frac{A}{T} = C \times R$$

2.6   Example

Using the earlier data, establish the cyclical variation, using the additive model.

2.7   Solution

Step 1   A table of the following type is drawn up:

Year	Period of moving averages	Sales (£'000) (A)	Trend figures (T)	Cyclical + Residual variation (A - T)
19X1	1	491	-	-
19X2	2	519	-	-
19X3	3	407	495	−88
19X4	4	452	533	−81
19X5	5	607	582	25
19X6	1	681	640	41
19X7	2	764	700	64
19X8	3	696	739	−43
19X9	4	751	797	−46
19Y0	5	802	849	−47
19Y1	1	970	890	80
19Y2	2	1,026	940	86
19Y3	3	903	−	−
19Y4	4	998	−	−

Notes on the calculation

The figures in the last column for the cyclical variation are just the differences between the actual sales and the trend figures, ie:

$$407 - 495 = -88$$
$$452 - 533 = -81$$
$$\vdots$$
$$1{,}026 - 940 = 86$$

The '+' and '−' signs are important since they show whether the actual figures are above or below the trend figures.

Step 2   To remove the residual component from $C + R$, another table must now be drawn up in order to establish the average cyclical variations.

	Period 1	Period 2	Period 3	Period 4	Period 5
Cyclical variation calculated above	−	−	−88	−81	25
	41	64	−43	−46	−47
	80	86	−	−	−
(i) Totals	121	150	−131	−127	−22
(ii) Average cyclical variation (= (i)/2)	60.5 ≈ 61	75	−65.5 ≈ −66	−63.5 ≈ −64	−11

The individual variations have been averaged out for each year of the cycle ie,

$$\text{Year 1 of each cycle} = \frac{41+80}{2} \qquad = \frac{121}{2} = 60.5, \text{rounded to 61};$$

$$\text{Year 2 of each cycle} = \frac{64+86}{2} \qquad = \frac{150}{2} = 75$$

etc.

 One more step is necessary because the cyclical variation should total to zero, and $61 + 75 + (-66) + (-64) + (-11) = -5$.

The adjustment is made by dividing the excess (-5 in this case) by the number of years in the cycle (5 in this case) and subtracting the result from each of the cyclical variations.

Adjustment is $-5 \div 5 = -1$

Cyclical variations within each cycle are:

Year 1	$61 - (-1)$	$=$	$61 + 1$	$=$	62
Year 2	$75 - (-1)$	$=$	$75 + 1$	$=$	76
Year 3	$-66 - (-1)$	$=$	$-66 + 1$	$=$	-65
Year 4	$-64 - (-1)$	$=$	$-64 + 1$	$=$	-63
Year 5	$-11 - (-1)$	$=$	$-11 + 1$	$=$	-10

(and just as a check, the revised cyclical variations do total zero: $62 + 76 - 65 - 63 - 10 = 0$)

2.8   Seasonal variations

When figures are available for a considerable number of years as in the example above, it is possible to establish the trend and the cyclical variations.

Often, however, monthly or quarterly figures are only available for a few years, 3 or 4, say. In this case, it is possible to establish the trend by means of a moving average or regression analysis. The span of the data is insufficient to find cyclical variations, but seasonal variations can be found.

2.9   Example

The following table gives the takings (£000) of a shopkeeper in each quarter of 4 successive years.

Qtrs	1	2	3	4
19X1	13	22	58	23
19X2	16	28	61	25
19X3	17	29	61	26
19X4	18	30	65	29

Calculate the trend figures and quarterly variations, using moving averages and the additive model and draw a graph to show the overall trend and the original data.

2.10   Solution

The data is now over too short a time for any cyclical component to be apparent, the model becomes:

A   =   T + S + R

1 Year & quarter	2 Takings (£'000) A	3 4 quarterly moving average	4 Centred value T	5 Quarterly + Residual variation S + R
1	13	-	-	-
2	22		-	-
19X1 3	58	29	30	28
4	23	30	31	−8
		31		
1	16	32	32	−16
2	28		33	−5
19X2 3	61	33	33	28
4	25	33	33	−8
		33		
1	17	33	33	−16
2	29	33	33	−4
19X3 3	61	33	34	27
4	26	34	34	−8
		34		
1	18	35	35	−17
2	30	35	36	−6
19X4 3	65	36	-	-
4	29	-	-	-

Notes on the calculation

Column 3

To smooth out quarterly fluctuations, calculate a 4-point moving average, since there are 4 quarters (or seasons) in a year.

ie, $\dfrac{13 + 22 + 58 + 23}{4}$ $= \dfrac{116}{4} =$ 29 then, advancing by one quarter:

$$\frac{22+58+23+16}{4} \quad = \quad \frac{119}{4} \quad = \quad 30 \quad \text{(rounding to nearest whole number)}$$

$$\frac{18+30+65+29}{4} \quad = \quad \frac{142}{4} \quad = \quad 36 \quad \text{(rounding to nearest whole number)}$$

But there is a problem, 29 is the average of the figures for the four quarters of 19X1 and so if plotted, would be at the mid-point of the interval from the end of the first quarter to the end of the fourth quarter ie, half-way through the third quarter of 19X1. But, to find A – T, it is essential that A and T both relate to the same point in time. The four-quarterly moving averages do not correspond with any of the A values, the first coming between the second and third A values and so on down. To overcome this, the moving averages are 'centred' ie, averaged in twos. The first centred average will then coincide with the third A value and so on.

Note: that this is necessary because the cycle has an even number of values (4) per cycle. Where there is an odd number of values per cycle, as in the previous example, the moving averages themselves correspond in time with A values, and centring should not be done.

Column 4

The centring is as follows:

$$\text{ie,} \quad \frac{29+30}{2} \quad = \quad 30 \quad \text{(rounding up)}$$

$$\frac{30+31}{2} \quad = \quad 31 \quad \text{(rounding up)}$$

$$\frac{35+36}{2} \quad = \quad 36 \quad \text{(rounding up)}$$

The first average now corresponds in time with the original value for the 3rd quarter, and so on.

These are the trend values.

Column 5

A – T = S + R, hence the figures for the quarterly + residual variations are the differences between the actual figures and the centred values.

$$\text{ie,} \quad 58-30 \quad = \quad 28$$
$$23-31 \quad = \quad -8$$

$$30-36 \quad = \quad -6$$

In order to establish the quarterly variation another table must be drawn up (as in the earlier example), to remove the residual variation *R*.

	Quarter 1	*Quarter* 2	*Quarter* 3	*Quarter* 4
	–	–	28	–8
	–16	–5	28	–8
	–16	–4	27	–8
	–17	–6	–	–
Totals	–49	–15	83	–24
Average Seasonal variation	–16	–5	28	–8

The individual variations have been averaged out for each quarter of the cycle:

ie,   Quarter 1 $\dfrac{-16+(-16)+(-17)}{3}$ $=$ $\dfrac{-49}{3}$ $=$ –16

Quarter 2 $\dfrac{-5+(-4)+(-6)}{3}$ $=$ $\dfrac{-15}{3}$ $=$ –5

The quarterly variations should total to zero again, but –16 + (–5) + 28 + (–8) = –1. However, the adjustment would only be –1 ÷ 4 ie, –0.25 which means using a spurious accuracy of two decimal places.   To avoid this one value only need be adjusted, choosing the greatest value as this will give the lowest relative adjustment error.

1st	Quarter	=			–16
2nd	Quarter	=			–5
3rd	Quarter	=	28 + 1	=	29
4th	Quarter	=			–8
					———
					0
					———

Draw the graph

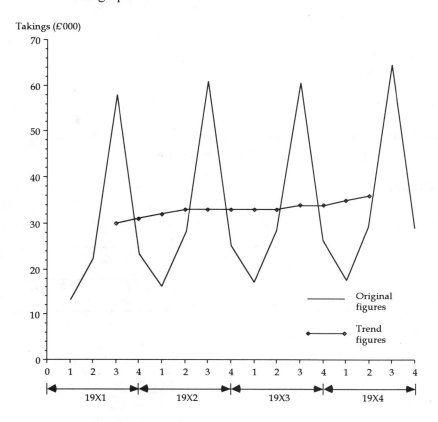

Comment

As can be seen from the calculations and the graph, the takings show a slight upward trend and the seasonal (quarterly) variations are considerable.

3   SEASONALLY ADJUSTED FIGURES

3.1   Introduction

A popular way of presenting a time series is to give the seasonally adjusted or de-seasonalised figures.

This is a very simple process once the seasonal variations are known.

For the additive model:

| Seasonally adjusted data | = | Original data | – | Seasonal variation | = | A – S |

For the multiplicative model:

| Seasonally adjusted data | = | Original data | ÷ | Seasonal indices | = | A ÷ S |

The main purpose in calculating seasonally adjusted figures is to remove the seasonal influence from the original data so that non-seasonal influences can be seen more clearly.

3.2   Example additive model

The same shopkeeper as in the last example found his takings for the four quarters of 19X5 were £19,000, £32,000, £65,000 and £30,000 respectively. Has the upward trend continued?

3.3   Solution

De-seasonalising the figures gives:

Seasonally adjusted figures (£'000)

Quarter 1	19 – (–16)	=	35
Quarter 2	32 – (–5)	=	37
Quarter 3	65 – 29	=	36
Quarter 4	30 – (–8)	=	38

So, as can be seen from comparing the seasonally adjusted figures with the trend figures calculated earlier, the takings are indeed still increasing ie, there is an upward trend.

3.4   Example multiplicative model

The following data will be seasonally adjusted using 'seasonal indices.'

| | Quarter | | | |
	1	2	3	4
Sales (£'000)	59	50	61	92
Seasonal variation	–2%	–21%	–9%	+30%

If $A = T \times S \times R$, the de-seasonalised data is A/S.

A decrease of -2% means a factor of 0.98. Similarly, an increase of 30% means a factor of 1.3. Hence the seasonal factors are   0.98,   0.79,   0.91,   1.30   respectively. The actual data, A, must be **divided** by these values to remove the seasonal effect. Hence:

A	*Seasonal factor (S)*	*Seasonally adjusted figure (= A/S)*
59	0.98	60
50	0.79	63
61	0.91	67
92	1.30	71

While actual sales are lowest in summer and highest in winter, the seasonally adjusted values show a fairly steady increase throughout the year.

4   TIME SERIES APPLIED TO FORECASTING MODELS

It has been shown in the above sections how data can be de-seasonalised in order to identify the underlying trend. However, it is often the case that predictions are required to be made about the future, but taking into account seasonal factors.

This can be done in two ways:

(a)   by fitting a line of best fit (straight or curved) by eye (preferably through the trend found by moving averages); or

(b)   by using linear regression. This was considered earlier in the text.

The line is then extended to the right in order to estimate future trend values. This 'trend' value is then adjusted in order to take account of the seasonal factors.

Hence, the forecast $= T_e + S$,   where T_e = extrapolated trend.

Residual variations are by nature random and therefore unforecastable.

4.1   Example

Using the data from the shopkeeper predict the takings of the shop for the first and second quarters of   19X5.

4.2   Solution

Takings (£'000)

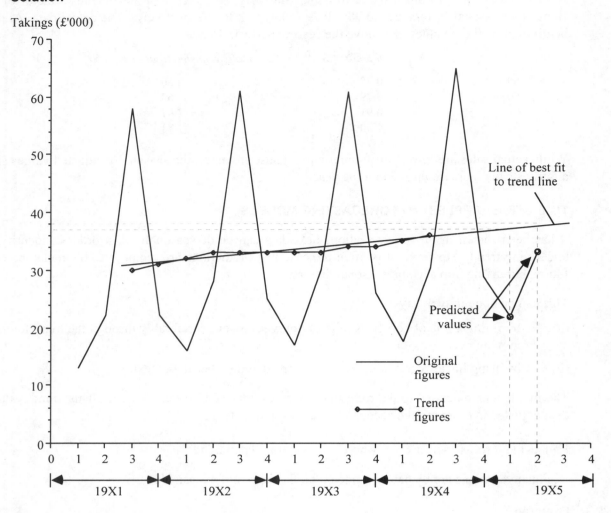

From the graph it can be seen that the trend line predicts values as follows:

Quarter in 19X5	(i) *Trend value*	(ii) *Seasonal variation*	(i) + (ii) *Final prediction*
1	37,000	−16,000	21,000
2	38,000	−5,000	33,000

The predicted values of £21,000 and £33,000 have been plotted on the graph.

For the multiplicative model, the extrapolated trend must be **multiplied** by the appropriate seasonal factor. Thus in the example in paragraph 2.14, if the predicted trend value for the first quarter of the following year was £65,000, the appropriate seasonal factor for this quarter being 0.98, the forecast of actual sales would be £65,000 × 0.98 = £64,000 (to the nearest £000).

4.3   Time series applied to forecasting models – alternative method

As we have seen in the previous chapter, an alternative method for making predictions is to use linear regression in order to establish the trend line in the first place (rather than using the method of moving averages), and then on the basis of this regression line it is possible to predict the figures for the underlying trend. These are then used to estimate seasonal variations and the extrapolated trend values are calculated from the regression equation.

5   CHAPTER SUMMARY

This was the second of the chapters looking at different forecasting techniques. In this chapter the use of time series was considered.

6   SELF TEST QUESTIONS

6.1   What is a time series analysis? (1.1)

6.2   Which axis is always the time axis? (1.1)

6.3   What is a seasonal variation? (1.3)

6.4   What is the formula for an additive time series model? (2.1)

6.5   What does the method of moving averages try and achieve? (2.2)

7   EXAMINATION TYPE QUESTION

7.1   Daily visitors to a hotel

The number of daily visitors to a hotel, aggregated by quarter, is shown below for the last three years.

Year	Quarter 1	Quarter 2	Quarter 3	Quarter 4
19X6	-	-	-	88
19X7	90	120	200	28
19X8	22	60	164	16
19X9	10	80	192	-

The following additive model is assumed to apply:

Actual value = Trend + Seasonal variation + Residual (irregular) variation

You are required:

(a)   to find the centred moving average trend;   **(5 marks)**

(b)   to find the average seasonal variation for each quarter;   **(5 marks)**

(c)   to plot the original data and the trend on the same time-series graph; **(5 marks)**

(d)   to predict the number of daily visitors for the fourth quarter of 19X9, showing clearly how this is calculated, and state any assumptions underlying this answer.   **(5 marks)**

                                                                                        (Total: 20 marks)

8   ANSWER TO EXAMINATION TYPE QUESTION

8.1   Daily visitors to a hotel

(a)   Trend using centred moving average

Note: you are given considerable help in finding the trend using moving averages, in that you are told to find a centred moving average. Set out the original data on every other line, then the first 4 quarter moving average corresponds to a time period half way between the first two and the next two quarters. By finding an 8 quarter moving average a trend figure is found that can be compared with the original data. It is worth finding the seasonal variations for part (b) at the same time.

Year	Quarter	Visitors	4-quarter total	8-quarter total	Centred trend (8-quarter average)	Variations (visitors-trend)
19X6	4	88				
19X7	1	90				
			498			
	2	120		936	117	3
			438			
	3	200		808	101	99
			370			
	4	28		680	85	-57
			310			
19X8	1	22		584	73	-51
			274			
	2	60		536	67	-7
			262			
	3	164		512	64	100
			250			
	4	16		520	65	-49
			270			
19X9	1	10		568	71	-61
			298			
	2	80				
	3	192				

(b)   Average seasonal variations

Year/Quarter	1	2	3	4	Total
19X7		+3	+99	-57	
19X8	-51	-7	+100	-49	
19X9	-61				
Total	-112	-4	+199	-106	
Mean	-56	-2	+99.5	-53	-11.5
Adjusted mean	-53	+1	+102	-50	0.0

Note: the adjusted mean is the seasonal variations. The original mean variations add up to 11.5 so 3 is added to each of these figures, except Q3, to ensure that the total is zero.

(c)   Graph of time series

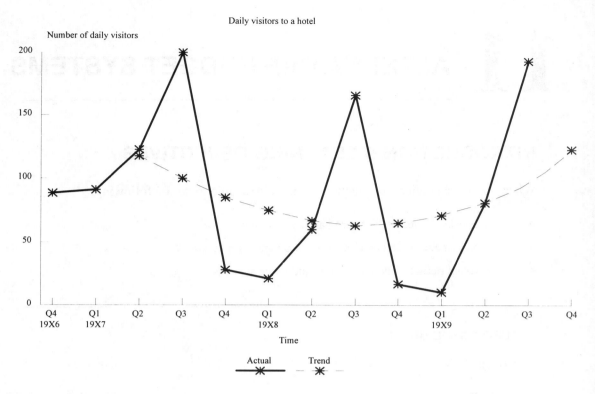

(d)   Forecast for quarter 4 in 19X9

The trend figure for quarter 4 in 19X9 is read from the graph as 120 visitors.

To this should be added the average seasonal variation for quarter 4 which, from (b), is −50.

This makes the best estimate for quarter 4 in 19X9.

$$120 - 50 = 70 \text{ visitors per day.}$$

The assumptions include:

-       the additive model is more appropriate than the proportional model;
-       the random variations for the quarter will not be material; and
-       there are no unusual events that will make the quarter atypical.

11 ALTERNATIVE BUDGET SYSTEMS

INTRODUCTION & LEARNING OBJECTIVES

When you have studied this chapter you should be able to do the following:

- Describe the features of zero based budgeting.
- Contrast zero based and incremental budgeting methods.
- Explain periodic and continuous budgeting systems.

1 ZERO BASED BUDGETING

1.1 Introduction

 A method of budgeting whereby all activities are re-evaluated each time a budget is set. Discrete levels of each activity are valued and a combination chosen to match funds available.

ZBB requires the budgeting of every part of an organisation from 'scratch' or 'base'. The technique forces managers to consider all the costs of an operation, consider the level of service provided and the costs of providing that service. Often the 'zero-option' is not feasible, nor desired, but different levels of operation are considered.

The costs of providing each level of service will be assessed against the level of service provided and the most appropriate chosen.

1.2 The technique of zero-based budgeting

The first requirement in a ZBB process which is most effective in controlling service department budgets is the development of a *decision package*.

This has been defined by its first proponent Peter A Pyhrr of Texas Instruments as:

'A document that identifies and describes a specific activity in such a manner that senior management can:

(a)   evaluate it and rank it against other activities competing for limited resources; and

(b)   decide whether to approve or disapprove it.'

Decision packages are developed by managers for their particular areas of responsibility.

Decision packages will contain information such as:

- the function of the department;
- a performance measure for the department;
- costs and benefits of operating a department at a range of different levels of funding;
- consequences of not operating at those levels.

The second requirement is the actual ranking of the decision packages, using cost/benefit analysis.

The result is a list of ranked projects or activities which senior management can use to evaluate needs and priorities in making budget approvals. The resources available to the organisation for the forthcoming budget period are thus allocated accordingly.

This in practice may be a formidable task, particularly with the interrelationships that exist within an organisation, and probably no organisation can afford to take the time to examine every activity in the necessary depth every year. A review cycle covering each activity once every three or four years may be more practical. ZBB is said to be particularly useful in local government. It may be easier to apply in that situation because it is possible to segregate and assess the benefits of each activity (eg, refuse collection, schools, road maintenance) and the complicated links often found in industry are minimal. In the private sector its most productive use would seem to be in the area of non-manufacturing costs. In this area efficiency standards are difficult to develop and costs often tend to mushroom.

1.3   Benefits of zero-based budgeting

Despite considerable practical problems associated with applying ZBB throughout the organisation, some important benefits are envisaged in its rationale:

(a)   it helps to create an organisational environment where change is accepted;

(b)   it helps management to focus on company objectives and goals;

(c)   it concentrates the attention of management on the future rather than on the past;

(d)   it helps to identify inefficient and obsolete operations within the organisation;

(e)   it provides a framework to ensure the optimum utilisation of resources by establishing priorities in relation to operational activity;

(f)   it should lead to a more logical and beneficial allocation of resources available to an organisation; and

(g)   it can assist motivation of management at all levels;

(h)   it provides a plan to follow when more financial resources become available;

(i)   it establishes minimum requirements from departments;

(j)   it can be done piecemeal.

It does have some disadvantages namely:

(a)   it takes more management time than conventional systems, in part because managers need to learn what is required of them;

(b)   there is a temptation to concentrate on short-term cost savings at the expense of longer-term benefits;

(c)   it takes time to show the real benefits of implementing such a system.

1.4   Example

ZBB Ltd has two service departments - material handling and maintenance, which are in competition for budget funds which must not exceed £925,000 in the coming year. A zero base budgeting approach will be used whereby each department is to be treated as a decision package and will submit a number of levels of operation showing the minimum level at which its service could be offered and two additional levels which would improve the quality of the service from the minimum level.

The following data have been prepared for each department showing the three possible operating levels for each:

Material handling department

Level 1. A squad of 30 labourers would work 40 hours per week for 48 weeks of the year. Each labourer would be paid a basic rate of £4 per hour for a 35 hour week. Overtime hours would attract a premium of 50% on the basic rate per hour. In addition, the company anticipates payments of 20% of gross wages in respect of employee benefits. Directly attributable variable overheads would be incurred at the rate of 12p per man hour. The squad would move 600,000 kilos per week to a warehouse at the end of the production process.

Level 2. In addition to the level 1 operation, the company would lease 10 fork lift trucks at a cost of £2,000 per truck per annum. This would provide a better service by enabling the same volume of output as for level 1 to be moved to a customer collection point which would be 400 metres closer to the main factory gate. Each truck would be manned by a driver working a 48 week year. Each driver would receive a fixed weekly wage of £155.

Directly attributable overheads of £150 per truck per week would be incurred.

Level 3. A computer could be leased to plan the work of the squad of labourers in order to reduce their total work hours. The main benefit would be improvement in safety through reduction in the time that work-in-progress would lie unattended. The computer leasing costs would be £20,000 for the first quarter (3 months), reducing by 10% per quarter cumulatively thereafter.

The computer data would result in a 10% reduction in labourer hours, half of this reduction being a saving in overtime hours.

Maintenance department

Level 1. Two engineers would each be paid a salary of £18,000 per annum and would arrange for repairs to be carried out by outside contractors at an annual cost of £250,000.

Level 2. The company would employ a squad of 10 fitters who would carry out breakdown repairs and routine maintenance as required by the engineers. The fitters would each be paid a salary of £11,000 per annum.

Maintenance materials would cost £48,000 per annum and would be used at a constant rate throughout the year. The purchases could be made in batches of £4,000, £8,000, £12,000 or £16,000. Ordering costs would be £100 per order irrespective of order size and stock holding costs would be 15% per annum. **The minimum cost order size would be implemented**.

Overheads directly related to the maintenance operation would be a fixed amount of £50,000 per annum.

In addition to the maintenance squad it is estimated that £160,000 of outside contractor work would still have to be paid for.

Level 3. The company could increase its maintenance squad to 16 fitters which would enable the service to be extended to include a series of major overhauls of machinery. The additional fitters would be paid at the same salary as the existing squad members.

Maintenance materials would now cost £96,000 per annum and would be used at a constant rate throughout the year. Purchases could be made in batches of £8,000, £12,000 or £16,000. Ordering costs would be £100 per order (irrespective of order size) and stock holding costs would now be

13.33% per annum. In addition, suppliers would now offer discounts of 2% of purchase price for orders of £16,000. The minimum cost order size would be implemented.

Overheads directly related to the maintenance operation would increase by £20,000 from the level 2 figure.

It is estimated that £90,000 of outside contractor work would still have to be paid for.

You are required to

(a)   Determine the incremental cost for each of levels 1, 2 and 3 in each department.

(b)   In order to choose which of the incremental levels of operation should be allocated the limited budgeted funds available, management have estimated a 'desirability factor' which should be applied to each increment. The ranking of the increments is then based on the 'incremental cost × desirability factor' score, whereby a high score is deemed more desirable than a low score. The desirability factors are estimated as:

	Material handling	*Maintenance*
Level 1	1.00	1.00
Level 2 (incremental)	0.60	0.80
Level 3 (incremental)	0.50	0.20

Use the above ranking process to calculate which of the levels of operation should be implemented in order that the budget of £925,000 is not exceeded.

1.5   Solution

(a)   **Material handling department**

Level 1:

		£	£
Wages cost:	30 × 40 hours × 48 weeks × £4		230,400
	30 × 5 hours × 48 weeks × £2		14,400
			244,800
Employee benefits	20% × £244,800		48,960
Variable overhead	30 × 40 hours × 48 weeks × 12p		6,912
Incremental cost			**300,672**

Level 2:

		£
Leasing:	10 trucks @ £2,000	20,000
Drivers' wages	10 drivers × 48 weeks × £155	74,400
Overhead	10 trucks × 48 weeks × £150	72,000
Incremental cost		**166,400**

Level 3:

Leasing:	(£20,000 + £18,000 + £16,200 + £14,580)		68,780

Savings:

(30 men × 40 hours × 48 weeks × 10% = 5,760 hours)

Wages cost:	5,760 hours × £4	23,040	
	2,880 hours × £2	5,760	
		28,800	
Employee benefits	20% × 28,800	5,760	
Variable overhead	5,760 hours × 12p	691	
			(35,251)

Incremental cost	**33,529**

Maintenance department

Level 1:

		£
Engineers' salaries	2 × £18,000	36,000
Outside contractors		250,000
Incremental cost		**286,000**

Level 2:

Engineers' salaries	2 × £18,000	36,000
Fitters' salaries	10 × £11,000	110,000
Materials		48,000
Ordering costs (W1)		600
Stockholding costs (W1)		600
Overheads		50,000
Outside contractors		160,000
		405,200
Less level one costs		(286,000)
Incremental cost		**119,200**

Level 3:

Engineers' salaries	2 × £18,000	36,000
Fitters' salaries	16 × £11,000	176,000
Materials		96,000
Ordering costs (W2)		600
Stockholding costs (W2)		1,045
Discount		(1,920)
Overheads		70,000
Outside contractors		90,000
		467,725
Less level two costs		(405,200)
Incremental cost		**62,525**

(b)   **Factor scores:**

		Material handling		Maintenance
Level 1:	(£300,672 × 1.00)	300,672	(£286,000 × 1.00)	286,000
Level 2:	(£166,400 × 0.60)	99,840	(£119,200 × 0.80)	95,360
Level 3:	(£33,529 × 0.50)	16,765	(£62,525 × 0.20)	12,505

The budget will be spent as follows:

			£
Material handling	-	Level 3	
		(£300,672 + £166,400 + £33,529)	500,601
Maintenance	-	Level 2	
		(£286,000 + £119,200)	405,200
			905,801

WORKINGS

(W1)

Order size	No. of orders	Average stock	Ordering cost	Holding cost	Total cost
£4,000	12	£2,000	£1,200	£300	£1,500
£8,000	6	£4,000	£600	£600	£1,200
£12,000	4	£6,000	£400	£900	£1,300
£16,000	3	£8,000	£300	£1,200	£1,500

(W2)

Order size	No. of orders	Average stock	Ordering cost	Holding cost	Total cost
£8,000	12	£4,000	£1,200	£533.2	£1,733.2
£12,000	8	£6,000	£800	£799.8	£1,599.8
£16,000	6	£8,000	£600	£1,066.4	£1,666.4

The discount of 2% is worth (2% × £96,000) = £1,920 per annum; therefore net cost if orders are placed for £16,000 each time is negative, orders will be placed at this level.

At stock is thereby reduced by 2% the stock-holding cost is also reduced by 2% to £1,045.07.

1.6   Conclusions on zero-based budgeting

Sound procedures for budgeting should always involve a careful and detailed evaluation of all the operating facets each time a budget is prepared. The ZBB approach is a relatively new procedure that can be adopted at the planning stage; it does not in itself change the underlying philosophy of planning and control in budgeting.

Theoretically ZBB is a very sound tool of management, and the likely success of such a system depends very largely on commitment to it in terms of management time and effort. This type of analytical approach to budgeting can be very costly in terms of time and money, and there should be some attempt to measure the benefits that could be obtained.

Under a traditional approach to budgeting, which accepts current levels of expenditure, budgeting is very often a time-consuming activity. Some large organisations in the UK begin the budgetary planning stage for the next year very early in the current year – and that is with a traditional approach. The adoption of a system of ZBB would undoubtedly lengthen the cycle considerably.

Few, if any, large organisations in this country have adopted ZBB for *all* their parts for *every* year, and it is doubtful whether this would ever be completely feasible. However, a selective approach as to which parts of the organisation are to be subjected to a ZBB procedure in any one year may be a practical compromise, even if by doing this some of the advantages may be clearly curtailed.

Given the resources in terms of people, time and money there is little doubt that the aims spelt out for a pure system of ZBB could be achieved but it is not seen to be practicable as a completely new approach. Some compromise approach would provide some benefits to an organisation but, as with all new management tools, the cost/benefit would need to be monitored carefully.

The following summary is taken from Horngren:

'Some generalisations concerning ZBB experiences

While it is difficult to conclude on the appropriateness and effectiveness of this technique in different organisational settings, the following comparative outline represents an attempt to integrate some of these experiences:

		Private sector	*Public sector*
(1)	Extent of use	The use of ZBB has spread rapidly in both sectors since the early 1970s. Furthermore, there is no indication that there is a levelling off of interest in ZBB or its use.	
(2)	Where and how it is primarily being used	As a management tool in planning for and controlling the staff and support functions. A ZBB review is normally conducted for a relatively small portion of a corporation's total budget.	As the main system of budget justification (and, in most cases, presentation) for all functions within an organisation.
(3)	Perceived effectiveness of ZBB as a tool in reducing costs/personnel and shifting resource allocations	There have been some examples of cost/personnel savings and shifts in resource allocation resulting from the use of ZBB, but these have not been widespread.	To date there have been no substantive examples of savings or shifts in resource allocation which resulted from the use of ZBB.
(4)	Most frequently mentioned benefit and problem associated with the use of ZBB	*Benefit* – Increased participation of managers in the budget preparation process. *Problem* – Time and effort required to develop, implement and operate the system.	
(5)	Incidence of post audits of ZBB	Many user organisations in both sectors have conducted a review of the process at various stages in its implementation and use. However, these reviews tend to be informal, providing limited insight into the 'real' cost-effectiveness of the process.	

The extent to which these observations are valid is still open to debate and the test of time. Due to the 'newness' of the technique the above comments are based on the short-run experiences of users.'

1.7   Zero based budgeting v incremental budgeting

Incremental budgeting is the technique of setting future budgets by adjusting earlier budgets or actual results. As a consequence the present position is accepted without justification.

As earlier paragraphs have explained, zero based budgeting makes no such assumptions. Every activity and cost must be justified if it is to be included in the budget.

This is the fundamental difference between the methods, ZBB should identify any budgeting slack and thus cause it to be eliminated whereas incremental budgeting is more likely to allow it to continue.

However ZBB is more costly to operate and, if not used with care, can result in the cessation of activities which are for the long-term benefit of the company.

2   PLANNING, PROGRAMMING, BUDGETING SYSTEMS

2.1   Introduction

Planning, programming, budgeting systems (PPBS) were specifically developed to overcome perceived deficiencies in traditional budgeting as applied to government organisations. These perceived deficiencies were:

(a)   confusion between budgets as short-term financial plans and long-term strategic planning. As a result budgets were often used for strategic planning in the absence of any coherent plan or objectives;

(b)   budgets failed to provide information on planned and actual accomplishments;

(c)   budgets failed to provide a sound basis for deciding on resource allocation.

It is this final difficulty which PPBS were particularly designed to deal with - allowing non-commercial organisations to make more informed decisions about resource allocation. The budgets that a local authority or non-profit making organisation traditionally produce will be drawn up along departmental lines with each departmental manager putting forward his or her own budget. Under a PPBS budgets are constructed on the basis of **programmes**, planned activities of an organisation which have been specified.

These programmes will cut across departmental barriers and once this philosophy has been accepted it will allow the scarce resources of an organisation, which may well be located in a single department, to be put to the best use. Identifying such scarce resources allows for the expansion of that critical department, possibly at the expense of departments now seen to be overstaffed. The approach also focuses people's minds on the long-term commitments of an organisation that those programmes represent.

It has been suggested that PPBS is best implemented within a 'matrix' type organisational structure, with programme managers responsible for specific programmes, and functional managers responsible for specific functions within all programmes.

Two organisations that have dabbled with PPBS are the American Forestry Service and their Department of Defence. A 'programme' that the former might wish to implement would be to increase access to the Forestry Service property over a two year period. This would involve effort from the publicity department to heighten awareness; the Forestry Service's roads department to make areas more accessible; maintenance departments would be required to equip picnic areas; building departments would have to provide kiosks or larger refreshment facilities. The service would produce a budget for its 'Increased Access' programme which would include the costs incurred on the programme by all these departments. The person responsible for 'driving' that programme would compare actual costs with his budget in the conventional way - this would require a more detailed costing system that would formerly have been used.

2.2   Conclusions on PPBS

PPBS were first used in the USA in the 1960's and initially were seen to be effective. Their advantages were seen as:

- providing management information that related more directly to the work of an organisation;

- allowing scarce resources to be identified, put to best use, and eliminated as a budgeting constraint;

- allowing programmes to be assessed in terms of their efficiency and effectiveness;

- highlighting long-term commitments of an organisation.

However after its initial apparent success it was felt that PPBS had contributed to the subsequent poor performance in the Department of Defence. The department, like the Forestry Service, modified the process adopting hybrid approaches to budgeting. Whether PPBS could be said to be entirely to blame is doubtful; some of the cause of criticism in these government agencies must be attributed to the difficulties of reconciling the different priorities of different political parties and special interest groups.

3   CONTINUOUS (ROLLING) BUDGETS

3.1   Introduction

Budgets are deemed by many organisations to be unchangeable and sacrosanct. The reasons are twofold:

(a)   How committed would management be to the budget preparation process if they knew that senior management accepted that their budgets would need to be adjusted before the end of the budget term?

(b)   The comparison of the original master budget with annual revenues and costs is a useful one - even if the organisation operated under very changed conditions from that originally planned. Also the use of 'revision variances' can be used to bridge the gap and produce meaningful management performance reports.

However there are circumstances in which management may consider that the initial master budget is inadequate as a forecast of future outturn and/or as a control benchmark, and where alternative measures are required. For example, the environmental suppositions upon which strategic and budget planning are based may prove to be very unlike those conditions encountered during the budget term.

If change in the budget is required the options available to management are:

(a)   to continue with the original budget, making allowances as necessary;
(b)   to adapt the original budget to reflect the changed circumstances;
(c)   to adopt a 'rolling budget' or forecast revision approach; or
(d)   to re-budget from scratch.

The decision is liable to rely partly upon the degree of error from the budgeted assumptions, and partly upon the ways management use the budget eg, as authority to spend, or limits on spending.

If environmental states are not considerably different from those budgeted for, it may be pragmatic to retain the original budget and expect middle and junior managers to **adapt to the changed situation within the structure of the original budget**. This policy would maintain the integrity of the budgeting procedures and most likely be a practical and economic approach.

If the different states evolved around only one or two assumptions (such as interest rates and a certain material input inflation), it might be wise and feasible to **adapt the master budget to the new situation**, particularly if the budgetary data are held in a sophisticated computer financial model. As the revised budget would be based on the original budget it is more likely to be accepted by managers who would appreciate the need to reflect new conditions.

Rolling (continuous) budgets (and forecast revisions) are more likely to be practised as a matter of routine managerial philosophy, rather than as a response to a particular or unexpected situation.

The bigger the divergence of actual conditions from those budgeted the more logical would be the decision to recognise the inadequacy of the original budget and the need to rebudget. Failure to do so might cause managers to waste limited resources or to use them inappropriately.

The many consequences of changing the annual budget can be reduced to a few major considerations:

(a)   a weakening of the importance placed on the budget system;
(b)   increased time spent by managers on budget preparation;
(c)   the problem of gaining budget acceptance;
(d)   the lack of clear financial objectives; and
(e)   the lack of meaningful management performance measures.

3.2   Preparation of rolling budgets

A rolling budget is defined as "a budget continuously updated by adding a further period, say a month or quarter and deducting the earliest period. Beneficial where future costs and/or activities cannot be forecast reliably". Rolling forecasts have been defined as "a continuously updated forecast whereby each time actual results are reported, a further period is added and intermediate period forecasts are updated".

A typical rolling budget might be prepared as follows:

(a)   A budget is prepared for the coming year (say January - December) broken down into suitable, say quarterly, control periods.

(b)   At the end of the first control period (31 March) a comparison is made of that period's results against the budget. The conclusions drawn from this analysis are used to update the budgets for the remaining control periods and to add a budget for a further three months, so that the company once again has budgets available for the coming year (this time April - March).

(c)   The planning process is repeated at the end of each three-month control period.

The budgeting options available to management who face a dynamic business environment have been discussed above. The views outlined there suggest that rolling budgets are not essential if an organisation is undergoing rapid change, although there may be advantages for a company adopting this approach to budgeting. These include the following:

(a)   Budgets are more realistic and achievable since they are continuously revised to reflect changing circumstances.

(b)   The **annual** disruption associated with the preparation of an annual budget is removed.

(c)   The pressures (and stress) placed on managers to achieve unrealistic budget targets are eased.

(d)   Variance feedback is more meaningful.

(e)   It tends to reduce budgetary bias.

(f)   It reduces the rigidity of the budget system and builds contingency and innovation into the preparation/feedback stages of the control system.

(g)   The assessment of objectives and plans is continuous rather than being a one-off exercise.

(h)   Without some form of budget revision, operational management may continue to invest and recruit etc, with the belief that management strategy holds firm.

(i)   It might help to increase management commitment to the budget.

(j)   The arbitrary and artificial distinction drawn between one financial year and the next is removed, since budgets always extend for a year ahead.

However the problems likely to be encountered with rolling budgets include the following:

(a)   If it is difficult to plan ahead accurately (and it always is!) when once a year managers spend a **lot** of time and effort on the task, how likely is it that managers can do the same forecasts more accurately every month or quarter when they are involved in other responsibilities?

(b)   There is a danger that the rolling budget will become the last budget 'plus or minus a bit' and will be representative of absolutely nothing in terms of corporate objectives and meaningless for performance control purposes.

(c)   Managers will be faced with a greater work load and additional staff may be required.

(d)   Managers may devote insufficient attention to preparing budgets which they know will shortly be revised.

(e)   The organisation might be required to operate annual budgets (such as enterprises operating in the public sector).

In conclusion it is worth noting that the relatively recent development of sophisticated computer budgeting models has increased the use of rolling budgets and similar concepts in organisations. Often figures are now revised by computers with minimal intervention by managers.

4   CHAPTER SUMMARY

This chapter has considered a number of different budgeting techniques. You should recognise that many organisations use a combination of these techniques when setting their budgets.

5   SELF TEST QUESTIONS

5.1   What steps are needed when carrying out a zero-based budgeting exercise? (1.2)

5.2 What is the major difference between PPBS budgets for a non-profit making organisation and conventional departmental budgets? (2.1)

6 EXAMINATION TYPE QUESTION

6.1 A manufacturing company

A manufacturing company intends to introduce zero base budgeting in respect of its service departments.

You are required:

(a) to explain how zero base budgeting differs from incremental budgeting and explain the role of committed, engineered and discretionary costs in the operation of zero based budgeting.
(8 marks)

(b) to give specific examples of committed, engineered and discretionary costs for each of the following service departments:

(i) safety;
(ii) maintenance; and
(iii) accounting.
(6 marks)

(c) to prepare a brief summary which explains ways in which profitability may improve by increasing the proportion of funds allocated to each of the service departments named in (b) above.
(6 marks)
(Total: 20 marks)
(ACCA June 91)

7 ANSWER TO EXAMINATION TYPE QUESTION

7.1 A manufacturing company

(Tutorial note: there is a lot to write in part (a) (assuming the knowledge is there!). Part (b) requires common sense (and a good imagination!).)

(a) Zero base budgeting may be defined as 'A method of budgeting whereby all activities are re-evaluated each time a budget is set'. It basically involves starting budget preparation with a 'clean sheet' and only including items in the budget if they can be justified and represent the most cost effective way of achieving the objective.

Incremental budgeting contrasts with this approach in that it involves using the previous year's budget as the starting point ie, last year's budget is implicitly assumed to be reasonable. Incremental adjustments are then made to last year's budget to allow for changes in volume and price level. The disadvantage of this latter approach is that it too easily takes previous budgets as still being valid, even though operating conditions may change, significantly affecting the budget in the next period.

Committed costs are costs which 'arise from having property, plant, equipment and a functioning organisation; little can be done in the short run to change committed costs' (Horngren). By their nature decisions regarding whether they are incurred are made on a long term basis - via preparation of the capital budgets. In the assumed context of annual operating budgets these costs would not be affected when zero based budgeting is used.

Engineered costs are 'costs that result from a clear-cut, measured relationship between inputs and outputs' (Horngren). These costs are therefore specific to the activity level achieved. The amount included under zero base budgeting will therefore be changed in line with the projected activity level.

Discretionary costs are costs, the level of which is a matter of policy (eg, research and development). The amount incurred is therefore not governed by the activity level. Here the manager, under zero base budgeting, must justify, perhaps using cost benefit analysis, the amount of expenditure to include in the budget.

(b)

		Committed	*Engineered*	*Discretionary*
(i)	Safety	Cost of meeting legal requirements, eg, guards on machines	Protective clothing	Expenditure on literature promoting safety awareness
(ii)	Maintenance	Cost of tools, etc. needed by maintenance staff	- Cost of spare parts - Cost of services needed at specific interval (eg, every 10,000 hours)	Cost of having the factory painted
(iii)	Accounting	Cost of maintaining statutory books and producing published accounts	- Invoicing and postage costs per order - Computer processing time	- Staff examination and training costs - Cost of management training

(c)   (*Tutorial note:* several points may be made here but there are only six marks!)

Ways in which profitability may be improved by the allocation of additional funds to the following areas:

(i)   **Safety**

- Less absenteeism (due to reduction in industrial accidents) and associated production time lost (labour and machine idle time);

- higher staff morale (feeling of well being due to safety procedures);

- may attract better staff and reduce labour turnover;

- reduction in insurance premiums if the number of industrial accidents is lower than average.

(ii)   **Maintenance**

- Improved reliability of machinery ie, less breakdowns, if there is planned maintenance and it will reduce idle time costs;

- may reduce material wastage;

- reduced power consumption if production is completed in a shorter time period;

- life of machines may be extended;

- shorter production lead times would improve quality of service provided to customers, possibly resulting in increased sales.

(iii)   **Accounting**

- Improved information eg, faster and more detailed, if computers are used resulting in better decisions;

- computer systems may enable number of staff to be reduced;

- more time available for credit control - reduce payment period taken by debtors;

- more time to improve stock control eg, identify slow moving items.

12 STANDARD COSTING

INTRODUCTION & LEARNING OBJECTIVES

This chapter considers the use of standard costing as an alternative to the use of budgets and budgetary control methods.

The concept of standard costs and the setting of standards is considered, and the difficulties of introducing standard costing into non-manufacturing and specific order environments are examined.

Finally the difficulties of ensuring that standards are meaningful and relevant is discussed.

When you have studied this chapter you should be able to do the following:

- Define standard costs.

- Explain the differences between different types of standard.

- Explain the relationship between standard costing and budgetary control.

- Recognise and explain the difficulties of using standard costing in non-manufacturing and specific order environments.

- Explain the importance and problems associated with ensuring that standards remain meaningful and relevant.

1 STANDARD COSTING

1.1 Introduction

Definition   A method of cost accounting which incorporates standard costs and variances into the ledger accounts of the organisation.

1.2 Standard cost

Definition   A standard cost is a standard expressed in money. It is built up from an assessment of the value of cost elements. Its main uses are providing bases for performance measurement, control by exception reporting, valuing stock and establishing prices.

1.3 Standard cost card

This shows the standard cost for a single unit of a product.

Standard cost card
Cost per unit of product X

		£
Raw materials:	5 kgs P @ £2/kg	10.00
	3 kgs Q @ £1.5/kg	4.50
Labour	4 hrs grade A @ £4/hr	16.00
	1 hr grade B @ £5.50/hr	5.50
		─────
		36.00
		─────

This standard cost is used as a basis of comparison with actual results.

1.4 The meaning of 'standard'

The term implies a fixed relationship which is assumed to hold good for the budget period or until it is deliberately revised. By the use of standards one measurement can be converted into another. When it is said that a journey of 90 miles from A to B takes three hours, a standard speed under prevailing traffic conditions of 30 miles per hour is assumed. It is thus possible to express distance in hours.

Therefore, if our standard speed of production is 50 items per hour, a transfer of 5,000 items into finished store may be said to represent 100 hours of work. Again, if the standard cost of raw materials is £2.50 per lb and the standard usage per item is 2 lb, the 5,000 items may be regarded either as representing 10,000 lb of raw material or as having a raw material content of £25,000.

A standard cost is calculated in relation to a prescribed set of working conditions ie, it reflects technical specifications and scientific measurement of the resources used to manufacture a product.

Standard costs represent target costs. As such they represent costs which are most likely to be useful for:

(a) planning;
(b) control;
(c) motivation.

However carefully costs are predetermined (and one authority has referred to them as 'scientifically' predetermined costs), in the end they must be **somebody's** best estimate.

Nevertheless in one sense standard costs go beyond a best estimate: standard costs have been adopted as the firm's target - they become a statement of policy. For this reason it is necessary to think carefully about what sort of standards should be set.

1.5 The standard hour

Output is measured in terms of standard hours. A standard hour is a hypothetical unit which represents the amount of work which should be achieved in one hour at standard performance. Thus, if 50 articles are estimated to be made in a 'clock' hour, an output of 150 should take three 'clock' hours and would be valued at the standard cost of those three hours, irrespective of the actual time taken to manufacture them.

1.6 Activity

XYZ Ltd manufactures three different sized fridges. The expected (standard) number of labour hours per fridge is as follows:

Small	5 hours
Medium	7 hours
Large	10 hours

During February the following output was produced by working 130 hours more than the budgeted number of hours which was 470 hours:-

Small	28
Medium	32
Large	30

Calculate the number of standard hours produced during February.

1.7   Activity solution

$$(28 \times 5) + (32 \times 7) + (30 \times 10) = 664 \text{ standard hours}$$

1.8   Control ratios

These ratios may be used as a means of reporting performance without attributing monetary values to the differences between the actual and target results.

For these purposes the budget is assumed to represent available capacity and to be based on efficiency rated at 100%.

There are three ratios:-

(a)   volume;
(b)   capacity;
(c)   efficiency.

1.9   Volume ratio

This compares the actual output (measured in standard hours) to the budget output (in standard hours) and expresses the ratio as a percentage.

Suppose the budget hours were 1,000 and the actual number of standard hours produced were 980. The ratio would be:-

$$\frac{\text{Standard hours produced}}{\text{Budget standard hours}} \times 100$$

$$= \frac{980}{1,000} \times 100 = 98\%$$

1.10   Capacity ratio

This measures the extent to which the budgeted capacity was actually used.

Suppose the actual hours worked in the above example were 950, the capacity ratio would be

$$\frac{\text{Standard worked}}{\text{Budget hours}} \times 100$$

$$= \frac{950}{1,000} \times 100 = 95\%$$

1.11   Efficiency (productivity) ratio

This measures the efficiency of the actual hours worked. Using the above data:

$$\frac{\text{Standard hours produced}}{\text{Actual hours worked}} \times 100$$

$$= \frac{980}{950} \times 100 = 103.16\%$$

1.12   Relationship between the ratios

The volume ratio is the overall effect of the capacity and efficiency ratios. This can be proven by multiplying the capacity and efficiency ratios to get the volume ratio:-

$$95\% \times 103.16\% = 98\%$$

1.13   Setting standards

In general, a standard cost will be set for each product, comprising:

(a)   **Direct materials:** standard quantity (kgs, litres etc) × standard price per unit (kg, litre etc.)

(b)   **Direct wages:** standard labour hours × standard hourly rate.

(c)   **Variable overhead:** standard hours (labour or machine) × standard rate per hour.

(d)   **Fixed overhead:** budgeted overhead for the period ÷ budgeted standard hours (labour or machine) for the period.

2   EVOLUTION OF STANDARDS

2.1   Continuous improvement

Organisations are continually seeking ways to improve efficiency, often by the installation of technologically superior equipment. When a standard costing system is in use the standard set is based upon the existing operating method.

If the method of operation changes the standard will be out of date and no longer relevant. A new standard is required which reflects the new method of working.

2.2   Keeping standards meaningful and relevant

An analysis of the causes of the variances between actual and standard performance may indicate the relevance of the standard to current operating conditions. In addition to the effects of method changes referred to earlier, significant price differences may affect the validity of the standard and affect its usefulness.

There is therefore an argument for revising the standard to reflect the present attainable conditions. However to do so presents difficulties:

(a)   the determination of the present attainable conditions as opposed to what is presently being attained; and

(b)   the implications for other parts of the planning process of frequent revisions to standard costs.

2.3   Performance evaluation

The purpose of standard costs as targets is to evaluate performance by making comparisons with actual results.

If the standard is no longer meaningful and relevant, then the results of comparing actual performance with those standards also has no meaning.

Variance reports which have been prepared following the comparison of actual results with existing standards may be used as the starting point in determining whether the present standards continue to be appropriate.

The reason or cause of the variance must be established and this may result in a recognition that the standard is no longer appropriate.

2.4   [Conclusion]   Standard costs need to be updated for changes in method as they occur, but changes in prices and similar factors are better highlighted through non-controllable variances if they occur during the planning period.

3   SOME ASPECTS OF IMPLEMENTATION AND OPERATION OF STANDARD COSTING

3.1   Standard costs and frequent price changes

Many organisations operating standard costing systems set standards on an annual basis, the standards for next year being based on estimated average prices. In times of high inflation this approach can lead to large price variances in any particular control period, such variances tending to be favourable in the early part of the budget year and adverse in the later months. In many instances the changes in price levels will have been foreseen and incorporated into the overall standard set for the coming year, so the variances which arise (because the actuals are being compared with the average annual standard each period) may mask other variances which should be highlighted for the attention of management. An alternative approach to the problems associated with the annual standard in periods of high inflation is for the organisation to adopt **current standards**.

3.2   Current standard

[Definition]   A standard established for use over a short period of time, related to current conditions.

3.3   Establishment of current standards

Current standards should be set before the start of the budget year for each month or accounting period. This approach would allow a fully-phased annual budget to be evaluated. In practice the annual budget is often established first and subsequently phased into the individual budgets for each period by recognising the timing of price changes.

Some businesses have a few significant items of cost for which individual estimates are made for the timing and quantification of price level changes eg, organisations with a small number of raw materials which are subject to volatile market conditions. However, most organisations will try and predict accurately the timing and effect of pay increases to their own work force. With labour intensive types of operations this element of cost and the consequent labour cost variances are important and significant.

3.4   Applying control techniques to practical situations

It is impractical, if not impossible, to lay down a standard approach and/or common principles which can be universally applied to the problems of planning and control systems as each individual case is different.

3.5   Relationship of standard costing to budgetary control

Historically, standard costing evolved as a parallel system to budgetary control, representing a different approach to the problem. Today, standard costing has become a subset of budgetary control, and is commonly used within an organisation as part of a budgetary control system.

Nevertheless, it is important to identify three factors that differentiate standard costing from other approaches to budgetary control:

(a)   Under standard costing, for costing purposes all stocks are valued at their standard costs.

(b)   Standard costs are incorporated in the ledger accounts; budgets are a memorandum record outside the ledger accounts.

(c)   Standard costs are set as unit costs; budgets tend to be set as total costs.

Thus although standard costing is a subset of budgeting, it has certain distinct features of its own.

4   CHAPTER SUMMARY

This chapter has explained how standard costing may be used to either supplement or replace a system of budgets and budgetary control.

The setting of different types of standard has been considered in terms of the uses of standard costs, and the difficulties of introducing standard costing into certain organisational environments examined.

Finally the evolution of standards was discussed.

5   SELF TEST QUESTIONS

5.1   What is standard costing? (1.1)

5.2   What is a standard cost? (1.2)

5.3   What is a standard hour? (1.5)

5.4   Identify the three control ratios (1.8)

5.5   What is the relationship between these control ratios? (1.12)

6   EXAMINATION TYPE QUESTION

6.1   Marketing cost budgets

(a)   Comment in detail on the factors you would observe and the steps you would take in constructing a marketing cost budget for a manufacturer of a widely distributed household durable product. Set out your points in brief numbered notes.

(b)   Arising from (a) above, what proposals can you make for setting standards to control such costs?

7   ANSWER TO EXAMINATION TYPE QUESTION

7.1   Marketing cost budgets

(a)   As a preliminary to constructing a marketing cost budget, the following factors require consideration:

    (i)   **Functional responsibilities**

        The organisation structure should be analysed to define the activities embraced by the marketing function eg, packing costs may be considered part of the production budget or credit control part of the administration function.

    (ii)   **Budget centres**

        Budget centres should be developed to facilitate analysis of the budget in relation to executive responsibility. Sales executives may be responsible for particular areas or for specific types of customer, whereas managers within the distribution function are more likely to be allocated product responsibilities.

(iii)   **Integration with other budgets**

Distribution costs will largely be budgeted in relation to sales, but selling costs (apart from commission) will be budgeted in relation to planned sales effort. The two elements of the marketing budget, therefore, require different approaches.

(iv)   **External influences**

The budget will be affected by many factors outside the control of the executive responsible. These factors, such as economic conditions, corporate policy, statutory regulations, etc., should be analysed to assess their effect on the budget.

As indicated by (iii) above, separate selling and distribution budgets would be constructed as follows:

(i)   **Selling**

Assuming that sales responsibility is divided by geographical area, separate budgets would be prepared for each area, together with a budget to cover central sales administration. Within each area budget costs could be grouped between salesmen and establishment expenses, the former set in relation to planned effort and the latter representing fixed selling costs. If practical, the total advertising and promotion expense authorised would be allocated to represent area budgets. The separate budgets would be summarised for review and authorisation as the selling cost budget.

(ii)   **Distribution**

Budget centres would be set up for the activities within the distribution function. A substantial part of the costs would represent packing and transport, and a flexible budgeting approach could be used to control those costs, since a definite relationship exists between the level of costs and sales volume. Fixed administration costs could represent one budget centre controlled by the senior executive within the function.

(b)   Possible standards to control selling and distribution costs would include:

(i)   **Selling**

Apart from commission, which could be expressed as a standard percentage of sales value, selling costs would need to be measured against appropriate work units eg:

Cost item	*Unit*
Travel expenses	Mile or visit
Order processing	Order
Credit control	Account

Standards could be further analysed by area or class of trade for more effective control if the level of costs justified the work involved.

(ii)   **Distribution**

Similarly, standard costs per unit could be developed for different activities eg,

Activity	*Unit*	*Sub-analysis*
Warehousing	£100 factory cost	Product group
Packing	Order	Order size
Delivery	Ton-mile	Type of transport

Separate standards for the major cost items within each activity could be developed, if justifiable.

The above standards would be used for budget preparation and cost control/reduction.

13 VARIANCE ANALYSIS

INTRODUCTION & LEARNING OBJECTIVES

When you have studied this chapter you should be able to do the following:

- Discuss what standard costing is and what it tries to achieve.
- Calculate elementary variances.
- Present operating statements.
- Provide various interpretations of causes of variances and discuss their interdependence.

1 NATURE OF STANDARD COSTING

1.1 A few definitions

Definition **Standard costing** - a control technique which compares standard costs and revenues with actual results to obtain variances which are used to stimulate improved performance.

This highlights the fact that variance analysis is one essential step in the operation of a standard costing system, the other two being the determining of standards and budgets and the recording of costs and transfers in cost ledger accounts. It also highlights the major purpose of operating a standard costing system: to provide a means of planning and controlling the day to day running of a business' activities - although there is also a subsidiary motivational function of operating such a system. This definition leads onto the second:

Definition **Variance analysis** - the analysis of performance by means of variances. Used to promote management action at the earliest possible stages.

This purpose of variance analysis, trying to eliminate inefficiencies, is returned to later. Both these definitions refer to a third:

Definition **Standard cost** - a predetermined measurable quantity set in defined conditions and expressed in money. It is built up from an assessment of the value of cost elements. Its main uses are providing bases for performance measurement, control by exception reporting, valuing stock and establishing selling prices.

This definition has provided another use of variance analysis namely to act as a basis for performance measurement. It also leads to the types of standard that may be set.

1.2 Types of standard

There is a whole range of bases upon which standards may be set within a standard costing system. This choice will be affected by the use to which the standards will be put.

- basic standard
- ideal standard
- attainable standard
- current standard.

Their definitions are as follows:

Definition   **Basic standard** - a standard established for use over a long period from which a current standard can be developed.

Definition   **Ideal standard** - a standard which can be attained under the most favourable conditions, with no allowance for normal losses, waste and machine downtime. Also known as potential standard.

Users believe that the resulting unfavourable variances will remind management of the need for improvement in all phases of operations. Ideal standards are not widely used in practice because they may influence employee motivation adversely.

Definition   **Attainable standard** - a standard which can be attained if a standard unit of work is carried out efficiently, a machine properly operated or material properly used. Allowances are made for normal losses, waste and machine downtime.

The standard represents future performance and objectives which are reasonably attainable. Beside having a desirable motivational impact on employees, attainable standards serve other purposes eg, cash budgeting, inventory valuation and budgeting departmental performance.

Definition   **Current standard** - a standard established for use over a short period of time, related to current conditions.

Given the stated uses of standard costs, the first two types of standard will be rarely used unless a firm wants demotivated staff and information that provides little guidance for performance measurement or cost control. The third type of standard, attainable standards, will be used when operating a standard costing system and for two of the purposes previously mentioned, stock valuation and as a basis for pricing decisions. Whilst variance analysis will initially be carried out by reference to these attainable standards, more useful information comes by comparing with current standards as will be explained later.

2   CALCULATION OF VARIANCES

2.1   Cost variances

Definition   A cost variance is a difference between planned, budgeted or standard cost and actual cost.

Cost variances occur when standard costs are compared to actual costs. There is one important feature of standard costing which must be remembered: standard costing carries out variance analysis using the normal, double entry ledger accounts. This is done by recording in the ledgers:

(a)   actual costs as inputs;
(b)   standard costs as outputs;
(c)   the difference as the variance.

2.2   **Direct material cost variances**

The purpose of calculating direct material cost variances is to quantify the effect on profit of actual direct material costs differing from standard direct material costs. This total effect is then analysed to quantify how much has been caused by a difference in the price paid for the material and how much by a difference in the quantity of material used.

2.3   **Example**

The following standard costs relate to a single unit of product X:

	£
Direct materials	10
Direct labour	8
Production overhead	5
	23

On the basis of the above standard costs if a unit of product X is sold for £30, the expected (or standard) profit would be £7 (£30 – £23).

However, if the **actual** direct material cost of making the unit of X were £12 then (assuming the other costs to be as per standard) the actual cost of product X would be:

	£
Direct materials	12
Direct labour	8
Production overhead	5
	25

Thus when the product is sold, the profit is only £5 (£30 – £25).

This reduction in profit is the effect of the difference between the actual and standard direct material cost of £2 (£12 – £10).

This simple example considered only one unit of product X, but it is the principle upon which variance calculations are made.

2.4   **Direct material total cost variance**

The purpose of this variance is to show the effect on profit for an accounting period of the actual direct material cost being different from the standard direct material cost.

2.5   **Example**

In July, 1,000 units of product X were manufactured, and sold for £30 each.

Using the data above,

(i)   the standard direct material cost of these 1,000 units of product X would be:

1,000 units × £10/unit = £10,000

(ii)   the actual direct material cost of these 1,000 units of product X would be:

1,000 units × £12/unit = £12,000

Assuming the other actual costs to be as expected in the standard, the actual profit and loss account would appear:

	£	£
Sales (1,000 × £30)		30,000
Direct materials (1,000 × £12)	12,000	
Direct labour (1,000 × £8)	8,000	
Production overhead (1,000 × £5)	5,000	
		25,000
Profit		5,000

The expected profit was £7 per unit (£30 – £23) so on sales of 1,000 units this would be:

1,000 units × £7/unit = £7,000.

Actual profit is £2,000 less than expected. Note that this is the same as the difference between the actual and standard direct material cost calculated earlier (£12,000 – £10,000).

This is known as the direct material total cost variance, and because it causes actual profits to be less than expected it is said to be an **adverse** variance.

Note that this total variance for the period can be shown to be equal to the difference of £2 per unit of X (calculated earlier) multiplied by 1,000 units.

2.6   Activity

The standard direct material cost of product A is £5. During August 600 units of product A were made, and the actual direct material cost was £3,200. Calculate the direct material total cost variance for the period.

2.7   Activity solution

	£
Standard direct material cost of 600 units: £5 × 600	3,000
Actual direct material cost	3,200
Direct material total cost variance - Adverse	200

2.8   Analysing the direct material total cost variance

When a standard material cost is determined for a unit of a product it is made up of two parts. These are estimates of:

(a)   the quantity of material to be used; and
(b)   the price to be paid per unit of material.

If we return to the earlier example concerning product X, the standard direct material cost per unit was stated to be £10. This was based on using 5 kg of a particular material to make each unit of product X and paying £2/kg for the material.

You should remember that the actual direct material cost incurred in making 1,000 units of product X was £12,000. The invoice for these costs shows:

4,800 kg @ £2.50/kg = £12,000.

It should be noted that this form of analysis corresponds to the two estimates which form the basis of the standard cost. It is this which allows the direct material total cost variance to be analysed.

2.9   Direct material price variance

The purpose of calculating this variance is to identify the extent to which profits will differ from those expected by reason of the actual price paid for direct materials being different from the standard price.

The standard price per kg of material was stated above to be £2/kg. This can be used to calculate the expected cost of the actual materials used to make 1,000 units of product X. On this basis the 4,800 kg of material should have cost:

> 4,800 kg × £2/kg = £9,600.

The actual cost of these materials was £12,000 which is £2,400 (£12,000 − £9,600) more than expected. Since the actual price was greater than expected this will cause the profit to be lower than expected. This variance, known as the direct material price variance, is adverse.

2.10   Activity

A raw material, used in the manufacture of product F has a standard price of £1.30 per litre. During May 2,300 litres were bought at a cost of £3,128. Calculate the direct material price variance for May.

2.11   Activity solution

	£
Standard cost of 2,300 litres: 2,300 litres × £1.30/litre	2,990
Actual cost of 2,300 litres	3,128
Direct material price variance - Adverse	138

2.12   Direct material usage variance

The purpose of this variance is to quantify the effect on profit of using a different quantity of raw material from that expected for the actual production achieved.

Returning to our example concerning product X, it was stated that each unit of product X had a standard direct material usage of 5 kgs. This can be used to calculate the amount of direct material (in kgs) which should be used for the actual production achieved.

> 1,000 units of X @ 5 kgs of direct material each = 5,000 kgs.

You should remember that the analysis of the actual cost showed that 4,800 kgs of direct material were actually used.

Thus a saving of 200 kgs (5,000 − 4,800) was achieved.

This saving of materials must be valued to show the effect on profit. If the original standard direct material cost were revised to reflect this saving of material it would become:

> 4.8 kgs (4,800/1,000) @ £2/kg = £9.60.

This is £0.40 per unit of product X less than the original standard and profit would therefore increase by this amount for every unit of product X produced. This has a total value of

1,000 units × £0.40 = £400.

We achieve the same result by multiplying the saving in quantity by the standard price:

200 kgs × £2/kg = £400.

In this case profits will be higher than expected because less material was used than expected in the standard. Therefore the variance is said to be **favourable**.

2.13 Activity

The standard direct material usage per unit of product K is 0.4 tonnes. The standard price of the material is £30/tonne.

During April 500 units of K were made using 223 tonnes of material costing £6,913. Calculate the direct material usage variance.

2.14 Activity solution

Standard usage of 500 units of K:	
500 × 0.4 tonnes	200 tonnes
Actual usage	223 tonnes
Excess usage	23 tonnes

Valued at standard price of £30/tonne:

Direct material usage variance is:

23 tonnes × £30/tonne = £690 Adverse

2.15 Raw material stocks

The earlier example has assumed that the quantity of materials purchased equalled the quantity of materials used by production. Whilst this is possible it is not always certain to occur. Where this does not occur profit will be affected by the change in the level of stock. The extent to which this affects the calculation of direct material variances depends on the methods chosen to value stock. Stocks may be valued either using:

(a)   the standard price for the material; or
(b)   the actual price (as applies from using FIFO, LIFO, etc).

2.16 Stocks valued at standard price

This is the most common method when using a standard costing system because it eliminates the need to record value based movements of stock on stores ledger cards (since all movements, both receipts and issues, will be valued at the standard price).

The effect of this valuation method is that price variances are calculated based on the quantity purchased rather than the quantity of materials used. This is illustrated by the following example.

2.17   Example

Product P requires 4 kg of material Z per unit. The standard price of material Z is £8/kg. During September 16,000 kgs of Z were bought for £134,400. There was no opening stock of material Z but at the end of September 1,400 kgs of Z remained in stock. Stocks of Z are valued at standard prices.

The price variance is based on the quantity purchased (ie, 16,000 kgs). The standard cost of these materials can be calculated:

	£
16,000 kgs × £8/kg	128,000
Actual cost of 16,000 kgs	134,400
Direct material price variance - Adverse	6,400

2.18   Stock account

Continuing the above example the issues of material Z of 14,600 kgs (16,000 − 1,400) would be valued at the standard price of £8/kg.

The value of the issues debited to work in progress would thus be:

14,600 kgs × £8/kg = £116,800.

The stock account would appear thus:

Raw material Z

	£		£
Creditor	134,400	Work in progress	116,800
		Price variance	6,400
		Bal c/d	11,200
	134,400		134,400

Note that the balance c/d comprises the closing stock of 1,400 kgs valued at the standard price of £8/kg.

1,400 kgs × £8/kg = £11,200.

The entry representing the price variance is shown as a credit in the raw material account because it is an adverse variance. The corresponding entry is made to a price variance account, the balance of which is transferred to profit and loss at the end of the year. The price variance account is as follows:

Raw material price variance

	£		£
Raw material Z	6,400		

2.19   Stocks valued at actual price

If this stock valuation method is used it means that any price variance is recognised not at the time of purchase but at the time of issue.

When using this method issues are made from stock at actual prices (using, FIFO, LIFO, etc) with the consequence that detailed stores ledger cards must be kept. The price variance is calculated based upon the quantity used.

2.20   Example

Using the data concerning material Z above, calculations of the value of issues and closing stock can be made as follows:

$$\text{Actual cost 1 kg} = \frac{£134,400}{16,000} \qquad = \quad £8.40$$

Value of issues (at actual cost)   =   14,600 kgs × £8.40
   =   £122,640

Closing stock value (at actual cost)   =   1,400 kgs × £8.40
   =   £11,760.

The direct material price variance based on the issues quantity can be calculated:

	£
Standard cost of 14,600 kgs:	
14,600 kgs × £8/kg	116,800
Actual cost of 14,600 kgs (above)	122,640
Direct material price variance - Adverse	5,840

2.21   Stock account

If stock is valued using actual prices, the stock account will be as follows:

Raw material Z

	£		£
Creditor	134,400	Work in progress	122,640
		Balance c/d	11,760
	134,400		134,400

Note that the closing balance comprises:

	£
1,400 kgs × standard price of £8/kg	11,200
Adverse price variance not yet recognised:	
1,400 kgs × (£8.40 – £8.00)	560
	11,760

The price variance is shown in the work in progress account with the corresponding entry as before:

Work in progress

	£		£
Raw material Z	122,640	Direct material price variance	5,840

2.22   Direct labour cost variances

The purpose of calculating direct labour cost variances is to quantify the effect on profit of actual direct labour costs differing from standard direct labour costs.

This total effect is then analysed to quantify how much has been caused by a difference in the wage rate paid to employees and how much by a difference in the number of hours.

2.23   Example

The following standard costs relate to a single unit of product Q:

	£
Direct materials	8
Direct labour	12
Production overhead	6
	26

On the basis of these standard costs if a unit of product Q is sold for £35, the expected (or standard) profit would be £9 (£35 − £26).

However, if the actual direct labour cost of making the unit of Q were £10, then (assuming the other costs to be as per standard) the actual cost of product Q would be:

	£
Direct materials	8
Direct labour	10
Production overhead	6
	24

Thus when the product is sold the profit is £11 (£35 − £24).

This increase in profit is the effect of the difference between the actual and standard direct labour cost of £2 (£12 − £10).

This simple example considered only one unit of product Q, but it is the principle upon which variance calculations are made.

2.24   Direct labour total cost variance

The purpose of this variance is to show the effect on profit for an accounting period of the actual direct labour cost being different from the standard direct labour cost.

2.25   Example

In August, 800 units of product Q were manufactured, and sold for £35 each.

Using the data above,

(i)   the standard direct labour cost of these 800 units of product Q would be:

   800 units × £12/unit = £9,600

(ii)   the actual direct labour cost of these 800 units of product Q would be:

   800 units × £10/unit = £8,000.

Assuming the other actual costs to be as expected in the standard, the actual profit and loss account would appear:

	£	£
Sales (800 × £35)		28,000
Direct materials (800 × £8)	6,400	
Direct labour (800 × £10)	8,000	
Production overhead (800 × £6)	4,800	
		19,200
Profit		8,800

The expected profit was £9 per unit (£35 – £26) so on sales of 800 units this would be:

800 units × £9/unit = £7,200.

Actual profit is £1,600 more than expected. Note that this is the same as the difference between the actual and standard direct labour cost calculated earlier (£9,600 – £8,000).

This is known as the direct labour total cost variance, and because it causes actual profits to be more than expected it is said to be a favourable variance.

Note that this total variance for the period can be shown to be equal to the difference of £2 per unit of Q (calculated earlier) multiplied by 800 units.

2.26   Activity

The standard direct labour cost of product H is £7. During January 450 units of product H were made, and the actual direct labour cost was £3,450. Calculate the direct labour total cost variance of the period.

2.27   Activity solution

	£
Standard direct labour cost of 450 units:	
£7 × 450	3,150
Actual direct labour cost	3,450
Direct labour total cost variance - Adverse	300

2.28   Analysing the direct labour total cost variance

When a standard labour cost is determined for a unit of a product it is made up of two parts. These are estimates of:

(a)   the number of hours required per unit; and
(b)   the hourly wage rate.

If we return to the example concerning product Q, the standard direct labour cost per unit was stated to be £12. This was based on 4 direct labour hours being required per unit of Q and paying a wage rate of £3/hour.

You should remember that the actual direct labour cost incurred in making 800 units of product Q was £8,000. An analysis of the payroll records shows:

   2,000 hours @ £4/hour = £8,000.

It should be noted that this corresponds to the two estimates which form the basis of the standard cost. It is this which allows the direct labour total cost variance to be analysed.

2.29 Direct labour rate variance

The purpose of calculating this variance is to identify the extent to which profits will differ from those expected by reason of the actual wage rate per hour being different from the standard.

The standard wage rate per hour was stated to be £3. This can be used to calculate the expected cost of the actual hours taken to make 800 units of product Q. On this basis the 2,000 hours should have cost:

   2,000 hours × £3/hour = £6,000.

The actual labour cost was £8,000 which is £2,000 (£8,000 – £6,000) more than expected.

Since the actual rate was greater than expected, this will cause the profit to be lower than expected. This variance, known as the direct labour rate variance, is adverse.

2.30 Direct labour efficiency variance

The purpose of this variance is to quantify the effect on profit of using a different number of hours than expected for the actual production achieved.

Continuing with our example concerning product Q, it was stated that each unit of product Q would require 4 direct labour hours. This can be used to calculate the number of direct labour hours which should be required for the actual production achieved.

   800 units of Q × 4 direct labour hours each = 3,200 direct labour hours

You should remember that the analysis of the actual cost showed that 2,000 hours were used.

Thus a saving of 1,200 direct labour hours (3,200 – 2,000) was achieved.

This saving of labour hours must be valued to show the effect on profit. We do this by multiplying the difference in hours by the standard hourly rate:

   1,200 direct labour hours × £3/hr = £3,600.

In this case profit will be higher than expected because fewer hours were used. Therefore the variance is favourable.

2.31 Activity

The following data relates to product C

Actual production of C (units)	700
Standard wage rate/hour	£4.00
Standard time allowance per unit of C (hours)	1.50
Actual hours worked	1,000
Actual wage cost	£4,200

Calculate the direct labour rate and efficiency variances from the above data.

2.32   Activity solution

		£
Expected cost of actual hours worked:		
1,000 hours × £4/hr		4,000
Actual wage cost		4,200
Direct labour rate variance - Adverse		200
Expected hours for actual production:		
700 units × 1.50 hours/unit		1,050
Actual hours		1,000
A saving (in hours) of		50

These are valued at the standard wage rate/hour.

Direct labour efficiency variance is:

50 hours × £4/hour = £200 Favourable.

3   VARIABLE OVERHEAD VARIANCES

3.1   Introduction

These variances are very similar to those for material and labour because, like these direct costs, the variable overhead cost also changes when activity changes.

The most common examination question assumes that variable overhead costs vary with labour hours worked. This results in the calculation of two variable overhead variances which are illustrated by the following example.

3.2   Example

K Limited has a budgeted variable overhead cost for August of £84,000. Budgeted production is 20,000 units of its finished product and direct labour hours are expected to be 40,000 hours.

During August the actual production was 20,500 units. Actual hours worked were 41,600 hours and the variable overhead cost incurred amounted to £86,700.

3.3   Variable overhead total variance

In order to calculate the total variance it is necessary to calculate the standard variable overhead cost for the actual production achieved.

The budgeted variable overhead cost per hour is calculated by:

$$\frac{\text{Budgeted cost}}{\text{Budgeted hours}} = \frac{£84,000}{40,000} = £2.10 \text{ per hour}$$

Actual production was 20,500 units which is the equivalent of 41,000 standard hours. (According to the budget each unit should require 2 hours ie, 40,000 hours/20,000 units.)

	£
The standard cost of 41,000 hours at £2.10 per hour is	86,100
Actual cost	86,700
Variance	600 (A)

The variance is adverse because the actual cost exceeded the standard cost and therefore profits would be lower than expected.

3.4   Variable overhead expenditure variance

This variance measures the effect on profit of the actual variable overhead cost per hour differing from the standard hourly cost.

The actual hours worked were 41,600.

	£
If these had cost £2.10/hour as expected the cost would have been	87,360
This is the standard cost of actual hours.	
The actual cost was	86,700
Variance	660 (F)

This results in a favourable expenditure variance of £660.

3.5   Variable overhead efficiency variance

This variance measures the effect on profit of the actual hours worked differing from the standard hours produced.

Standard hours produced	41,000
Actual hours worked	41,600
Difference	600

This difference in hours is valued at the standard variable overhead cost/hour:

$$600 \times £2.10 = £1,260 \text{ (A)}.$$

The variance is adverse because actual hours exceeded standard hours.

3.6   Proof of total variance

Note that the sum of these sub-variances, representing expenditure and efficiency equals the total variance:

$$£660 \text{ (F)} + £1,260 \text{ (A)} = £600 \text{ (A)}.$$

3.7   When variable overhead cost varies with volume

If variable overhead cost changes not as a result of a change in direct labour hours, but as a result of a change in production volume it is not possible to calculate the sub-variances illustrated above.

Instead only the total variance can be calculated using the standard variable overhead cost/unit:

$$\frac{\text{Budgeted cost}}{\text{Budgeted units}} = \frac{£84,000}{20,000} = £4.20 \text{ per unit}$$

	£
Standard cost of actual production 20,500 units × £4.20/unit	86,100
Actual cost	86,700
Total variance (as before)	600 (A)

4   FIXED OVERHEAD VARIANCES

4.1   Introduction

These variances show the effect on profit of differences between actual and expected fixed overhead costs. By definition these costs do not change when there is a change in the level of activity, consequently many of the variances are calculated based upon budgets; however, the effect on profit depends upon whether a marginal or absorption costing system is being used. In the variance calculations which follow firstly an absorption costing system is assumed. These are then compared with the variances which would arise if a marginal costing system were used.

4.2   Marginal v absorption costing - a reminder

The difference between these costing methods lies in their treatment of fixed production overheads. Whereas absorption costing relates such costs to cost units using absorption rates, marginal costing treats the cost as a period cost and writes it off to profit and loss as it is incurred.

4.3   Fixed overhead total variance

Assuming an absorption costing system, this is the effect on profit of there being a difference between the actual cost incurred and the amount absorbed by the use of the absorption rate based on budgeted costs and activity. This is illustrated by the following example.

4.4   Example

Q Limited has completed its budget for October; the following data have been extracted:

Budgeted fixed overhead cost	£100,000
Budgeted production	20,000 units
Budgeted machine hours	25,000

A machine hour absorption rate is used.

The actual fixed overhead cost incurred was £98,500. Actual production was 20,300 units using 25,700 machine hours.

4.5   Solution

The absorption rate per machine hour (based upon the budget) is given by:

$$\frac{\text{Budgeted fixed overhead cost}}{\text{Budgeted machine hours}}$$

$$= \frac{£100,000}{25,000} = £4 \text{ per machine hour}$$

This would be used to determine the fixed overhead cost absorbed (ie, attributed to the actual production achieved).

In a standard costing system the actual production achieved is measured in standard hours, in this case standard machine hours.

According to the budget 20,000 units should require 25,000 machine hours, this is the equivalent of 1.25 machine hours per unit (25,000/20,000).

Thus the actual production of 20,300 units is equivalent to

$20,300 \times 1.25 = 25,375$ standard machine hours.

The amount absorbed is therefore:

25,375 standard machine hours × £4/machine hour = £101,500

This is the standard cost of the actual production (using absorption costing). It is compared with the actual cost to find the total variance:

	£
Standard cost	101,500
Actual cost	98,500
Variance	3,000 (F)

Since the actual cost is less than the standard cost it is a favourable variance.

4.6   Over/under absorptions and the total variance

The comparison of actual fixed overhead cost incurred and the amount of fixed overhead cost absorbed is not new, it was used in your earlier studies to determine the extent of any under/over absorption. Often this is done using a fixed production overhead control account which is shown below based upon the above figures:

Fixed production overhead control a/c

	£		£
Creditors	98,500	Work in progress	101,500
P & L (over absorption)	3,000		
	101,500		101,500

You should note that the over absorption is equal to the total variance.

4.7   Activity

TP has the following data concerning its fixed production overheads:

Budget cost	£44,000
Budget production	8,000 units
Budget labour hours	16,000
Actual cost	£47,500
Actual production	8,450 units
Actual labour hours	16,600

Calculate the fixed overhead total variance assuming an absorption system based upon labour hours.

4.8   Activity solution

$$\text{Absorption rate} = \frac{\text{Budgeted cost}}{\text{Budgeted hours}} = \frac{£44,000}{16,000} = £2.75$$

Actual output in standard hours = $8,450 \times \dfrac{16,000}{8,000} =$	16,900
Amount absorbed = 16,900 × £2.75 =	£46,475
Actual cost =	£47,500
Variance	1,025 (A)

4.9   Analysing the total variance

In the same way that any over/under absorption can be analysed into the causes known as expenditure and volume, the same analysis can be made of the total variance. The same terminology is used, and the method of calculation is the same as you learnt earlier in this text. The example we used earlier (reproduced below) will be used to show this.

4.10   Example

Q Limited has completed its budget for October, the following data have been extracted:

Budgeted fixed overhead cost	£100,000
Budgeted production	20,000 units
Budgeted machine hours	25,000

A machine hour absorption rate is used.

The actual fixed overhead cost incurred was £98,500. Actual production was 20,300 units using 25,700 machine hours.

4.11   Fixed overhead expenditure variance

This variance shows the effect on profit of the actual fixed overhead expenditure differing from the budgeted value:

	£
Budgeted expenditure	100,000
Actual expenditure	98,500
	———
Variance	1,500 (F)

The variance is favourable because the actual expenditure is less than that budgeted.

4.12   Fixed overhead volume variance

This variance measures the difference between the amount actually absorbed based upon actual production (in standard hours) compared to the amount expected to be absorbed based upon budgeted production (in standard hours).

Budgeted production (standard machine hours)	25,000
Actual production (standard machine hours)	25,375
	———
Difference	375

This difference of 375 standard machine hours is valued at the absorption rate of £4/hr:

375 hours × £4/hr = £1,500 (F).

This variance is favourable because the actual output exceeded the expected output. Since the cost is fixed, the actual cost/unit is lowered by making greater production and profits will therefore increase.

4.13   Fixed overhead capacity and efficiency variances

Some authors advocate analysing the fixed overhead volume variance into a separate capacity variance and efficiency variance so that the full analysis is as follows:

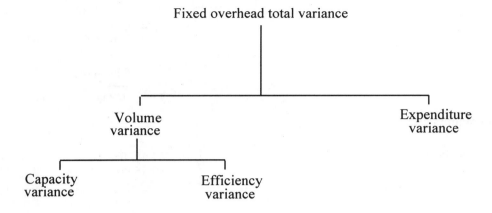

The capacity variance measures whether the workforce worked more or less hours than budgeted for the period:

Capacity variance = (Actual hours worked − Budgeted hours worked) × Absorption rate

The efficiency variance measures whether the workforce took more or less time than expected in producing their output for the period:

Efficiency variance = (Standard hours worked for actual production − Actual hours worked) × Absorption rate

Together, these two sub-variances explain why the level of activity was different from that budgeted ie, they combine to give the fixed overhead volume variance.

Using the figures in the example above for Q Limited:

Capacity variance = (25,700 − 25,000) × £4/hr = £2,800 (F)

Efficiency variance = (25,375 − 25,700) × £4/hr = £1,300 (A)

Naturally, the sum of the capacity variance and the efficiency variance equals the volume variance, and the sum of the expenditure variance and the volume variance equals the total variance.

4.14   Activity

Analyse the total variance you calculated in the previous activity into the fixed overhead expenditure and volume variances. (The data is reproduced below for convenience.)

TP has the following data concerning its fixed production overheads:

Budget cost	£44,000
Budget production	8,000 units
Budget labour hours	16,000
Actual cost	£47,500
Actual production	8,450 units
Actual labour hours	16,600

4.15 Activity solution

Fixed overhead expenditure variance:

	£
Budget cost	44,000
Actual cost	47,500
	3,500 (A)

Fixed overhead volume variance:

Budget production (labour hours)	16,000
Actual production (standard hours)	16,900
	900

900 hours × £2.75 = £2,475 (F)

Proof of total:

£3,500 (A) + £2,475 (F) = £1,025 (A)

4.16 Fixed overhead variances and marginal costing

As was stated earlier, marginal costing does not relate fixed production overhead costs to cost units. The amount shown in the profit and loss account is the cost incurred. Since the cost is a fixed cost it is not expected to change when activity changes thus the expected cost of any level of production is always the budgeted cost.

The purpose of variance analysis is to calculate the effect on profit of actual performance differing from that expected, consequently, under marginal costing this will be the difference between the actual and budgeted expenditure.

Thus under marginal costing the total fixed production overhead variance will always equal the fixed production overhead expenditure variance which is calculated in the same way as for absorption costing systems (above).

5 NON-PRODUCTION OVERHEADS

5.1 Introduction

Since the purpose of variance analysis is to show the effect on profit of actual results differing from those expected, it is also necessary to compare the costs of non-production overheads such as selling, marketing and administration.

5.2 Non-production overhead variances

These costs are not related to the cost unit (even in an absorption costing system) so the calculation of variances for these items is exactly the same as that for fixed production overheads in a marginal costing system.

In other words the only variance is expenditure which is simply the difference between actual and budgeted expenditure. It is usual for separate variances to be calculated for each function (ie, selling, marketing, administration).

6   SALES VARIANCES

6.1   Introduction

The purpose of calculating sales variances is to show their effect when a comparison is made between budget and actual profit. There are two causes of sales variances, a difference in the selling price and a difference in the sales volume.

6.2   Sales price variance

This variance shows the effect on profit of selling at a different price from that expected. The following example is used to illustrate its calculation.

6.3   Example

TZ has the following data regarding its sales for March:

Budgeted sales	1,000 units
Budgeted selling price	£10/unit
Standard variable cost	£6/unit
Budgeted fixed cost	£2/unit*

* based upon annual fixed costs and activity levels

Actual sales	940 units
Actual selling price	£10.50/unit

If the actual sales volume had been sold at the budgeted selling price the sales revenue would have been

940 units × £10 =	£9,400
But actual sales revenue was	
940 units × £10.50 =	£9,870
Variance	470 (F)

The variance is favourable because the higher actual selling price causes an increase in revenue and a consequent increase in profit.

6.4   Sales volume variance

The purpose of this variance is to calculate the effect on profit of the actual sales volume being difference from that budgeted. The effect on profit will differ depending upon whether a marginal or absorption costing system is being used.

Under absorption costing all production costs are attributed to the cost unit, and the fixed production overhead volume variance accounts for the effects of actual volumes differing from those expected, whereas under marginal costing contribution is emphasised (ie, the difference between the selling price and the variable cost).

This affects the calculation of the sales volume variance, under absorption costing any difference in units is valued at the standard profit per unit, whereas under marginal costing such a difference in units is valued at the standard contribution per unit.

In neither case is the standard selling price used. This is because when volumes change so do production costs and the purpose of calculating the variance is to find the effect on profit.

6.5   Sales volume variance - absorption costing

Using the data from the example above:

Budgeted sales	1,000 units
Actual sales	940 units
Difference	60 units

These 60 units are valued at the standard profit of £2/unit (£10-£6-£2)

60 units × £2 = £120 (A).

The variance is adverse because actual sales volume was less than expected.

6.6   Sales volume variance - marginal costing

The difference of 60 units (as above) is valued at the standard contribution of £4/unit (£10-£6):

60 units × £4 = £240 (A).

6.7   Reconciling the sales volume variances under absorption and marginal costing

Using the above example:

Variance under		
	- absorption costing	£120 (A)
	- marginal costing	£240 (A)

There is a difference between these variances of £120 (A).

Earlier in this chapter we learnt how to calculate fixed overhead variances. These too were affected by the choice of costing method. Absorption costing required the calculation of both an expenditure and a volume variance, whereas marginal costing only required an expenditure variance.

Continuing with the data from the above example there is a volume difference of 60 units. The fixed cost is absorbed at a rate equivalent to £2/unit.

Thus the fixed production overhead volume variance would be

60 units × £2/unit = £120 (A)

The variance would be adverse because actual volume was less than expected and, since the cost is fixed this would increase the cost per unit and so decrease profit.

Thus when reconciling the profits, the absorption and marginal systems would show:

	Absorption	*Marginal*
Variances:		
Sales volume	£120 (A)	£240 (A)
Fixed production overhead volume	£120 (A)	Not applicable
	£240 (A)	£240 (A)

All other cost variances and the sales price variance would be identical under both systems.

The reconciliation of profits is covered in more depth later in this chapter.

6.8   Activity

Budgeted sales	500 units
Actual sales	480 units
Budgeted selling price	£100
Actual selling price	£110
Standard variable cost	£50/unit
Budgeted fixed cost	£15/unit

Calculate:

(i)   the selling price variance;
(ii)   the sales volume variance assuming an absorption costing system;
(iii)   the sales volume variance assuming a marginal costing system.

6.9   Activity solution

(i)   480 units × (£110 − £100) = £4,800 (F)
(ii)   20 units × (£100 − 50 − 15) = £700 (A)
(iii)   20 units × (£100 − 50) = £1,000 (A)

7   RECONCILIATION OF BUDGET AND ACTUAL PROFITS - OPERATING STATEMENTS

7.1   Introduction

The purpose of calculating variances is to identify the different effects of each item of cost/income on profit compared to the expected profit. These variances are summarised in a reconciliation statement.

7.2   The reconciliation statement

The example which follows shows how such a statement reconciles the budget and actual profit of a period, based on absorption costing.

The statement commences with the budgeted profit which is based upon budgeted cost and activity levels.

This is then adjusted by the sales volume variance to reflect any difference in actual and budgeted activity. The result, which is referred to as the 'Standard profit on actual sales' represents the profit which would be achieved if:

(i)   the selling price was as budgeted; and
(ii)   all variable costs were as per the standard unit cost; and
(iii)   all fixed costs were as budgeted.

The selling price and cost variances are then included under the headings of adverse and favourable as appropriate. The total of these should reconcile the actual profit to the standard profit on actual sales.

7.3   Example

The following example illustrates the variances defined above.

Chapel Ltd manufactures a chemical protective called Rustnot. The following standard costs apply for the production of 100 cylinders:

		£
Materials	500 kgs @ 80p per kg	400
Labour	20 hours @ £1.50 per hour	30
Fixed overheads	20 hours @ £1.00 per hour	20
		450

The monthly production/sales budget is 10,000 cylinders. Selling price = £6 per cylinder.

For the month of November the following production and sales information is available:

Produced/sold	10,600 cylinders
Sales value	£63,000
Material purchased and used 53,200 kgs	£42,500
Labour 2,040 hours	£3,100
Fixed overheads	£2,200

You are required to prepare an operating statement for November detailing all the variances.

7.4   Solution

	£
Budgeted profit (10,000 cylinders) (W(a))	15,000
Add: Sales volume variance (W(f))	900
Standard profit on actual sales (10,600 cylinders) (W(c))	15,900

Less: Variances (W(f) – (i)):	Adv. £	Fav. £
Sales price (f)	600	
Material price (g)		60
Wages rate (h)	40	
Fixed overhead expenditure (i)	200	
Material usage (g)	160	
Labour efficiency (h)		120
Fixed overhead volume (i)		120
	1,000	300
		700
Actual profit (W(b))		15,200

WORKINGS

		£	£
(a)	**Budgeted profit**		
	10,000 cylinders @ £1.50		15,000
(b)	**Actual profit**		
	Sales		63,000
	Less: Materials	42,500	
	Labour	3,100	
	Fixed overheads	2,200	
			47,800
			15,200

(c) **Actual units/standard profit**

Sales value 10,600 × £6	63,600
Less: Standard cost of sales 10,600 × £4.50	47,700
	15,900

(d) **Standard hours**

10,600 cylinders × 0.2 hours = 2,120 hours

(e) **Budgeted hours**

10,000 × 0.2 = 2,000 hours

Variances

(f) **Sales**

The budgeted selling price is £6 per cylinder. Actual sales were 10,600 cylinders for £63,000. If the actual cylinders sold had been sold at the budgeted selling price of £6 then sales would have been

10,600 × £6 = £63,600.

Thus the difference in selling price resulted in a lower sales value by £600. This is an adverse selling price variance.

The budgeted volume was 10,000 cylinders costing £4.50 each. At the budgeted selling price of £6 each this is a budgeted profit of £1.50 per cylinder.

Actual sales volume was 10,600 cylinders, 600 more than budget. These extra 600 cylinders will increase profit by

600 × £1.50 = £900.

This is a favourable sales volume variance.

(g) **Raw materials**

The standard price of the raw material is £0.80 per kg. If the actual quantity of 53,200 kg had been bought at the standard price this would have been

53,200 kg × £0.80/kg = £42,560.

The actual cost was £42,500. This is a saving caused by price, it is a favourable price variance of £60.

Each 100 cylinders should use 500 kgs of material. Therefore the 10,600 cylinders produced should use

10,600 × 500 kg/100 = 53,000 kgs

The actual usage was 53,200 kgs. These additional 200 kgs of material have a value (using standard prices) of

200 kgs × £0.80 = £160.

This is an adverse material usage variance.

(h)   **Labour**

The standard labour rate is £1.50 per hour. The actual labour hours was 2,040 hours, so if they had been paid at the standard rate per hour, the wage cost would have been

2,040 × £1.50 = £3,060.

The actual wage cost was £3,100. This extra £40 is the adverse wage rate variance.

Each 100 cylinders should take 20 hours to produce. The actual production was 10,600 cylinders so these should have taken

10,600 × 20/100 = 2,120 hours

Actual hours were 2,040 hours, a saving of 80 hours. These hours (valued at the standard rate) are worth

80 × £1.50 = £120.

This is a favourable labour efficiency.

(i)   **Fixed overheads**

The standard fixed overhead cost is £20 per 100 cylinders. Monthly production is budgeted at 10,000 cylinders. Therefore the budgeted fixed overhead cost is

10,000 × £20/100 = £2,000.

The actual cost was £2,200. The extra cost of £200 is an adverse fixed overhead expenditure variance.

But the actual production was 10,600 cylinders, 600 more than budgeted. This extra volume of 600 units (valued at the standard absorption rate of £20/100 units) is

600 × £20/100 = £120

This is a favourable fixed overhead volume variance.

7.5   Marginal costing reconciliation

The above presentation was based on absorption costing; on a marginal costing basis it would appear as:

			£
Budgeted profit			15,000
Add: Sales volume variance (j)			1,020
Standard contribution on actual sales (Wj)			16,020

Less: Variances (W(f)-(i)):	Adv £	Fav £	
Sales price (f)	600		
Material price (g)		60	
Wages rate (h)	40		
Fixed overhead expenditure (i)	200		
Material usage (g)	160		
Labour efficiency (h)		120	
	1,000	180	
			820
Actual profit (W(b))			15,200

WORKING

(a) to (i) are as in the previous example.

(j) $600 \times$ contribution of £1.70 each = £1,020 (F)

Contribution/unit $= £6 - \left(\dfrac{£400 + £30}{100} \right)$ $=$ £1.70/unit

8   CAUSES AND INTERDEPENDENCE OF VARIANCES

8.1   Causes of variances

The calculation of variances is only the first stage. Management wants information to plan and control operations. It is not sufficient to know that a variance has arisen: we must try to establish why. The figures themselves do not provide the answers, but they point to some of the questions that should be asked. Possible causes of the individual variances are now discussed.

Bromwich has proposed four general causes of variances:

- bad budgeting;
- bad measurement or recording;
- random factors;
- operational factors.

The following list concentrates on examples of the fourth of these causes.

(a)   **Material price variance**

This could be due to:

(i)   different source of supply;
(ii)   unexpected general price increase;
(iii)   alteration in quantity discounts;
(iv)   substitution of a different grade of material;
(v)   standard set at mid-year price so one would expect a favourable price variance in the early months and an adverse variance in the later months of the year.

(b)   **Material usage variance**

This could be due to:

(i)   higher/lower incidence of scrap;
(ii)   alteration to product design;
(iii)   substitution of a different grade of material.

(c)   **Wages rate variance**

Possible causes:

(i)   unexpected national wage award;
(ii)   overtime or bonus payments different from plan;
(iii)   substitution of a different grade of labour.

    (d)   **Labour efficiency variance**

        (i)   improvement in methods of working conditions including better supervision;
        (ii)   consequences of the learning effect;
        (iii)   introduction of incentive scheme or staff training;
        (iv)   substitution of a different grade of labour.

    (e)   **Variable overhead**

        (i)   unexpected price changes for overhead items;
        (ii)   incorrect split between fixed and variable overheads.

    (f)   **Fixed overhead expenditure**

        (i)   changes in prices relating to fixed overhead items eg, rent increase;
        (ii)   seasonal effect eg, heat/light in winter. (This arises where the annual budget is divided into four equal quarters or thirteen equal four-weekly periods without allowances for seasonal factors. Over a whole year the seasonal effects would cancel out.)

    (g)   **Fixed overhead volume**

        (i)   change in production volume due to change in demand or alterations to stockholding policy;
        (ii)   changes in productivity of labour or machinery;
        (iii)   production lost through strikes, etc.

    (h)   **Operating profit variance due to selling prices**

        (i)   unplanned price increase;
        (ii)   unplanned price reduction eg, to try and attract additional business.

    (i)   **Operating profit variance due to sales volume**

        This is obviously caused by a change in sales volume, which may be due to:

        (i)   unexpected fall in demand due to recession;
        (ii)   additional demand attracted by reduced prices;
        (iii)   failure to satisfy demand due to production difficulties.

8.2   Interdependence of variances

The cause of a particular variance may affect another variance in a corresponding or opposite way, eg:

    (a)   If supplies of a specified material are not available, this may lead to a favourable price variance (cheaper material used), an adverse usage variance (cheaper material caused more wastage), an adverse fixed overhead volume variance (production delayed while material was unavailable) and an adverse sales volume variance (unable to meet demand due to production difficulties).

    (b)   A new improved machine becomes available which causes an adverse fixed overhead expenditure variance (because this machine is more expensive and depreciation is higher) offset by favourable wages efficiency and fixed overhead volume variances (higher productivity).

    (c)   Workers trying to improve productivity (favourable labour efficiency variance) might become careless and waste more material (adverse material usage variance).

In each of these cases, if one variance has given rise to the other, there is an argument in favour of combining the two variances and ascribing them to the common cause. In view of these possible interdependencies, care has to be taken when implementing a bonus scheme. If the chief buyer is rewarded if he produces a favourable price variance, this may bring about trouble later as shoddy materials give rise to adverse usage variances.

9   CHAPTER SUMMARY

You should now be happy with the meaning and purpose of standard costing, calculating elementary variances and presenting operating statements. The interpretation of the reasons for variances has been introduced which requires a degree of practical common sense. Some structure to any discussion has been given by identifying Bromwich's suggestion of four general reasons for variances:

- bad budgeting;
- bad measurement or recording;
- random factors;
- operational factors.

10   SELF TEST QUESTIONS

10.1   What is a definition of standard costing? (1.1)

10.2   What are four types of standard? (1.2)

10.3   How can a material cost variance be calculated? (2.5)

10.4   What are the various splits of a total fixed production overhead cost variance? (4.9)

10.5   What are the differences between operating statements based on standard absorption and standard marginal costing principles? (7.4, 7.5)

10.6   Give examples of possible causes of the labour efficiency variance. (8.1)

10.7   Give illustrations of likely variance interdependencies. (8.2)

11   EXAMINATION TYPE QUESTION

11.1   Department X

The following statement has been produced for presentation to the general manager of Department X.

	Month ended 31 October 19X9		
	Original budget £	*Actual result* £	*Variance* £
Sales	600,000	550,000	(50,000)
Direct materials	150,000	130,000	20,000
Direct labour	200,000	189,000	11,000
Production overhead:			
Variable with direct labour	50,000	46,000	4,000
Fixed	25,000	29,000	(4,000)
Variable selling overhead	75,000	72,000	3,000
Fixed selling overhead	50,000	46,000	4,000
Total costs	550,000	512,000	38,000
Profit	50,000	38,000	(12,000)
Direct labour hours	50,000	47,500	
Sales and production units	5,000	4,500	

Note: there are no opening and closing stocks.

The general manager says that this type of statement does not provide much relevant information for him. He also thought that the profit for the month would be well up to budget and was surprised to see a large adverse profit variance.

You are required:

(a)   to re-draft the above statement in a form which would be more relevant for the general manager;   **(6 marks)**

(b)   to calculate all sales, material, labour and overhead variances and reconcile these to the statement produced in (a);   **(9 marks)**

(c)   to produce a short report explaining the principles upon which your re-drafted statement is based and what information it provides.   **(7 marks)**
                                                                               (Total: 22 marks)

12   ANSWER TO EXAMINATION TYPE QUESTION

12.1   Department X

(a)   **Revised statement**

A flexed budget corresponding with an output of 4,500 units is required.

	Budget			
	Original	Flexed	Actual	Variance
Units	5,000	4,500	4,500	
	£	£	£	£
Sales	600,000	540,000	550,000	10,000 F
Direct materials	150,000	135,000	130,000	5,000 F
Direct labour	200,000	180,000	189,000	9,000 A
Variable production overheads	50,000	45,000	46,000	1,000 A
Variable selling overheads	75,000	67,500	72,000	4,500 A
Total variable costs	475,000	427,500	437,000	9,500 A
Contribution	125,000	112,500	113,000	500 F
Fixed costs:				
Production overhead	25,000	25,000	29,000	4,000 A
Selling overhead	50,000	50,000	46,000	4,000 F
Total costs	550,000	502,500	512,000	9,500 A
Profit	£50,000	£37,500	£38,000	£500 F

Variance of flexed budget against original budget: 37,500 − 50,000 =   12,500 A
Variance of actual against flexed budget: 500 F

Variance of actual against original budget: £12,000 A

(b)   **Variances**

   (i)   Preliminary calculations

		Standard
Hours		50,000

Selling price $\dfrac{£540,000}{4,500} = £120$

Direct labour rate/hr. $\dfrac{£200,000}{50,000} = £4.00$

Standard hours per unit $\dfrac{50,000}{5,000} = 10 \text{ hours}$

Var. prod. overhead cost/hour $\dfrac{£45,000}{45,000} = £1.00$

Var. selling overhead cost/unit $\dfrac{£67,500}{4,500} = £15$

Profit per unit $\dfrac{£50,000}{5,000} = £10$

Fixed production overhead costs per hour $\dfrac{£25,000}{50,000} = £0.5$

Fixed selling overhead cost per unit $\dfrac{£50,000}{5,000} = £10$

   (ii)   Variances from flexible budget

	£	*From (a)*
Selling price = £550,000 − 4,500 × £120		10,000 F
Direct materials = £135,000 − £130,000		5,000 F
Direct labour:		
Rate = £4.00 × 47,500 − £189,000	1,000 F	
Efficiency = (45,000 − 47,500) × £4	10,000 A	
Total		9,000 A
Variable production overhead:		
Expenditure = £1 × 47,500 − £46,000	1,500 F	
Efficiency = (45,000 − (1 × 47,500) × £1	2,500 A	
Total		1,000 A
Variable selling overhead:		
£15 × 4,500 − £72,000		4,500 A
Fixed cost expenditure:		
Production overhead		
£25,000 − £29,000		4,000 A
Selling overhead		
£50,000 − £46,000		4,000 F
		£500 F

(iii)   Variance of flexible budget from original budget

Sales volume profit
  (4,500 – 5,000) × £10   5,000 A
Fixed production overhead
    Capacity
      (47,500 – 50,000) × £0.50   1,250 A
    Efficiency
      (4,550 × 10 – 47,500) × £0.5   1,250 A
Fixed selling overhead volume
  (4,500 – 5,000) × £10   5,000 A
                             £12,500 A   12,500 A

(c)   **Report**

To: The General Manager

From: The Management Accountant

Revised Budget Statement, month ending 31 October

The cause of the high adverse profit variance was the low volume of actual output. The budget statement has now been flexed to correspond with the actual volume produced so as to separate this effect. This has assumed that there is a linear relationship between volume of output, sales revenue and variable costs. Fixed costs, being independent of output volume, remain unchanged. A marginal costing approach has been used to show the contribution. The revised variances show a favourable profit variance of those variances controllable by the department; direct materials costs now have a favourable variance, direct labour and variable overheads have reduced adverse variances; although labour efficiency variances need investigating; the direct selling overheads variance is greater. The analysis does not show the causes of the variances nor of the failure to achieve the budget volume of output.

Note: various alternative presentations would be acceptable; in particular an absorption costing approach to part (a) could have been used.

14 MIX AND YIELD VARIANCES

INTRODUCTION & LEARNING OBJECTIVES

When you have studied this chapter you should be able to do the following:

- Calculate mix and yield variances for materials.
- Calculate mix and yield variances for sales.

1 MATERIALS MIX AND YIELD VARIANCES

1.1 Relationship to direct material price and usage variances

In many industrial situations, more than one material is used in the manufacturing cycle for a single product. If the various materials used cannot be substituted in any way for each other, the approach is to continue to look at each material quite separately. However, in many circumstances the materials used are to some extent substitutes for each other ie, the mix of materials used in the manufacturing can be altered without noticeably affecting the end product. It is in this situation that the calculation of a mix variance becomes appropriate.

1.2 Mix and yield variances as a sub-set of the usage variance

The following data will be used to show this approach:

Standard cost for 990 tonnes of production:

Material	Tonnes	Price per tonne £	£
A	550	6.00	3,330
B	330	5.00	1,650
C	220	4.50	990
	1,100		5,940
Less: Normal process loss (10%)	110		-
Standard cost for	990	=	5,940

This represents a standard product cost per tonne of £6.00.

Actual material cost and usage to produce 990 tonnes:

Material	Tonnes	Price per tonne £	£
A	444	7.50	3,330
B	446	6.00	2,676
C	240	4.50	1,080
	1,130		7,086
Less: Process loss	140		-
Standard cost for	990		7,086

The following statements can be derived from the data:

Material	Actual quantity used at standard prices				Actual quantity used in standard proportions (mix) at standard prices		
	Tonnes	Standard price per tonne £	£		Tonnes	Standard price per tonne £	£
A	444	6.00	2,664		565	6.00	3,390
B	446	5.00	2,230		339	5.00	1,695
C	240	4.50	1,080		226	4.50	1,017
	1,130		5,974		1,130		6,102

The variance analysis is as follows:

£

Actual tonnes
Actual mix
Actual cost   7,086

Actual tonnes
purchased (and used)   Price variance
Actual mix   £1,112A
Standard cost   5,974

Direct material mix variance

= (Total material input in a standard mix × standard prices) − (Actual material input × standard prices)

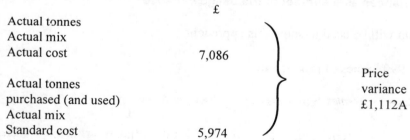

=   A $\begin{pmatrix} 565 \times 6 \\ 339 \times 5 \\ 226 \times 4.50 \end{pmatrix}$ − $\begin{pmatrix} 444 \times 6 \\ 446 \times 5 \\ 240 \times 4.50 \end{pmatrix}$
    B
    C

= 6,102 − 5,974

= £128 (F)

Direct material yield variance

= (Standard quantity of materials specified for actual production × standard prices) − (Actual total material input in standard proportions × standard prices)

$$= \begin{matrix} A \\ B \\ C \end{matrix} \begin{pmatrix} 990 \times \dfrac{550}{990} \times 6 \\ 990 \times \dfrac{330}{990} \times 5 \\ 990 \times \dfrac{220}{990} \times 4.50 \end{pmatrix} - \begin{pmatrix} 565 \times 6 \\ 339 \times 5 \\ 226 \times 4.50 \end{pmatrix}$$

= 5,940 − 6,102

= 162 (A)

∴ **Usage variance** = 128 − 162 = 34 (A)

The mix and yield variances can be interpreted as follows:

(a) the mix variance of £128F arises because, compared with the standard, less of the more expensive material (A) has been used and more of the cheaper materials (B and C);

(b) the yield variance represents the fact that 1,130 tonnes of material in total were input into the process and, with a normal loss of 10%, the expected yield of good production was 1,017 tonnes (0.9 × 1,130). However, good production only amounted to 990 tonnes. The yield was lower than expected by 27 tonnes which, evaluated at the standard product cost of £6 per tonne, gives a yield effect of £162A.

These two variances are probably interrelated and should, therefore, be considered together. It is likely that the change to a cheaper mix of materials has resulted in the yield of good production being down compared with standard. The net effect of the two is an overall adverse usage variance for direct material of £34.

1.3   Mix variances related to individual material inputs

The worked example in the previous section produced a direct material mix variance of £128F in total. It is possible to show the build-up of this figure for materials A, B and C separately, as follows:

Material	Actual quantity used tonnes	Actual quantity used in standard mix tonnes	Mix variance tonnes	Standard price per tonne £	Mix variance £
A	444	565	121 F	6.00	726 F
B	446	339	107 A	5.00	535 A
C	240	226	14 A	4.50	63 A
	1,130	1,130	Nil		128 F

The same total favourable mix variance (£128) is made up of favourable and adverse sub-variances. A reduction in the proportion of the relatively expensive material A has given rise to a favourable variance and the increased usage of the relatively cheaper materials has given adverse variances for B and C.

The mechanics of the calculations are quite clear but how would a manager receiving such a breakdown of the total mix variance interpret the analysis? The manager might conclude that it was a good idea to reduce the proportion of A used as this produces a favourable variance, but a bad thing to increase the proportions of B and C with their resultant adverse effects. The two aspects are interrelated so perhaps the manager should concentrate on the net effect of the changes in the mix ie, the total direct material mix variance.

There is an alternative method of calculation for the mix sub-variances so that if the total variance is favourable so will each of the components. Such an approach makes use of the *average* standard price of the input.

Using the same example, the average standard price of the input is:

$$\frac{£5,940}{1,100} \quad = \quad £5.40 \text{ per tonne}$$

The alternative analysis would evaluate the variances as follows:

Material	*(1)* Standard price per tonne £	*(2)* Average standard price per tonne £	*(3)* Actual quantity used in standard mix tonnes	*(4)* Actual quantity used tonnes	*(5)* Mix variance £
A	6.00	5.40	565	444	72.60 F
B	5.00	5.40	339	446	42.80 F
C	4.50	5.40	226	240	12.60 F
			1,130	1,130	128.00 F

The mix variance (column (5)) is obtained by the following calculation indicated by column numbers $((1) - (2)) \times ((3) - (4))$.

This method acknowledges that it is the deviation from a standard mix that is being evaluated. Material A variance is favourable because less of an expensive material has been used. The increased usage of the relatively cheaper materials B and C would tend to reduce the overall cost of the mix and so produce the favourable variances. This approach is clear-cut; the effect of the change in the mix, compared with the standard, is favourable because it has reduced the overall average cost of the mix.

The total effect on the yield of good production is an interrelated consideration. Although it is possible to sub-analyse the yield variance doing so is unlikely to produce any more meaningful information to management than the total yield variance on its own does. The yield variance is a measure of whether more or less good production has been achieved from the actual input, compared with the standard. Therefore, the yield is related more to output than to individual material inputs.

In summary, there is some doubt about the usefulness to management of any breakdown in the direct material mix or yield variances. If an analysis of the mix variances is undertaken, there are two methods of calculation. The approach using the comparison with the average standard input price seems to produce logical and unequivocal variances, but it should be noted that some authorities prefer the other approach which can produce a mixture of adverse and favourable sub-variances.

1.4   Mix and yield variances – a summary

The whole subject of direct material mix and yield variances can be confusing because there are many acceptable methods for their calculation. It is easy to concentrate too much attention on the mechanics of the various methods of calculation and to overlook the fact that variance analysis is a way of presenting information to management so that individual managers can take decisions on the most appropriate courses of action. In any organisation the method of variance analysis adopted should be the most meaningful in all the circumstances involved. It is important that the manager receiving the variance report should understand the meaning of any mix and yield variances in it.

1.5   Activity

The Acton company produces a product by mixing three chemicals X, Y, Z in the proportions 4, 3, 3 respectively. Minor variations on these proportions are acceptable. The standard prices for the chemicals are:

X   £3.20/litre
Y   £2.50/litre
Z   £3.60/litre

There is a 5% normal loss.

Last month's output was 210,000 litres.

The inputs were:

X   70,200 litres at £3.30
Y   69,800 litres at £2.45
Z   60,200 litres at £3.70

Calculate the material price, the material mix, the material yield and the material usage variances. Hence check the relationship between the mix, yield and usage variance.

1.6   Activity solution

Material price variance
= (Actual price – standard price) × Actual quantity

$$£$$

X (3.30 – 3.20) × 70,200   =   7,020 A
Y (2.45 – 2.50) × 69,800   =   3,490 F
Z (3.70 – 3.60) × 60,200   =   6,020 A

Price variance   9,550 A

Material mix variance
(Actual mix – standard mix of actual) × Standard price

$$£$$

.4	X	(70,200 – 80,080) × 3.20	=	31,616 F
.3	Y	(69,800 – 60,060) × 2.50	=	24,350 A
.3	Z	(60,200 – 60,060) × 3.60	=	504 A

200,200   200,200   6,762 F = Mix variance

Material yield variance

=   (Standard input for actual output − Actual mix in standard proportions) × Standard price

				£
.4	X	$(88,421 − 80,080) × 3.20$	=	26,691 F
.3	Y	$(66,316 − 60,060) × 2.50$	=	15,640 F
.3	Z	$(66,316 − 60,060) × 3.60$	=	22,522 F
		221,053 200,200		64,853 F = Yield variance

$$\text{Standard input for actual output} = \frac{100}{95} \times 210,000 = 221,053$$

Material usage variance

(Standard input for actual output − Actual mix) × Standard price

		£
X $(88,421 − 70,200) × 3.20$	=	58,307 F
Y $(66,316 − 69,800) × 2.50$	=	8,710 A
Z $(66,316 − 60,200) × 3.60$	=	22,018 F
		71,615 F	= usage variance

Check: mix variance   +   yield variance   =   usage variance

            6,762 F +   64,853 F   =   71,615 F

2   SALES MIX AND QUANTITY VARIANCE

2.1   Introduction

Where more than one product is sold, it is likely that each will have a different profit. If they are sold in a mix different from that budgeted, a sales mix profit variance will result. Even though the products are not substitutes, a change of sales mix may indicate a change in emphasis of selling effort by sales staff or marketing resources.

Example

Note: the profit figure used will be the standard profit (assuming an absorption costing system).

The Omega company sets the following sales budgets for three products:

			Budgeted profit
			£
A	400	units at a standard profit of £8	3,200
B	600	units at a standard profit of £6	3,600
C	1,000	units at a standard profit of £4	4,000
	2,000	units	£10,800

The company expects to sell A, B and C in the proportion of 4 : 6 : 10 respectively. Actual sales are achieved at the standard selling price:

			Actual profit
			£
A	300	units @ £8	2,400
B	700	units @ £6	4,200
C	1,200	units @ £4	4,800
	2,200	units	£11,400

There are many different ways of determining the effect of any change in the sales mix ie, the proportion of the total sales each product represents. The methods compared here rely on taking the actual total quantity sold and determining the quantity of each product that would have been sold had the standard mix been achieved.

2.2   Method

In this example any differences in selling price have been ignored. If products are sold for anything other than their standard selling price this variance should be calculated **separately** first. Thereafter the calculation of the sales volume variance can be done at a standard margin (profit, as here, or contribution) per unit. A tabular approach, analogous to that used for materials is strongly recommended, although other approaches will be shown. The column headings for the relevant tables are:

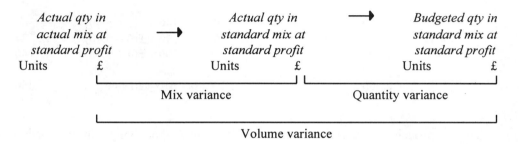

2.3   Solution

The previous figures show a favourable variance of £600 (£11,400 − £10,800) attributable to a change in sales volume which can be split into mix and quantity. A useful working is the average standard profit per unit

$$= \quad \frac{£10,800}{2,000} \quad = \quad £5.40$$

The table then shows:

	Actual qty in actual mix at standard profit			Actual qty in standard mix at standard profit			Budgeted qty in standard mix at standard profit	
	Units	£		Units	£		Units	£
A	300	2,400						
B	700	4,200		at £5.40				
C	1,200	4,800						
	2,200	£11,400		2,200	£11,880		2,000	£10,800

					£	
Sales mix variance	=	£11,400 − £11,880	=		480	(A)
Sales quantity variance	=	£11,880 − £10,800	=		1,080	(F)
Sales volume variance	=	£11,400 − £10,800	=		£600	(F)

Since the net effect of the quantity changes is always zero (ie, we are considering the mix with the total sales of 2,200 units) the overall mix variance will be favourable if more products with a higher profit per unit are sold in place of products with a lower profit per unit ie, in this case the proportion of B and C, which have a lower profit per unit has been increased whereas A, which yields a higher profit per unit, has been reduced. Hence an overall adverse mix variance.

2.4   An alternative approach

If any split of the mix variance is deemed necessary the following approach is suggested although the low additional information content of the split makes the exercise rather futile. This approach is the method outlined in *Horngren*. The basic idea is to assess the effect of the change in proportion of each product by reference to the weighted average contribution earned if the standard mix is sold ie, as per budget (£5.40).

Actual quantity in standard mix		*Actual quantity in actual mix*			£	
A	440	300	=	$140 \times £(8 - 5.40)$	= 364	A
B	660	700	=	$40 \times £(6 - 5.40)$	= 24	F
C	1,100	1,200	=	$100 \times £(4 - 5.40)$	= 140	A
	2,200	$\Leftarrow$	2,200	Mix variance	480	A

This approach specifically demonstrates whether the change in proportion of each individual product increases or decreases the weighted average profit earned.

Hence in the case of A, as contribution is higher than the weighted average, the reduction in proportion of A will depress profits. With product C the profit per unit (£4) is below average. Hence an increase in proportion of C is *not* beneficial as it will reduce the weighted average contribution earned.

2.5   Approach

(a)   **Sales mix profit variance**

=   (Total actual sales units × budgeted weighted average standard profit per unit) – (Actual sales units × individual standard profit per unit)

Where sales value is more appropriate for calculating the mix variance, the calculation is:

=   (Turnover* @ standard selling prices × budgeted weighted profit to sales ratio) – (Actual sales @ standard selling prices × individual profit to sales ratios)

* Turnover can be defined as actual sales volume.

In this example:

$$= \quad (2{,}200 \times 5.40) - \begin{bmatrix} \text{A:} & 300 \times 8 \\ \text{B:} & 700 \times 6 \\ \text{C:} & 1{,}200 \times 4 \end{bmatrix}$$

=   £480 (A)

This version of the formula excludes any 'analysis' of the mix variance between products and is therefore easier. This version can be used in the examination.

(b)   **Sales quantity profit variance is defined as:**

(Budgeted sales units × standard profit per unit) – (Total actual sales units × budgeted weighted average standard profit)

The quantity variance is the overall increase/decrease in volume valued at the weighted average contribution, ie:

$$\begin{pmatrix} A: & 400 \times 8 \\ B: & 600 \times 6 \\ C: & 1{,}000 \times 4 \end{pmatrix} - \quad (2{,}200 \times 5.40)$$

=   10,800 – 11,880

=   1,080

or:

Budgeted quantity		Actual quantity				
2,000	–	2,200	=	200 units @ £5.40	=	£1,080 F

(c)   **Sales volume profit variance**

This is the total variance and compares standard quantity, standard mix with actual quantity, actual mix:

Standard quantity, standard mix		Actual quantity, actual mix				£	
A	400 × 8	300 × 8	=	100 × £8	=	800	A
B	600 × 6	700 × 6	=	100 × £6	=	600	F
C	1,000 × 4	1,200 × 4	=	200 × £4	=	800	F
	2,000	2,200		Volume profit variance		600	F

These variances are summarised as follows:

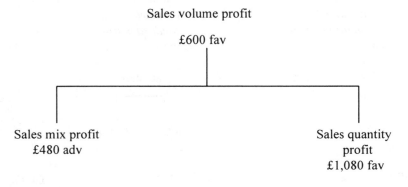

2.6   Usefulness of the sales mix variance

Variances are calculated for the purpose of control. Managers are provided with a variance analysis of their areas of responsibility so that they can improve their decisions. The sales margin mix variance must be judged by this objective.

Two situations are possible:

(a)   The manager is responsible for two or more products which are to some extent substitutes for each other eg, ranges of cheap and expensive cosmetics.   Since the mix variance represents shifts in demand between the product ranges, it has significance.   As stated before, it is even relevant for non-substitutes.

(b)   The manager is responsible for one line of products;   other managers are responsible for other totally different product lines.   In this situation, to provide a product manager with a mix variance when he can control only one product is meaningless.

2.7   Activity

From the following information provide a comprehensive sales margin variance analysis:

		Product X	Product Y	Product Z
Budget:				
	Sales price	£20	£20	£10
	Cost	£10	£15	£8
	Units	100	700	200
	Total profit	£1,000	£3,500	£400
Actual:				
	Sales price	£21	£24	£7
	Units sold	200	700	100

2.8   Activity solution

Sales price variance
= (Actual price − Standard price) × Actual quantity sold

Product		£
X	(£21 − £20) × 200	= 200 (F)
Y	(£24 − £20) × 700	= 2,800 (F)
Z	(£7 − £10) × 100	= 300 (A)
		£2,700 (F)

	Actual qty in actual mix at standard margin		→	*Actual qty in standard mix at standard margin*	→	*Budgeted qty in standard mix at standard margin*	
	Units	£		Units	£	Units	£
X	200	2,000					
Y	700	3,500		at £4.90			
Z	100	200					
	1,000	£5,700		1,000	£4,900	1,000	£4,900

Budgeted profits	=	£1,000 + £3,500 + £400	=	£4,900
Average profit/unit	=	£4,900 ÷ 1,000	=	£4.90

				£	
Sales mix variance	=	£5,700 − £4,900	=	800	(F)
Sales quantity variance	=	£4,900 − £4,900	=	-	
Sales volume variance	=	£5,700 − £4,900	=	£800	(F)

2.9   Sales mix variance - alternative basis for calculation

As if there weren't enough ways already of finding sales mix variances, other approaches are often discussed. Sales mix variances have been calculated by standardising the units sold. There may be circumstances where the prices are so different (eg, transistor radios and colour TVs) that it would be inappropriate to base the comparison on units. Instead the sales mix may be found by standardising it in terms of £ value of sales, rather than unit sales.

Example

Three products – A, B and C – are sold. During a period the budget and actual sales are as follows:

	Units	Price £	Sales £	Profit £	Total profit £	Units	Price £	Sales £	Profit £	Total profit £
Product A	200	10	2,000	3	600	150	10	1,500	3	450
Product B	300	5	1,500	2	600	260	5	1,300	2	520
Product C	500	3	1,500	1	500	400	3	1,200	1	400
Total	1,000		£5,000		£1,700	810		£4,000		£1,370

(a)   **Variances calculated on basis of units (ie, as earlier)**

(i)   **Sales mix profit variance**

$$(810 \times \frac{£1,700}{1,000}) - (150 \times £3 + 260 \times £2 + 400 \times £1)$$

=   £1,377 – £1,370

=   £7 (A)

(ii)   **Sales quantity profit variance**

$$£1,700 - \left(810 \times \frac{£1,700}{1,000}\right)$$

=   £1,700 – £1,377

=   £323 (A)

(iii)   **Sales volume profit variance**

=   £1,700 – £1,370

=   £330 (A)

(b)   **Variances calculated on basis of sales value**

(i)   **Sales mix profit variance**

=   (Turnover @ standard selling prices × budgeted weighted profit to sales ratio) – (Actual sales @ standard selling prices × individual profit to sales ratios)

$$\left(£4,000 \times \frac{£1,700}{£5,000}\right) - \left(£1,500 \times \frac{3}{10} + £1,300 \times \frac{2}{5} + £1,200 \times \frac{1}{3}\right)$$

=   £1,360 – £(450 + 520 + 400)

=   £1,360 – £1,370

=   £10 (F)

(ii)   **Sales quantity profit variance**

= (Budgeted sales × standard profit to sales ratios) – (Total actual sales @ standard selling prices × budgeted weighted profit to sales ratio)

$$= \left(£2,000 \times \frac{3}{10} + £1,500 \times \frac{2}{5} + £1,500 \times \frac{1}{3} \right) - \left(£4,000 \times \frac{£1,700}{£5,000} \right)$$

= £1,700 – £1,360

= £340 (A)

(iii)   **Sales volume profit variance** (as before): £330 (A)

The approach that will normally be adopted is to base the mix variance analysis on unit sales rather than £ sales.

2.10   Sales variance analysis - a summary

The size of each of the following variances will remain the same whichever method or approach is adopted:

(a)   selling price variance;

(b)   sales volume profit variance.

The volume variance can be sub-divided into quantity and mix variances where there is more than one product involved and products are to some extent interchangeable. If the concept of the standard mix is used to calculate these, it can be based on either:

(a)   the physical units in the budget; or

(b)   the sales value of products in the budget.

Each will lead to different mix and quantity variances, but in each case they will net to the same result (the volume profit variance).

3   CHAPTER SUMMARY

This chapter has explained how mix and yield variances may be calculated and interpreted by management. In doing so you should remember that two valuation bases may be used, they both result in the same total variance but the values of each item in the mix are different.

4   EXAMINATION TYPE QUESTION

4.1   Chemical company

A chemical company has the following standards for producing 9 gallons of a machine lubricant:

5 gallons of material P @ £0.70 per gallon
5 gallons of material Q @ £0.92 per gallon.

No stocks of raw materials are kept. Purchases are made as needed so that all price variances relate to materials used. Actual results showed that 100,000 gallons of material were used during a particular period as follows:

			£
45,000	gallons of material P at an actual cost per gallon used of £0.80		36,000
55,000	gallons of material Q at an actual cost per gallon used of £0.97		53,350
100,000			£89,350

During the period 92,070 gallons of the machine lubricant were produced.

You are required:

(a)   to calculate the total material variance and analyse it into its price, yield and mix components.   **(11 marks)**

(b)   to explain the circumstances under which a material mix variance is relevant to managerial control.   **(4 marks)**

(Total: 15 marks)

5   ANSWER TO EXAMINATION TYPE QUESTION

5.1   Chemical company

(a)   **Variance calculations**

Standard cost card

Materials	*Gallons*	*£/gallon*	*£*
P	5	0.70	3.50
Q	5	0.92	4.60
Input	10 gallons	(at £0.81)	8.10
Normal loss	1 gallon		-
Output	9 gallons	(at £0.90)	£8.10

Standard cost of actual production

$$= \quad 92,070 \times £0.90 \quad = \quad £82,863$$

Actual qty in actual mix at actual price		*Actual qty in actual mix at standard price*		*Actual qty in std. mix at standard price*		*Std. qty in std. mix at standard price*	
Gallons	£	Gallons	£	Gallons	£	Gallons	£
45,000	36,000	45,000	31,500				
55,000	53,350	55,000	50,600	at 81p			
100,000	£89,350	100,000	£82,100	100,000	£81,000		£82,863

Materials cost variances:

			£	
Mix	£81,000 – £82,100	=	1,100	(A)
Yield	£82,863 – £81,000	=	1,863	(F)
Usage	£82,863 – £82,100	=	763	(F)
Price	£82,100 – £89,350	=	7,250	(A)
Total	£82,863 – £89,350	=	£6,487	(A)

(b)   **Usefulness of mix variances**

Manufacturing processes often entail the combination of a number of different materials to obtain one unit of finished product. Examples of such processes are chemicals, paints, plastics, fabrics and metal alloys.

The basic ingredients can often be combined in a variety of proportions (or mixes), without perhaps affecting the specified quality characteristics or properties of the finished product.

The sub-analysis of variances into mix and yield components can provide a valuable aid to management decisions as these two variances are often interrelated. The use of a different mixture of raw materials may reduce the cost of the mix but could produce an adverse yield effect. However, a yield variance can arise for reasons other than a change in the mixture of raw materials, for example due to poor management supervision or deliberate wastage of materials by operatives.

A change in the mixture of raw materials may also affect other variances, in particular labour and variable overhead efficiency variances.

A study of mix variances (and of other related variances) may be particularly important when management is experimenting with the introduction of a material substitute.

15 DECISION MAKING

INTRODUCTION & LEARNING OBJECTIVES

When you have studied this chapter you should be able to do the following:

- Recognise the information needed for planning and decision making.

- Recognise relevant costs and revenues.

- Solve simple decision making problems.

- Present clear reports to management.

1 USE OF RELEVANT, OPPORTUNITY AND NOTIONAL COSTS

1.1 Structure of a decision

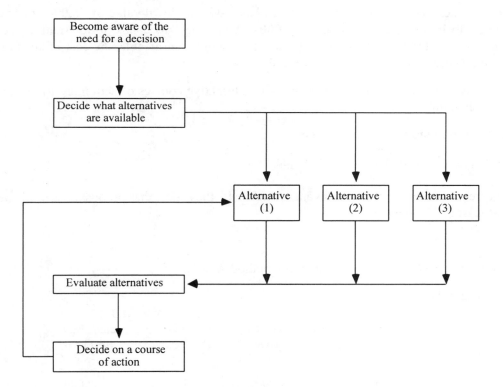

Although the cost accountant may be involved in all four stages, the main concern is with the evaluation process. Three types of cost may be involved:

Definition Relevant costs are those costs appropriate to a specific management decision.

Definition Opportunity cost is the value of a benefit sacrificed in favour of an alternative course of action.

Definition Notional cost is the value of a benefit where no actual cost is incurred.

1.2   Quantitative and qualitative factors

In an evaluation of the alternatives the manager will take account of factors of two types:

(a)   those which may be quantified in monetary terms;

(b)   those which may not as easily be quantified eg, effect on customer relations.

1.3   Short and long term decisions

The decisions faced by management may affect the future of the business in the long term, the short term or both.

Factors which are relevant in the short term may be irrelevant in the long term or *vice versa;* but in evaluating the factors, only the revenues and costs which are affected by the decision are relevant.

Factors which are **not** relevant to decision-making include:

(a)   **Sunk costs.** Costs which have already been incurred eg, costs already incurred in market research. The information gained from the research will be useful in making the decision, but the costs are irrelevant as the decision will not change them.

(b)   **Book values and accounting depreciation.** Both of these figures are determined by accounting conventions. For decision-making purposes it is the economic considerations which are important.

Illustration

A machine which cost £10,000 four years ago has a written down value of £6,000 and the depreciation to be charged this year is £1,000. Assuming that it has no alternative use, could be sold now for £3,000, but in one year's time will be unsaleable, the cost of keeping it and using it for a further year will be £3,000.

(c)   **Common costs.** Costs which are common to all alternative courses of action are irrelevant to decision-making.

1.4   General approach to decision-making problems

In the examples which follow, remember the key question:

Do the relevant revenues exceed the relevant costs?   If they do, the proposals are to be recommended, at least on financial grounds.

1.5   Example

A decision has to be made whether to use production method A or B.

The cost figures are as follows:

	Method A		Method B	
	Costs last year	Expected costs next year	Costs last year	Expected costs next year
	£	£	£	£
Fixed costs	5,000	7,000	5,000	7,000
Variable costs per unit:				
Labour	2	6	4	12
Materials	12	8	15	10

Which costs are relevant to the decision?

(a)   First, reject past costs (though in practice they may be used as a guide to future costs).

(b)   Second, reject expected fixed costs because, although they are not past, they are the same for both alternatives and may therefore be ignored.

(c)   Hence the only relevant costs are:

	Method A £	*Method B* £
Expected future variable costs:		
Labour	6	12
Materials	8	10
	14	22

It is concluded that the analysis should eliminate all irrelevant figures ie, those unaffected by the decision.

This, of course, considerably simplifies the decision, because it eliminates from consideration many irrelevant costs.

Note that fixed costs are not always irrelevant. If they vary between decision alternatives, they are relevant and must be taken into account.

1.6   Problems of uncertainty

The approach presupposes that the relevant costs and revenues are known. In fact, it is never possible to know future costs or revenues with certainty. Estimates may have varying degrees of confidence attached to them.

The examples in this chapter will use single figure estimates of costs and revenues. In practice it may be more desirable to use a range of figures, and to give probability weightings to the various values.

The techniques available for measuring uncertainty are outside the scope of this syllabus.

1.7   Determining the relevant costs of materials

In any decision situation the cost of materials relevant to a particular decision is their opportunity cost. This can be represented by a decision tree:

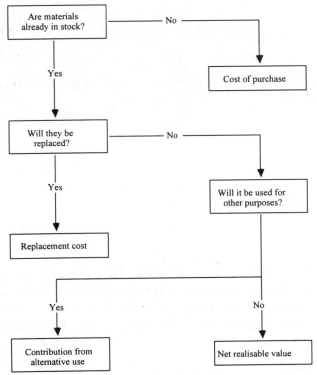

This decision tree can be used to identify the appropriate cost to use for materials.

1.8   Determining the relevant cost of labour

A similar problem exists in determining the relevant costs of labour. In this case the key question is whether spare capacity exists and on this basis another decision tree can be produced:

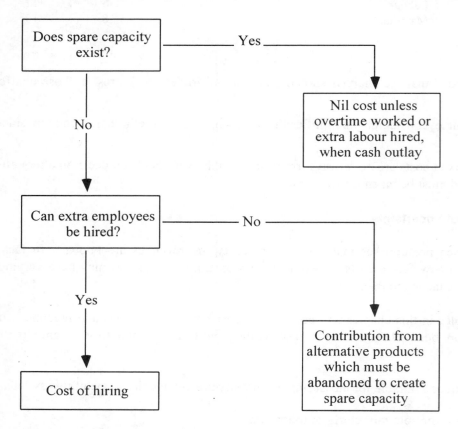

Again this can be used to identify the relevant opportunity cost.

1.9   Activity

Z Ltd has 50kg of material P in stock which was bought five years ago for £70. It is no longer used but could be sold for £3/kg.

Z Ltd is currently pricing a job which could use 40kg of material P. What is the relevant cost of P which should be included in the price?

1.10   Activity solution

40kg @ £3/kg = £120

2   CONTRIBUTION IN DECISION MAKING

2.1   Introduction

It is considered more informative to present comparison statements on a contribution basis. The term **contribution** describes the amount which a product provides or contributes towards a fund out of which fixed overhead may be paid, the balance being net profit. Where two or more products are manufactured in a factory and share all production facilities, the fixed overhead can only be apportioned on an arbitrary basis.

2.2   Example

A factory manufactures three components – X, Y and Z – and the budgeted production for the year is 1,000 units, 1,500 units and 2,000 units respectively. Fixed overhead amounts to £6,750 and has been apportioned on the basis of budgeted units: £1,500 to X, £2,250 to Y and £3,000 to Z. Sales and variable costs are as follows:

	Component X	Component Y	Component Z
Selling price	£4	£6	£5
Variable cost	£1	£4	£4

The budgeted profit and loss account based on the above is as follows:

	Component X		Component Y		Component Z		Total	
Sales units	1,000		1,500		2,000		4,500	
	£	£	£	£	£	£	£	£
Sales value		4,000		9,000		10,000		23,000
Variable cost	1,000		6,000		8,000		15,000	
Fixed overhead	1,500		2,250		3,000		6,750	
		2,500		8,250		11,000		21,750
Net profit/(loss)		1,500		750		(1,000)		1,250

Clearly there is little value in comparing products in this way. If the fixed overhead is common to all three products, there is no point in apportioning it. A better presentation is as follows:

	Component X	Component Y	Component Z	Total
Sales units	1,000	1,500	2,000	4,500
	£	£	£	£
Sales value	4,000	9,000	10,000	23,000
Variable cost	1,000	6,000	8,000	15,000
Contribution	3,000	3,000	2,000	8,000
Fixed cost				6,750
Net profit				1,250

Analysis may show, however, that certain fixed costs may be associated with a specific product and the statement can be amended to differentiate specific fixed costs (under products) from general fixed costs (under total).

2.3 Activity

Gadgetry Ltd manufactures a single product which is marketed in three grades of finish – Presentation, De Luxe and Standard. The variable cost of the basic unit is £6 and the cost of finishing and packing is as follows:

Presentation model	£4
De Luxe model	£2
Standard model	£1

The selling prices are:

Presentation model	£15
De Luxe model	£12
Standard model	£10

The marketing manager has estimated demand for next year as follows:

Presentation model	20,000 units
De Luxe model	30,000 units
Standard model	40,000 units

The production manager has estimated the production capacity of the factory at 150,000 pa. Fixed costs have been estimated at £100,000 for the forthcoming year.

An enquiry has been received from a manufacturer who is considering using the basic unit as a sub-assembly in his own product and who, at an acceptable price, would be willing to buy 30,000 units a year.

The company's pre-taxation profit objective for the next year is £300,000.

You are required to:

(a)   calculate the lowest price which could be quoted for the supply of the 30,000 units; and

(b)   comment upon any business policy matters that you consider relevant in these circumstances.

2.4 Activity solution

(a)   The lowest acceptable price, based on the company's profit objective for next year, is calculated as follows:

	Contribution per unit	Estimated sales units	Contribution £
Presentation model	£5	20,000	100,000
De Luxe model	£4	30,000	120,000
Standard model	£3	40,000	120,000
			340,000
Fixed costs			100,000
Estimated net profit			240,000
Balance required to meet objective			60,000
Profit objective			300,000

To achieve the profit objective, the 30,000 additional units need to obtain a contribution of £60,000 ie, £2 per unit. Thus, the lowest selling price will be the variable cost of the basic unit, £6 plus £2 contribution = £8 per unit.

(b)   Relevant policy matters to be considered by Gadgetry Ltd would include

   (i)   any price in excess of £6 per unit would increase the net profit of Gadgetry;

   (ii)   the requirement for Gadgetry's basic unit implies that the manufacturer's product may be in competition with Gadgetry's products;

   (iii)   the special order represents an increase of one-third of estimated output - it is likely that such a substantial increase would necessitate a reappraisal of estimated costs;

   (iv)   the special order would raise Gadgetry's production to 80% of capacity - if demand for Gadgetry's products suddenly increased, the company would be unable to take advantage and would lose sales of its more profitable products.

3   BREAK-EVEN ANALYSIS

3.1   The conventional break-even chart

Definition   Break-even is the point where sales revenue equals total cost ie, there is neither a profit nor a loss. Profit (or loss) is the difference between contribution and fixed costs. Thus the break-even point occurs where contribution equals fixed costs.

The conventional break-even chart plots total costs and total revenues at different output levels:

Conventional break-even chart

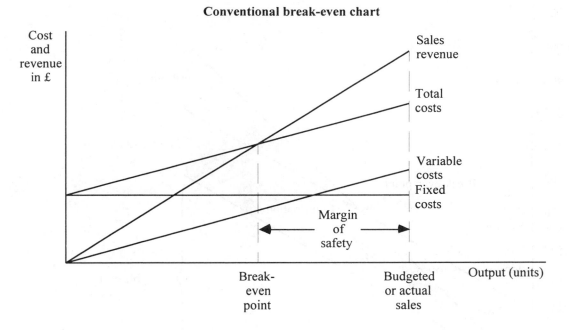

The chart or graph is constructed by:

(a)   plotting fixed costs as a straight line parallel to the horizontal axis;
(b)   plotting sales revenue and variable costs from the origin;
(c)   total costs represent fixed plus variable costs.

The point at which the sales revenue and total cost lines intersect indicates the break-even level of output. The amount of profit or loss at any given output can be read off the chart.

The chart is normally drawn up to the budgeted sales volume.

The difference between the budgeted sales volume and break-even sales volume is referred to as the margin of safety.

3.2   Usefulness of charts

The conventional form of break-even charts was described above. Many variations of such charts exist to illustrate the main relationships of costs, volume and profit. Unclear or complex charts should, however, be avoided as a chart which is not easily understood defeats its own object.

Generally, break-even charts are most useful to:

(a)   Compare products, time periods or actual versus plan.

(b)   Show the effect of changes in circumstances or to plans.

(c)   Give a broad picture of events.

3.3   Contribution break-even charts

A contribution break-even chart may be constructed with the variable costs at the foot of the diagram and the fixed costs shown above the variable cost line.

The total cost line will be in the same position as in the break-even chart illustrated above; but by using the revised layout it is possible to read off the figures of contribution at various volume levels, as shown in the following diagram:

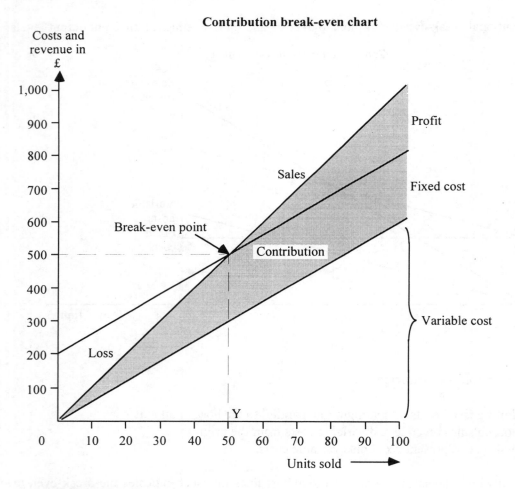

Contribution break-even chart

3.4   Contribution target

It has been seen that unit contribution can be assumed to be constant for all levels of output in the relevant range. Similarly, fixed costs can be assumed to be a constant amount in total.

The relationships may be depicted thus:

(a)   Unit contribution   = Selling price per unit – variable costs per unit.

(b)   Total contribution   = Volume × (Selling price per unit – variable costs per unit).

(c)   Contribution target   = Fixed costs + Profit target.

(d)   Volume target $= \dfrac{\text{Contribution target}}{\text{Unit contribution}}$

Bearing in mind the concept of **relevant range**, the formulae can be useful in simplifying predictions for planning and decision making.

3.5   Applications of break-even analysis

To illustrate the application, an example is used.

3.6   Example

Company	:	Widgets Ltd
Product	:	Widgets
Selling price	:	£3 per unit
Variable costs	:	Raw materials, £1 per unit
Fixed costs	:	Factory rent, £500 pa.

(a)   How many widgets must be sold per annum to break-even?

$$\text{Volume target} = \frac{\text{Contribution target}}{\text{Selling price - variable costs per unit}}$$

$$= \frac{£500 + £0}{£3 - £1} = 250 \text{ widgets.}$$

At sales volume of 250 units per annum, Widgets Ltd will make nil profit or loss:

		£
Sales	250 × £3	750
Variable costs	250 × £1	250
		‾‾‾
		500
Fixed costs		500
		‾‾‾
Profit/(loss)		Nil

(b)   If rent goes up by 10% and Widgets Ltd aims to make £200 pa profit, what annual output is needed?

$$\text{Volume target} = \frac{\text{Contribution target}}{\text{Unit contribution}} = \frac{£500 + £50 + £200}{£3 - £1} = 375 \text{ widgets}$$

(c)   Assuming the maximum possible output of Widgets Ltd is 250 widgets pa, what selling price would achieve the required profit target of £200 (assuming the increased rent)?

Contribution target	=	Fixed costs + Profit target
	=	£550 + £200 = £750

and

$$\text{Total contribution} = \text{Volume} \times (\text{Selling price per unit} - \text{Variable costs per unit})$$

$$\therefore \quad 750 = 250 \times (SP - 1)$$
$$750 = 250\,SP - 250$$
$$1{,}000 = 250\,SP$$

The required selling price (SP) is therefore, £4 per unit, giving:

			£
Sales	:	250 widgets × £4 =	1,000
Variable costs	:	250 × £1	250
Contribution			750
Fixed costs:			550
Profit			200

The simple example above illustrates that, given the cost/selling price structure, a range of alternative predictions can be easily calculated. Any change in selling price or variable costs will alter unit contribution; changes in fixed costs or profit required will affect the contribution target.

3.7 Contribution to sales ratio

In the above illustration, it was assumed that Widgets Ltd had sold only one product. If it had produced three products, say widgets, gidgets and shmidgets and the unit contribution of each product was different, then it would be uninformative to assess total volume in terms of units.

If, however, the relative proportion of each product sold could be assumed to remain similar or if each product has the same ratio of contribution to sales value, then similar calculations could be made for the business as a whole. Output would be expressed in terms of sales revenue rather than numbers of units, ie:

$$\text{Contribution to sales ratio (C/S ratio)} = \frac{\text{Contribution in £}}{\text{Sales in £}}$$

Note: students may encounter the term profit to volume (or P/V) ratio, which is synonymous with the contribution to sales ratio. Profit to volume is an inaccurate description, however, and should not be used. The C/S ratio is conveniently written as a percentage.

3.8 Example

Widgets Ltd operating statement for year 3 shows:

	Widgets	*Gidgets*	*Schmidgets*	*Total*
Sales units	100	40	60	200
	£	£	£	£
Sales value	400	240	300	940
Variable costs	220	130	170	520
Contribution	180	110	130	420
Fixed costs				350
Profit				70
C/S ratio	45%	46%	43%	44½%

Break-even volume in sales value $= \dfrac{\text{Fixed costs}}{\text{C / S ratio}}$

$$= \dfrac{£350}{44\frac{1}{2}\%} = £786.50$$

Thus, the business must sell about £790 of a mixture of widgets, gidgets and shmidgets before it starts to make a profit. The calculation in this instance would be acceptably accurate because the three products have almost identical C/S ratios. If the ratios were significantly different, however, use of the total C/S ratio would imply that the proportions of widgets, gidgets and schmidgets to total sales remained the same over the range of output considered.

3.9   Margin of safety

The difference between budgeted sales volume and break-even sales volume is known as the **margin of safety**. It indicates the vulnerability of a business to a fall in demand. It is often expressed as a percentage of budgeted sales.

3.10   Example

Budgeted sales	:	80,000 units
Selling price	:	£8
Variable costs	:	£4 per unit
Fixed costs	:	£200,000 pa

Break even volume $= \dfrac{200,000}{8-4}$

$\qquad\qquad\qquad = 50,000$ units

$\therefore$ Margin of safety $= 80,000 - 50,000$

$\qquad\qquad\qquad\quad = 30,000$ units or $37\frac{1}{2}\%$ of budget.

The margin of safety may also be expressed as a percentage of actual sales or of maximum capacity.

Students should note the relationship between the margin of safety when expressed as a percentage of actual sales and the C/S and profit to sales (P/S) ratio.

$\qquad$ P/S ratio $\qquad =$ Margin of safety $\times$ C/S ratio.

3.11   Example

	£
Sales	10,000
Variable costs	6,000
	4,000
Fixed costs	2,500
	1,500

(a) $\quad$ P/S ratio $\qquad = \dfrac{1,500}{10,000}$

$\qquad\qquad\qquad\qquad\quad = 15\%$

(b)   C/S ratio $= \dfrac{4,000}{10,000}$

$= 40\%$

(c)   Break-even sales $= \dfrac{2,500}{0.4}$

$= £6,250$

Excess sales $= 3,750$

Margin of safety $= \dfrac{3,750}{10,000}$

$= 37.5\%$

$\therefore$ P/S ratio $= 37.5\% \times 40\%$

$= 15\%$

3.12   Limitations of break-even analysis

Break-even analysis is useful insofar as it either meets or approximates to the requirements of the model. These requirements are:

(a)   Costs can be classified as either fixed or variable.

(b)   Over the time scale and activity range under review, unit variable costs remain constant and total fixed costs remain constant.

(c)   Unit sales price remains constant.

(d)   The costs and relationships are known.

Despite the obvious limitations these requirements impose, break-even analysis is of great practical importance. This is not just for itself, but because of the understanding it gives of cost behaviour patterns for decision purposes, considered further below.

3.13   Profit-volume chart

Break-even charts usually show both costs and revenues over a given range of activity and they do not highlight directly the amounts of profits or losses at the various levels. A chart which does simply depict the net profit and loss at any given level of activity is called a **profit-volume chart (or graph)**.

Profit-volume chart (1)

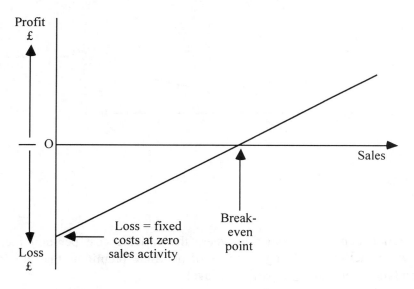

From the above chart the amount of net profit or loss can be read off for any given level of sales activity.

The points to note in the construction of a profit-volume chart are:

(a)   The horizontal axis represents sales (in units or sales value, as appropriate). This is the same as for a break-even chart.

(b)   The vertical axis shows net profit above the horizontal sales axis and net loss below.

(c)   When sales are zero, the net loss equals the fixed costs and one extreme of the 'profit volume' line is determined - therefore this is one point on the graph or chart.

(d)   If variable cost **per unit** and fixed costs **in total** are both constant throughout the relevant range of activity under consideration, the profit-volume chart is depicted by a straight line (as illustrated above). Therefore, to draw that line it is only necessary to know the profit (or loss) at one level of sales. The 'profit-volume' line is then drawn between this point and that determined in (c) and extended as necessary.

(e)   If there are changes in the variable cost per unit or total fixed costs at various activities, it would be necessary to calculate the profit (or loss) at each point where the cost structure changes and to plot these on the chart. The 'profit-volume' line will then be a series of straight lines joining these points together, as simply illustrated as follows:

Profit-volume chart (2)

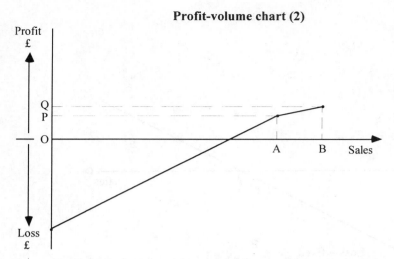

This illustration depicts the situation where the variable cost per unit increases after a certain level of activity (OA) eg, because of overtime premiums that are incurred when production (and sales) exceed a particular level.

Points to note:

(a)   the profit (OP) at sales level OA would be determined and plotted;

(b)   similarly the profit (OQ) at sales level of OB would be determined and plotted;

(c)   the loss at zero sales activity (= fixed costs) can be plotted;

(d)   the 'profit-volume' line is then drawn by joining these points, as illustrated.

3.14   Calculations for decisions

The kinds of decisions where break-even analysis is appropriate may be illustrated by the following example.

Example

Reprographics Ltd manufactures a document reproducing machine which has a variable cost structure as follows:

	£
Material	40
Labour	10
Overhead	4
	54
Selling price	£90

Sales and fixed costs during the current year are expected to be £1,350,000 and £140,000 respectively.

Under a wage agreement, an increase of 10% is payable to all direct workers from the beginning of the forthcoming year. Materials costs are expected to increase by 7.5%, overheads by 5% and fixed costs by 3%.

You are required to state:

(a)   The new selling price if the current C/S ratio is to be maintained.

(b)   The quantity to be sold during the forthcoming year to yield the same amount of profit as the current year, assuming the selling price is to remain at £90.

Note: you may ignore the question of stocks and work-in-progress and may assume that the fixed cost is fixed to a production level up to 20,000 machines.

(a)   **New selling price**

Current C/S ratio = $\dfrac{90-54}{90}$ =   40%

Revised variable costs per machine

			£
Materials	£40 + 7.5%	=	43.00
Labour	£10 +10%	=	11.00
Overhead	£4 + 5%	=	4.20
			58.20

Selling price (SP) to maintain C/S ratio:

$\dfrac{SP-58.2}{SP}$ =   40%

∴ SP   =   £97

(b)   **Target quantity**

Current year sales   =   £1,350,000 ÷ 90 = 15,000 machines

Current year profit   =   15,000 × £(90 − 54) − 140,000 = £400,000

New fixed costs   =   £140,000 + 3% = £144,200

Target quantity   = $\dfrac{\text{Contribution target}}{\text{Contribution per unit}}$

= $\dfrac{400,000+144,200}{90-58.20}$ = 17,113 machines

3.15   Activity

The following details relate to a shop which currently sells 25,000 pairs of shoes annually

Selling price per pair of shoes	£40
Purchase cost per pair of shoes	£25

Total annual fixed costs

	£
Salaries	100,000
Advertising	40,000
Other fixed expenses	100,000

You are required:

Answer each part independently of data contained in other parts of the requirement.

(a)   Calculate the break-even point and margin of safety in number of pairs of shoes sold.

(b)   Assume that 20,000 pairs of shoes were sold in a year.

Calculate the shop's net income (or loss).

(c)   If a selling commission of £2 per pair of shoes sold was to be introduced, how many pairs of shoes would need to be sold in a year in order to earn a net income of £10,000?

(d)   Assume that for next year an additional advertising campaign costing £20,000 is proposed, whilst at the same time selling prices are to be increased by 12%.

What would be the break-even point in number of pairs of shoes?

3.16 **Activity solution**

(a) Break-even point $= \dfrac{\text{Total fixed costs}}{\text{Contribution per pair}}$

Contribution per pair $=$ Selling price $-$ Variable cost $= 40 - 25 = 15$

Break-even point $= \dfrac{100,000 + 40,000 + 100,000}{15}$

$= \underline{16,000 \text{ pairs}}$

Margin of safety $=$ Current level of sales $-$ Break-even sales

$= 25,000 - 16,000$

$= \underline{9,000 \text{ pairs}}$

(b) Net income from sale of 20,000 pairs:

	£
Contribution: $20,000 \times 15$	300,000
Less: Fixed costs	240,000
Net profit	60,000

(c) Sales volume for a required profit $= \dfrac{\text{Total fixed cost } + \text{ Required profit}}{\text{Contribution per pair}}$

$= \dfrac{240,000 + 10,000}{15 - 2}$

Sales volume for a net income of £10,000 $= \underline{19,231 \text{ pairs}}$

Note: because of the need for a whole number answer, actual net income will be [$19,231 \times 13 - 240,000$] ie, £10,003.

(d) Break-even point $= \dfrac{240,000 + 20,000}{\left(15 + \left(40 \times \dfrac{12}{100}\right)\right)}$

Break-even point $= \dfrac{260,000}{19.8}$ $= \underline{13,132 \text{ pairs}}$

Note: again this whole number answer results in just above break-even point being achieved ie,

Contribution: $13,132 \times 19.8 =$	260,013.6
Less: Fixed costs	260,000.0
Net income	13.6

3.17   Conclusion

Consider the following companies:

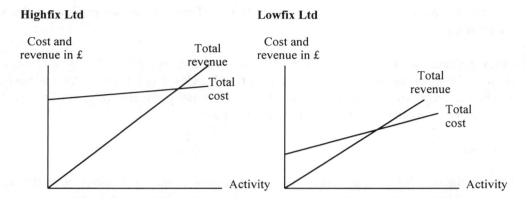

At a glance it may be seen that these two firms have entirely different cost/revenue structures.

Highfix Ltd has high fixed and low variable costs. Lowfix Ltd has low fixed and high variable costs.

Highfix Ltd is the higher risk firm. Losses increase rapidly as output falls below break-even point because of the relatively high fixed costs. On the other hand, as output rises above break-even, profits increase rapidly because of the high contribution ratio.

Lowfix Ltd is in the contrary situation. It is relatively low risk because most costs are variable. On other hand, it will find it much more difficult to make high profits.

4   PRODUCT SALES PRICING AND MIX DECISIONS

4.1   Economic theory

The economic theory of pricing states that in order to increase demand (and therefore sales) there has to be a reduction in price. It follows from this that profit is maximised when marginal costs equal marginal revenues.

4.2   Pricing and decision making

In the context of decision making, many of the earlier examples have used a single price for the product. Whilst it is accepted that this is too simplistic according to the economic model, it should be realised that in the context of short-term decision making within the boundaries of the relevant range it is probably acceptable.

However, this should be borne in mind when advising management on decision making situations which have price implications.

4.3   Sales mix

If an organisation produces more than one product, the products may be complementary to one another or they may be substitutes for each other. It is likely that each will yield different profits.

In the context of product pricing a factor which should be considered is the relationship between the products in multi-product organisations.

4.4   Limiting factors

All businesses which aim to maximise profit find that the volume of output and sales is restricted. For many, sales demand is the limiting factor and therefore the business will seek to make the maximum profit by concentrating its selling efforts on those products which yield high contributions.

Other limiting factors may prevent sales growth eg, shortage of building space, machine capacity, skilled labour, or the necessary materials. In such cases it is important for the business to obtain maximum profit by concentrating its efforts on those products which yield high contributions relative to the amount of the limiting factor they consume.

4.5   Example

Two products - Alpha and Gama - are given a final finish by passing them through a spraying process. There is considerable demand for both products but output is restricted by the capacity of the spraying process. The product details are as follows:

	Alpha £	*Gama* £
Selling price	10.00	15.00
Variable cost	6.00	7.50
Contribution	4.00	7.50
Finishing time in spraying process	1 hour	3 hours

Without any restriction in the capacity of the spraying process, Gama is the more profitable product and should be promoted (assuming that the sales of each product do not affect the other). However, as the spraying process is the limiting factor, it is important for the business to use the capacity of the process as profitably as possible ie, to earn the maximum profit for each spraying hour. The contributions per spraying hour are £4.00 for Alpha and £2.50 for Gama and, therefore, it is Alpha which should be promoted. This can be proved by assuming a fixed number of spraying hours per week, say 45:

	Alpha	*Gama*
Number of units to be sprayed in 45 hours	45	15
Contribution per unit	£4.00	£7.50
Total contribution	£180.00	£112.50

4.6   Differential cost approach

The proof in the above example illustrates an application of differential costing, a technique in which only cost and income differences between alternative courses of action are considered.

The difference between the two alternatives (viz product Alpha alone and product Gama alone) is £67.50.

4.7   Other considerations regarding limiting factors

(a)   In the long run management must seek to remove the limiting factor. In the example above, management should be attempting to increase the capacity of the spraying process. Thus, any one limiting factor should only be a short term problem. However, as soon as it is removed, it will be replaced by another limiting factor.

(b)   Even in the short run management may be able to find ways round the bottleneck eg, overtime working or sub-contracting might be solutions to the situations described.

(c)   It may not always be easy to identify the limiting factor. In practice, as already stated, several limiting factors may operate simultaneously. Even in examination questions where there is only one limiting factor, it may be necessary to investigate several possible limiting factors.

(d)   Other parameters may set minimum production levels eg, there may be a contract to supply Gama so that certain minimum quantities must be produced.

4.8   Example

X Ltd makes three products - A, B and C - of which unit costs, machine hours and selling prices are as follows:

	Product A	Product B	Product C
Machine hours	10	12	14
	£	£	£
Direct materials £1 per lb	14 (14 lbs)	12 (12 lbs)	10 (10 lbs)
Variable overhead	18 (12 hours)	12 (8 hours)	6 (4 hours)
Marginal cost	38	30	22
Selling price	50	40	30
Contribution	12	10	8

Sales demand for the period is limited as follows:

A	4,000
B	6,000
C	6,000

However, as a matter of company policy it is decided to produce a minimum of 1,000 units of Product A. The supply of materials in the period is unlimited but machine hours are restricted to 200,000 and direct labour hours to 50,000.

Indicate the production levels that should be adopted for the three products in order to maximise profitability, and state the maximum contribution.

Solution

First, determine which is the limiting factor. At potential sales level:

	Sales potential (units)	Total machine hours	Total labour hours
Product A	4,000	40,000	48,000
Product B	6,000	72,000	48,000
Product C	6,000	84,000	24,000
		196,000	120,000

Thus the limiting factor is the labour hours. The next stage is to calculate contribution per labour hour:

Product A $\frac{£12}{12} = £1.00$

Product B $\frac{£10}{8} = £1.25$

Product C $\dfrac{£8}{4} = £2.00$

Thus, production should be concentrated on C up to maximum available sales, then B and finally A.

However, a minimum of 1,000 units of A must be produced. Taking these factors into account, the production schedule becomes:

	Units produced	*Labour hours*	*Cumulative labour hours*	*Limiting factor*
Product A	1,000	12,000	12,000	Policy to produce 1,000 units
Product C	6,000	24,000	36,000	Sales
Product B	1,750	14,000	50,000	Labour hours

4.9   Shadow prices

A shadow price is the loss or gain in contribution which would occur if the availability of a scarce resource were to change by one unit of that resource.

Using the example of X Ltd above, the loss or gain of one labour hour would affect the production of product B.

Product B takes 8 hours to produce and yields a contribution of £10 per unit. An alteration in the labour hours available by one would therefore alter production of B by one-eighth of a unit, and change contribution by $\frac{1}{8}$th of £10 or £1.25 (ie, B's contribution per hour).

The shadow price therefore also represents the maximum amount which should be paid in order to obtain an extra hour or avoid losing an hour. In this example this is £1.25 (or very slightly less) since this is the value in contribution terms of the hour. This is, of course, in addition to the normal cost of one hour because this has already been included in the marginal cost of the product.

5   MAKE OR BUY DECISIONS

5.1   Types of make or buy decisions

Occasionally a business may have the opportunity to purchase, from another company, a component part or assembly which it currently produces from its own resources.

In examining the choice, management must first consider the following questions:

(a)   Is the alternative source of supply available only temporarily or for the foreseeable future?
(b)   Is there spare production capacity available now and/or in the future?

5.2   Spare capacity

If the business is operating below maximum capacity, production resources will be idle if the component is purchased from outside. The fixed costs of those resources are irrelevant to the decision in the short term as they will be incurred whether the component is made or purchased. Purchase would be recommended, therefore, only if the buying price were less than the variable costs of internal manufacture.

In the long term, however, the business may dispense with or transfer some of its resources and may purchase from outside if it thereby saves more than the extra cost of purchasing.

5.3   Example

A company manufactures an assembly used in the production of one of its product lines. The department in which the assembly is produced incurs fixed costs of £24,000 pa. The variable costs of production are £2.55 per unit. The assembly could be bought outside at a cost of £2.65 per unit.

The current annual requirement is for 80,000 assemblies per year. Should the company continue to manufacture the assembly, or should it be purchased from the outside suppliers?

5.4   Solution

A decision to purchase outside would cost the company £(2.65 - 2.55) = 10p per unit, which for 80,000 assemblies would amount to £8,000 pa. Thus, the fixed costs of £24,000 will require analysis to determine if more than £8,000 would actually be saved if production of the assembly were discontinued.

5.5   Other considerations affecting the decision

Management would need to consider other factors before reaching a decision. Some would be quantifiable and some not:

(a)   **Continuity and control of supply.** Can the outside company be relied upon to meet the requirements in terms of quantity, quality, delivery dates and price stability?

(b)   **Alternative use of resources.** Can the resources used to make this article be transferred to another activity which will save cost or increase revenue?

(c)   **Social/legal.** Will the decision affect contractual or ethical obligations to employees or business connections?

5.6   Capacity exhausted

If a business cannot fulfil orders because it has used up all available capacity, it may be forced to purchase from outside in the short term (unless it is cheaper to refuse sales). In the longer term management may look to other alternatives, such as capital expenditure.

It may be, however, that a variety of components is produced from common resources and management would try to arrange manufacture or purchase to use its available capacity most profitably. In such a situation the limiting factor concept makes it easier to formulate the optimum plans; priority for purchase would be indicated by ranking components in relation to the excess purchasing cost per unit of limiting factor.

5.7   Example

Fidgets Ltd manufactures three components used in its finished product. The component workshop is currently unable to meet the demand for components and the possibility of sub-contracting part of the requirement is being investigated on the basis of the following data:

	Component A	*Component B*	*Component C*
	£	£	£
Variable costs of production	3.00	4.00	7.00
Outside purchase price	2.50	6.00	13.00
Excess cost per unit	(0.50)	2.00	6.00
Machine hours per unit	1	0.5	2
Labour hours per unit	2	2	4

You are required:

(a)   to decide which component should be bought out if the company is operating at full capacity

(b)   to decide which component should be bought out if production is limited to 4,000 machine hours per week

(c)   to decide which component should be bought out if production is limited to 4,000 labour hours per week

5.8   Solution

(a)   Component A should always be bought out regardless of any limiting factors, as its variable cost of production is higher than the outside purchase price.

(b)   If machine hours are limited to 4,000 hours:

	Component B	Component C
Excess cost	£2	£6
Machine hours per unit	0.5	2
Excess cost per machine hour	£4	£3

Component C has the lowest excess cost per limiting factor and should, therefore, be bought out.

Proof:

	Component B	Component C
Units produced in 4,000 hours	8,000	2,000
	£	£
Production costs	32,000	14,000
Purchase costs	48,000	26,000
Excess cost of purchase	16,000	12,000

(c)   If labour hours are limited to 4,000 hours:

	Component B	Component C
Excess cost	£2	£6
Labour hours	2	4
Excess cost per labour hour	£1	£1.50

Therefore, component B has the lowest excess cost per limiting factor and should be bought out.

Proof:

	Component B	Component C
Units produced in 4,000 hours	2,000	1,000
	£	£
Production costs	8,000	7,000
Purchase costs	12,000	13,000
Excess cost of purchase	4,000	6,000

6   **EVALUATING PROPOSALS**

6.1   **Volume and cost structure changes**

Management will require information to evaluate proposals aimed to increase profit by changing operating strategy. The cost accountant will need to show clearly the effect of the proposals on profit by pin-pointing the changes in costs and revenues and by quantifying the margin of error which will cause the proposal to be unviable.

6.2   **Example**

A company produces and sells one product and its forecast for the next financial year is as follows:

	£'000	£'000
Sales 100,000 units @ £8		800
Variable costs:		
Material	300	
Labour	200	
		500
Contribution (£3 per unit)		300
Fixed costs		150
Net profit		150

As an attempt to increase net profit, two proposals have been put forward:

(a)   to launch an advertising campaign costing £14,000. This will increase the sales to 150,000 units, although the price will have to be reduced to £7;

(b)   to produce some components at present purchased from suppliers. This will reduce material costs by 20% but will increase fixed costs by £72,000.

Proposal (a) will increase the sales revenue but the increase in costs will be greater:

	£'000
Sales 150,000 × £7	1,050
Variable costs	750
	300
Fixed costs plus advertising	164
Net profit	136

6.3   **Solution**

Proposal (a) is therefore of no value and sales must be increased by a further 7,000 units to maintain net profit:

Advertising cost	=	£14,000
Contribution per unit	=	£2
∴ Additional volume required	=	7,000 units

Proposal (b) reduces variable costs by £60,000 but increases fixed costs by £72,000 and is therefore not to be recommended unless the total volume increases as a result of the policy (eg, if the supply of the components were previously a limiting factor). The increase in sales needed to maintain profit at £150,000 (assuming the price remains at £8) would be:

Reduced profits at 100,000 units	=	£12,000
Revised contribution per unit	=	£3.60
∴ Additional volume required	=	3,333 units

6.4   Utilisation of spare capacity

Where production is below capacity, opportunities may arise for sales at a specially reduced price, for example, export orders or manufacturing under another brand name (eg, 'St Michael'). Such opportunities are worthwhile if the answer to two key questions is 'Yes':

(a)   Is spare capacity available?

(b)   Does additional revenue (Units × Price) exceed additional costs (Units × Variable cost)?

However, the evaluation should also consider:

(i)   Is there an alternative more profitable way of utilising spare capacity (eg, sales promotion, making an alternative product)?

(ii)   Will fixed costs be unchanged if the order is accepted?

(iii)   Will accepting one order at below normal selling price lead other customers to ask for price cuts?

The longer the time period in question, the more important are these other factors.

6.5   Example

At a production level of 8,000 units per month, which is 80% of capacity, the budget of Export Ltd is:

	Per unit £	8,000 units £
Sales	5.00	40,000
Variable costs:		
Direct labour	1.00	8,000
Raw materials	1.50	12,000
Variable overheads	0.50	4,000
	3.00	24,000
Fixed costs	1.50	12,000
Total	4.50	36,000
Budgeted profit	0.50	4,000

An opportunity arises to export 1,000 units per month at a price of £4 per unit.

Should the contract be accepted?

6.6   Solution

(a)   Is spare capacity available?   Yes

			£
(b)	Additional revenue	1,000 × £4	4,000
	Additional costs	1,000 × £3	3,000
			1,000

Increased profitability

Therefore, the contract should be accepted.

Note that fixed costs are not relevant to the decision and are therefore ignored.

6.7   Special contract pricing

A business which produces to customer's order may be working to full capacity. Any additional orders must be considered on the basis of the following questions:

(a)   What price must be quoted to make the contract profitable?
(b)   Can other orders be fulfilled if this contract is accepted?

In such a situation the limiting factor needs to be recognised so that the contract price quoted will at least maintain the existing rate of contribution per unit of limiting factor.

6.8   Example

Oddjobs Ltd manufactures special purpose gauges to customers' specifications. The highly skilled labour force is always working to full capacity and the budget for the next year shows:

	£	£
Sales		40,000
Direct materials	4,000	
Direct wages 3,200 hours @ £5	16,000	
Fixed overhead	10,000	
		30,000
Profit		10,000

An enquiry is received from XY Ltd for a gauge which would use £60 of direct materials and 40 labour hours.

(a)   What is the minimum price to quote to XY Ltd?

(b)   Would the minimum price be different if spare capacity were available but materials were subject to a quota of £4,000 per year?

6.9   Solution

(a)   The limiting factor is 3,200 labour hours and the budgeted contribution per hour is £20,000 ÷ 3,200 hours = £6.25 per hour. Minimum price is therefore:

	£
Materials	60
Wages 40 hours @ £5	200
	260
Add: Contribution 40 hours @ £6.25	250
Contract price	510

At the above price the contract will maintain the budgeted contribution (check by calculating the effect of devoting the whole 3,200 hours to XY Ltd.)

Note, however, that the budget probably represents a mixture of orders, some of which earn more than £6.25 per hour and some less. Acceptance of the XY order must displace other contracts, so the contribution rate of contracts displaced should be checked.

(b)   If the limiting factor is materials, budgeted contribution per £ of materials is £20,000 ÷

4,000 = £5 per £1.

Minimum price is therefore:

	£
Materials/wages (as above)	260
Contribution £60 × 5	300
Contract price	560

Because materials are scarce, Oddjobs must aim to earn the maximum profit from its limited supply.

6.10   Closure of a business segment

Part of a business may appear to be unprofitable. The segment may, for example, be a product, a department or a channel of distribution. In evaluating closure the cost accountant should identify:

(a)   loss of contribution from the segment;

(b)   savings in specific fixed costs from closure;

(c)   penalties eg, redundancy, compensation to customers etc;

(d)   alternative use for resources released;

(e)   non-quantifiable effects.

6.11   Example

Harolds department store comprises three departments - Menswear, Ladies' Wear and Unisex. The store budget is as follows:

	Mens Ladies £	Unisex £	Total £	£
Sales	40,000	60,000	20,000	120,000
Direct cost of sales	20,000	36,000	15,000	71,000
Department costs	5,000	10,000	3,000	18,000
Apportioned store costs	5,000	5,000	5,000	15,000
Profit/(loss)	10,000	9,000	(3,000)	16,000

It is suggested that Unisex be closed to increase the size of Mens and Ladies.

What information is relevant or required?

6.12   Solution

Possible answers are:

(a)   Unisex earns £2,000 net contribution (store costs will be re-apportioned to Mens/Ladies).

(b)   Possible increase in Mens/Ladies sales volume.

(c)   Will Unisex staff be dismissed or transferred to Mens/Ladies?

(d)   Reorganisation costs eg, repartitioning, stock disposal.

(e)   Loss of custom because Unisex attracts certain types of customer who will not buy in Mens/Ladies.

6.13   Comparing segment profitability

When presenting information for comparing results or plans for different products, departments etc, it is useful to show gross and net contribution for each segment. The information in the example above would be presented in the following form.

	Menswear	Ladies Wear	Unisex	Total
	£'000	£'000	£'000	£'000
Sales	40	60	20	120
Direct cost of sales	20	36	15	71
Gross contribution	20	24	5	49
Department costs	5	10	3	18
Net contribution	15	14	2	31

Note that the store costs if shown would only appear in the total column. In addition, the statement should include performance indicators relevant to the type of operation. For a department store, such indicators would include:

(a)   C/S ratios (based on **gross** contribution);

(b)   gross and net contribution per unit of floor space;

(c)   gross and net contribution per employee.

For a manufacturing company, more relevant indicators would include:

(a)   contribution per labour/machine hour;

(b)   added value/conversion cost per hour;

(c)   added value/conversion cost per employee.

6.14   Temporary shut-down

When a business has experienced trading difficulties which do not appear likely to improve in the immediate future, consideration may be given to closing down operations temporarily. Factors other than cost which will influence the decision are:

(a)   suspending production and sales of products will result in their **leaving the public eye;**

(b)   dismissal of the labour force will entail bad feeling and possible difficulty in recruitment when operations are restarted;

(c)   danger of plant obsolescence;

(d)   difficulty and cost of closing down and restarting operations in certain industries eg, a blast furnace.

The temporary closure of a business will result in additional expenditure eg, plant will require protective coverings, services will be disconnected. In the same way, additional expenditure will be incurred when the business restarts.

On the other hand, a temporary closure may enable the business to reorganise efficiently to take full advantage of improved trading conditions when they return.

In the short term a business can continue to operate while marginal contribution equals fixed expenses. In periods of trading difficulty, as long as some contribution is made towards fixed expenses, it will generally be worthwhile continuing operations.

6.15   Example

A company is operating at 40% capacity and is considering closing down its factory for one year, after which time the demand for its product is expected to increase substantially. The following data applies:

	£
Sales value at 40% capacity	60,000
Marginal costs of sales at 40% capacity	40,000
Fixed costs	50,000

Fixed costs which will remain if the factory is closed amount to £20,000. The cost of closing down operations will amount to £4,000.

Prepare a statement to show the best course of action.

Statement of profit or loss

Continuing operation	£	Temporary closure	£
Sales	60,000	Fixed expenses	20,000
Marginal cost of sales	40,000	Closing down costs	4,000
Contribution to fixed costs	20,000		
Fixed costs	50,000		
Net loss	(30,000)		(24,000)

Ignoring non-cost considerations, the company will minimise its losses by closing down for one year.

Students should note that the marginal contribution of £20,000 does not cover the difference between existing fixed costs and those that remain on closure (ie, £(50,000 − 24,000) = £26,000 compared to £20,000).

7   PRESENTATION OF INFORMATION

7.1   Report writing

Accountants are used to dealing with figures, but they must also learn to express themselves clearly in words. This is important not only for the passing of examinations, but also in professional work. Accountants are (or should be!) well prepared for the degree of precision and organisation required in report writing, but may need practice to improve their written style.

The following guidelines for report writing should be observed both in examinations and in practical situations:

(a)   **Reporting objectives**

Every report has several objectives. Generally these will be to:

- define the problem;
- consider the alternatives; and
- make a reasoned recommendation for a specific alternative.

(b) **Recipient**

The writer should consider the position of the recipient and design the report accordingly. Some recipients will require detailed calculations; others will have little time to study a lengthy report and should therefore be given one of minimum length consistent with providing the required information.

In the examination you should write in a professional report style, pretending that you are writing to a client or to a senior manager.

(c) **Heading**

Each report should be headed to show who it is from and to, the subject and the date.

(d) **Paragraph point system – each paragraph should make a point; each point should have a paragraph**

This simple rule should always be observed. Important points may be underlined.

(e) **Jargon and technical terms**

The use of jargon should be avoided at all times. If it is necessary to use technical terms, these should be fully explained, as should any techniques with which the recipient may be unfamiliar eg, decision trees, linear programming, marginal costing, etc.

(f) **Conclusion**

A report should always reach a conclusion. This should be clearly stated at the end of the report, not in the middle. The report should make it clear why you have arrived at the stated conclusion: it is not enough merely to state all the alternatives and then to recommend one of them without supportive reasoning.

(g) **Planning**

The report must be properly planned so that all the points appear in the most logical order. In practice a report can be prepared in draft form and then amended. In the examination there is not enough time for this, so the initial planning is of paramount importance. Witness this extract from an examiner's report:

... if only candidates had their hands tied behind their backs for five minutes before being permitted to start writing, in many cases the marks that they might then have obtained could well be significantly higher.

(h) **Figures**

All detailed figures and calculations should be relegated to appendices, only the main results appearing in the body of the report. Remember that comparative figures will often be useful. The report should be made as visually stimulating as possible, for instance by the use of graphs and charts instead of, or to supplement, figures.

8   CHAPTER SUMMARY

This chapter has shown examples of the different kinds of decisions which must be made in order to maximise profitability.

Relevant costs for decisions have been identified and the techniques used to evaluate decision options illustrated.

The application of cost behaviour to marginal costing, contribution theory and break-even analysis has been explained.

Finally this chapter has explained the styles of report which may be used to present information to management.

9   SELF TEST QUESTIONS

9.1   What is a notional cost? (1.1)

9.2   How can you determine the relevant cost of materials? (1.7)

9.3   Explain 'contribution' (2.1)

9.4   Why is a contribution target important in decision making? (3.4)

9.5   Explain 'contribution to sales ratio' (3.7)

9.6   Explain the limitations of breakeven analysis (3.12)

9.7   What is a limiting factor? (4.4)

9.8   What is a shadow price? (4.9)

9.9   In a closure decision, name five factors that should be considered (6.10)

9.10   What factors should be considered when writing reports? (7.1)

10   EXAMINATION TYPE QUESTIONS

10.1   Jen Ltd

Jen Ltd manufactures three products, J, E and N, which undergo similar production processes and use similar materials and types of labour. The company's forecast profit statement for the forthcoming year, as submitted to the board, is as follows:

	Product J £	Product E £	Product N £	Total £
Sales	1,344,000	840,000	680,000	2,864,000
Direct material	336,000	294,000	374,000	1,004,000
Direct labour	201,600	168,000	136,000	505,600
Variable overhead	268,800	168,000	204,000	640,800
	806,400	630,000	714,000	2,150,400
Contribution	537,600	210,000	(34,000)	713,600
Fixed overhead				113,600
Profit				600,000

At a board meeting, a decision was made to discontinue the production of Product N as demand was falling and there was no possibility of increasing the selling price. Prospects for the other two products, however, were bright and the company had, in the past, been unable to meet the demand. It was decided, therefore, that the labour force released should be used to increase production of Products J and E; 60% of the budgeted labour for Product N being transferred to J and the remainder to E. The increased production of J and E is not expected to change their cost/selling price relationships.

You are required to prepare the revised forecast profit statement and to comment briefly upon the effect of the Board's decision.

(20 marks)

10.2   Hard and soft

A company produces a hard grade and, by additional processing, a soft grade of its product.

A market research study for next year has indicated very good prospects not only for both the hard and soft grades but also for a light grade produced after still further processing.

The raw material is imported and there is a possibility that a quota system will be introduced allowing only a maximum of £300,000 pa of material to be imported.

The company's marketing policy has been to sell 60% of its capacity (or of its allocation of material if the quota is introduced) in the most profitable grade. It has been decided that this policy should continue if it is to produce three grades, but that only 15% of its capacity (or material allocation) should be sold in the least profitable grade.

The budgeted prime costs and selling prices per ton for each grade are as follows:

	Hard £	*Soft* £	*Light* £
Selling price	70	95	150
Direct material cost	15	20	25
Direct wages (@ £2.50 per hour)	15	25	45

For next year the company's annual production capacity is 225,000 direct labour hours and its fixed overhead is £500,000. Variable overhead is 20% of direct wages.

Fixed overhead is at present absorbed by a rate per ton produced.

You are required:

(a) to state which of the three grades of product will be most profitable and which will be least profitable in the short term assuming that such volume as can be produced can be sold:

   (i)   if the materials quota does not operate;
   (ii) if the materials quota does come into force.

(b) if the materials quota does come into force, to calculate the budgeted profit for next year from the company's marketing policy if:

   (i)   only light grade is produced;
   (ii) all three grades are produced in accordance with present policy.

11 ANSWERS TO EXAMINATION TYPE QUESTIONS

11.1 Jen Ltd

Note: a variable cost is a cost which changes in direct proportion with changes in the volume of production or sales. In this example we have to apply this definition in reverse ie, if we increase the direct labour cost (assumed to be variable) by a certain percentage, then the production volume will increase by the same percentage.

Revised profit statement

	Product J £	*Product E* £	*Total* £
Sales	1,888,000	1,112,000	3,000,000
Direct materials	472,000	389,200	861,200
Direct labour	283,200	222,400	505,600
Variable overhead	377,600	222,400	600,000

	1,132,800	834,000	1,966,800
Contribution	755,200	278,000	1,033,200
Fixed overhead			113,600
Profit			919,600

The following points are relevant to the Board's decision:

(a)   The change results in a substantial profit increase of £319,600;

(b)   It is necessary to consider whether there is sufficient additional demand for Products J and E to meet such large increases in volume;

(c)   If the products are at all complementary this may result in sales of Product J and E being adversely affected by not selling Product N;

(d)   Although the products use 'similar' labour it is necessary to confirm that the changes are acceptable to the employees and unions.

(e)   Also, is it reasonable to assume that the same level of efficiency will be maintained by the employees switching from Product N?

WORKINGS

	Product J £	*Product E* £
Additional direct labour		
£136,000 × 60%	81,600	
£136,000 × 40%		54,400
Existing direct labour	201,600	168,000
Percentage increase	$\frac{81,600}{201,600} \times 100$	$\frac{54,400}{168,000} \times 100$
	= 40.476%	= 32.381%

As direct labour is a variable cost and assuming the same level of efficiency the production and sales volume of Product J and Product E will increase by these respective percentages.

11.2   Hard and soft

(a)   In the short term, whatever decision the company makes regarding the mix of products to be produced and sold, the fixed overhead can be assumed to remain the same. It is necessary, therefore, to base the decision on the contribution earned by each product.

	Hard £ £	*Soft* £ £	*Light* £ £
Selling price	70	95	150
Direct material	15	20	25
Direct wages	15	25	45
Variable overhead	3	5	9
	33	50	79
Contribution	37	45	71
Hours per unit	6	10	18
Contribution per hour	£6.167	£4.500	£3.944
Contribution per £1 material	£2.467	£2.25	£2.84

(i)   If the materials quota does not operate, the company's production capacity is limited to 225,000 labour hours, in which case it must seek to obtain the greatest contribution for each labour hour. The hard grade gives the greatest contribution per hour and therefore this is the most profitable.

(ii)   If the materials quota comes into force, the company must obtain the maximum contribution from each £1 spent on material. The light grade gives the greatest contribution per £1 of material and this is therefore the most profitable.

Note: this applies only if the materials quota provides production which is within the production capacity of 900,000 hours. To test this:

$$\frac{£300,000}{£25} \times 18 = 216,000 \text{ hours}$$

As this is within the labour constraint, conclusion (ii) is correct.

(b)   (i)

	Light
Material	£300,000
Budgeted units	12,000
Contribution per unit	£71
	£
Total contribution	852,000
Fixed overhead	500,000
Budgeted profit for year	352,000

(ii)

	Hard	*Soft*	*Light*	*Total* £
Material allocation	£75,000 (25%)	£45,000 (15%)	£180,000 (60%)	300,000
Budgeted units	5,000	2,250	7,200	
Contribution per unit	£37	£45	£71	
Total contribution	£185,000	£101,250	£511,200	797,450
Fixed overhead				500,000
Budgeted profit for year				297,450

16 ECONOMIC OBJECTIVES AND FISCAL POLICY

INTRODUCTION & LEARNING OBJECTIVES

The remaining chapters cover financial management. The economic environment in which an organisation operates affects all financial management decision making, thus we shall deal first with the economic environment before going on to financial management decisions in Chapter 20.

When you have studied this chapter you should be able to do the following:

- Identify and explain the main macroeconomic objectives

- Explain the main features of recent UK economic performance

- Consider the impact of economic policy on business

---

1 GOVERNMENT MACROECONOMIC OBJECTIVES

1.1 Macroeconomic policy: objectives, targets and instruments

> **Definition**   Management of the economy refers to the conduct of economic policy in such a way as to influence the performance and behaviour of the economy as a whole.

For much of the post-war period UK governments have engaged in economic policies designed to manage the economy. The emphasis placed upon different macroeconomic objectives has changed over time and the changes in economic theory have led to changes in the instruments of policy used. Nonetheless, the important distinctions between objectives, targets and instruments of policy have remained:

- objectives of policy are those overall characteristics of the economy which are generally deemed to be desirable eg, price stability

- these objectives become targets of policy when they are given particular values and time periods eg, an inflation target of 1-4% for the next 3 years

- instruments of policy are those particular policies which governments use in order to achieve their policy targets.

It should be noted however that these distinctions sometimes break down in practice: some government policies may have the characteristics of both instruments and objectives. Two examples are given:

(a)   A government may have a policy of shifting the burden of taxation from one group in society to another: this may be partly an objective reflecting the government's perception of the appropriate distribution of income but may also be seen as an instrument of policy designed to alter incentives for individuals.

(b)   The external exchange rate for the currency is not an objective in itself and in a world of floating exchange rates would be allowed to change according to market pressures: however, government have sometimes come to see a particular exchange value for sterling as an objective in itself and have adopted policies to support that exchange rate.

1.2   The objectives of macroeconomic policy

The principal objectives of UK macroeconomic policy have been to achieve the following:

(a)   Full employment of resources especially of the labour force.

(b)   Price stability.

(c)   Economic growth.

(d)   Balance of payments equilibrium.

(e)   An appropriate distribution of income and wealth.

Full employment has been an objective of all recent UK governments. However, the concept of full employment is complex and has undergone some changes in recent years. Full employment cannot mean that everyone has full time employment: until the late 1970s full employment effectively meant an unemployment rate below 3% of the labour force. Since then, full employment has been downgraded as a policy objective with Governments claiming that the level of employment reflects a wide range of factors some of which, like the wage rate, are outside of their control. Instead governments have emphasised that long term full employment may be best achieved by the avoidance of inflation. There is however agreement that unemployment is undesirable since it involves:

*   loss of economic output and welfare;
*   direct economic consequences for the unemployed;
*   heavy government expenditure to support the unemployed.

The pursuit of price stability is the oldest of government policy objectives dating back to the 19th century. Inflation is seen to be undesirable because it may:

*   damage the UK's international competitiveness and hence cause both employment and balance of payments problems;

*   make business planning and decision making difficult hence reducing the volume of investment;

*   discourage saving and distort investment away from productive assets towards those providing a hedge against inflation;

*   distort the distribution of income and wealth in an arbitrary manner.

Economic growth is a relatively recent addition to the list of macroeconomic policy objectives. A high and stable rate of growth as measured by output and income per person (eg, gross national product per capita) is desired for its ability to provide for a rising standard of living. However, the pursuit of economic growth has encountered difficulties:

*   possible conflicts with other objectives eg, price stability;

*   the difficulty of construction of an effective growth policy - economic theory is of limited value here;

*   the growing awareness of possible environmental constraints on long term economic growth.

The objective of external balance is also problematic. While it is clear that a country cannot run balance of payments deficits where imports exceed exports indefinitely, it is not clear that a balance of payments surplus is especially desirable. It might be better to regard the balance of payments as a constraint on policy rather than a real objective: governments must conduct policy in the light of the long term impact of that policy on the balance of payments.

The distribution of wealth and income is clearly of interest to governments even if different political parties may disagree as to what constitutes an appropriate distribution. Its importance lies not so much in the way in which the economy as a whole is managed but in the way policy instruments are used. Issues of government expenditure and the levels and forms of taxation are strongly influenced by concern for their impact on income distribution.

1.3   Conflicts in macroeconomic policy

Both economic theory and the experience of managing the economy suggest that the simultaneous achievement of all macroeconomic objectives may be extremely difficult. Two examples of possible conflict are:

(a)   There may be conflict between full employment and price stability; the original Phillips Curve suggested that inflation and employment were inversely related and the achievement of the former may lead to excessive inflation through an excess level of aggregate demand in the economy.

(b)   Rapid economic growth may, in the short term at least, have damaging consequences for the balance of payments since rapidly rising incomes may lead to a rising level of imports.

Thus the conduct of macroeconomic policy involves trade-offs; governments may have to sacrifice the achievement of some objective in order to achieve another. The identification of targets for policy should reflect this; government reputation and business confidence will both be damaged if the government is seen to be pursuing policy targets which are widely regarded as incompatible.

Conclusion   Policy objectives may conflict and hence governments have to consider trade-offs between objectives.

1.4   Activity

Identify the arguments which might be used to determine whether full employment or low inflation should have priority in government policy objectives.

2   THE PERFORMANCE OF THE UK ECONOMY

2.1   Introduction

In recent years the UK economy has experienced periods of severe recession and periods of rapid economic growth. These swings in economic performance are important.

(a)   They are themselves indicators of some failure of macroeconomic policy. One concern of policy is to achieve stability; that is to avoid the worst consequences of the trade cycle and the impact this has on growth, employment and price stability.

(b)   They make the assessment of the performance of the economy difficult. When measuring some aspect of performance the choice of starting and finishing dates crucially affects the assessment of how well the economy has performed. If growth were measured from the low point of one recession to the high point of the following recovery, it would greatly overstate the underlying rate of economic growth.

Thus the data concerning economic performance, especially when used as a comparison with other countries, must be interpreted carefully.

2.2   UK economic performance in historical perspective

The following table indicates how well the UK economy has performed over time with respect to the main objectives of macroeconomic policy.

Annual averages	*1960-69*	*1970-79*	*1980-89*	*1990-4*
Unemployment (% of labour force)	1.8	4.1	11.4	8.5
Inflation (% rise in RPI)	3.5	12.6	7.5	5.2
Growth (% rise in GDP)	3.1	2.0	2.1	0.3
Balance of payments (current account as % of GDP)	-0.2	-0.4	-0.1	-1.9

Source: CSO Economic Trends, Annual Abstract of Statistics 1995

It is clear from this data that inflation and unemployment have been serious problems in recent years; although government policy has brought down inflation from the high levels of the 1970s, the cost has been in terms of higher unemployment and slower economic growth.   The main features of UK economic performance in the recent past reveal the difficulties involved in conducting macroeconomic policy.

(a)   The attempt to participate in the exchange rate mechanism (ERM) of the European Monetary System (EMS) failed.   The UK entered in 1990 and was therefore obliged to conduct policy to maintain a fixed rate of exchange between sterling and other European Union currencies.   The UK was forced to leave the ERM in September 1992 and sterling was devalued by about 15%.   This failure was the result of:

- Entering the ERM at too high an exchange rate: this damaged UK international competitiveness and contributed to the severity of the UK recession 1990-93.

- Unwillingness of the UK government to maintain interest rates high enough to attract sufficient foreign capital to the UK and thus maintain the demand for and hence rate of exchange of sterling.   This highlighted the issue of the interdependence of economies and of macroeconomic policy between countries.

(b)   The UK experienced a very severe recession in 1990-92 with rising unemployment and contracting GDP.   The recession was the result of a variety of factors.

- All economies show a distinct trade cycle and the recession was the downswing part of this process.

- The government attempted to slow down the inflation caused by the previous boom (1984-89); this involved deflationary monetary policy which contributed to the severity of the recession.

• The overvalued exchange rate for sterling when the UK entered the ERM in October 1990 deflated the economy by discouraging exports and encouraging imports.

The economy began to recover following the abandonment of government policy and its withdrawal of sterling from the ERM. This led to a fall in the exchange rate which encouraged exports and permitted lower interest rates which promoted both consumption and investment. The subsequent recovery showed rapid economic growth especially in 1994; however this soon began to generate inflationary pressures and the government reacted by raising interest rates from the autumn of 1994.

2.3 Economic performance in the industrial economies

Other G7 countries have also experienced problems with macroeconomic policy and performance in recent years. We may compare the recent performance of the main world economies by looking at the objectives of macroeconomic policy.

1995 averages	*Unemployment*	*Inflation*	*Growth*
UK	8.3%	2.8%	2.4%
Germany	9.4%	2.0%	2.1%
France	11.6%	1.7%	2.4%
Italy	12.0%	5.5%	3.3%
United States	5.6%	2.4%	2.0%
Japan	3.2%	0.4%	0.7%

CANADA

Source: LBS Economic Outlook May 1996

This data shows that all the G7 countries have experienced macroeconomic problems in recent months; this is not surprising since major recessions such as the one which affected the UK recently are now international in character and few economies completely escape their effects. Nonetheless, the UK performance does not look very good in comparison to other G7 economies.

(a) In terms of unemployment, the UK has a relatively high level, along with the other EU countries.

(b) Inflation in the UK has also been worse than the G7 average and only Italy has experienced a higher rate.

(c) The UK achieved reasonable growth in 1995, but this was from a low base point after the recent recession.

Thus the industrialised countries show some common economic problems but this should not hide the seriousness of the difficulties of macroeconomic policy in the UK.

2.4 Activity

Construct a 'misery index' (unemployment + inflation - growth rate) for the main world economies and rank them by this index.

3   MACROECONOMIC POLICY AND THE INTERDEPENDENCE OF ECONOMIES

3.1   The nature of economic interdependence

> [Definition]   Economic interdependence occurs when changes in one economy whether induced by policy or not, have an economic impact on other economies.

Economies are linked together such that changes in any one economy are likely to have an impact on other economies especially those with whom they have a high level of international trade. These links may take two broad forms.

(a)   Real links via international trade. Thus a rise in economic activity in one economy raises its level of imports; this raises the exports of its trading partners and this affects the level of economic activity in those economies.

(b)   Monetary links via the movement of capital between economies. Internationally mobile capital will flow towards economies with high interest rates; thus if the UK reduces interest rates there may be an outflow of capital and downward pressure on the sterling exchange rate.

The degree of interdependence between economies has increased over recent years as a result of:

•   larger trade flows between major economies;

•   increasing mobility of capital between countries due to the reduction in government controls and the globalisation of banking;

•   increasing economic integration especially between the member states of the European Union.

3.2   Economic interdependence and macroeconomic policy

The increasing interdependence of economies has important implications for the conduct of macroeconomic policy. In particular, policy is constrained by the recognition of two aspects of interdependence.

(a)   Governments have to recognise that their policy actions have consequences for other countries and these may not always be desirable. Therefore governments need to consider this and behave in an internationally responsible way. Examples of this include:

•   deflationary policy by one country to prevent inflation imparts deflationary shocks to its trading partners, possibly leading to rises in unemployment in those economies;

•   a devaluation of the currency eg, sterling, to increase international competitiveness automatically means a rise in other currencies relative to sterling and hence a loss of competitiveness for other economies.

(b)   The ability of governments to conduct an independent economic policy may be limited by interdependence. Thus governments which have relatively open economies cannot conduct a monetary policy that is seriously out of line with its main partners since this would lead to large inflows or outflows of short term capital with resulting upward or downward pressure on the exchange rate. Only a genuine floating exchange rate would permit such a policy.

> [Conclusion]   Macroeconomic policy is constrained by the interdependence of economies and thus a degree of policy co-ordination between countries may be desirable.

3.3   Activity

Explain why and how a policy in one country to alter its exchange rate affects that country's trading partners.

4   MACROECONOMIC POLICY AND THE BUSINESS SECTOR

4.1   Introduction

In order for macroeconomic policy to work, its instruments must have an impact on economic activity: this means it must affect the business sector.   It does so in two broad forms; macroeconomic policy may

(a)   influence the level of aggregate demand and thus activity in the economy as a whole;

(b)   influence the costs of the business sector.

4.2   Business and aggregate demand

Definition   Aggregate demand is the total demand for goods and services in the economy.

The broad thrust of macroeconomic policy is to influence the level of aggregate demand (AD) in the economy.   This is because the level of AD is central to the determination of the level of unemployment and the rate of inflation.   If AD is too low, unemployment might result; if AD is too high, inflation induced by excess demand might result.   Changes in AD will affect all businesses to varying degrees.   Thus effective business planning requires that businesses can:

*   predict the likely thrust of macroeconomic policy in the short to medium term;

*   predict the consequences for sales growth of the overall stance of macroeconomic policy and any likely changes in it.

The more stable government policy is, the easier it is for businesses to plan especially in terms of investment, employment and future output capacity.

4.3   Business costs and macroeconomic policy

Not only will the demand for goods and services be affected by macroeconomic policy.   The instruments of macroeconomic policy have important implications for the costs of businesses. Three important areas may be identified.

(a)   Macroeconomic policy may involve changes in exchange rates eg, the devaluation of sterling in September 1992.   This will have the effect of raising the sterling price of imported goods.   Most businesses use some imported goods in the production process; hence this leads to a rise in production costs.

(b)   Fiscal policy involves the use of taxation: changes in tax rates or the structure of taxation will affect businesses.   For example, a change in the employer's national insurance contribution will have a direct effect on labour costs for all businesses.   Changes in indirect taxes (for example a rise in VAT or excise duties) will either have to be absorbed or the business will have to attempt to pass on the tax to its customers.

(c)   Monetary policy involves changes in interest rates; these changes will directly affect firms in two ways:

    *   costs of servicing debts will change especially for highly geared firms;

    *   the viability of investment will be affected since all models of investment appraisal include the rate of interest as one of, if not the main, variable.

Conclusion   Both business costs and sales may be affected by macroeconomic policy.

4.4   Activity

Identify the factors which will determine the overall effect on a company's costs of a large rise in interest rates.

5   CHAPTER SUMMARY

This chapter has been concerned with the objectives and conduct of macroeconomic policy.

(a)   The objectives of economic policy and the distinction between objectives, targets and instruments of macroeconomic policy and the possibility of conflicts between objectives.

(b)   The relative performance of the UK economy compared to the G7 with respect to the main objectives of macroeconomic policy. The UK performance appears to have been poorer than most in recent years.

(c)   The nature of economic interdependence between economies: its origins and its potential effects on the conduct of macroeconomic policy.

(d)   The impact of macroeconomic policy on the business sector.

6   SELF TEST QUESTIONS

6.1   Distinguish between objectives, targets and instruments of economic policy. (1.1)

6.2   Identify and explain the principal objectives of economic policy. (1.2)

6.3   Compare and contrast recent UK macroeconomic performance with that of other G7 economies. (2.3)

6.4   Define economic interdependence and give examples. (3.1, 3.2)

6.5   Define aggregate demand and explain how changes in it affect business planning. (4.2)

Note re examination style questions

The economics part of this syllabus is likely to be examined either as background to other questions or as part of another question. It is not therefore really possible to produce examination style questions for chapters 16, 18 and 19. We have included questions at the end of chapter 17 as this is basic theory that could be examined - however even these topics may be examined as background or part of a fuller question.

17 MONETARY AND FISCAL POLICY

INTRODUCTION & LEARNING OBJECTIVES

When you have studied this chapter you should be able to do the following:

- Explain the purpose and nature of monetary and fiscal policy
- Discuss the main features of the supply of money and the demand for money
- Explain the determination of the rate of interest
- Identify the link between monetary and fiscal policy
- Discuss the problems and limitations of monetary and fiscal policy

1 THE ROLE OF MONETARY POLICY

1.1 The role of money in the economy

Definition Money is any financial asset which has liquidity and fulfils the task of a medium of exchange.

All modern economies use money because money fulfils a range of essential economic functions. The alternative would be a system of barter in which goods and services were exchanged directly for other goods and services; this would entail all sorts of difficulties, the most notable of which are:

- the need for two participants in exchange to have exactly what the other wants (the 'double coincidence of wants')

- the absence of a common measure of values; hence the impossibility of establishing a system of prices

- the difficulty of deferring consumption by saving a part of income.

Societies soon develop systems of money to overcome these problems. The principal functions of money in a modern economy are:

(a) A medium of exchange. This is the most important function of money since it overcomes the problems involved in barter. Without money the process of specialisation by which individuals, organisations, regions and even countries specialise in a narrow range of economic activities would be greatly hampered. Specialisation has been a fundamental source of economic progress and rising incomes over time.

(b) A unit of account. Since money acts as a means of exchange it also becomes a measure of the relative economic value of goods and services, that is prices are possible. Money provides a common unit by which all economic transactions can be measured. Without this, the price system with prices acting as signals in the resource allocation process, would be impossible.

(c)   A store of value. While it is possible to defer consumption ie, to save in the absence of money, it is clearly difficult and inconvenient to do so. The principal reason for this is the lack of liquidity; other assets have varying degrees of liquidity, money has complete liquidity. Thus the shorter the time period for saving, the more likely that money will be used as a store of value.

(d)   A standard of deferred payment. When credit transactions take place, it is necessary for those involved to agree on the size of the future payments; this is done by using money as the unit of account but for future as opposed to current transactions.

These functions of money can only be fulfilled efficiently by a financial asset which has certain attributes. If a particular form of money loses these attributes the economy will either find a substitute form of money or resort to barter. The required characteristics of money are:

•   Acceptability by those engaged in economic transactions.

•   Stability of value. If money rapidly loses value through the process of inflation it will lose acceptability and cannot function as a store of value.

•   Portability, divisibility and durability.

Provided that money has these features it can fill the roles assigned to it. In a modern economy money thus becomes central to the way economies work. Since money is used both for spending (medium of exchange) and for saving (store of value) the volume of money in the economy and how it is used will have significant effects on the way the economy functions.

1.2   The nature of monetary policy

Definition   Monetary policy is concerned with influencing the overall monetary conditions in the economy.

It is clear that money is crucial to the way in which a modern economy functions. It is for this reason that government macroeconomic policy may wish to concern itself with monetary conditions in the economy: monetary policy is concerned with influencing the monetary conditions in an economy. In particular, monetary policy may be concerned with:

(a)   The volume of money in circulation. The stock of money in the economy (the 'money supply') is believed to have important effects on the volume of expenditure in the economy; this in turn may influence the level of output in the economy or the level of prices.

(b)   The price of money. The price of money is the rate of interest. If governments wish to influence the amount of money held in the economy or the demand for credit, it may attempt to influence the level of interest rates.

It should be noted that the monetary authorities (the Treasury and the Bank of England) may be able to control either the supply of money in the economy or the level of interest rates but it cannot do both simultaneously. They can either fix the supply of money, in which case the level of interest (like any price) will be determined by the interaction of demand with that fixed supply; or the rate of interest can be fixed and the supply and demand for money allowed to adjust to it.

In order to understand the conduct of monetary policy it is necessary to consider how the market for money works. Like any market, the price (the rate of interest) is determined by the interaction of demand for, and supply of the commodity. Thus the demand for money ('demand for money balances') and the supply of money (the money stock) must be explained.

| Conclusion | Monetary policy can aim to influence either the stock of money in the economy or the rate of interest but not both. |

1.3   Activity

Explain why a central bank could determine the price of money or the stock of money but not both.

2   THE DEMAND FOR MONEY AND THE RATE OF INTEREST

2.1   Introduction

| Definition | The demand for money is the amount of liquid assets that economic agents wish to hold at any point in time. |

In analysing the demand for money it is important to note that money and income are not the same thing. Income is the flow of purchasing power over time; money is a stock of liquid assets held at any one time. Thus the demand for money or demand for money balances is the amount of money households and firms wish to hold at any one time. The demand for money can be analysed, like the demand for any commodity, using the concept of a demand curve. This therefore raises two issues:

(a)   What are the reasons why money is held and how does this affect the position of the demand curve and the factors which would lead to a shift in that demand curve?

(b)   How elastic the demand curve is. That is, how does the demand for money respond to changes in the rate of interest?

The nature of the demand for money is the subject of considerable controversy within economics. There are major differences between the views of Keynesian and monetarist economists. These divergences of view have important implications for our understanding of how the economy functions and hence for the role and effectiveness of macroeconomic policy.

2.2   The demand for money: the Keynesian approach

Keynes referred to the demand for money as liquidity preference. He argued that we can keep our financial assets either in a liquid form (eg, cash or bank current accounts) or in non liquid forms (eg, deposit accounts, stocks and shares). To the latter Keynes used the collective name of 'bonds' but they include a whole range of financial assets. The distinction between liquid assets and bonds is, in principle, clear:

*   liquid assets earn no interest (eg, cash)

*   bonds earn a rate of interest (eg, government securities).

However, the development of financial institutions and financial instruments has meant that the distinction between liquid, non-interest earning assets and non-liquid, interest earning assets has become blurred. For example, building society accounts may be highly liquid but may still earn a rate of interest. Nonetheless for purposes of explanation it is convenient to maintain this distinction. The effect of this is that we can regard the price of liquidity as the rate of interest since this is the income forgone by holding assets in a liquid rather than in a non-liquid form.

Given that the holding of money involves a cost, why should there be a demand for money? Keynes identified three motives for holding liquid assets.

(a)   The transactions motive. Households and firms need to hold money to finance day to day transactions involving purchases in cash or by cheque. The amount of money held will be largely a function of the level of income and the frequency of payment of that income. Thus a rise in household income will result in a rise in transactions demand and a shift to the left in the demand for money curve. However, although the transactions demand for money may be affected slightly by changes in the rate of interest, it is generally accepted that the transactions demand for money is inelastic with respect to the rate of interest.

(b)   The precautionary motive. Money may be held both by households and firms to meet unforeseen contingencies. Again this will be mainly a function of the level of income and is unlikely to be greatly affected by changes in the rate of interest.

(c)   The speculative motive. Money is held as part of a portfolio of financial assets; sometimes the preference is to hold money, sometimes the preference is to hold what Keynes called bonds. The question is what factors will influence the balance of assets held in these liquid and non-liquid forms. Keynes argued that the willingness to hold bonds depended on expectations of future changes in bond prices since this would determine whether bond holders experience capital gains or losses. In turn bond prices will be related to changes in interest rates since bond prices and interest rates are inversely related: a rise in interest rates will cause a fall in bond prices, a fall in interest rates will cause a rise in bond prices. Keynes thus argued that:

- when interest rates are high, expectations are that the next move in interest rates is more likely to be downwards than upwards and hence bond prices are expected to rise. In these circumstances, the demand for money will be low, the demand for bonds will be high.

- when interest rates are very low, expectations are that the next move in interest rates is more likely to be upwards than downwards and hence bond prices are expected to fall. In these circumstances the demand for money will be high and the demand for bonds will be low.

Thus the speculative demand for money is highly elastic with respect to the rate of interest.

These motives for holding money can be illustrated using the Keynesian liquidity preference curve - the Keynesian demand curve for money.

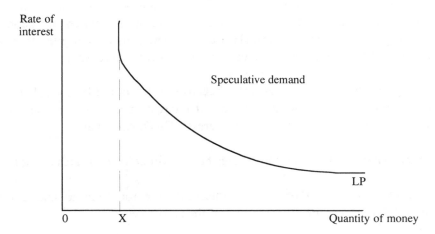

LP is the demand for money curve (Liquidity Preference). OX money is demanded for transactions and precautionary purposes and is largely unaffected by the rate of interest but the speculative demand for money is affected. Indeed at very low rates of interest the demand for money becomes almost perfectly elastic: this Keynes called the 'liquidity trap'.

<u>Conclusion</u> The Keynesian model of the demand for money is based on three motives and implies that the demand for money will vary with the rate of interest.

2.3   Money demand, money stock and the rate of interest

The Keynesian approach argues that the rate of interest is determined by the interaction of the demand for money and the supply of money. Let us assume for the moment that the supply of money can be controlled by the monetary authorities, notably the central bank, and is therefore given at any one time. This will determine the rate of interest and changes in the supply of money will lead to a change in interest rates.

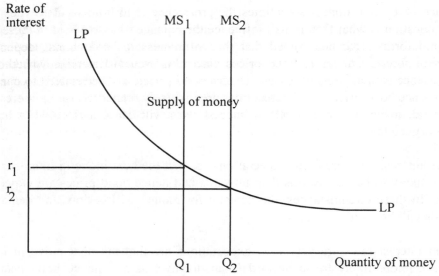

If the supply of money is MS_1, the rate of interest will be r_1. An increase in the supply of money will lead to a reduction in the rate of interest to r_2. This raises the question of the impact on the economy of a change in either the demand for money or supply of money.

First we may consider a change in the supply of money. If there was an increase in the supply of money, this would lead to a fall in the rate of interest. This fall in interest rates might be expected to lead to a rise in aggregate monetary demand in the economy since it should lead to a rise in credit based consumer demand and more importantly, a rise in business investment. This would imply that monetary policy might be an appropriate and effective policy when the economy is in a recession and suffering from unemployment. However Keynesians have argued that policy might be ineffective in getting the economy out of severe recessions for two reasons:

(a)   It may be difficult to reduce interest rates because of the 'liquidity trap'. If the demand for money has become very elastic at low rates of interest, increases in money supply will be ineffective in further reducing the rate of interest. This means that

* there may be a floor to interest rates below which interest rates cannot be forced;

* this minimum level of interest rates may be too high to encourage sufficient investment to get the economy out of the recession.

(b)   The demand for investment may be insensitive to changes in interest rates. Keynes argued that investment intentions were determined largely by the general state of business confidence and by expectations of future demand for the product. In recessions business confidence may be so poor that even large falls in interest rates may do very little to encourage business investment.

Thus Keynesian economists have argued that fiscal policy may be a more effective tool of macroeconomics management than monetary policy especially in very severe recessions.

Secondly we may consider a change in the demand for money. The criticism of the use of fiscal policy to raise aggregate monetary demand when the economy is in recession is the danger of crowding out. The use of an expansionary fiscal policy will lead to an increase in the demand for money. For example, the government may reduce income tax. This raises the disposable income of taxpayers and their transactions demand for money will rise. This rise in the demand for money, with the supply of money fixed, must lead to a rise in interest rates. This in turn, reduces private investment and hence expansionary fiscal policy has crowded out some private expenditure. The Keynesian response to this is twofold.

(a)   The increase in the demand for money may have only a small effect on interest rates because of the liquidity trap. If the supply of money crosses the liquidity preference curve where the demand is elastic and the curve horizontal, a rightward shift in the curve will have no effect on interest rates.

(b)   The demand for investment is relatively inelastic with respect to changes in interest rates. Thus, even if interest rates rise as a result of expansionary fiscal policy, the subsequent fall in investment will be relatively small.

Thus for Keynesians the nature of the demand for money and the low sensitivity of investment to changes in interest rates means that crowding out is not a significant problem and fiscal policy remains a useful macroeconomic tool especially when the economy is in a serious recession.

| Conclusion | The Keynesian view of the demand for money means that fiscal policy is a more effective tool of macroeconomic policy than monetary policy especially in a recession. |

2.4   Money demand, money stock and the rate of interest: the monetarist view

The monetarist view (particularly associated with the work of Milton Friedman) of how the market for money works differs in significant ways from that of Keynesians. The monetarist approach can be looked at through their view of the nature of the demand for money and through the quantity theory of money.

Monetarists argue that the demand for money can be seen as part of a wider demand for assets of all kinds from money through other financial assets to durable goods such as houses, cars etc. Thus individuals will hold a portfolio of assets of which cash is merely the most liquid. The demand for money is held to be solely for transactions purposes; monetarists deny that there is a speculative demand for money. The consequence of this is that the demand for money is a stable function of income since it is incomes that determine the transactions demand for money. Thus the demand for money curve will shift if incomes shift but will be very inelastic with respect to the rate of interest. The importance of this can be illustrated by looking at the consequences of the use of fiscal and monetary policy.

(a)   If, in a recession, the government was to increase public expenditure as part of an expansionary fiscal policy, the level of incomes would rise. This would set off a series of effects:

- as income rose the demand for money would rise ie, the demand for money curve would shift to the right

- with a fixed supply of money this would lead to a steep rise in interest rates

- the rise in interest rates would reduce private investment which, according to monetarists is very sensitive to changes in interest rates.

Thus there is a process of crowding out: private investment has been crowded out by increasing public expenditure and the level of aggregate monetary demand is unchanged.

(b)   If the government attempted to finance a public sector borrowing requirement by borrowing on an unfunded basis, the money supply would expand. The result of this would be:

- the stock of money in the economy would rise and interest rates will fall

- individuals and organisations would now hold more money that they had wished to hold; since the demand for money is interest rate inelastic, the fall in interest rates does not significantly raise the amount of money held

- individuals and organisations adjust their portfolio of assets by spending any excess money they hold; this according to the quantity theory of money, will only result in rising prices.

Thus modern monetarist thinking about the nature of the demand for money provides theoretical support for the quantity theory of inflation. This will be discussed in more detail in the chapter on inflation.

Conclusion   monetarists hold that the demand for money is a stable function of income and inelastic with respect to the rate of interest.

2.5   Activity

Identify the circumstances under which an increase in money supply or an increase in money demand has no effect on interest rates.

3   THE STOCK OF MONEY

3.1   Introduction

The analysis in the previous section shows that both for Keynesian and monetarist economists the stock of money in the economy is of considerable importance.

(a)   For Keynesians, changes in the money stock will alter interest rates to varying degrees; only in the circumstances of a very severe recession with the supply of money in the zone where the liquidity trap operates will changes in the money stock have no effect on interest rates. In turn, changes in interest rates will indirectly affect the level of spending in the economy.

(b)   For monetarists, changes in the money stock will always have significant effects on the rate of interest. Moreover, changes in the money stock will directly affect spending since the demand for money is primarily for transactions purposes.

Thus for all economists, but especially for monetarists, monetary policy - influencing the size of the money stock or the level of interest rates - is of considerable importance. To conduct monetary policy successfully the monetary authorities must:

- be able to identify the most appropriate measure of the stock of money in the economy in order that it can be targeted in the conduct of monetary policy

- have a range of policy instruments which can be used to control the stock of money in the economy.

3.2   Measures of the money stock

If the government is to conduct a successful monetary policy it must be able to identify an appropriate measure of the money stock. This measure must be one which

- has a definite and stable relationship to the economic variables that monetary policy is designed to influence, such as the rate of interest or the level of expenditure in the economy

- can be closely controlled by the instruments of monetary policy that are available to the monetary authorities.

The difficulty for the government is that there is a large number of alternative measures of the money stock that could be used as a monetary target. This wide range of measures arises from the development of the range of financial assets available to the economy and to developments in the institutions and technology of the banking system. In principle, the most appropriate measure would be one which included all those financial assets which influenced the ultimate objectives of monetary policy. If the objective of monetary policy was to influence the aggregate level of spending in the economy, the appropriate measure of the money stock would have to include all those assets used to finance current spending but exclude those financial assets used primarily for the purposes of saving. The assets which appear to be used primarily for transactions purposes include:

- cash
- current accounts held in banks
- deposit accounts held at banks and building societies.

However, accounts at building societies have varying degrees of liquidity and hence have varying relationships with the current level of spending by households. Clearly the measures of the money stock are bound to be, to some extent, arbitrary. This is reflected in the variety of measures of the money stock which are recorded by the Bank of England on behalf of the government. However, within this range of measures there is an important distinction:

- narrow money: essentially notes, coins, retail (less than £100k) accounts in banks and building societies

- broad money: notes and coins plus all sterling deposits (including certificates of deposit) at retail banks and building societies

During the 1980s, the emphasis in monetary policy shifted from focusing on broad money as the target to focusing on narrow money. The details of narrow and broad money are given in the table below.

3.3   Measure of money stock in the UK

UK Monetary Aggregates

Narrow money measures

M0	1	Notes and coins in circulation with the public
	2	Till money held by banks and building societies
	3	Operational balances held by commercial banks at the Bank of England
M2	1	Notes and coins in circulation with the public
	4	Retail sterling deposits held by the private sector at UK banks and building societies

Broad money measures

M4   1   Notes and coins in circulation with the public
     5   All sterling deposits (including certificates of deposit) held by the private sector at
            UK banks and building societies

M3H 1   Notes and coins in circulation with the public
     5   All sterling deposits (including certificates of deposit) held by the private sector at
            UK banks and building societies
     6   Non-sterling currency deposits of UK residents with UK banks and building
            societies
     7   Sterling and foreign currency deposits of UK public corporations with UK banks
            and building societies.

The components of these measures require some explanation:

- 1   notes and coins held by the public are clearly for transactions but are only a very
         small proportion of the money stock - about 8% on total M2

- 2   all banks and building societies hold some cash for meeting customers' demands

- 3   commercial banks have accounts at the Bank of England which are used for
         settlement of interbank debts

- 4   retail deposits are all cheque accounts of less than £100k held by the private sector
         - individuals and businesses

- 5   all sterling deposits consist of deposits of any value denominated in sterling and
         held by the private sector

- 6   these are accounts held by the UK sector with the UK banking system but
         denominated in currencies other than sterling

- 7   accounts of public corporations (eg, nationalised industries) held in UK banks and
         building societies.

In the early 1980s, M4 was the favoured monetary target for UK government policy. Now only M0 is given a specific target rate of growth although other, broader, measures of money stock are monitored by the Bank of England. M3H is a standard measure of money stock used in the European Union. The rate of growth of M3H is expected to be broadly similar to that of M4. The sizes and growth rates of these aggregates are given below.

Monetary aggregates: March 1996

	£ billion	annual growth
M0	23.1	5.7%
M4	640.0	9.8%

Source: ONS Financial Statistics May 1996

Conclusion   There is a wide range of measures of money stock ranging from narrow to broad money.

3.4   Activity

Outline the criteria that might be used to determine whether a financial asset should be considered part of the money stock.

4   CONTROL OF THE MONEY STOCK

4.1   Control of the money stock

Whatever measure of money stock the government decides to target, it needs to employ a set of instruments to control its size if effective monetary control is to be exercised. In order to do this the government needs to establish control over the sources of change in the money stock. Since most of the money stock consists not of cash but of accounts in the banking system this is not obviously an easy task. In theory, the government and the Bank of England operating on its behalf, have a choice of two broad approaches.

- Since the ability of the banking system to create additional credit (ie, lend out deposits) depends on the volume of liquid assets it holds, the government could attempt to control the volume of liquid assets in the system.

- Alternatively, the government could seek to control the ability of the banking system to create credit from any given volume of liquid assets it holds.

4.2   Monetary control before 1979

In the early 1970s, the emphasis was on controlling the growth of bank assets on which credit could be created. This was known as Competition and Credit Control and involved a variety of methods by which the money stock was to be controlled.

(a)   Bank reserve ratios. The Competition and Credit Control regulations required that all banks should maintain a minimum of eligible reserve (ie, liquid) assets relative to liabilities. This Reserve Assets Ratio was set at 12.5%. Thus if the bank's holdings of liquid assets fell, they would, in theory, have to reduce their deposits by a multiple of eight.

(b)   Special Deposits. The Bank of England could require the banks to deposit a certain percentage of their eligible liabilities in a special deposit account at the Bank of England. These deposits could not be counted as part of the Reserve Assets Ratio of the commercial banks and hence their ability to create credit would be reduced.

(c)   Open Market Operations. In its ordinary operations of borrowing on behalf of the government, the Bank of England engages in open market operations in which it buys and sells government securities (gilts) on the open market. In selling gilts the Bank of England could reduce the liquid assets of the banks since these would be paid for out of the commercial banks' balances at the Bank of England. Again, the banks' eligible reserve assets would fall and they would be forced to contract their lending.

In principle, the system of Competition and Credit Control was one in which the emphasis was on the control of the money supply and interest rates were allowed to find their own level. In practice the Bank of England also exercised some control over the level of interest rates via the Minimum Lending Rate (MLR). By its actions in the gilt market, the government via the Bank of England could create a situation in which banks and discount houses became short of cash; the Bank would lend this cash ('lender of last resort') but only at the higher MLR. In this way the Bank could induce a rise in interest rates throughout the banking system.

The system of controlling the money stock through the instruments of Competition and Credit Control ran into serious difficulties in the later 1970s. These included:

- the unwillingness to have no control over interest rates as implied by the original approach of only controlling the stock of money

- the growth of secondary banking outside the Competition and Credit Control regulations

- large budget deficits and the need to finance them made the use of open market operations ineffective since governments needed to issue large amounts of gilts to finance the PSBR.

4.3   Monetary control after 1979

The initial response was to introduce quantitative controls on banks. These involved direct ceilings on the growth of bank deposits (the 'corset') with financial penalties on banks which exceeded some monthly figure. Clearly however, a new approach was required. This was contained in the Medium Term Financial Strategy adopted in 1980. This approach had several elements.

(a)   Quantitative controls and reserve assets requirements were abandoned. This was probably necessary since in 1979 the government had abolished all exchange controls (ie, controls on the movement of capital in and out of the UK) and this meant that banks could always acquire liquid assets by borrowing from abroad.

(b)   In the long term the growth of the money stock was to be limited by reducing government borrowing. If the government finances the Public Sector Borrowing Requirement (PSBR : discussed later in this chapter) by selling government securities to the banking system, this increases the liquid assets of the system and enables them to increase their lending. Thus a progressive reduction in the size of the PSBR would imply a progressive reduction in the rate of growth of the money stock.

(c)   In the shorter run, the Bank of England would use interest rate policy to discourage borrowing. In this approach it was felt that banks would create assets (ie, loans) if the demand from customers - households and business - was there. This demand could be reduced by raising interest rates. Interest rates could be influenced by the Bank of England operating in the money markets as the ultimate provider of cash in the banking system.

The new system of controlling the money stock experienced a range of difficulties since the early 1980s. The most important of these were:

- the difficulty of reducing the size of the PSBR as planned; this was especially true during the severe recessions of 1980-83 and 1990-93 when tax receipts fell and expenditure on unemployment related social security rose steeply;

- large rises in interest rates seemed to have limited effects on the demand for credit from the private sector: very large increases were required and these had undesirable consequences such as for the level of investment and the exchange rate.

As a result of these difficulties target rates of growth for the money stock were regularly exceeded and the gap between official targets and outcomes was wider than in the 1970s. The government response was to shift the attention of monetary policy to a narrow measure of money M0; this measure seemed to behave better in that it grew less rapidly than other measures of the money stock. In addition the government began to target the exchange rate for sterling. By this interest rates were managed so as to keep the exchange rate for sterling at a particular level. This became official in 1990 when the UK entered the exchange rate mechanism (ERM) of the European Monetary System. This, in turn was abandoned when the UK was forced out of the ERM in 1992.

By 1993 governments only had official targets for M0 and the instruments of control over the growth of the money stock included a variety of techniques including funding the PSBR, open market operations and interest rate policy. Policy had become one of using a variety of instruments to generally influence monetary conditions in the economy with an overall objective of achieving price stability.

Conclusion │ The means by which the money stock is controlled depends on the ability to control the liquid assets on the banking system and the use of interest rates to discourage private sector borrowing.

4.4   Activity

Explain the relationship between the PSBR and the growth of the money stock.

4.5   Impact of changes in monetary policy on business decision making

Changes in monetary policy will influence:

(a)   the availability of finance. Credit restrictions achieved via the banking system or by direct legislation will reduce the availability of loans. This can make it difficult for small or medium sized and new businesses to raise finance. The threat of such restrictions in the future will influence financial decisions by companies, making them more likely to seek long term finance for projects.

(b)   the cost of finance. Any restrictions on the stock of money, or on credit restrictions will raise the cost of borrowing, making fewer investment projects worthwhile and discouraging expansion by companies. Also, any increase in the level of general interest rates will increase shareholders' required rate of return, so unless companies can increase their return share prices will fall as interest rates rise. Thus, in times of 'tight' money and high interest rates organisations are less likely to borrow money and will probably contract rather than expand operations.

(c)   the level of consumer demand. Periods of credit control and high interest rates reduce consumer demand. Individuals find it more difficult and more expensive to borrow to fund consumption, whilst saving becomes more attractive. This is another reason for organisations to have to contract operations.

(d)   the level of inflation. Monetary policy is often used to control inflation. Rising price levels, and uncertainty as to future rates of inflation make financial decisions more difficult and more important. As prices of different commodities change at different rates the timing of purchase, sale, borrowing and repayment of debt become critical to the success of organisations and their projects.

(e)   the level of exchange rates. Monetary policy which increases the level of domestic interest rates is likely to raise exchange rates as capital is attracted into the country. Very many organisations now deal with both suppliers and customers abroad and thus cannot ignore the effect of future exchange rate movements. Financial managers must consider methods of hedging exchange rate risk and the effect of changes in exchange rates on their positions as importers and exporters.

5   THE PROBLEMS OF MONETARY POLICY

5.1   Introduction

The previous section considered some of the difficulties of implementing monetary policy, notably the difficulty of identifying the appropriate measure of money stock to target and the problems of actually controlling the targeted monetary measure. In addition there are some other problems with the use of monetary policy. The most important of these are:

- the problem of lags
- the choice of targeting the stock of money or the rate of interest
- the effects of interest rates changes.

5.2   Lags in monetary policy

Definition   Lags in macroeconomic policy are the time gaps between the implementation of policy and the resulting effects on economic variables.

As with all macroeconomic policy there are lags between the implementation of policy and the effects on the economic variables that are the ultimate target of monetary policy. These lags in monetary policy arise out of:

- time taken for the data to confirm the need for a change in the monetary policy of the government

- time taken in implementing changes in policy: for example large changes in interest rates in a short period are avoided because of the danger of destabilising financial markets

- time taken for households and firms to respond to changes in monetary conditions.

Moreover, the size of the eventual response to changes in monetary conditions is unpredictable. In the case of changes in interest rates, the monetary authorities cannot be sure how much consumer spending and investment spending will fall by in response to a given rise in interest rates. The conduct of monetary policy has been likened to pulling a brick across a table with an elastic band: for a long time nothing happens then the brick moves all of a sudden.

Thus there is a clear danger that monetary policy might be destabilising in the short run. Because of lags it might be counter-cyclical, restricting the growth of demand when the need to do so has passed and because of the uncertain size of its effects, the policy may be excessive even if the timing is correct. For these reasons, monetarists have argued that monetary policy should be seen as a medium term macroeconomic policy.

Monetarists argue that the economy has a greater degree of short term stability than is generally recognised. Continuous shifts in fiscal and monetary policy are likely to damage the inherent stability of the economy. Instead, monetary policy should be designed to achieve long term price stability in the economy. In doing this, the monetary authorities would maintain a steady growth in the money stock. The rate of growth of the money stock should be equal to the long term rate of growth of real national income. According to monetarists this would have two advantages:

- control of the long term growth of the money stock at this rate would ensure long term price stability according to the quantity theory of money.

- the stability of policy would influence the expectations in the economy; this itself would enhance the stability of the economy and promote price stability.

This rule by which monetary policy might be conducted over the medium to long run is sometimes known as the monetarist 'golden rule'.

Conclusion   The 'golden rule' suggests that the growth of the money stock should be restricted to the long term growth of real national income.

5.3   The choice of targets

A fundamental problem of monetary policy concerns the choice of variable to operate on. The ultimate objective of monetary policy is to influence some important variable in the economy - the level of demand, the rate of inflation, the exchange rate for the currency etc. However monetary policy has to do this by targeting some intermediate variable which, it is believed, influences, in some predictable way, the ultimate object of the policy.

The broad choice here is between targeting the stock of money or the rate of interest. If the government wished to undertake a deflationary monetary policy it could:

(a)   attempt to reduce the money stock by open market operations, funding the PSBR etc. This would shift the stock of money curve to the right and interest rates would rise. How much interest rates would rise would depend on the elasticity of demand for money curve and this is largely unknowable by the monetary authorities.

(b)   force up interest rates to some target level by appropriate actions in managing the money market and the banks' needs for cash. This would produce a subsequent fall in the demand for credit based purchases of consumer goods and in the demand for investment. The size of this effect is, however, unpredictable.

The problem for the monetary authorities is that controlling the level of interest rates is rather easier than controlling the overall stock of money but the effects of doing so are less certain.

5.4   The effects of interest rate changes

If governments choose to target interest rates as the principal means of conducting monetary policy this may have a series of undesirable effects. These principally relate to the indiscriminate nature of interest rate changes and to the external consequences of monetary policy.

When interest rates are changed it is expected that the general level of demand (AMD) in the economy will be affected. Thus a rise in interest rates will discourage expenditure by raising the cost of credit. However, the effects will vary.

(a)   Investment may be affected more than consumption. The rate of interest is the main cost of investment whether it is financed by internal funds or by debt. However, most consumption is not financed by credit and hence is less affected by interest rate changes. Since the level of investment in the economy is an important determinant of economic growth and international competitiveness there may be serious long term implications arising from high interest rates.

(b)   Even where consumption is affected by rising interest rates, the effects are uneven. The demand for consumer durable goods and houses is most affected since these are normally credit based purchases. Hence active interest policy may induce instability in some sectors of business.

The second problem arises out of the openness of modern economies and their economic interdependence. There is now a very high degree of capital mobility between economies: large sums of short term capital move from one financial centre to another in pursuit of higher interest rates. Changes in UK interest rates relative to those in other financial centres will produce large inflows and outflows of short term capital. Inflows of capital represent a demand for sterling and hence push up the exchange rate; outflows represent sales of sterling and hence depress the exchange rate. This presents no problem for the conduct of monetary policy providing the government is unconcerned about movements in the exchange rate. There are two circumstances when this will not be the case.

(a)   If a country is in a fixed exchange rate system (eg, the ERM) it is required to keep the exchange rate for its currency within a narrow band. In such cases, interest rates cannot be allowed to become significantly different from those of other major economies: an independent monetary policy is virtually impossible.

(b)   If a country has a large trade ratio (the ratio of trade to gross domestic product), changes in the exchange rate will have very significant domestic implications:

•   a falling exchange rate will raise the domestic price of imports and this may result in inflationary pressures in the economy

- a rising exchange rate will raise the foreign exchange price of exports and reduce the domestic price of imports; this loss of international competitiveness has serious implications for both domestic output and employment and for the balance of payments.

For the UK with a very large trade ratio and a high degree of integration into world capital markets these problems are very serious. It is doubtful if the UK can operate a genuinely independent interest rate policy even it if were to remain outside of the ERM element of the European Monetary System.

Conclusion   An independent monetary policy is no longer possible given the high degree of capital movement between economies.

5.5   Activity

Consider how the re-entry of the UK into the ERM would affect UK interest rate policy.

6   FISCAL POLICY AND PUBLIC EXPENDITURE

6.1   Introduction

Definition   Fiscal policy is the manipulation of the government budget in order to influence the level of activity in the economy.

All governments engage in public expenditure although levels vary somewhat from country to country. This expenditure must be financed either by taxation or by borrowing. Thus the existence of public expenditure itself raises issues of policy, notably how to tax and whom to tax. But, in addition, the process of expenditure and taxation permits the use of fiscal policy in a wider sense: the government budget can be manipulated to influence the level of aggregate demand in the economy and hence the level of economic activity.

The principal issues related to fiscal policy are therefore:

- how is government expenditure financed?
- what are the consequences of government borrowing?
- what are the functions of fiscal policy?
- what are the limitations and problems of fiscal policy?

It should be borne in mind that fiscal policy is an area of considerable debate and dispute between economists; economists of a Keynesian persuasion regard fiscal policy as an important and effective part of macroeconomic policy while monetarists regard fiscal policy as largely ineffective with undesirable side effects.

6.2   Public finance

Issues of public finance arise out of the need to engage in and pay for public expenditure. There has been a long run tendency for the levels of public expenditure to rise in all economies; in the UK total public expenditure is now in the order of 40% of national income and this is typical of industrialised economies. The two main categories of public expenditure are:

(a)   Expenditure on goods and services. The government directly purchases goods and services; these in turn fall into two broad types:

- public goods which are those goods and services that cannot be provided by the private sector because of the difficulty of ensuring that all those who benefit would pay eg, public administration, law and order, defence;

- merit goods which are those which can be provided by the private sector but would be under consumed because of the failure to take into account social benefits eg, education and health provision.

(b)   Transfer payments. The government transfers income from taxpayers to other groups in society through the payments of eg, pensions, social security and unemployment benefits.

The UK government has experienced serious fiscal problems in recent years as a result of large increases in expenditure on transfer payments. This has resulted in large budget deficits and the need to engage in levels of borrowing. The increase in transfer payments has been partly the result of some structural changes in the UK economy: the increasing proportion of elderly people has led to increased payments of pensions and increased pressure for expenditure in the health service. However, the major problem has been the rise in unemployment; this automatically raises public expenditure on social security while at the same time reducing tax receipts. Thus in the recession of 1990-93, government finances deteriorated alarmingly and the budget deficit approached £50bn in 1993.

| Conclusion | Public expenditure must be financed either by taxation or by government borrowing. |

6.3   Taxation

The obvious means by which public expenditure can be financed is by taxation. The government receives some income from direct charges in the public sector (eg, health prescription charges) and from trading profits of some public sector undertakings, but the bulk of its income comes from taxation.

Taxes are divided into broad groups:

(a)   Direct taxes: these are taxes levied directly on income receivers whether they are individuals or organisations. These include income tax, national insurance contributions, corporation tax, inheritance tax. These taxes in turn may be

- progressive where the proportion of income paid in tax rises as income rises;
- proportional where the proportion of income paid in tax is constant as income rises;
- regressive where the proportion of income paid in tax falls as income rises.

Most direct taxes are progressive but regressive ones are not unknown; the Community Charge ('poll tax') was a regressive tax.

(b)   Indirect taxes: these are levied on one set of individuals or organisations but may be partly or wholly passed on to others and are largely related to consumption not income. These include VAT and excise duties. By their very nature, indirect taxes tend to be regressive.

Taxation can raise very large flows of income for the government: in 1995 in the UK taxation amounted to £250 billion, 42.8% of GDP. However, there are some limits to the levels of taxation that can be imposed upon an economy in normal circumstances. Excessive taxation may have undesirable economic consequences. Those most frequently cited are:

(i)   Personal disincentives to work and effort; this may be related mainly to the form of taxation eg, progressive income tax rather than the overall level of taxation but some economists eg, Milton Friedman claim that indirect as well as direct taxes damage incentives.

(ii)   Discouragement to business, especially the incentive to invest and engage in research and development, which results from high business taxation.

(iii)   Disincentive to foreign investment: multinational firms may be dissuaded from investing in economies with high tax regimes.

(iv)   A reduction in tax revenue may occur if taxpayers are dissuaded from undertaking extra income generating work and are encouraged to seek tax avoidance schemes. This was suggested by the American economist Arthur Laffer and resulted in the Laffer Curve:

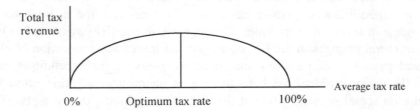

Thus if the tax rate exceeds a certain level, the total tax revenue falls. It should be noted that these disincentive effects, while apparently clear in principle, are difficult to identify in the real world and hence their impact is uncertain.

6.4   Activity

Explain the case for shifting taxation from direct to indirect taxes and identify the drawbacks of such a policy.

7   THE GOVERNMENT BUDGET AND PUBLIC BORROWING

7.1   The government budget

The government budget (including central and local government) is a statement of public expenditure and income over a period of one year. Expenditure can be financed either by taxation or by borrowing. In recent years the UK government has also used the receipts from privatisation to help finance public expenditure. The relationship of expenditure to taxation indicates the state of the budget. Three budget positions can be identified.

(a)   A balanced budget: total expenditure is matched by total taxation income.

(b)   A deficit budget: total expenditure exceeds total taxation income and the deficit must be financed by borrowing.

(c)   A surplus budget: total expenditure is less than total taxation income and the surplus can be used to pay back public debt incurred as a result of previous deficits.

To the extent that the government can raise funds by privatisation, this will reduce the need for either taxation or borrowing to finance public expenditure. However there are limits to the effectiveness of privatisation as a means of raising income:

•   it cannot be done indefinitely as public assets can only be sold once;

•   it may reduce future revenue since the profits of the industries privatised are no longer part of the income of the public sector.

The government may have a deficit budget for one of two main reasons; a budget deficit may be intended by the government as part of fiscal policy designed to boost the level of aggregate demand in the economy. Some economists have argued that this would be the appropriate policy when the economy is moving into a recession and the level of economic activity is contracting. This is associated with the 'Keynesian' view of how the economy works. Other economists, mainly 'monetarists', deny this is a useful way of conducting fiscal policy.

However, a budget deficit may also be unintended. The levels of public expenditure and taxation are affected directly by policy decisions but also indirectly affected by the state of the economy. If the economy moves into a recession this will reduce taxation income since incomes and spending will contract, and it will raise public expenditure as the level of unemployment rises. Thus a recession pushes the budget towards a deficit without any action by the government; conversely, recovery in the economy will move the budget towards a surplus, again without any action being taken by the government.

In either case, the budget will be in deficit. This will have to be financed by government borrowing: in effect the government will have a public sector borrowing requirement.

7.2   The PSBR (Public Sector Borrowing Requirement)

Definition   The PSBR is the amount of borrowing by the government needed to finance the excess of public expenditure over taxation income in a given period.

Should the income of the public sector as a whole (local government, central government, nationalised industries) be less than its income, the difference - the PSBR - will have to be met by borrowing. Should there be a surplus - a PSDR (Public Sector Debt Repayment) - no new borrowing will be needed and previous debt can be repaid. The recent experience of the UK is as follows:

PSBR (+), PSDR (-)	£ billion
1985	+7.4
1986	+2.5
1987	−1.4
1988	−11.9
1989	−9.3
1990	−2.1
1991	+7.7
1992	+28.7
1993	+42.5
1994	+37.9
1995	+35.5

Source: ONS Financial Statistics May 1996

The changes in government finances shown in this table reflects two main processes:

(a)   Finances are affected by the state of the economy. When there is rapid economic growth the PSBR contracts and is replaced by a PSDR. The budget moves into surplus and debt can be repaid as between 1987 and 1990. However, when the economy moves into recession the budget moves into deficit and a positive PSBR appears as in the period 1991-1995.

(b)   Finances are affected by government policy: the UK government engaged in a policy of tax cutting in the mid to late 1980s. This may have reduced the tax base and thus made the deterioration in public finances caused by the recession that much worse.

Whatever the source of a government budget deficit, it has to be financed by borrowing. This is principally conducted in the UK although overseas institutions and even individuals may purchase some government debt when it is offered. Broadly the government can undertake two types of borrowing:

(a)   It can borrow directly or indirectly from the public by issuing relatively illiquid debt. This includes national savings certificates, premium bonds, long term government stock. This is referred to as 'funding' the debt.

(b)   It can borrow from the banking system by issuing relatively liquid debt such as Treasury Bills. This is referred to as 'unfunded' debt.

The balance between these two forms of borrowing is important as these will have different effects on the economy. The funded part of government borrowing is clearly in competition with other potential borrowers and this raises the possibility that these other borrowers may be 'crowded out' with significant consequences for the economy. The 'unfunded' part of government borrowing is unlikely to have this effect; however, since it increases the liquid assets held by the banking system it may enable banks to increase the amount of credit they can create - in effect there is an increase in the money supply in the economy with possible inflationary consequences.

7.3   The PSBR and Macroeconomic Policy

In recent years there has been a growing concern about the PSBR and much effort in macroeconomic policy has been directed at limiting the size of the PSBR. The basis of this concern was threefold:

(a)   A large PSBR implied a rapidly growing national debt: this debt would have to be serviced (ie, interest paid upon it) and this would eventually become a significant part of public expenditure and would require taxation to pay this. Given the belief that levels of taxation were already unacceptably high, government macroeconomic policy was directed more and more towards the progressive reduction in the PSBR.

(b)   From the mid to late 1970s, governments progressively adopted a macroeconomic policy designed to limit the growth of the money supply in order to reduce the rate of inflation. This became known as 'monetarism'. Many economists believed that unfunded government borrowing would be a major source of expansion in the money supply; control of the money supply thus required control of the PSBR.

(c)   Part of the changes in thought about macroeconomic policy associated with monetarism was the belief that active fiscal policy was ineffective as a means of altering the level of employment in the economy. This was partly because of the notion of crowding out: government borrowing when unfunded would lead to a rise in interest rates and this, in turn, would lead to reduced private sector investment. Thus extra government spending would 'crowd out' private spending. If this were the case government borrowing would involve all sorts of problems but with no advantages in terms of reducing the level of unemployment.

Thus much recent macroeconomic policy has been directed to reducing or eliminating the PSBR. This is illustrated by:

(a)   Privatisation. Much of the impetus behind the programme of privatisation has been the recognition that this was a way of financing public expenditure without resort to borrowing. Although this cannot be the basis of a long term strategy, it is undoubtedly effective as a source of revenue in the short to medium term.

(b)   The MTFS. In 1980 the government announced the Medium Term Financial Strategy (MTFS) which specified progressive reductions in the PSBR and in the growth of the money supply. These targets for the PSBR and money supply were regularly updated; the government's success in achieving these targets has been mixed however. This is mainly because, as we have seen, the size of the PSBR is affected not merely by deliberate policy but also by the levels of activity in the economy.

(c)   Budgets in 1993 and 1994. The budgets in these two years saw very large increases in taxation. The combined effect of these two budgets was to produce a rise in taxation as a proportion of national income which was unprecedented in UK post-war policy. The government was clearly determined to reduce the PSBR despite its previous policy of tax reduction.

Conclusion   The conduct of fiscal policy is now severely constrained by the problems arising from the need to finance budget deficits.

7.4   Activity

Explain how the size of the PSBR is related to the trade cycle in economic activity.

8   THE CONDUCT OF FISCAL POLICY

8.1   Introduction

Fiscal policy is made possible and arises out of the existence of the government budget. The original point of fiscal policy was a purely financing one: how to pay for government expenditure. Indeed, prior to the First World War, the size of the government budget was probably too small to have much effect on the economy and hence active fiscal policy was not possible. However since then two important changes have occurred.

(a)   The size of the government budget has grown to the point where changes in it are likely to have a significant impact on the economy as a whole.

(b)   Developments in economic theory, associated with the work of JM Keynes, suggested that the budget could be used to influence the level of economic activity in the economy.

The combination of these led to the use of active fiscal policy in UK macroeconomic management. This raises issues about the way in which fiscal policy can be used and two broad areas can be identified:

*   the effect of the overall balance of the budget (balance, surplus, deficit) on economic activity as a whole;

*   the effect of particular taxes and particular forms of expenditure on specific aspects of economic activity.

8.2   Fiscal policy and aggregate demand

The work of the economist JM Keynes suggested that the level of employment in the economy was a function of the total demand for goods and services in the economy - aggregate monetary demand (AMD). The principal components of AMD are:

*   private consumption
*   investment
*   government expenditure
*   net exports.

Keynes showed that there was no automatic reason for the level of AMD to be sufficient to employ all the available resources and hence general ('demand deficient') unemployment was possible. It followed from this that the government might be able to influence expenditure in such a way as to maintain AMD close to the full employment level. It could do this by:

(a)   Altering its own level of expenditure: it could increase public investment in construction (schools, roads) for example. Thus there would be an increase in demand and the creation of useful social infrastructure.

(b)   Reducing taxation: this raises the disposable income of taxpayers whether individuals or business organisations and they in turn would raise their expenditure - either consumption or private investment.

In either case, the government would move to a deficit budget in order to boost expenditure in the economy. If the level of AMD was too high and the problem was not unemployment but inflation caused by excess demand, the government could reduce its expenditure and/or raise taxation and move towards a surplus budget. Thus governments came to believe that they could, by regular adjustments in the budget stance, keep the level of AMD at some point where unemployment was largely eliminated but without excessive inflationary pressure. This policy, adopted in the 1950s, became known as 'fine-tuning'.

However, this approach to macroeconomic policy came under severe criticism from the early 1970s. The criticism was based partly on debates about the effectiveness of fiscal policy in general and partly because of practical problems in the implementation of such fiscal policy.

(a)   The practical problems arose largely out of the existence of lags. These lags include:

- information lags: time taken for data to clearly show the need for and adjustment in fiscal stance;

- implementation lags: time taken to decide upon and take action especially when annual budgets are employed;

- impact lags: changes in fiscal stance would not take effect immediately.

Some economists argued that these lags were so large that fiscal policy might end up operating in the wrong direction and become destabilising.

(b)   Monetarists argued that fiscal policy was, in any case, ineffective as a means of controlling the level of unemployment. This was because expansionary fiscal policy would involve budget deficits (ie, a positive PSBR). The result of this would be either:

- no net effect on output and employment because of the 'crowding out' effect, or

- inflation because borrowing had not been funded and this had produced an expansion of the money supply.

Thus there was a decline in active fiscal policy from the late 1970s. This was highlighted in the 1982 budget which raised taxation and reduced expenditure (ie, was deflationary/contractionary) in the middle of the severest recession for 50 years. This was the opposite of the fiscal policy that would have been recommended previously. Instead, fiscal policy in recent years has emphasised the importance of limiting government borrowing and the use of fiscal policy not to influence AMD as a whole, but to influence particular aspects of economic behaviour. Much of this is associated with the term 'supply side' policy.

Conclusion   The role of fiscal policy as a tool for managing total demand in the economy has given way to its use in 'supply side' policy.

8.3   Problems of fiscal policy: crowding out

Two difficulties associated with fiscal policy have dominated debates about macroeconomic management in recent years: the problem of crowding out and the incentives effects of taxation. Both have had a major impact on the way in which fiscal policy has been conducted especially in the UK and USA.

Economists have argued that crowding out has taken several forms: the original model suggested that a growing public sector producing output that was not marketed (eg, education, health, law and order) would inevitably employ resources that could not then be employed in the private sector. Thus the private sector activity would be 'crowded out' by a sheer lack of resources. It was argued that the contraction of manufacturing ('deindustrialisation') was the result. This model is no longer accepted after the experience of the 1980s when, despite large scale unemployment and a contraction of employment in the public sector, the manufacturing sector continued to contract.

This model of crowding out was superceded by one of 'financial crowding out' whereby government borrowing led to a fall in private investment since it would lead to higher interest rates. This model too has come in for some criticism:

(a)   While it is true that government borrowing must represent an additional demand for funds, it is not the only demand and not necessarily the largest demand. Thus its impact on interest rates is problematic; during the period following the withdrawal of the UK from the ERM in September 1992, government borrowing rose to very high levels yet the general level of interest rates fell.

(b)   The level of private investment is affected by a whole range of factors of which the rate of interest is only one. The marginal efficiency of investment curve, which shows the relationship between investment and the rate of interest, may be inelastic. Moreover the position of the curve may reflect business expectations and an expansionary fiscal policy may encourage business to raise rather than reduce investment.

(c)   With the globalisation of banking and the abolition of controls on the flow of capital, interest rates may be determined by world interest rates more than purely domestic monetary processes.

| Conclusion | Doubts exist over the likely size of any crowding out effect but a very large PSBR may well lead to a fall in private investment. |

8.4   Problems of fiscal policy: incentives

It is likely that all taxes have some effect; indeed, the structure of taxes is designed to influence particular economic activities: in particular, taxes on spending are used to alter the pattern of consumption:

•   high excise duties on alcohol and tobacco products reflect UK social and health policy priorities;

•   the recent decision to use excise duties to raise the real price of petrol over time is designed to discourage the use of private cars because of the environmental effects.

Thus taxes as instruments of fiscal policy can fulfil a variety of useful functions.

However there has been a growing concern among some economists that taxes have undesirable side effects on the economy, notably on incentives. It is argued that high taxes, especially when they are steeply progressive act as a disincentive to work and effort. The relative price of leisure is income forgone; high taxes reduce the net income from work ie, reduce the price of leisure. Rational individuals would work less and take more leisure. Moreover some taxes have more specific effects eg, employer national insurance payments raise the cost of labour and probably reduce employment.

The effects of these arguments on fiscal policy has been to shift emphasis from the management of total demand in the economy to improving the ability of the economy to generate output: supply side policy. This approach has had implications for a wide range of government policy including education, industrial relations, and the social security system. The principal effects on fiscal policy have been as follows.

(a)   The pressure to reduce public expenditure has increased since this would permit a reduction in the general level of taxation and hence reduce disincentive effects overall.

(b)   There has been a major shift in taxation from direct taxation (eg, income tax) towards indirect taxation (eg, VAT): this is justified on the grounds that direct taxes, related to income, have strong disincentive effects which are absent from indirect taxes.

One consequence of this approach has been to produce a major change in income distribution which has become much less equitable. This has generated much debate both about its morality but also about its effectiveness in making the economy more dynamic. Inevitably, very high marginal rates of tax will have disincentive effects for those who are affected by them: whether this can be generalised to the whole tax system and the majority of tax payers is subject to more controversy.

| Conclusion | Emphasis in fiscal policy has shifted from the management of demand towards the improvement of the supply capability of the economy. |

9   THE RELATIONSHIP BETWEEN FISCAL AND MONETARY POLICY

So far monetary and fiscal policy have been discussed as if they were independent and could be conducted without reference to each other. However, this is, in practice, not the case. Effective macroeconomic policy needs a degree of co-ordination between fiscal and monetary policy. Two broad alternatives are possible:

(a)   Monetary policy may be accommodating to fiscal policy. If a government wished to conduct an active fiscal policy as the principal part of macroeconomic policy it would be faced with the problems that a PSBR might have for the level of interest rates:

•   private investment: the crowding out effect

•   the exchange rate in a relatively open economy.

To avoid this, the government could operate an accommodating monetary policy in which it expanded or contracted the money stock in order to keep interest rates reasonably stable. The conduct of monetary policy would thus be determined by the needs of fiscal policy. It has been said that this was the basis of monetary policy in the UK between 1945 and the early 1970s.

(b)   Alternatively, fiscal policy could be made subservient to monetary policy. If a government wished to see monetary policy as the main element of macroeconomic policy it would need to conduct fiscal policy in the light of its effects on the growth of the money stock. This is because the size of the PSBR and the way in which it is financed will affect the liquidity of the banking system and hence the growth of bank deposits. A large PSBR implies either:

•   that it will be unfunded and financed by sales of securities to the banking system and hence there will be a large increase in the stock of broad money (M4)

•   that it will be funded and financed by sales of government debt directly to the general public and hence this will lead to upward pressure on interest rates as the government competes with other borrowers.

In either case, monetary conditions in the economy are crucially affected by the fiscal stance. In consequence, if governments wish to conduct an active monetary policy it may have to take steps to reduce the PSBR to levels consistent with its monetary targets. The Medium Term Financial Strategy (MTFS) which operated in the 1980s was an attempt to reduce the PSBR and make it consistent with monetary targets.

Thus there is a close relationship between fiscal and monetary policy and the principal targets within each must be consistent with each other.

Conclusion   Fiscal and monetary policy are interdependent and monetary and budgetary targe
must be made consistent.

10   CHAPTER SUMMARY

This chapter has considered monetary and fiscal policy. It has emphasised:

(a)   The demand for money and how differences of view about this influence the importance of changes in the money stock.

(b)   The supply of money and how the money stock may be measured.

(c)   How the interaction of the demand for money and the supply of money determines the rate of interest.

(d)   The different ways the monetary authorities may attempt to control the growth of the money stock and the difficulties these methods encounter.

(e)   The problems of conducting monetary policy: the difficulty of controlling the stock of money and the undesirable consequences for the economy of some aspects of monetary policy.

(f)   The nature of fiscal policy and public finance and a consideration of the effects of taxation on incentives.

(g)   The importance of the government budget and the financing of the PSBR. The significance of the size of the PSBR and the way it is funded was emphasised.

(h)   The conduct of fiscal policy was considered with an explanation of the problems of conducting fiscal policy with special emphasis on the notion of crowding out.

(i)   The links between fiscal and monetary policy especially with respect to the relationship between the PSBR and the growth of the money stock.

11   SELF TEST QUESTIONS

11.1   Identify the principal functions of money. (1.1)

11.2   Define monetary policy and explain its principal elements. (1.2)

11.3   Compare and contrast the Keynesian and monetarist models of the demand for money. (2.2, 2.4)

11.4   Distinguish between narrow and broad measures of the money stock. (3.2)

11.5   Show how open market operations can influence the stock of money. (4.2)

11.6   Explain what is meant by lags and show how they occur in monetary policy. (5.2)

11.7   What are the disadvantages of using interest rates as the main instrument of monetary policy? (5.4)

11.8   Distinguish between public goods and merit goods. (6.2)

11.9   Explain what is meant by progressive, proportional and regressive taxes. (6.3)

11.10   Explain what is meant by the PSBR. (7.2)

11.11   Show how a government could use the budget to influence the level of aggregate demand in the economy. (8.2)

11.12   Explain what is meant by 'crowding out' and show how it may occur. (8.3)

11.13   Why can governments not regard fiscal and monetary policy as being independent of each other? (9)

...ty preference

...ain the Liquidity Preference Theory of interest rate determination.   **(20 marks)**

12.2   PSBR

(a)   Explain the term the public sector borrowing requirement (PSBR) and show how it might be financed.   **(8 marks)**

(b)   Why might the size of the PSBR change over time?   **(12 marks)**

          (Total: 20 marks)

13   ANSWERS TO EXAMINATION TYPE QUESTIONS

13.1   Liquidity preference

The Liquidity Preference Theory was suggested by Keynes as a means of explaining the determination of the rate of interest. He saw an interest rate as the price of borrowing money, paid by the borrower to the lender and, like any other price, determined in a free market by the interaction of the demand for and the supply of money.

Keynes distinguished between money which possessed the property of liquidity and which does not earn interest, and bonds which are fixed interest-bearing securities. (This distinction was used as a simplification in the explanation). Liquidity can be defined as the ease and speed with which an asset can be turned into cash without significant loss of value ie, it is readily convertible into spending power. Keynes argued that if people do not hold their resources in the form of money, they put it into bonds; he identified three motives or reasons why people will hold money (ie prefer liquidity) rather than investing in bonds, and it is these motives which determine the demand for money.

The transactions motive: people need money to pay for their day-to-day needs eg food, electricity, rent etc. There is a minimum demand for money for these purposes regardless of income, but the demand for money for transactions purposes will rise as income rises. It is not connected directly with the rate of interest.

The precautionary motive: people demand money in order to have it available in case of emergencies. This will also depend on income and is also not directly determined by the rate of interest.

The speculative motive. Bonds are fixed interest securities (a fixed amount of interest is paid on a bond whatever its price). The percentage yield varies inversely with the price of the bond eg if its price rises, the fixed amount of interest earned now becomes a lower percentage of the higher price. People hold money for as long as it is unfavourable to buy bonds (having already set aside sums for the transactions and precautionary motives). It is unfavourable to buy bonds when their price is high and the interest rate low. This is because high bond prices are more likely to fall than rise. However if their price is low and the interest rate high, people switch from money to bonds. The speculative demand for money is therefore interest-rate determined and it is higher when interest rates are low and vice versa.

The following graph illustrates liquidity preference which is the sum of the three motives. The shape of the curve is given by the speculative motive.

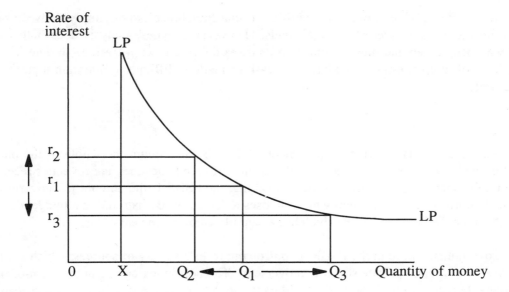

OX is the minimum amount of money demanded in order to satisfy the transactions and precautionary motives and it is independent of the rate of interest. The curve starts to fall at this point and shows that the higher the rate of interest, the lower the quantity of money demanded and vice versa. The curve will become more elastic at lower interest rates because people will give up proportionately large quantities of bonds in exchange for money in response to a proportionately small change in the rate of interest. The demand for money therefore has a normal negatively-sloping curve (but it becomes increasingly interest rate elastic and eventually becomes perfectly so).

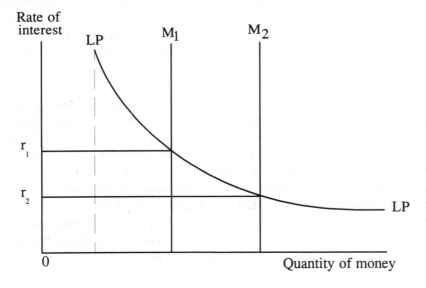

The supply of money, as far as Keynes was concerned, is determined by the government and has no relationship with the prevailing rate of interest; ie the supply of money is perfectly interest-inelastic.

The initial money stock is M_1 and the rate of interest r_1. If the government now decides to increase the money supply it will cause the supply of money to shift to M_2. Some individuals will now speculate that bond prices are as high as they ever will be and will choose to hold this additional money; however others speculate that bond prices can continue to rise and will therefore purchase bonds. This pushes up the price of bonds, reducing market yields and interest rates. Thus, an increase in the money supply will cause interest rates to fall, and vice versa.

Today we see that the general level of interest rates is primarily determined by government policy and it may seem that this theory is not very useful, especially in view of the fact that modern financial systems offer a wide variety of securities so that the choice is not simply between non-interest bearing money and interest-bearing bonds. However, Keynes' analysis does help us to understand why people demand money, and it emphasises the role of **expectations** in determining the general level of interest rates. This has on occasions made it difficult to maintain a particular interest rate strategy.

13.2   PSBR

(a)   The Public Sector Borrowing Requirement (PSBR) is the amount the whole of the public sector needs to borrow each year to make up the difference between tax revenues received and public sector expenditure. Loosely speaking, the PSBR is the amount the government needs to borrow. A government which chooses to have a PSBR is running a budget deficit. The National Debt is the PSBR which has accumulated over the years.

The government can fund the PSBR by borrowing from a variety of sources, which include banks, the non-bank private sector and overseas. The borrowing can be in the form of both marketable and non-marketable debt. Marketable debt consists of securities which can be bought and sold on the financial markets. The securities may be short term, in which case they are described as Treasury Bills, although these are used more for the purposes of monetary control than for funding borrowing requirements. Long-term securities issued by the government are government bonds, called gilt-edged stock. They are fixed interest bearing securities which are issued to fund the PSBR, rather than as part of the government's short-term monetary policy.

Non-marketable debt in the United Kingdom takes the form of National Savings Certificates and premium bonds, which cannot be resold by their owner to a third party.

(b)   The size of the PSBR may change because the government is using it to carry out its economic policies, or the change may be due to an unplanned excess of expenditure over tax receipts.

Considering first a discretionary change, the government may adopt a Keynesian policy of demand expansion via increased public expenditure and a budget deficit. Keynesian policies hinge on managing aggregate monetary demand (AMD) as a way of controlling or influencing the level of national income (NI). AMD is made up of private sector consumption and investment expenditure, government expenditure and net exports. All these factors are injections into the circular flow of funds and, if increased, will increase national income in the Keynesian model. The government may therefore decide to raise national income towards a level of full employment by increasing its own expenditure, without increasing taxes; alternatively, it could lower taxes and maintain the level of government expenditure. Either method would result in a PSBR.

Figure 1 shows the effect of running a budget deficit.

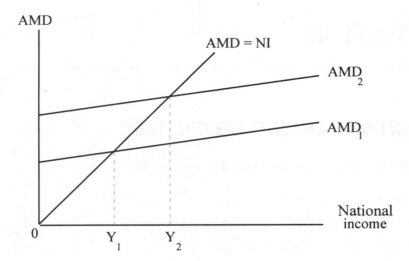

Figure 1 Increasing the level of national income

In Figure 1 the level of national income is Y_1, below the full-employment level of Y_2. The government can move Y_1 to Y_2 by increasing AMD from AMD_1 to AMD_2, since the economy will settle at an equilibrium given by any point of intersection between the AMD line and the line AMD =NI. There are many ways in which AMD could be increased, but the one relevant for this question is for the government to spend more than it receives in taxes, running a budget deficit.

Turning now to a non-discretionary, or unplanned, PSBR, changes in the level of government borrowing may simply occur because the government receives less money in taxes than it had planned, or spends more than it had planned to do. Both these effects may occur in a recession, when people's incomes are falling, so less income tax is paid, and the government is having to fund very high levels of unemployment benefit.

18 INFLATION

INTRODUCTION & LEARNING OBJECTIVES

When you have studied this chapter you should be able to do the following:

- Define inflation and show how it may be measured
- Explain the domestic and international consequences of inflation
- Explain and evaluate the main theories of inflation
- Consider how households and firms may limit the impact of inflation
- Explain the effect of inflation on company performance and evaluation.

1 THE DEFINITION AND MEASUREMENT OF INFLATION

1.1 What is meant by inflation?

Definition   Inflation is the rise in the general level of prices over time.

The term inflation refers to the process by which the general level of prices in the economy rises over time. The process does not require that the prices of all goods and services increase over time, nor that the increase in prices is uniform between different goods or different periods of time. The rate of inflation may vary between extremes:

- creeping inflation where the price level rises by a few percentage points per year eg, the UK in the 1950s and 1960s

- hyperinflation where the price level rises exceptionally rapidly and money quickly loses its purchasing power eg, the great German inflation of 1922-3 when prices rose to one billion times their 1914 level.

An alternative way of looking at inflation is to regard it as the process by which money loses its value or purchasing power over time. Since money is denominated in nominal terms ie, it has a fixed face value, any change in prices will influence the amount which can be bought with a fixed sum of money. Inflation will reduce its purchasing power, disinflation (falling price levels) will raise its purchasing power. The extent to which the purchasing power of money falls during inflation depends on two variables:

(a)   The rate of price increase for different goods and services. Not all goods and services experience the same rate of inflation. In recent years in the UK the price of some services have risen faster than average whereas house prices have hardly risen at all; the prices of some electronic goods have actually fallen.

(b)   The pattern of consumption. If the prices which are rising fastest are for those goods which make up a large proportion of one's expenditure this will have a greater effect in reducing the purchasing power of money than if they were for goods that make up a small proportion of total expenditure.

The fact that price changes are widely different for different goods and services, and because expenditure patterns vary from person to person and over time, the measurement of inflation is a complex process.

1.2   The measurement of inflation

In order to produce a single figure for the rate of inflation in an economy it is necessary to combine the effects of all price rises (and any price falls) into a single measure. This is done by constructing a single index of the overall price level. The index most commonly used in the UK is the retail price index (RPI). This is constructed by:

- regular monitoring of changes in the prices of a whole range of consumer goods and services at the retail level

- constructing an index of retail prices in which the weights given to any one good or service are determined by their relative importance in consumer budgets. This data is derived from the Family Expenditure Survey. Thus weightings given to food, energy and motoring expenditure are relatively high, that given to newspapers and periodicals is relatively low.

The resulting index provides a measure of the rate of retail inflation over time. Recent changes in the price indices are given below:

The UK Retail Price Index
(Annual averages, Jan 1987 = 100)   *Index of*

	Food prices	*Non food prices*	*All retail prices*
1987	101.4	102.0	101.9
1988	105.7	107.3	106.9
1989	111.9	116.1	115.2
1990	120.9	127.4	126.1
1991	128.6	135.1	133.5
1992	132.6	140.5	138.5
1993	136.1	142.6	140.7
1994	138.5	146.5	144.1
1995	143.9	151.4	149.1

Source: ONS Monthly Digest of Statistics May 1996

The table shows that the prices of foodstuffs have risen less rapidly than those of non-foodstuffs and that the overall level of prices rose by 49.1% between 1987 and 1995. The RPI is usually expressed as an index but the rate of inflation in % terms can be easily derived from the data. Thus the rate of inflation, as measured by the RPI, between 1991 and 1992 was 3.75%:

$$\frac{138.5 - 133.5}{133.5} \times 100 = 3.75\%$$

1.3   Limitations of the RPI

The RPI provides a good measure of the rate of inflation in an economy as it affects consumers. However, it has some serious weaknesses.

(a)   The weightings used within the RPI basket of goods have to be periodically changed as the pattern of consumption changes. This is a technical difficulty but of no great consequence for the validity of the RPI as a measure of inflation. But there are further technical problems:

- the RPI cannot reflect changes in quality: thus the price of cars may rise but their quality may have improved

- the RPI cannot easily deal with new products or with products which cease to be consumed since neither have prices at both the start and the end of the period under consideration

(b)   The RPI measures the rate of inflation for a typical basket of consumption; but consumption patterns will vary a great deal from person to person. Hence the RPI may overstate or understate the rate of inflation experienced by any one person. Thus if food and energy prices rise faster than other prices, the rate of inflation experienced by the poor (including pensioners) will be higher than that indicated by the RPI since these commodities form a larger proportion of their expenditure than for the average consumer.

(c)   The RPI only measures changes in the level of retail prices and ignores the prices on other goods and services eg, capital goods purchased by business, imported goods and services purchased by business. To get an indication of the rate of inflation for the economy as a whole, the government uses the gross domestic product (GDP) deflator. This may be a better guide to overall inflationary pressure in the economy.

(d)   The apparent rate of inflation may be misleading as to the underlying rate of inflation in the economy because of the content of the RPI basket of goods and services. In the UK the rate of interest charged on mortgages is included in the RPI calculations. Thus if government were to raise interest rates to dampen inflationary pressures, this has the perverse effect of raising the RPI and hence the headline rate of inflation. It might be argued that measures of the underlying rate of inflation should exclude the effect of government policy in this way. The UK government now announce the figure for underlying inflation excluding mortgage interest and has recently started publishing an index excluding the effect of increases in indirect taxes as well. Government targets for inflation are now expressed in the figure for underlying inflation.

Thus there are a variety of ways of measuring the rate of inflation in the economy. Which measures one uses depends on the reasons for wanting a measure of inflation.

- If the concern is with the potential impact on living standards then the RPI would be the appropriate measure;

- if the concern was with the long run competitiveness of the economy then the GDP deflator might be more appropriate.

Clearly governments are concerned with inflation since price stability is a long standing objective of macroeconomic policy. This raises the question of what are the economic effects of inflation?

1.4   Activity

Consider how the expenditure patterns of retired people differ from the average and how this influences the rate of inflation experienced by this group.

2   THE GENERAL ECONOMIC CONSEQUENCES OF INFLATION

2.1   Introduction

In a closed economy with no international trade there is no immediately obvious reason why inflation should have undesirable economic effects. Society, as a whole, cannot be made poorer by inflation since a rise in the price of a good/service must represent a rise in the money incomes of the individuals or organisations that produced those goods and services. So long as money incomes rise faster than prices then real incomes - the purchasing power of incomes as a whole, will continue to rise.

Indeed there have only been a few years since 1945 when average money incomes have risen less rapidly than prices: the normal experience of inflation is that prices rise but less rapidly than money incomes.

If this is the case why should inflation be seen as a problem and its avoidance a major objective of government policy? The answer is that inflation has other domestic effects that are deemed undesirable. The most important of these are that inflation may:

- damage the ability of money to fulfil its functions
- distort the distribution of income in arbitrary ways
- distort or reduce investment
- affect other economic variables such as interest rates and exchange rates.

2.2   Inflation and functions of money

The first problem concerns the role of money in the economy since inflation can be seen as a process by which the value (purchasing power) of money is reduced. Money has a crucial role to play in the efficient functioning of a modern economy and there would be serious consequences if inflation reduced its ability to fulfil its functions. How might inflation affect the acceptability of money?

- money loses its value as a result of inflation and hence its effectiveness as a store of value is reduced

- money may become an ineffective standard of deferred payment: this will produce particular problems for long term contracts

- money may become a poor unit of account if there are varying rates of inflation for different goods and services.

These problems will become more acute the more rapid is the inflationary process. If inflation becomes excessive (hyperinflation) then it may lose all acceptability and be no longer able even to fulfil its function of a means of exchange. Resort will be had to barter or a substitute form of money will be employed eg, the use of cigarettes as money in Germany immediately after the war.

For most countries the experience of inflation is such that there is unlikely to be much effect on the use of money. However the cumulative effect of inflation can still be considerable: inflation of 4% a year will double the price level in less than 18 years. This may well produce other economic consequences.

2.3   Inflation and the distribution of income

Even relatively slow rates of inflation are likely to lead to a change in the distribution of income and wealth. Only if all money prices and money incomes were indexed so that they rose in line with the general level of prices would this problem be avoided. Two particular cases should be noted.

(a)   For those on fixed incomes or those who are in weak bargaining positions, inflation may erode the purchasing power of their incomes: money incomes would be stable (and might even rise) but real incomes would fall. Some of this may be avoided eg, by linking state pensions to changes in the price level but many instances may be unavoidable.

(b)   Since inflation reduces the value of money, it will reduce the real value of assets denominated in money. The real value of loans will fall: this will shift wealth from lenders to borrowers. Thus when inflation occurs, those who have large financial debts eg, mortgage holders or businesses with large debts tend to gain at the expense of net lenders.

Thus the distribution of income and wealth is affected by the process of inflation. Governments may wish to avoid this consequence for two reasons:

- it may produce unwanted and unpredictable changes in the distribution of income and wealth

- it may produce reactions eg, by potential savers which have undesirable consequences.

However, it should be noted that such effects may not be all bad: the redistribution of income from savers to borrowers may, in effect, shift income from those who save to those who spend and invest - this may not be undesirable if full employment and economic growth is desired.

2.4   Inflation: the effects on saving and investment

As inflation reduces the value of money, potential savers may be discouraged unless the rate of interest contains an element to offset inflation. If this is not so, savers may prefer the acquisition of non-financial assets in the hope that these will act as a hedge against inflation. In the UK property has in the past been seen as a better long term outlet for savings than lending. The experience of stagnation in the property market in 1990-1995 may have indicated that this is not necessarily the case. If the long term flow of savings is reduced, this may reduce the level of investment which such savings finance with consequential effects on the rate of economic growth.

Even if savings are not affected, inflation may have direct effects on business investment.

(a)   Inflation introduces a degree of uncertainty into business decision making: the prospect of future inflation which cannot be accurately predicted makes the estimation of the profitability of investment projects difficult. As a result businesses may well not undertake marginally profitable investments.

(b)   Inflation may distort the pattern of investment. Because of the uncertainty associated with inflation and because of its effects on the real value of future profits, investors may prefer:

- short term investment to long term investment since the shorter the payback period the less the uncertainty;

- investment in assets other than productive capital equipment if their prices are expected to rise eg, in the property booms of the early 1970s and late 1980s.

The effect of inflation may therefore be to reduce the overall level of investment. This may have short term macroeconomic effect, making it harder to achieve full employment as well as long term effects on the rate of economic growth.

2.5   Inflation and the rate of interest

There are debates about the factors which determine the rate of interest but clearly interest is paid:
- as a reward to lenders for forgoing the liquidity of retaining cash
- as a reward for risk.

Thus lenders require a rate of return measured as a percentage rate on the loans/investments. Since inflation reduces the real value of money, this will have to be incorporated into the rate of return required by lenders. Thus we may distinguish between the real and nominal rate of return on a loan.

Example: if a lender of a sum of £100 requires a real rate of return of 6% this implies a desired money value of £106 after one year.

If inflation is expected to be 10% then the nominal return will have to be such that the return produces a purchasing power equivalent to £106 when inflation was zero.

This return will be $1.06 \times 1.10 = 1.166$
ie, the required rate of return has become 16.6%

This inflation effect on the nominal rate of return is called the Fisher Effect. This raises important issues:

- how far are inflation expectations built into nominal interest rates especially for long term lending when estimates of future inflation become more problematic?

- how does this affect investment planning since borrowers need to build an element of inflation into projections of rates of return?

Conclusion   Inflation has serious effects for income distribution and savings and investment which become more serious as the rate of inflation rises.

2.6   Activity

Consider whether the prospect of inflation has affected your own savings/expenditure patterns and in what ways.

3   THE EXTERNAL CONSEQUENCES OF INFLATION

3.1   Inflation and international competitiveness

It is possible that within countries individuals, businesses and governments could take action to limit the impact of inflation. However, this could not remove the external impact of inflation on international competitiveness. If one country has a rate of inflation that exceeds that of its main trading partners it will become relatively uncompetitive. There are two main consequences of this.

(a)   Declining competitiveness will affect the balance of payments: the level of exports of goods and services would tend to decline while that of imports would rise. The size of the effect would depend on the price elasticity of demand; the higher this is, the larger the effect. Since it is not possible to finance a balance of payments deficit indefinitely, this would require remedial action by the government.

(b)   Loss of exports and increased import penetration implies declining domestic output and rising unemployment. Any attempt to cure this by expansionary fiscal policy may only make the balance of payment problems worse because rising aggregate monetary demand will lead to higher levels of imports.

One possible solution to this is that the exchange rate for the country's currency could fall to offset the domestic inflation: this implies that one function of the exchange rate is to offset price differences between countries.

3.2   Inflation and the rate of exchange

The main function of an exchange rate is to provide a mechanism for translating prices expressed in one currency into prices expressed in another currency: the implication is that the rate of exchange will be determined by these differences in prices. This arises from the Law of One Price.

The law of one price states that in a free market with no barriers to trade and no transport or transactions costs, the competitive process will ensure that there will only be one price for any given good or service. If price differences occurred they would be removed by arbitrage; entrepreneurs would buy in the low price market and resell in the high price market. This itself would eventually eradicate price differences.

If this law is applied to the case of international trade, it suggests that exchange rates will always adjust to ensure that one price exists between countries where there is relatively free trade. Thus if a typical set of consumer goods cost $1,000 in the USA and £500 in the UK, free trade between them would produce an exchange rate of £1 to $2. This is known as the purchasing power parity (PPP) theory of exchange rates:

$$\text{Exchange rate (£/\$)} = \frac{\text{average price level in UK}}{\text{average price level in USA}}$$

The clear implication of this is that inflation in one country will produce a fall in that country's exchange rate:

- inflation in UK reduces US demand for UK goods and raises UK demand for USA goods

- UK has a trade deficit, USA has a trade surplus

- relative demand for £ and $ to finance trade leads to exchange rate for £ falling.

The evidence is that while the PPP theory is useful in explaining long term movements in exchange rates, it is less useful in explaining short term movements. This is probably because:

- it ignores the effect of capital movements on exchange rates

- governments may 'manage' exchange rates eg, by interest rate policy

- trade and therefore exchange rates will reflect only the prices of goods that enter into trade and not the general price level since this includes non-tradeables (eg, inland transport).

Nonetheless, the general principle is clear: if a country has a rate of inflation consistently above that of its trading partners, it will tend to run a persistent and possibly increasing trade deficit. Since this cannot be financed indefinitely , the currency will eventually depreciate.

3.3   Activity

How important have price pressures been in your own company's ability to compete internationally in the recent past?

4   THE EFFECTS OF INFLATION ON COMPANIES

4.1   Cash flow and profit

It is possible to identify two main categories of effect on companies of a sustained rate of inflation:

- real effects on the level of profits and the cash flow position of the company

- effects on the ability to assess the real performance of the company when nominal values are different from real values.

The first of these largely depends on the form that inflation is taking and the nature of the markets in which the company is operating. One way of categorising inflation is to distinguish between:

(a)   Demand pull inflation. This might occur when excess aggregate monetary demand in the economy and hence demand for particular goods and services enables companies to raise prices and expand profit margins.

(b)   Cost push inflation.   This will occur when there are increases in production costs independent of the state of demand eg, rising raw material costs or rising labour costs. The initial effect is to reduce profit margins and the extent to which these can be restored depends on the ability of companies to pass on cost increases as price increases for customers.

One would expect that the effect of cost push inflation on company profits and cash flow would always be negative but that with demand pull inflation, profits and cash flow might be increased, at least in nominal terms and in the short run. In practice however even demand pull inflation may have negative effects on profits and cash flow.

(a)   Even if aggregate monetary demand is relatively high, some companies may be working in highly competitive markets where the ability to raise prices may be limited. This is especially true when markets are international.

(b)   Even if profit margins are expanded in the short run, the inflation will induce cost rises in the long run eg, as wage rates rise in response to rises in the RPI.

(c)   Demand pull inflation may in any case work through cost. This is especially true if companies use pricing strategies in which prices are determined by cost plus some mark-up. In these circumstances demand pull inflation may work via costs:

•   excess demand for goods leads companies to expand output

•   this leads to excess demand for factors of production especially labour and hence costs (eg, wages) rise

•   companies pass on the increased cost as higher prices.

Conclusion   In most cases inflation will reduce profits and cash flow especially in the long run.

4.2   The assessment of company performance

The success of a company may be measured by comparing its capital as shown on its balance sheet at the start and at the end of some accounting period. The difficulty arises because there is the need to use a common unit of measure for both different types of capital asset and for the same capital asset over time. It is money's function of a measure of value and unit of account that provides this common unit. Provided that the value of money is constant and there is no inflation or deflation, there is no problem. The process of inflation does, however, cause problems.

In a world of zero inflation, the conventional accounting procedure of valuing assets at historic cost produces no difficulty.

•   Assets and liabilities are measured in terms of their original money values and the difference between the two is regarded as the net capital of the company.

•   Other things being equal, an increase in the net capital of the company is indicative that it is running at a profit.

However if historic cost accounting is used when prices are rising, the information may be misleading. Thus if a company maintains a constant level of stocks in physical terms but their costs have risen between the opening balance sheet and the closing balance sheet, it will look as if the assets of the company have increased. If no other changes have occurred in the assets of the company, it will appear to have earned a profit when the real situation has not changed. This may produce two difficulties:

- difficulty of assessing, from both inside and outside the company, the true profitability of the company

- taxation may be based on changes in nominal accounts and not the real changes: hence the need for measures of stock relief for company taxation in periods of rapid inflation.

Because of the problems inherent in historic cost accounting there have been attempts to provide an alternative basis for accounting in periods of inflation:

(a)   Current purchasing power (CPP) was proposed in Provisional SSAP 7 (PSSAP 7) in 1974. This proposed that since all assets must be measured in terms of a common unit but that nominal money values were misleading when prices changed, the unit used should be the purchasing power of nominal money values. Thus the values of incomes and assets would be based on historic cost adjusted for the general rate of inflation over the accounting period. This approach was not adopted however.

(b)   Current cost accounting. This was proposed by SSAP 16 (1980). This contained the notion that capital should be measured in terms of its ability to maintain output. Thus if the capital stock of a company was such that the ability to produce output was maintained but not increased over the accounting period this would be shown in the accounts even if the nominal values of assets had increased because of inflation. SSAP 16 was eventually withdrawn in 1988.

Clearly the assessment of company performance is made more difficult by inflation but the accounting solution to this is not easy. Provided that inflation is relatively slow the effects may be limited and the slower inflation from the early 1980s onwards might be the reason for the declining interest in alternative accounting approaches.

Conclusion   Historic cost accounting may give a misleading picture of company performance especially in periods of rapid inflation.

4.3   Activity

Identify the ways in which inflation has affected your organisation's profit and cash flow.

5   COPING WITH INFLATION

5.1   Introduction

If inflation were persistent, one would expect that both individuals and organisations might seek means to protect themselves from the effects of inflation. This would imply the need to:

- protect the value of money assets against the fall in the value of money

- protect the value of money incomes so that increases in money income match the rise in the price level.

The ability to do this might be a reflection of the economic power that individuals or organisations have. For example

(a)   individuals who have powerful employee organisations may be able to ensure that money incomes are regularly raised at least in line with the rate of inflation. Trade unions might be seen to have this function on behalf of their members.

(b)   companies with a degree of market power and who are facing relatively inelastic demand curves for their products may be able to pass on cost increases without significant loss of sales.

These sorts of factors may well explain the differential ability of households and companies to avoid the worst effects of inflation but they are clearly somewhat arbitrary and variable. The alternative is to devise institutional arrangements which provide a measure of protection against inflation. The obvious mechanism is for the payment of interest.

5.2   Interest

One way in which net savers can protect the value of financial assets against the effects of inflation is to invest in interest-bearing investments. Thus there will be a nominal rate of interest and a real rate of interest. The real rate of interest will be the nominal rate minus the rate of inflation over the relevant period. Provided that the real rate is positive it would appear that the investor has protected himself/herself from the effects of inflation. However there are reasons for supposing that the nominal rate of interest does not always fully reflect inflation:

(a)   Interest rates are fixed periodically and are subject to a range of forces. Some investments have interest rates that are fixed over relatively long periods of time. Inflation however is continuous. Thus unless inflation expectations are entirely accurate, money markets may fix nominal interest rates at either too high or too low a level. In the latter case the investor will not be fully compensated for the effects of inflation.

(b)   At certain times the real rate of interest has been negative: the nominal rate of interest has been less than the rate of inflation. For example, if the nominal rate of interest is 5%:

> £1 invested for a year becomes £1.05

But, if inflation was 7% the investor needs £1.07 to be 'as well off'. Receiving just £1.05 means the investor is 'worse off' ie, the real interest rate is negative. Thus the value of investments has fallen in real terms. Since we would never expect that, in the absence of inflation, interest rates would be negative, it is clear that in such cases, the interest rate has not fully protected the investor against the effects of inflation.

> **Conclusion**   Interest rates reflect a range of economic factors and will not always fully reflect the rate of inflation.

5.3   Indexing

> **Definition**   Indexing is the process by which money values are regularly raised in line with an appropriate measure of inflation.

If the payment of interest is seen as an unreliable means of protecting the value of assets against inflation, the alternative might be indexing. When capital values are indexed the nominal value is periodically raised in line with the rise in the general price level. The common example is index linked National Savings Certificates. These have the effect of providing absolute protection of the value of savings against the effects of inflation. These are most valuable and most popular when inflation is rapid since it is then that nominal interest rates are most likely to be less than the rate of inflation. In periods of low inflation such index linking is less popular and, indeed, less necessary.

Indexing has also been used in other cases where inflation generates problems. This is especially so in the case of taxation. If there is a progressive taxation system inflation may bring tax payers into higher tax brackets because money incomes have risen even if real incomes have not. As a result inflation tends to raise government revenue; this process is known as fiscal drag. To avoid this, some figures used in taxation computations are index linked:

- personal tax allowances
- costs of assets subject to capital gains tax.

Thus the Chancellor of the Exchequer is obliged to raise annually personal tax allowances by an amount equal to the rate of inflation unless specifically excluded by a clause in the Finance Act.

Indexing may therefore be used in a variety of ways to limit the impact of inflation. It is even possible to extend such a system to a much wider range of cases where real values may be reduced by inflation. In Italy a system known as the 'scala mobile' was devised in the 1970s in which a range of money values including most wage rates were indexed to the rate of inflation. This had the effect of protecting most incomes against the effects of inflation. However, its disadvantage is that it ensures the continuance of inflation and reduces the pressure to conduct economic policy to reduce the rate of inflation. This may have serious implications for international competitiveness and the balance of payments. For this reason the 'scala mobile' was eventually abandoned.

Thus indexing may be a means of protecting individuals against the effects of inflation and is clearly useful where money incomes are determined by administrative action (eg, pensions, social security payments) rather than by economic forces. The clear danger of indexing, especially if adopted on a wide scale, is that inflation becomes built in to the economic system. The longer term solution to the problem is to reduce inflationary pressures. To do that requires an understanding of the causes of inflation.

| Conclusion | Indexing may ameliorate the effects of inflation but is an inadequate substitute for long term price stability.

5.4   Activity

List as many as you can of the prices/payments which are currently indexed linked in the UK.

6   THE CAUSES OF INFLATION

6.1   Introduction

For an individual the effects of inflation are the same whatever might be the cause of inflation. Nonetheless, the identification of the possible causes of inflation is of concern for two reasons:

- the effects on company profits and cash flows might vary

- if a policy towards inflation is to be effective, it needs to reflect the underlying cause of inflation.

The explanation of inflation is therefore an important task for economics. Unfortunately the causes of inflation have been the source of much debate and argument within the economics profession and there is no clear consensus over the precise nature of the causes of inflation even if there is some degree of general agreement. Moreover, at any one time it is possible that more than one source of inflation is at work thus complicating the task of identifying the cause of inflation.

The debate over the causes of inflation was first conducted around two broad categories of inflationary pressure.

(a)   Cost push inflation was seen to be the process by which prices are forced upwards by independent increases in the costs of production.

(b)   Demand pull inflation was seen to be a process by which excessive aggregate monetary demand in the economy pulled up prices independently of what was happening to costs of production.

Although this distinction has weaknesses, notably that costs are, after all, really just another set of prices, it is useful for clarifying the issues involved. Another distinction that should be noted is that between

- inflationary shocks: the initial pressure on prices eg, the oil price rises of 1974 and 1979

- the transmission mechanism by which an initial shock to prices becomes a process of continuous inflation in the economy as a whole.

With these distinctions in mind we may analyse the causes of inflation.

6.2   Cost push inflation

Definition   Cost push inflation occurs when prices rise as a result of autonomous increases in costs.

For a company to stay in business it is ultimately necessary that the income it receives for its output exceeds its costs of production. Any rise in production costs which cannot be easily offset by productivity increases must therefore place upward pressure on prices of final output. This process has been termed cost push inflation. For genuine cost push inflation to occur these rises in costs must be autonomous ie, not caused by excessive demand/short supply of the factor of production, raw material etc whose price is rising. The question that is raised is why should costs rise in this fashion? Several possibilities can be identified.

(a)   Wage cost inflation. If wage rates rise irrespective of the state of demand for labour in general or that type of labour in particular, then cost push inflation may occur. An autonomous rise in wages may be related to:

- trade union power: trade unions or professional associations may have the ability to secure wage/salary increases irrespective of the demand for labour

- expectations: if groups of workers expect inflation to occur in the future this will be incorporated into the wage bargaining; this may produce a wage price spiral and, in effect, expectations have become part of the transmission process for inflation.

(b)   Import cost inflation. An autonomous rise in import prices may induce a process of cost push inflation. If the price of imported raw materials, components, capital goods rise then this raises production costs directly. If the price of imported consumer goods rises this will be an inflationary shock to the economy which may generate inflation via expectations and a wage price spiral. Two sources of rising import prices can be identified:

- a general rise in world prices or in the prices of significant products eg, the inflationary impact of the oil price rises of 1974 and 1979

- a depreciation of the currency: when sterling depreciates against other currencies, the sterling price of imports will rise. This is the main concern with using devaluation as a means of correcting a balance of payments deficit.

(c)   Taxation. It is possible that increases in indirect taxation will impart a cost push shock to the economy. A large rise in VAT (eg, when VAT was raised from 8% to 15% in 1980) will have a significant effect on a wide range of consumer prices. Whether this produces a process of inflation rather than a once for all price rise depends on the existence of a transmission mechanism. Clearly a wage price spiral based on expectations following a rise in indirect taxation must be considered a possibility.

Cost push inflation presents difficulties for governments because it is not clear what appropriate action could be taken. Until 1979 incomes policies were seen as a means of limiting wage cost push inflation but fell into disuse after that time. Part of the reason for this was that inflation was believed to be largely of a different sort: demand pull inflation.

6.3   Demand pull inflation

> **Definition**   Demand pull inflation is the result of excessive aggregate demand in the economy.

One of the problems of the notion of cost push inflation - especially of the wage push type - was to explain why costs should rise autonomously. What conferred market power on trade unions to secure wage increases? The implication was that trade unions were powerful when the demand for labour was high: in effect the principal cause of inflation was excess demand in the economy which pulled prices upwards.

The formal analysis of the process is the result of the work of the economist JM Keynes. The Keynesian model suggests that the opposite of unemployment is not full employment but inflation. Why and when would demand pull inflation occur? Keynesian economists argue that as the total demand for goods and services in the economy (aggregate monetary demand or AMD) rises it would produce a supply response so long as there was spare capacity (ie, some unemployment of resources) in the economy. However, once the space capacity had been used, further increases in demand would not produce increases in output; prices would rise instead. The probable mechanism would be:

- companies respond to demand for goods and services by attempting to increase output

- this could lead to excess demand for factors of production, especially labour

- excess demand for labour leads firms to bid up wage rates and for trade unions to exploit their market power.

Thus the apparent cause of inflation is a rise in costs, especially wage costs: the real cause is excessive aggregate demand in the economy.

The inflationary process may start before full employment is reached but will tend to become faster the closer to full employment is the level of demand. This may be illustrated by the aggregate demand and supply diagram.

Aggregate demand and supply

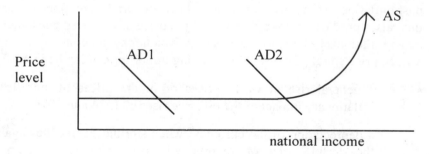

If the level of aggregate demand rises from AD1 to AD2 then the level of national income rises (and unemployment falls) but the level of prices also begins to rise.

The theory has two implications for the conduct of policy with respect to demand pull inflation:

- demand pull inflation could be prevented by using fiscal and monetary policy to restrain the level of aggregate monetary demand in the economy

- the price of preventing demand pull inflation would be higher unemployment.

This latter possibility appeared to be confirmed by the work of AW Phillips who discovered a strong statistical relationship between the level of unemployment and the rate of increase in money wage rates and hence in the rate of inflation.

The Phillips curve

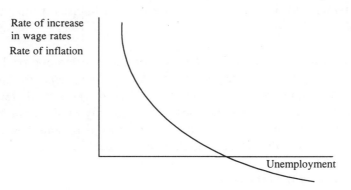

The Phillips curve relationship implied that there was a trade-off between inflation and unemployment: the pursuit of price stability might imply an unacceptable level of unemployment. The search for effective incomes policies in the 1960s and 1970s might be seen as an attempt to circumvent the Phillips curve relationship and to reduce the amount of inflation that would normally be implied by low levels of unemployment.

However, the very nature of the Phillips curve relationship came under serious doubt in the 1970s. This was reflected in:

- evidence that unemployment was rising simultaneously with rising inflation: something that could not happen in the original Phillips curve

- monetarist economic theory which claimed that the Phillips curve was, in fact, vertical and that the sole source of inflation was excessive expansion of the money supply.

6.4   Inflation and the money stock

Monetarist economists argue that inflation is a monetary phenomenon and is always the result of excessive demand in the economy. Cost push inflation cannot exist in a monetarist world unless an initial cost shock to the economy is transmitted through the economy by an increase in the money supply. The monetarist approach to explaining inflation and its relationship to unemployment has two main elements: the effect of an increase in money supply and the operation of the labour market.

Monetarists argue that the only motive for holding money is the transactions motive. If we assume that we start from a position of equilibrium in the money market then the supply of money will be equal to the amount that economic agents - households and companies - wish to hold. If there is now an increase in the supply of money, households and companies will have more money than they wish to hold: the result is that this extra money will be spent. This increase in demand will result in:

- some deterioration in the balance of payments since some of the increased expenditure will be on imported goods

- an increase in the price level: demand pull inflation.

This approach has its origins in the Quantity Theory of Money. This stated that:

$$MV = PT$$

where: M   is the stock of money
               V   is the velocity of circulation (the rate at which money can be used)
               P   is the price level
               T   is the number of transactions (ie, the level of output in the economy)

Monetarists argue that the velocity of circulation is stable and that the economy is normally at some full employment level; hence if M, the money stock, rises it must lead directly to a rise in P, the price level.

Clearly this is not necessarily at odds with the Keynesian approach. Keynesians economists also argued that, at full employment, excess demand will lead to inflation. However, monetarist economists have gone on to argue that this effect will be felt whatever the level of unemployment: in the long run increased aggregate demand leads only to higher inflation, not to some combination of increased output and higher inflation. The reason for this lies with the second element of the monetarist argument: the nature of the labour market.

6.5   Expectations and the labour market

For monetarists, the long run Phillips curve is vertical. This is the result of building in expectations of inflation into the model. It is argued that workers bargain for, and work for a given real wage not for a money wage and this changes the nature of the Phillips curve. Let us suppose that the level of unemployment is seen by governments as unacceptably high and they therefore adopt expansionary fiscal policy to reduce unemployment.

(a)   The initial effect is a reduction of unemployment as with the original Phillips curve. Money wages rise as a result and this encourages workers to take up the extra employment on offer.

(b)   However workers eventually recognise that the increase in money wages will produce inflation, that is they have expectations of inflation. This means that there will be no increase in the real wage rate even if money wage rates rise: workers who took up jobs when it appeared that money and real wages were rising now cease to do so and unemployment rises back to the original level but at a higher rate of inflation.

(c)   If governments persist in attempting to reduce unemployment below the original level, the effect is to continually boost the rate of inflation without raising real wage rates and hence without reducing unemployment.

Thus the 'expectations augmented Phillips curve' of monetarist theory is vertical at some 'natural' level of unemployment. This natural rate of unemployment is better seen as the non-accelerating inflation rate of unemployment (NAIRU): provided governments do not attempt to reduce unemployment below this level, inflation will be stable and not accelerating.

In the diagram below each Pe curve shows a different expectation of inflation and is short run only. Pc is the long run Phillips curve at the natural rate of unemployment. For example, if there is no inflation (Pe = 0) and the government, through its fiscal policy, tries to reduce unemployment to U_1, there will be excess demand in the labour market and wages will rise by (say) 5% which becomes price inflation of 5% and thus expectations of inflation become as shown by Pe = 5 and unemployment returns to the 'natural rate' but with inflation of 5%.

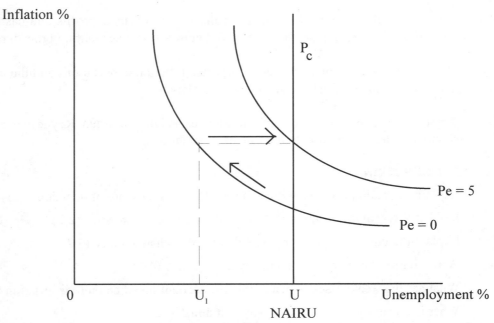

The monetarist approach therefore blames inflation on governments attempting to reduce unemployment below NAIRU and adopting expansionary fiscal policy involving the growth of the money supply. For monetarists, appropriate policy is to:

- use fiscal and monetary policy to reduce the growth and the money supply and to dampen inflationary expectations

- use supply side policies (tax incentives, reductions in unemployment support, retraining etc) to reduce the level of unemployment.

Much of government policy in the 1980s since 1979 has been based on the monetarist view of inflation and the experience has shown that, as with its Keynesian predecessor, the facts did not quite fit the theory: inflation fell in the mid 1980s despite rapid growth of the money supply. Nonetheless, we now know that we have to add the money supply and expectations to cost shocks and excess aggregate demand as possible causes of inflation.

[Conclusion]   Monetarist theory emphasises the crucial role of expectations and excessive growth in the money stock in the inflation process.

6.6   **Activity**

What do you expect will happen to the rate of inflation in the next year and why? How should business organisations react to such inflationary expectations?

7   **CHAPTER SUMMARY**

This chapter has considered the causes of inflation and the problems inflation may cause. It has emphasised:

(a)   The problems of measuring inflation using the conventional retail price index.

(b)   The domestic effects of inflation especially the impact on the distribution of income and the patterns of savings and investment.

(c)   The effects of inflation on international competitiveness and the rate of exchange for the currency.

(d)   The effects of inflation on companies: the impact on their profits and cash flow and the difficulties of assessing performance using conventional accounting procedures.

(e)   The extent to which interest rates incorporate inflation expectations and the use of indexing to overcome some of the consequences of inflation.

(f)   The debates over the causes of inflation especially between Keynesian and monetarist economists and in relation to the role of expectations.

8   SELF TEST QUESTIONS

8.1   Explain the main problems with using the RPI as a measure of inflation. (1.3)

8.2   In what ways might inflation distort the distribution of income? (2.3)

8.3   Explain the purchasing power parity theory of exchange rates. (3.2)

8.4   Will inflation raise or lower company cash flows? (4.1)

8.5   What are the weaknesses of historical cost accounting when there is inflation? (4.2)

8.6   What is meant by 'indexing' and why is it done? (5.3)

8.7   Explain the principal sources of cost push inflation. (6.2)

8.8   When is demand pull inflation most likely to occur? (6.3)

8.9   Explain the Phillips curve. (6.3)

8.10   Why are expectations important in the process of inflation? (6.5)

19 GOVERNMENT INTERVENTION IN INDUSTRIES AND MARKETS

INTRODUCTION & LEARNING OBJECTIVES

When you have studied this chapter you should be able to do the following:

- Identify the sources of market failure and explain the government approach to such problems

- Explain the ways in which government provides financial support for business

- Consider the case for 'green' policies and evaluate alternative green policies

- Explain what is meant by 'supply-side policy' and identify current supply side problems and policies.

1 COMPETITION POLICY

1.1 Barriers to competition and market failure

Definition Barriers to competition are those mechanisms which prevent existing or new firms from competing in a market.

The economist Pareto identified the conditions under which full economic efficiency ('Paretian optimality') would be achieved. Full economic efficiency he defined as the situation where no reallocation of resources could raise one person's or group's welfare without reducing that of others. The principal conditions for achieving this are:

- universal competition in all markets
- the absence of externalities
- perfect knowledge.

However, the real economy may display a range of problems that may prevent this fully efficient use of resources.

(a) There may be an absence of competition. Some markets are characterised by various degrees of market power whereby producers become price makers rather than price takers:

- oligopoly: markets dominated by a small number of large firms
- monopoly: markets dominated by single large firms.

(b) There may be externalities. Externalities are costs or benefits which occur in either the production or consumption process which are not borne or received by the producers or consumers themselves. These are not therefore taken into account when making production or consumption decisions. Pollution is an obvious example of an external cost.

(c) There may be a lack of information which prevents markets from operating efficiently: information may not be available to individuals or is costly to obtain. This may be of particular significance with respect to the quality and safety of consumer products. An example would be the recent disquiet about the selling of personal pension schemes.

Even if these imperfections did not exist, there remains the question of equity. There is no guarantee that an allocation of resources which maximises efficiency in a Paretian sense will also produce a distribution of income that is regarded as ideal or even acceptable. Markets may fail to produce equity even when they produce efficiency.

1.2   Monopoly and efficiency

Definition   Monopoly is where a firm has a sufficient share of a market to enable it to restrict output and raise prices.

The absence of competition is seen by all economists to be a source of economic inefficiency. This inefficiency has two components.

(a)   Allocative inefficiency. This occurs if firms are using resources to produce an output somewhere on their cost curve other than at lowest average cost. Economic theory predicts that firms with a degree of monopoly power will tend to restrict output and produce at less than optimum(ie, cost minimising) output.

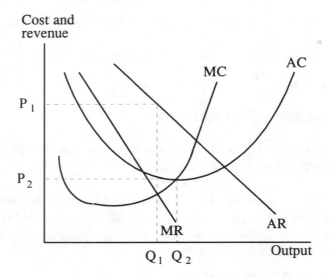

If we assume the firm is attempting to profit maximise, it will aim to produce where MC = MR ie, at Q_1 and Price P_1. This is less than the cost minimising output of Q_2 at Price P_2.

(b)   X-inefficiency. This occurs when the firm's costs are higher than they need be given the current state of knowledge, technology etc. This is seen to be the result of lack of competition which encourages a degree of managerial 'slack' in the organisation. Here the whole average cost curve is shifted upwards.

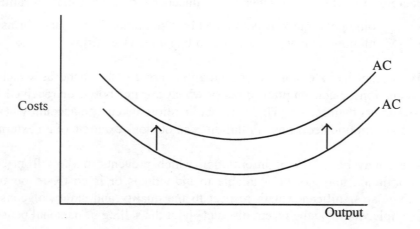

In addition to these arguments about efficiency, it may be that there are other disadvantages of firms having monopoly power:

- monopolies may be able to engage in price discrimination: charging different prices to different customers for the same good or service eg, peak and off peak pricing. This may act against the interests of customers

- disincentive to innovate: the absence of competition may reduce the incentive to develop new products or new production processes

- pricing practices: monopolies may adopt pricing practices to make it uneconomic for new firms to enter the industry (eg, 'limit pricing') thus reducing competition in the long run.

These potential problems of companies with monopoly power must be considered in the light of some possible advantages that may be associated with such firms.

(a)   Large firms may secure economies of scale. It is possible that there are significant economies of scale, reducing production costs, but that these require large firms and hence the number of firms in an industry is restricted. In this case the benefits of economies of scale may offset the allocative and X-inefficiencies involved.

(b)   The special case of natural monopolies. This is the case where the economies of scale in the provision of some basic infrastructure are so great that only one producer is feasible. This may be the case of the public utilities in energy and water.

(c)   Research and development: it may be that monopoly profits are both the reward for, and the source of finance for technological and organisational innovation. Thus some static welfare losses have to be accepted in order to ensure a dynamic and innovatory business sector.

Conclusion   Economic theory concludes that, other things being equal, economic welfare is maximised when markets are competitive.

1.3   Fair competition: regulation and public provision

The response to the problems associated with monopoly power can take a variety of forms. The first of these is public provision. This is where an economic activity is nationalised. The advantages of this are:

- unfair pricing practices and/or excessive prices can be eliminated
- cost advantages of economies of scale can be reaped.

Traditionally, public utilities have presented the most convincing case for nationalisation because they are natural monopolies. However, nationalised industries may have disadvantages, notably a greater potential for X-inefficiency. Moreover governments may be tempted to use them as a form of hidden taxation via their pricing policy. Recent UK policy has been to transfer productive assets back to the private sector via privatisation.

The alternative response is regulation.

There are two forms of regulation of business behaviour:

- self regulation
- government regulation.

Self regulation is common in many professions where the profession itself establishes codes of conduct and rules of behaviour (eg, the Law Society, the BMA). Self-regulation has also been used to cover certain financial activities: activity on the stock exchange is regulated by the Stock Exchange Council and the Securities and Investments Board regulates the behaviour of major financial intermediaries. This form of regulation has certain advantages, notably one of reducing the public cost of regulation. However in recent years doubts have grown about the effectiveness of such forms of self regulation: the failure to deal with insider dealing on the Stock Exchange and the problems associated with the sale of private pensions have highlighted these doubts.

The alternative is some form of public or legal regulation. The obvious example in the UK is the establishment of regulatory bodies for the privatised utilities such as OFTEL and OFGAS. These were established in recognition of the monopoly power of the privatised utilities and have a degree of power over both prices and services in these industries. This may be a more effective form of regulation but this too has its disadvantages:

- costs of regulation: these additional costs fall on both the taxpayer (the cost of running the regulatory body) and on the firms in the industry (cost of conforming to the regulations)

- possibility of 'regulatory capture': the regulatory body becomes dominated by the firms to be regulated and regulation becomes ineffective or even counter productive

- behavioural effects: regulation may produce changes in business behaviour in ways that were unintended or unexpected eg, the possibility that the enforcement of competition in the gas supply industry may lead to price rises for many customers.

These are real problems with the use of regulation. An alternative approach would be to prevent the growth of monopoly business power rather than attempt to manage them via regulation. This is the basis of competition policy in the UK.

1.4   Fair competition: the control of monopoly

Formal competition policy in the UK has centred upon two broad issues:

- monopolies and mergers
- restrictive practices.

The concern for monopolies is with firms which have a degree of monopoly power (defined as having more than 25% of the market for a good or service) or with mergers which may produce a new company with more than 25% of market share. The underlying presumption is that monopolies are likely to be allocatively inefficient and may act against the interest of customers.

The concern for restrictive practices is with trading practices of firms which may be deemed to be uncompetitive and act against the interests of consumers. To conduct public policy on competition there is both a legislative framework and an institutional framework.

(a)   The main elements of the legislative framework are:

- 1948 Monopolies and Restrictive Practices Act which set up the Monopolies Commission which could investigate and report on monopoly companies

- 1956 Restrictive Trade Practices Act by which all restrictive trade practices had to be registered with, and could be investigated by, the Restrictive Practices Court

- 1965 Monopolies and Mergers Act which allowed the Monopolies and Mergers Commission (MMC) to investigate mergers likely to create monopolies

- 1973 Fair Trading Act which set up the Office of Fair Trading (OFT) to oversee restrictive trade practices

- 1976 Restrictive Trade Practices Act which largely consolidated previous legislation

- 1976 Resale Prices Act which prohibited resale price maintenance

- 1980 Competition Act which empowers the OFT to investigate any anti-competitive activity and refer it, if necessary to the MMC.

(b)   This legislation has created an institutional framework, the main elements of which are indicated below:

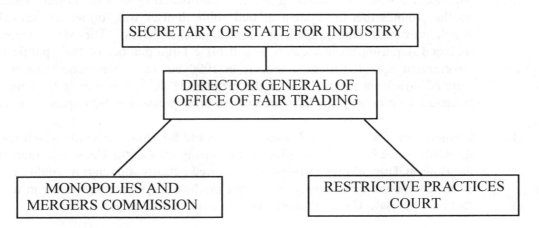

1.5   Monopolies and mergers: the work of the MMC

The Director General of fair trading can refer to the MMC any company which has at least 25% of a market for a good or service or a merger proposal likely to produce such an outcome. Its report is presented to the Secretary of State for Industry who may or may not act upon its recommendations.

The task of the MMC is to decide whether or not the monopoly is acting 'against the public interest'. The exact meaning of this is not specified in the legislation but is generally taken to mean activity against the interest of the consumer. The MMC recognises two types of monopoly:

- scale monopoly where a single firm has at least 25% of the market for a good or service

- complex monopoly where a group of firms collectively controlling at least 25% of a market behave as if they were a single monopoly.

Within this general framework the MMC recognises that a monopoly in itself is not necessarily against the public interest but it has tended to look particularly unfavourably on:

- entry barriers to new firms since this limits new competition
- vertical integration since this may lead to unfair competition for unintegrated firms
- aggressive competition designed to discourage new entrants.

After investigation, the MMC makes recommendations to the OFT. These may take a variety of forms from structural changes eg, the removal of entry barriers, to changes in behaviour eg, a requirement for price cuts. However, the decision to implement these recommendations rests with the Secretary of State for Industry.

Progressively, the MMC has become more concerned with mergers: the emphasis has shifted away from dealing with the consequences of monopoly power towards attempting to prevent its growth in the first place. The Director General of the OFT is empowered to refer to the MMC any merger which

- will create a monopoly firm with over 25% of the market, or
- involves the transfer/acquisition of more than £30m of assets.

In its report the MMC will make recommendations to the Secretary of State which may or may not be acted upon.

The work of the MMC can be illustrated through three examples:

(a)   Monopoly Power. The brewing industry, dominated by 6 large brewers was investigated, on the grounds that the system of tied public houses was formed of vertical integration which prevented fair competition from smaller brewers. The MMC recommendations included requiring these brewers to sell off a large number of their public houses. The government accepted these proposals in 1990 but the recommendations were gradually watered down until very little of the original MMC report was left. Some argued this reflected the power of the firms involved to bring pressure to bear upon the government.

(b)   Mergers. In 1985 Imperial Tobacco made a bid for United Biscuits which was referred to the MMC since it would have given the company 45% of the UK snacks market. However, the Hanson Trust bid for Imperial was allowed because although it would produce a much larger conglomerate company, it did not produce the monopoly power in a given market that the Imperial - United Biscuit merger would have done.

(c)   Public Sector Businesses. Since the 1980 Act, the MMC has had the power to make efficiency audits of public sector activities. Some 15 took place in the early 1980s with a wide range of recommendations largely related to increased efficiency: this may be seen as an attempt to reduce the degree of X-inefficiency in public monopoly firms.

It is difficult to evaluate the success of the MMC in encouraging fair competition and protecting consumer interests. Relatively few mergers now seem to be investigated by the MMC but mergers likely to create monopolies may have been discouraged by the possibility of MMC investigation. Also, the MMC is often perceived to be lacking in real power: the serious weakening of its recommendations in the case of brewing has been cited by some as evidence of this.

Conclusion   The MMC has large powers of investigation but this does not imply that intervention always results.

1.6   Restrictive practices: the work of the Restrictive Practices Court

There is a legal requirement for all companies to register restrictive practices with the Restrictive Practices Court. These include all agreements between companies relating to

- the prices of goods/services
- the conditions of sale of goods/services.

The obvious example would be a price fixing cartel arrangement.

The Director General of the OFT can decide whether an agreement should be considered by the Court: within the Court the agreement is deemed to be undesirable and therefore illegal, unless it can be shown otherwise. The onus is thus on the firms concerned to demonstrate that the agreement does not operate against the public interest. There are two elements to this process:

(a)   There are 8 so-called 'gateways' which would allow the companies to claim that the agreement should not be deemed illegal. For example they include the arguments that the agreement is needed to protect employment or to protect the safety of the public. If it is accepted by the Court that the agreement meets the requirements of one of the gateways it can be retained provided it meets the 'tailpiece'.

(b)   The 'tailpiece' requires that the demonstrated public benefits of the agreement outweigh any disadvantages to the public. Thus it is not sufficient to show that there is some public benefit to retain an agreement; companies have to show an overall benefit to the public.

An example of the work of the Court was the 1983 report on the ABTA agreement among travel agents. This agreement between travel agents and holiday tour operators limited price competition. This was outlawed by the Court since it led to higher prices. However the long term effect might be to lead to fewer firms and less short term stability in the market. However, the ABTA exclusive dealing arrangement between ABTA agents and ABTA tour operators was allowed to be retained since it maintained quality of service and protected customers from company failures.

As with the work of the MMC, it is difficult to evaluate the success of the Restrictive Practices Court. The bulk of the 5,000 or so agreements registered with the Court have either been voluntarily abandoned or deemed illegal by the Court. This would suggest a considerable success for the Court. There is however the possibility that many agreements have not been registered with the Court or have taken on a more informal character in order to avoid detection.

1.7   Competition policy in the European Union

Increased integration within the European Union (EU) has added a further dimension to competition policy in the UK. UK firms are now subject to EU law on competition and can be investigated by the European Commission. On the whole EU competition law is rather more restrictive than UK law. The Commission can investigate:

- unfair competition by any firm with a 'dominant position' in the market

- restrictive practices

- mergers where combined EU wide sales would exceed a certain level (about £175m).

Examples of recent EU competition policy affecting UK firms include:

- the pricing policy of Distillers which sold whisky at higher prices in France than in the UK and then restricted the ability of UK buyers to resell in France

- the membership of ICI in a cartel to fix the EU wide prices of polypropylene

- the payments to British Aerospace to encourage it to take-over the Rover Group.

As the degree of European integration increases, it is likely that EU law and procedures will steadily replace UK law as the basis for competition policy.

1.8   Activity

Identify an area of UK business which you believe should be considered by the MMC and outline your reasons.

2   DEREGULATION AND PRIVATISATION

2.1   Deregulation in the UK

Definition   Deregulation is the removal of any form of regulation which has the effect of restricting competition in the market.

During recent years there has been a movement in all advanced economies but especially in the UK and the USA to attempt to liberalise markets by the reduction or removal of state or other regulations which were seen to be inhibiting the competitive process. The reasons for doing so were much the same as those which had motivated the desire to control monopolies. It was believed that increased competition would:

- improve allocative efficiency since activity would shift to more efficient providers of the good or service

- reduce X-inefficiency since regulations would have protected some producers against the full rigours of competition.

Although there are economic dangers in unregulated competition such as potential threat to quality of provision and the danger of economic waste in the duplication of service, the prevailing government view has been that there are significant net benefits from deregulation.

Examples of deregulation include:

(a)   Bus and coach travel. There is now free entry into this industry in most parts of the UK. The result has been an increased number of firms and increased competition in the industry.

(b)   The removal of monopoly power in some professions eg,

- the supply of spectacles only by registered opticians

- the conduct of house conveyancing only by solicitors.

(c)   Compulsory competitive tendering (CCT) in the public sector. This requires that local authorities and health authorities have to contract out certain services previously supplied internally if a competitive bid is received from a private contractor.

(d)   Another area for deregulation in the UK has been labour markets where government intervention (eg, via Wage Councils) has been progressively reduced. The unwillingness of the UK government to sign up to the Social Chapter of the Maastricht Treaty can be seen as further evidence of a desire to reduce rather than increase labour market regulation.

(e)   **Deregulation of capital markets**

Since the early 1980s, international governments have tried to create a more efficient market place for capital instruments by repealing strict government rules and leaving markets to the control of market forces. The hope is that market discipline should replace the dead hand of government and encourage innovation in market practices. Uncompetitive practices have been swept away in the hope that ultimately all participants in the market should benefit.

Deregulation in UK capital markets

The influences of deregulation in capital markets in the UK can be looked at separately in:

- the stock market
- the gilts market
- banks and building societies.

The London Stock Exchange's 'Big Bang' of October 1986 swept in an enormous raft of deregulatory measures. Fixed commissions were abandoned, restrictions on ownership of stock exchange firms were lifted, the old distinction between jobbers and brokers was blurred and anyone could see the latest share prices by putting a computer screen on their desk.

Statutory regulation of the new stock exchange system centred around the Financial Services Act 1986 in which the government devolved direct responsibility to the Securities and Investments Board (SIB) to oversee the new system and ensure that the London Stock Exchange acted responsibly as a Recognised Investment Exchange (RIE).

Big Bang also introduced a new system for trading gilt-edged securities (gilts ie, UK government bonds), largely modelled on the United States Treasury bond market. The old single-capacity system involved brokers (acting for their client) approaching jobbers on the floor of the Stock Exchange and seeking the best prices to satisfy their client's order. However by 1985 there were only eight jobbing firms dealing in gilts so that the liquidity of the market could not be assured. By introducing dual-capacity screen-based trading the number of Gilt-edged market-makers (GEMMs) has been substantially increased and transparency introduced into the trading market.

The Banking Act 1987 and Building Societies Act 1986 introduced new statutory frameworks for banks and building societies respectively, giving each far greater commercial freedoms. For example building societies were permitted for the first time to make unsecured loans and to own and develop land. This opened up the possibility of their incorporation, a route started by Abbey National and now being followed by most of the large building societies.

Deregulation in the 1990s

Although the main deregulatory provisions took place in the late 1980s, the continuing Conservative UK governments of the 1990s have tried to continue the push for deregulation. Building societies now offer almost an identical range of services to banks, and commissions charged on the London Stock Exchange and gilts market remain low. However the effectiveness of the supervisory regime must be questioned in the light of developments such as the failure of Barings Bank.

| Conclusion | Deregulation has increased competition in many activities and has led to structural change in the financial sector. |

2.2   Privatisation

| Definition | Privatisation is the process of transferring the ownership of productive assets from the public sector to the private sector. |

In the last decade the UK government has undertaken an extensive programme of privatisation. The major privatisations have been of the public utilities: gas, water, electricity and telephones. However others have been in other areas of activity such as British Airways, the Rover Group and Cable and Wireless. This policy has been the subject of much debate especially concerning the privatisation of the utilities.

The advantages of privatisation are that:

(a)   If the privatisation leads to increased competition this should encourage better services and lower prices ie, improved allocative efficiency. The impact of competition on BT may be cited as an example of this.

(b)   The transfer of ownership and control from the state to shareholders may provide more incentive for the companies to become more efficient. Thus the problem of X-inefficiency would be reduced.

(c)   Greater dynamism: increased commercial freedom may encourage the companies to show more innovation than they would have done in the public sector.

(d)   Commercial pressures will force the companies to become more responsive to the interests of consumers and less dominated by the interests of producer groups (eg, the labour force).

(e)   Privatisation provides an easy source of public finance as an alternative to borrowing or extra taxation.

Although these advantages appear to be substantial, the privatisation programme, especially of the public utilities, has produced considerable criticism. The main disadvantages of the policy appear to be:

(a)   The absence of any real pressure to become more efficient unless privatisation increases competition. While increased competition is possible in some areas, in others eg, provision of water services, it is clearly not. Hence public monopolies may have become private monopolies.

(b)   The profit motive may lead companies to reduce the quality of service especially in less profitable areas. Thus a privatised British Rail may be less willing to maintain loss making rural lines even if a social need for them exists.

(c)   Possible loss of the benefits of economies of scale in the pursuit of competition. Thus British Gas has claimed that the requirement for increased competition in the industry will raise prices for some customers.

The evidence on the effectiveness of the privatisation policy is mixed. In some areas real prices have been reduced for many services and there does seem to be a wider range of services and products available. On the other hand, recent evidence suggests that labour productivity rose faster over the 1980s in the public sector industries than in private sector industries thus denying the importance of the profit motives. By the mid 1990s privatisation had become less popular: this may have been a reaction to the very large increases in the financial rewards for directors in these industries and a fear that privatised concerns would ignore social needs and priorities. The latter played an important role in the defeat in Parliament in 1994 of the government's plan to privatise the Post Office.

| Conclusion | The effectiveness of privatisation depends heavily on whether or not genuine competition is created.

2.3   Activity

Use the arguments for and against privatisation to evaluate the case for privatising British Rail.

3   OFFICIAL AID SCHEMES

3.1   Introduction

UK governments have for many years undertaken to provide financial support for firms in the UK. This has been done on the belief that there would be benefits to the economy as a whole and this justifies the use of public funds. The aid provided has generally been part of a wider approach to supporting industry and commerce and has fallen into one of two broad categories:

•   as a part of regional policy

•   as a part of policy designed to help particular types of firms eg, small businesses.

The amount of this assistance is however declining. This partly reflects a decline in the belief in the value of regional policy; the government has come to rely more and more on market processes to deal with regional economic problems. However, it is also partly the result of the increasing impact of European Union competition policy which is progressively limiting the financial aid that national governments, as opposed to EU bodies, can give to private companies.

3.2 Regional assistance to companies

Definition Assisted Areas are those parts of the UK with specified economic problems and hence eligible for government financial assistance for companies within them.

The two main sources of support for companies in the Assisted Areas of the UK are:

(a) Regional Selective Assistance. These are grants that can be made on a selective basis to companies locating or expanding within Assisted Areas. They can be used to contribute to the costs of capital investment or training. They have been used to encourage inward investment from overseas companies especially Japanese manufacturing firms.

(b) The European Regional Development Fund (ERDF). This provides funds from the EU budget to be allocated to the poorer regions of the EU to support investment, especially infrastructure projects. The funds are allocated directly to the national governments concerned.

The funding on a regional basis has tended to decline in recent years. There is the criticism that ERDF funding, although intended to be additional to national funding, has often merely replaced that funding leading to little net increase in the total funding.

3.3 Other assistance

Other assistance to companies in the UK has tended to reflect a perception that some companies especially small ones, may have special problems which require a governmental response. This is reflected in some of the forms that assistance is given:

(a) The Loan Guarantee Scheme (1981) helps small businesses to obtain loans from banks without the normal security that banks would require.

(b) The Enterprise Investment Scheme (1994) encourages investment in the shares of unquoted companies by providing tax relief for the individual purchasing the shares up to a specified limit.

(c) Venture Capital Trusts (1993) provide tax relief on dividends and capital gains in investment trusts which devote a large proportion of their investments to small and unquoted companies.

These forms of assistance show a belief that the UK financial system is a poor provider of funds for small businesses. This has been a persistent complaint from small businesses and a long standing criticism of UK capital markets. The main weakness of this policy is that the tax relief measures merely subsidise activities that might well have taken place anyway. Moreover, financial flows may be distorted by tax relief away from areas where the return is greatest towards areas with lower returns but where tax relief is available.

Conclusion Official assistance schemes demonstrate a belief that market forces do not always function efficiently in the financing of companies.

4   'GREEN' POLICIES: THE PROBLEM OF EXTERNALITIES

4.1   Externalities

Definition   Externalities are costs (benefits) which are not paid (received) by the producers or consumers of the product but by other members of society.

One of the conditions under which a Pareto optimal allocation of resources would occur was the absence of externalities. In reality, externalities do exist and take two forms:

(a)   External social costs. These are costs which are not paid by those involved in the production or consumption of a good but are inflicted on society as a whole. These may occur in either

- production: an example would be river pollution from various manufacturing processes

- consumption: an example would be motor vehicle emissions causing air pollution and health hazards.

(b)   External social benefits. These are economic benefits which do not accrue to the producer or consumer of the good but are received by society as a whole. These may be in either

- production: an example would be when a company trains employees who subsequently move to other companies

- consumption: an example would be education where the recipient becomes more productive but not all of this is reflected in higher salary.

Thus the total cost of producing goods is the resource costs incurred by the producer (private cost) plus external costs: this total is referred to as social cost (ie, the total cost to society as a whole). The total benefit of a good or service is the utility derived by the consumer of that good (private benefit) plus any external benefit. This total is called social benefit.

Conclusion   Not all costs and benefits are incurred/enjoyed by the private producers or consumers.

4.2   Externalities and resource allocation

If external costs and benefits exist in the production or consumption process and if they are large in relation to private costs and benefits, the price system may be a poor mechanism for the allocation of resources. This is because private producers and consumers ignore (and indeed may be unaware of) the external effects of their activities:

- supply reflects the private costs of production

- demand reflects the private utility gained from consumption.

Thus the price system, in which prices are determined by the interaction of supply and demand and which determines the allocation of resources, may lead to a misallocation of resources.

This can be demonstrated using conventional demand and supply analysis. In this we will assume that there are external costs which raise the social cost of production above the private cost. Since the supply reflects cost, it would be different if these external costs were internalised into the supplier's costs.

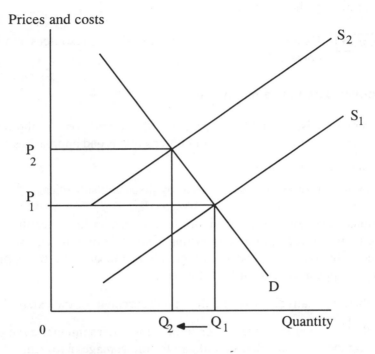

Thus in a market system, the quantity demanded and supplied would be Q_1 at a price P_1. If external costs were taken into account, the relevant supply curve would be S_2 rather than S_1 and the quantity produced and sold would fall to Q_2 and the market price would rise to P_2.

The general conclusions of this analysis are:

- where social cost exceeds private cost the price system will lead to output and consumption to be greater than is economically desirable

- where social benefit exceeds private benefit the price system will lead to output and consumption to be lower than is economically desirable.

These difficulties may affect a whole range of goods and services. However, there may be extreme cases where the production or consumption of goods produces very large externalities.

(a)   Public goods. This is where the external benefits are so large that private producers are unable to capture those benefits in terms of prices charged to the beneficiaries, for example law and order, street lighting.

(b)   Merit goods. This is where although there is a large private benefit there are also large benefits to society as a whole of which the consumer is largely unaware and therefore disregards. In this case there would be serious under consumption of the good or service. Education is normally cited as the chief example of a merit good.

(c)   Pollution. A major and growing concern is over the effects of production and consumption on the environment especially the issue of air pollution related to the use of motor vehicles. It is now recognised that vehicle pollution is a major health hazard and hence the consumption process involves large external costs.

These problems raise the issue of how governments should respond. Most governments have taken the view that they alone can effectively provide public goods and these are therefore provided in the public sector and financed by taxation. In the case of merit goods governments have taken a similar approach with much provision in the public sector, mainly in the areas of education and health.

This leaves the question of externalities which affect the environment: the issue of 'green' policies and the form they should take.

| Conclusion | Externalities lead to a misallocation of resources and imply the need for policies to correct this.

4.3   Green policies and the environment

If governments wish to tackle the problem of external costs in the form of environmental damage arising from production or consumption it has two broad approaches it can take:

- the use of regulations

- modification of the price system by taxes and subsidies.

Regulations have long been used in certain areas where health and safety are concerned, for example there are regulations concerning vehicle emissions and waste disposal by manufacturing companies. In some circumstances regulations appear to be the appropriate form of intervention. Regulations appear to be most useful where:

- there is relatively easy and direct measurement of the external cost involved

- the intention is to prevent or limit some environmental damage rather than merely wishing that those responsible should pay for the damage involved.

Regulations clearly impose cost upon the companies involved who are required to find alternative ways of waste disposal or to adopt different and presumably more costly production techniques. This is acceptable given the reality of external cost. However, there is an additional administrative cost in policing the regulations and this is the main drawback of this approach.

The alternative approach is to work through the price mechanism via taxes and subsidies.

(a)   Subsidies might be used to encourage the use of production techniques or forms of consumption that are less damaging to the environment. Examples include:

- subsidies given to householders for house insulation thus reducing the need to produce energy

- subsidies for public transport to encourage its use rather than private motor vehicles.

However, in many cases subsidies may be inappropriate: subsidising companies to replace polluting technology with more environmentally friendly technology raises the income of the producers and may reduce prices and hence encourage the consumption of a good which has serious external costs.

A better approach would be on the principle that the 'polluter should pay'. Thus indirect taxes could be used to discourage the consumption and production of goods with large external costs. This would have the effect of shifting the supply curve upwards and to the left, raising the price to the consumer. As with any indirect tax, this has two effects:

- there is a price rise which discourages consumption

- not all of the tax can be passed on to customers; thus some of the burden is borne by the producer whose profits fall and hence production is discouraged.

It is likely that such policies will become more and more common as concern for the environment increases. The UK already has a differential tax on leaded and unleaded petrol and the government has taken the decision to use taxes to raise the real price of petrol each year. There is also the continuing debate in the EU over the possible introduction of a wider 'carbon tax'.

Conclusion   Taxes appear to be the most appropriate response to the problem of pollution and such policies will become more common.

4.4   Activity

What combination of policies could the government use to reduce pollution from motor vehicle use?

5   SUPPLY SIDE POLICY

5.1   The nature of supply-side policy

Definition   Supply-side policies are concerned with raising the capacity of the economy to respond to increased demand with increased output.

Until relatively recently emphasis within macroeconomic policy was on managing the level of total demand for goods and services - aggregate monetary demand. However in recent years there has been a shift in both economics and in government policy towards what is known as supply side policy. This has been the result of:

(a)   The experience of inflation in market economies which could be explained in terms of increasing demand running into supply constraints which leads to rising prices rather than rising output.

(b)   The argument that in the long run, the level of output in an economy and the standard of living are a function of the supply capacity and characteristics of the economy.

(c)   The claim that government intervention in the economy has weakened its ability and incentive to respond to demand with increasing supply. In effect, regulation has made the economy less dynamic.

(d)   The need to compete with dynamic and low cost producers of manufactured goods especially in South East Asia requires that the economy become more cost conscious and more flexible in response to competitive challenges.

If supply side policies were successful, they would change the nature of the aggregate supply curve which shows how responsive is the economy as a whole to an increase in demand. Thus the aggregate supply curve might be shifted out to the right or made more elastic. In either case the result is that the economy can

- run at the same level of AMD but with a lower price level
- run at a higher level of AMD with the same price level.

This is illustrated below:

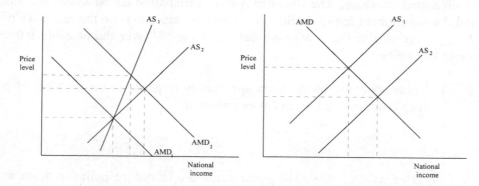

In the first diagram the aggregate supply curve has become more elastic and hence the shift from AMD_1 to AMD_2 produces a smaller price rise than would have been the case. In the second diagram the aggregate supply curve has shifted to AS_2 thus reducing the price level.

5.2   The forms of supply side policy

In recent years the UK government has developed a range of supply side policies to deal with a perceived set of problems. The most important of these have been:

- the impact of government regulations on supply
- the incentive implications of the tax system
- the operation of labour markets
- the quality of the labour force.

(a)   Concern for the impact of regulations on the supply capacity and responsiveness of the economy have led to the policy of deregulation. This was discussed in detail earlier.

(b)   Government policy on the structure of taxation has reflected the implications of the Laffer curve. This suggests that if taxes rise above a certain level the disincentive effects are so strong that total tax revenue falls. This is discussed in detail in an earlier chapter.

(c)   Much of recent government supply side policy has concentrated on the operation of the labour market. It was argued that the labour market did not function as a proper market and hence wages were inflexible because of:

- the impact of trade unions which limited wage flexibility in a downwards direction

- employment protection legislation which discouraged employers from taking on employees in the first place

- unemployment benefit which limited workers' willingness to accept employment at lower wage rates in periods of unemployment.

Attempts to deal with these difficulties have included the reform of industrial relations and a reduction in the powers of trade unions, the reduction in employment protection and a reduction in unemployment pay relative to average earnings. Those in favour of this approach claim that the result is a more flexible labour market and the creation of additional employment. The critics point to the deterioration in job security and the growth of part time employment at the expense of full time employment.

(d)   Government policy has also been directed at attempting to improve the quality of the labour force. The need to compete internationally requires lower labour cost: this may be achieved by either:

- reducing wage rates, or
- increasing labour productivity.

Education and training are seen as the keys to long term increase in labour productivity. Many recent policies may be interpreted as attempts to meet the education and skills requirements of the labour force:

- introduction of a national curriculum in schools
- shift towards vocational education
- the development of training schemes for the unemployed
- the expansion of higher education.

The problem is that these are very expensive in terms of the use of current resources and the success or otherwise of the policy is not evident except after a long period of time.

| Conclusion | Supply side policies are directed at improving the long term supply capacity of the economy: their success is therefore difficult to judge in the short run. |

5.3   Activity

From your own experience, identify the main supply side constraints on your company.

6   CHAPTER SUMMARY

This chapter has considered ways in which the government might manage the economic activity in the economy in ways other than through the management of aggregate demand. The emphasis has been on:

(a)   Government policy towards monopoly and restrictive practices and the form that intervention has taken.

(b)   The policies of deregulation and privatisation and possible effects that these have.

(c)   The various systems of financial assistance to firms especially on a regional basis or for small companies.

(d)   The need for governments to respond to externalities in order to improve resource allocation and the form that such policies could take with special emphasis on environmental or 'green' issues.

(e)   Supply-side policies designed to improve the ability of the economy to respond to increases in demand and the particular areas of the economy where such policies might be most usefully directed.

7   SELF TEST QUESTIONS

7.1   Explain the economic rationale for a policy of encouraging competition. (1.1, 1.2)

7.2   What are the principal ways in which the government can discourage the misuse of monopoly power? (1.3 - 1.6)

7.3   Explain the arguments in favour of a policy of deregulation. (2.1)

7.4   Outline the advantages and disadvantages of privatising public utilities. (2.2)

7.5   Describe the principal sources of financial assistance available to companies in the UK. (3.2, 3.3)

7.6   Explain, with examples, what is meant by the term 'externalities'. (4.1)

7.7   How might governments attempt to reduce the level of pollution caused by manufacturing firms? (4.3)

7.8   Explain what is meant by 'supply-side policy'. (5.1)

7.9   What are the main problems to which recent UK supply-side policy has been directed? (5.2)

20 THE NATURE AND SCOPE OF FINANCIAL MANAGEMENT

INTRODUCTION & LEARNING OBJECTIVES

Financial management is concerned with managing a company's finances, ie

- setting financial objectives
- planning and acquiring the optimum finance to meet those objectives
- seeing that fixed and working capital are effectively managed.

This chapter starts by examining the objectives of organisations, whether large and publicly owned, or small and owned by its managers. A company's objective is usually assumed to be to maximise the wealth of its shareholders, but you will see that there are other objectives to be satisficed at the same time. Most of the remainder of the chapter is concerned with ratio analysis as a method of measuring corporate financial performance.

When you have studied this chapter you should be able to do the following:

- Distinguish between maximising and satisficing objectives.

- Explain the interests of the various stakeholders in a company.

- Discuss the objectives of small companies and not-for-profit organisations.

- Calculate relevant ratios from a set of accounts and interpret their values.

- Discuss the concept of environmental reporting.

---

1   BUSINESS MOTIVATION

1.1   Introduction

Unfortunately there are no clear-cut answers to the question of appropriate company objectives. Many academic papers have been written over the years discussing the objectives of organisations, but none has come anywhere near defining a single all-embracing corporate objective.

1.2   Maximising and satisficing

The concept of **maximising** involves the seeking of the best possible outcome. On the other hand, **satisficing** involves finding a merely adequate outcome.

Thus, management could on the one hand, constantly seek the maximum level of profitability, even though this might involve exposure to risk and much higher management workloads. On the other hand, management might decide to hold profits at a satisfactory level, avoiding risky ventures and reducing workloads.

Within a company, management will seek to maximise the return to some groups (eg, shareholders) and satisfy the requirements of other groups (eg, employees). The discussion about objectives is really about which group's returns management is trying to maximise.

The issue is clouded by the fact that the management may itself be unclear about the difference between maximising and satisficing. Thus management may believe that it is, say, maximising shareholder returns, when in fact it has reduced effort and accepted a merely satisfactory level of shareholder return.

Nevertheless, the objectives, if not the applications of maximising as compared with satisficing should be clear.

1.3   Maximising whose returns?

The question is whose returns should be maximised rather than satisficed. The alternatives are examined below:

(a)   **The community at large**

Laudable, but hardly practical as an objective for the management of a company. There are also problems of measurement - what are returns to the community at large?

(b)   **Company employees**

Obviously, many trade unionists would like to see their members as the beneficiaries from any surplus the company creates. Certainly, there is no measurement problem: returns = wages or salaries. However, maximising the returns to employees does assume that risk finance can be raised purely on the basis of satisficing.

(c)   **Equity investors (ordinary shareholders)**

Within any economic system, the equity investors provide the risk finance. In the UK, it is usually ordinary shareholders, or sometimes the government. There is a very strong argument for maximising the wealth of equity investors. In order to attract funds, the company has to compete with other risk-free investment opportunities eg, government securities. The attraction is the accrual of any surplus to the equity investors. In effect, this is the risk premium which is essential for the allocation of resources to relatively risky investments in companies.

Although most financial management theory is developed subject to the assumed objective of maximising shareholder wealth it is important to realise that in the real world companies may be working toward other objectives.

1.4   Objectives of other parties

We have already noted that other parties with interests in the organisation (eg, employees, the community at large, creditors, customers etc,) have objectives that differ from those of the shareholders. As the objectives of these other parties are likely to conflict with those of the shareholders it will be impossible to maximise shareholder wealth and satisfy the objectives of other parties **at the same time.** In this situation the firm will face **multiple, conflicting objectives,** and **satisficing** of interested parties' objectives becomes the only practical approach for management. If this strategy is adopted then the firm will seek to earn a satisfactory return for its shareholders while at the same time (for example) paying reasonable wages to satisfy employees and being a 'good citizen' by not polluting the environment through effluent or smoke of the community in which it operates for example.

1.5   Managerial objectives

Neither should we forget that the managers of the firm will have their own objectives which could conflict with those of the shareholders and other interested parties. For example, managers could be interested in maximising the sales revenue of the firm or the number of employees so as to increase their own prestige and improve their career prospects.   Alternatively they could be interested in maximising their short-term financial return by increasing salaries or managerial 'perks'. It is also important to note that different groups of managers may be following differing objectives.   Marketing management may be interested in maximising sales revenue, whilst production managers may be more interested in developing the technological side of the firm as far as possible.

Although the firm is owned by the shareholders the day-to-day control is in the hands of the managers (the **divorce of ownership and control)** and they are in an ideal position to follow their own objectives at the expense of other parties.   Whilst in theory shareholders can replace the management of a company by voting out the directors at the AGM, in practice the fragmented nature of shareholdings makes this unlikely.

Specific examples of the conflicts of interest that might occur between managers and shareholders include:

(a)   **Take-overs**

Victim company managers often devote large amounts of time and money to 'defend' their companies against take-over. However, research has shown that shareholders in companies that are successfully taken over often earn large financial returns.   On the other hand managers of companies that are taken over frequently lose their jobs. This is a common example of the conflict of interest between the two groups.

(b)   **Time horizon**

Managers know that their performance is usually judged on their short-term achievements, shareholder wealth on the other hand is affected by the long-term performance of the firm. Managers can frequently be observed to be taking a short-term view of the firm which is in their own best interest but not in that of the shareholders.

(c)   **Risk**

Shareholders appraise risks by looking at the overall risk of their investment in a wide range of shares. They do not have 'all their eggs in one basket' and can afford a more aggressive attitude toward risk-taking than managers whose career prospects and short-term financial remuneration depend on the success of their individual firm.

(d)   **Gearing**

As managers are likely to be more cautious over risk than shareholders they might wish to adopt lower levels of financial gearing than would be optimal for the shareholders.

1.6   Non-financial objectives

The influence of the various parties with interests in the firm results in firms adopting many non-financial objectives, eg:

(a)   growth
(b)   diversification
(c)   survival
(d)   maintaining a contented workforce
(e)   becoming research and development leaders
(f)   providing top quality service to customers
(g)   maintaining respect for the environment.

Some of these objectives may be viewed as specific to individual parties (eg, engineering managers may stress research and development), whereas others may be seen as straight surrogates for profit, and thus shareholder wealth (eg, customer service). Finally areas such as respect for the environment may be social constraints rather than objectives.

Conclusion	In the real world organisations undoubtedly follow objectives other than the maximisation of shareholder wealth. The return to equity holders will be an important consideration in financial decisions but it is unlikely to be the only one.

It is important, however, not to overplay the above conflicts. Most managers know that if they let the shareholders down share prices will fall and this could result in difficulty in raising further finance, unwanted take-over bids and the end of managerial careers. Also the increasing concentration of shares in the hands of institutional investors such as insurance companies and pension funds means that the divorce of ownership and control is far from complete. Institutional investors, because of their large shareholdings, are considered to hold great potential power over company management. Actions of institutions, particularly in times of take-over bids, can determine the future of the firm and their objectives must be carefully considered by managers.

A compromise view of corporate objectives would be that for a listed company shareholder wealth will be the paramount objective but it will be tempered by the influences and objectives of other parties.

1.7   The influence of 'green' policies

In recent years the strength of the environmental lobby in society has grown enormously, so that no company today can carry on its business without having regard to the effects of its activities on the environment. These effects go much wider than simply considering the effects of pollution and effluents on the local community. Companies must now consider

(a)   their recycling of consumable outputs. For example, letters and price lists can be printed on recycled paper, and components from obsolete/scrapped products can be extracted to be used in new products.

(b)   energy usage. Many offices are kept unnecessarily hot in the UK regardless of the temperature outside. Energy usage can be reduced by turning thermostats down, insulating ceilings, etc and money will be saved at the same time as prolonging non-renewable energy resources.

(c)   their attitude to employees working at home. Huge amounts of time and energy are wasted in employees driving to work each day and then driving home. Modern technology permits many jobs to be carried out at home without the company having to pay for a huge head office.

You should appreciate from the above examples that there is much more benefit to companies from 'going green' than simply earning a better image for the company from society, leading to happier customers. The green initiatives can save money at the same time and lead to higher profits and enhanced shareholder wealth.

1.8   Corporate social responsibility

Some writers use the term corporate social responsibility to describe the duties that a company owes to each of the stakeholders involved in its business. These responsibilities can be summarised as follows

Stakeholder	*Responsibility*
Shareholders	Pay dividends
	Seek to enhance the share price
	Hold AGMs etc to comply with company law
Loan creditors	Pay interest on time
	Return principal as agreed
	Avoid excessive risk
Employees	Comply with health and safety obligations
	Pay wages
	Involvement in the decision-making process
Customers	Meeting quality requirements
	Honest dealings
Suppliers	Paying on time
	Not abusing large purchasing power
The public	Green concerns
	Not abusing monopoly status (especially relevant to newly privatised utilities)
The government	Paying taxes on time
	Complying with all laws scrupulously

Note that the term 'stakeholder' is much wider than the shareholders in a company. Anyone who is directly affected by the activities of a company is called a stakeholder in that company.

2   BUSINESS MOTIVATION: PROFIT-MAKING AND NOT-FOR-PROFIT ORGANISATIONS

2.1   Objectives of small firms

Most of the above discussion of objectives centres around large stock market listed companies. Unlisted companies will differ in two major ways:

(a)   Their owners will often be their managers and hence many of the agency problems referred to above will not apply.

(b)   As they are not listed on the stock market the value of shareholder wealth is not directly observable by reference to share prices. It is not unreasonable to assume, however, that the objective of the owners would be the maximisation of owners' wealth (tempered perhaps by the desire to remain independent).

2.2   Financial objectives in the public sector

This category of organisation includes such bodies as nationalised industries and local government organisations. They represent a significant part of the UK economy. The major problem here lies in obtaining a measurable objective.

For a stock market listed company we can take the maximisation of shareholder wealth as a working objective and know that the achievement of this objective can be monitored with reference to share price and dividend payments. For a public corporation the situation is more complex. The two questions to be answered are:

(a)   in whose interests are they run? and
(b)   what are the objectives of the interested parties?

Presumably such organisations are run in the interests of society as a whole and therefore we should seek to attain the position where the gap between the benefits they provide to society and the costs of their operation is the widest (in positive terms). The cost is relatively easily measured in accounting terms. However, many of the benefits are intangible. The benefits of such bodies as the National Health Service or Local Education Authorities are almost impossible to quantify.

Economists have tried to evaluate many public sector investments through the use of cost benefit analysis, with varying degrees of success: however, problems are usually encountered in evaluating all the benefits. Value for money audits are conducted in the public sector but these concentrate on monetary costs rather than benefits.

Because of the problem of quantifying the non-monetary objectives of such organisations most public bodies operate under government (and hence electorally) determined objectives such as obtaining a given accounting rate of return, cash limits, meeting budget, or breaking even in the long run.

Finally a word of caution. Although it is true that certain financial management techniques are transferable from the private to the public sector, care must be taken in using their results. For example, it is unlikely that NHS hip replacement operations would show a good rate of return in accounting terms, but we must appreciate that the benefits of such operations are other than purely financial.

2.3   The search for value for money

Value for money (VFM) is a notoriously elusive concept and yet it is assumed that everyone recognises it when they see it. The term is frequently bandied about but rarely defined. VFM can simply be described as 'getting the best possible combination of services from the least resources' ie, to maximise the benefits available at the lowest cost to the tax-payer. It is generally taken to mean the pursuit of economy, efficiency and effectiveness.

What do the words 'economy', 'effectiveness' and 'efficiency' mean?

A diagram helps to explain

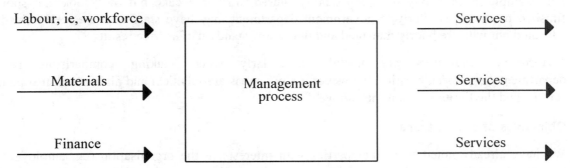

'Economy' is a measure of inputs to achieve a certain service or level of service.

'Effectiveness' is a measure of outputs ie, services/facilities.

'Efficiency' is the optimum of economy and effectiveness ie, the measure of outputs over inputs.

The three terms can be defined as follows:

Definition   **Economy** is the terms and conditions under which the authority acquires human and material resources. An economical operation acquires resources of the appropriate quality and provides a service to the appropriate standard at the lowest cost.

Definition   **Effectiveness** is the extent to which a programme achieves its established goals or other intended effects.

> **Definition** **Efficiency** is the relationship between the goods or services produced and the resources used to produce them. An efficient operation produces the maximum output for any given set of resource inputs; or, it has minimum inputs for any given quantity and quality of services provided.

The three 'E's' are the fundamental prerequisites of achieving VFM. Their importance cannot be over-emphasised, so much so that external auditors in some parts of the public sector ie, local government, are now charged with the responsibility of ensuring that bodies have made adequate arrangements for securing economy, effectiveness and efficiency in the use of public funds.

The problem of accurately measuring VFM cannot be fully resolved in the public sector. Unlike the private sector, there is no profit yardstick against which to measure success; and, in most areas of public service provision, no commercial pressure to respond to. Certain indicators have been developed, the following being a few typical examples:

(a)   Cost in providing a certain service per unit (per week/per '000 population/per mile, etc)

eg, cost of providing secondary education per '000 population, or operating expenses per train mile.

(b)   Service provided per unit (per week/per '000 population etc)

eg, home help hours per '000 population.

(c)   Inputs compared to outputs

eg, administrative costs per metre of steel produced

(d)   Other

eg, percentage of trains cancelled compared to total timetable, complaints received.

Care must be taken, however, not to derive false meanings from limited data. Qualitative judgements about services provided must not be attempted from input information, other factors must be considered.

For example, a chef may have top quality ingredients for a cake but over-cook and spoil the finished product. Similarly, a government department may have staff who are well-trained and educated but who are poorly managed and thus a low standard of service results.

Performance indicators are useful, particularly when making comparisons between departments/regions/authorities. However, no two areas are identical and allowance must be made for this and the limitations outlined above.

2.4   Objectives of other parties

We have already noted that other parties with interests in the organisation (eg, employees, the community at large, creditors and customers) have objectives that differ from those of the shareholders. As the objectives of these other parties are likely to conflict with those of the shareholders it will be impossible to maximise shareholder wealth and satisfy the objectives of other parties *at the same time*. In this situation the firm will face *multiple, conflicting objectives,* and *satisficing* of interested parties' objectives becomes the only practical approach for management. If this strategy is adopted then the firm will seek to earn a satisfactory return for its shareholders while at the same time (for example) paying reasonable wages and being a 'good citizen' of the community in which it operates.

2.5   The distinction between long and short-term objectives

Note the example above where managers' short-term objectives could be different from shareholders' long-term objectives.   The assumed objective of financial managers is the maximisation of long-term shareholder value but it would be foolish to ignore short-term influences. The minimum short-term objective that managers seek would be stability: risks would be eliminated wherever possible and large movements in the share price avoided.

If a company encounters a recession it may find that it starts to make losses and may have to reassess its objectives; the long-term objective continues to be to report a steady growth in earnings per share but the short-term objective is simply to survive.

Some writers concentrate on the alleged incompatibility of short-term and long-term objectives, for example highlighting cases where companies have reduced their research budgets to be able to report high short-term profits, while long-term prospects are damaged.   In the final analysis, however, the long-term is nothing more than a series of short-term periods so this argument can be exaggerated.

2.6   Limitations of financial accounting data

When measuring the achievement of objectives in organisations it is important to remember that financial accounting data may be of only limited use in that

(a)   it cannot reflect unquantifiable costs and benefits, such as damage to or protection of the environment.

(b)   it reflects historical data only. Costs and benefits to future generations are not included in accounting data.

(c)   it is not based on opportunity cost. Financial accounting data reflects historical book costs and values and accounting policies as opposed to the more relevant, incremental cashflows.

3   CONSTRAINTS TO POLICY FORMULATION AND ACTION

3.1   Introduction

The above discussion concluded that the maximisation of shareholder wealth could generally be taken as the primary objective of companies, tempered by the influences and objectives of other parties.   This section briefly examines the constraints that exist on companies formulating their policies.   These constraints can be divided into internal constraints and external constraints.

3.2   Internal constraints

Self-imposed constraints confine the company to act other than to the widest possible range of activities, but may still be routes to long-term prosperity.   For example a company might concentrate on gaining a good reputation in environmental/green issues.   Although this costs money, the good public reputation achieved should increased the company's customer base and bring in long-term profits.

Other internal constraints might be in the area of funding policy and gearing levels. We will see later in the text that high gearing levels involve a high degree of risk; it will always be possible in theory to issue more and more loan stock at higher and higher interest costs to compensate the lenders for the risk. Most companies will however choose not to exceed a certain gearing level as a matter of policy. Similarly although it might be possible to negotiate a higher and higher overdraft limit at the bank by promising greater security and paying a higher interest rate, in practice companies will not wish to exceed some particular overdraft limit.

3.3   External constraints

Constraints to policy formulation and action that arise outside the company might be due to any of the following.

- Government legislation;
- Accounting concepts and conventions;
- Other regulatory decrees.

The Companies Acts 1985 and 1989 are the principal statutory influences on the actions of companies.   They lay down the relationships between directors and shareholders and offer protection to the shareholders, for example by requiring financial statements to be audited.   Other Acts govern companies which operate in specific areas eg, the Financial Services Act 1986 for companies carrying on investment business.

In the UK it is the task of the Accounting Standards Board to publish accounting standards which must be obeyed if companies' accounts are to give a true and fair view.   These Statements of Standard Accounting Practice (SSAPs) and Financial Reporting Standards (FRSs) limit the methods of accounting for transactions that can be chosen by directors and can have a direct effect on the companies' activities.   For example SSAP 21 requires obligations under finance leases to be shown on the lessee's balance sheet, while FRS 5 requires quasi-subsidiaries to be included in consolidated accounts.   Both of these may increase a company's reported gearing ratio and make further debt finance more expensive to raise.

4   PERFORMANCE

4.1   Methods of analysing financial performance

The financial performance of a company can be assessed by reference to itself over a period of time or by comparison with its competitors. There are various methods which can be used to achieve either of these aims. The methods are largely common sense but it is useful to classify the methods that can be adopted.

Horizontal analysis

Horizontal analysis is a line-by-line comparison of the current year's accounts with those of the previous year.

Example

Horizontal analysis of profit and loss account:
Mack plc

	19X3 £m	19X4 £m	% change
Turnover	951.9	1,156.5	+21.5
Cost of sales	617.1	739.0	+19.8
Gross profit	334.8	417.5	+24.7
Distribution costs	39.1	48.3	+23.5
Marketing, selling and administrative expenses	226.5	280.0	+23.6
Other operating income	(4.2)	(4.6)	+9.5
Trading profit	73.4	93.8	+27.8
Interest paid less received	12.2	19.3	+58.2
Profit before taxation	61.2	74.5	+21.7
Taxation	28.4	28.0	−1.4
Profit attributable to holding company	32.8	46.5	+41.8
Dividends	15.7	18.4	+17.2
Added to reserves	17.1	28.1	+64.3

Trend analysis

Extending the horizontal analysis over a number of years provides **trends**. To see more clearly the trend, the figure in the first year of the series is given a value of 100. Subsequent years' figures are related to this base.

Example

Trend analysis: Mack plc

	19X0	*19X1*	*19X2*	*19X3*	*19X4*
Turnover (£m)	629.8	688.0	770.5	951.9	1,156.5
Index (19X0 base = 100)	100.0	109.2	122.3	151.1	183.6
Trading profit (£m)	44.8	48.0	55.9	73.4	93.8
Index (19X0 base = 100)	100.0	107.1	124.8	163.8	209.4

If inflation is taken account of, the figures or the indices could be restated. Suppose in the above example the average RPI for each of the years was:

	19X0	*19X1*	*19X2*	*19X3*	*19X4*
RPI	130	136	146	140	160

The figures could be converted into 19X4 £m.

	19X0	*19X1*	*19X2*	*19X3*	*19X4*
Turnover (19X4 £m)	775.1	809.4	844.4	1,087.9	1,156.5
Trading profit (19X4 £m)	55.1	56.5	61.3	83.9	93.8

The working is:

$$\text{Figure} \ \times \ \frac{\text{RPI 19X4}}{\text{RPI for year figure taken from}}$$

Or the index could be adjusted.

	19X0	*19X1*	*19X2*	*19X3*	*19X4*
Turnover index	100.0	109.2	122.3	151.1	183.6
Adjusted for inflation	100.0	104.4	108.9	140.3	149.2

The working is:

$$\text{Index for the year} \ \times \ \frac{\text{RPI for base year}}{\text{RPI for the year}}$$

Vertical analysis

'Common size' balance sheets or profit and loss accounts can be prepared. Each balance sheet item is expressed as a percentage of the balance sheet total and each profit and loss account item as a percentage of sales (or earnings).

Example

Vertical analysis of a balance sheet: Mack plc

	19X3 £m	19X4 £m	Common size statements 19X3 %	19X4 %
Fixed assets				
Land and buildings	156.9	169.0	32.2	30.4
Plant and machinery	202.8	239.5	41.6	43.2
	359.7	408.5	73.8	73.6
Current assets				
Stocks, debtors	305.0	344.0	62.5	62.0
Other creditors				
(due within 1 year)	(163.5)	(181.6)	(33.5)	(32.7)
Creditors (due over 1 year)	(13.5)	(16.0)	(2.8)	(2.9)
	487.7	554.9	100.0	100.0
Capital and reserves				
Share capital	82.0	83.0	16.8	14.9
Reserves	267.0	309.6	54.8	55.8
Shareholders' funds	349.0	392.6	71.6	70.7
Minority interests	0.1	0.1	-	-
Deferred taxation	-	6.0	-	1.1
Other provisions	9.5	15.6	1.9	2.8
Loan capital	99.9	148.6	20.5	26.8
Short-term borrowings (funds)	29.2	(8.0)	6.0	(1.4)
	487.7	554.9	100.0	100.0

Ratio analysis

Ratios can be produced by comparing one item in a balance sheet or profit and loss account with another for the same period, or with the current price of the company's shares.

Earnings per share and gearing are two ratios which are given particular importance by the financial community. A financial manager will thus be very interested in maintaining and growing the EPS of the company and showing a reasonable gearing not only because of their inherent importance in managing the finances of a business but also because of the interest shown in them by outsiders.

A quotation from the chairman of an investment broker illustrates the overriding importance given to EPS.

'At 8.15 each weekday morning the security salesmen and analysts at my firm meet to consider the ideas that will be put to our 300 or so institutional customers during the day. Analysts ... give their recommendations for specific shares: buy, hold or sell.'

'It is these recommendations, together with similar conclusions reached at twenty or so other security houses, that collectively drive share prices in the market. The single most important figure affecting the analysts' – and hence the markets' view – is forecast earnings per share.' Ian Hay Davison, chairman of CL Alexanders Laing & Cruickshank.

The Accounting Standards Board (ASB) dislikes the overriding use of EPS as the single indicator used to assess a company's financial performance, so has required profit and loss accounts to present more information concerning continuing activities and discontinued activities. Financial Reporting Standard 3 (FRS 3) now requires that all published profit and loss accounts should give this additional information and the ASB hopes that accounts will start to be interpreted on the basis of many factors, not just the EPS. In the meantime, however, earnings per share remains an extremely important ratio for the whole investment community.

5 ANALYSIS OF ACCOUNTING STATEMENTS AND USE OF RATIOS

5.1 Basis for decision making

Up to this point only the preparation and underlying theory of financial statements have been considered. However, many users of accounts need to draw conclusions which will form the basis for decisions in the future. Much of this information will be gathered by calculating ratios and making comparisons with:

(a)   the performance of the business in previous years;
(b)   the budgeted or planned performance in the current year;
(c)   the performance of similar businesses.

The ratios themselves do not tell one what to do, but they do help to point one in the right direction. Ratios should, therefore, make it easier to make better decisions.

5.2 Limitations of historical cost accounting

The majority of financial statements are based on historical cost accounting. Historical cost accounts are subject to many limitations during periods of changing prices. In certain circumstances they may even be misleading.

When using ratios based on historical cost accounts, it is necessary to remember that the ratios themselves are subject to any weaknesses and limitations present in the underlying financial statements.

5.3 What information does a user require?

The various users of financial statements require information for quite different purposes. There are a large number of ratios, not all of which will be relevant to a particular situation. It is therefore important to determine the precise information needs of the user, and the decisions he has to take after analysing the relevant information.

The needs of three particular users may be summarised:

User	*Required for*
Management	Control of costs, improved profitability
Lenders	Borrowing and credit purposes
Shareholders and investment analysts	Investment decisions – buying and selling shares

Ask yourself the questions 'What decision is being made?' and 'What information is relevant to that decision?'

5.4 Types of ratios

Ratios fall into several groups, the relevance of particular ratios depending on the purpose for which they are required. The groups to be considered here are:

(a)   profitability ratios;
(b)   short term liquidity ratios;

(c)   working capital efficiency;
(d)   medium and long term solvency ratios;
(e)   investor ratios.

5.5   Illustration

The above ratios will be illustrated by reference to the following. Assume that a limited company has a reasonably detailed trading and profit and loss account (published accounts might not provide this amount of detail).

Summarised balance sheets at 30 June

	19X7		19X6	
	£'000	£'000	£'000	£'000
Fixed assets (net book value)		130		139
Current assets:				
Stock	42		37	
Debtors	29		23	
Bank	3		5	
	74		65	
Creditors: amounts falling due within one year:				
Trade creditors	36		55	
Taxation	10		10	
	46		65	
Net current assets		28		—
Total assets less current liabilities		158		139
Creditors: amounts falling due beyond one year:				
5% secured loan stock		40		40
		118		99
Ordinary share capital (50p shares)		35		35
8% Preference shares (£1 shares)		25		25
Share premium account		17		17
Revaluation reserve		10		-
Profit and loss account		31		22
		118		99

Summarised profit and loss account for the year ended 30 June

	19X7 £'000	19X7 £'000	19X6 £'000	19X6 £'000
Sales		209		196
Opening stock	37		29	
Purchases	162		159	
	199		188	
Closing stock	42		37	
		157		151
Gross profit		52		45
Interest	2		2	
Depreciation	9		9	
Sundry expenses	14		11	
		25		22
Net profit		27		23
Taxation		10		10
Net profit after taxation		17		13
Dividends:				
Ordinary shares	6		5	
Preference shares	2		2	
		8		7
Retained profit		9		6

5.6   Profitability ratios

There are several ratios which attempt to assess the profitability of a business. These are more conveniently expressed in percentage form and include:

(a)   The gross profit percentage

This is a very popular ratio and is used by even the smallest of businesses. Gross profit is expressed as a percentage of sales. In the illustration the ratios for the two years are as follows:

$$
\begin{array}{cc}
\textit{19X7} & \textit{19X6} \\
\dfrac{52}{209} \times 100 = 24.9\% & \dfrac{45}{196} \times 100 = 23.0\%
\end{array}
$$

What can be learned from these figures? Clearly, the gross profit percentage has improved, a higher figure means a better return for investors, but it is not known why. Nor is it obvious whether these figures are better or worse than those which would be expected in a similar type of business. Before coming to definite conclusions one would need further information. For example, most businesses sell a wide range of products, usually with different gross profit percentages (or profit margins). It may be that in 19X7 the **sales mix** changed and that a larger proportion of items with a high profit percentage were sold, thus increasing the overall gross profit percentage of the business.

Percentage change in sales

It is relevant to consider the change in sales at this point. The percentage growth in sales is:

$$\frac{209 - 196}{196} \times 100 = 6.6\%$$

This is not a significant increase. A larger increase might have given some evidence of the type of changes in trading conditions that may have occurred. An increase could be due to a larger quantity being sold, or to price increases.

(b)   **Net profit as a percentage of sales**

19X7	*19X6*
$\frac{27}{209} \times 100 = 12.9\%$	$\frac{23}{196} \times 100 = 11.7\%$

What conclusions can be drawn from this apparent improvement? Very few! Since net profit equals gross profit less expenses, it would be useful to tabulate, for each of the two years, the various expenses and express them as a percentage of sales. A suitable tabulation might be:

	19X7		*19X6*	
	£'000	%	£'000	%
Sales	209	100.0	196	100.0
Cost of sales	157	75.1	151	77.0
Gross profit	52	24.9	45	23.0
Interest	(2)	(1.0)	(2)	(1.1)
Depreciation	(9)	(4.3)	(9)	(4.6)
Sundry expenses	(14)	(6.7)	(11)	(5.6)
Net profit	27	12.9	23	11.7

Given a detailed trading and profit and loss account, the above type of summary could be very useful. Care must be taken in interpreting the results, particularly since sales (£) are used as the denominator and an increase in sales (£) could be due to a combination of price and quantity effects.

Gross profit margin and net profit margin levels and how they change give an indication of how well an organisation is controlling its costs or increasing selling prices or quantities. If the two measures move in parallel, it may indicate stable efficiency but divergence suggests that cost structures are changing.

(c)   **Return on capital employed (ROCE)**

This is an important ratio as it relates profit to the capital invested in a business. Finance for a business is only available at a cost – loan stock finance requires interest payments and further finance from shareholders requires either the immediate payment of dividends or the expectation of higher dividends in the future. Therefore a business needs to maximise the profits per £ of capital employed.

Due to its importance the ROCE is sometimes referred to as the **primary ratio**.

There are several ways of measuring ROCE, but the essential point is to relate the profit figure used to its capital base eg,

Total capital employed in the business

$$\frac{\text{Profit before interest and tax}}{\text{Share capital} + \text{Reserves} + \text{Long term liabilities}} \times 100$$

The denominator could alternatively be calculated as total assets less current liabilities.

Equity shareholders' capital employed

$$\frac{\text{Profit after interest and preference dividend but before tax}}{\text{Ordinary share capital} + \text{Reserves}} \times 100$$

The denominator could alternatively be calculated as net assets less preference shares.

Although it is better to base the calculation on average capital employed during the year, the calculation is often based on year-end capital employed (because there is insufficient data for all years to compute an average).

An increase in ROCE is considered good for shareholders, since the more profit is generated by the capital in a business the more is available each year either to distribute to investors (as dividend or interest) or to invest in making the business even more profitable.

5.7   Activity

Calculate ROCE for 19X6 and 19X7 using each of these alternatives.

5.8   Activity solution

Total capital employed

19X7	19X6
$\dfrac{(27+2)}{158} \times 100 = 18.4\%$	$\dfrac{(23+2)}{139} \times 100 = 18.0\%$

Equity capital employed

19X7	19X6
$\dfrac{27-2}{118-25} \times 100 = 26.9\%$	$\dfrac{23-2}{99-25} \times 100 = 28.4\%$

There is a slight improvement in total ROCE and a falling off in equity ROCE.

A reason for the variation is the revaluation of fixed assets during the year. This has the effect of increasing the denominator in 19X7 relative to 19X6 and creates an unfair comparison as it is likely that the fixed assets were worth more than their book value last year as well. It is not common, however, for UK companies to revalue their assets every year so that comparisons from year to year can be difficult.

The differences in returns for equity compared to total capital employed are large. It means that equity shareholders have had a significant increase in their return because of the company's using fixed interest finance to enlarge the capital employed in the business.

5.9   Structure of profitability ratios

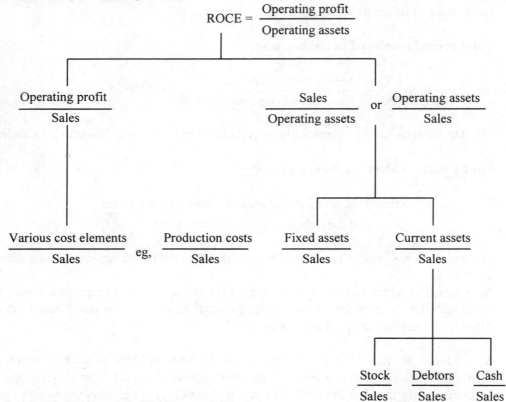

5.10   Factors affecting return on capital employed

There are two:

(a)   Profitability of sales.
(b)   Rate of asset utilisation.

Note: that the product of these two gives the return on capital employed:

$$\frac{\text{Operating profit}}{\text{Sales}} \times \frac{\text{Sales}}{\text{Operating assets}} = \frac{\text{Operating profit}}{\text{Operating assets}} = \text{ROCE}$$

In the example for 19X7:

$$\frac{\text{Operating profit}}{\text{Sales}} = \frac{£29,000}{£209,000} = 13.9\%$$

$$\frac{\text{Sales}}{\text{Operating assets}} = \frac{£209,000}{£158,000} = 1.32$$

Note:

$13.9\% \times 1.32 \times 100 = 18.3\%$ ie, ROCE subject to a rounding difference.

One may, in turn, subdivide these into their component elements.

5.11   Factors affecting operating profit/sales

This ratio may be subdivided as far as detail in our profit and loss account permits, since:

$$\frac{\text{Operating profit}}{\text{Sales}} + \frac{\text{Cost elements}}{\text{Sales}} = 1$$

Cost elements may include production, marketing, distribution, administration and so on.

5.12 Factors affecting operating assets/sales

In the first place, operating assets may be subdivided into fixed and current assets, since:

$$\frac{\text{Operating assets}}{\text{Sales}} = \frac{\text{Fixed assets}}{\text{Sales}} + \frac{\text{Current assets}}{\text{Sales}}$$

Each of these may be appropriately subdivided, eg:

Fixed assets = plant and machinery + Freehold land + etc

Current assets = stock + debtors + cash + etc

Thus, two of the ratios give the months' stock and debtors carried by the company.

> **Conclusion** From the analysis it becomes clear that the subdivision of the key ratio, return on capital employed, is limited only by the detail in the data available. The important point to remember is that in each case the ultimate result is directly related to each individual ratio by the pyramid, ie, there is an arithmetical relationship between all the pyramid ratios, so it is possible to determine the effect that a change in one of the ratios will have on the key ratio – return on capital employed.

6 LIQUIDITY, WORKING CAPITAL AND SOLVENCY

6.1 Short term liquidity ratios

The two main ratios are:

(a) **The current ratio** – the ratio of current assets to current liabilities

19X7	*19X6*
$\frac{74}{46} = 1.61$	$\frac{65}{65} = 1.0$

The current ratio is sometimes referred to as the working capital ratio.

(b) **The liquidity** (or **quick** or **acid test**) **ratio** – the ratio of current assets excluding stock to current liabilities

19X7	*19X6*
$\frac{32}{46} = 0.7$	$\frac{28}{65} = 0.43$

Both of these ratios show a strengthening.

The extent of the change between the two years seems surprising and would require further investigation.

It would also be useful to know how these ratios compare with those of a similar business, since typical ratios for supermarkets are quite different from those for heavy engineering firms.

What can be said is that in 19X7 the current liabilities were well covered by current assets. Liabilities payable in the near future (creditors), however, are only half covered by cash and debtors (a liquid asset, close to cash).

Conventional wisdom has it that an ideal current ratio is 2 and an ideal quick ratio is 1. It is very tempting to draw definite conclusions from limited information or to say that the current ratio **should** be 2, or that the liquidity ratio **should** be 1. However, this is not very meaningful without taking into account the type of ratio expected in a similar business.

In general, high current and liquidity ratios are considered 'good' in that they mean that an organisation has the resources to meet its commitments as they fall due.

However a high current or liquidity ratio is not necessarily a good thing. It may indicate that working capital is not being used efficiently, for example that there is too much idle cash that should be invested to earn a return.

6.2   Elements of working capital

It is necessary to consider three ratios concerned with current assets and current liabilities:

(a)   **Stock turnover ratio**

Companies have to strike a balance between being able to satisfy customers' requirements out of stock and the cost of having too much capital tied up in stock. The stock turnover ratio is the cost of sales divided by the average level of stock during the year. Using the example:

$$\textit{19X7} \qquad\qquad\qquad\qquad \textit{19X6}$$

$$\frac{157}{\frac{1}{2}(37\ +\ 42)} = 4.0 \text{ times pa} \qquad\qquad \frac{151}{\frac{1}{2}(29\ +\ 37)} = 4.6 \text{ times pa}$$

The stock turnover ratio has fallen.

In general, the higher the stock turnover ratio the better. It is very expensive to hold stock and thus minimum stock holding usually points to good management. However, not all industries can operate a just-in-time stock policy and unless the nature of the business is known, it is not possible to say whether either 4.6 or 4.0 is satisfactory or unsatisfactory. A jeweller will have a low stock turnover ratio, but it is hoped that a fishmonger selling fresh fish has a very high turnover ratio.

An alternative calculation of the stock turnover ratio is to show the result in days. The calculation is:

$$\frac{\text{Average stock during the accounting period}}{\text{Cost of sales}} \times 365 \text{ (ie, length of accounting period)}$$

$$\textit{19X7} \qquad\qquad\qquad\qquad \textit{19X6}$$

$$\frac{\frac{1}{2}(37\ +\ 42)}{157} \times 365 = 92 \text{ days} \qquad\qquad \frac{\frac{1}{2}(29\ +\ 37)}{151} \times 365 = 80 \text{ days}$$

(b)   **Debt collection period (or average period of credit allowed to customers)**

Businesses which sell goods on credit terms specify a credit period. Failure to send out invoices on time or to follow up late payers will have an adverse effect on the cash flow of the business.

The debt collection period relates closing trade debts to the average daily credit sales.

In the example:

	19X7	*19X6*
Credit sales per day	$\dfrac{£209,000}{365} = £573$	$\dfrac{£196,000}{365} = £537$
Closing trade debtors	£29,000	£23,000
Debt collection period	$\dfrac{£29,000}{£573} = 50.6$ days	$\dfrac{£23,000}{£537} = 42.8$ days

Compared with 19X6 the debt collection period has worsened in 19X7.

If the average credit allowed to customers was, say, thirty days, then something is clearly wrong. Further investigation might reveal delays in sending out invoices or failure to 'screen' new customers.

The quickest way to compute the debt collection period is to use the formula:

$$\frac{\text{Closing trade debtors}}{\text{Credit sales for year}} \times 365$$

19X7	*19X6*
$\dfrac{29,000}{209,000} \times 365 = 50.6$ days	$\dfrac{23,000}{196,000} \times 365 = 42.8$ days

In general, the shorter the debtor period the better because debtors are effectively 'borrowing' from the company, but, remember, the level of debtors reflects not only the ability of the credit controllers but also the sales and marketing strategy adopted, and the nature of the business. Any change in the level of debtors must therefore be assessed in the light of the level of sales.

(c) **Average period of credit allowed by suppliers**

This relates closing creditors to average daily credit purchases.

In the example:

	19X7	*19X6*
Credit purchases per day	$\dfrac{£162,000}{365} = £444$	$\dfrac{£159,000}{365} = £436$
Closing trade creditors	£36,000	£55,000
Average period of credit allowed by suppliers	81.1 days	126.3 days

The average period of credit allowed has fallen substantially from last year. It is however, in absolute terms still a high figure.

Often, suppliers request payment within thirty days. The company is taking nearly three months. Trade creditors are thus financing much of the working capital requirements of the business which is beneficial to the company.

An increase in creditor days may be good in that it means that all available credit is being taken, but there are three potential disadvantages of extending the credit period.

(i)   Future supplies may be endangered.

(ii)   Possibility of cash discounts is lost.

(iii)   Suppliers may quote a higher price for the goods knowing the extended credit taken by the company.

The quick calculation is:

$$\frac{\text{Closing trade creditors}}{\text{Credit purchases for year}} \times 365$$

19X7

$$\frac{36,000}{162,000} \times 365 = 81.1 \text{ days}$$

19X6

$$\frac{55,000}{159,000} \times 365 = 126.3 \text{ days}$$

6.3   The working capital cycle

The investment made in working capital is largely a function of sales and, therefore, it is useful to consider the problem in terms of a firm's working capital (or **cash operating**) cycle.

The cash operating cycle

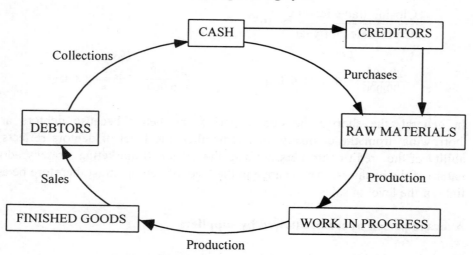

The cycle reflects a firm's investment in working capital as it moves through the production process towards sales. The investment in working capital gradually increases, firstly being only in raw materials, but then in labour and overhead as production progresses. This investment must be maintained throughout the production process, the finished goods holding period and up to the final collection of cash from trade debtors. Note that the net investment can be reduced by taking trade credit from suppliers.

The faster a firm can 'push' items around the operating cycle the lower its investment in working capital will be.

With some fairly basic financial information it is possible to measure the length of the working capital cycle for a given firm.

Example

Extracts from the profit and loss account for the year and the balance sheet as at the end of the year for a company show:

	£
Sales	250,000
Cost of goods sold	210,000
Purchases	140,000
Debtors	31,250
Creditors	21,000
Stock	92,500

Note: assume all sales and purchases are on credit terms.

Calculate the working capital cycle.

Solution

(1)   Creditors:

Average payment collection period

$$= \left(365 \times \frac{\text{Creditors}}{\text{Purchases}}\right) \qquad 365 \times \frac{21}{140} = \qquad (55 \text{ days})$$

(2)   Debtors:

Average collection period

$$= \left(365 \times \frac{\text{Debtors}}{\text{Sales}}\right) \qquad 365 \times \frac{31.25}{250} = \qquad 46 \text{ days}$$

(3)   Stock turnover:

$$= 365 \times \frac{\text{Stock}}{\text{Cost of goods sold}} \qquad 365 \times \frac{92.5}{210} = \qquad 161 \text{ days}$$

Length of working capital cycle   152 days

The length of the cycle depends on the efficiency of management and the nature of the industry. The optimum level is the amount that results in no idle cash or unused stock, but does not put a strain on liquid resources. Trying to shorten the cash cycle may cause detrimental effects elsewhere with the organisation lacking the cash to meet its commitments and lost sales since customers will generally prefer to buy from suppliers who are prepared to extend trade credit, and who have items held in stock when required.

6.4   Medium and long term solvency ratios

Consider the various forms of long term finance. The table below lists their priorities as regards the distribution of profits and repayment on liquidation. These priorities will be specified in the articles of association:

Source of finance	Priority in relation to profit	Priority on liquidation
Secured loan stock (debentures)	Interest must be paid whether or not the company makes a profit	Secured by a fixed or floating charge – first claim on assets
Unsecured loan stock	Interest must be paid whether or not the company makes a profit	Ranks as unsecured creditor
Preference share capital (assumed non-participating)	If the company makes a profit, the preference dividend has a priority over the ordinary dividend	Cannot be repaid until all liabilities have been met. Has priority over ordinary shareholders
Ordinary share capital	Dividends paid after debenture interest and fixed preference dividends have been paid	Ranks behind all the above but usually entitled to surplus assets in a liquidation

The various ratios can now be considered.

6.5   Capital gearing

Gearing is one of the most widely-used terms in accounting. Unfortunately it can be defined and calculated in several different ways. It is essential to state the definition used.

Gearing is relevant to the long term financial stability of a business. Two possible definitions will be considered, both based on book values of assets. Both of these consider the relationship between:

(a)   ordinary shareholders' funds (or equity interest);
(b)   fixed return capital – comprising long term loans and preference share capital.

6.6   Equity gearing

$$\frac{\text{Preference share capital plus loans}}{\text{Ordinary share capital and reserves}}$$

$$\begin{array}{cc} 19X7 & 19X6 \\ \frac{25+40}{118-25} \times 100 = 69.9\% & \frac{25+40}{99-25} \times 100 = 87.8\% \end{array}$$

6.7   Total gearing

$$\frac{\text{Preference share capital plus loans}}{\text{Total long term capital}}$$

$$\begin{array}{cc} 19X7 & 19X6 \\ \frac{65}{158} \times 100 = 41.1\% & \frac{65}{139} \times 100 = 46.8\% \end{array}$$

There is no real difference between the two types of calculation as the components of the numerator remain the same. Some prefer to use the equity gearing as it shows a more pronounced change if either fixed return capital or equity capital changes. Most use the second calculation as it is perhaps clearer to note the relationship of fixed interest finance to **total** finance.

It is also possible to include short term debt in the gearing ratio; indeed, this should be done if short term loans (such as overdrafts) are being used continuously by a business and thus are really part of the long term financing of the organisation even though they are renegotiated on a regular basis.

There is no immediate cut-off between a low-geared company and a highly-geared company. Gearing is a matter of degree.

Gearing may have an important effect on the distribution of profits. For example, consider two companies with the same profit record but different capital structures. The return of the ordinary shareholders can vary considerably.

	A Ltd £	B Ltd £
Capital structure:		
10% Loan stock	20,000	-
Ordinary share capital and reserves	10,000	30,000
	30,000	30,000

	Highly geared £	No gearing £
Year 1 – Profits £4,000 before interest		
∴ Returns:		
10% Interest	2,000	-
Ordinary shares – balance	2,000	4,000
	4,000	4,000
Year 2 – Profits double to £8,000 before interest		
∴ Returns:		
10% Interest	2,000	-
Ordinary shares – balance	6,000	8,000
	8,000	8,000
Therefore, increase in return to ordinary shareholders	3 times	2 times

Thus, the doubling of the profits in year 2 has the effect of tripling the return to the equity shareholders in the highly-geared company. The effect would be even more dramatic if the profits fell below £2,000 because then there would be no return at all to the ordinary shareholders in A Ltd. Thus an investment in ordinary shares in a highly-geared company is a far more speculative investment than a purchase of ordinary shares in a low-geared company.

What is the 'best' level of gearing for an organisation? In general, because debt is secured and interest is paid before dividends, debt is cheap and thus some gearing is good. As long as the gearing ratio is small, investors will be confident that there will be adequate profits to pay both loan interest and a dividend. But as gearing increases, there will come a point where shareholders worry about the company's ability to pay a dividend because of all the interest that must be paid first; at this point it is likely that both equity and debt holders will want a higher return for their now risky investment. Thus too high a level of gearing is not good. What is a good level of gearing will depend on how variable the earnings of the company are and how good the management is perceived to be by investors.

6.8   Interest cover

Interest on loan stock (debenture stock) must be paid whether or not the company makes a profit. The ratio emphasises the cover (or security) for the interest by relating profit before interest and tax to interest paid.

19X7

$$\frac{52-9-14}{2} = \frac{29}{2} \text{ ie, 14.5 times}$$

19X6

$$\frac{45-9-11}{2} = \frac{25}{2} \text{ ie, 12.5 times}$$

From the point of view of medium and long term solvency, the company is in a strong position as regards the payment of interest. Profit would have to drop considerably before any problem of paying interest arose. Thus in general, a high level of interest cover is 'good' with shareholders confident that profit is sufficient to pay interest and their dividend. But, a high interest cover may also be interpreted as a company failing to exploit gearing opportunities to fund projects at a lower cost than from equity finance.

6.9   The importance of net debt in interpretation of accounts

As interest rates rose at the end of the 1980s, those companies with large floating rate borrowings (eg, a large bank overdraft), or who had to refinance borrowings at a higher rate than previously, found their profits squeezed. Several of the highly geared management buyouts of the early 1980s found that they simply could not afford to pay the higher interest charges and they went bust. All businesses with significant debt found themselves under pressure to reduce their debt levels, by applying cash inflows from operations to repaying borrowings, or by raising new equity funds (eg, by a rights issue).

A key statistic when reporting financial performance in the early 1990s became the level of net debt, measured as total overdrafts and borrowings less cash balances held. A successful company would be expected to report a fall in net debt each year to reduce the financial risk of the business.

However in the mid 1990s interest rates have fallen to low levels, so it is no longer considered such a bad thing for a company to have high borrowings. Memories seem to be short and the attention that was paid to net debt has moved on to other ideas such as unbundling conglomerates. A lower emphasis is therefore now placed on reporting a falling level of net debt than was the case five or so years ago.

7   STOCK EXCHANGE RATIOS

7.1   Information required by investors

An investor is interested in the income earned by the company for him and the return on his investment (the income earned related to the market price of the investment).

An investor in ordinary shares can look to the earnings of the company available to pay the ordinary dividend or to the actual ordinary dividend paid as a measure of the income earned by the company for him. The ratios he would compute in each case would be:

Dividends	*Earnings*
Dividends per share Times covered Dividend yield	Return on equity Earnings per share Price earnings ratio

In general, the higher each of these ratios is, the more attractive the shares will be to potential investors, who will be increasingly confident about the return the shares will give.

Suppose that the company in the illustration in section 5.5 is quoted on the Stock Exchange and that the market value of each ordinary share is 204 pence. Tax credits are 20/80ths.

(a)   **Dividend per share**

This relates to ordinary shares:

19X7	19X6
$\dfrac{£6,000}{70,000} = 8.6$ pence per share	$\dfrac{£5,000}{70,000} = 7.1$ pence per share

(b)   **Dividend cover**

This is calculated by dividing profit available for ordinary shareholders by the dividend for the year (ie, interim plus final):

19X7	19X6
$\dfrac{£17,000 - £2,000}{£6,000} = 2.5$ times	$\dfrac{£13,000 - £2,000}{£5,000} = 2.2$ times

Note: that the profits available for ordinary shareholders are after the deduction of the preference dividend. The cover represents the 'security' for the ordinary dividend – in this company the cover is reasonable.

(c)   **Dividend yield**

This expresses dividend per share as a percentage of the current share price. The net yield at today's date is:

$$\frac{8.6p}{204p} \times 100 = 4.2\%$$

On the stock market the dividend yield is normally stated **gross** of tax (ie, the tax credit is added to the dividend). This enables the yield on shares to be compared with yields on interest stocks (company and government stocks).

$$\frac{8.6p \times \frac{100}{80}}{204p} \times 100 = 5.3\%$$

or compute the net yield and adjust for the tax credit:

$$4.2\% \times \frac{100}{80} = 5.3\%$$

(d)   **Return on equity**

This is a profitability ratio similar to ROCE explained earlier, but of particular relevance to the ordinary shareholders of a company. It is defined as

$$\text{Return on equity} = \frac{\text{Profit after tax and preference dividends}}{\text{Ordinary shareholders' funds}} \times 100\%$$

For 19X7 this equals: $\dfrac{17-2}{118-25} \times 100 = 16.1\%$

(e)   **Earnings per share (EPS)**

When a company pays a dividend, the directors take many factors into account, including the need to retain profits for future expansion. Earnings per share looks at the profits which could in theory be paid to each ordinary shareholder.

Earnings are profits after tax, minority interests, extraordinary items and preference dividends, but before ordinary dividends.

The denominator is:

The number of equity shares in issue and ranking for dividend in the accounting period.

SSAP 3 requires earnings per share to be disclosed on the face of the profit and loss account of quoted companies.

19X7	*19X6*
$\dfrac{£17,000 - £2,000}{70,000} = 21.4\text{p per share}$	$\dfrac{£13,000 - £2,000}{70,000} = 15.7\text{p per share}$

(f)   **Price earnings ratio (P/E ratio)**

This is regarded as the most important investment ratio. It expresses the current share price (market value) as a multiple of the earnings per share. For 19X7, the price earnings ratio is:

$$\frac{204\text{p}}{21.4\text{p}} = 9.5$$

The ratio of 9.5 implies that if the current rate of EPS is maintained it will take nine and a half years to repay the cost of investing. The higher the PE ratio the longer the payback period. Thus we could conclude that the lower the PE ratio, the better investment it is. However, this is not generally the case. **High** PE ratios are generally viewed as better than low ones.

The apparent paradox is resolved if the forward looking nature of stock exchange investments is considered. The PE ratio is based on **current** EPS but the stock market is pricing the share on expectations of **future** EPS. If the market considers that a company has significant growth prospects, the market price of the share will rise.

(g)   **Earnings yield**

This term is not often referred to these days. It expresses the earnings per share as a percentage of the current share price, ie:

$$\text{Earnings yield} \quad = \quad \frac{21.4\text{p}}{204\text{p}} \times 100$$

$$= \quad 10.5\%$$

It is merely the reciprocal of the PE ratio:

$$\frac{1}{\text{PE ratio}} \quad = \quad \text{Earnings yield}$$

$$\frac{1}{9.5} \quad = \quad 0.105 \text{ ie, } 10.5\%$$

8   BASIC INTERPRETATION AND REPORTING TO MANAGEMENT

8.1   Introduction

The examiner lays great emphasis on the ability of students to make use of accounting data, not merely to prepare the data. Unfortunately it is a difficult area for which to prepare, as a wide variety of situations can be encountered. The key points to remember are:

(a)   If a ratio is computed, define what items have been included in the numerator and denominator, as for some ratios definitions vary.

(b)   Only compute a few ratios. Ratios are only a means to an end, ie, they are computed in order that a comment can be made. The marks are gained by making the comments.

(c)   Show the ratio in the 'normal' form, eg, a ratio based on a profit figure is normally expressed as a percentage.

(d)   Do not be frightened of making what may be regarded as an obvious comment. Thus, a statement that 'the gross profit to sales ratio has increased from last year' is stating something important – that the business is more profitable. It is only an obvious comment because the computation of a ratio made it so obvious. That is the main point of ratios – to highlight trends.

8.2   Reporting to management

It must be emphasised that accounting ratios are only a means to an end; they are not an end in themselves. By comparing the relationship between figures, they merely highlight significant features or trends in the accounts. Indeed, they may well create more problems than they solve. The real art of interpreting accounts lies in defining the reasons for the features and fluctuations disclosed. To do this effectively more information may be needed.

If the analysis is of the company of which you are the management accountant, this further information will probably be available. However you may be required to comment on other businesses which your management is interested in (eg, a possible purchase). In such a situation, there may be a significant amount of missing or potentially misleading information.

8.3   Possible problems of interpretation

The following general points should be borne in mind.

(a)   The date at which the accounts are drawn up. Accurate information can only be obtained with any degree of certainty from up-to-date figures. Furthermore, seasonal variations in the particular trade should be taken into account. Final accounts tend to be drawn up at the end of seasonal trade when the picture they present is of the business at its strongest point financially.

(b)   The accuracy of the position shown in the balance sheet. The arrangement of certain matters can be misleading and present a more favourable picture, eg, such 'window-dressing' operations as:

(i)   making a special effort to collect debts just before the year-end in order to show a larger cash balance and lower debtors than is normal;

(ii)   ; ordering goods to be delivered just after the year-end so that stocks and creditors can be kept as low as possible.

(c)   Interim accounts. Whenever possible interested parties should examine accounts prepared on a monthly basis, as a clearer picture of the trends and fluctuations will emerge from these than from the annual financial statements.

(d)   Accounting ratios are based on accounting information and are, therefore, only as accurate as the underlying accounting information. At a time, as at present, when traditional accounting procedures are coming in for heavy criticism, students should remember that ratios based on those procedures can be easily criticised.

(e)   The accounting ratios of one company must be compared with those of another similar company in order to draw meaningful conclusions. These conclusions will only be so if that other company's trade is similar.

8.4   Example of a report to management

The following is a past examination question. Note the layout adopted for the report and the division of the report into appropriate sections.

Machine Tool

G plc is a holding company with subsidiaries that have diversified interests. G plc's board of directors is interested in the group acquiring a subsidiary in the machine tool manufacturing sector. Two companies have been identified as potential acquisitions, A Ltd and B Ltd. Summaries of both these companies' accounts are shown below:

Profit and loss accounts for the year ended
30 April 19X8

	A Ltd £'000	B Ltd £'000
Turnover	985	560
Cost of goods sold		
Opening stock	150	145
Materials	255	136
Labour	160	125
Factory overheads	205	111
Depreciation	35	20
Closing stock	(155)	(140)
	650	397
Gross profit	335	163
Selling and administration expenses	(124)	(75)
Interest	(35)	(10)
Profit before taxation	176	78
Taxation	65	25
Profit after taxation	111	53

Balance sheets at 30 April 19X8

	A Ltd		B Ltd	
	£'000	£'000	£'000	£'000
Fixed assets		765		410
Current assets				
Stock	155		140	
Debtors	170		395	
Bank	50		45	
	375		580	
Current liabilities				
Trade creditors	235		300	
Other	130		125	
	365		425	
Net current assets		10		155
Debentures		(220)		(70)
		555		495
Share capital		450		440
Profit and loss account		105		55
		555		495

You are required to prepare a report for the board of G plc assessing the financial performance and position of A Ltd and B Ltd. Your report should be prepared in the context of G plc's interests in these two companies and should be illustrated with financial ratios where appropriate. You should state any assumptions you make as well as any limitations of your analysis.

8.5   Solution

REPORT

To: The board of G plc

From: XXX

Date: XXX

Subject: Acquisition of subsidiary in the machine tool manufacturing sector

The investigation has been based on the accounts of companies A Ltd and B Ltd and should be viewed as preliminary in nature since more detailed information about the two companies will be required before any decision is made.

Assumptions

It is assumed that the two companies use similar accounting policies and the balance sheets are representative of the companies' normal levels of trading.

Limitations of analysis

(a)   The analysis is dependent on the assumptions being valid. Further work should be carried out to determine whether the assumptions are reasonable.

(b)   As the accounts are (presumably) prepared under the historical cost convention, the capital employed in the two companies is probably not stated in comparable terms ie, the fixed assets may have been purchased at different dates by the two companies (and thus at different prices).

Profitability

The Appendix shows various profitability ratios. The performance of A Ltd is better than B Ltd in terms of profitability to sales and profitability to assets employed. This is due to the markedly high sales per fixed assets employed.

Gearing

A Ltd is significantly more highly geared than B Ltd (see Appendix). However, in income terms the interest of A Ltd is six times covered by profits which would indicate the advantage that has accrued to A Ltd by investing in assets through debt financing.

Liquidity/working capital efficiency

The current ratio and acid test ratio are lower for A Ltd than for B Ltd. The industry averages should be examined to determine whether A Ltd or B Ltd is in a stronger position. The debtor collection periods and stock turnover ratios indicate that it is A Ltd. B Ltd has a very long debtor collection period which indicates a complete lack of credit control.

Conclusion

From the above analysis it would appear that A Ltd is a stronger and more profitable company. Subject to further and detailed investigation and the expected cost of acquisition it may be considered the best option. However, there is ample scope to improve B Ltd's performance by tightening up controls over working capital. Thus B Ltd may be a better purchase if the cost of acquisition is significantly lower than for A Ltd.

Appendix - Calculation of ratios

	A Ltd	*B Ltd*
Profitability		
Return on capital employed		
$\dfrac{\text{Profit before tax and interest}}{\text{Total assets less current liabilities}} \times 100$	$\dfrac{211}{775} \times 100$	$\dfrac{88}{565} \times 100$
	= 27.2%	= 15.6%
$\dfrac{\text{Gross profit}}{\text{Sales}} \times 100$	$\dfrac{335}{985} \times 100$	$\dfrac{163}{560} \times 100$
	= 34%	= 29%
$\dfrac{\text{Net profit}}{\text{Sales}} \times 100$	$\dfrac{176}{985} \times 100$	$\dfrac{78}{560} \times 100$
	= 18%	= 14%
$\dfrac{\text{Sales}}{\text{Fixed assets}}$	$\dfrac{985}{765} = 1.3$	$\dfrac{560}{410} = 1.4$

	A Ltd	B Ltd

Gearing

Capital

$$\frac{\text{Debentures}}{\text{Total assets less current liabilities}} \times 100 \qquad \frac{220}{775} \times 100 \qquad \frac{70}{563} \times 100$$

$$= 28.4\% \qquad = 12.5\%$$

Interest cover

$$\frac{\text{Profit before tax and interest}}{\text{Interest}} \qquad \frac{211}{35} \qquad \frac{88}{10}$$

$$= 6.0 \text{ times} \qquad = 8.8 \text{ times}$$

Liquidity

Current ratio

$$\frac{\text{Current assets}}{\text{Current liabilities}} \qquad \frac{375}{365} \qquad \frac{580}{425}$$

$$= 1.0 \qquad = 1.4$$

Acid test

$$\frac{\text{Current assets - stock}}{\text{Current liabilities}} \qquad \frac{200}{365} \qquad \frac{440}{425}$$

$$= 0.6 \qquad = 1.0$$

Debtors collection period

$$\frac{\text{Debtors}}{\text{Sales}} \times 365 \qquad \frac{170}{985} \times 365 \qquad \frac{395}{560}$$

$$= 63 \text{ days} \qquad = 257 \text{ days}$$

Stock turnover

$$\frac{\text{Cost of sales}}{\text{Average stock}} \qquad \frac{650}{0.5(150+155)} \qquad \frac{397}{0.5(145+140)}$$

$$= 4.3 \text{ times pa} \qquad = 2.8 \text{ times pa}$$

8.6   Environmental reporting

It was stated earlier than companies are increasingly reviewing their methods of operation and implementing 'greener' ways of doing things, both to improve their reputation amongst customers and to reduce costs. Examples are using recycled materials wherever possible and reducing energy bills.

Many commentators then suggest that each company's annual report and accounts should be required to include an environmental report in which the company must state its policy and actions in environmental activities so that readers of the accounts can judge whether the company is fulfilling its responsibilities to society. However the UK accounting profession has been extremely slow in bringing forward proposals in this area. Neither the ASB nor the APB has established a task force to gather ideas for possible standards on environmental reporting. The UK is not alone in being slow; no other European country currently has standards in place to require the publishing of annual environmental reports.

Future progress in this area is likely to originate from the European Commission, which has two initiatives in hand, the Community Eco-management and Audit Scheme (EMAS) and the Action Programme on the Environment. Both will promote improvements in the environmental performance of industrial companies; they may lead to significant developments in the near future.

9   CHAPTER SUMMARY

The number of ratios that can be calculated from a set of accounts may easily lead to confusion. Try to organise your thoughts in this area by mentally using the categories into which this chapter is broken down: operating ratios; liquidity, working capital and solvency; and stock exchange ratios.

Remember above all that the ratios are not an end in themselves. The examiner is interested in your ability to draw conclusions from accounts. Calculating a ratio is not the same as drawing a conclusion, but it can point you towards a conclusion.

10   SELF TEST QUESTIONS

10.1   Name three different user groups of financial statements and state the particular interests of each group. (1.3)

10.2   Give three examples of value for money indicators for public organisations. (2.3)

10.3   How do you calculate the return on capital employed for a company? (5.6)

10.4   Show how two important ratios can be multiplied together to give the return on capital employed. (5.10)

10.5   What are the two key ratios to assess a company's liquidity? (6.1)

10.6   How would you assess whether a company's debt collection procedures were improving or deteriorating? (6.2)

10.7   Which is the more risky investment, in a highly geared company or a company with low gearing? (6.7)

10.8   What is the formula to calculate a gross dividend yield? (7.1)

10.9   How does SSAP 3 (as revised) define the earnings of a company? (7.1)

10.10   What is meant by environmental reporting? (8.6)

11   EXAMINATION TYPE QUESTION

11.1   Ratios – B Ltd

The following are the summarised accounts for B Ltd, a company with an accounting year ending on 30 September:

Summarised balance sheets

	19X6		19X7	
	£'000	£'000	£'000	£'000
Tangible fixed assets – at				
cost less depreciation		4,995		12,700
Current assets:				
Stocks	40,145		50,455	
Debtors	40,210		43,370	
Cash at bank	12,092		5,790	
	92,447		99,615	
Creditors – Amounts falling due				
within one year:				
Trade creditors	32,604		37,230	
Taxation	2,473		3,260	
Proposed dividend	1,785		1,985	
	36,862		42,475	
Net current assets		55,585		57,140
Total assets less current liabilities		60,580		69,840
Creditors – Amounts falling due after				
more than one year:				
10% debentures 20X6/20X9		19,840		19,840
		40,740		50,000
Capital and reserves:				
Called up share capital of				
25p per share		9,920		9,920
Profit and loss account		30,820		40,080
Shareholders' funds		40,740		50,000

Summarised profit and loss accounts

	19X6	19X7
	£'000	£'000
Turnover	486,300	583,900
Operating profit	17,238	20,670
Interest payable	1,984	1,984
Profit on ordinary activities before taxation	15,254	18,686
Tax on profit on ordinary activities	5,734	7,026
Profit for the financial year	9,520	11,660
Dividends	2,240	2,400
	7,280	9,260
Retained profit brought forward	23,540	30,820
Retained profit carried forward	30,820	40,080

You are required:

(a) to calculate, for each year, **two** ratios for **each** of the following user groups, which are of particular significance to them:

 (i) shareholders;
 (ii) trade creditors;
 (iii) internal management; **(12 marks)**

(b) to make brief comments upon the changes, between the two years, in the ratios calculated in (a) above. **(8 marks)**

(Total: 20 marks)

12 ANSWER TO EXAMINATION TYPE QUESTION

12.1 Ratios – B Ltd

(a) (i) **Ratios of particular significance to shareholders**

	19X6	*19X7*
Earnings per share	$\dfrac{9,520}{39,680} \times 100$	$\dfrac{11,660}{39,680} \times 100$
	= 23.99p	= 29.39p
Dividend cover	$\dfrac{9,520}{2,240}$	$\dfrac{11,660}{2,400}$
	= 4.25 times	= 4.86 times

(Tutorial note:

$$\text{Earnings per share} = \frac{\text{Net profit for year after tax, preference dividends,}}{\text{No of equity shares in issue and ranking for dividend}}$$

$$\text{Dividend cover} = \frac{\text{Profit for the financial year}}{\text{Ordinary dividend}})$$

(ii) **Ratios of particular significance for trade creditors**

	19X6	*19X7*
Current ratio	$\dfrac{92,447}{36,862}$	$\dfrac{99,615}{42,475}$
	= 2.51	= 2.34
Quick ratio	$\dfrac{92,447 - 40,145}{36,862}$	$\dfrac{99,615 - 50,455}{42,475}$
	= 1.42	= 1.16

(Tutorial note:

$$\text{Current ratio} = \frac{\text{Current assets}}{\text{Current liabilities}}$$

$$\text{Quick ratio} = \frac{\text{Current assets excluding stock}}{\text{Current liabilities}})$$

(iii)   **Ratios of particular significance for internal management**

	19X6	*19X7*
Return on capital employed	$\dfrac{15,254}{40,740} \times 100\%$	$\dfrac{18,686}{50,000} \times 100\%$
	$= 37.4\%$	$= 37.4\%$
Turnover/Fixed assets	$\dfrac{486,300}{4,995}$	$\dfrac{583,900}{12,700}$
	$= 97.36$ times	$= 45.97$ times

(Tutorial note:

$$\text{Return on capital employed} = \frac{\text{Profit before taxation}}{\text{Share capital and reserves}}$$

It could also be calculated as:

$$\frac{\text{Profit before interest and taxation}}{\text{Share capital and reserves and long- term liabilities}}$$

$$\text{Turnover/Fixed assets} = \frac{\text{Turnover}}{\text{Tangible fixed assets (NBV)}}$$

Other management ratios include Operating profit/Sales and Debtors/Sales.*)*

(b)   Earnings per share has increased by 22.5% due to improved profits. There has been no change in share capital. The dividend cover (the number of times the ordinary dividend is covered by the available profits) has increased because the percentage of profits paid out as a dividend has decreased. The dividend itself has gone up 7% which is clearly not as much as the earnings improvement. The company is adopting a cautious policy but the dividend looks secure.

The current ratio is decreasing but it is still at an acceptable level. The quick ratio (measure of the company's liquidity) is also decreasing and at a faster rate due to the increasing investment in stock (current ratio is down approximately 7% and the quick ratio about 18%). The quick ratio is above the generally desired level of 1 but the company should watch this area carefully.

Return on capital employed has remained constant. The ratio of turnover to fixed assets has reduced dramatically due to the high investment in fixed assets. These should help increase turnover and profitability in future years.

21 THE FINANCIAL MANAGEMENT FRAMEWORK

INTRODUCTION & LEARNING OBJECTIVES

There are a large number of available types of investment and different types of participant in both the UK money market (ie investing for the short term) and the UK capital market (investing for the long term). This chapter explains these types of investment and describes the players in each of the markets.

When you have studied this chapter you should be able to do the following:

- explain the role of financial intermediaries.

- appreciate the implications of the Efficient Markets Hypothesis to the pricing of securities on stock markets.

- discuss the influences on interest rate levels.

- discuss different types of security.

- explain the workings of the international money and capital markets.

---

1 FINANCIAL INTERMEDIARIES

Definition The term 'intermediation' refers to the process whereby potential borrowers are brought together with potential lenders by a third party, the intermediary.

1.1 Major UK financial intermediaries

(a) Clearing banks

The familiar High Street banks provide a payment and cheque clearing mechanism. They offer various accounts to investors and provide large amounts of short to medium-term loans to the business sector and the personal sector. They also offer a wide range of financial services to their customers.

(b) Merchant banks

Merchant banks, whether independent, subsidiary to clearing banks, or part of a large financial group, form an important part of the British banking system.

The largest of the merchant banks are members of the Accepting Houses Committee, although acceptance business is now only a small part of their operation. They now concentrate upon the following:

(i) Financial advice to business firms

Few manufacturing or commercial companies of any size can now afford to be without the advice of a merchant bank. Such advice is necessary in order to obtain investment capital, to invest surplus funds, to guard against takeover, or to take over others. Increasingly, the merchant banks have themselves become actively involved in the financial management of their business clients and have had an influence over the direction these affairs have taken.

(ii)   **Providing finance to business**

Merchant banks also compete in the services outlined earlier of leasing, factoring, hire-purchase and general lending. They are also the gateway to the capital market for long-term funds because they are likely to have specialised departments handling capital issues as 'issuing houses'.

(iii)   **Foreign trade**

A number of merchant banks are active in the promotion of foreign trade by providing marine insurance, credits, assistance in appointing foreign agents and in arranging foreign payments.

Not all merchant banks are large and not all offer a wide range of services: the term is now rather misused. However, it is expected that a merchant bank will operate without the large branch network necessary for a clearing bank, it will work closely with its business clients, and will be more ready to take business risks and promote business enterprise than a clearing bank. It is probably fair to say that a merchant bank is essentially in the general business of creating wealth and of helping those who show that they are capable of successful business enterprise.

(c)   **Savings banks**

The National Savings Bank operates through the Post Office system and is used to collect funds from the small personal saver which are mainly invested in government securities. The Trustee Savings Bank fulfils a similar role but in the last few years has expanded its role until its operations more closely resemble those of the clearing banks.

(d)   **Building societies**

These take deposits from the household sector and lend to individuals buying their own homes. They have recently grown rapidly and now provide many of the services offered by the clearing banks. They are not involved, however, in providing funds for the business sector.

(e)   **Finance companies**

These come in three main varieties.

(i)   Finance houses, providing medium-term instalment credit to the business and personal sector. These are usually owned by business sector firms or by other financial intermediaries. The trend is toward them offering services similar to the clearing banks.

(ii)   Leasing companies, leasing capital equipment to the business sector. They are usually subsidiaries of other financial institutions.

(iii)   Factoring companies, providing loans to companies secured on trade debtors, are usually bank subsidiaries. Other debt collection and credit control services are usually on offer.

(f)   **Pension funds**

These collect funds from employers and employees to provide pensions on retirement or death. As their outgoings are relatively predictable they can afford to invest funds for long periods of time.

(g)   **Insurance companies**

These use premium income from policyholders to invest mainly in long-term assets such as bonds, equities and property. Their outgoings from their long-term business (life assurance and pensions) and their short-term activities (fire, accident, motor etc) are once again relatively predictable and therefore they can afford to tie up a large proportion of their funds for a long period of time.

(h)   **Investment and unit trusts**

Investment trusts are limited liability companies collecting funds by selling shares and bonds and investing the proceeds, mainly in the ordinary shares of other companies. Funds at their disposal are limited to the amount of securities in issue plus retained profits, hence they are often referred to as 'closed end funds'. Unit trusts on the other hand, although investing in a similar way, find their funds vary according to whether investors are buying new units or cashing in old ones. Both offer substantial diversification opportunities to the personal investor.

(i)   **The discount houses**

Holders of interest rate-sensitive investment instruments such as bills of exchange and certificates of deposit can sell them, ie discount them, to a discount house before the instrument's maturity date. Discount houses make their money by buying and selling such instruments.

(j)   **Others**

Many other intermediaries exist. For example, the 3i Group provides equity and debt finance to medium-sized firms. The Export Credits Guarantee Department, originally wholly owned by the government, provides insurance and short-term finance for exporters.

1.2   Financial markets

These are not actually a sector of the economy but rather 'places' where surplus and deficit units can meet. Specialist traders usually operate in these market places buying and selling financial claims on their own account to smooth over temporary excesses or shortages of funds. Two types of activity are usually recognised within each market.

(a)   **Primary markets**, which deal in new issues of loanable funds. These raise new finance for deficit units.

(b)   **Secondary markets**, which do not provide new funds for deficit units but allow existing holders of financial claims to sell them to other investors.

Primary markets provide a focal point for borrowers and lenders to meet. The forces of supply and demand should ensure that funds find their way to their most productive usage.

Secondary markets allow holders of financial claims to realise their investment before the maturity date by selling them to other investors. They therefore increase the willingness of surplus units to invest their funds. A well-developed secondary market should also reduce the price volatility of securities, as regular trading in 'second-hand' securities should ensure smoother price changes. This should further encourage investors to supply funds.

1.3   Role of financial intermediaries in financial markets

Financial markets help investors achieve the following ends.

(a)   **Diversification**

By giving investors the opportunity to invest in a wide range of enterprises it allows them to spread their risk. This is the familiar 'Don't put all your eggs in one basket' strategy.

(b)   **Risk shifting**

Deficit units, particularly companies, issue various types of security on the financial markets to give investors a choice of the degree of risk they take. For example company loan stocks secured on the assets of the business offer low risk with relatively low returns, whereas equities carry much higher risk with correspondingly higher returns.

(c)   **Hedging**

> **Definition**   Hedging is the reduction or elimination of risk and uncertainty.

Financial markets offer participants the opportunity to reduce risk through hedging which involves taking out counterbalancing contracts to offset existing risks. For example, if a UK exporter is awaiting payment in francs from a French customer he is subject to the risk that the French franc may decline in value over the credit period. To hedge this risk he could enter a counterbalancing contract and arrange to sell the French francs forward (agree to exchange them for pounds at a fixed future date at a fixed exchange rate). In this way he has used the foreign exchange market to insure his future sterling receipt. Similar hedging possibilities are available on interest rates and on equity prices.

(d)   **Arbitrage**

> **Definition**   Arbitrage is the process of buying a security at a low price in one market and simultaneously selling in another market at a higher price to make a profit.

Although it is only the primary markets that raise new funds for deficit units, well-developed secondary markets are required to fulfil the above roles for lenders and borrowers. Without these opportunities more surplus units would be tempted to keep their funds 'under the bed' rather than putting them at the disposal of deficit units although the emergence of *disintermediation* and *securitisation* where companies lend and borrow funds directly between themselves has provided a further means of dealing with cash flow surpluses and deficits.

2   THE COMMERCIAL BANKS

2.1   The primary banks

The primary banks are also known as retail banks, and consist of all banks who participate in the Bank of England's clearing system which was described above. The main commercial banks are the big high street ones (Barclays, Lloyds, Midland and Nat West), together with the Northern Ireland Banks, the Trustee Savings Bank, Girobank and the Abbey National, which was previously a building society.

2.2   Secondary banks

These are principally the merchant banks, foreign banks and consortium banks, and almost all of them are London-based. They are sometimes also referred to as the wholesale banks because they have few, if any, branches and deal only in very large amounts of money obtained either directly from personal, business and public sector customers or via brokers in the City money markets. They are involved only to a minor extent in the payments mechanism and so their volume of sight deposits to total deposits is very small. They have relatively few customers, mostly major companies, and deal mainly in large term deposits and loans.

The London money markets are an important source of the wholesale deposits that make up the deposit base of the secondary banks and of the large term lending that is their chief characteristic. The activities of the secondary banks are far more heavily involved with foreign currency than are those of the primary banks - British merchant banks typically have over 50% of their assets and liabilities in foreign currency, while the figure can be over 90% for foreign and consortium banks.

The secondary banks are highly competitive and work on more narrow margins than the primary banks, but with no extensive branch networks their costs are lower; this means that though they pay more for their funds than the primary banks - they have very little low cost current account money available to them - their rates on loans and deposits are still attractive to customers.

The distinction between primary/retail and secondary/wholesale banks has become increasingly blurred over time as a result of the diversification of services and the acquisition or setting up of subsidiary institutions. In particular the primary banks, and notably the London clearers, have moved into those forms of business (eg, term lending) that were previously the preserve of the secondary banks, have increased their foreign currency transactions, and have become extensively involved in the parallel money markets. These and other activities may be carried out either directly or through subsidiaries and associates. In a similar way many secondary banks, especially the merchant banks, have expanded their range of activities, though with the exception of one or two foreign banks hardly any have gone so far as to attempt to establish substantial numbers of retail branches with the large-scale introduction of services aimed principally at the personal customer.

2.3   The clearing banks

The six members of the London Bankers' Clearing House are closely linked with the Scottish Clearing Banks. The Clearing Houses are systems for simplifying daily payments so that all the thousands of individual customer payments are reduced to a few transfers of credit between the members. The great bulk of the business is transacted by the big four - Barclays, Lloyds, Midland and National Westminster. Most of the payments made by transfers of bank credit within the UK pass through the various clearing systems of these banks.

The work of these institutions can best be understood through a consideration of the main items in their balance sheets.

(a)   **Liabilities**

The money for which the banks are responsible comes chiefly from their customers' sight and time deposits - mostly current and deposit accounts with which most people are familiar. An important additional item relates to Certificates of Deposit. These are issued generally for a minimum amount of £50,000 and a maximum of £500,000 with an initial term to maturity of from three months to five years.

(b)   **Assets**

Customers' money, as already explained, is re-lent in a variety of ways. The main aim of the banks is to have a range of lending instruments of varying terms so that money can be recovered quickly and yet, at the same time, earn the maximum return. Some funds, however, have to be kept in balances at the Bank of England for use in settling inter-bank debts through the Clearing House.

Commercial banks' lending takes the following main forms:

(i)   **Money at call and short notice**

This is money lent to a group of institutions known as discount houses, which operate in the short-term **money market**. Discount houses originally dealt as specialist houses discounting commercial bills of exchange ie, lending money on the security of approved bills. They now operate not only in commercial bills but much more widely in any first class security with a short maturity period. They fulfil a useful function in borrowing money at call and very short notice and re-lending at longer periods in the knowledge that not all the money will be re-called at the same time. If they have to repay money they do not have, they possess the right to borrow from the Bank of England at the Bank's Minimum Lending Rate which is usually higher than the normal current market rate for short-term funds.

(ii)   **Treasury bills**

The clearing banks and discount houses also hold the Government's own short-term securities - Treasury bills, which operate in much the same way as commercial bills.

(iii)   **Commercial or trade bills**

These constitute a definite agreement to pay a certain sum of money at an agreed place and time. A bill is really a sophisticated IOU which is of very great value in foreign trade because it allows exporters to give credit to foreign buyers and yet obtain payments from banks as soon as goods are shipped. The necessary arrangements are nearly always handled by merchant banks. A commercial bill can be held until payment is due (unusual), discounted with a bank or discount house (normal), or used to pay another debt (not common in modern practice).

(iv)   **Loans to customers**

The clearing banks lend widely to individuals, private business customers, companies and organisations in the public sector. They do so by overdraft term facilities and loans repayable in instalments during an agreed period. Until recently, they were reluctant to lend directly for more than short periods, but increasingly they have become involved in the longer-term (up to about eight years) for business firms and even, under American influence, in the long term mortgage market.

(v)   **Trade investments**

There are many specialist financial and lending activities that the banks are reluctant to handle through their general branches. They prefer to finance these indirectly through the ownership and overall control of specialist subsidiaries. Such activities include:

•   **Hire purchase**, much of it for the purchase of motor vehicles.

- **Leasing** ie, hiring vehicles or equipment as opposed to purchase or hire-purchase, a practice encouraged by the peculiarities of the British taxation system.

- **Factoring and invoice discounting** ie, lending to business firms on the security of approved trade debts or taking over responsibility for the collection of trade debts; this is a method that allows a firm to give credit in competitive markets and still be paid for goods in order to keep necessary cash flowing through the firm.

3   THE CREATION OF MONEY

3.1   Introduction

This section considers the process for creating money under a modern banking system.

3.2   Money creation under a fractional reserve system

A **fractional reserve system** is one where banks only keep part of their assets in the form of cash to repay investors. The rest of the assets are in the form of investments which cannot easily be converted into cash eg,

Bank Z - Balance sheet at Day 1

	£		£
Share capital	100	Fixed assets	100
Customer deposits	1,000	Cash	1,000
	1,100		1,100

In this simple example, share capital finances fixed assets, and so can be ignored. The customer deposits represent current accounts of customers. The bank therefore has a liability to repay all of these on demand.

However, since not all customers want their cash out at once, the bank only has to hold say 1/10 (£100) in the form of 'cash' (in practice, mainly deposits at the central bank). The rest can be loaned to other customers. If the bank loans £900 to customers, the balance sheet will look as follows:

Bank Z - Balance sheet at Day 2

	£		£
Share capital	100	Fixed assets	100
Customer deposits	1,000	Loans	900
		Cash	100
	1,100		1,100

Note that there is now only £100 cash in the bank, the remaining £900 is in circulation and will eventually be spent and deposited back with the bank. The balance sheet will now look as follows:

Bank Z - Balance sheet at Day 3

	£		£
Share capital	100	Fixed assets	100
Customer deposits (1,000 + 900)	1,900	Loans	900
		Cash (100 + 900)	1,000
	2,000		2,000

3.3 . How much money is there in the above system?

The vital point to grasp is that the economy in the above example started with £1,000 cash, (ignoring the cash used to subscribe for the share capital and buy the fixed assets). This cash was held outside the banking system and could be spent. There was therefore £1,000 money in the economy in the form of cash.

Day 1

When that cash is deposited in the bank in day 1, the **money** in the economy becomes the £1,000 of **deposits**. Remember that money is what can be spent - it is the means of exchange. Thus when the cash is in the bank it is not the **cash** that will be spent but the **customer deposits** - people will write out cheques and spend their bank balance - their deposits.

Day 2

When the bank loans out £900 in day 2, the amount of **money** in the economy is £1,900 - the £1,000 of deposits as above plus the £900 cash that is now back in circulation and can be spent.

Day 3

When this £900 is deposited back at the bank the money in the economy is still £1,900 - the amount of customer deposits at the bank.

Day 4 to say 20

We can now extend the example because the bank only needs to keep 10% of its deposits in the form of cash. The bank can continue to lend money, have it redeposited and then lend it again until customer deposits reach £10,000. The balance sheet will now be:

Bank Z - Balance sheet at Day 20

	£		£
Share capital	100	Fixed assets	100
Customer deposits	10,000	Loans	9,000
		Cash	1,000
	10,100		10,100

The money in the economy is now £10,000 - the customer deposits.

Conclusion
- One definition of money in a modern economy comprises deposits in the banking system plus cash held outside the banking system.

- The banks **create money**. In the above example they created £9,000 of money out of an initial £1,000.

- Money is whatever can be spent. In the above examples it was bank deposits and cash outside the system. Clearly there are other forms of money - building society accounts, liquid investments of various sorts, etc.

4   THE MAIN FINANCIAL MARKETS

The following are the major financial markets in the UK, both offering primary and secondary markets.

4.1   The capital markets

These are concerned with trading in financial claims with lives of more than one year. The bulk of this business is conducted on the Stock Exchange, which includes the main market and the Unlisted Securities Market. The major types of securities are as follows:

(i)   Public sector and foreign stocks;

(ii)   Company securities; and

(iii)   Eurobonds

Definition   Eurobonds are bonds denominated in a currency other than that of the national currency of the issuing company (nothing to do with Europe!)

As the Stock Exchange is of crucial importance in meeting the financial needs of business and government, its operation is dealt with in more detail later.

4.2   The money markets

These are wholesale markets for funds, largely between financial institutions. No physical location exists, transactions being conducted by telephone or telex. On the discount markets discount houses borrow funds short-term (overnight or on demand) largely from the clearing banks and invest them in Treasury, Local Authority and Commercial Bills and various short-term securities. The parallel money markets trade in a range of unsecured financial claims the interest rates of which move closely together. The major participants are the banks, local authorities, building societies and industrial and commercial companies. This market also deals in Eurocurrency ie, currency held on deposit or invested outside its country of origin.

4.3   Classifying sources of finance

In order to provide a framework for study of sources of finance, they must be classified in an appropriate way. There are a number of possible classifications, but for the purposes of this text one distinction is of particular importance - namely the distinction between the money and capital markets.

The following classification is therefore applied:

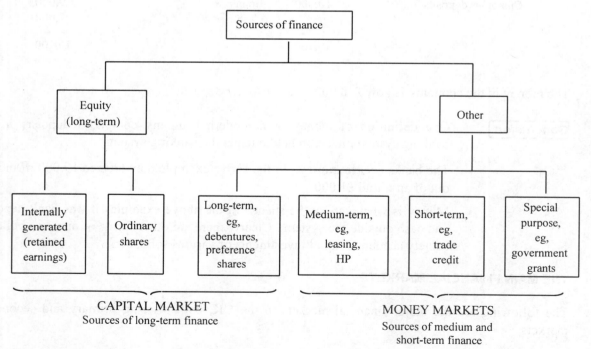

Each of these categories of finance will need to be considered in more detail as the text progresses.

Definitions of long-term, medium-term and short-term are somewhat elastic but as a rough guide the following durations can be taken.

Short-term	Up to one year
Medium-term	1 year to 5 years
Long-term	5 years or more

4.4   The money market and money market instruments

The money market is a market mainly for short-term and very short-term loans, in both sterling and foreign currencies, though some longer-term transactions are also undertaken. In fact, it is not one single market but a number of different markets which closely inter-connect with each other. The main participants in these markets are the Bank of England, the commercial banks and the discount houses. Other participants include the finance houses, building societies, investment and unit trusts, local authorities, large companies, and some private individuals.

5   THE STOCK EXCHANGE

5.1   Introduction

The Stock Exchange is the institution that embodies many of the processes of the capital market. The Stock Exchange is essentially the market for the issued securities of public companies, government bonds, local authority and other publicly owned institution loans and for some overseas stocks. Without the ability to sell long-term securities easily few people would be prepared to risk making their money available to business or public authorities. This is why a public company which wishes its securities to be 'marketable' cannot proceed with an issue until it knows that it is acceptable to the Stock Exchange.

The Stock Exchange assists the allocation of capital to industry; if the market thinks highly of a company that company's shares will rise in value and it will be able to raise fresh capital through the new issue market at relatively low cost. On the other hand, less popular companies will have difficulty in raising new capital. Thus, the Stock Exchange helps successful firms to grow and the unsuccessful to contract.

5.2   The role of speculation

Any consideration of the Stock Exchange has to face up to the problem of speculation ie, gambling. For many, the idea of people gambling with the ownership of firms in which people have invested their working lives, skills and ambitions is understandably offensive. On the other hand, it is claimed that speculation assists the working of the capital market and so improves the economic opportunities of thousands of workers. It is suggested that speculation can perform the following functions:

(a)   It smoothes price fluctuations Speculators, to be successful, have to be a little ahead of the rest of the market. The skilled speculator will be buying when others are still selling and selling when others are still buying. The speculator, therefore, removes the peaks and troughs of inevitable price fluctuations and so makes price changes less violent.

(b)   Speculation ensures that shares are readily marketable. Almost all stock can be quickly bought and sold, at a price. Without the chance of profit there would be no professional operator willing to hold stock or agree to sell stock that is not immediately available. The fact that there are always buyers and sellers is of considerable importance to the ordinary individual investor who may have to sell unexpectedly at any time with little warning.

Nevertheless, these advantages, whilst very real for a market containing mostly individual investors, begin to look less persuasive when it is remembered that the proportion of ordinary shares held by private individuals has now fallen to under a quarter.

5.3   Share ownership

During much of the post war period share ownership on the part of private individuals has been in decline. As a proportion of personal sector gross wealth shares have fallen from 25% in 1966 to about 10% currently. The growth of contractual savings schemes, particularly pension funds and life assurance policies, has resulted in dominance of the stock market by institutional investors. The most significant factor influencing share ownership during the post-war period was the collapse of the stock market in the mid 1970s which led to a sharp fall in private ownership of the shares - falling in fact by 50% 1971-1976. Even after privatisation issues, over 75% of shares are now held by financial institutions.

There are several reasons put forward to explain this trend including unfavourable tax treatment for shareholdings and related gains, minimum broking commissions and low business profits in the mid 1970s. Since 1979 government policy has favoured the development of individual shareholdings and is supported by the following:

(a)   **The privatisation programme**. A number of large government owned organisations have been privatised with particular arrangements being made to encourage employees and small investors to purchase shares. This has not only directly stimulated the wider ownership of shares but has also raised public awareness and interest.

(b)   **Personal Equity Plans** (to be replaced by ISAs in April 1999). These were introduced in the 1986 budget to enable people to invest in shares entirely free of tax on reinvested dividends and capital gains. The scheme came into operation on 1 January 1987 and was designed to be simple and encourage small investors to enter the equity market.

The scheme now allows PEPs to be based solely upon unit trusts thereby contributing to wider stock market investment by private individuals.

Peps are administered by financial institutions such as banks and unit trust managers who:

- arrange the buying and selling of shares/unit trusts;
- hold share certificates on behalf of investors;
- keep detailed records; and
- effect all dealings with the tax authorities.

Factors which are likely to encourage further developments in individual share ownership include the future privatisation programme, reductions in brokerage fees, the expansion of 'money shops', the further entry of building societies and insurance companies into the market for unit trusts and the recommencement of a bull stock market. Indeed it is the latter which is likely to be the most important single demand determinant for shares held by the personal sector.

Share ownership has increased steadily throughout the 1980s - about 20% of the adult population now hold shares. However, a majority of these holdings are relatively small and relate to privatisation issues - only about 5% of the population hold a wide range of shares, excluding privatisation stocks.

5.4   Buying and selling shares

An investor will contact a **broker** in order to buy and sell shares. The broker may act as agent for the investor by contacting a **market-maker** (see below) or he may act as principal if he makes a market in (ie, buys and sells on his own behalf) those shares (ie, he is a **broker-dealer**).

Market-makers maintain stocks of securities in a number of quoted companies, appropriate to the level of trading in that security, and their income is generated by the profits they make by dealing in securities. This profit is approximately framework by the difference between the 'bid' and 'offered' price for a given security - the price at which a market-maker is prepared to buy the stock and the price at which he would be prepared to sell it.

Certain deals are carried out on the Stock Exchange for purely speculative reasons. There are two types of speculative dealers, bulls and bears.

(Definition)   A **bull** believes that share prices will rise. He buys securities in the hope that he will be able to sell them for more than he bought them for.

(Definition)   A **bear** believes that share prices will fall. He sells securities which he does not at present own, in the hope that he can buy them at a lower price later.

From this, it follows that a general rise in share prices will favour bulls whereas a general fall will favour bears.

5.5   Determining share prices

As stated above, dealers quote prices for shares when requested. These quotations are based on expectations of the general marketability of the shares and, as such, will probably vary constantly. For example, assume a quotation in respect of a fictitious company, Clynch plc.

The dealer might quote 145, 150.

This means he will buy the shares at £1.45 each and sell at £1.50 each.

If the investor wants to buy 10,000 shares, the dealer might decide to raise his prices to encourage people to sell and thereby ensure that he will have sufficient shares to meet the order he has just received. Thus, his next quote might be 150, 155.

Conversely, if the investor wants to sell 10,000 shares, the dealer will be left with that number of additional shares, and he may wish to reduce his quotation to encourage people to buy: thus he may quote 140, 145.

If sufficient numbers of people wish to buy and sell the shares of Clynch plc, eventually a price will be found at which only marginal transactions are taking place.

If the general economic climate is reflected by each company's shares, it follows that there will be times when in general people wish to sell shares and hence prices drop, and other times when in general people are buying shares and prices rise.

6   OTHER CAPITAL MARKET INSTITUTIONS

6.1   Introduction

In this section we shall consider the other institutions that comprise the capital markets. These will include not only the processes or the institution in which the processes occur (eg, the Unlisted Securities Market) but also the participants in the market.

6.2   The Unlisted Securities Market

From about 1973 the Stock Exchange had not been attracting the small to medium-sized companies which previously would have regarded a listing as a natural step in their growth. The main reasons were high interest rates and inflation but increased regulation, resulting in higher costs of obtaining a listing, were also a factor.

When the Wilson Committee's interim report in 1978 emphasised the importance of encouraging the growth of small and medium-sized businesses, the Stock Exchange responded by publicising the arrangements already in existence for dealings in unlisted securities. The interest aroused and the concern for more effective control over these dealings eventually led to the establishment of the Unlisted Securities Market in 1980.

Companies had to satisfy certain conditions before they were allowed to join the USM eg, at least 10% of the company's shares had to be offered for sale. During the 1980s the USM went from strength to strength, with more than 800 companies joining, and many graduating from the USM to a full listing.

However the 1990s saw a reduction in the number of new companies joining. The recession played a part in this, since there were fewer small companies growing strongly, but the major problem was new EC directives which drove up the costs of floating on the USM to a degree that they were only slightly less than the costs of a full listing, so new companies tended to go straight for a listing.

The Stock Exchange acted by preventing new companies from joining the USM after 1994 and it wound up the USM at the end of 1996. In its place is a new Alternative Investment Market (AIM).

6.3   The Alternative Investment Market

Trading on the AIM began in June 1995. It is designed as a separate market for the shares of smaller growing companies that are not yet ready for a full listing; for example some former USM companies joined the AIM when the USM was wound up.

There are no requirements governing the size of a company's market capitalisation, the length of its trading history or the minimum proportion of shares which must be in public hands before a company can join the AIM. To be admitted, a company must publish the information required in the Public Offers of Securities Regulations 1995, must have a nominated adviser (recognised by the Stock Exchange) to help it through the admission procedure and to meet the ongoing requirements, and must have a nominated broker who will try and find matching business in the company's shares.

The nominated adviser can be anyone authorised to carry on investment business under the Financial Services Act 1986, such as a firm of accountants.

The Stock Exchange's planned rules for the AIM have been broadly welcomed by the investment community, and the early years of the AIM appear to have been as successful as was the USM in its early years.

6.4   Over the counter market

The USM's initial rapid growth was matched by that of its smaller rival, the over-the-counter market (OTC).

The OTC is really a collection of telephone share markets. There are no centrally collected figures - regulation is one of the OTC's greatest problems - but it was estimated that at its peak in the mid 1980s there were 15 leading market makers quoting prices in more than 150 companies' shares.

There were two main reasons for the growth of the OTC.

(a)   Business Expansion Scheme relief (now terminated) was available to OTC companies, but not to quoted companies including USM companies.

(b)   A willingness to deal in the shares of companies whose trading records were too short even to qualify for the USM.

The OTC has declined in recent years as first the USM established itself and then the **Financial Services Act** created restrictions. Currently there is little activity in the OTC.

7   FINANCIAL MARKET EFFICIENCY

7.1   The efficiency of financial markets

The efficiency of a financial market may be examined in various ways; the most relevant here being in terms of information processing.

> **Definition**   **Information processing efficiency -** this reflects the extent to which information regarding the future prospects of a security is reflected in its current price.

If all known information is reflected in a security's price then investment becomes a 'fair game'. All investors have the same chance, even if some of them have access to more information, because under this concept of efficiency all information that can be known is already reflected in the share price. Consider for example a pension fund manager who discovers that a particular company has made a scientific breakthrough that will lead to its expected profit doubling in the next few years. If the market were not efficient the manager could buy shares in the company at a cheap price from small investors who had not yet discovered the firm's new circumstances. In this situation the informed investor is gaining at the expense of the uninformed investor. In an efficient market, however, the share price of the company would reflect all information that could be known on the company and hence the informed investor would have to pay a 'fair' price for the shares.

The idea of 'fairness' is important as it encourages individuals to invest. This is not to say that there is no risk involved in investment, but it means the risks are fair in that returns received by investors should be proportionate to risks taken. Also it means that firms with the best apparent future prospects will command the highest share prices and therefore find it easier to attract new funds. Overall this should ensure allocative efficiency.

Information processing efficiency is of great importance to financial management as it means that the results of management decisions will be quickly and accurately reflected in share prices. For example, if a firm undertakes an investment project which will generate a large surplus then in an efficient market it should see the value of its equity rise. Accordingly there have been many tests of the so-called Efficient Market Hypothesis (EMH) for the USA and the UK stock markets.

> **Definition**   The Efficient Market Hypothesis argues that stock markets are efficient, in that information is reflected in share prices accurately and rapidly.

For the purposes of testing, the EMH is usually broken down into three categories, as follows.

(a)   The weak form;
(b)   The semi-strong form; and
(c)   The strong form.

These are examined in the following sections. Each concerns the **type** of information which is reflected in share prices.

7.2   Efficient market hypothesis - weak form

> **Definition**   The weak form of the hypothesis states that share prices fully reflect information included in historic share price movements and patterns.

If this hypothesis is correct, then it should be impossible to predict future share price movements from historic patterns. For example, if a company's share price had increased steadily over the last few months to a current price of £2.50, this price will already fully reflect the information about growth. The next change in share price could be either upwards or downwards, with equal probability.

Because of this randomness in share price movements, this is frequently referred to as the **random walk hypothesis**. This means that the movements of share prices over time approximate to a random walk. It also follows that because the current share price fully reflects past information about price changes it is the best estimate of the share's value. Thus it makes no sense to talk about a share being 'below' its normal value just because its present price is less than the former. There is no evidence to suggest that the price will climb to its so called 'normal' level rather than fall still further.

There is strong evidence to support the random walk view, and hence the weak form of the efficient market hypothesis.

7.3   Efficient market hypothesis - semi-strong form

Definition   The semi-strong form of the hypothesis states that current share prices reflect not only historic share price information but also current publicly available information about the company.

This hypothesis can be tested by examining the way in which the market reacts to new information about a company eg, share splits, interim results, and so on.

The evidence also tends to confirm the semi-strong form of the hypothesis.

7.4   Efficient market hypothesis - strong form

Definition   The strong form of the hypothesis states that current share prices reflect not only historic share price patterns and current public knowledge, but also all possible (ie, inside) information about the company.

This hypothesis can be tested by analysing market response to the release of previously confidential information about the company. If the hypothesis is correct then the mere publication of the information should have no impact on the share price, consequently it should not be possible to make profits by dealing in response to 'inside' information. (This would be insider dealing and is illegal in both the UK and the USA.)

The evidence is that the market does react when information is published. Profits could therefore be made by insider dealing, and thus it would appear that the strong form of the Efficient Market Hypothesis is not correct.

7.5   Implications of the EMH for financial managers

The above tests demonstrate that although the stock market is not completely efficient it is largely so. This has significant implications for financial management.

(a)   **Timing of financial policy**

Some financial managers argue that there is a right and a wrong time to issue new securities. New share issues should only be made when the market is at a high rather than a low. However, if the market is efficient how are financial managers to know if tomorrow's prices are going to be higher or lower than today's? Today's 'low' could turn out to be the highest the market will stand for the next five years. All current information is already reflected in share prices and unless the financial manager knows something the rest of the market does not then it is impossible to say in which direction the market will turn.

(b)   **Project evaluation**

When evaluating new projects financial managers usually use required rates of return drawn from securities traded on the capital market. For example, the rate of return required on a particular project may be determined by observing the rate of return required by shareholders of firms investing in projects of similar risks. This assumes that securities are fairly priced for the risk they carry - in other words that the stock market is efficient. If this is not the case then financial managers could be appraising projects on the wrong basis and therefore making bad investment decisions.

(c)   **Creative accounting**

In an efficient stock market share prices are based upon the expected future cash flows offered by securities and their level of risk. In turn these expectations reflect all current information. There is little point in firms attempting to distort current information to their advantage as investors will quickly see through any such attempts.

One American test of the semi-strong form of the hypothesis by Kaplan and Roll examined the impact on share prices of companies moving from accelerated to straight-line depreciation. This change only increased reported accounting earnings: actual cash flows remained unaltered as tax allowable depreciation remained unchanged. Initially share prices rose, possibly because the investors were not immediately informed of the changes, but within three months share prices fell as investors concluded that the cosmetic alterations to earnings were a sign of weakness rather than strength.

Other studies support this conclusion and it seems unlikely that investors can be 'fooled' by the manipulation of accounting profit figures or changes in capital structure resulting from capitalisation issues. Eventually (and usually sooner rather than later) investors will realise the cash-flow consequences and alter share prices appropriately.

(d)   **Mergers and takeovers**

If shares are correctly priced this means that the purchase of a share is a zero NPV transaction. In other words the expected returns when discounted to present value will equal the current price of the security. This does not mean that the share is a bad investment but merely that it is fairly priced - its price is commensurate with its risk and return.

If this is true the rationale behind many mergers and takeovers may be questioned. If companies are acquired at their current equity valuation then the purchasers are effectively breaking even. If they are to make a significant gain on the acquisition then they must rely upon operating economies or rationalisation to provide the savings. If the acquirer pays current equity value plus a premium of 50% (which is not uncommon) these savings would have to be considerable to make the takeover attractive.

(e)   **Validity of current market price**

If the market is efficient, statements such as 'XYZ shares are under-priced' are meaningless. The market reflects all known information in existing share prices and investors therefore know that if they purchase a security at current market price they are receiving a fair risk and return combination for their money. Financial managers should also know that if they sell new equities at current market prices they are raising funds at a fair cost.

Therefore there should be no need for substantial discounts on new issues: if the current price is fair investors will need no great extra incentive to purchase the securities as in an efficient capital market they are unlikely to find better buys elsewhere.

8   THE RISK-RETURN TRADE-OFF

We have just concluded that if the stock market is efficient then share prices will reflect a fair risk and return combination. We now need to consider this risk-return relationship in more detail, and then consider how it is reflected in market prices.

8.1   The relationship between risk and return

In considering return, the tradeoff with risk is of fundamental importance. In this context risk refers not to the possibility of total loss, but rather to the likelihood of actual returns varying from those forecast.

Consider four investment opportunities A, B, C, and D. These may be described on the following risk and return graph:

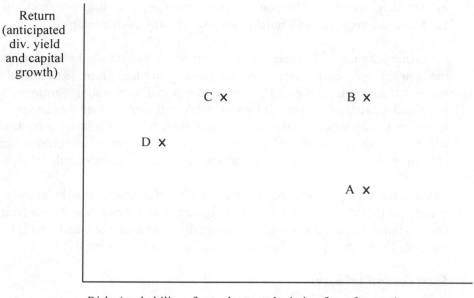

Note that: Risk A   =   Risk B

Return B   =   Return C

In choosing between the investment opportunities:

B is preferable to A - higher return, same risk
C is preferable to B - same return, lower risk

The question is whether D is preferable to C – lower return, lower risk. This question can only be answered if the tradeoff between risk and return is known.

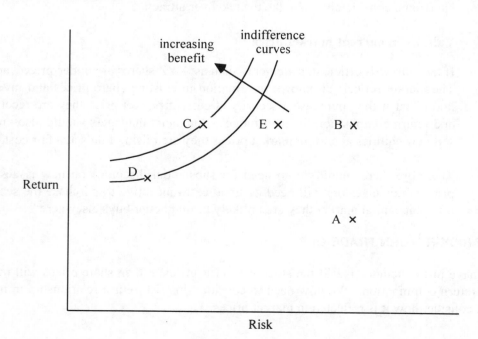

The indifference curves represent alternative combinations of risks and return between which the investor is indifferent. Obviously each investor will have different indifference curves, but they will tend to be of the slope indicated above. This is because most investors are averse to risk, and will demand a higher return to compensate.

Thus, the indifference curves represent the tradeoff between risk and return for an individual investor. In this example, the investor would prefer C to D as it is on a higher indifference curve - the lower level of risk for D does not adequately compensate for the lower level of return.

8.2   Activity

By drawing a third indifference curve onto the diagram above, determine whether the investor would prefer E to C.

8.3   Activity solution

The indifference curve will lie below the lower of the two curves already given. Since C is on a higher indifference curve than E, the investor will prefer C, not E.

9   THE PATTERN OF INTEREST RATES

9.1   Introduction

The pattern of interest rates refers to the variety of interest rates on different financial assets. It is thus different from the **general level** of interest rates. How can the pattern of interest rates be explained?

The answer lies in several factors.

(a)   **The duration of the loan** - This is referred to as the term structure and is examined in more detail a little later.

Though they usually move up and down together, short-term interest rates (ie, those for loans up to three months) are normally lower than longer term rates of interest. The simple reason for this is that the longer the period of a loan the more the risk for the lender - uncertainty is greater and the possibility of default increases, hence he will want a higher rate of return to compensate him for this enhanced degree of risk on a longer-term loan. However, it is possible for short-term interest rates to be temporarily higher than longer-term rates eg, as the result of a foreign exchange crisis. It is also possible for even overnight money to become extremely expensive when expressed as an annual rate: this phenomenon can occur as a consequence of the need for banks and other institutions in the money markets to balance their books at the end of each day.

(b)   **Risk**

There is a trade-off between risk and return. Higher-risk borrowers will have to pay higher yields on their borrowing, to compensate lenders for the greater risk involved.

For this reason, a bank will charge a higher rate of interest on loans to borrowers from a high-risk category than to a low-risk category borrower. Banks will assess the creditworthiness of the borrower, and set a rate of interest on its loan at a certain mark-up above its base rate or LIBOR. In general, larger companies are charged at a lower rate of interest than smaller companies.

(c)   **The need to make a profit on re-lending**

Financial intermediaries make their profits from re-lending at a higher rate of interest than the cost of their borrowing. Intermediaries must pay various costs out of the differences, including bad debts and administration charges. What is left will be profit.

For example:

(i)   the interest rate charged on bank loans exceeds the rate paid on deposits;

(ii)   the mortgage rate charged by building societies exceeds the interest rate paid on deposits.

(d)   **The size of the loan or deposit**

The yield on assets might vary with the size of the loan or deposit.

(i)   Time deposits above a certain amount will probably attract higher rates of interest than smaller-sized time deposits. The intermediary might be prepared to pay extra for the benefit of holding the liability as a single deposit (greater convenience of administration).

(ii)   The administrative convenience of handling wholesale loans rather than a large number of small retail loans partially explains the lower rates of interest charged by banks on larger loans. (The greater security in lending to a low-risk borrower could also be a factor.)

(e)   **Different types of financial asset**

Different types of financial asset attract different rates of interest. This is partly because different types of asset attract different sorts of lender/investor. For example, bank deposits attract individuals and companies, whereas long-dated government securities are particularly attractive to various institutional investors.

(f)   **International factors**

International interest rates will differ from country to country because of the different risks involved. The main risk is that the exchange rate may move against the investor reducing the capital value of the investment.

9.2   Illustration - world interest rates

Money rates

	Over night	One month	Three mths	Six mths	One year
Belgium	$5\frac{1}{8}$	$5\frac{5}{16}$	$5\frac{9}{16}$	$5\frac{13}{16}$	$6\frac{1}{16}$
France	$5\frac{3}{8}$	$5\frac{1}{2}$	$5\frac{5}{8}$	$5\frac{3}{4}$	$6\frac{1}{8}$
Germany	4.95	4.95	4.95	4.95	5.13
Italy	8	$8\frac{3}{16}$	$8\frac{3}{8}$	$8\frac{5}{8}$	$9\frac{1}{8}$
US	$4\frac{1}{4}$	$4\frac{7}{16}$	$4\frac{11}{16}$	5	$5\frac{9}{16}$
Japan	$2\frac{1}{16}$	$2\frac{1}{16}$	$2\frac{1}{8}$	$2\frac{3}{16}$	$2\frac{9}{16}$
UK	5	$5\frac{1}{16}$	$5\frac{3}{16}$	$5\frac{1}{2}$	$6\frac{1}{4}$

(Source: Financial Times)

Note the very considerable variety of rates across countries and also how the rate increases as the term of the loan is longer.

9.3 Illustration - UK gilt yields

Shorts (Lives up to 5 years)	Yield
Exch $12\frac{1}{2}$pc 1994	5.10
Treas 9pc 1994	5.16
12pc 1995	5.22
Exch 3pc Gas 90-95	4.99
$10\frac{1}{4}$pc 1995	5.89

Five to Fifteen Years	Yield
Exch $12\frac{1}{4}$pc 1999	8.41
Treas $10\frac{1}{2}$pc 1999	8.40
Treas 6pc 1999	8.17

Over Fifteen Years	
Treas 8pc 2009	8.45
Treas $6\frac{1}{4}$pc 2010	8.26
Conv 9pc Ln 2011	8.42

(Source: Financial Times)

Note again the increased yield for the longer dated gilts.

10 THE TERM STRUCTURE OF INTEREST RATES - YIELD CURVES

10.1 The meaning of term structure

Definition The term structure of interest rates refers to the way in which the yield of a security varies according to the term of the security ie, to the length of time before the borrowing will be repaid.

Analysis of term structure is normally carried out by examining risk-free securities such as UK government stocks, also called gilts. Newspapers such as the **Financial Times** show the gross redemption yield (ie, interest yield plus capital gain/loss to maturity) and time to maturity of each gilt on a daily basis.

For example, at the time of writing the yields on three gilts were as follows

Name of gilt	*Gross redemption yield*
Treasury 12% 1995	5.28
Treasury 13% 2000	7.75
Treasury 8% 2009	7.81

These three exhibit the typical situation, with yields rising as the term to maturity increases. A graph can be drawn of the yield for each gilt against the number of years to maturity; the best curve through this set of points is called the yield curve.

At the current time the yield curve looks as follows:

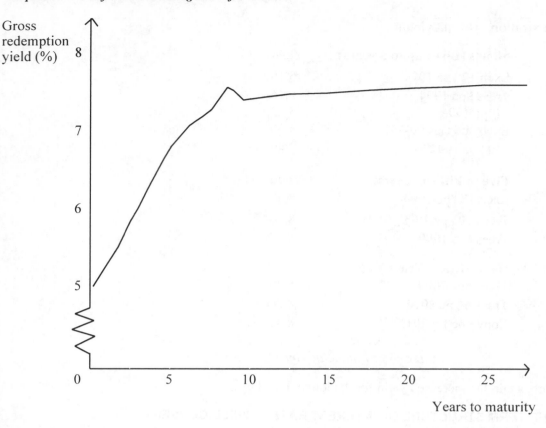

The redemption yield on shorts is less than the redemption yield of mediums and longs, and there is a 'wiggle' on the curve between 5 and 10 years.

10.2   Explanations for the shape of the yield curve

The shape of the yield curve at any particular point in time is generally believed to be a combination of three theories acting together:

- expectations theory
- liquidity preference theory
- market segmentation theory.

Expectations theory

This theory states that the shape of the yield curve varies according to investors' expectations of future interest rates. A curve that rises steeply from left to right indicates that rates of interest are expected to rise in future. There is more demand for short-term securities than long-term securities since investors' expectation is that they will be able to secure higher interest rates in the future so there is no point in buying long-term assets now. The price of short-term assets will be bid up, the price of long-term assets will fall, so the yields on short-term and long-term assets will respectively fall and rise.

A falling yield curve (also called an inverted curve, since it represents the opposite of the usual situation) implies that interest rates are expected to fall. For much of the period of sterling's membership of the ERM, high short-term rates were maintained to support sterling and the yield curve was often inverted since the market believed that the long-term trend in interest rates should be lower than the high short-term rates.

A flat yield curve indicates expectations that interest rates are not expected to change materially in the future.

Liquidity preference theory

Investors have a natural preference for holding cash rather than other investments, even low risk ones such as government securities. They therefore need to be compensated with a higher yield for being deprived of their cash for a longer period of time. The normal shape of the curve as being upwards sloping can be explained by liquidity preference theory.

Market segmentation theory

This theory states that there are different categories of investor who are interested in different segments of the curve. Typically, banks and building societies invest at the short end of the market while pension funds and insurance companies buy and sell long-term gilts. The two ends of the curve therefore have 'lives of their own', since they might react differently to the same set of new economic statistics.

Market segmentation theory explains the 'wiggle' seen in the middle of the curve where the short end of the curve meets the long end - it is a natural disturbance where two different curves are joining and the influence of both the short-term factors and the long-term factors is weakest.

10.3   Significance of yield curves to financial managers

Financial managers should inspect the current shape of the yield curve when deciding on the term of borrowings or deposits, since the curve encapsulates the market's expectations of future movements in interest rates.

For example, a yield curve sloping steeply upwards suggests that interest rates will rise in the future. The manager may therefore wish to avoid borrowing long-term on variable rates, since the interest charge may increase considerably over the term of the loan. Short-term variable rate borrowing or long-term fixed rate borrowing may instead be more appropriate.

11   CAPITAL MARKET INSTRUMENTS

11.1   Introduction

We repeat below the chart showing the connections between the different sources of finance.

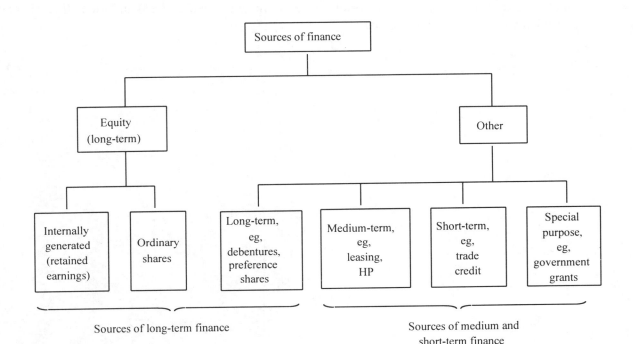

The capital markets are concerned with long-term finance and these are described below.

11.2   Ordinary shares

These usually represent permanent capital because British company law does not normally allow companies to repay ordinary shares although this is possible. Companies try to obtain as much money as possible through shares because the immediate cost can be low (if shareholders accept a low rate of dividend in the expectation of rising share values in the future) and because dividend payment is not guaranteed at any definite rate. Failure to keep to forecast dividends does, of course, damage a company's reputation and make it difficult to raise any further money. However, it is often only possible to issue new shares when capital markets are favourable ie, when share prices are generally high. Unfortunately many companies may then be queuing up to make issues. For an existing public company it is normal to make a new issue of ordinary shares through a **rights issue**. This means that the new shares are first offered to existing shareholders at a favourable price. If the shareholders do not wish to buy the shares they can sell their 'rights' to others through the capital market. The reason for this is that any increase in the number of shares **dilutes** the value of existing shares because the future profit has to be shared out more thinly. It is only fair, therefore, to compensate the shareholders for this dilution by offering them some immediate benefit.

11.3   Preference shares

These pay a fixed dividend but in a period of inflation they are not popular unless there are definite taxation advantages. There are circumstances when preference shares are suitable but under modern conditions they are not now in common use. They are divided into cumulative and non-cumulative preference shares as described in the table below.

11.4   Debentures

This general term covers any loan from the public that can be exchanged on much the same conditions as shares. Today there are secured and unsecured loans and also loans that carry a right to be exchanged for ordinary shares under agreed conditions. The firm has the advantage of a fixed rate of interest which becomes progressively cheaper during inflation and payment of interest is made before calculation of profit for tax purposes - it is an expense which is allowable against tax. On the other hand, the interest has to be paid regardless of profit and debenture holders can sue for unpaid interest and insist on any secured property being sold. In practice only large companies can issue unsecured loan stock. As investors have continued to suffer from inflation, fixed interest investments have declined in popularity.

11.5   Summary of Instruments

Type of capital	Security or voting rights	Income	Amount of capital
Ordinary shares	Usually have voting rights in general meetings of the company. Rank after all creditors and preference shares in liquidation.	Dividends payable at the discretion of the directors (subject to sanction by shareholders) out of undistributed profits remaining after senior claims have been met. Amounts available for dividends but not paid out are retained in the company on behalf of the ordinary shareholders.	The right to all surplus funds after prior claims have been met.
Cumulative preference shares	Right to vote at a general meeting only when dividend is in arrears or when it is proposed to change the legal rights of the shares. Rank after all creditors but usually before ordinary shareholders in liquidation.	A fixed amount per year at the discretion of the directors subject to sanction of shareholders and in accordance with rules regarding dividend payments; arrears accumulate and must be paid before a dividend on ordinary shares may be paid. Note that unlike other forms of debt, the dividend paid on preference shares is not corporation tax deductible.	A fixed amount per share.
Non-cumulative preference shares	Likely to have some voting rights at all times rather than in specified circumstances as in the case of cumulative. Rank as cumulative in liquidation.	A fixed amount per year, as above; arrears do not accumulate.	A fixed amount per share.

Secured debentures and loan stock	The charge is on one or more specific assets, usually land and buildings, which are mortgaged - or a floating charge over all assets. On default, the assets are sold; any surplus adds to the assets of the company available for the satisfaction of creditors; if there is a deficit, the company is liable for the unsatisfied balance. No voting rights.	A fixed annual amount, usually expressed as a percentage of nominal value.	A fixed amount per unit of loan stock or debenture.
Unsecured debentures and loan stock	None; holders have the same rights as ordinary creditors. No voting rights.	A fixed annual amount, usually expressed as a percentage of nominal value.	A fixed amount per unit of loan stock or debenture.

11.6   Convertible loans and preference shares

Convertible stocks are fixed return securities - either secured or unsecured - which may be converted at the option of the holder, into ordinary shares in the same company. Prior to conversion the holders have creditor status, although their rights may be subordinated to those of trade creditors. The conversion rights are either stated in terms of a conversion ratio (ie, the number of ordinary shares into which £100 stock may be converted) or in terms of a conversion price (ie, the right to convert into ordinary shares at a price of Xp) eg, '£100 of stock may be converted into 25 ordinary shares' is a conversion ratio; 'stock may be converted into shares at a value of 400p per share' is the equivalent conversion price.

Sometimes, the conversion price increases during the convertibility - this is done to stimulate early conversion. Another variation is to issue partly convertible stocks whereby only a portion of the stock - usually 50% - may be converted. Conversion rights usually cater for an adjustment in the event of capitalisation, rights issues, etc. Convertible preference shares are also possible.

From the investor's point of view, convertible stocks offer a low-risk security with the added advantage of an opportunity to study share price movements before deciding whether to invest in the equity.

The benefits to the issuing company are as follows.

(a)   Obtaining finance at a lower rate of interest than on ordinary debentures (provided that prospects for the company are good).

(b)   Encouraging possible investors with the prospect of a future share in profits.

11.7   Derivatives

Derivatives are instruments that derive from another instrument - typically an equity share. An option is a typical derivative and is described briefly below.

Definition   An **option** is a right to buy or sell shares at a specified price up to a specified date in the future.

There are two groups of options which can be bought or sold: **traditional options** and **traded options.** We shall only describe traditional options here as derivatives are rather marginal as far as this syllabus is concerned.

Traditional options, as their name implies, have existed since the early days of the Stock Exchange. There are two main types which are described below:

(a) **Put option**

An investor who buys a put option buys the right (but not the obligation) to sell shares at a given price (the **exercise price**) until the expiry date of the option. The two parties to the option are known as the **giver** and the **taker**; the giver buys the right to **'put'** the shares onto the taker who is usually an institution. The exercise price or **striking price** will be the market maker's bid price at the time the option was agreed.

(b) **Call option**

Under this option the giver would be able to **'call'** on the taker to supply the shares; in other words, the giver would buy the right to buy shares at the exercise price. In this case, the exercise price would be the market maker's offer price at the time the option was agreed.

12   MONEY MARKET INSTRUMENTS - HOW BUSINESSES BORROW

12.1   Finance for business

Companies need funds to bridge the gap between paying for production of finished goods and receiving money from their customers. They also need them for buying the fixed assets with which they operate. The former type of finance is known as working capital and includes buying materials, paying labour and overheads associated with running the business. The latter type of finance is fixed capital and will pay for items such as machinery, land and buildings.

The general rule is that the term of borrowed funds should match that of the assets which they buy. So funds to finance working capital should be short-term, as they will be replenished when the stocks are sold and debtors make their payments. On the other hand, money raised to buy a piece of equipment with a ten year life, should not need repayment before the ten years are up.

The major source of finance for companies is retained profits, which can be used both for working capital and fixed assets, as they are funds which permanently belong to the business. However, these are insufficient for financing a business, particularly a new one, which has not yet had the opportunity to build up reserves of retained profits.

Short- or medium-term finance is obtained from the money markets as explained below. The way in which a company can obtain long-term finance is by using the capital markets and issuing shares or debentures.

12.2   Loans and overdrafts

Two of the most common forms of borrowing are loans and overdrafts. The main difference between them is that overdrafts are (or should be) of a short-term nature and fluctuate in amount, whereas loans are arranged for specific periods, generally short- to medium-term, and are for specific amounts.

Overdrafts are an extremely expensive way of borrowing and should be avoided. Loans generally carry a lower rate of interest than do overdrafts.

12.3   Trade credit

Borrowing from one's creditors is a less obvious way of obtaining funds. By delaying payments to creditors a company obtains the use of the funds owed for an extended period. It may seem that this is a costless way of borrowing money, but eventually the costs will be passed on in the form of higher prices. In fact, the business sector often complains that certain companies with histories of slow payment are costing their creditors large sums of money; there are frequent requests that charging interest on late payments should be made the legal right of any business which wishes to do so.

However, trade credit taken within reasonable limits is vital for the smooth flow of production and trade; almost all industries have standard credit terms, which allow customers to pay after goods or services have been received.

For example, a manufacturer must buy raw materials and process them into finished goods before selling them. If he sells to the public, he may extend credit to his customers and if he sells to other traders, they will take trade credit. The time between purchasing the raw materials and receiving final payment can be very long indeed, and credit from his suppliers is vital if he is not to go out of business. It is also to his suppliers' benefit to allow credit, otherwise he would be unable to produce more goods until the first ones had been sold and demand for their product would be erratic and unpredictable.

12.4   Hire purchase (HP) and finance leases

Both of these are forms of agreement whereby a company wishing to buy an asset can rent it from an HP or a finance company over a given period, paying a nominal sum at the end of the hire or lease period to obtain ownership of the asset. The effect of such agreements is that the company hiring the asset essentially owns it, but pays for it in instalments; in other words, it borrows money from the HP or lease company to finance the purchase of the asset.

12.5   Bills of exchange

An alternative to (covertly) borrowing from its creditors, a company might decide to use a bill of exchange (a bill).

Definition   A bill of exchange is an unconditional promise to pay a certain amount of money at a given future date (often three months' hence).

A bill of exchange is therefore just like an IOU or a post-dated cheque.

The system of using bills of exchange is fairly complex, so there follows a simplified description, illustrated by Figure 1.

(a)   The first transaction to take place is that a supplier sends goods to a customer, who sends a bill of exchange back to the supplier. Assume that the promise is to pay £100 in three months' time.

(b)   This gives the supplier a little more security than if he had no bill at all, but is no guarantee that the customer will honour the debt. To give more security, the supplier may insist that the customer gets the bill 'accepted'.

Definition   A bill is accepted when a third party, such as a bank, guarantees to honour the bill if the customer defaults.

The customer will have to pay a fee to the bank for accepting (guaranteeing) his bill.

(c)   The supplier could just wait for three months and then collect the £100 from the customer, or from the accepting bank if the customer defaults. Alternatively, he can use the bill to obtain money immediately by selling it, just like any other asset.

The supplier would go to a bank or 'discount house' and 'discount' the bill.

Definition   Selling a bill to a third party at less than its face value is called 'discounting' the bill. Discount houses are involved in buying discounted bills, both those of the government and of private sector firms.

For example, the supplier might sell the bill to a discount house for £98 (ie, at a discount to its true value).

(d)   When the three months are up, the discount house will go to the customer and present the bill for payment. If the customer defaults, the accepting bank will pay the discount house.

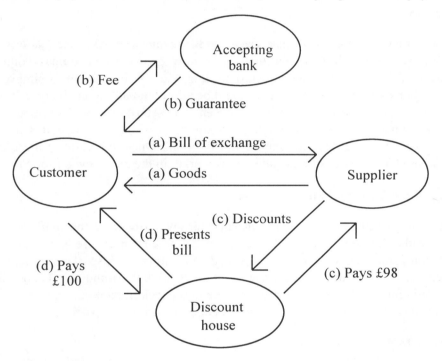

Figure 1 Using bills of exchange

Note that the discount house has effectively earned £2 (=£100 - £98) 'interest' on a three-month loan of £98. It gave the supplier £98 at the beginning of the period and then, after three months, received payment of £100 from the supplier.

Conclusion   Bills of exchange do not, strictly speaking, pay interest. However, when they are discounted, there is a rate of interest implied by the amount of the discount.

In this example, the discount house earned £2/£98 $\approx$ 2.04% interest for a three-month loan.

12.6   Activity

A discount house discounts a £200 three-month bill for £194. What is the implied rate of interest for the three months?

12.7   Activity solution

The discount house pays £194 at the beginning of the period and receives £200 at the end of the period. The £200 can be seen as representing £194 capital, plus £6 interest. The implied rate of interest is therefore £6/£194 ≈ 3.09%.

13   INTERNATIONAL CAPITAL MARKETS - EUROMARKETS AND FOREIGN BOND MARKETS

13.1   Introduction

An international financial market exists where domestic funds are supplied to a foreign user or foreign funds are supplied to a domestic user. The currencies used need not be those of either lender or borrower.

The most important international markets are the 'Euromarkets' and the foreign bond markets.

13.2   The Euromarkets

The term 'Euromarkets' is somewhat misleading, but the name has stuck. The markets originated in the 1950s, dealing in Eurodollars, but they have now grown to encompass other currencies including Euro-yen, Euro-Deutschmarks, Euro-sterling, etc. A Eurodollar is simply a US dollar deposited with a bank outside the USA. This could be a foreign bank or an overseas branch of a US bank. A similar definition would apply to Euro-yen, Euro-sterling, etc. Note that these deposits need not be with European banks, although originally most of them were, and active Euromarket centres exist in New York, Tokyo, Singapore and Bahrain. Once in receipt of these Eurodeposits, banks then lend them to other customers and a Euromarket in the currency is formed.

13.3   The attraction of the Euromarkets

The key factor in guaranteeing the long-run survival and growth of the markets is the narrow interest rate spreads. Lending rates are low as many of the customers are banks, governments and multinational companies who have impeccable credit ratings. Also the market is essentially wholesale, dealing in very large sums (usually at least $500,000) and this keeps administrative overheads to a minimum. Deposit rates are high due to the lack of banking regulations, interest rate restrictions and freedom of interest from domestic taxation until it is repatriated.

13.4   Types of Euromarket

The short- to medium-term end of the Euromarket is known as the **Eurocurrency market.** Various types of deposits and loans are available. Deposits vary from overnight to five years. Deposits can be in the form of straight-term deposits, with funds placed in a bank for a fixed maturity at a fixed interest rate: however, these carry the problem of interest rate penalties if early repayment is required. Alternatively, deposits can be made in the form of negotiable **Certificates of Deposit** (CDs). There is an active secondary market in CDs and investors are therefore able to have access to their funds when required. CDs come in several varieties including fixed rate CDs, floating rate CDs and discount CDs which are issued at a discount and then redeemed at par. Deposits can be made in individual currencies or in the form of 'currency cocktails' to allow depositors to take a diversified currency position. One common cocktail is the Special Drawing Right consisting of US dollars, Deutschmarks, yen, French francs and sterling.

Euromarket loans may be in the form of straight bank loans, lines of credit (similar to overdraft facilities) and revolving commitments (a series of short-term loans over a given period with regular interest rate reviews). Small loans may be arranged with individual banks, but larger ones are usually arranged through syndicates of banks.

Much of the business on the Eurocurrency market is interbank, but there are also a large number of governments, local authorities and multinational companies involved. Firms wishing to use the market must have excellent credit standing and wish to borrow (or deposit) very large sums of money.

In recent years many nations have borrowed to finance balance of payments deficits, and the concern over the ability of countries such as Mexico, Brazil and Argentina to meet their commitments is well publicised. Default by any of these nations could cause a collapse of many Western banks – hence the frequent restructuring of their loan repayment schedules.

To give some impression of the size of the Eurocurrency market it is estimated that the amount of funds involved is over four times higher than the UK money supply (M4).

The long-term end of the Euromarkets is the Eurobond Market.

The bonds can be privately placed through the banks or quoted on stock exchanges and they may run for periods of between three and twenty years. Traditionally fixed rate issues were made, but in order to make them more attractive in periods of high inflation floating rate bonds were also introduced. Convertible Eurobonds (similar to domestic convertible loan stocks) and Option Eurobonds (giving the holder the option to switch currencies for repayment and interest) are also used.

The major borrowers are large companies, international institutions like the World Bank, and the EC. The most common currencies are the US dollar, the Swiss franc, the Deutschmark, and to a smaller extent sterling.

13.5   Foreign bond market

Foreign bonds are, unlike Eurobonds, only traded in the market in which they are issued. As any such issues will be subject to local regulations they have proved less popular with borrowers than the Eurobond Market. The US, UK, Swiss, West German and Japanese capital markets have proved the most frequent venues for such issues.

14   SELF TEST QUESTIONS

14.1   Give five examples of financial intermediaries. (1.1)

14.2   Distinguish between the primary market and the secondary market for securities. (1.2)

14.3   What is arbitrage? (1.3)

14.4   What are the benefits deriving from the existence of speculators on the Stock Exchange? (5.2)

14.5   What has recently replaced the USM? (6.3)

14.6   Explain the expectations theory for explaining the shape of a yield curve. (10.2)

14.7   Do preference shares offer a fixed or a variable dividend? (11.3)

14.8   What are the rights of ordinary shareholders on winding up a company? (11.5)

14.9   What is a convertible loan? (11.6)

14.10   What is the disadvantage of using trade credit as a source of business finance? (12.3)

14.11   What is a bill of exchange? (12.5)

15   EXAMINATION TYPE QUESTIONS

15.1   Financial intermediaries

(a)   Identify the major financial intermediaries.   **(8 marks)**

(b)   Why does a modern economy require financial intermediaries?   **(12 marks)**
                                                                                                (Total: 20 marks)

15.2   Stock markets

Explain briefly how stock markets work and assess their usefulness to business as a source of long-term capital.   **(20 marks)**

16   ANSWERS TO EXAMINATION TYPE QUESTIONS

16.1   Financial intermediaries

(a)   Financial intermediaries can be divided into those which are banks and those which are non-banks. However, there is increasingly some blurring of the distinction between both types of institution as many have expanded their functions and the services they provide, as a result of the increasing competition in the financial services sector and the globalisation of their markets.

The main bank financial intermediaries are the following:

- Commercial banks, which offer both primary services (ie, those of money transmission) and secondary services (ie, accepting deposits and making loans) as well as a variety of other financial services to both the retail sector (small transactions) and the wholesale sector (large transactions).

- Discount houses, which deal in the secondary bill market - this means that in effect they do wholesale business on a short-term basis.

- The National Savings Bank, which accepts deposits predominantly from the retail sector and lends to the public sector.

- Overseas banks in the UK, which take part in the Euro-currency and Eurobond markets.

- Consortium banks are large conglomerates which lend money in very large amounts to finance major industrial projects.

- The Bank of England, which is the central bank of the UK and as such plays a supervisory and monitoring role in the economy. It does perform some banking functions insofar as it intermediates between the commercial banks and also between the government and the private sector.

The main non-bank financial intermediaries are the following:

- Building societies, which deal predominantly with the retail sector, although their wholesale business is expanding. On the whole they accept deposits from savers and lend to finance house purchase, but they now offer a much wider range of 'banking' services than previously, including primary money transmission facilities.

- Insurance companies and pension funds, which accept money on a very long-term basis from those paying into life assurance and pension schemes, and use the money to make a wide range of investments.

- Unit trusts and investment trusts in which people buy shares and which invest in a wide-ranging portfolio of investments.

(b)   Both bank and non bank financial institutions have one thing in common: they bring together the surplus sector of the economy with the deficit sector; they borrow money from those individuals and companies which have more money than they currently need and lend it to those who have less than they currently need. This is the basic principle of financial intermediation. In doing this they eliminate certain problems which would otherwise prevent the funds of the surplus sector from becoming available to the deficit sector.

Such institutions make links between different groups of people who would not otherwise know each other - the lender who deposits money in a bank does not have to look for someone who wants to borrow the money, but lets the bank complete the transaction indirectly. The **information gap** is therefore bridged by the intermediary.

The existence of large institutions also allows **aggregation** to take place. Many borrowers want more money than single small savers can provide, but a bank, or other intermediary, is able to accept a very large number of smaller deposits and aggregate these into larger amounts for loan purposes.

Financial institutions provide **risk transformation**. Many people with surplus funds would be unwilling to lend all their savings to one or two borrowers because of the risk of non-repayment - they would be reluctant to 'put all their eggs into one basket'. A bank, however, provides a relatively risk-free place to deposit savings. As a bank it lends its total deposits to a very large number of borrowers, and because it is a huge company with considerable reserves, it can calculate, and withstand, likely bad debts and ensure that it receives back, with interest, the money it has lent. Insurance companies are another good example of companies which 'pool' risks.

Financial institutions carry out **maturity transformation**. Another obstacle to lending and borrowing without the presence of intermediaries is (in many cases) the desire on the part of the lender to receive the money back sooner than the borrower wishes or is able to repay it. A financial intermediary is able to give liquidity to those depositors who want it and at the same time to allow many borrowers a longer time to repay - a building society is a good example of this, as much of its lending is done on a very long-term basis. The intermediary is thus able to combine short-term liabilities with longer-term assets. It can do this as long as it has an adequate reserve of liquid assets, based on its knowledge of how much money it needs to repay daily, on average, to those depositors who require liquidity. Many depositors are happy to leave their money for long periods of time, and the intermediary uses this money.

If financial intermediaries were not present in the economy individual savers would not know who to lend to, would not be able to supply the required amount nor be willing to accept the risk and the loss of liquidity. The intermediaries thus ensure that lending and borrowing take place on a much larger scale than could be possible without them.

It is of vital economic importance that such lending and borrowing should take place. From the viewpoint of surplus units in the economy, it is important that people with money to lend should be able to find a safe place to put their savings, which will give them the liquidity they need and at the same time pay them a rate of interest. Many individuals and companies rely on the income they receive from interest payments.

On the other hand from the viewpoint of intended deficit units it is vital that people who need to borrow should be able to do so. Economic growth is based on investment; ie, the expansion and modernisation of industry and commerce, and investment comes from borrowed funds. Governments need to borrow to be able to finance important areas of public expenditure; companies need to borrow to finance expansion, purchases of new equipment etc, and also to finance short-term trading imbalances; and individuals need to borrow to be able to buy houses and to enable them to consume much of the output of industry which would otherwise remain unsold. Borrowing leads to employment and growth.

16.2   Stock markets

The Stock Market is a financial intermediary which brings together individuals with different financial requirements. One of its functions is to enable those who need funds to be matched with those who have a surplus of funds. One example of this might be when a private company goes public, the owner realising some of his assets by selling off part or all of his interest in the company. Alternatively, companies needing money to carry out investment projects can raise the funds by issuing securities in the primary market.

The secondary market is the other most important role carried out by the Stock Exchange. This refers to the purchase and sale of second-hand shares and bonds, those which are already held by investors, rather than newly-issued securities.

Long-term capital can be defined in a number of ways, but the usual period over which long-term funds are lent is ten years or more. There are very many types of long-term capital which a company may issue, but essentially it has a choice of three basic categories: ordinary shares, preference shares or loan stock.

Ordinary shares, or equity, are held by the owners of the company. Each share represents a share in the assets of the company and entitles its owner to a dividend, paid out of the profits of the company. The dividend is variable both upwards and downwards, although in practice, dividends per share tend to rise slowly over time. In general, ordinary shares also confer the right to vote on their owner.

Preference shares do not represent ownership of the company, nor do they carry votes. They are entitled to a fixed dividend, which must be paid before the ordinary shareholders receive a dividend. If profits are not high enough to pay the dividend, it remains unpaid, although if the shares are cumulative, all unpaid dividends must be paid as soon as the company makes sufficient profits. Preference shares are more akin to loan stock than they are to equity.

Loan stock has many different names, the most familiar ones being debentures or bonds. This is debt capital, normally carrying fixed rate interest. The loan is usually made for a specific number of years, after which it is repaid (although a company may issue irredeemable loan stock, which is never repaid). This is different from ordinary and preference shares, which are usually not redeemed by the company; investors wishing to realise their investment sell their shares on to other investors.

The main advantage of raising long-term funds on the Stock Market is the fact that it provides a regulated and ordered way of finding individuals or organisations with money they want to lend. In addition to this function, the secondary market gives assurance to investors that they will be able to realise their investments when they need to. As large volumes of securities are traded on the Stock Market every day, people are relatively safe in tying up their money for apparently long periods of time. Should they need funds, they can liquidate their investments by selling the securities on to somebody else. This means that companies do not have to find investors who are willing to lend money indefinitely or for many years at a time.

Raising equity or debt both have advantages and disadvantages. Equity is useful as the dividends paid depend on profits, so can be reduced or cancelled in times of difficulty. On the other hand, bringing in new shareholders dilutes the control of the company and subjects the original owners to controls and regulations which they may find onerous.

Debt receives a fixed interest payment which is tax deductible, unlike dividends. This makes debt a fairly cheap form of finance, as the payment of interest is offset to a certain extent by the saving of tax. However, debt agreements usually carry with them the right of the debt holders to force the company into liquidation if interest payments are not met.

One of the main criticisms levelled at the Stock Market and those who provide funds through it, is the short-termism. Share ownership, although perhaps wider than it once was, is concentrated in the hands of a few large institutions, such as pension funds, insurance companies and investment and unit trusts. These institutions are often accused of being interested only in short-term gains, concentrating on dividend payouts and fast capital growth. This means that companies are forced into making short-term decisions to satisfy the institutions, rather than considering the longer term and, for example, carrying out research and development, which may use up cash in the present, but will increase future profits. This problem is one of the reasons behind the recent spate of public companies going private, such as Richard Branson's Virgin Group.

Another area of complaint which was noted many years ago by the Wilson Committee, and still continues is the lack of funds available for risky or small ventures. Not only are the big institutions reluctant to make such investments, but the cost of raising money on the Stock Exchange makes it prohibitive for all but the largest companies. Other sources of capital, in particular venture capital companies, are needed.

Finally, a company always risks not having its shares fully subscribed by the public, although issues are usually underwritten to ensure that shares can be placed with some investor. The most notorious underwriting problem was encountered by the Government, when it sold off shares in British Petroleum around the time of the Stock Market crash in October 1977. The issue was under-subscribed, forcing the Government to turn to the underwriters, who were extremely reluctant to fulfil their role of buying the outstanding shares.

22 WORKING CAPITAL MANAGEMENT: GENERAL ISSUES

INTRODUCTION & LEARNING OBJECTIVES

'Working capital' is the capital available for conducting day-to-day operations of an organisation. It is usually defined as net current assets.

The managers of an organisation have the responsibility to manage the levels of working capital in the best interests of the owners. This chapter examines the general issues that are involved in the management of working capital. The next chapter then examines the techniques that are appropriate for managing each constituent of the working capital total ie, stocks, debtors, cash and creditors.

When you have studied this chapter you should be able to do the following:

- Discuss the traditional and the modern approaches to financing working capital

- Explain the range of possible sources of short and medium-term finance.

- Appreciate the difference between cash flow and profits.

- Explain the role of the treasury function.

- Discuss illiquidity and corporate collapse.

- Discuss the management and financing of debtors.

- Discuss the problems of extending credit to overseas customers.

1 WORKING CAPITAL MANAGEMENT

1.1 Definition and introduction

As mentioned above, *working capital* normally refers to short-term net assets – stock, debtors, cash less creditors.

Working capital management is used to refer to the management of all aspects of both current assets and current liabilities, to minimise the risk of insolvency while maximising the return on assets.

Typically, current assets represent more than half the assets of companies. They tend to be of particular importance to small firms. There is substantial historical evidence of small business failure as a result of failing to control working capital investment and business liquidity. There is a very direct link between sales growth and working capital management.

Surveys, not unnaturally, indicate that financial managers spend a considerable amount of their time on working capital management.

All of this leads to the conclusion that working capital management, although introducing no major new concepts, is a subject of importance.

The two fundamental questions to be answered in the area of working capital management are the following.

(a)   How much should the firm invest in working capital? and

(b)   How should the investment in working capital be financed?

1.2   Activity

A business has annual sales of £2.4 million and a gross profit margin of 40%. It intends to delay paying its trade creditors by a month longer than usual. By how much will its cash balance benefit?

1.3   Activity solution

Step 1   Calculate cost of sales, using the cost structure.

	%	£m
Sales	100	2.40
Cost of sales	60	1.44
Gross profit	40	0.96

Step 2   Calculate one month's purchases. If £1.44m is the annual cost of sales, one month's purchases must be $\frac{1}{12}$ of this ie, £0.12m.

This is the value of one month's extra trade credit. The cash balance will therefore benefit by £120,000.

1.4   The traditional approach to financing working capital

Traditionally current assets were seen as fluctuating, originally with a seasonal agricultural pattern. Current assets would then be financed out of short-term credit, which could be paid off when not required, whilst fixed assets would be financed by long-term funds (debt or equity).

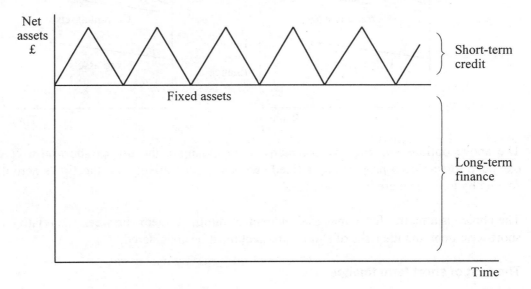

This approach to the analysis is rather simplistic. In most businesses a proportion of the current assets are fixed over time being thus expressed as 'permanent'. For example, certain base levels of stock are always carried, cash balances never fall below a particular level, and a certain level of trade credit is always extended. If growth is added to this situation a more realistic business picture would be as follows:

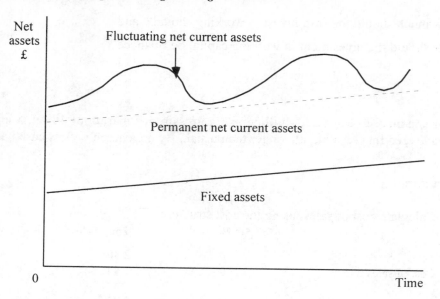

1.5   The modern approach to working capital funding

Given the permanent nature of a large proportion of current assets, it is generally felt prudent to fund a proportion of net current assets with long-term finance. The question is generally one of the extent to which such funding occurs. The possibilities include the following.

Option (1) - some permanent current net assets financed by short-term credit

Option (2) - all permanent and some fluctuating current net assets financed by long-term credit.

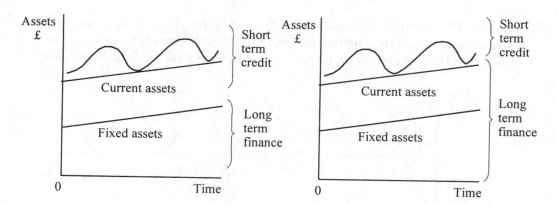

The above options are only two of many. For example, the use of short-term credit could be extended to finance a proportion of fixed assets, or, alternatively, all the firm's activities could be funded by long-term credit.

The choice is a matter for managerial judgement but the tradeoff between the relative cheapness of short-term debt and the risks of short-term debt must be considered.

1.6   The cost of short-term finance

Short-term finance is usually cheaper than long-term finance. This is largely due to the risks taken by creditors. For example, if a bank were considering two loan applications, one for one year and the other for 20 years, all other things being equal it would demand a higher interest rate on the 20 year loan. This is because it feels more exposed to risk on long-term loans as more could go wrong with the borrower over a period of twenty years than a period of one year.

It should be noted that occasionally this situation is reversed, with rates of return being higher on short-term finance. This occurs most often when the market expects interest rates to fall in the long run. It is also possible where the term of funding is very short and the initial set up costs of the lender render percentage return rates high.

Short-term finance also tends to be more flexible. For example, if funds are raised on overdraft and used to finance a fluctuating investment in current assets they can be paid off when not required and interest saved. On the other hand, if funds were borrowed long-term early repayment may not be possible, or, if allowed, early repayment penalties may be experienced. The flexibility of short-term finance may, therefore, reduce its overall cost.

Short-term finance includes items such as trade creditors, which are normally regarded as low cost funds, whereas long-term finance will include debt and equity. Equity finance is particularly expensive, its required returns being high, and non tax deductible.

1.7 Sources of short and medium-term finance

Previous sections have examined the possible approaches to financing the firm's investment in working capital, and highlighted the importance of short-term funds to many firms. No hard and fast definitions hold in this area and authorities disagree on what constitutes 'short-term' and 'medium-term'. As a rough guide up to three years can be seen as short-term, and three to ten years as medium-term, but many firms would apply different definitions. For example, three years might be short-term in a business where the gestation period of new investment is very long (eg, electricity generation) but for a fast moving industry (eg, consumer electronics) it could be considered long-term. Accordingly it is always possible to dispute whether a particular source of funds is short to medium-term, or long-term.

The most widely-used sources of short and medium-term funds are the following.

(a)   Bank overdrafts and loans;
(b)   Private loans;
(c)   Trade and expense credit;
(d)   Leasing and instalment credit; and
(e)   Various forms of debtor related finance, including factoring of debts and invoice discounting.

1.8 The risks of short-term finance

Short-term financing has already been established as generally 'the cheaper option'. However, the price paid for reduced cost is increased risk for the borrower. There may be the following problems.

(a)   **Renewal problems**

Short-term finance may need to be continually renegotiated as various facilities expire. In some situations, either because of economic conditions (eg, a credit squeeze) or because of the financial situation of the company, it may be difficult to obtain renewal of a short-term finance facility. This could leave the firm in a very embarrassing position. Even if no renewal problem is encountered, the cost of negotiations in terms of management time may be high, and must be considered.

(b)   **Stability of interest rates**

If the company is constantly having to renew its funding arrangements it will be at the mercy of fluctuations in short-term interest rates.

1.9   Conclusions on the financing decision

No ideal financing package can be recommended. Much will depend upon the risk-return tradeoff for individual companies. The 'textbook' rule of thumb is that 'long-term assets should be financed by long-term funds and short-term assets by short-term funds'. This approach matches up the maturity of the finance with the duration of the investment and hence avoids many of the renewal problems. However, many companies choose to break this rule, often with great success.

1.10   Investment in working capital

Management of the investment in working capital can be considered at the individual current asset or liability level or in terms of total working capital requirement. For now, the total investment in working capital will be considered. Management of individual current asset and liability elements (ie, stocks, debtors, cash and creditors) will be considered later.

Overall investment in working capital largely concerns tradeoff. Here, the firm must consider the cost of investing in working capital (largely the financing cost) against the benefits it brings. With no investment in working capital there would be no stocks and no debtors, which would probably result in few sales and, therefore, little profit.

Cash flow is the lifeblood of the thriving business. Effectual (effective and efficient) management of the working capital investment is essential to maintaining control of business cash flow. Management must have full awareness of the profitability versus liquidity tradeoff. Healthy trading growth typically produces two factors.

(a)   Increased profitability; and

(b)   Requirement for increased investment in

- fixed assets and
- working capital.

There is a tradeoff under which trading growth and increased profitability squeezes cash. Ultimately, if not properly managed, increased trading can carry with it the spectre of overtrading and inability to pay the business creditors.

1.11   The difference between cash flow and profits

It is worthwhile stressing the difference between cash flow and profits. Companies fail, not because they are reporting insufficient profits, but because they have run out of cash to pay their liabilities (wages, amounts due to suppliers, overdraft interest, etc).

Some examples of transactions that have a different effect on cash flows and on profits are as follows:

(a)   purchase of fixed assets for cash. The cash will be paid in full to the supplier when the fixed asset is delivered. However profits will be charged gradually over the life of the asset in the form of depreciation charges.

(b)   sale of goods on credit. Profits will be credited in full once the sale has been confirmed; however the cash may not be received for some considerable period afterwards.

(c)   some payments such as tax and dividend payments have no effect on profits but do constitute a cash outflow.

Clearly management will need to monitor cash balances and cash flows just as closely as trading profits. The need for adequate cash flow information is vital to enable management to fulfil this responsibility. In large organisations management may decide to set up a separate department, a 'treasury' department to help them monitor the group cash position.

2 THE ROLE OF THE TREASURY FUNCTION

2.1 The importance of cash within a business

The term 'treasurer', and therefore 'treasurership department', is an old one that has been resurrected in a modern context. This modern term is an import from the USA and essentially covers the following activities:

(a) Banking and exchange;
(b) Cash and currency management;
(c) Investment in short term assets;
(d) Risk and insurance; and
(e) Raising finance.

These roles have always existed, but the modern concept is to bring them all together and combine them under a corporate treasurer. All the areas above are concerned with managing the liquidity of a business. A business must maintain an inflow of cash in order to survive and a further inflow of funds if it is to expand. Cash can be regarded as equally as important as profits. Certainly the business must be profitable in its existing and prospective activities, but the profitability objectives can only be achieved within the constraints imposed by funding requirements.

2.2 Reasons for the development of the treasurership department

As indicated above, the functions carried out by the corporate treasurer have always existed, but have been absorbed within other finance functions. A number of reasons may be identified for the development of a separate treasurership department.

(a) Size and internationalisation of companies. These add to both the scale and the complexity of the treasury functions.

(b) Size and internationalisation of currency, debt and security markets. These make the operations of raising finance, handling transactions in multiple currencies and investing much more complex. They also present opportunities for greater gains.

(c) Sophistication of business practice. This process has been aided by modern communications, and as a result the treasurer is expected to take advantage of opportunities for making profits or minimising costs which did not exist a few years ago.

For these reasons, most large international corporations have moved towards setting up a separate treasurership department.

2.3 The role of the treasurer

The treasurer reports to the finance director, with a specific emphasis on borrowing, cash and currency management.

In addition, although the major responsibility is held by the finance director, the treasurer will have a direct input into the former's management of debt capacity, debt and equity structure, resource allocation, equity strategy and currency strategy.

Finally, often in common with the controller (chief accountant) and management accountant, the treasurer will be involved in the investment appraisal process; and the finance director will often consult the treasurer in matters relating to the review of acquisitions and divestments, dividend policy and defence from takeover.

In summary, treasurers work closely with finance directors in key aspects of the latter's specific responsibilities, and with important decision-making responsibilities of their own. These responsibilities will vary slightly from group to group, but the underlying themes of borrowing, investment, cash and currency management will remain the same.

2.4   Establishing a treasurership department

Traditionally in the UK the corporate treasurer, in common with other senior finance personnel, has been drawn from the ranks of qualified accountants. This contrasts with the USA, where only a minority of treasurers and finance directors are qualified accountants. However, even in the UK the position is changing against the accounting profession, and more corporate treasurers are drawn from other sources eg, MBA and the corporate treasury department of a multinational company.

Treasurership departments are not large, since they are not involved in the detailed recording of transactions. They tend to rely heavily on new technology for information.

2.5   The centralisation of treasury activities

The question arises in a large international group of whether treasury activities should be centralised or decentralised. If centralised, then each operating company holds only the minimum cash balance required for day to day operations, remitting the surplus to the centre for overall management. If decentralised, each operating company must appoint an officer responsible for that company's own treasury operations.

Advantages of centralisation

(i)   No need for treasury skills to be duplicated throughout the group. One highly trained central department can assemble a highly skilled team, offering skills that could not be available if every company had their own treasury.

(ii)   Necessary borrowings can be arranged in bulk, at keener interest rates than for smaller amounts. Similarly bulk deposits of surplus funds will attract higher rates of interest than smaller amounts.

(iii)   The group's foreign currency risk can be managed much more effectively from a centralised treasury since only they can appreciate the total exposure situation. A total hedging policy is more efficiently carried out by head office rather than each company doing their own hedging.

(iv)   Bank charges should be lower since a situation of carrying both balances and overdraft in the same currency should be eliminated.

Advantages of decentralisation

(i)   Greater autonomy leads to greater motivation. Individual companies will manage their cash balances more attentively if they are responsible for them rather than simply remitting them up to head office.

(ii)   Local operating units should have a better feel for local conditions than head office and can respond more quickly to local developments.

3   SHORT-TERM INVESTMENT MANAGEMENT PRINCIPLES

3.1   Introduction

Investments may be classified into long-term and short-term. Long-term investments are committed to projects which will meet the strategic objectives of the company. Land, property, plant and shares are typical examples.

Short-term investment opportunities present themselves when cash surpluses arise. Companies may hold cash not only for transaction needs, but also for precautionary and speculative motives. The company's attitude to risk and working capital management will determine the planned cash holdings. Companies with an aggressive working capital policy will plan to minimise funds held, and borrow whenever cash is needed. Those with a defensive policy will set aside cash in an investment portfolio, which can be drawn upon when the need arises.

This section deals with the practical aspects of the management of a portfolio of short-run investments.

3.2   Investing surplus cash

In this section surplus cash is defined as liquid balances held by a business which are neither needed to finance current business operations nor held permanently for short-term investment. Their availability is temporary, awaiting employment either in existing operations or in new investment opportunities (whether already identified or not).

The 'temporary' period can be of any duration from one day to the indefinite future date at which the new investment opportunity may be identified and seized.

The significance of this concept of balances held temporarily for conversion to other, more important business uses is the absolute priority which must be given to the avoidance of risk over maximising returns. The usual principle of finding the optimal mix between risk and return does not apply here because the investment is secondary and incidental to the ultimate business use of the asset, not an end in itself.

3.3   How does surplus cash arise?

Broadly, surplus cash can become available in the following ways:

(a)   Overfunding; or
(b)   A reduction in operating or other assets; or
(c)   A surplus of retained earnings over the increase in net assets employed.

Overfunding can be deliberate or unintended. For example if a company finds its market growing, its fixed assets and working capital should also be growing over the years, and it may from time to time fund this growth of assets from share or long-term debt issues. If the company deliberately funds more than its current short-term debt so as to make the issue a worthwhile sum, then it will have surplus cash until the growth of its net operating assets catches up with its long-term funding.

A reduction in net operating assets occurs annually in all seasonal trades, or more irregularly where a trade runs into a more serious decline or indeed where the company deliberately reduces its working capital by improved efficiency or by a financial device like factoring its receivables.

These are just a few illustrations of how surplus cash can become available.

A common problem is the build-up of surplus funds in an overseas subsidiary where local tax or exchange control regulations make the remittance of these funds to other parts of the group either illegal or uneconomic. Very often these problems are aggravated by economic or regulatory barriers to expansion projects which would absorb the funds. If no cure is visible, the cash may be outside the above definition of surplus cash.

3.4   Objectives in the investment of surplus cash

The objectives can be categorised as follows:

(a)   Liquidity: the cash must be available for use when needed.

(b)   Safety: no risk of loss must be taken.

(c)   Profitability: subject to (a) and (b) above, the aim is to earn the highest possible after tax returns.

Each of these objectives raises problems which will be explored now.

3.5   Liquidity

This problem is at first sight simple enough. If a company knows that it will need the funds in three days (or weeks or months), it simply invests them for just that period at the best rate available with safety. The solution is to match the maturity of the investment with the period for which the funds are surplus.

There are however, complications.

(a)   The exact duration of the surplus period is not always known. It is of course known if the cash is needed to meet a loan instalment, a large tax payment or a dividend, but it will not be known if the need is unidentified, or depends on the build-up of inventory (stock), the progress of construction work, or the hammering out of an acquisition deal.

(b)   It will be seen below that the maturity of investments can also depend on the view taken of future trends in interest rates.

(c)   The options are extended (and therefore complicated) by the possibility of borrowing to bridge the gap between the time when the cash is needed and the subsequent date on which the investment matures.

(d)   Finally, an investment may not need to be held to maturity if either an earlier withdrawal is permitted by the terms of the instrument without excessive penalty, or if there is a secondary market and its disposal in that market causes no excessive loss. A good example of such an investment is a certificate of deposit where the investor 'lends' the bank a stated amount for a stated period, usually between one and six months. As evidence of the debt and its promise to pay interest the bank gives the investor a certificate of deposit (CD) which is a negotiable instrument. If the investor needs the money before maturity, they can sell the CD to another investor. When the loan matures the new owner presents the CD to the bank and receives payment. There is an active market for CDs issued by the commercial banks and turning a CD into cash is easy and cheap.

3.6   Example

IH has purchased a three-months (92 days) £100,000 certificate of deposit (CD) maturing on 31 October 19X3. The interest rate is 9.5% pa, so the total sum of principal and interest due to IH on 31 October is £102,394.52 (as there are 365 days in a year).

However, IH unexpectedly needs the cash on 21 October, ten days before maturity. Its only alternatives are to borrow on overdraft at 10.5%, or to sell the CD in the secondary market. The cost of borrowing £102,394.52 for 10 days at 10.5% is £294.56 (£102,394.52 $\times$ 10.5% $\times$ $\frac{10}{365}$). It therefore pays IH to sell the CD, provided it can sell it for more than (£102,394.52 − £294.56 =) £102,099.96. If not, it would be better to overdraw for the ten days.

3.7   Safety

Safety means no risk of loss. Superficially this again looks simple. The concept certainly includes the absence of credit risk. For example, not depositing with a bank which might conceivably fail within the maturity period and thus fail to repay the amount deposited.

But now suppose that IH is holding the surplus cash with the express purpose of paying for a new capital asset like a freehold factory, the ultimate cost of which depends on building costs. IH has not yet negotiated a fixed money price for it, and construction contractors are unwilling to accept a price which is not subject to a cost escalation clause. IH is interested in any investment instrument which will (after tax) maintain its purchasing power against domestic price inflation. In that case a safer instrument might be an index-linked gilt-edged bond with a maturity date about the expected date of the capital payment.

Again, suppose the surplus cash is held specifically against a payment due in a foreign currency like the D-mark. For example, against a deferred credit payment for a capital asset bought from a German supplier. In that case the only riskless investment would be one denominated in DM. This may give a lower nominal return, but its DM value would not be exposed to exchange rate fluctuation. Moreover, in practice it would pay IH to ask its German supplier to quote for a discounted immediate cash price and compare the after-tax saving on this with the after-tax return on the most favourable D-mark investment.

So safety is not necessarily to be defined as the certainty to get the original investment repaid at 100% of its original *sterling* money value. This may be correct, but if the purpose for which the surplus cash is held is not itself fixed in sterling, then other criteria of safety may apply.

3.8   Activity

A UK company needs to pay a German supplier DM20,000 in three months' time. The current exchange rate is £1 = DM2.67. It is expected that the exchange rate will be £1 = DM 2.65 in three months' time. The current sterling deposit interest rate is 10% pa. The company can either invest sufficient sterling now to pay the supplier DM20,000 at the forecast future exchange rate; or convert sterling into D-marks today, investing sufficient D-marks to pay the bill in three months' time.

What must the German interest rate be for the company to be indifferent between these two actions?

3.9   Activity solution

To be indifferent, the current sterling cost of each method must be the same. In each case, the company will invest slightly less than the final required amount, as the principal will accumulate interest over the deposit period.

Investing sterling

The final sum required will be $\dfrac{20,000}{2.65} \approx £7,547.17$, if the predicted exchange rate is correct.

The deposit will earn $\dfrac{10\%}{4} = 2.5\%$ interest over the period.

Therefore the amount which must be invested is $\dfrac{£7,547.17}{1.025} = £7,363.09.$

Investing D-marks

Let the German interest rate be $x\%$ pa. The D-mark deposit will earn $\dfrac{x\%}{4} = 0.25\,x\%$ interest over the period. Therefore the D-mark amount which must be invested is DM $\dfrac{20{,}000}{1+0.0025x}$. The current sterling cost of this is $\dfrac{1}{2.67} \times \dfrac{20{,}000}{1+0.0025x}$. For indifference, this must equal £7,363.09.

Solving for x, we obtain $x \approx 6.9\%$ pa.

3.10   Profitability

This objective too looks deceptively simple at first: go for the highest rate of return subject to the overriding criteria of safety and liquidity. However, here there are even more complications.

(a)   Fixed or variable rates?

(b)   What maturity?

(c)   Timing of interest receipts.

(d)   Tax effects.

(e)   Use of other currencies.

(f)   Difficulties in forecasting available funds.

(g)   Ascertaining the most favourable rates.

These questions can be answered by an approach similar to that explained above.

4   THE IMPORTANCE OF CORPORATE LIQUIDITY TO SURVIVAL

4.1   Introduction

A flow of cash is essential to enable an undertaking to carry out the day-to-day transactions which form its business activity. Some cash payments (eg, to small creditors) can be delayed without endangering the company's prospects but others must be paid on time.

- If debenture interest is not paid, the trust deed may allow the debenture holders to appoint a receiver to sell sufficient assets for the debenture to be repaid.

- Employees must be paid their wages and salaries on time, otherwise they will leave and the business will cease to function.

A major responsibility of the financial manager is to ensure that an adequate flow of cash is available to enable the business to operate efficiently. Cash must be in place to meet obligations as they fall due. If insufficient cash is available, the company will suffer from illiquidity. At the extreme, the company may be forced into failure due to an illiquidity position. A lot of academic research work has been carried out in recent years to try and develop warning indicators that suggest the risk that a company might be going to fail through illiquidity, particularly by Professor Altman in developing Z-scores.

Profit earned will, to a certain extent, alleviate the effect of cash delay factors, but the strain on operating cash flow will be accentuated by the need to provide for the items below:

(a)   Future of the business ie, by investing in fixed assets.

(b)   Rewards of the providers of capital ie, dividends and interest.

(c)   Taxation.

Management of cash flows therefore involves the interrelationship of the following items:

(a)   Profits.
(b)   Working capital levels.
(c)   Capital expenditure.
(d)   Dividend policy.
(e)   Taxation.

Capital expenditure control and dividend policy are discussed in detail elsewhere and taxation planning is largely outside the scope of this text. The emphasis in this section of the text, therefore, is on the control of levels of working capital.

4.2   Short-term cash control

Control of cash over short periods is best achieved by preparing short-term forecasts for comparison with actual results. If the cash forecast shows an unacceptable cash balance or a cash deficit, then it will be necessary to review a number of items:

(a)   Profit levels, including changes in selling price or improvements in operating efficiency.

(b)   Working capital requirements ie, stockholdings, credit periods given and taken, invoice processing procedures, etc.

(c)   Fixed asset requirements, having regard to the timing and amounts of capital projects.

(d)   Dividend policy.

4.3   Over-capitalisation v overtrading

A company's managers must strike a balance between over-capitalisation and overtrading.

Definition   A company is overcapitalised if a company's working capital is excessive for its needs. Excessive stocks, debtors and cash will lead to a low return on investment, with long-term funds tied up in non-earning short-term assets.

Overcapitalisation can normally be identified by poor accounting ratios (such as liquidity ratios being too high or stock turnover periods too long).

Definition   A company is overtrading if it is trying to carry on too large a volume of activities with its current levels of working capital.

Often a company may try to grow too fast, reporting increasing profits while its overdraft soars. Remember that more companies fail when the economy is recovering from a recession than when the economy is entering a recession.

5   THE MANAGEMENT OF DEBTORS

5.1   Level of trade credit

The optimum level of trade credit extended represents, as always, a balance between two factors.

(a)   Profit improvement from sales obtained by allowing credit; and
(b)   The cost of credit allowed.

A lenient credit policy may well attract additional custom, but at a disproportionate increase in cost.

Management will be anxious to do the following.

(a)   Establish a credit policy in relation to normal periods of credit and individual credit limits;

(b)   Develop a system which will control the implementation of credit policy;

(c)   Prescribe reporting procedures which will monitor the efficiency of the system.

5.2   Credit policy

The period of credit extended will be set by reference to the factors below.

(a)   Elasticity of demand for the company's products;

(b)   Credit terms offered by competitors;

(c)   Considered risk of bad debts resulting from extended credit periods;

(d)   Financing costs and availability of finance;

(e)   Costs of administering the credit system.

Individual credit limits are dependent on an assessment of the creditworthiness of a particular customer: in the first instance, whether the customer would be allowed credit at all; and secondly, the maximum amount that should be allowed.

Assessment involves analysis of the prospective customer's current business situation and credit history, derived from information obtained from any available sources.

Credit policy will, of necessity, be reasonably flexible to reflect changes in economic conditions, actions by competitors and marketing strategy (eg, the desire to 'kill off' a new competitor in the market).

5.3   Activity

A study of the debtors of XYZ Co Ltd has shown that it is possible to classify all debtors into certain classes with the following characteristics:

Category	Average collection period (days)	Bad debts %
A	15	0.5
B	20	2.5
C	30	5.0
D	40	9.5

The average standard profit/cost schedule for the company's range of products is as follows:

	£	£
Selling price		2.50
Less: Material	1.00	
Wages	0.95	
Variable cost	0.30	
Fixed cost	0.05	2.30
Profit		0.20

The company has the opportunity of extending its sales by £1,000,000 per annum, split between categories C and D in the proportions 40:60. The company's short-term borrowing rate is 11½% per annum on a simple interest basis.

Evaluate the effect of the proposed increase in sales by carrying out the steps below.

Step 1   Calculate the additional contribution from the extra sales, split between the different categories of debtor.

Assume that the contribution per £ of sales will be as shown on the standard cost card.

Step 2   For each category of debtor work out the bad debts arising from the sales, using the given percentages. Deduct the bad debts from the additional contribution worked out in Step 1.

Step 3   For each category of debtor work out the (absolute) interest cost of allowing credit over the relevant period.

The cost equals

Annual interest rate × Additional debtors, where

Additional debtors =

$$\text{Additional annual sales} \times \frac{\text{Average collection period (days)}}{365}$$

Deduct this cost from the net additional contribution derived in Step 2.

The final result is the net profit or loss from expanding sales.

5.4   Activity solution

	Ref to Steps	£	Category C £	£	Category D £
Additional contribution	(1)		40,000		60,000
Less: Additional costs:					
Bad debts	(2)	20,000		57,000	
Funding debtors	(3)	3,781	23,781	7,561	64,561
Additional profit and loss			16,219		(4,561)

Therefore, total additional profit = £16,219 − £4,561 = £11,658.

NB: It has been assumed that fixed costs will not increase as a result of the sales expansion.

Steps

(1)   **Additional contribution** (average per unit   =   £2.50 − (1.00 + 0.95 + 0.30)
                              =   £0.25)

	Category C £	Category D £
Additional sales	40% × 1,000,000 = 400,000	60% × 1,000,000 = 600,000
Additional contribution	$\frac{0.25}{2.50} \times 400,000$ = 40,000	$\frac{0.25}{2.50} \times 600,000$ = 60,000

(2)   **Bad debts**

Category C	5% × £400,000 =	£20,000
Category D	9.5% × £600,000 =	£57,000

(3)   **Funding debtors**

Additional debtors

$$\frac{30}{365} \times 400,000 \qquad\qquad \frac{40}{365} \times 600,000$$

$$= 32,876 \qquad\qquad\qquad = 65,753$$

Cost of funding debtors =
11½% × Additional debtors   = 3,781   = 7,561

It can be seen that additional profit is halved as a result of the additional financing required. In fact, the financing cost represents 1.26% of the sales value of Category D, while the bad debts represent 9.5%, a total of 10.76%.

5.5   Implementing credit policy

To ensure the effectiveness of the credit control system, the following aspects of credit should be considered.

(a)   **Accepting credit customers**

As indicated previously, procedures should be laid down to assess creditworthiness before a new customer is extended credit terms. Sources of information are listed below.

(i)   **Trade references**

The potential customer is asked to give names of two existing suppliers who will testify to the firm's credit standing. Note that there is a danger that firms will nominate only suppliers that are paid on time.

(ii)   **Bank references**

Permission is sought to approach the customer's bank to discuss his creditworthiness. Note, however, that banks are often reluctant to give their customers bad references.

(iii)   **Credit agencies and credit associations**

These bodies will provide independent assessments of creditworthiness for a fee. Short reports may be obtained from regularly updated registers or special more detailed reports may be commissioned. Dun and Bradstreet are probably the most well-known credit agency in this area.

(iv)   **Reports from salesmen**

Salesmen are often the only representative of the supplying firm that actually meets the potential customer's staff and sees the premises. They are therefore in a unique position to provide information on customer creditworthiness.

(v)   **Information from competitors**

In 'close-knit' industries competing suppliers often exchange credit information on potential customers.

(vi)   **Financial statement analysis**

Recent accounts may be analysed to determine the customer's ability to pay.

(vii)   **Credit scoring**

Definition   Credit scoring is a technique which enables companies to apply a systematic approach to the granting of credit.

It can be applied in all circumstances where credit is under consideration, but is more applicable where sales are direct to the public, and the use of the above evaluations are either not possible or are too expensive.

Example

A sample of past customers would identify the factors associated with bad debts. Age, sex, marital status, family size, occupation etc, may be significant factors.

The company may allocate a points score to potential customers as follows:

Factor	*Points score*
Aged over 40	15
Married with fewer than three children	20
Home owner	20
At same address for over three years	15
At existing job for over two years	20
Car owner	10
Total	100

Past records may show that there had been no records of payment difficulties with customers with a score of 80 or over, bad debts of 10% for scores between 35 and 80, and bad debts of 25% where customers had a score of less than 35. A 'cut-off' point of 35 would probably be established, and credit refused to any potential customer with a score of less than 35.

It may be considered worthwhile to carry out some further form of credit evaluation for potential customers with scores between 35 and 80, to reduce the bad debts below 10%. The costs of the further analysis would have to be compared with the financial benefits from the reduction in bad debts.

The factors which are considered most likely to influence creditworthiness are of course a matter of judgement, as are the respective weights which should be attached to each factor.

(b)   **Preventing credit limits from being exceeded**

Control of credit limits should be directed at the order processing stage ie, the customer's ledger account will be adapted to reflect orders in the pipeline as well as invoiced sales.

(c)   **Prompt invoicing**

The customer's period of credit will relate to receipt of invoice, so it is essential to minimise the time-lag between despatch and invoicing eg, by streamlining authorisation and administrative procedures.

(d)   **Collection of overdue debts**

The longer a debt is allowed to run, the higher the probability of eventual default. Thus, a systematic progression of follow-up procedures is required, bearing in mind the risk of offending a valued customer to such an extent that their business is lost.

Techniques for 'chasing' overdue debts include the following.

(i)   **Reminder letters**

These are often regarded as being a relatively poor way of obtaining payment, as many customers simply ignore them. Sending reminders by fax is usually more productive than simply using the normal postal service.

(ii)   **Telephone calls**

These are more expensive than reminder letters but where large sums are involved they can be an efficient way of speeding payment.

(iii)   **Withholding supplies**

Putting customers on the 'stop list' for further orders or spare parts can encourage rapid settlement of debts.

(iv)   **Debt collection agencies and trade associations**

These offer debt collection services on a fixed fee basis or on 'no collection no charge' terms. The quality of service provided varies considerably and care should be taken in selecting an agent.

(v)   **Legal action**

This is often seen as a last resort. A solicitor's letter often prompts payment and many cases do not go to court. Court action is usually not cost effective but it can discourage other customers from delaying payment.

5.6   Monitoring the credit system

Management will require regular information to facilitate corrective action and measurement of the impact of credit allowed on working capital investments.

Typical reports will include the following points.

(a)   Age analysis of outstanding debts.

(b)   Ratios, compared with the previous period or target, to indicate trends in credit levels and the incidence of overdue and bad debts.

(c)   Statistical data to identify causes of default and the incidence of bad debts among different classes of customer and types of trade.

5.7   Settlement discounts

A company may offer settlement discounts to its customers, that is it allows debtors to pay less than their full debt if they pay sooner than the end of their credit period. The company must ensure that offering the discount is financially sensible, with the benefit of receiving the cash early exceeding the cost of the discount.

The mathematics of offering settlement discounts are very similar to the decision as to whether discounts should be taken from suppliers; this decision is examined later.

6   FINANCING FROM DEBTORS

6.1   Methods

The following methods are used for obtaining finance from debtors.

(a)   Expediting payments by debtors.

(b)   Releasing working capital tied up in debtors, as follows:

    (i)   Factoring of debts;
    (ii)   Undisclosed factoring;
    (iii)   Invoice discounting;
    (iv)   Block discounting of hire-purchase debtors; and
    (v)   Bills of exchange and acceptance credits.

Each of these is considered below.

6.2   Expediting payment by trade debtors

This usually involves the installation of a sound credit control and reminder system. The cost of not collecting debts within the credit period allowed by one's competitors could be argued to be either one of the following:

(a)   The same as the cost which the selling business has to pay on any bank overdraft which it is using; or

(b)   The rate of return which could be earned by the business with funds released by its debtors - ie, the opportunity cost.

6.3   Factoring of debts

Factoring involves turning over responsibility for collecting the company's debts to a specialist institution. Factoring companies offer the following services:

(a)   Taking over the running of clients' sales ledgers.

(b)   Offering 100% protection against bad debts, provided excessive credit was not allowed by the client (often known as non-recourse factoring).

(c)   Providing financing by means of advances, the security for which would be the debtors' balances owing.

A company may take advantage of some or all of these services. To take over the running of the sales ledger and the bad debts protection, the factor company will require a fee of about 1.5 – 2.5% of turnover. The factoring company would pay the client company for the debts on a calculated average settlement date.

To provide the finance described under (c) above, the factoring company will require a fee of about 2.5% above base rates. It will normally advance about 75 – 90% of the book value of the debts, the remaining amount (less the fee) being paid when the debtors are collected.

6.4   Activity

A company has a sales ledger totalling some £80,000, which represents two months' sales. A factoring company will run the sales ledger on a non-recourse basis for 1.8% of turnover. It is felt that using the factor will cause some customers to go to a competitor as they will assume that the company is in financial difficulty. Sales will fall by an estimated £14,000 per annum. If the factor is used, administrative savings of £13,000 will be made. Bad debts currently run at 2% of turnover.

Advise whether the company should use the factor's services.

6.5   Activity solution

	£	£
Cost of using the factor:		
Fee: $1.8\% \times [(\pounds 80,000 \times \frac{12}{2}) - \pounds 14,000]$		8,388
Loss in sales	14,000	
Less: Bad debts 2% × £14,000	(280)	
		13,720
		22,108
Benefits of using the factor:		
Administrative savings		13,000
Bad debts saved $2\% \times [(\pounds 80,000 \times \frac{12}{2}) - \pounds 14,000]$		9,320
		22,320

It is therefore just worth using the factor.

6.6   Benefits of factoring

One of the reasons why factoring was initially slow to take off in the UK may have been the fear that a customer may regard the intervention of the factoring company as an indication of the client company's financial instability, with a resulting loss of goodwill.

However, the popularity of factoring has grown and nowadays most of the clearing banks operate debt factoring subsidiaries and it is generally regarded as a 'respectable' source of finance.

The benefits of factor finance provision are likely to vary between companies, but it should be noted that factor finance charges are generally higher than overdraft rates. Much will depend upon other sources of funds available and the improved cash flow offered by the factor.

Factoring is most suitable for small and medium-sized companies, which cannot afford sophisticated credit control and sales accounting systems, and for those companies which are expanding rapidly. These latter companies often have substantial working capital investments which can be eased by factoring debts. Factoring is particularly useful where overseas debts are concerned and many companies that do use factoring will only factor their export sales debts.

6.7   Invoice discounting

This is a system of obtaining finance against the security of sales debtors but, unlike the service offered by factoring companies, companies which provide an invoice discounting service only supply finance. They do not provide a sales ledger service or protection against bad debts ie, the finance provided is **with recourse** to the client company.

For a typical system, the discounting organisation immediately advances 75% of the value of invoices bought, controls receipts of cash settling those invoices and passes on the remaining 25% when received. The fee for the service is about 1% per month.

6.8   Block discounting of HP debtors

When a company sells consumer goods on hire-purchase terms, it can obtain finance on the security of those hire-purchase debts. A block of hire-purchase agreements can be sold to a finance house, usually in return for an immediate advance of 75% of the debts. The advance is repaid, over the average unexpired period of the discounted hire-purchase agreements, by the repayments made by hire-purchase debtors.

7   EXPORT CREDIT AND FINANCE

7.1   Export credit risk

Export credit risk is the risk of failure or delay in collecting payments due from foreign customers. Possible causes of loss include the following.

(a)   Illiquidity or insolvency of the customer. This also of course occurs in domestic trading. But when an export customer cannot pay, suppliers have extra problems in protecting their positions in a foreign legal and banking system.

(b)   Bankruptcy or failure of a bank in the remittance chain.

(c)   A poorly specified remittance channel.

(d)   Inconvertibility of the customer's currency, and lack of access to the currency in which payment is due. This can be caused by deliberate exchange controls or by an unplanned lack of foreign exchange in the customer's central bank.

(e)   Political risks. Their causes can be internal (change of regime, civil war) or external (war, blockade) to the country concerned.

These causes apply to all export trade, of whatever size.

7.2   Protection against export credit risks

Exporters can protect themselves against these risks by the following means.

(a)   By using banks in both countries to act as the collecting channel for the remittance and to control the shipping documents so that they are only released against payment or acceptance of negotiable instruments (bills of exchange or promissory notes);

(b)   By committing the customer's bank through an irrevocable letter of credit (ILC);

(c)   By requiring the ILC to be confirmed (effectively guaranteed) by a first class bank in the exporter's country. This makes the ILC a confirmed ILC (CILC);

(d)   Obtaining support from third parties eg,

   (i)   guarantee of payment from a local bank,

   (ii)   letter from local finance ministry or central bank confirming availability of foreign currency.

(e)   By taking out export credit cover.

(f)   By using an intermediary like a confirming, export finance, factoring or forfaiting house to handle the problems on their behalf; or possibly by giving no credit or selling only through agents who accept the credit risk (del credere agents) and are themselves financially strong.

None of these devices will enable the exporter to escape from certain hard facts of life.

(a)   The need to avoid giving credit to uncreditworthy customers. Weak customers cannot obtain an ILC from their own bank, nor would they be cleared for credit by a credit insurer or intermediary.

(b)   The need to negotiate secure payment terms, procedures and mechanisms which customers do not find congenial. An ILC and especially a CILC are costly to customers, and restrict their flexibility: if they are a bit short of cash at the end of the month, they must still pay out if their bank is committed.

(c)   Exporters can only collect under a letter of credit if they present exactly the required documents. They will not be able to do this if they have sent the goods by air and the credit requires shipping documents; nor if they need to produce the customer's inspection certificates and the customer's engineer is mysteriously unavailable to inspect or sign.

(d)   The need to insist that payment is in a convertible currency and in a form which the customer's authorities will permit to become effective as a remittance to where the exporters need to have the funds, usually in their own country. Often this means making the sale subject to clearance under exchange controls or import licensing regulations.

7.3   Transaction exposure

This relates to the gains or losses to be made when settlement takes place at some future date of a foreign currency denominated contract that has already been entered into. These contracts may include import or export of goods on credit terms, borrowing or investing funds denominated in a foreign currency, receipt of dividends from overseas, or unfulfilled foreign exchange contracts. Transaction exposure can be protected against by adopting a hedged position – ie, entering into a counterbalancing contract to offset the exposure, or by internal methods of risk management such as netting, leading and lagging, and matching. The possibilities therefore include:

(a)   **Hedge in the forward foreign exchange market**

   Buy foreign currency forward to guarantee the cost of the currency.

(b)   **Netting** involves offsetting the group's debtors and creditors in the same currency and only covering the net position. For example there is no point in one subsidiary hedging a $1m receivable at the same time as another subsidiary is hedging a $1m payable. The parent company treasury department can assess the overall group position and only cover the group's net exposure.

(c)   **Leading and lagging**

'Leading' and 'Lagging' are terms relating to the speed of settlement of debts.

'Leading' refers to an immediate payment or the granting of very short term credit, whereas 'Lagging' refers to the granting (or taking) of long-term credit.

In relation to foreign currency settlements, additional benefits can be obtained by the use of these techniques when currency exchange rates are fluctuating (assuming one can forecast the changes).

If the settlement is in the payer's currency, then 'leading' would be beneficial to the payer if this currency were weakening against the payee's currency. 'Lagging' would be appropriate for the payer if the currency were strengthening.

If the settlement was to be made in the payee's currency, the position would be reversed.

In either case, the payee's view would be the opposite.

(d)   **Matching**

Matching of foreign currency receipts and payments is common in multi-national enterprises. Assuming a foreign subsidiary has both payments and receipts from a third country, then payments and settlements are made directly by the subsidiary.

Eg, a French subsidiary makes purchases from, and sales to Italy. It may open a currency account into which it receives lira, and from which it makes payments in lira, without converting into francs.

Possible advantages:

Transaction costs are virtually eliminated.

Transaction exposure is eliminated, except for any balancing figure.

Where the time-scale is significant, care must be exercised to ensure that large balances are not left idle, or unnecessary and expensive overdrafts incurred.

8   SELF TEST QUESTIONS

8.1   What is the traditional approach to financing working capital? (1.4)

8.2   Give examples of transactions that have a different effect on profits than on cash flows. (1.11)

8.3   For which activities is a corporate treasurer responsible? (2.1)

8.4   State three objectives in the investment of surplus cash. (3.4)

8.5   Distinguish between overcapitalisation and overtrading. (4.3)

8.6   Explain the term 'credit scoring'. (5.5)

8.7   Describe the main features of debt factoring. (6.3)

23 WORKING CAPITAL MANAGEMENT: SPECIFIC TECHNIQUES

INTRODUCTION & LEARNING OBJECTIVES

The previous chapter looked at the general issues involved in the management of a company's working capital and considered debtors in more detail. This chapter concentrates on the detail of how best to manage each of the stock, creditors and cash balances, giving practical advice as well as theoretical principles.

When you have studied this chapter you should be able to do the following:

- Explain the principles of stock control, including the EOQ model.

- Identify the benefits and potential dangers of using creditors as a form of finance.

- State the advantages and disadvantages of bank overdrafts as compared with bank loans.

- Optimise the level of cash held.

---

1 CONTROL OF WORKING CAPITAL

1.1 Working capital ratios

The adequacy of net working capital will only be determined by a detailed analysis of current resources and requirements; but a broad indication at any point in time may be obtained by calculating the *current ratio* and the *quick (acid test or liquid) ratio*.

Definition
$$\text{The current ratio} = \frac{\text{Current assets at end of period}}{\text{Current liabilities at end of period}}$$

The quick ratio is the relationship between assets quickly convertible into cash and the liabilities payable on the same time scale. When calculated from published accounts, it will normally be the relationship between debtors and cash (ie, current assets less stocks and work-in-progress) and total current liabilities.

Short-term investments would normally be treated as a liquid asset unless they were specifically earmarked for investment in fixed assets.

1.2 Activity

A company's annual sales are £8 million with a mark-up on cost of 60%. It normally pays creditors two months after purchases are made, holding one month's worth of demand in stock. It allows debtors 1½ months' credit and its cash balance currently stands at £1,250,000. What are its current and quick ratios?

1.3   Activity solution

Step 1   Calculate annual cost of sales, using the cost structure.

	%	£m
Sales	160	8
Cost of sales	100	5
Gross profit	60	3

Step 2   Calculate creditors, debtors and stock.

$$\text{Creditors} = \frac{2}{12} \times \text{annual COS} = \frac{2}{12} \times £5m = £0.833m$$

$$\text{Debtors} = \frac{1.5}{12} \times \text{annual sales} = \frac{1.5}{12} \times £8m = £1m$$

$$\text{Stock} = \frac{1}{12} \times \text{annual COS} = \frac{1}{12} \times £5m = £0.417m$$

Step 3   Calculate the ratios.

$$\text{Current ratio} = \frac{\text{Stock} + \text{debtors} + \text{cash}}{\text{Creditors}} = \frac{0.417 + 1 + 1.25}{0.833}$$

$$= 3.2$$

$$\text{Quick ratio} = \frac{\text{Debtors} + \text{cash}}{\text{Creditors}} = \frac{1 + 1.25}{0.833}$$

$$= 2.7$$

1.4   Control of stocks and work-in-progress

The dream of production managers is likely to be a situation where their company allows them to produce all products on a stock basis to enjoy the benefits of producing in long runs. Operations can then be mechanised, perhaps automated, setting time is cut to a minimum, inspection is simplified and quality improved at reduced cost. On the other hand, the sales manager seeks to increase product variety in order to satisfy every whim of the customer, and would like substantial stocks of all products and parts to provide immediate delivery. Such policies will probably lead to high stock levels and may result in obsolescence, stock deterioration, shortage of storage space and excessive investment.

There is no reason why stocks of new materials and finished components cannot be kept to a minimum, reasonably long production runs obtained and a reasonable service still given to customers, because this is the function of a production planning and control department. Management must recognise that a policy of providing a wide variety of products is not conducive to keeping low stock levels; the objective of the policy may be achieved, for example, by stocking only basic designs and incorporating the customers' full specifications on final assembly.

The production or material controller will need to set up a formal stock control procedure, setting maximum, minimum, and re-order levels for major items of stock material. Before doing so, the need to keep the material in stock at all must be verified. If supplies can easily be obtained and adequate notice is normally given before the material is required, perhaps a stock is not needed. Other factors, however, need to be considered eg, bulk discounts and ordering costs.

It is important to recognise that stock is built up in anticipation of demand. Therefore, current stocks need to be related to future ie, budgeted, sales.

1.5   Control of debtors

A company must establish a policy for credit terms given to its customers. The accountant would want to obtain cash with each order delivered, but that is impossible unless substantial cash discounts are offered as an inducement. It must be recognised that credit terms are part of the company's marketing policy. If the trade or industry has adopted a common practice, then it is probably wise to keep in step with it.

Where no particular custom applies, the business must consider the time it takes to produce sales invoices and statements, and also the normal time taken by its customers in passing those invoices for payment.

A business in liquidity difficulties may give cash discounts, although that can be an expensive way of obtaining finance.

The main features of control over debtors' balances are to do the following.

(a)   Express monthly balances in terms of the previous month's sales to indicate the average credit taken by customers.

(b)   Analyse the debts by age, itemising old ones for special action.

(c)   Ensure that no additional orders are accepted from customers who are badly in arrears.

(d)   Send reminders when payments are overdue.

1.6   Control of creditors

A proportion of the company's suppliers will normally offer cash discounts which should be taken up where possible by ensuring that special clearing treatment is given where cash discount is allowed. However, if the company is short of funds, it might wish to make maximum use of the credit period allowed by suppliers regardless of the cash discounts offered. It is, of course, a mistake to reduce working capital by holding on to creditors' money for a longer period than is allowed as, in the long term, this will affect the supplier's willingness to supply goods and raw materials, and cause further embarrassment to the company. Favourable credit terms will be one of several factors which will influence the choice of a supplier. Furthermore, the act of accepting cash discounts has an opportunity cost ie, the cost of finance obtained from another source to replace that not obtained from creditors.

1.7   Control of cash

Cash and bank balances should be kept to a minimum, as they earn nothing for the company, but care must be taken to ensure that the company's activities are not restricted through a shortage of cash to pay employees and creditors. Finance must be set aside to meet taxation liabilities, pay dividends and invest in capital expenditure. However, until such payments become due, the money may be profitably invested in short-term investments.

1.8   Control of orders received

Overtrading can cause grave financial problems, so it may be vital to limit the amount of business accepted. There are various matters to which management must give its attention in limiting orders. Each order must be analysed to discover the following.

(a)   Its effect on factory capacity.

(b)   The amount of money tied up in the order.

(c)   The length of time for which the company must provide finance.

(d)   The estimated profit or contribution of the order.

Management will wish to select the most profitable orders and could perhaps formulate a selection factor relating the contribution to the total order value and the total financing period, eg,

$$\frac{\text{Contribution}}{\text{Order value} \times \text{Financing period}}$$

It might also be possible to limit the orders taken by a salesman to a certain order value, with an overall ceiling any month. Beyond this, the salesman must obtain approval from the sales manager. In that way, a profitable mix of orders could be selected which can be handled comfortably by the company. Another aspect of orders is the relationship between quotations sent and orders received: if, say, 90% of quotations are accepted and firm orders received, the company may be under-pricing its products.

1.9   Control of purchase commitments

Since the firm's creditors are able to put the firm into liquidation if their demands for settlement are not satisfied, it is clearly important to apply controls to the routines which create the liabilities ie, purchasing of material and plant, etc. The purchasing manager should verify that materials to be purchased will be resold within a reasonable time – say two months. In many cases this factor should carry greater weight than the savings that can be made by bulk-buying. The purchasing manager should, however, seek to negotiate with suppliers in an attempt to obtain bulk discounts by placing larger orders, but taking delivery over a long period – thereby reducing the total initial liability.

2   INVESTMENT IN INVENTORY (STOCK)

2.1   Inventory economics

It may be asserted that the object of holding stocks is to increase sales and thereby increase profit. The implications of stockholding are that a wider variety of products is offered and that customer demand is more immediately satisfied because the product is available: both implications should prevent prospective customers from going elsewhere.

Although the above assertion is more identifiable when related to finished goods, the benefits of stockholding of materials and components may be similarly postulated.

Holding stock is an expensive business - it has been estimated that the cost of holding stock each year is one-third of its cost. Holding costs include interest on capital, storage space and equipment, administration costs and leases.

On the other hand, running out of stock (known as a stock-out) incurs a cost. If, for example, a shop is persistently out of stock on some lines, customers will start going elsewhere. Stock-out costs are difficult to estimate, but they are an essential factor in inventory control.

Finally, set-up or handling costs are incurred each time a batch is ordered. Administrative costs and, where production is internal, costs of setting up machinery will be affected in total by the frequency of orders.

The two major quantitative problems of re-order levels and order quantities are essentially problems of striking the optimum balance between two of the three costs categories above.

Essentially, three inventory problems need to be answered under either of two assumptions.

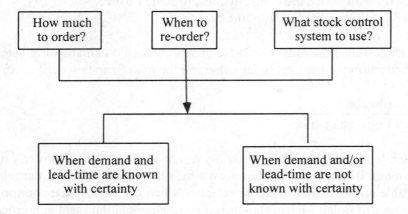

Definition   Lead-time is the time between placing an order and delivery of the goods.

2.2   Pattern of stock levels

When new batches of an item in stock are purchased or made at periodic intervals the stock levels will exhibit the following pattern over time.

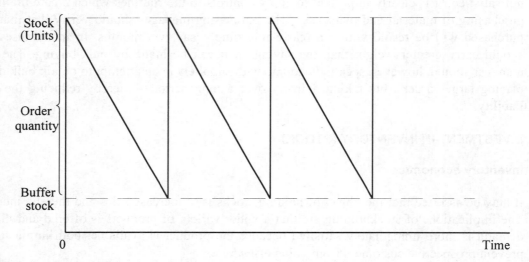

Definition   Buffer stock is a basic level of stock held for emergencies.

The questions asked are as follows.

(a)   **How much to order?**

Large order quantities cut ordering and set up costs each year. On the other hand, stock volumes will on average be higher and so holding costs increase. The problem is balancing one against the other.

It is worth noting that the economic order quantity is not affected by uncertainty of demand and lead-times as long as the demand is independent of stock levels.

Definition   Economic order quantity(EOQ) is the quantity of stock ordered each time which minimises annual costs.

(b)   **When to re-order?**

A gap (the lead-time) inevitably occurs between placing an order and its delivery. Where both that gap and the rate of demand are known with certainty, an exact decision on when to re-order can be made. In the real world both will fluctuate randomly and so the order must be placed so as to leave some buffer stock if demand and lead-time follow the average pattern. The problem is again the balancing of increased holding costs if the buffer stock is high, against increased stock-out costs if the buffer stock is low.

2.3   Order quantities

Calculation involves two distinct problems.

(a)   How much to order when production/delivery is instantaneous.

(b)   How to evaluate bulk order discounts.

The problems are examined in the following example.

2.4   Illustration - Estimating lowest cost order quantity

Consider the following situation. Watallington Ltd is a retailer of beer barrels. The company has an annual demand of 30,000 barrels. The barrels are purchased for stock in lots of 5,000 and cost £12 each. Fresh supplies can be obtained immediately, ordering and transport costs amounting to £200 per order. The annual cost of holding one barrel in stock is estimated to be £1.20.

The stock level situation could be represented graphically as follows:

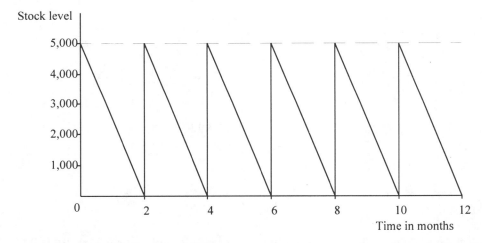

Thus Watallington Ltd orders 5,000 barrels at a time and these are used from stock at a uniform rate.

Every two months stock is zero and a new order is made. The average stock level is $\dfrac{5,000}{2}$ barrels ie, half the replenishment level.

Watallington's total annual inventory costs are made up as follows.

		£
Ordering costs	$\dfrac{30,000}{5,000} \times £200$	1,200
Cost of holding stock	$\dfrac{5,000}{2} \times £1.20$	3,000
Total inventory costs		4,200

30,000 barrels are purchased annually in lots of 5,000. If each order costs £200, the total ordering costs are £1,200. The cost of holding each barrel in stock was estimated at £1.20. With the average stock being half the replenishment level, the annual stockholding costs are £3,000 when ordering six times a year.

2.5   The EOQ formula

You should remember from your previous studies that such situations offer minimum total stock costs when the order quantity is set at

$$x = \sqrt{\frac{2CD}{H}}$$

where   C = fixed costs per batch
         D = expected annual sales volume
         H = holding cost per stock unit per annum

Thus, for Watallington, EOQ $= \sqrt{\dfrac{2 \times 200 \times 30,000}{1.20}}$

$= \quad$ 3,162 barrels

Total annual costs for the company will be

Holding costs + Reordering costs

$= \quad$ (Average stock $\times$ H) $+$ (Number of reorders pa $\times$ C)

$= \quad \left(\dfrac{x}{2} \times H\right) \quad\quad\quad + \quad\quad \left(\dfrac{D}{x} \times C\right)$

$= \quad \left(\dfrac{3,162}{2} \times £1.20\right) \quad + \quad \left(\dfrac{30,000}{3,162} \times £200\right)$

$= \quad$ £1,897.20 $+$ £1,897.53

$\approx \quad$ £3,795

2.6   Activity

Demand for a company's product is about 600,000 per annum. It costs £3 to keep one unit in stock for one year. Each time an order is placed, administrative costs of £40 are incurred.

How many units should the company order at a time?

2.7   Activity solution

Use the formula   EOQ $= \sqrt{\dfrac{2CD}{H}}$

Here   C = £40
        D = 600,000
        H = £3

So EOQ $= \sqrt{\dfrac{2 \times 40 \times 600,000}{3}}$

$= \quad$ 4,000 units

2.8   Large order discounts

Frequently, discounts will be offered for ordering in large quantities. The problem is that if the order quantity to obtain the discount is above what would otherwise be the EOQ, is the discount still worth taking? The problem may be solved by the following procedure.

Step 1   Calculate EOQ, ignoring discounts.

Step 2   If this is below the level for discounts, calculate total annual stock costs.

Step 3   Recalculate total annual stock costs using the order size required to just obtain the discount.

Step 4   Compare the cost of steps 2 and 3 with the saving from the discount, and select the minimum cost alternative.

Step 5   Repeat for all discount levels.

2.9   Example

In the Watallington illustration, suppose, additionally, that a 2% discount is available on orders of at least 5,000 barrels and that a 2.5% discount is available if the order quantity is 7,500 barrels or above. With this information, would the economic order quantity still be 3,162?

2.10   Solution

	£
Steps 1 and 2 have already been carried out, and it is known that total annual cost at 3,162 barrels/batch =	3,795

Step 3   At order quantity 5,000 total costs

$$= \frac{xH}{2} + \frac{CD}{x} = \frac{5,000 \times £1.2}{2} + \frac{30,000 \times £200}{5,000}$$ 4,200

Extra costs of ordering in batches of 5,000	(405)
Less: Saving on discount 2% × £12 × 30,000	7,200

Step 4   Net cost saving   6,795

Hence batches of 5,000 are worthwhile.

Similarly, purchasing in batches of 7,500 results in:

Total costs $\frac{7,500 \times £1.2}{2} + \frac{30,000 \times £200}{7,500}$	5,300
Costs at 5,000 batch size	4,200
Extra costs	1,100
Saving on extra discount (2.5 − 2)% × £12 × 30,000	1,800
Net cost saving	700

It is concluded that a further saving can be made by ordering in batches of 7,500.

*(**Tutorial note:** often the 'holding cost' will reduce where quantity discounts are taken - because this cost often relates to the original cost of buying an item.)*

2.11   When to re-order

The second problem in inventory is when to re-order. When demand and lead-time are known with certainty this may be calculated exactly.

2.12   Activity

Return to the original Watallington example. Assume that the company adopts the EOQ as its order quantity and that it now takes two weeks for an order to be delivered. How frequently will the company place an order? How much stock will it have on hand when the order is placed?

2.13   Activity solution

(a)   Annual demand is 30,000.

EOQ is 3,162.

The company will therefore place an order once every $\frac{3,162}{30,000} \times 365$ days ≈ 38 days.

(b)   The company must be sure that there is sufficient stock on hand when it places an order, to last the two weeks' lead-time. It must therefore place an order when there is two weeks' worth of demand in stock:

ie, $\frac{2}{52} \times 30,000 \approx 1,154$ units.

2.14   Re-order level with variable demand or variable lead-time

Definition   The re-order level (ROL) is the quantity of stock on hand when an order is placed.

As the previous activity demonstrated, the ROL is easy to determine when demand and lead-time are known. It equals demand during lead-time.

On this basis, as the next delivery is made the last unit of stock is being sold. However, in the real world, this ideal cannot be achieved. Demand will vary from period to period, and re-order levels must allow some buffer, or safety, stock.

The size of the buffer stock is a function of three factors.

(a)   Variability of demand.
(b)   Cost of holding stocks.
(c)   Cost of stock-outs.

The problem may be solved by calculating costs at various decision levels, by the following procedure.

Step 1   Estimate cost of holding one extra unit of stock for one year.

Step 2   Estimate cost of each stock-out.

Step 3   Calculate expected number of stock-outs per order associated with each level of stock.

Step 4   Calculate EOQ, and hence number of orders per annum.

Step 5   Calculate the total costs (stock-outs plus holding) per annum associated with each level of buffer stock, and select minimum cost options.

2.15   Example

Autobits Ltd is one of the few suppliers of an electronic ignition system for cars, and it sells 100 units each year. Each unit costs £40 from the manufacturer, and it is estimated that each order costs £10 to handle and that the cost of holding one unit in stock for one year is 25% of the cost price. The lead-time is always exactly one week. The weekly demand for units follows a probability distribution with a mean of 2, as follows.

Demand	Probability of demand
0	0.14
1	0.27
2	0.27
3	0.18
4	0.09
5	0.04
6	0.01

Autobits estimates that the stock-out cost, the cost of not being able to meet an order, is £20 per unit.

Autobits must estimate when orders should be placed.

2.16   Solution

Step 1   Cost of holding one unit: £10 (£40 × 25%)

Step 2   Cost of stock-out: £20

The *normal* level of demand in the lead time is 2 (average, or mean, demand). Define buffer stock as re-order level minus 2. For example, if buffer stock were zero, reordering would take place when stock fell to 2.

Buffer stock of 4 (6 − 2) would mean that, on the basis of the observations, a stock-out would never occur. Thus, the range of buffer stock options is between 0 and 4 units ie, re-order levels between 2 and 6.

The pay-off table between buffer stock and actual demand in terms of stock-outs is as follows:

Pay-off table in terms of stock-outs

Re-order level	2	3	4	5	6
Actual demand during lead-time					
2 or less	0	0	0	0	0
3	1	0	0	0	0
4	2	1	0	0	0
5	3	2	1	0	0
6	4	3	2	1	0

Multiplying, then, by the probability of that level of demand occurring, the expected number of stock-outs is:

Expected number of stock-outs

		Re-order level	2	3	4	5	6
Demand	Probability						
2 or less	0.68 *		0	0	0	0	0
3	0.18		0.18	0	0	0	0
4	0.09		0.18	0.09	0	0	0
5	0.04		0.12	0.08	0.04	0	0
6	0.01		0.04	0.03	0.02	0.01	0
Total = Expected stock-outs per order			0.52	0.20	0.06	0.01	Nil

* calculated as 0.14 + 0.27 + 0.27 = 0.68

Step 4

$$EOQ = \sqrt{\frac{2CD}{H}}$$

$$= \sqrt{\frac{2 \times 10 \times 100}{10}}$$

$$= \sqrt{200}$$

$$= 14.142$$

$$= 14 \text{ to the nearest whole number.}$$

$$\text{Orders per annum} = \frac{100}{14}$$

$$= 7.142$$

Step 5

		2	3	4	5	6
(i)	Re order level	2	3	4	5	6
(ii)	Buffer stocks ((i) −2)	0	1	2	3	4
(iii)	Annual cost of holding buffer stock ((ii) × £10)	0	£10	£20	£30	£40
(iv)	Stock-outs per order (per step 3)	0.52	0.20	0.06	0.01	Nil
(v)	Annual cost of stock outs ((iv) × 7.142 × £20) (where 7.142 is number of orders pa)	£74.28	£28.57	£8.57	£1.43	Nil
(vi)	Total buffer stock cost ((iii) + (v))	£74.28	£38.57	£28.57	£31.43	£40

Therefore the minimum cost solution is to hold a buffer stock of 2 ie, re-order when stocks fall to 4.

Conclusion   From the above analysis, it is apparent that increasing buffer stock is worthwhile if the following apply.

Reduction in annual stock-out costs   >   Unit holding cost or

$$\text{Stock-out cost} \times \text{Orders per annum} \times \text{Decrease} \quad > \quad \text{Unit holding cost}$$
in expected number of stock outs per order

2.17   Inventory control systems - two bin system

Under this system the existence of two bins is assumed, say A and B. Stock is taken from A until A is empty. A is then replenished with the economic order quantity. During the lead-time stock is used from B. The standard stock for B is the expected demand in the lead-time, plus the buffer stock. When the new order arrives, B is filled up to its standard stock and the rest placed in A. Stock is then drawn as required from A, and the process repeated.

The same sort of approach is adopted by some firms for a single bin. In such cases a red line is painted round the inside of the bin, such that when sufficient stock is removed to expose the red line, this indicates the need to re-order. The stock in the bin up to the red line therefore represents bin B, and that above the red line bin A.

In considering the costs of stock control, the actual costs of operating the system must be recognised. The costs of a continual review as implied by the two-bin system may be excessive, and it may be more economic to operate a *periodic review system.*

2.18   Periodic review system

Under this system the stock levels are reviewed at fixed intervals eg, every four weeks. The stock in hand is then made up to a predetermined level, which takes account of likely demand before the next review and during the lead-time. Thus a four-weekly review in a system where the lead-time was two weeks would demand that stock be made up to the likely maximum demand for the next six weeks.

This system is described in some textbooks as the *constant order cycle system.*

2.19   Physical stocks and recorded stocks

The systems described above assume that physical stock counts are taken to arrive at re-order levels. Under the two-bin system this may be so, but increasing reliance is placed on stock records such as bin cards to show when the re-order point is reached. It is frequently found during physical stock checks that recorded stocks bear no relation to stocks actually held. The reason for differences include the following.

(a)   Breaking of bulk;
(b)   Pilferage;
(c)   Poor record-keeping.

The consequence of differences between physical and recorded stocks will be that the use of stock records for re-order purposes will be inadequate. Every effort must therefore be made to ensure that stock records are as accurate as possible, otherwise the stock control model will be rendered unreliable. However, more frequent stock counts will raise the cost of stockholding and the model will require further review.

The use of computers in business has resulted in increasing reliance on stock records as opposed to physical stock counts.

2.20   Two-bin versus periodic review

Advantages of two-bin system	*Advantages of periodic review system*
Stock can be kept at a lower level because of the ability to order whenever stocks fall to a low level, rather than having to wait for the next re-order date.	Order office load is more evenly spread and easier to plan. For this reason the system is popular with suppliers.

2.21   'Just in time' methods (JIT)

Just in time methods of inventory control are becoming increasingly popular in certain industries, in particular the motor car industry, because of increasing influence by Japanese management.

The aim of JIT is to have particular parts delivered only hours before they are required in the production process, thus stocks of these components need not be held. Clearly, for this system to work, there needs to be very close liaison between supplier and purchaser, to the extent that the supplier is made aware of the purchasers' production scheduling. Also, the supplier needs to be reliable, since if a vital component is not delivered as scheduled there is no 'slack' in the system to take account of this.

Arguably, as a technique, it is appropriate to industries where purchasers behave in an authoritative, paternalistic fashion - they agree to support the supplier in the long run and not to 'chop and change'. In return they expect very high standards of quality and loyalty from the suppliers, and often expect to have some influence over the suppliers' manufacturing methods to ensure this is the case.

2.22   Total quality management and stock control

In recent years may companies have put particular effort into trying to raise the quality of the goods and services that they offer to their customers. A total quality management (TQM) philosophy has been instilled into UK business.

TQM has been defined as the continuous improvement in quality, productivity and effectiveness obtained by establishing management responsibility for processes as well as outputs. Every process has an identified process owner and every person in the company operates within a process and contributes to its improvement, striving towards a zero defect culture.

JIT stock systems need TQM procurement methods, otherwise the company will suffer repeated stockouts leading to a loss of business. The company must be able to rely on its suppliers delivering stock exactly when promised.

2.23   Control levels

In a system where order quantities are constant, it is important to identify alterations to the estimates on which the EOQ was based. Thus, a reporting mechanism is incorporated whereby the stock controller is notified when the stock level exceeds a maximum or falls below a minimum.

Maximum level would represent the normal peak holding ie, buffer stocks plus the re-order quantity. If the maximum is exceeded, a review of estimated demand lead-time is implied.

Minimum level usually corresponds with buffer stock. If stock falls below that level, emergency action to replenish may be required.

The foregoing levels would be subject to modification according to the relative importance/cost of a particular stock item.

2.24   Slow-moving stocks

Certain items may have a high individual value, but subject to infrequent demands. Generally, it is suggested that about 20% of items stocked should make up 80% of total usage. Slow-moving items may be ordered only when required, unless a minimum order quantity were imposed by the supplier.

A regular report of slow-moving items is useful in that management is made aware of changes in demand and of possible obsolescence. Arrangements may then be made to reduce or eliminate stock levels or, on confirmation of obsolescence, for disposal.

3   CONTROL OF CREDITORS

3.1   Trade credit

Trade credit is the term used to describe the situation whereby a company is able to obtain goods (or services) from a supplier without immediate payment, the supplier accepting that the company will pay for the goods at a later date.

3.2   Credit periods

Trade credit periods vary from industry to industry and each industry will have what is a generally accepted norm which would be from seven days upwards. The usual terms of credit range from four weeks to the period between the date of purchase and the end of the month following the month of purchase. However, considerable scope for flexibility exists and longer credit periods are sometimes offered, particularly where the type of business activity requires a long period to convert materials into saleable products eg, farming.

Where businesses do not confine the period of credit taken to that allowed by suppliers, they are able to delay their demand for finance still further. Suppliers may attempt to stop their customers taking extended credit by refusing future supply, quoting COD (cash on delivery) terms, or by incorporating an incentive to pay on time in their standard sales terms eg, a discount.

3.3   Cost of trade credit

In order to compare the cost of different sources of finance, all costs are usually converted to a rate **per annum** basis. The cost of extended trade credit is usually measured by loss of discount, but the calculation of its cost is bedevilled by such variables as the number of alternative sources of supply, and the general economic condition.

Certain assumptions have to be made concerning (a) the maximum delay in payment which can be achieved before the supply of goods is withdrawn by the supplier, and (b) the availability of alternative sources of supply.

Example

A business is buying £1,000 worth of goods per month and can take 2.5% discount if it settles accounts within one month. It will lose that source of supply if it delays payment for more than three months.

It has a supplying industry that is organised in such a way that an alternative supply of goods will be difficult to obtain in the event of the business obtaining a bad name.

To work out the cost to the business of taking the extra two months' credit and losing the discount, carry out the following steps.

Step 1   Work out the discount available and the amount due if the discount were taken.

Discount available = 2.5% × £1,000 = £25
Amount due after discount = £1,000 – £25 = £975.

Step 2   The effective interest cost of not taking the discount is

$$\frac{\text{Discount available}}{\text{Discounted amount due}}$$

This applies to the maximum credit period available after losing the discount (ie, three months – one month).

Interest cost of taking two months' credit = $\frac{£25}{£975} \approx 0.0256$ for a two month period.

The idea here is that the business is effectively borrowing £975 from the supplier for two months, and paying £1,000 back at the end, an interest charge of £25 on the 'loan'.

Step 3   Calculate the equivalent annual rate. For simple interest, this will be

Interest cost for period × number of periods in a year × 100%.

For compound interest, the rate will be

$(1 + \text{interest cost for period})^n - 1$, where 'n' is the number of periods in a year.

As there are approximately six, sixty day periods in a year the simple annual cost would be: 0.0256 × 6 × 100% ≈ 15.4%. The compound annual cost is:

$$\left(1 + \frac{25}{975}\right)^6 - 1 = 0.164 \text{ or } 16.4\%$$

It should also be noted that this calculation contains only the explicit costs of trade credit. The implicit costs of delaying payment to the three month point should also be considered. For example, although suppliers may not cut off future supplies they may put a low priority on the quality of service given to late paying customers.

3.4   Activity

Work out the equivalent simple and compound annual costs of the following credit terms. 1.75% discount for payment within three weeks; alternatively, full payment must be made within eight weeks of the invoice date. Assume there are 50 weeks in a year.

Hint: Consider a £100 invoice.

3.5   Activity solution

Step 1   Work out the discount available and the amount due if the discount were taken.

Discount available on a £100 invoice = 1.75% × £100 = £1.75.
Amount due after discount = £100 – £1.75 = £98.25.

Step 2 The effective interest cost of not taking the discount is $\dfrac{£1.75}{£98.25} \approx 0.018$ for a $(8-3)$ five-week period.

Step 3 Calculate the equivalent annual rate. There are ten five-week periods in a year.

The simple interest annual rate is therefore $0.018 \times 10 \times 100\% = 18\%$.

The compound interest annual rate is $(1 + 0.018)^{10} - 1 \approx 0.195$ or 19.5%.

4   TECHNIQUES FOR CONTROLLING CASH

4.1   Example of the cash operating cycle

Definition The cash operating cycle is the length of time which elapses between a business paying for its raw materials and the business's customers paying for the goods made from the raw materials. It equals the debtors' collection period plus the length of time for which stocks are held, less the creditors' payment period.

Analyse the following information from the viewpoint of its implications for working capital policy.

	Position as of now	*Budget position one year from now*
	£	£
Sales	250,000	288,000
Cost of goods sold	210,000	248,000
Purchases	140,000	170,000
Debtors	31,250	36,000
Creditors	21,000	30,000
Raw materials stock	35,000	60,000
Work-in-progress	17,500	30,000
Finished goods stock	40,000	43,000

Assume all sales and purchases are on credit terms.

4.2   Solution to example

Analysis of the figures (which is detailed below) shows that working capital investment is being increased. Debtor balances are moving pro-rata with sales, the current and budgeted collection period both being 46 days. However, some additional finance will be taken from creditors as a result of the payment period being increased from 55 days to 64 days. This increase represents about 16% and is not particularly significant unless creditors demand payment within 60 days, or offer discounts for payment within that time (which will be lost).

A significant change in the turnover of stock levels is anticipated. Raw materials stocks turnover will be decreased by 29% and work-in-progress by 31%, while finished goods stock turnover will increase by 10%. The implication is that production will increase while sales will fall; in the period following the budget, stocks will be very high. The overall impression is that unnecessarily high investment in raw materials and work-in-progress is being undertaken. A reappraisal of the situation should be made to see if these stocks can be reduced, thereby releasing funds for other uses. It may also be possible to reduce debtors to their current levels.

WORKINGS

			Current	Budget

(W1)   Creditors

Average payment period

$= (365 \times \dfrac{\text{Creditors}}{\text{Purchases}})$ $365 \times \dfrac{21}{140} =$ (55 days) $365 \times \dfrac{30}{170} =$ (64 days)

(W2)   Debtors

Average collection period

$= 365 \times \dfrac{\text{Debtors}}{\text{Sales}}$ $365 \times \dfrac{31.25}{250} = 46$ days $365 \times \dfrac{36}{288} = 46$ days

(W3)   Finished stock turnover

$= \dfrac{\text{Cost of goods sold}}{\text{Finished goods stock}}$ $\dfrac{210}{40}$ $\dfrac{248}{43}$

= 5.25 times pa or 70 days   = 5.8 times pa or 63 days

(W4)   Raw materials stock turnover

$= \dfrac{\text{Purchases}}{\text{Raw materials stock}}$ $\dfrac{140}{35}$ $\dfrac{170}{60}$

= 4 times pa or 91 days   = 2.83 times pa or 129 days

(W5)   Work-in-progress turnover

$= \dfrac{\text{Cost of goods sold}}{\text{Work - in - progress stock}}$ $\dfrac{210}{17.5}$ $\dfrac{248}{30}$

= 12 times pa or 30 days   = 8.26 times pa or 44 days

Length of cash operating cycle   182 days   218 days

*(**Tutorial note:** calculation of work-in-progress turnover assumes no change in finished goods stock.)*

4.3   Activity

A company generally pays its suppliers six weeks after receiving an invoice, while its debtors usually pay within four weeks of invoicing. Raw materials stocks are held for a week before processing, which takes three weeks, begins. Finished goods stay in stock for an average of two weeks.

How long is the company's operating cycle?

4.4   Activity solution

The operating cycle equals debtors' collection period plus raw materials' stock-holding period and processing time plus finished goods' stock-holding period less the creditors' payment period

= 4 + 1 + 3 + 2 − 6 = 4 weeks.

4.5   Financing the operating cycle

A common source of short-term financing for many businesses is a bank overdraft. These are mainly provided by the clearing banks and represent permission by the bank to write cheques even though the company has insufficient funds deposited in the account to meet the cheques. A limit (the overdraft limit) will be placed on this facility, but provided that the limit is not exceeded, the company is free to make as much or as little use of the overdraft as it desires. Interest is charged by the bank on amounts outstanding at any one time, and the bank may also require repayment of an overdraft at any time.

The advantages of overdrafts are the following.

(a)   Flexibility - they can be used as required.

(b)   Cheapness - interest is usually 2-5% above base rate (and all loan interest is a tax deductible expense).

The disadvantages are as follows.

(a)   The overdraft is legally repayable on demand. Normally, however, the bank will give customers assurances that they can rely on the facility for a certain time period, say six months.

(b)   Security is usually required by way of fixed or floating charges on assets or sometimes in private companies by personal guarantees from owners.

(c)   Interest costs vary with bank base rates.

Overall, bank overdrafts are one of the most important sources of short-term finance for industry. Although the banks reserve the right to recall them on demand (eg, in times of a credit squeeze or if the firm's financial position is deteriorating) this right is seldom exercised. The banks know that they have little to gain from putting such pressure on customers.

4.6   Bank loans

Bank loans represent a formal agreement between the bank and the borrower, that the bank will lend a specific sum for a specific period (one to seven years being the most common). Interest must be paid on the whole of this sum for the duration of the loan. The source is, therefore, liable to be more expensive than the overdraft and is less flexible, but, on the other hand, there is no danger that the source will be withdrawn before the expiry of the loan period. Interest rates and requirements for security will be similar to overdraft lending.

4.7   Comparison of bank loans and overdrafts

The difference in interest charges can be shown as follows.

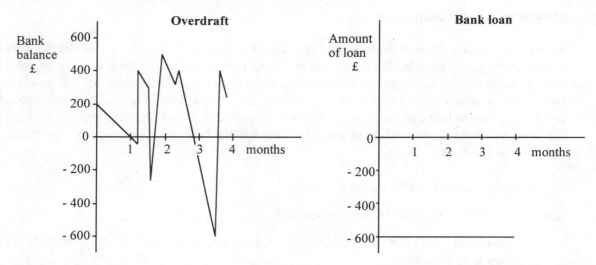

The company requires a maximum of £600, over the next four months. However, it is only halfway through month four that it actually requires the full amount. For the remainder of the period it will pay interest on an overdraft of substantially less than that. If it borrows £600 by way of a bank loan, it must pay interest for four months on the amount borrowed despite the fact that it rarely requires the full sum.

Interest rates on bank loans and overdrafts are normally variable ie, they alter in line with base rates. Fixed rate loans are available, but are less popular with firms (and providers of finance).

4.8   Cash management models

A number of different mathematical models have been developed for managing cash balances, based on the EOQ approach of inventory control. Baumol's model suggests that a fixed cost can be identified with each time cash is raised and a variable cost can be estimated as the opportunity cost of holding cash per time period. The usual EOQ formula can then be used to estimate the optimum amount of cash to raise. A more sophisticated model is the Miller-Orr model.

4.9   The Miller-Orr model

It is considered unlikely that a calculation question would ever be set on this model but a knowledge of its workings could be required.

The model takes into account uncertainty and both receipts and payments of cash. It is best explained with reference to the following diagram:

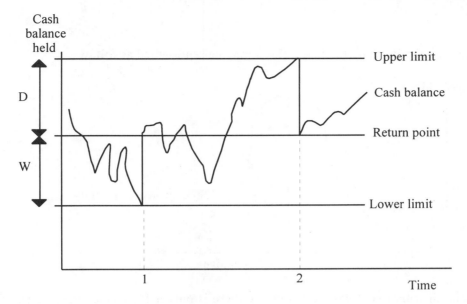

All cash receipts and payments are met from the cash balance and, as can be seen from the diagram, the cash balance of the firm is allowed to wander freely between two limits. The lower limit has to be specified by the firm and the upper limit is calculated by the model. If the cash balance on any day goes outside these limits action must be taken.

At point 1 the cash balance reaches the lower limit and must be replenished in some way eg, by the sale of marketable securities or withdrawal from a deposit account. The size of this withdrawal is indicated on the diagram (W), and it is the distance between the return point (calculated by the model) and the lower limit.

At point 2 the cash balance reaches the upper limit and an amount (D) must be invested in marketable securities or placed in a deposit account. Again, this is calculated by the model as the distance between the upper limit and the return point.

The minimum cost return point and upper limit are calculated by reference to brokerage costs, holding costs and the variance of cash flows. The model has some fairly restrictive assumptions eg, normally distributed cash flows but, in tests, Miller and Orr found it fairly robust and claim significant potential cost savings for companies.

In practical terms, the model closely follows stochastic models for inventory control.

4.10   Probability based models

Probability distributions of daily net cash inflows can be helpful in determining the minimum cash balance to hold.

Example

On the basis of past observations a firm discovers that its daily net cash outflow has a mean of zero with a standard deviation of £20,000 and is normally distributed.

Assuming that it is only prepared to accept a one-in-a-hundred chance of running out of cash, what is the minimum cash balance it must hold at the start of any day?

Solution

The probability distribution of net cash flows may be represented as follows:

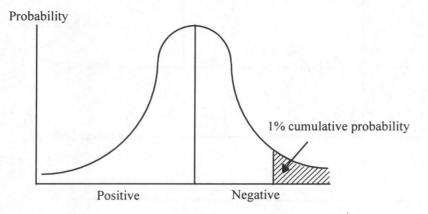

From normal distribution tables we know that there is only a 1% chance that the net cash outflow will exceed:

$$\text{Mean} + (2.326 \times \text{Standard deviation}) = £0 + (2.326 \times £20,000)$$

$$= £46,520$$

Therefore, if at the start of each day the firm has a cash balance of £46,520, there is only a 1% chance that it will run out of cash.

It is, of course, possible to have successive daily net cash outflows but it is assumed that the cash balance is brought back to this level, £46,520, daily.

4.11   Cash budgets

The objectives of cash budgets are:

(a)   To integrate and appraise the effect of operating budgets on the company's cash resources.

(b)   To anticipate cash shortages and surpluses, and to allow time to plan how to deal with them.

(c)   To provide a basis for comparison with actual, to identify unplanned occurrences.

4.12   Relationship of forecast to budget

The cash budget is an integral part of the master budget of the business. It reflects the impact on cash resources of budgeted sales, costs and changes in asset structure, and is also confirmation that the plans are financially viable. It is important to distinguish between a budget and a forecast. A cash forecast is an estimate of cash receipts and payments for a future period under existing conditions before taking account of possible actions to modify cash flows, raise new capital, or invest surplus funds.

A cash budget is a commitment to a plan for cash receipts and payments for a future period after taking any action necessary to bring the preliminary cash forecast into conformity with the overall plan of the business. Cash forecasts and cash budgets can both be prepared in any of the ways described.

4.13   Scope

The period covered by the budget and the frequency with which it is revised will depend on the purpose for which it is made.

A cash budget may be *long-term* or *short-term*, or may be made in connection with a particular contract or project. A long-term cash budget will be made in connection with the long-term corporate plan, typically covering a period of three to five years. In some companies, however, the time horizon of budgeting may be less than a year, while in others (particularly those concerned with the exploitation of natural resources) budget periods in excess of five years may be necessary. A short-term cash budget relates to current operations. In a business which by choice or necessity gives very detailed attention to cash management, the shortest-term budget may be prepared daily or weekly and may cover perhaps one week or one month or more ahead.

A project cash budget may be prepared in connection with a project or contract which is part of the business operations, but which needs to be assessed separately from the point of view of the cash resources it requires and its ability to pay for the use of those resources. Particular examples of this requirement are capital expenditure projects, research and development programmes and special marketing campaigns. In a business which undertakes major long-term contracts it could be important to forecast the pattern of cash flows on each contract so that the average balance of unrecovered outlays could be minimised, and the fee or price recoverable could include an interest charge on those outstanding balances.

4.14   Method of preparation

An example showing the preparation of a cash receipts and payments budget was fully explained in the earlier chapter of this text dealing with 'Budget preparation'.

4.15   Payment systems using new technology

Traditionally bills have been paid in the UK by putting a cheque in the post when payment was due, for example 30 days after the invoice date. The advent of cheap computer power means that much closer control can now be maintained over cash balances.

Throughout this section the banking system will be described as it is in the UK; the student is not expected to know the often very different functioning of banking systems outside the UK. Occasional references to other systems will be clearly attributed to the countries concerned.

The previous sections pointed out the benefits of optimising the net working capital. The process involves *optimising* those elements of working capital which contribute to profit (like giving customers competitive or even attractive credit terms) and *eliminating* wasteful elements which do not contribute to profit, like obsolete or unbalanced inventory, or paying payables (creditors) prematurely when no cash discount is obtainable.

In the previous sections the emphasis was on the balance sheet. This section focuses on the process of making and receiving payments through the banking system.

If a customer's payment is delayed in the banking system, it can be either before or after the accounting system transfers the amount from receivables (debtors) to cash.

4.16   Example

International Harps plc (IH) receives a cheque for £10,000; it will in its own books debit cash and credit receivables. However, the £10,000 will not be available as an increment in IH's spending power until it becomes 'cleared value' in IH's bank account. In accounting terms the delay in the clearing of this cheque must be described as a difference between the company's book balance and the bank's cleared balance in the bank account: it is a part of the 'uncleared cheques' in the reconciliation between IH's books and the cleared bank balance.

The delay could however occur before IH transfers the £10,000 from receivables to cash. If the payment were by direct bank transfer, the accounting entry would not be made until IH has been told of its arrival by the bank. This could occur either before or after the receipt has become cleared value. During the period between arrival at the bank and notification to IH the receivables would be £10,000 higher than they would have been without that delay.

The example illustrates that the impact of the time taken by money transmission is not unequivocally attributable to any particular balance sheet item as it appears in the reporting system. Performance measurement in this field cannot wholly rely on accounting data.

4.17   The objectives of money transmission management

Money transmission is one of the operating spheres in which financial managers play the major part in their company. In doing this they will be concerned to optimise profitability and liquidity, emphasising whichever is currently of primary concern. They will discharge this function by doing the following.

(a)   Cutting out avoidable waste in 'bank float' time: the time which a remittance spends in the banking and clearing system without being available to the payer or the payee as good, usable funds.

(b)   Optimising those aspects of money transmission which affect commercial performance and relations rather than bank float.

Strictly, even (a) is a process to be optimised, for the elimination of unnecessary bank float can often be achieved by incurring modest extra costs like telex charges, and there is obviously a minimum size of payment below which the benefit in interest saved or in extra liquidity is outweighed by that cost.

Objective (b) is concerned with those payment delays which benefit the payer at the expense of the payee. There is the well-known instance of the US treasurer who arranged bank accounts all over the country, and paid each supplier from the most distant account, thus achieving a number of extra value days before the payments reduced his company's cleared balances. Such a policy can be taken economically only to the point where the gain in interest or liquidity is balanced by the adverse reactions of the suppliers. It is in this overall business sense that transmission management must be optimised.

4.18   The clearing period

Most business payments are made through the banking (or postal giro) system.

Some payments of course are between parties holding bank accounts in the same branch of the same bank, but the more normal case is where the payer and the payee have their accounts with different banks, perhaps in different locations, or even different countries. The process of making the payment involves the debiting of the payer's bank account and the crediting of the payee's bank account.

Generally, therefore, the banks each day have a large number of mutual remittances to execute. As between the banks each will have receipts and payments to make. In a closed system, for instance in the domestic system of one country for inland remittances only, the total net sum would be zero, but each bank within the system would normally be a net payer or payee each day. This net settlement process between the banks, and within each bank's internal branch network is called the 'clearing'.

The time taken depends on whether the country has a national clearing system (not the case in the USA or Italy), the communications used by that system (such as the mail or on-line electronic means), how quickly the mechanism works, and by what means the system operates.

There is therefore a period, the clearing period, during which the payee's bank has the cheque, has credited the payee's *ledger* account with its value, but cannot yet without loss give the payee 'good value' for that cheque. 'Good' or 'cleared' value here means two things.

(a)   That payees can draw on funds if they are near their overdraft limit (or if the balance is near zero and there is no agreed overdraft facility).

(b)   That payees' overdrawn balances on which they are charged interest for that night, are reduced by that cheque.

4.19   Value dating and float time

Strictly the clearing period ends for each cheque when the bank has collected the funds through the clearing system. However, specific remittances can for various reasons take different times to clear, and there would be a considerable extra cost to the banks in collecting and using that information for each remittance. Banks therefore classify collections by geographical distances, and negotiate arbitrary, but not unrealistic 'value dates' with each customer. Thus a corporate customer with an account within the City of London might negotiate same day value for 'town' cheques, and two or perhaps three days for country cheques ie, other cheques drawn on accounts in England, Wales and Scotland.

All this refers to collections by the bank on behalf of its customers. On payments, the bank's customers lose cleared value from the moment their branch has the cheque presented to it or initiates a direct bank transfer at their request.

Bank float occurs whenever the payee obtains 'cleared' value on a date after the payer has lost cleared value. Float time is the time during which the banking system, and not the parties to the transaction, has the use of the money. Float time occurs with most remittances. In the UK float time is measured in days, in Italy in weeks.

4.20   Cleared balances

The bank credits its customer's accounts as soon as the incoming cheque is lodged, which is usually *before* the cheque is 'good value'. The resulting balance is the bank's 'book' or ledger balance, which is shown on the familiar bank statements issued by UK banks to each customer. Those statements do not normally show *cleared* balances.

So where cheques have been lodged but not yet 'cleared', there are three conflicting balances.

(a)   The payee company's own book balance (which would for example credit cheques received by the company but not yet in the possession of the bank).

(b)   The bank's book balance (which would credit cheques lodged with the bank but not yet cleared).

(c)   The bank's 'cleared' balance, which represents the effective position between the company and the bank.

It is (c), which is not normally shown on bank statements, which counts against facility limits and for interest and bank charges.

Banks nowadays have computer programmes which enable them to supply a customer with statements in terms of cleared balances. Cleared balances for the previous night can also be notified to corporate customers by telephone by say 10 am on the following morning. This is vital information to a financial manager.

For large corporate customers some banks can now (for a suitable charge) provide online real time computer access to cleared balances. The banks' ability to offer this is spreading very rapidly.

4.21   The clearing process

In the UK the clearing process has traditionally been conducted in a single place, the 'Bankers' Clearing House', originally by the physical handling in that place of all the cheques, direct transfers and other payment instruments. Gradually this system is being replaced by automated, computerised systems. The BACS (Bankers' Automated Clearing System) has handled many remittances (for example direct debits) by magnetic tape since the mid-1970s. In 1984 CHAPS (Clearing House Automated Payment System) began to operate - this gives same day value for remittances of £10,000 or more. For international remittances there is SWIFT (Society for Worldwide Interbank Financial Telecommunications). All the electronic systems are collectively described as EFTS (electronic funds transfer systems).

In many American states and in many other countries there is no organised multilateral clearing system. This makes for a much slower clearing process, much more bank float, and a much higher cost to the users of the money transmission process. At present there is no significant federal (interstate) clearing in the US.

4.22   Delays in the remittance process

Delays in the remittance process can be analysed into those where the payer's and the payee's interests conflict and those where they do not conflict. Generally, their interests do not conflict where the delay is due to bank float – where one or both parties' loss is the banking system's gain. On the other hand in the choice between bank transfer and cheque there is a clear conflict of interest between payer and payee. The payer gains from a cheque, the payee from a direct transfer.

Moreover, even the apparently external delays in the time a cheque spends in the mail, are a benefit to the payer at the expense of the payee.

The student should carefully note this distinction between delays where the interests of the two parties either do or do not conflict. For the relationship between payers and payees is usually commercial and contractual. Payers face a complex problem in optimising their policy, depending on whether payees will be sensitive to the delay, and if so how strong the relative bargaining positions are in that relationship. If buyers have any weakness at all, they may find that their next order will be turned down or priced more highly to allow for the financing cost of the delay. What matters is that the coexistence of the commercial and financial aspects of the decision are recognised.

Moreover, payers and payees will much more easily co-operate where their common interests conflict with those of the banking system.

Cash apart, remittance delays can occur in the following ways.

(a)   Outside the banking process, mainly through delays in transmitting documents by mail or other means. This applies particularly to cheques from the time a cheque is drawn to the time it reaches the payee's bank. The payer could be slow to post it, the mail could be slow to transmit it to the payee, and the payee's system might be dilatory in lodging it with the bank, or perhaps use the mail again to convey it to the bank.

(b)   Searching time in the banking process. This must happen whenever the bank which initiates the remittance process (payer's bank for a bank transfer, payee's bank for a cheque) does not know the other bank's correspondent bank. More importantly it occurs when the paying bank of a bank transfer has not been notified of the payee's bank and branch.

Example

A German customer remits DM 120,000 to a supplier Fornitore SpA in Bologna. The customer's bank (Commerzbank) remits DM 120,000 to the main branch in Bologna of its correspondent bank (say Credito Italiano). This is done by crediting Credito Italiano's account. Credito Italiano, Bologna only knows Fornitore's address and writes to Fornitore by post requesting the bank and branch which holds the 'benestare bancario' (bank certificate which has to be issued for each export and retained by the issuing bank until payment is received by that branch). The Italian post has at times taken three weeks to deliver such letters. When Fornitore receives this, it may well inform Credito Italiano by telephone that the benestare is held by a particular branch in Bologna of Banca Commerciale Italiana (Comit). There is then further scope for delay before the DM 120,000 are made available by Credito Italiano to Comit.

(c)   Advice to payee. Time can be lost between receipt of good value and telling the payee that the funds are available. In the UK corporate customers can ascertain their overnight cleared balances each morning, but in most Southern European countries this can take many days.

These are the main stages at which delay can occur in the remittance process. There are, of course, other delays which occur when the parties themselves act negligently, deliberately, or through lack of funds so as to delay a remittance. However, that is part of the problem of credit control rather than money transmission.

4.23   How can the payee manage the remittance process better?

This involves the following.

(a)   Informing the payer of the desired remittance channel, and of the location and number of the payee's bank account, so as to cut down bank float.

(b)   Negotiating with the payer and asking for payment by direct transfer, and by telex, so long as the monetary inducement is worthwhile under the break-even formula, so as to overcome the conflict of interest and to shorten the remittance delays other than bank float.

(c)   Establishing distant collection accounts, known as lock boxes in the US, for example a dollar collection account with an international bank in New York. This greatly speeds up collections from New York State customers; instant video terminal access to that account can be arranged if the volume of such collections warrants the cost.

(d)   Ensuring that collection accounts are drawn upon (where this is locally permitted) if the company's overall net liquid position is overdrawn. This ensures that all remittances save interest from the moment they become cleared value in the collection account.

(e)   Making the most rapid possible arrangements for advice by the bank of remittances received. This is particularly profitable where accounts may not be overdrawn and credit balances bear no interest, as is the case in many postal giro systems.

(f)   Ensuring instant internal handling of collections. It is self-evident that cheques must not be kept in a drawer pending entry in the reporting system or resolution of queries. It is equally wasteful to delay before acting on advice from the bank or bank transfers collected, if the funds can be used more profitably elsewhere.

(g)   Ensuring the speediest possible banking of cash collections. If the postal giro is the only way to do this on a Saturday, it probably pays to open a giro account.

(h)   Optimising the banking arrangements. A company or group with many bank accounts in the UK can make three types of arrangement.

(i)   To have all accounts cleared every night to a central account; or

(ii)   To have all accounts at the same branch of the same bank with an agreement that the bank will pool them for interest and limit purposes; or

(iii)   To have such an arrangement with the bank across all its UK branches where substantial accounts are kept.

4.24   How can the payer manage the remittance process better?

Payers are in the doubly strong position that they are both the customer and the initiator of the remittance process. It will not be worth abusing this tactical advantage so as to make the supplier either bankrupt or reluctant to accept future orders at the usual prices. Subject to this, payers have the power to select the remittance process which results in the slowest loss of cleared value. This is normally the cheque. Great delays have been achieved by drawing cheques in the supplier's currency on a bank in the customer's own country, such as a dollar cheque drawn on a London clearing bank. However, short-term gains can be more than balanced by long-term commercial disadvantages. A financial manager would be ill advised to use these delaying tactics without the knowledge and cooperation of the purchasing manager.

5   SELF TEST QUESTIONS

5.1   What are the four main ways in which debtors can be controlled? (1.5)

5.2   State the standard EOQ formula. (2.5)

5.3   What are the advantages and disadvantages of bank overdrafts? (4.5)

5.4   What steps should be followed in the preparation of a receipts and payments cash forecast? (4.14)

6   EXAMINATION TYPE QUESTIONS

6.1   Cash management

(a)   'Cash is no different from any other asset - if it is not being utilised properly it is going to result in lower profits.'

Discuss this statement in particular referring to the motives for holding cash.

(b)   The AB Credit Collection Company Ltd employs agents who collect hire purchase instalments and other outstanding accounts on a door to door basis from Monday to Friday. The agents bank the cash collected to be remitted to head office once per week at the end of the week. The budget for next year shows that the total collections will be of the order of £5,200,000 and that the estimated bank overdraft rate is 9%. The collection manager has suggested that a daily remitting system should be introduced for collectors.

You are required to comment on the significance of this stating clearly any assumptions you are required to make.

(20 marks)

6.2   Cuckoo plc

Cuckoo plc is a retailer of hardware; one of its best selling lines is the midget. Daily sales of midgets have the following probability distribution.

Number	Probability
5	0.5
7	0.5

The shop is open 300 days pa.

Midgets are purchased from one supplier at a cost of £8 each. They are sold for £10 each. Operating costs allocated to the sale of midgets (rent, assistant's wages, etc.) are £2,250 pa.

Cuckoo sets a minimum reorder level for each product ie, a continuous record is kept of the actual stock level and an order is placed when actual stock falls to the reorder level. It has been estimated that ordering costs amount to £17.60 per order and that it costs £4.40 to hold a unit of the product in stock for one year. The lapse of time between the placing of an order and the availability of the goods for sale is described by the following probability distribution.

Days	Probability
1	0.30
2	0.50
3	0.20

If the firm is out of stock when a customer asks for an item, it is likely that the sale will be lost to a competitor.

You are required:

(a)   To estimate the optimal order size for midgets;

(b)   To estimate the optimal size of the minimal reorder level, as far as possible given the above information assuming that Cuckoo wishes to maximise the expected value of cash flows (consider the range 15-21); and

(c)   To discuss the practical difficulties involved in estimating relevant costs for purposes of the calculation of the minimum re-order level.   **(25 marks)**

7   ANSWERS TO EXAMINATION TYPE QUESTIONS

7.1   Cash management

(Tutorial note: part (a) requires a fairly standard discussion of the motives for and costs of, holding cash. In part (b) speeding up banking will effectively reduce a firm's overdraft requirement. In this question there are no extra costs of banking daily but they can exist and should be mentioned in your discussion.*)*

(a)   The reasons for holding cash are as follows.

    (i)   **The transaction motive**

        Cash will be required for the day-to-day operations of the business eg, to pay creditors, to buy stocks or to make dividend payments.

(ii)   **The speculative motive**

The company will need cash to finance risky business ventures eg, the purchase of a machine to carry out a speculative project.

(iii)   **The precautionary motive**

Contingent losses may materialise eg, legal claims against the company or the dishonour of a bill of exchange which the company has accepted. Cash will need to be held to satisfy such contingencies as they arise.

The company must, therefore, maintain a sufficient level of cash to satisfy the above three requirements. However, any cash in excess of this level will result in lower profits. It is true that surplus cash can be invested in the short term to earn a return in the form of interest. In this respect cash is different from other assets. However, such returns will nearly always be less than the return which can be earned on the business's other assets. Thus, in general, cash is really the same as any other working capital assets and should be subject to similar management and control. Surplus cash which can only be invested at low short-term interest rates or, worse still, which is lying idle, is not being properly utilised and will result in decreased profitability.

On the other hand, if the company is holding too little cash it may encounter liquidity problems. Such a shortage of cash could mean that the company is forced to reject certain worthwhile investment opportunities owing to lack of funds, or that its very survival is threatened. It should be realised that several profitable companies have been forced into liquidation purely as a consequence of cash flow problems.

Proper cash budgeting and planning procedures should ensure that a company does not fall into the trap of holding too little or too much cash.

(b)   **AB Credit Collection Co**

Annual collections	$= £5,200,000$
$\therefore$ Weekly collections (average)	$= \dfrac{5,200,000}{52}$
	$= £100,000$
$\therefore$ Average daily collections	$= \dfrac{£100,000}{5}$
	$= £20,000$
Annual overdraft rate	$= 9\%$
$\therefore$ Daily overdraft rate	$= \dfrac{9\%}{365}$

Cost of not banking

$$= \text{Sums not banked} \times \text{days not banked} \times \text{daily rate}$$

£

Monday   : £20,000 × 4 days × $\dfrac{9\%}{365}$ =   19.73

Tuesday   : £20,000 × 3 days × $\dfrac{9\%}{365}$ =   14.79

Wednesday   : £20,000 × 2 days × $\dfrac{9\%}{365}$ =   9.86

Thursday   : £20,000 × 1 day × $\dfrac{9\%}{365}$ =   4.93

Friday   : No change to banking pattern   -

Total cost of not banking daily   49.31

Annual cost   = £49.31 × 52

             = £2,564

Assumptions

(i)   There are fifty-two weeks in a year, five days each week, and collections are made on each of these days.

(ii)   Takings are evenly spread daily and weekly.

(iii)   Bankings are used to reduce the overdraft and thus the overdraft rate is suitable for calculating the annual cost of weekly banking. If the company were able to make use of the funds released in other ways then a different rate may be appropriate. For example, if the company had available investment opportunities, then the cost of capital should be used.

It appears that a daily remitting system would save the company £2,564 pa. However, this must be assessed in the light of the possible effects on agents. At present they may be earning interest prior to remitting collections to head office and might resent the change in company policy. Also, what effect will the new system have on the number of agent defaults?

7.2   Cuckoo plc

(a)   **Optimal order size**

Expected sales volume per day   = $(0.5 × 5) + (0.5 × 7)$

                                         =   6

Expected sales volume pa, D   = $6 × 300$

                                         =   1,800

Fixed costs per batch, C   =   £17.60

Stockholding per unit pa, H   =   £4.40

∴ The optimal order size for midgets   = $\sqrt{\dfrac{2CD}{H}}$

                                         = $\sqrt{\dfrac{2 × 17.60 × 1,800}{4.40}}$

                                         =   120

Chapter 23   *Working capital management: specific techniques*

(b)   **Optimal size of minimum re-order level**

(Tutorial note: suppose that the lapse of time between the placing of an order and availability of the goods for sale is one day. During one day the maximum demand for midgets will be 7. If the gap is two days, the maximum demand will be 14. Considering the range of the minimum re-order level from 15 to 21, the only time that contribution will be lost as a result of goods not being available for sale will be when the gap is three days or more, since the demand for midgets over three days will be at the minimum 15 and the maximum 21.*)*

The problem may now be solved in a series of steps as follows.

Step 1   Construct the probability distribution of demand over three days.

Possible patterns of sales over a 3 day period.

Demand day	1	2	3	Total	Probability	
	5	5	5	15	0.125	
	5	5	7	17	0.125	
	5	7	5	17	0.125	0.375
	7	5	5	17	0.125	
	5	7	7	19	0.125	
	7	5	7	19	0.125	0.375
	7	7	5	19	0.125	
	7	7	7	21	0.125	
					1.000	

Step 2   Construct a matrix for stock outs and loss of contribution (£2 per midget not sold over three days).

		Minimum re-order level							
Demand	Probability	15		17		19		21	
		Stock-outs	EV	Stock-outs	EV	Stock-outs	EV	Stock-outs	EV
		£	£	£	£	£	£	£	£
15	0.125	0	0	0	0	0	0	0	0
17	0.375	4	1.5	0	0	0	0	0	0
19	0.375	8	3.0	4	1.5	0	0	0	0
21	0.125	12	1.5	8	1	4	0.5	0	0
Expected loss of contribution (£)			6.0		2.5		0.5		0

(Tutorial note: the figures in the matrix are the number of stock-outs at £2 each eg, for a re-order level of 15 and a demand of 17 two stock outs will occur costing £2 each. This has an expected value of £4 × 0.375 = £1.50*)*

Step 3   Estimate the loss of contribution *per year* from the possible re-order level policies.

Probability of a 3-day lag for any order = 0.2

$$\text{No. of orders per year} \quad = \quad \frac{\text{Expected sales volume}}{\text{Optimal batch size}}$$

$$= \quad \frac{1{,}800}{120}$$

$$= \quad 15$$

Of these orders, the number subject to a 3-day delay

$$= \quad 0.2 \times 15$$

$$= \quad 3$$

The expected loss of contribution per year will be three times the expected loss from an order which lags by three days.

Step 4 Evaluate loss of contribution against stock-holding pa.

	Re-order level	15	17	19	21
(a)	Cost of stock-outs for three day lead time (step 2)	£6.00	£2.50	£0.50	£0.00
(b)	No. of three day lead times p.a. (Step 3)	3	3	3	3
		£	£	£	£
(c)	Annual cost of stock-outs ((a) × (b))	18.00	7.50	1.50	0.00
(d)	Cost of holding stock above 15 units * (re-order level − 15) × £4.40	0.00	8.80	17.60	26.40
	Total costs ((c) + (d))	18.00	16.30	19.10	26.40

* the use of 15 is quite arbitrary and does not affect the solution. It is the difference in stock levels between policies that counts.

Hence, costs are minimised if the minimum re-order level is set at 17 units.

(Tutorial note: the above calculations can be performed in several ways. In step 1 the probabilities of a particular level of demand are calculated **given** a 3 day lead time. Alternatively we could have specified the overall probability of a given level of demand.)

Step 1 **Demand**

Less than	15		$1 - 0.2$	$= 0.8$
	15		0.2×0.125	$= 0.025$
	17		0.2×0.375	$= 0.075$
	19		0.2×0.375	$= 0.075$
	21		0.2×0.125	$= 0.025$
				$\overline{1.000}$

Step 2

		Minimum re-order level							
Demand	Probability	15		17		19		21	
		Stock-outs	EV	Stock-outs	EV	Stock-outs	EV	Stock-outs	EV
		£	£	£	£	£	£	£	£
Less than 15	0.8	0	0	0	0	0	0	0	0
15	0.025	0	0	0	0	0	0	0	0
17	0.075	4	0.3	0	0	0	0	0	0
19	0.075	8	0.6	4	0.3	0	0	0	0
21	0.025	12	0.3	8	0.2	4	0.1	0	0
Expected loss of contribution (£)			1.2		0.5		0.1		0

Step 3   Loss of contribution per year.

There are $\frac{1,800}{120}$ = 15 orders per year. Therefore the annual cost of stock-outs will be

Re-order level	Expected cost per year	£
15	£1.2 × 15	18
17	£0.5 × 15	7.5
19	£0.1 × 15	1.5
21	0 × 15	0

Step 4   As above

(c)   **Practical difficulties in estimating relevant costs**

The practical application of the techniques used in parts (a) and (b) above is hampered by the difficulties of making accurate cost estimates. The problem may be examined by considering the three cost estimates involved.

(i)   **Stock-holding costs**

Holding stock is expensive but how expensive? Such costs will comprise the following.

(1)   Interest on capital tied up in stock.
(2)   Cost of storage space.
(3)   Administrative and handling costs.
(4)   Cost of obsolescence and deterioration.

Against these costs may be offset the gain which arises through holding stock in a period of inflation. These factors are amenable to estimate. The main problem concerns the *fixity* of the costs. For example, if stock is reduced, there may be no alternative use for a warehouse on a long lease. Over a long enough period, however, all such costs tend to be variable.

(ii)   **Re-order costs**

Since there is no question of bulk order discounts, this simply refers to the administrative cost of placing an order. Again, the problem is one of opportunity costs ie, what else will be done with the time saved by placing fewer orders? Only if there is either a real cash saving, or an opportunity for increased cash contribution, should such costs be considered.

(iii)   **Stock-out costs**

In this example the stock-out cost is simply taken to be the contribution lost. For a realistic analysis, it would be necessary for an analysis to be made of customer behaviour when an item cannot be supplied from stocks. There are three possibilities.

(1)   The customer buys this item from a competitor, but returns for the next purchase, or

(2)   The customer buys this item from a competitor, and continues to give custom to the competitor, or

(3)   The customer waits until the item is in stock.

Clearly the distinction is important and will vary between customers and over time. This makes the estimation of *stock-out costs* a matter of considerable practical difficulty.

24 LONG-TERM FINANCE: INVESTOR RETURNS

INTRODUCTION & LEARNING OBJECTIVES

This chapter considers a number of ways in which a company can gain a stock market listing to enhance the marketability of its shares and hence enhance shareholder value. The various forms in which investors may receive returns from a company are examined, together with the dividend valuation model which gives a theoretical valuation for a share's value. This ties in with the discounted cash flow techniques that you have already studied and explains how share prices are in theory directly derived from expected future dividend levels.

When you have studied this chapter you should be able to do the following:

- Explain the various methods of raising equity finance.

- Discuss the particular problems faced by smaller companies in raising equity finance.

- Appreciate the implications of stock market ratios that can be calculated.

- Understand the dividend valuation model, both with and without any assumed growth in dividend levels.

---

1 RAISING EQUITY FINANCE (ORDINARY SHARE CAPITAL)

1.1 Share issues

There is a variety of methods of issuing new shares according to the circumstances of the company.

Type of company	Company requirement	Method of issue	Type of investor
Unquoted	Finance without an immediate quotation.	Private negotiation or placing; EIS (see below) and OTC.	Individuals, merchant banks, finance corporations.
Unquoted Quoted	Finance with an immediate quotation. Finance with a new issue.	Stock Exchange or AIM placing; direct invitation; offer for sale; offer for sale by tender.	The investing public, pension funds, insurance companies and other institutions.
Quoted or Unquoted	Limited finance without offering shares to non-shareholders.	Rights issue.	Holders of existing shares.

1.2 Unquoted companies

Traditionally, unquoted companies obtained their funds from owner proprietors or rich patrons who were prepared to take a risk in order to show an above average return.

This century it has become progressively more difficult for small unquoted companies to raise equity finance from outside shareholders. The tax system has channelled individual investors' money into institutions, and institutions are generally unenthusiastic about investing in unquoted companies for a number of reasons.

(a)   The shares are not easily realisable.

(b)   Costs can be kept down by investing in large parcels of shares rather than spreading investment over many small companies.

(c)   Small firms are regarded as more risky (for example they may lack proper financial control systems).

However, it is possible to arrange a placing of shares with an institution. Generally this is when there is at least a prospect of eventually obtaining a quotation on the Stock Exchange.

Following the Wilson report which highlighted small firm problems, the government set up its Business Start up Scheme which was later widened to become the Business Expansion Scheme and has now become the Enterprise Investment Scheme. The provisions of this scheme are dealt with later, but broadly the idea is to stimulate investors to give help to small unquoted businesses by allowing them to deduct the price paid for shares from their taxable income.

The provision of the **Companies Act 1985** which allows companies to issue redeemable ordinary shares has also played a part in making unquoted shares more liquid and therefore more attractive.

The small firm equity finance problem is dealt with in detail later in this chapter.

1.3   Becoming quoted (listed)

A company will wish to become listed on the stock exchange to increase its pool of potential investors. Only by being listed can a company offer its shares to the public.

The natural progression in recent years has been to seek a quotation on the USM (now replaced by the Alternative Investment Market (AIM)) followed by a full listing on the Stock Exchange.

The possible methods of obtaining a stock exchange listing are:

(a)   **Offer for sale by prospectus**

Shares are offered at a fixed price to the general public (including institutions). The prospectus contains information about the company's past performance and future prospects as specified by the stock exchange rules in the 'Yellow Book'.

(b)   **Offer for sale by tender**

Shares are offered to the general public (including institutions) but no fixed price is specified. Potential investors bid for shares at a price of their choosing. The 'striking price' at which the shares are sold is determined by the demand for shares.

(c)   **Placing**

A placing may be used for smaller issues of shares (up to £15m in value). The bank advising the company selects institutional investors to whom the shares are 'placed' or sold.

If the general public wish to acquire shares, they must buy them from the institutions.

(d)   **Introduction**

An introduction is used where there is no new issue of shares and the public already holds at least 25% of the shares in the company (the minimum requirement for a stock exchange listing). The shares become listed and members of the public can buy shares from the existing shareholders.

1.4   Rights issue

A rights issue can be made by a quoted or an unquoted company. It is an offer to the existing shareholders to subscribe for more shares, in proportion to their existing holding, usually at a relatively cheap price. Company legislation now requires an offer to be made to existing shareholders before it can be made to the public. This has always been a Stock Exchange requirement but now applies in company law to any company. If a public offer is to be made, the shareholders must first pass an ordinary resolution allowing the offer.

The prospectus requirements for a rights issue are restricted thus saving costs, and savings are made on advertising, but the offer is usually underwritten, even though it is possible to argue that this is unnecessary.

1.5   Costs of raising finance

A rights issue for a quoted company is more expensive than a placing, but less expensive than a public offer. For example, for a Stock Exchange listed company with ordinary share capital total capitalisation £10 million, wishing to sell £3 million worth of shares the relative costs are approximately:

	£'000	% of amount raised
Placing	200	6.6%
Rights issue	250	8.3%
Public offer	300	10.0%

These costs comprise underwriting fees, capital taxes, accountants' fees etc. Note that in a rights issue if the existing shareholders do not wish to 'take up their rights' to subscribe for shares, they can sell their rights to outside investors.

(*Tutorial note:* It should be noted that the majority of costs associated with raising finance are 'fixed' in nature, and therefore as the amount raised increases, the percentage 'lost' in transaction costs reduces.)

1.6   Pricing of rights issues

Rights issues are usually priced at below the current market price to give the shareholders an incentive to take up their rights. The result of issuing these shares at an effective discount is to reduce the market value of all the shares in issue.

The new share price after the issue is known as the theoretical ex-rights price and is calculated as follows:

$$\text{Ex-rights price} = \frac{\left(\begin{array}{c}\text{Market value of old shares}\\ \text{before rights issue}\end{array}\right) + \left(\text{Proceeds of rights issue}\right)}{\text{Number of shares ex-rights}}$$

1.7   Example

Alpha plc, which has an issued capital of 1,000,000 shares, having a current market value of £1 each, makes a rights issue of one new share for two existing shares at a price of 40p, raising £200,000. The ex-rights price is 80p each, calculated as follows:

$$\frac{(\text{Market value of old shares}) + (\text{Proceeds of rights issue})}{\text{Number of shares ex-rights}} = \frac{1,000,000 + 200,000}{1,500,000}$$

$$= 80p$$

This formula assumes the following.

(a)   There is no change in expectations for growth in equity earnings in the future;

(b)   The return to the company of the new issue will be the same as that previously enjoyed by the company; and

(c)   No costs of issue are incurred.

The shareholders' options with a rights issue are to do one of the following.

(i)   Take up their rights by buying the specified proportion at the price offered;
(ii)   Renounce their rights and sell them in the market;
(iii)   Renounce part of their rights and take up the remainder; and
(iv)   Do nothing.

Consequences of these four options are as follows.

(i)   Purchasing further shares at a reduced price compensates shareholders for the drop in the ex-rights price of their existing shares.

(ii)   The sale of the shareholders' rights compensates them for the drop in the ex-rights price of their existing shares eg, the right to participate in Alpha's rights issue is worth (80p − 40p) = 40p ie, the difference between the rights price and the market value ex-rights.

(iii)   This results in a combination of (i) and (ii) above.

(iv)   If the shareholders took no action at all they would be left with their original holding, which now has a reduced market value.

Shareholders must take some action on a rights issue if they are not to lose out as a result.

1.8   Example - rights issues

A shareholder in Alpha plc (previous example) holds 100 shares before the rights issue. Indicate the effect on the value of his shareholding if he:

(i)   takes up all his rights; or
(ii)   sells his rights; or
(iii)   takes up his rights on 60 old shares, sells them on 40 old shares; or
(iv)   takes no action.

1.9   Solution

Had the previous example not been done, the first step would be:

$\boxed{\textbf{Step 1}}$ Calculate the theoretical ex-rights price.

$\boxed{\textbf{Step 2}}$ Calculate the value of the rights per share.

Value of right =   theoretical ex-rights price – cost of taking up the right

=   80p – 40p = 40p.

This is the price which the market will pay for each right.

$\boxed{\textbf{Step 3}}$ Evaluate the options.

		£
(i)	Value of shareholding before rights issue	100
	Subscribed for rights issue $\dfrac{100}{2} \times 40\text{p}$	20
	Value of shareholding ex rights, $150 \times 80\text{p}$	120
(ii)	Value of shareholding before rights	100
	Less: Proceeds of sale of rights $\dfrac{100}{2} \times 40\text{p}$	20
	Value of shareholding ex rights, $100 \times 80\text{p}$	80

		£
(iii)	Value of shareholding before rights	100
	Subscribed for rights $\dfrac{60}{2} \times 40\text{p}$	12
		112
	Less: Proceeds of sale of rights $\dfrac{40}{2} \times 40\text{p}$	8
	Value of shareholding ex-rights, $130 \times 80\text{p}$	104
(iv)	Value of shareholding before rights	100
	Value after rights issue, $100 \times 80\text{p}$	80

1.10   Capitalisation issues

$\boxed{\textbf{Definition}}$ A capitalisation issue (or scrip issue or bonus issue) is the capitalisation of the reserves of a company by the issue of additional shares to existing shareholders in proportion to their holdings. Such shares are normally fully paid up with no cash called for from the shareholders.

A capitalisation issue is a method of altering the share capital without raising cash. It is done by changing the company's reserves into share capital.

The rate of a capitalisation issue is normally expressed in terms of the number of new shares issued for each existing share held eg, one for two (one new share for each two shares currently held). In North America, capitalisation issues are usually expressed in terms of the number of shares held following the issue compared with the number previously held. Thus, a one for two scrip issue will be termed a **three for two split**. The student should be familiar with both UK and US terminology, as the majority of studies on this subject are to be found in American textbooks.

Example

UK terminology	Before	New	After	US terminology
1 for 2 scrip	2	1	3	3 for 2 split
2 for 5 scrip	5	2	7	7 for 5 split
3 for 10 scrip	10	3	13	13 for 10 split

A capitalisation issue does not change the shareholders' proportionate ownership of the company.

Do not confuse a scrip issue with a scrip dividend. Many companies allow shareholders to opt to receive their dividend entitlements in the form of new shares rather than in cash. This is called a scrip dividend. The advantage to the shareholder is that he can painlessly increase his shareholding in the company without having to pay broker's commissions or stamp duty on a share purchase. The advantage to the company is that it does not have to find the cash to pay a dividend and in certain circumstances it can save tax.

1.11   Activity

J Bloggs holds 1,000 shares in Deucalion plc which has a total issued capital of 4,000,000 shares. The directors decide to capitalise some of the revenue reserves by making a 1 for 4 scrip issue. Calculate J Bloggs' percentage share in the company before and after the scrip issue.

1.12   Activity solution

	Before	After
J Blogg's shareholding	1,000 shares	1,250 shares
Total issued capital	4,000,000 shares	5,000,000 shares
J Bloggs' percentage holding	0.025%	0.025%

1.13   Capitalisation issues, the balance sheet and investors' returns

The effect of a capitalisation issue on a company's balance sheet and on an investor's return is shown in the following example.

Example

Pyrrha plc has issued share capital of one million shares of 10p each. It generally pays a total dividend of £12,000. The company decides to issue bonus shares in the ratio of one for every two held. Note that the market value of the company will not change.

	Before bonus issue	After 1 for 2 bonus issue
Number of shares	1,000,000	1,500,000
Nominal value	10p	10p
Issued capital	100,000	150,000
Reserves (change into share capital after bonus issue)	100,000	50,000
Net assets	200,000	200,000
Net assets per share	20p	13.3p
Market capitalisation	£150,000	£150,000

Market price (market capitalisation/number of shares	15p	10p
Dividend per share	1.2p	0.8p
Dividend yield (ignoring income tax)	8.0%	8.0%

Since a capitalisation issue does not increase the total dividend received by investors, or the total value of each one's holding or the total net assets of the company attributable to each holding, what is its purpose? It is argued that it can be used for the following reasons.

(a)   To increase the marketability of the shares, since it will increase the number of shares in issue and hence reduce the market value of each share (in our example, from 15p to 10p each).

(b)   To increase the amount of permanent capital of the business in line with growth in its assets.

(c)   To provide a return to shareholders without having to pay out cash.

Students should appreciate that argument (c) is totally spurious, assuming that investors have more than a modest amount of sense. There may be some merit in (b), although it could also be argued that most shareholders would in any event, never expect the entire figure for 'retained earnings' in a balance sheet to be paid out by way of dividend. The first point is the most common reason, and is peculiar to the UK. In the USA and Germany, for example, it is not uncommon to have single shares which are quoted at a price of the equivalent of several hundred pounds.

1.14   Share split

Like a capitalisation issue, a share split (also called a stock split) does not raise extra cash. A share split simply involves the division of existing shares into smaller denominations, making the share capital more marketable eg, a company whose shares have a nominal value of £1 each but a market value of £10 each may decide to split each £1 share into 10 shares of 10p each. The market value of each share then becomes £1.

The reverse procedure might be appropriate where the market value of a company's share is very low. This procedure is known as a **consolidation** of shares.

1.15   Offers for sale by tender

The main feature which distinguishes an offer for sale by tender is that the investing public are not invited to apply for shares at a fixed price but are invited to tender for shares at the price they are willing to pay. A minimum price, however, is set by the issuing company and tenders must be at or above the minimum.

Once all tenders are received, the actual issue price is set. The issue price will be one of the following.

(a)   The highest price at which the entire issue is sold, all tenders at or above this price being allotted in full.

(b)   A price lower than that in (a) but with tenders at or above this price receiving only a proportion of the shares tendered for. This is to prevent the concentration of shares in the hands of one party.

Whichever method is adopted the shares are issued at only one price and not at a variety of prices. Hence investors who make tenders at high prices will usually pay less than the amount tendered.

1.16   Activity

A company is issuing 10,000 shares using an offer for sale by tender. It will use one of the methods described above.

The directors believe that were they to set a striking price, the demand for the shares would be as follows.

Price per share £	Total number of shares sold
7	5,000
6	8,000
5	10,000
4	15,000
3	19,000

If method (a) is adopted, what will be the issue price? What will be the difference between the price paid by investors and the price they were willing to pay? If method (b) is chosen, with an issue price of £4, how many shares will be issued at each tender level? In both cases, assume that investors tender the highest price they are willing to pay according to the demand schedule given above.

1.17   Activity solution

Step 1 Calculate the number of shares tendered for at each price. For example, 8,000 shares could be sold at £6, while only 5,000 could be sold at £7. Therefore, the 'top slice' of investors will be willing to pay a maximum of £7 per share for 5,000 shares; the next tranche of investors will be willing to pay a maximum of £6 per share for a further 8,000 – 5,000 = 3,000; and so on.

Price per share £	Number tendered for
7	5,000
6	3,000
5	2,000
4	5,000
3	4,000

Step 2 Method (a): From the original table, it can be seen that all shares will be sold at a price of £5.

Identify tenders at or above £5. Calculate the total price paid for the shares and the total price originally tendered.

Price per share £	Number of shares tendered for	Total price paid (at £5) £	Total price originally tendered £
7	5,000	25,000	35,000
6	3,000	15,000	18,000
5	2,000	10,000	10,000
		50,000	63,000

The difference is £63,000 – £50,000 = £13,000.

Step 3   Method (b):

Identify the proportion of shares issued to shares tendered for.

At £4, 15,000 shares will be tendered for and 10,000 shares will be issued, a proportion of $\frac{2}{3}$.

Step 4   Calculate the number issued at each level, using the relevant proportion.

Price per share £	Number of shares tendered for	Number issued
7	5,000	3,333
6	3,000	2,000
5	2,000	1,333
4	5,000	3,334
	15,000	10,000

1.18   When a tender issue is made

The circumstances where a tender issue is appropriate mainly concern those cases where there is significant difficulty in determining an appropriate issue price. Reasons for this include the following.

(a)   The company has not previously had a quotation.

(b)   The market is extremely volatile and prices are likely to change significantly between the time of setting the issue price and carrying out the issue procedure.

In such cases a tender issue will help safeguard against setting an issue price which later proves inappropriate and it may also, in a rising market, assist in raising more capital for the issuing company than would be the case with a fixed price issue.

Example

If a company offers 10,000 shares to the public, and 10,000 investors offer £1 or more for the shares, then all the shares will be sold if the price is set at £1. It is possible that, in total 20,000 investors offered £0.75 or above for the shares but the 10,000 who offered between £0.75 and £1 will not receive an allocation.

As demonstrated in the previous activity, shareholders do not necessarily have to pay the price they offered for the shares: 1,000 of the investors may have offered as much as £2 for the shares, but they will only have to pay a price of £1 per share because this was the price which cleared the issue. The Stock Exchange watches this method of issue very carefully to prevent abuse. It will not allow a multi-tiered price structure; that is more than one price at which the shares are to be issued. Only one striking price is allowed.

1.19   Issuing houses

A company wishing to raise capital by direct invitation or offer for sale would first get in touch with one of the issuing houses which specialise in this kind of business.

An **issuing house** is a commercial concern specialising in the issue in the capital market of shares and debentures of companies. In some cases, the issuing house earns a fee by organising public issues; in others, it purchases outright a block of shares from a company and then makes them an 'offer for sale' to the public on terms designed to bring in a profit. There are between 50 and 60 members of the Issuing House Association, including all the important merchant banks. The fact that an issue is launched by one of these banks or other houses of high reputation is in itself a factor contributing to the chance of success of such a venture.

1.20   The role of merchant banks

The UK merchant banks perform the functions of underwriting, marketing and pricing new issues.

(a)   **Underwriting** - the merchant bank making the issue arranges with financial institutions to underwrite a new share issue. If the shares are not fully subscribed, the underwriters collect a commission on the value of the shares taken by the underwriters.

(b)   **Marketing** - the marketing and selling of a new issue is a business activity in its own right. The merchant bank provides the expertise.

(c)   **Pricing** - one of the most difficult decisions in making a new issue is that it should be priced correctly. If the price is too low, the issue will be over-subscribed, and existing shareholders will have had their holdings diluted more than is necessary. If the price is too high and the issue fails, the underwriters are left to subscribe to the shares. This will adversely affect the reputation of the issuing house and the company.

Correct pricing is important, and the merchant bank will be able to offer advice based on experience and expertise. One way round the issue price problem is an issue by tender.

2   FINANCING PROBLEMS OF SMALL FIRMS AND NON-CORPORATE ENTITIES

2.1   Equity capital problems

Equity finance provided by wealthy individuals once formed an important source of expansion funds for the small business. More recently, however, such firms have found themselves cut off from this source of capital for two main reasons.

(a)   The increasing expense and difficulty of obtaining a quotation on the Stock Exchange.

    The attractiveness of a speculative equity investment in a company is much increased if there is a reasonable chance of a quotation, which gives the opportunity of selling the shares.

(b)   The UK tax system has encouraged individuals to save with large institutions. For a variety of reasons these institutions prefer to invest in the shares of large companies rather than small ones or in non-corporate entities.

These reasons include the following.

(a)   Investments in large companies are more easily marketable. An investment in a small company or a non-corporate business would need to be long-term.

(b)   The general belief that small enterprises are more risky than large companies.

(c)   The administrative costs of investing in a limited number of large businesses will be less than those involved in investing in a large number of small ones.

Thus, wealthy individuals, who once provided a major source of venture capital (see below) for small businesses have been persuaded by the tax system to channel their funds indirectly into large companies.

The Wilson Committee on the provision of funds to industry and trade, summarised the position in 1979, as follows:

> 'Compared to large firms, small firms are at a considerable disadvantage in financial markets . . . External equity is more difficult to find and may only be available on relatively unfavourable terms. Venture capital is particularly hard to obtain . . . Proprietors of small firms do not always have the same financial expertise as their larger competitors and information and advice about finance may not be easily accessible.'

2.2   Equity capital - attempted solutions

The increasing difficulties of financing small firms have attempted to be countered by direct attacks on the two main problems.

(a)   **Making the shares marketable**

The most important developments have been the Unlisted Securities Market, its successor, the Alternative Investment market and the Over The Counter market described above.

In addition, there are the provisions of the *Companies Act 1985*, which allows companies to purchase their own shares. This should lead to shares of small private companies being more easily realisable and hence more attractive to the small investor. The position where a minority shareholder becomes trapped in such a company can now be avoided.

(b)   **Tax incentives**

The Wilson Committee made a number of recommendations to cope with the small firm problems. Specifically as regards equity finance, it suggested the formation of a new form of investment trust to be known as Small Firms Investment Companies. Purchase of shares in SFICs should attract tax relief. These ideas eventually led to the Business Expansion Scheme and then the Enterprise Investment Scheme.

The Business Expansion Scheme

The BES offered tax relief, at their highest rate of income tax, to individuals who invested up to £40,000 new equity capital in an unquoted UK trading company. However a large proportion of the funds raised under the BES bought properties to be let out under assured tenancies rather than genuine new entrepreneurial trading, so the BES was wound up at the end of 1993 and replaced by the EIS.

The Enterprise Investment Scheme

The EIS is the successor to the BES. Individuals may invest up to £100,000 each tax year and qualify for 20% tax relief. Any gain on disposing of EIS shares is exempt from capital gains tax. Income or capital gains tax relief will be available on losses.

The scheme applies to any company trading in the UK and enables companies to raise up to £1m a year. Participating investors can become a paid director of the company and still qualify for the relief.

Relief is available to investments in shares issued after 1 January 1994.

The venture capital scheme

The objective of this scheme is to encourage individuals to hold a portfolio of unquoted shares (including AIM and OTC shares), by allowing any losses on amounts subscribed to attract tax relief at the highest marginal rate. For example, individuals who pay tax at 40% marginal rate risk only £600 for every £1,000 invested. A similar relief is available for investment companies.

Share incentive schemes

There are three schemes designed to encourage employees to hold shares in companies by which they are employed. All such schemes require Inland Revenue approval.

Other tax incentives

These include the following.

(i)   Indexation of capital gains.
(ii)   Tax relief on loans to purchase shares in a closely controlled company.
(iii)   Reduced rates of corporation tax for small companies; and
(iv)   Higher VAT registration threshold.

The combination of increasing the prospective marketability of small company shares and tax relief schemes has led to the proliferation of venture capital funds which are described in the next section.

2.3   Venture capital funds

[Definition]   The term venture capital simply means equity capital for small and growing businesses.

One of the original, and still one of the best known, venture capital institutions is the Industrial and Commercial Finance Corporation, now part of the 3i Group. It will take a continuing interest in its client enterprises and will not require to withdraw the capital after, say, a five year period.

However, in recent years, most major sources of business finance have in some way become involved in the provision of venture capital, usually by setting up or participating in specialist 'venture capital funds'. The main spur to their growth has come from the incentives described above.

The result is that there is now no real shortage of venture capital for viable projects. The range of possible funds include those run by the following bodies.

(a)   Investment trusts (ie, public limited companies set up specifically to take equity in other companies) (eg, Electra Risk Capital).

(b)   Merchant banks (eg, County Fund, Charterhouse Fund).

(c)   Clearing banks (eg, Barclays Development Capital).

(d)   Overseas banks.

(e)   Pension funds.

(f)   Syndicates of institutions, banks, etc (eg, Equity Capital for Industry).

(g)   Individuals with experience of banking and high-risk ventures and who have good contacts with institutional investors.

(h)   Local authorities.

(i)   Development agencies.

In addition, many of these organisations have separate subsidiaries for dealing specifically with EIS funds.

2.4   Evaluation of a new project by a venture capital fund

The information required by a venture capital fund when assessing the viability of a new project can be classified as follows.

(a)   **Financial aspects**

  (i)   **Project viability**

  The investor would wish to see cash flow and profit projections for at least two years to ensure that the expansion stands a good chance of success, together with balance sheets for each year end. NPV calculations and sensitivity analysis would be useful.   However, usually the best indicators of project viability are non-financial, and are dealt with below (part (b)).

  (ii)   **Financing requirement**

  Cash flow projections should show the total financing requirement but not specify in detail how that funding requirement is to be met. The provider of funds will wish to devise the best package.

  (iii)   **Accounting system**

  The investor will require regular management accounting information to monitor the progress of the investment, and will wish to evaluate the existing or proposed accounting system.

  (iv)   **Availability of other sources of finance, including loans and grants from government bodies.**

  (v)   **Future policy as regards dividends and retention of profits**

  This will affect investors' tax positions and the future growth of the firm. Most venture funds are looking for high growth.

  (vi)   **The intentions of eventually obtaining a quotation**

  This will be important in encouraging investors who eventually wish to realise their investment. A typical time-scale for achieving a quotation is seven to ten years.

  (vii)   **The percentage stake which is offered in the firm**

  This will affect the influence which is exercised over the company, and the size of the investor's risk.

(b)   **Additional information affecting the proposal**

  For most venture funds, evaluating financial information comes second to evaluating the credibility of the firm's management. A view must be formed as to whether the existing team has sufficient expertise to manage a growing firm, or whether specialist talent needs to be added.

The investor would then wish to see evidence that thorough studies of the firm's markets had been made, so that projected sales budgets were realistic. The single most common cause of failure in this sort of situation is over-optimism in sales projections. Relevant information includes market research, orders in hand, letters from potential customers and general projections of the market's prospects.

Information on technical aspects of the firm's products would then be useful, especially new designs which have not yet been tested.

The investor would also be interested in knowing how much influence it is envisaged it will have on the management decision-making in the firm. Nearly all venture funds will want a seat on the board.

2.5   Loan capital - problems

Traditionally, small businesses have borrowed by means of loans and overdrafts from clearing banks. The main problems have always been the security required by the bank for granting the loan, and the risk averse attitude of the banks when faced with a decision relating to a new and untested project. A bank will often require personal guarantees from the proprietors to cover the loan or overdraft advance. This requirement has inhibited the expansion of many small businesses and contributed towards the problem of British ideas being developed abroad.

2.6   Loan capital - solutions

The government's policy is that finance for firms should be provided through the private sector as far as possible and one of its major innovations has been the **Loan Guarantee Scheme** in which the repayment of a high proportion of a loan is guaranteed by the government, in situations where the project is regarded as commercially viable and the only thing which prevents the granting of a normal medium-term loan is lack of sufficient security.

However in practice, the loan guarantee scheme has hardly been used. The interest rate is higher than on similar loans (because of the premium) and banks are reluctant to promote it.

2.7   Preference shares

These pay a fixed dividend but in a period of inflation they are not popular unless there are definite taxation advantages. There have been circumstances in the past when preference shares have been suitable for small firms' fundraising but under modern conditions they are not now in common use.

2.8   Small firm advice

The problem of the lack of advice available to small firms, which was highlighted by the Wilson Report, has now been solved by numerous initiatives.

The DTI has set up eleven Small Firms Centres over the country. There are also more than fifty area counselling offices. Free advice is available by telephone or by personal visit.

In addition, grants are available for smaller firms to assist with advice on product improvement, new technology feasibility studies, export advice, energy saving advice, etc.

The British Chambers of Commerce offer a range of services to small firms, and local business communities have set up a network of 'Enterprise Agencies', which are sponsored by both private and public sector money. Their services include the provision of information and advice, training and trade fair promotions. A few enterprise agencies (eg, St Helen's Trust), have set up venture capital funds.

3   STOCK MARKET RATIOS

The key stock market ratios were defined and discussed in an earlier chapter. Be sure that you are familiar with each of:

- dividend per share
- dividend cover
- dividend yield
- return on equity
- earnings per share
- PE ratio

and that you can relate their values to an assessment of past, current and future investor returns.

4   THE DIVIDEND VALUATION MODEL FOR SHARES

4.1   The rate of return on shares

The anticipated rate of return on a share acquired in the market consists of two components.

> Component 1 - Dividends paid until share sold
> Component 2 - Price when sold

Applying the concept of discounted cash flow, in making a purchase decision it is assumed that the investor discounts future receipts at a personal discount rate (or personal rate of time preference). For the illustration below define this rate as 'i'.

In order to make a purchase decision, the shareholder must believe the price is below the present value of the receipts ie,

$$\text{Current price, } P_0 < \frac{\text{Dividends to sale } + \text{ Sale price}}{\text{Discounted at rate i}}$$

Algebraically, if the share is held for n years
then sold at a price P_n
and annual dividends to year n are $D_1, D_2, D_3, \dots D_n$

Then

$$P_0 < \frac{D_1}{1+i} + \frac{D_2}{(1+i)^2} + \frac{D_3}{(1+i)^3} + \dots + \frac{D_n + P_n}{(1+i)^n}$$

By similar logic, the seller of the share must believe that

$$P_0 > \frac{D_1}{1+i} + \frac{D_2}{(1+i)^2} + \frac{D_3}{(1+i)^3} + \dots + \frac{D_n + P_n}{(1+i)^n}$$

These different views will occur for two reasons.

(a)   Different forecasts for D_1, D_2, etc, and for P_n by the different investors.
(b)   Different discount rates being applied by different investors.

However, since the price of shares is normally in equilibrium, for the majority of investors who are not actively trading in that security:

$$P_0 = \frac{D_1}{1+i} + \frac{D_2}{(1+i)^2} + \frac{D_3}{(1+i)^3} + \dots + \frac{D_n + P_n}{(1+i)^n}$$

Conclusion   The dividend valuation model states that the value of a security equals the future expected returns from that security, discounted at the security holders' required rate of return.

4.2   Problems and assumptions in the above valuation model

It is important to appreciate that there are a number of problems and specific assumptions in this model.

(a)   **Anticipated values for dividends and prices** - all of the dividends and prices used in the model are the investors' estimates of the future.

(b)   **Assumption of investor rationality** - the model assumes investors act rationally and make their decisions about share transactions on the basis of financial evaluation.

(c)   **Application of discounting** - it assumes that the conventional compound interest approach equates cash flows at different points in time.

(d)   **Dividends are paid annually** with the next dividend payable in one year.

4.3   A general model

In the basic model developed above, each year's dividend must be forecast separately. This is both cumbersome and probably unrealistic as a representation of the investors' value forecasts.

The most convenient assumptions are that dividends either remain constant, or grow at some constant annual rate, g.

If we also accept that shares are in effect perpetuities (individuals may buy and sell them, but only very exceptionally are they actually redeemed), then the equilibrium share price, P_0, can be expressed in relatively simple terms as the sum of a perpetuity.

With constant dividends:

$$P_0 = \frac{d}{i} \qquad \text{or} \qquad i = \frac{d}{P_0}$$

With dividends growing at a constant annual rate, g:

$$P_0 = \frac{d(1+g)}{i-g} \qquad \text{or} \qquad i = \frac{d(1+g)}{P_0} + g$$

where P_0 is the price of shares ex-div
        d   is the size of the dividend just paid (per share)
        i   is the equity investors' anticipated rate of return.

In this model it is assumed that dividends are paid at annual intervals and that it is a year till the next payment.

4.4   Points to note

There are obvious flaws in such simple models of anticipated dividend behaviour. In particular note the following.

(a)   g must be less than i.

If g equals i, the share price becomes infinitely high, a nonsense result. But note that a growth rate this high **to perpetuity** is impossible. It implies a company which would very soon swallow up the entire world.

(b)   In practice companies are likely to experience periods of varying growth rates.   More sophisticated models have been developed to cope with such forecasts, but they do not need to be considered computationally.

4.5   Activity

Use the formulae above to answer the following questions.

(a)   A company's shares are quoted at £2.50 ex-div. The dividend just paid was £0.50. No growth in dividends is expected. What rate of return, i, do the investors anticipate?

(b)   As (a), but with an anticipated growth rate in dividends of 10% pa.

(c)   Investors in a company are known to require a rate of return of 15%. Current dividends are 30p per share, just paid. No increase is anticipated. Estimate the share price, P_0.

(d)   As in (c), but dividends are expected to growth at 5% pa.

4.6   Activity solution

(a) $i = \dfrac{d}{P_0}$

$= \dfrac{£0.50}{£2.50}$

$= 0.2$ or 20%.

(b) $i = \dfrac{d(1+g)}{P_0} + g$

$= \dfrac{£0.50(1.1)}{£2.50} + 0.1$

$= 0.32$ or 32%

(c) $P_0 = \dfrac{d}{i}$

$= \dfrac{£0.3}{0.15}$

$= £2$

(d) $P_0 = \dfrac{d(1+g)}{i-g}$

$= \dfrac{£0.3(1.05)}{0.15-0.05}$

$= £3.15$

4.7   Cum-div and ex-div share prices

Definition   If a dividend is just about to be paid on a share, an investor buying the share cum-div is entitled to the dividend. An investor buying the share ex-div is **not** entitled to the dividend. The seller of the share receives the dividend.

Dividends are paid periodically on shares. During the period prior to the payment of dividends, the price rises in anticipation of the payment. At this stage the price is **cum-div**.

Some time after the dividend is declared the share becomes **ex-div**, and the price drops. This may be expressed diagrammatically:

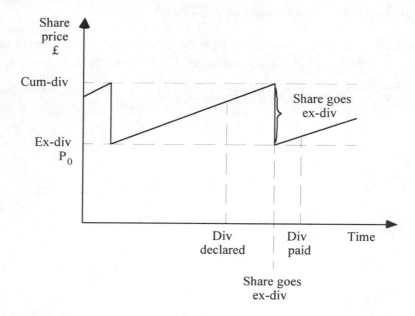

This share price profile is easily proved. Consider example (c) above with, for simplicity, a shareholder rate of time preference that does not change with time (ie, which remains at 15%).

$$\text{Share price (\textbf{ex-div}) now} = \frac{£0.3}{0.15} = £2$$

$$\text{Expected share price (\textbf{ex-div}) a year from now} = \frac{£0.30}{0.15} \quad \text{(expected returns pa from year 2 as a perpetuity)}$$
$$= £2$$

Thus, expected share price, **cum-div** = £2.30   (value of the share **ex-div** plus the dividend a purchaser would get at year 1 if **cum-div**)

Similarly, **cum-div** prices just before dividend payments could be expected to be £2.30 every year, with £2 as the price as the share goes **ex-div**. Hence the share price profile in the diagram.

Conclusion   Ex-div share price + dividend just about to be paid = cum-div share price.

4.8   Activity

A share is quoted **cum-div** at £4.50. The dividend has been declared at £0.50. What is the probable **ex-div** price?

4.9   Activity solution

The problem may be viewed diagrammatically:

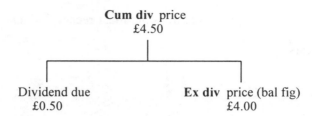

Hence the forecast **ex-div** price is £4.00. After all, a person buying the share **ex-div** would expect to receive all the value that would be obtained from a **cum-div** purchase **except** the present year dividend.

> **Conclusion**   The share goes **ex-div** shortly before the dividend is paid. Any person acquiring the share after this point in time will not receive the dividend, which will be paid to the original shareholder. The reason is that the time it takes for the company to amend its register of members requires a cutoff point somewhat before the dividend is paid.

Thus, when a share is quoted **cum-div**, the price includes both the underlying **ex-div** value of the share (P_0), and the dividend due shortly (d). Use of the dividend valuation model and the formulae developed thus far assumed the share was ex-div (ie, there is one year to wait before the dividend stream is received).

5   DIVIDEND GROWTH

5.1   Estimating growth rates - historic pattern

The anticipated growth rate, g, is an unknown, representing a subjective estimate made by individual investors. It cannot be calculated precisely, but an important factor in the investors' estimate will be the historical pattern of growth in dividends and earnings.

Thus, a growth rate may be estimated, given sufficient data, from:

$$d_0(1 + g)^n = d_n$$

where d_0 is a dividend in the past and d_n is the current dividend.

Example

A company currently pays a dividend of 32p; five years ago the dividend was 20p.

Estimate the annual growth rate in dividends.

Solution

$$20p \times (1 + g)^5 \quad = \quad 32p$$

or $(1 + g)^5 \qquad = \quad \dfrac{32}{20}$

$$= \quad 1.60$$

$\therefore\ 1 + g = 1.6^{1/5} \approx 1.1$, so g = 0.1 or 10%.

Earnings may be used instead of (or as well as) dividends to estimate growth from historic trends.

Conclusion   The future average growth rate, g, can be estimated from past dividends using the following formula.

$$1 + g = \left(\frac{d_n}{d_0}\right)^{\frac{1}{n}}$$, where d_n is the most recent dividend and d_0 is the dividend paid n years ago.

5.2   Activity

A company is just about to pay a dividend of 40p. Four years ago its dividend was 28p. What was the average annual growth rate over the four years?

5.3   Activity solution

Step 1   The most recent dividend , d_4, is 40p.

Step 2   The historic dividend, d_0, is 28p.

Step 3   Applying the formula:

$$1 + g = \left(\frac{40}{28}\right)^{\frac{1}{4}} \approx (1.43)^{\frac{1}{4}} \approx 1.09$$

$$\therefore g = 0.09 \text{ or } 9\%$$

5.4   Alternative growth model (Gordon growth model or earnings retention model)

A growth rate for equity-financed companies may be estimated as rb, where r is the current accounting rate of return and b is the proportion of profits retained for reinvestment.

The model is based on the premise that the higher the company's level of retentions, the greater is the potential growth rate. Although students will appreciate that this reliance on accounting profits is dubious, the model is not totally unreasonable. It follows from looking at the rate of growth of retained profits (for a wholly equity financed company). If all measures are constant, then it may be shown that 'g' the rate of growth of dividends is equal to the rate of growth of profits is equal to the rate of growth of share prices and so on.

Example

Consider the following summarised financial statement for XYZ plc

Balance sheet as at 31 December 19X1

	£		£
Assets	200	Ordinary shares	100
		Reserves	100
	200		200

Profits after tax for the year ended 31 December 19X2	£20
Dividend (a 40% payout)	£8

Balance sheet as at 31 December 19X2

	£		£
Assets	212	Ordinary shares	100
		Reserves 100 + (20 – 8)	112
	212		212

If the company's accounting rate of return and earnings retention rate remain the same what will be the growth in dividends in the next year?

Solution

Profit after tax as a % of capital employed will be $\dfrac{20}{200}$ = 10%.

10% × asset value at 31 December 19X2 = 10% × £212 = £21.20.

Dividends will therefore be 40% × £21.20 = £8.48.

This represents a growth of 6% on the year.

Normally this is more directly calculated by the following equation:

$$g \ = \ \text{r (accounting rate of return)} \times \text{b (the earnings retention rate)}$$
$$= \ 10\% \times 60\%$$
$$= \ 6\%.$$

Note: that the accounting rate of return is calculated with reference to opening balance sheet values.

Conclusion   Using the Gordon growth model, the annual growth in dividends, g, is estimated as g = rb, where r is the accounting rate of return and b is the proportion of funds retained by the company each year.

As stated above, the major problem with this model is its reliance on accounting profits and the assumption that r and b will be constant. Inflation can substantially distort the accounting rate of return if assets are valued on an historic cost basis.

6   SELF TEST QUESTIONS

6.1   What is an offer for sale by prospectus? (1.3)

6.2   Give three reasons for making a bonus issue. (1.10)

6.3   What are the three main functions of merchant banks in new share issues? (1.20)

6.4   Describe the main features of the Enterprise Investment Scheme. (2.2)

6.5   What is a cum-div share price? (4.7)

6.6   Describe the Gordon growth model. (5.4)

7   EXAMINATION TYPE QUESTION

7.1   Trendy and Jumbo

You are given the following information about two companies, which are both financed entirely by equity capital.

	Trendy Ltd	Jumbo Ltd
Number of ordinary shares of £1 ('000)	150,000	500,000
Market value per share, ex-div (£)	3.42	0.65
Current earnings (Total) (£'000)	62,858	63,952
Current dividend (Total) (£'000)	6,158	48,130
Balance sheet value of capital employed (£'000)	315,000	293,000
Dividend five years ago (Total) (£'000)	2,473	37,600

Both companies are in the same line of business and sell similar products.

(a)   Estimate the shareholders' required rate of return for both companies, using growth models.

(5 marks)

(b)   Describe, giving your reasons, any additional evidence to which you would refer in order to increase your confidence in the estimates of the rate of return required in practice.

(5 marks)

(Total: 10 marks)

8   ANSWER TO EXAMINATION TYPE QUESTION

8.1   Trendy and Jumbo

(Tutorial note: dividend growth is an important variable in this question. In general terms try to use both the approaches we have developed if the data is available.*)*

(a)   The shareholders' required rate of return can be estimated using the dividend valuation model involving predicted growth in dividends.

$$V = \frac{d(1+g)}{i-g}$$

where V =   market value per share at present, ex-dividend
         d =   dividend per share just paid
         g =   predicted constant growth rate in dividends
         i =   shareholders' required rate of return.

Rearranging

$$i = \frac{d(1+g)}{V} + g$$

The first step involves estimating the shareholders' prediction of the future growth rate. This might be taken from the past rate of growth, or by using accounting information and the Gordon growth model.

Estimates of g

(i)   **Past growth rate**

	Trendy Ltd	*Jumbo Ltd*
$\dfrac{\text{Current dividend}}{\text{Dividend five years ago}}$	$\dfrac{6,158}{2,473} = 2.49$	$\dfrac{48,130}{37,600} = 1.28$
Growth rate $(1 + g)^5$ from compounding tables	20%	5%

(ii)   **Gordon growth model**

$g = rb$

where   r = average rate of return on funds reinvested
            b = proportion of profits reinvested.

According to Gordon, r might be estimated by shareholders as the return on capital employed from the published accounts.

	Trendy Ltd	*Jumbo Ltd*
$r = \dfrac{\text{Current earnings}}{\text{Capital employed}}$	$\dfrac{62,858}{315,000} = 0.1995$	$\dfrac{63,952}{293,000} = 0.2183$
$b = \dfrac{\text{Current earnings less current dividend}}{\text{Current earnings}}$	$\dfrac{62,858 - 6,158}{62,858}$	$\dfrac{63,952 - 48,130}{63,952}$
	$= 0.902$	$= 0.2474$
$g = rb$	0.18 or **18%**	0.054 or **5.4%**

Rates of return

	Trendy Ltd	*Jumbo Ltd*
$i = \dfrac{d(1+g)}{V} + g$		
g from past growth rate	$\dfrac{6,158 \times 1.2}{150,000 \times 3.42} + 0.2$	$\dfrac{48,130 \times 1.05}{500,000 \times 0.65} + 0.05$
	$= 21.44\%$	$= 20.55\%$
g from Gordon model	$\dfrac{6,158 \times 1.18}{150,000 \times 3.42} + 0.18$	$\dfrac{48,130 \times 1.054}{500,000 \times 0.65} + 0.054$
	$= 19.42\%$	$= 21.01\%$

Despite the difference in dividend policies and growth rates between the two companies it can be seen that their rate of return to shareholders is roughly equal. If the companies are in the same type of business and have the same level of risk, these results are in line with the prediction of the dividend valuation model.

(b)   **Additional evidence which might increase confidence in the estimates**

(i)   The structure of interest rates at present - in order to see whether the figures are of a reasonable order of magnitude. The return to shareholders should be equal to the 'risk-free' rate of interest (estimated from short-dated government stocks) plus a 'risk premium' which depends on the risk of the company.

(ii)   Movements of market value of the shares over the last five years. It is assumed that the current market value is an equilibrium value which has resulted from steady growth over the period. If market values are abnormally high or low at the moment (eg, because a takeover bid is expected) the calculations will be invalid.

(iii)   Dividends for each of the last five years for more confidence in the past growth rate. Similar figures for earnings and market value should give roughly the same growth rate.

(iv)   Details of any published plans for the companies which might alter shareholders' expectations.

25 LONG-TERM FINANCE: DEBT AND HYBRIDS

INTRODUCTION & LEARNING OBJECTIVES

This chapter revises the features of the different sources of debt finance which have already been identified earlier in this text. The analysis here goes further, looking at warrants and deep discount bonds in addition to the more common instruments such as preference shares and straight debentures. The implications of convertibles and option rights on a company's earnings per share are also considered.

When you have studied this chapter you should be able to do the following:

- Identify the defining characteristics of each possible source of long-term debt finance available to a company.

- Appreciate the advantages of debt over equity.

- Calculate earnings per share figures, particularly for a company with convertibles or options in issue.

---

1 SOURCES OF LONG-TERM FINANCE

1.1 Introduction

We repeat below the chart showing the connections between the different sources of finance.

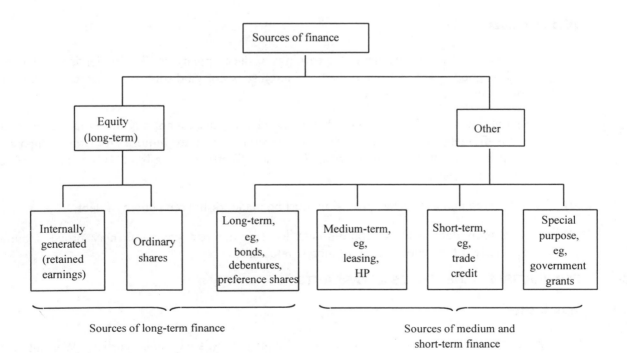

The defining characteristics of each of the sources of long-term finance were discussed earlier in this text. The previous chapter looked at equity finance in greater depth; this chapter turns to other forms of long term finance.

2 LONG TERM CORPORATE BONDS AND DEBENTURES

2.1 Introduction

Long term debt is frequently used by companies as a way of raising long term finance for their operations. It is an alternative to equity finance. Bonds (or debentures) may be secured on the assets of the business; if the company defaults on the payment of interest then the bond holders can, with the consent of the court, appoint a receiver to administer the assets until the interest is paid.

2.2 Characteristics of long term debt

From the viewpoint of the investor:

(a)   Debt is viewed as low risk

      (i)   it has a definite maturity and the holder has priority in interest payments and on liquidation

      (ii)   income is fixed, so the holder receives the same interest whatever the earnings of the company.

(b)   Debt holders do not usually have voting rights. Only if interest is not paid will holders take control of the company.

From the viewpoint of the company:

Advantages

(a)   Debt is cheap. Because it is less risky than equity for an investor, debt holders will accept a lower rate of return than shareholders. Also, debt interest is an allowable expense for tax.

(b)   Cost is limited to the stipulated interest payment.

(c)   There is no dilution of control when debt is issued.

Disadvantages

(a)   Interest must be paid whatever the earnings of the company, unlike dividends which can be paid in good years and not in bad. If interest is not paid, the trustees for the debenture holders can call in the receiver.

(b)   Shareholders may be concerned that a geared company cannot pay all its interest and still pay a dividend and will raise the rate of return that they require from the company to compensate for this increase in risk. This may effectively put a limit on the amount of debt that can be raised.

(c)   With fixed maturity dates, provision must be made for the repayment of debt.

(d)   Long term debt with its commitment to fixed interest payments may prove a burden especially if the general level of interest rates falls.

3 CONVERTIBLE DEBENTURES & WARRANTS

3.1 Introduction

Convertible debentures are a hybrid of debt and equity as was explained earlier. Warrants have many similarities to convertibles and will also be considered.

3.2   Definitions

Warrant - an option to buy shares in a company at a stated price, usually within a stated period.

Convertible debenture - a debenture which at the option of the holder may be converted into shares in a company, under specific conditions.

Thus, whereas a warrant is merely an option, a convertible debenture combines an option with a debenture ie, a warrant is not linked to an underlying security.

Warrants are commonly issued as 'sweeteners' with an issue of loan stock.

Note that in both cases there is no compulsion on the holders to exercise their rights. However, if they choose to do so the firm must oblige.

Example

(1)   Raybeck plc issues 8% unsecured loan stock 19X1/X5 as part of the consideration for the acquisition of companies. With the loan stock are subscription rights (warrants) on the basis that holders of £100 loan stock could subscribe for up to 30 ordinary shares in Raybeck at a price of £8.75 per share. The option could be exercised any time between 19X2 and 19X5.

(2)   Associated Engineering plc issues 7% convertible loan stock 19X8/X9. The conversion option is 80 ordinary shares for each £100 loan stock, and is exercisable between 19X1 and 19X5. If the option is not exercised, the debentures are redeemable at par between 19X8 and 19X9.

Comment

Note the difference between these two issues. In the Raybeck case, the option is separate from the loan stock, which continues to exist whether or not the option is exercised. Also, the exercise of the option costs money. On the other hand, conversion of Associated Engineering loan stock is an actual replacement of the loan stock by shares, with no cash effect.

It should be noted that there are a number of variations on the theme of conversion rights, including, for example, convertible preference shares. There is no need for you to memorise all the possibilities.

3.3   Attractions of convertibles as a source of finance

Convertibles offer a number of advantages to the company as follows.

Advantage	*Comment*
Immediate finance at low cost	Because of the conversion option, the loans can be raised at below normal interest rates.
Attractive, if share prices are depressed	Where companies wish to raise equity finance, but share prices are currently depressed, convertibles offer a 'back-door' share issue method.
Self-liquidating	Where loans are converted into shares, the problem of repayment disappears.
Exercise of warrants related to need for finance	Options would normally only be exercised where the share price has increased. If the options involve the payment of extra cash to the company, this creates extra funds when they are needed for expansion.

3.4   The decision to exercise

Investors will exercise their rights to convert if it is profitable to do so.

If firstly we examine the warrants issued by Raybeck plc we can see that they would be worth exercising if the share price of Raybeck were above £8.75. For example if the share price rose to £10 then the value of the warrant would be:

Current market price − Exercise price = £10 − £8.75 = £1.25

If share prices fell below £8.75 the warrant would be worthless. The above calculation is referred to as the formula value of the warrant.

Conclusion   The formula value of a warrant = current market price of share less exercise price of warrant (where current market price exceeds exercise price); or zero otherwise.

If we now consider the convertible we can see that the conversion option is worth exercising if the share price rises above:

$$\frac{\text{Value of £100 loan stock}}{80 \text{ shares}}$$

Above this price, shareholders would receive equity of greater value than the £100 loan stock. Unlike a warrant, however, below this share price the value of the convertible does not fall to zero, but would settle at the market value of the security as a straight debenture.

Example

Rexel plc has in issue a convertible debenture with a coupon rate of 12%. Each £100 unit may be converted into 20 ordinary shares at any time until the date of expiry and any remaining debentures will be redeemed at £100. The debenture has five years left to run. Investors would normally require a rate of return of 8% per annum on a five year debt security.

Should investors convert if the current share price is:

(a)   £4.00;
(b)   £5.00;
(c)   £6.00?

Solution

Value as debt

If the security is not converted it will have the following value to the investor:

	PVF @ 8%	PV £
Interest £12/year for 5 years	3.993	47.916
Redemption £100 in 5 years	0.681	68.100
		116.016

Note the present value is calculated at 8% - the required rate of return on a straight debt security.

Value as equity

Market price £	Value as equity
4.00	£80 (ie, 20 × £4)
5.00	£100
6.00	£120

If the market price of equity rises to £6.00 the security should be converted, otherwise it is worth more as debt. The 'break-even' conversion price is £5.80 per share (£116/20 shares).

The value of a convertible is the higher of its value as debt and its converted value. This is also known as its formula value.

Conclusion   The formula value of a convertible is the higher of its value as debt and its converted value.

3.5   Activity

A company has a 7% redeemable debenture in issue, quoted at £140. It is redeemable in six years' time at £140. It also has a 10% convertible debenture, which has six years to run. The terms of conversion are 30 shares per £100 debenture. If the debenture is not converted, it will be redeemed at £106. At what current share price would a debenture holder be indifferent between converting the debenture now, or holding on to it?

3.6   Activity solution

Step 1   Calculate debenture holders' required rate of return, using the figures relating to the 7% debenture.

Since the market price equals the redemption price, the irredeemable debenture formula can be used.

$$\text{Required return} = \frac{7\% \times £100}{£140} = 5\%$$

Step 2   Calculate the value of the convertible debenture if it is not converted.

The value equals the future flows discounted at 5%:

$$(\pounds 10 \times a \,\overline{6} \mid 5\% \;) + \frac{\pounds 106}{1.05^6} \;=\; (\pounds 10 \times 5.076) + (\pounds 106 \times 0.746)$$

$$=\; \pounds 129.84$$

Step 3   Calculate the equivalent current share price

Each debenture could be converted into 30 shares. For the investor to be indifferent, the shares must be worth $\dfrac{\pounds 129.84}{30} = \pounds 4.33$ each.

3.7   Formula values and market values

In practice convertibles often trade at considerably above their formula value. This excess is known as the **conversion premium**.

Definition   The conversion premium of a convertible debenture is the difference between the debenture's formula value and its market value.

4   OTHER TYPES OF DEBT

4.1   Deep discounted bonds and zero coupon bonds

Definition   Deep discounted bonds are those where the coupon rate being offered is below the market rate at the time of issue. There might even be no annual interest payment, these being referred to as zero coupon bonds.

The attractions of these bonds to the company are as follows.

(a)   The initial financing cash outflows are small.

(b)   The discount element of the bond is amortised and allowed annually against corporation tax.

From the investors' viewpoint, there are two other advantages.

(a)   There is little chance of the bond being called early, as this would prove very expensive to the firm.

(b)   Although the Revenue amortise the discount element for tax purposes, the tax on this element of return to the investor is not normally payable until redemption.

5   CALCULATION OF EARNINGS PER SHARE

5.1   Introduction

Earnings per share (EPS) is a widely used measure of a company's performance, particularly over a number of years, and is a component of the very important Stock Exchange yardstick – the price earnings (PE) ratio. A key objective in the financial management of a quoted company is to record an increase in EPS over successive accounting periods.

The importance of EPS was reinforced by the early issue of an accounting standard *SSAP 3*.

The objective of *SSAP 3* is to ensure that earnings per share is prominently disclosed in the published accounts, and that the basis on which it is computed is comparable, within one company over a period of time, and between companies. The computation of EPS was amended in 1992 on the publication of *FRS 3* **Reporting financial performance**.

Computation

$$\text{Earnings per share (in pence)} = \frac{\text{Net profit for the year after tax, minority interests, extraordinary items and preference dividends}}{\text{Number of equity shares in issue and ranking for dividend}}$$

5.2   Activity

M plc has the following summarised profit and loss account for 19X2.

	£'000
Profits before tax	6,000
Less: Tax	(1,300)
Profits after tax	4,700
Less: Minority interests	(700)
Profit for the financial year	4,000
Less: Dividends	(270)
Retained profit	3,730

An extract from the balance sheet as at 31 December 19X2 showed that issued share capital had been constant throughout the year as follows.

	£'000
£1 7% preference shares, fully paid	1,000
£1 ordinary shares, 75p paid	9,000
	10,000

Calculate the earnings per share for the year.

5.3   Activity solution

Earnings = Profit after tax, minorities, extraordinaries and preference dividends

= $4,000 - (7\% \times 1,000)$

= 3,930 thousand pounds.

$$\text{Number of issued equity shares} = \frac{\text{£9 million}}{75p} = 12 \text{ million}.$$

$$\text{Therefore the earnings per share} \quad = \quad \frac{\text{£3.93m}}{12\text{m shares}}$$

= 32.75p.

5.4   Fully diluted EPS

SSAP 3 requires full disclosure of fully diluted EPS in addition to EPS where the fully diluted EPS is more than 5% away from the EPS. In the financial management of a company, use is often made of **potential** share issues at a future date.

Examples are as follows.

(a)   Convertible loan stock.
(b)   Convertible preference shares.
(c)   Options and warrants.

The principles of convertible loan stock and convertible preference shares are similar and will be dealt with together.

5.5   Convertibles

Example

On 1 April 19X7, the company issued by way of rights or otherwise £1,250,000 8% convertible unsecured loan stock for cash at par. Each £100 nominal of the stock will be convertible in 20X3/X6 into the number of ordinary shares set out below.

On 31 December 20X3	124 shares
On 31 December 20X4	120 shares
On 31 December 20X5	115 shares
On 31 December 20X6	110 shares

Relevant information

Issued share capital:

£500,000 in 10% cumulative preference shares of £1;

£1,000,000 in ordinary shares of 25p = 4,000,000 shares.

Corporation tax is 45%.

Trading results for the year ended 31 December

	19X8 £	19X7 £
Profit before interest and tax	1,100,000	991,818
Interest on 8% convertible unsecured loan stock	100,000	75,000
Profit before tax	1,000,000	916,818
Corporation tax	450,000	412,568
Profit after tax	550,000	504,250

Calculation of earnings per share

		19X8 £	19X7 £
(1)	Basic earnings per share		
	Profit after tax	550,000	504,250
	Less: Preference dividend	50,000	50,000
	Earnings	500,000	454,250
	Earnings per share based on 4,000,000 shares	12.5p	11.4p

(2) Fully diluted earnings per share

	£	£	£	£
Earnings as above		500,000		454,250
Add: Interest on the convertible unsecured loan stock	100,000		75,000	
Less: Corporation tax	45,000		33,750	
		55,000		41,250
Adjusted earnings		555,000		495,500
Earnings per share based on 5,550,000 shares (19X7 – 5,162,500)		10p		9.6p

Notes:

(A)   Up to 20X2 the **maximum** number of shares issuable after the end of the financial year will be at the rate of 124 shares per £100, viz: 1,550,000 shares, making a total of 5,550,000.

(B)   The weighted average number of shares issued and issuable for 19X7 would have been one-quarter of 4,000,000 plus three-quarters of 5,550,000 ie, 5,162,500.

5.6   Options and warrants to subscribe

The problem here is similar to the above. For the dilution calculation, *SSAP 3* requires the earnings figure to be increased by the amount of interest which would have been earned by investing the subscription monies required on exercise of the option in a particular government stock, 2½% consolidated stock.

Example

On 1 April 19X7, in connection with a licensing scheme, the company executed an option agreement under which the licensers, at their option exercisable on or before 31 December 20X2, could call on the company to issue to them 1,000,000 ordinary shares of 25p (or 20% of the equity after such issue) on payment of the subscription monies of £1,000,000.

Relevant information

Issued share capital:

£500,000 in 10% cumulative preference shares of £1;

£1,000,000 in ordinary shares of 25p = 4,000,000 shares.

	19X8 £	19X7 £
Profit after tax for the year ending 31 December	550,000	450,000

Assumption:

The published yield on 2½% consols on 1 January 19X8 was 9.09% gross, equivalent to 5% net of corporation tax, and 10.20% gross (5.6% net) on 1 April 19X7.

Calculation of earnings per share

		19X8 £	19X7 £
(1)	Basic earnings per share		
	Profit after tax	550,000	450,000
	Less: Preference dividend	50,000	50,000
	Earnings	500,000	400,000
	Earnings per share based on 4,000,000 shares	12.5p	10p

		19X8 £	19X7 £
(2)	Fully diluted earnings per share		
	Earnings as above	500,000	400,000
	Assumed yield subscription monies:		
	$5.6\% \times \frac{9}{12} \times £1,000,000$		42,000
	5% on £1,000,000	50,000	
	Adjusted earnings	550,000	442,000
	Earnings per share based on 5,000,000 shares (19X7 – 4,750,000)	11p	9.3p

---

5.7   Activity

G plc had earnings for 19X2 of £300,000 and 2m ordinary shares in issue. Options were created on 1 April 19X2 for 150,000 shares to be issued @ £1.50 per share in future years. You are told that corporation tax is at 30% and that 2½% Consols are quoted at 25.

What is the basic and fully diluted earnings per share for 19X2?

5.8   Activity solution

Basic eps $= \dfrac{£300,000}{2m} = 15p$

Full diluted eps $= \dfrac{300,000 + (150,000 \times 1.50 \times \frac{9}{12} \times 70\% \times \frac{2.5}{25})}{(\frac{3}{12} \times 2m) + (\frac{9}{12} \times 2.15m)}$

$= \dfrac{311,812.5}{2,112,500}$

$= 14.76p.$

6   SELF TEST QUESTIONS

6.1   What is a convertible debenture? (3.2)

6.2   What is the formula value of a warrant? (3.4)

6.3   What is a deep discounted bond? (4.1)

6.4   Define the earnings of a company. (5.1)

6.5   How is EPS calculated for a year in which options have been granted? (5.6)

7   EXAMINATION TYPE QUESTION

7.1   Lavipilon plc

The managing director of Lavipilon plc wishes to provide an extra return to the company's shareholders and has suggested these three possibilities.

(1)   A 2 for 5 bonus issue (capitalisation issue) in addition to the normal dividend.
(2)   A 1 for 5 scrip dividend instead of the normal cash dividend.
(3)   A 1 for 1 share (stock) split in addition to the normal dividend.

Summarised balance sheet of Lavipilon plc (as at the end of last year)

	£m
Fixed assets	65
Current assets	130
Less current liabilities	(55)
	140

	£m
Ordinary shares (50 pence par value)	25
Share premium account	50
Revenue reserves	40
Shareholders' funds	115
11% debenture	25
	140

The company's shares are trading at 300 pence cum div and the company has £50,000,000 of profit from this year's activities available to ordinary shareholders of which £30,000,000 will be paid as a dividend if option (1) or option (3) is chosen. None of the £40,000,000 revenue reserves would be distributed. This year's financial accounts have not yet been finalised.

(a)   **You are required** to discuss reasons why a company might wish to make a scrip dividend;

(8 marks)

(b)   **You are required** to summarise the advantages to a company of issuing convertible loan stock rather than ordinary shares or debenture stock.   **(10 marks)**

(c)   **You are required** to state the circumstances under which there could be advantages to lenders and to borrowers respectively from issues of

(i)   debentures with a floating rate of interest;
(ii)   zero-coupon bonds.

Ignore taxation.   **(8 marks)**
(Total: 26 marks)

8   ANSWER TO EXAMINATION TYPE QUESTION

8.1   Lavipilon plc

(a)   Scrip dividend

The reasons for making a scrip dividend include the following:

(i)   A scrip dividend is a means of paying a return to shareholders without any cash transfer being made. Effectively, it converts retained profits into issued share capital. It therefore represents a means of transferring profits to the shareholders without actually making a cash dividend payment. Thus the company's liquidity position is preserved.

A scrip dividend is therefore beneficial for companies which wish to use all their internally generated funds for future investment.

(ii)   A scrip dividend may indicate to the market that the company has identified worthwhile profitable investments for which it requires substantial funds. As a result the share price might rise.

(b)   The advantages to a company of issuing convertible loan stock may be summarised as follows.

Advantages over ordinary shares

(i)   Convertible loan stock is much cheaper than equity finance. This is due to the security associated with its status as debt, making it very low risk, together with the attractiveness of the option to convert to equity if conditions are favourable.

(ii)   It shares initially all the other advantages of debt finance such as the interest being corporation tax deductible and the issue costs being less than those for an issue of new equity.

(iii)   Until conversion takes place, the existing shareholders' control of the company will be unaffected.

Advantages over debenture stock

(i)   Convertibles are cheaper than ordinary debentures since they have all the advantages of debt but in addition the attraction of conversion to equity. They therefore bear only upside risk until after conversion has taken place.

(ii)   Because its term as debt is likely to be only short-term its conditions of issue will be less restrictive.

(iii)   Provided conditions are favourable and conversion takes place, convertible debt is self-liquidating. In other words redemption effectively takes place with no cash flow implications for the company.

(c)   (i)   Debentures with a floating rate of interest

Such debentures are likely to be advantageous to both borrowers and lenders in circumstances where the market interest rates are volatile. The coupon rate of the debenture may be adjusted to reflect the current market rate of interest. Therefore, if interest rates fall the borrower's costs also fall due to a decreasing of the coupon rate and the borrower avoids being committed to a high fixed rate of interest. On the other hand, if interest rates rise this will be reflected in an increase in the coupon rate and higher interest payments to lenders.

Due to the matching of the coupon rate to the market rate of interest, the market price of the debentures will be much more stable. This may be attractive to lenders and therefore such debentures will be a means for borrowers of readily obtaining required funds.

(ii)   Zero-coupon bonds

As with the floating rate debentures, zero-coupon bonds are attractive in times of volatile interest rates. No interest is payable on the bonds, but the interest is effectively accrued and accounted for in the redemption value of the bond, or reflected in its current market value. Therefore the lender may sell the bond at any time during its life and recover an amount of interest which reflects the current market rates applicable during the period of ownership. The lender has therefore not been locked in to a low fixed rate of interest, but has been able to participate in higher rates, if there had been an interest rate rise since the issue of the bonds. Similarly the cost to the borrower will reflect the interest rates prevailing during the period of issue, as such interest rates will be incorporated in the final redemption value.

The cash flow effect of zero-coupon bonds represents another advantage to the borrower.

Short-term cashflows are preserved since no interest payments are made during the life of the bond.

26 LONG-TERM FINANCE: THE CAPITAL STRUCTURE DECISION

INTRODUCTION & LEARNING OBJECTIVES

A company's capital structure decision is concerned with its optimal gearing ratio. Financial gearing is a company's mix of equity and fixed return capital; the more debt is issued, the higher the interest payments that must be paid before any remaining earnings can be paid out to equity shareholders in the form of dividends. Operating gearing is a company's mix of variable costs and fixed costs; if a company has mostly fixed costs then any increase in turnover will feed substantially directly through to profits.

When you have studied this chapter you should be able to do the following:

- Calculate and discuss different gearing ratios.
- Discuss the links between financial gearing, operating gearing and combined gearing.

1 CALCULATION OF GEARING RATIOS

1.1 Illustration

This chapter requires a detailed analysis of a company's gearing. The basic idea of calculating gearing ratios from a set of accounts was explained earlier in this text and is included here again for revision purposes. This is the technique of investigating a company's **financial gearing.** Consider the set of accounts shown below:

Summarised balance sheet at 30 June

	19X7		19X6	
	£'000	£'000	£'000	£'000
Fixed assets (net book value)		130		139
Current assets:				
Stock	42		37	
Debtors	29		23	
Bank	3		5	
	74		65	
Creditors: amounts falling due within one year:				
Trade creditors	36		55	
Taxation	10		10	
	46		65	

Net current assets	28	-
Total assets less current liabilities	158	139
Creditors: amounts falling due beyond one year:		
5% secured loan stock	40	40
	118	99
Ordinary share capital (50p shares)	35	35
8% Preference shares (£1 shares)	25	25
Share premium account	17	17
Revaluation reserve	10	-
Profit and loss account	31	22
	118	99

Summarised profit and loss account for the year ended 30 June

	19X7		19X6	
	£'000	£'000	£'000	£'000
Sales		209		196
Opening stock	37		29	
Purchases	162		159	
	199		188	
Closing stock	42		37	
		157		151
Gross profit		52		45
Interest	2		2	
Depreciation	9		9	
Sundry expenses	14		11	
		25		22
Net profit		27		23
Taxation		10		10
Net profit after taxation		17		13
Dividends:				
Ordinary shares	6		5	
Preference shares	2		2	
		8		7
Retained profit		9		6

1.2   Capital gearing

Gearing is one of the most widely-used terms in accounting. Unfortunately it can be defined and calculated in several different ways. Capital gearing is calculated from a company's financing structure as shown in its balance sheet; it is essential to state the particular definition used.

Gearing is relevant to the long term financial stability of a business. Two possible definitions of capital gearing will be considered, both based on book values of assets. Both of these consider the relationship between:

(a)   ordinary shareholders' funds (or equity interest);

(b)   fixed return capital – comprising loans and preference share capital.

1.3   Equity gearing

$$\frac{\text{Preference share capital plus loans}}{\text{Ordinary share capital and reserves}}$$

19X7

$$\frac{25+40}{118-25} \times 100 = 69.9\%$$

19X6

$$\frac{25+40}{99-25} \times 100 = 87.8\%$$

1.4   Total gearing

$$\frac{\text{Preference share capital plus loans}}{\text{Total long term capital}}$$

19X7

$$\frac{65}{158} \times 100 = 41.1\%$$

19X6

$$\frac{65}{139} \times 100 = 46.8\%$$

There is no real difference between the two types of calculation as the components of the numerator remain the same. Some prefer to use the equity gearing as it shows a more pronounced change if either fixed return capital or equity capital changes. Most use the second calculation as it is perhaps clearer to note the relationship of fixed interest finance to **total** finance.

There is no immediate cut-off between a low-geared company and a highly-geared company. Gearing is a matter of degree.

Gearing may have an important effect on the distribution of profits. For example, consider two companies with the same profit record but different capital structures. The return of the ordinary shareholders can vary considerably.

	A Ltd £	B Ltd £
Capital structure:		
10% Loan stock	20,000	-
Ordinary share capital and reserves	10,000	30,000
	30,000	30,000

	Highly geared £	No gearing £
Year 1 – Profits £4,000 before interest		
∴ Returns:		
10% Interest	2,000	-
Ordinary shares – balance	2,000	4,000
	4,000	4,000

Year 2 – Profits double to £8,000 before interest
∴ Returns:

10% Interest	2,000	-
Ordinary shares – balance	6,000	8,000
	8,000	8,000

Therefore, increase in return to ordinary shareholders	3 times	2 times

Thus, the doubling of the profits in year 2 has the effect of tripling the return to the equity shareholders in the highly-geared company. The effect would be even more dramatic if the profits fell below £2,000 because then there would be no return at all to the ordinary shareholders in A Ltd. Thus an investment in ordinary shares in a highly-geared company is a far more speculative investment than a purchase of ordinary shares in a low-geared company.

2   OPERATING GEARING

2.1   Introduction

Definition   Operating gearing is the relationship between fixed and variable costs.

Firms with high financial gearing are risky as fixed interest payments must be made no matter the level of earnings.

Operating gearing (also called operational gearing) measures the cost structure (fixed and variable) of the firm. Firms with high levels of fixed costs are usually described as having high operating gearing.

Operating gearing can be measured as the percentage change in earnings before interest and tax for a percentage change in sales; or as the ratio of fixed to variable costs.

2.2   Example

Consider two firms.

	Firm A £m	Firm B £m
Sales	5	5
Variable costs	3	1
Fixed costs	1	3
EBIT (Earnings before interest and tax)	1	1

What would be the impact of a 10% increase in sales volume on the EBIT of each firm?

Firm A New EBIT = (5m − 3m) × 1.1 − 1 = £1.2m   ie, a 20% increase.
Firm B New EBIT = (5m − 1m) × 1.1 − 3 = £1.4m   ie, a 40% increase.

Operating gearing

	Firm A	Firm B
$\dfrac{\% \text{ change in EBIT}}{\% \text{ change in sales}}$	$\dfrac{20\%}{10\%} = 2$	$\dfrac{40\%}{10\%} = 4$

Alternatively

	Firm A	Firm B
$\dfrac{\text{Fixed costs}}{\text{Variable costs}}$	$\dfrac{1}{3} = 0.33$	$\dfrac{3}{1} = 3$

B carries a higher operating gearing because it has higher fixed costs. Its operating earnings are more volume sensitive.

2.3   Relationship between financial and operating gearing

[Definition]   Financial gearing (known in the US as leverage) is the proportionate relationship between borrowings and total capital.

(a)   **Operating gearing** may be defined as the percentage change in EBIT for a percentage change in sales (the former divided by the latter).

(b)   **Financial gearing** can be measured by the percentage change in earnings available to equity for a percentage change in EBIT (the former divided by the latter).

(c)   **Combined gearing** is the percentage change in earnings available to equity for a percentage change in sales.

These definitions will be used to explore the relationship between financial and operating gearing in the next activity.

2.4   Activity

Plato plc has the following profit and loss account.

	£'000
Sales	10,000
Costs:	
Fixed	(2,000)
Variable	(4,000)
EBIT	4,000

Suppose that £9m of 10% debentures are issued at par. Corporation tax is payable at 40%.

Calculate the three gearing ratios just described, now that the debentures have been issued.

In each case use a 10% increase in sales.

2.5   Activity solution

	Original £'000	Inc 10% £'000	Difference £'000
Sales	10,000	11,000	1,000
Costs:			
Fixed	(2,000)	(2,000)	-
Variable	(4,000)	(4,400)	(400)
EBIT	4,000	4,600	600
Interest	(900)	(900)	-
Profit before tax	3,100	3,700	600
Corporation tax @ 40%	(1,240)	(1,480)	(240)
Earnings available to equity	1,860	2,220	360

Calculation of ratios

$$\text{Operating gearing} = \frac{600 \div 4,000}{1,000 \div 10,000} = \frac{0.15}{0.10} = 1.5 \text{ or } 150\%$$

$$\text{Financial gearing} = \frac{360 \div 1,860}{600 \div 4,000} \approx \frac{0.19}{0.15} = 1.27 \text{ or } 127\%$$

$$\text{Combined gearing} = \frac{360 \div 1,860}{1,000 \div 10,000} \approx \frac{0.19}{0.10} = 1.9 \text{ or } 190\%$$

Note that the combined gearing = Operating gearing × financial gearing

= 1.5 × 1.27

= 1.9 or 190%

Conclusion   It is apparent that there is a tradeoff between operating and financial gearing. If a firm has a high degree of operating gearing, then unless sales were very stable it would prefer to avoid financial gearing, and vice versa.

3   RISK

3.1   The concept of financial risk

When investing in a business an investor faces two types of risk.

(a)   **Business (or operating) risk**

The variability in earnings before interest and tax associated with the industrial sector in which the firm operates. For example an oil prospecting venture would carry more business risk than a property company.

(b)   **Financial risk**

The additional risk introduced by the use of gearing as shareholders become concerned that the company will be unable to pay interest and still have sufficient left to pay a dividend.

Investors will want a return for both types of risk.

4   SELF TEST QUESTIONS

4.1   How is a company's operating gearing measured? (2.1)

4.2   How is a company's combined gearing measured? (2.3)

4.3   What is business risk? (3.1)

5   EXAMINATION TYPE QUESTION

5.1   Netherby plc

Netherby plc manufactures a range of camping and leisure equipment, including tents. It is currently experiencing severe quality control problems at its existing fully-depreciated factory in the south of England. These difficulties threaten to undermine its reputation for producing high quality products. It has recently been approached by the European Bank for Reconstruction and Development, on behalf of a tent manufacturer in Hungary, which is seeking a UK-based trading partner which will import and distribute its tents. Such a switch would involve shutting down the existing manufacturing operation in the UK and converting it into a distribution depot. The estimated exceptional restructuring costs of £5m would be tax-allowable, but would exert serious strains on cash flow.

Importing, rather than manufacturing tents appears inherently profitable as the buying-in price, when converted into sterling, is less than the present production cost. In addition, Netherby considers that the Hungarian product would result in increased sales, as the existing retail distributors seem impressed with the quality of the samples which they have been shown. It is estimated that for a five-year contract, the annual cash flow benefit would be around £2m pa before tax.

However, the financing of the closure and restructuring costs would involve careful consideration of the financing options. Some directors argue that dividends could be reduced as several competing companies have already done a similar thing, while other directors argue for a rights issue. Alternatively, the project could be financed by an issue of long-term loan stock at a fixed rate of 12%.

The most recent balance sheet shows £5m of issued share capital (par value 50p), while the market price per share is currently £3. A leading security analyst has recently described Netherby's gearing ratio as 'adventurous'. Profit-after-tax in the year just ended was £15m and dividends of £10m were paid.

The rate of corporation tax is 33%, payable with a one-year delay. Netherby's reporting year coincides with the calendar year and the factory will be closed at the year end. Closure costs would be incurred shortly before deliveries of the imported product began, and sufficient stocks will be on hand to overcome any initial supply problems. Netherby considers that it should earn a return on new investment projects of 15% pa net of all taxes.

Required

(a)   Is the closure of the existing factory financially worthwhile for Netherby?   **(5 marks)**

(b)   Explain what is meant when the capital market is said to be information-efficient in a semi-strong form.

        If the stock market is semi-strong efficient and without considering the method of finance, calculate the likely impact of acceptance and announcement of the details of this project to the market on Netherby's share price.   **(6 marks)**

(c) Advise the Netherby board as to the relative merits of a rights issue rather than a cut in dividends to finance this project. **(6 marks)**

(d) Explain why a rights issue generally results in a fall in the market price of shares.

If a rights issue is undertaken, calculate the resulting impact on the existing share price of issue prices of £1 per share and £2 per share, respectively. (You may ignore issue costs.) **(6 marks)**

(e) Assuming the restructuring proposal meets expectations, assess the impact of the project on earnings per share if it is financed by a rights issue at an offer price of £2 per share, and loan stock, respectively.

(Again, you may ignore issue costs.) **(4 marks)**

(f) Briefly consider the main operating risks connected with the investment project, and how Netherby might attempt to allow for these. **(8 marks)**
(Total: 35 marks)

6 ANSWER TO EXAMINATION TYPE QUESTION

6.1 Netherby plc

(a) Assuming that the restructuring cost is a revenue item, and that all costs are incurred in year 0, the estimated cash flow profile is:

Cash flow profile (£m)

Item	0	1	2	3	4	5	6
				Year			
Closure costs	(5)						
Tax saving		1.65					
Cash flow increase		2.00	2.00	2.00	2.00	2.00	
Tax payment			(0.66)	(0.66)	(0.66)	(0.66)	(0.66)
	(5)	3.65	1.34	1.34	1.34	1.34	(0.66)

$$\text{NPV (£m)} = -5 + 1.65(\text{PVIF}_{15,1}) + 2(\text{PVIFA}_{15,5}) - 0.66(\text{PVIFA}_{15,6} - \text{PVIFA}_{15,1})$$

$$= -5 + 1.65(0.870) + 2(3.352) - 0.66(3.784 - 0.870)$$

$$= -5 + 1.44 + 6.70 - 1.92 = +1.22 \text{ (ie, } +\text{£1.22m)}$$

Hence, the restructuring appears worthwhile.

(b) A semi-strong efficient capital market is one where security prices reflect all publicly-available information, including both the record of the past pattern of share price movements and all information released to the market about company earnings prospects. In such a market, security prices will rapidly adjust to the advent of new information relevant to the future income-earning capacity of the enterprise concerned, such as a change in its chief executive, or the signing of a new export order. As a result of the speed of the market's reaction to this type of news, it is not possible to make excess gains by trading in the wake of its release. Only market participants lucky enough already to be holding the share in question will achieve super-normal returns.

In the case of Netherby, when it releases information about its change in market-servicing policy, the value of the company should rise by the value of the project, assuming that the market as a whole agrees with the assessment of its net benefits, and is unconcerned by financing implications.

Net present value of the project = £1.22m

Number of 50p ordinary shares in issue = £5m × 2 = 10m shares

Increase in market price = £1.22m/10m = 12.2p per share.

(Alternatively, the answer could be expressed in terms of Netherby's price-earnings ratio. This would necessitate an assumption about Netherby's sustainable future earnings per share after tax).

(c)   Arguments for and against making a rights issue include the following:

For

(i)   A rights issue enables the company to at least maintain its dividends, thus avoiding both upsetting the clientele of shareholders, and also giving negative signals to the market.

(ii)   It may be easy to accomplish on a bull market.

(iii)   A rights issue automatically lowers the company's gearing ratio.

(iv)   The finance is guaranteed if the issue is fully underwritten.

(v)   It has a neutral impact on voting control, unless the underwriters are obliged to purchase significant blocks of shares, and unless existing shareholders sell their rights to other investors.

(vi)   It might give the impression that the company is expanding vigorously, although this appears not to be the case with Netherby.

Against

(i)   Rights issues normally are made at a discount, which usually involves diluting the historic earnings per share of existing shareholders. However, when the possible uses of the proceeds of the issue are considered, the *prospective* EPS could rise by virtue of investment in a worthwhile project, or in the case of a company earning low or no profits, the interest earnings on un-invested capital alone might serve to raise the EPS.

(ii)   Underwriters' fees and other administrative expenses of the issue may be costly, although the latter may be avoided by applying a sufficiently deep discount.

(iii)   The market is often sceptical about the reason for a rights issue, tending to assume that the company is desperate for cash. The deeper the discount involved, the greater the degree of scepticism.

(iv)   It is difficult to make a rights issue on a bear market, without leaving some of the shares with the underwriters. A rights issue which 'fails' in this respect is both bad for the company's image and may also result in higher underwriters' fees for any subsequent rights issue.

(v)   A rights issue usually forces shareholders to act, either by subscribing direct or by selling the rights, although the company may undertake to reimburse shareholders not subscribing to the issue for the loss in value of their shares. (This is done by selling the rights on behalf of shareholders and paying over the sum realised, net of dealing costs.)

(d)   (***Note:***   candidates are not expected to display a knowledge of SSAP 3 which is the province of Paper 10).

A rights issue normally has to be issued at a discount in order, firstly, to make the shares appear attractive, but more importantly, to safeguard against a fall in the market price below the issue price prior to closure of the offer. If this should happen, the issue would fail as investors wishing to increase their stakes in the company could do so more cheaply by buying on the open market. Because of the discount, a rights issue has the effect of diluting the existing earnings per share across a larger number of shares, although the depressing effect on share price is partly countered by the increased cash holdings of the company.

The two possible issue prices are now evaluated:

(i)   *A price of £1*

It is assumed that to raise £5m, the company must issue £5m/£1 = 5m new shares at the issue price of £1.

In practice, it is possible that the number of new shares required might be lower than this, as the post-tax cost of the project is less than £5m due to the (delayed) tax savings generated. The company might elect to use short-term borrowing to bridge the delay in receiving these tax savings, thus obviating the need for the full £5m.

Ignoring this argument, the terms of the issue would be '1-for-2' ie, for every two shares currently held, owners are offered the right to purchase one new share at the deeply-discounted price of £1.

The ex-rights price will be:

[Market value of 2 shares before the issue + cash consideration]/3

= [(2 × £3) + £1]/3 = £7/3 = £2.33

(ii)   *Similarly, if the issue price is £2*, the required number of new shares = £5m/£2 = 2.5m, and the terms will have to be '1-for-4'

The ex-rights price will be [(4 × £3) + £2]/5 = £14/5 = £2.80.

Clearly, the smaller the discount to the market price, the higher the ex-rights price.

(e)   Ignoring the impact of the benefits of the new project:

The rights issue at £2 involves 2.5m new shares.

The EPS was £15m/10m = £1.50p per share.

Hence, EPS becomes $\dfrac{£15m}{10m + 2.5m} = £1.20$

With the debt financing, the interest charge net of tax = $[12\% \times £5m].[1 - 33\%] = £0.40m$

Hence, EPS becomes $\dfrac{£15m - £0.40m}{10m} = £1.46$

Allowing for the benefits of the new project

The annual profit yielded by the proposal, after tax at 33% = $(£2m \times 0.67) = £1.34m$, although the cash flow benefit in the first year is £2m due to the tax delay.

After the rights issue, the prospective EPS will become:

$$[£15m + £1.34m]/12.5m = £1.31 \text{ per share}$$

With debt finance, the financing cost, net of tax relief, of £0.40m pa reduces the net return from the project to $(£1.34m - £0.40m) = £0.94m$ pa.

(In the first year, the cash flow cost will be the full pre-tax interest payment. Thereafter, Netherby will receive annual cash flow benefits from the series of tax savings.)

The EPS will be: $£15.94m/10m = £1.59$ per share.

Therefore, in terms of the effect on EPS, the debt-financing alternative is preferable, although it may increase financial risk.

(f)   A range of factors could be listed here. Among the major sources of risk are the following:

(i)   *Reliability of supply.* This can be secured by inclusion of penalty clauses in the contract, although these will have to be enforceable. The intermediation of the European Bank for Reconstruction and Development may enhance this.

(ii)   *The quality of the product.* Again, a penalty clause may assist, although a more constructive approach might be to assign a UK-trained total quality management (TQM) expert to the Hungarian operation to oversee quality control.

(iii)   *Market resistance to an imported product.* This seems less of a risk, if retailers are genuinely impressed with the product, and especially as there are doubts over the quality of the existing product.

(iv)   *Exchange rate variations.* Netherby is exposed to the risk of sterling depreciating against the Hungarian currency, thus increasing the sterling cost of the product. There are various ways of hedging against foreign exchange risk, of which use of the forward market is probably the simplest. Alternatively, Netherby could try to match the risk by finding a Hungarian customer for its other goods.

(v)   *Renewal of the contract.* What is likely to happen after five years? To obtain a two-way protection, Netherby might write into the contract an option to renew after five years. If the product requires re-design, Netherby could offer to finance part of the costs in exchange for this option.

27 INVESTMENT DECISIONS

INTRODUCTION & LEARNING OBJECTIVES

This chapter introduces the topic of capital investment appraisal which you should already be familiar with from your earlier studies. It begins by defining investment and stresses that a positive net present value is not all that is sought in investment appraisal; some strategic justification for a project to be accepted must also exist. The simple appraisal methods of payback and ROCE (also called ARR) are then revised. The appendix contains a revision of net present value and internal rate of return calculations.

When you have studied this chapter you should be able to do the following:

- Define investment and relate the concept to the ideas of capital and revenue expenditure.
- Discuss the strategic aspect of investment appraisal.
- Calculate and discuss payback periods of investments.
- Calculate and discuss return on capital employed of investments.
- Calculate net present values and internal rates of return (appendix).

---

1 THE MEANING OF INVESTMENT

1.1 Definition

Investment has been defined as any application of funds which is intended to provide a return by way of interest, dividend or capital appreciation. The idea is that funds are paid out now in the expectation of returns in the future.

Accountants divide up a company's expenditure into capital expenditure and revenue expenditure. Capital expenditure results in the acquisition of a fixed asset and is an investment. Revenue expenditure is charged to the profit and loss account, deriving either from the trade that the company cROCEies on or from maintaining the existing fixed assets.

Some writers also refer to revenue investment, meaning expenditure whose benefit is long-term but which is charged to the profit and loss account as a matter of accounting convention. Examples would be training costs and advertising costs.

1.2 Approaches to financing fixed assets and working capital

Earlier in this text two approaches to the financing of fixed and current assets were examined:

- the traditional approach
- the modern approach

These approaches are explained again here for revision purposes.

1.3   The traditional approach to financing working capital

Traditionally current assets were seen as fluctuating, originally with a seasonal agricultural pattern. Current assets would then be financed out of short-term credit, which could be paid off when not required, whilst fixed assets would be financed by long-term funds (debt or equity).

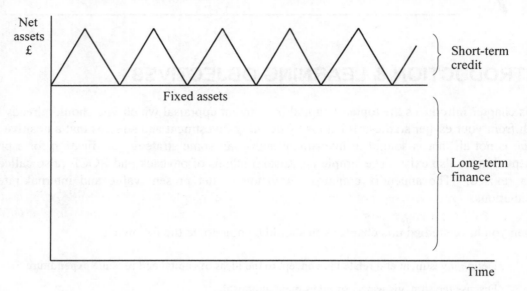

This approach to the analysis is rather simplistic. In most businesses a proportion of the current assets are fixed over time being thus expressed as 'permanent'. For example, certain base levels of stock are always cROCEied, cash balances never fall below a particular level, and a certain level of trade credit is always extended. If growth is added to this situation a more realistic business picture would be as follows:

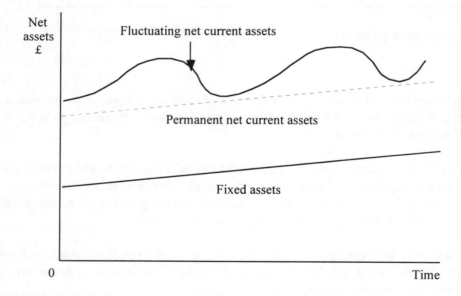

1.4   The modern approach to working capital funding

Given the permanent nature of a large proportion of current assets, it is generally felt prudent to fund a proportion of net current assets with long-term finance. The question is generally one of the extent to which such funding occurs. The possibilities include the following.

Option (1) - some permanent current net assets financed by short-term credit

Option (2) - all permanent and some fluctuating current net assets financed by long-term credit

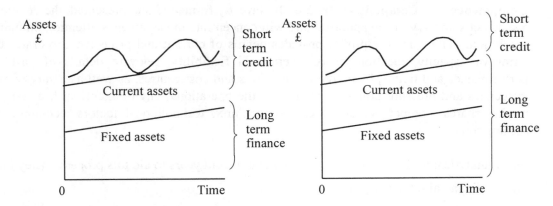

The above options are only two of many. For example, the use of short-term credit could be extended to finance a proportion of fixed assets, or, alternatively, all the firm's activities could be funded by long-term credit.

The choice is a matter for managerial judgement but the tradeoff between the relative cheapness of short-term debt and the risks of short-term debt must be considered.

2 STRATEGIC ANALYSIS

2.1 Introduction

A company will be faced at any one time with a vast choice of possible investment opportunities and must develop a means of deciding which investment proposals to accept and which to reject. There is much more to this decision than simple investment appraisal techniques such as calculations of the net present value (NPV) of investments. The company must have some idea of the long-term strategic direction it wants to go in and must tailor its choice of investments accordingly.

Academic writers such as Ansoff have proposed methods of cROCEying out such strategic analysis. One common way of structuring a corporate appraisal is to cROCEy out a SWOT analysis.

2.2 The concept

To assist in closing the gap between its predicted and desired performance, the organisation's strengths, weaknesses, opportunities and threats need to be ascertained. The work involved draws on the data obtained about objectives, current position, extrapolated position, gaps and environmental forecasts, and is sometimes called **corporate appraisal**.

Definition   'A critical assessment of the strengths and weaknesses, opportunities and threats **(SWOT analysis)** in relation to the internal and environmental factors affecting an entity in order to establish its condition prior to the preparation of the long term plan.

The factors involved in SWOT analysis are wide ranging and include decision variables which strengthen or constrain the operational powers of the company, such as the size of its markets, the competitive forces in the markets, opportunities for new products, availability of skilled labour, control of vital raw materials and access to additional capital.

2.3   Competence and competitive profile

The appraisal process will raise serious questions and may produce surprises. The findings need to be compiled into a presentation format which will take the form of what Ansoff refers to as a **Competence and Competitive Profile**. If correctly formatted and presented, the document will be a succinct summary of the appraisal and will concentrate management's attention on main areas for resolution. The company profile provides details of current and projected corporate resources in terms of capacity, location, costs, operational flexibility, relevant details of past operational performances and trends, by activities, divisions and cost centres, as well as a survey of the major influences and pressure points impacting on the operational environment, such as target markets, market shares, competitive activities, product mix, technological factors, economic trends and assumptions.

Many analytical tools have been developed over recent years to aid this process. They include:

(a)   financial ratio analysis;

(b)   product-market matrix displays;

(c)   product-life cycle analysis.

Here we consider the overall corporate appraisal without delving into all the individual techniques that might aid its process. The following table adapted from Ansoff's **Corporate Strategy** shows how a company's skills, facilities etc, can be analysed both in relation to competitors in its own industry and more widely. Ansoff suggests that in assigning the relative ratings some companies might use a simple two-valued strength or weakness classification. Others would prefer to rank the capabilities as outstanding, average or weak.

	Facilities	Personnel	Organisational skills	Management skills
Finance & general management	Data processing equipment.	Depth of GM and Fin. skills to cope easily.	Divisional structure. Planning & control.	(a) Investment management control. (b) Centralised. Decentralised.
Research & Development	Special equipment test facilities.	Special technical skills.	Product development industrial & consumer products.	Cost-performance optimisation
Operations	Machine shop automated products.	Machine operation. Close tolerance work.	Mass production. Batch & jobbing. Quality control.	Tight scheduling. Cost control.
Marketing	Warehousing Retailing	Types of selling expertise.	Direct sales. Retail. Industrial service.	Industrial marketing. Consumer marketing.

The competence profile will serve three separate uses for assessment.

(a)   **Assessment of internal strengths and weaknesses**

The competence profile can be used to assess the company's internal resources and to determine the areas in which the company is either very good or very poor.

(b)   **Assessment of competitiveness**

A part of the appraisal will conduct a competence profile of each of the company's main competitors. Superposition of the company's competence profile with the respective competitive profiles measures the company's competitiveness and determines those areas where the company excels or is deficient.

(c)   **Assessment of external opportunities and threats**

Another part of the appraisal will conduct a competence profile of the company's industry and outside industries. Superposition of these profiles measures the attractiveness, or otherwise, of the company's present industry and other industries. It will also measure the company's 'fit' with its existing industry, and its 'fit' with other industries thus indicating the chances of a successful entry.

2.4   Portfolio planning techniques

Portfolio planning is a phrase used to describe the methods of expressing a product/market relationship in a manner meaningful for management decision-making. There are two main aims:

- to ascertain, through factual analysis, the current strengths and weaknesses of an organisation's products/services, their position in the market and the state of attractiveness of each of those markets.

- to indicate a strategy that would emphasise the strengths and remedy the weaknesses.

The Boston Consulting Group (BCG) developed a matrix which categorises a company's products in terms of cash generation and demands with the two aspects of market growth and market share.

This formula operates on the assumption that the experience curve is operating and therefore, the company with the largest relative share will be the largest cost producer. Therefore 'big' is 'good'.

The portfolio BCG matrix would be expressed as:

High	**STAR** Moderate, safe, positive cash flow	**QUESTION MARK/ PROBLEM CHILD** Large negative cash flow
Relative market growth **Low**	**CASH COW** Large positive cash flow	**DOG** Modest positive or negative cash flow
	High Low	

Relative market share

The logic of the portfolio is that cash cows are the financiers of the other segments. Ideally, some question marks are selected to become stars; this will require demands for capital which will be provided by the cash cows. As a star matures and the market growth slows so it becomes a cash cow for future products. Question marks not selected should be managed to generate cash until they become dogs. Dogs should be harvested or divested from the portfolio.

BCG suggests a company should manage its portfolio of products or business units to maintain this desirable sequence.

3   IMPLICATIONS OF CAPITAL INVESTMENT

When considering whether a project is worthwhile, a company must consider its implications. Any potential investment is likely to affect:

(a)   the liquidity of the company. All projects involve cashflows in and out. The size and timing of such flows should be considered when appraising projects. If an aim of investment appraisal is to satisfy shareholders, then it is important to remember that if a company has no cash it cannot pay a dividend.

(b)   the reported profit and earnings. All projects will change the revenues, expenses and asset values shown in the financial accounts. If shareholders are concerned about such statistics as earnings per share then the effect of investments on reported figures must be part of the investment appraisal.

(c)   the variability of cash flows and earnings. Investors are concerned about the variability of returns from their investments. The greater the variability, the greater the risk, and therefore the greater the return they will require. Thus, when appraising potential projects managers should consider not only the likely size and direction of cashflows and profits but also whether they are likely to add to or reduce the variability of such flows. To take an extreme example, an ice cream manufacturer should look favourably on a project to manufacture umbrellas as whatever the weather his cashflow and profits would be stable. However a project to manufacture sandals would increase the variability of cashflow and profits and thus increase the risk perceived by investors in the company.

So the choice of investment appraisal method should reflect how the project affects:

- cash flow
- reported profits, earnings and asset values
- variability of cashflow and profits.

The methods covered in this syllabus are:

- payback
- return on capital employed
- discounted appraisal methods.

4   PAYBACK PERIOD

4.1   Introduction

[Definition]   The period, usually expressed in years, which it takes the cash inflows from a capital investment project to equal the cash outflows.

When deciding between two or more competing projects the usual decision is to accept the one with the shortest payback. Payback is commonly used as a first screening method. It is a rough measure of liquidity and not of profitability.

The term payback period is almost self-explanatory and the rider to the definition that it is a useful screening process that assesses liquidity is worth noting. A recent survey showed that it was slightly more popular in UK practice than the accounting rate of return; but, as will be shown later, it has weaknesses and should not be used as the main decision criterion (and certainly not for choosing between alternative investment opportunities).

In the simplified case of a project with equal annual cash inflows, it is easy to find the payback period.

$$\text{Payback period} = \frac{\text{Initial payment}}{\text{Annual Cash Inflow}}$$

Eg, if £2m is invested to earn £500,000 per annum for 7 years (these being net cash earnings) the payback period (P) is given by:

$$P = \frac{£2,000,000}{£500,000} = \textbf{4 years}$$

However, if cash inflows are uneven (a more likely state of affairs), the payback has to be calculated by working out the cumulative cash flow over the life of a project.

4.2   Payback period with uneven cash flows

At this stage a convention needs to be introduced, cash outflows will be shown as negative figures (in brackets) and cash inflows or receipts shown as positive figures.

Illustration

A project has the following cash flows.

You are required to calculate the project payback period.

Year	Cash flow	Cumulative cash flow
	£'000	£'000
0	(2,000)	(2,000)
1	500	(1,500)
2	500	(1,000)
3	400	(600)
4	600	Nil
5	300	300
6	200	500

The payback period is exactly 4 years.

For such a project it is possible that the payback period does give a realistic measure of its 'worthwhileness' – the point being that no account is taken of the time value of money (explained later). As far as payback is concerned, the shorter the payback period the better the project. However, the limitations of the technique can be seen when it is used to appraise several projects together and hence compare them.

Further illustration

Year		Cash flow					
Project		A	B	C	D	E	F
0		(100)	(100)	(100)	(100)	(80)	(80)
1		10	10	40	40	40	40
2		20	20	30	30	(20)	40
3		30	30	20	20	30	30
4		40	40	10	10	10	20
5		-	10	10	40	20	20
6		-	40	40	10	40	(40)
Payback period (years)		4	4	4	4	4 or 5	2?

The payback period for all of projects A, B, C and D is four years – and thus in terms of this measure the four projects are equivalent. However, since there is a time value to money (as explained later) the projects are not equivalent. In particular:

B is preferred to A because of the extra receipts in years 4 and 5.

C is preferred to B because the cash receipts in years 1, 2, 3 and 4 are received more rapidly.

D is preferred to C because the post payback period receipts are greater in the earlier years.

Additional problems arise when determining the payback for projects E and F. For project E, the payback may be deemed to be four years – the length of time taken for the cash receipts to cover the initial outlay, or five years, the length of time before cumulative cash flows are zero. For project F the initial outlay is recovered by the end of the second year but it seems very imprudent to totally ignore the cash flow arising at the end of year 6 (of course in line with the nature of conservative accountants positive cash flows arising after the payback period have been ignored in projects B to E also.)

4.3   Merits of payback period as an investment appraisal technique

(a)   **Simplicity**

As a concept, it is easily understood and is easily calculated.

(b)   **Rapidly changing technology**

If new plant is likely to be scrapped in a short period because of obsolescence, a quick payback is essential.

(c)   **Improving investment conditions**

When investment conditions are expected to improve in the near future, attention is directed to those projects which will release funds soonest, to take advantage of the improving climate.

(d)   **Payback favours projects with a quick return**

It is often argued that these are to be preferred for three reasons:

(i)   Rapid project payback leads to rapid company growth – but in fact such a policy will lead to many profitable investment opportunities being overlooked because their payback period does not happen to be particularly swift.

(ii)   Rapid payback minimises risk (the logic being that the shorter the payback period, the less there is that can go wrong). Not all risks are related to time, but payback is able to provide a useful means of assessing time risks (and only time risk). It is likely that earlier cash flows can be estimated with greater certainty.

(iii)   Rapid payback maximises liquidity – but liquidity problems are best dealt with separately, through cash forecasting.

(e)   **Cash flows**

Unlike the other traditional methods it uses cash flows, rather than profits, and so is less likely to produce an unduly optimistic figure distorted by assorted accounting conventions which might permit certain costs to be cROCEied forward and not affect profit initially.

4.4   Weaknesses of payback period

(a)   **Project returns may be ignored**

In particular, cash flows arising after the payback period are totally ignored.

(b)   **Timing ignored**

Cash flows are effectively categorised as pre-payback or post-payback – but no more accurate measure is made. In particular, the time value of money is ignored.

(c)   **Lack of objectivity**

There is no objective measure as to what length of time should be set as the minimum payback period. Investment decisions are therefore subjective.

(d)   **Project profitability is ignored**

Payback takes no account of the effects on business profits and periodic performance of the project, as evidenced in the financial statements. This is critical if the business is to be reasonably viewed by users of the accounts.

4.5   Conclusions on payback

Payback is best seen as an initial screening tool – eg, no project with a payback of more than ten years is to be considered.

It is an appropriate measure for relatively straightforward projects eg, those which involve an initial outlay followed by constant long term receipts.

However in spite of its weaknesses and limitations the payback period is one of the most common initial methods of investment appraisal in use in the UK. It is not, however, often used exclusively - rather in conjunction with other methods.

Various variations on the basic payback calculation are occasionally seen:

Discounted payback - determining how long it takes to recoup the initial capital investment from the present value of the cash inflows.

Payback reciprocal - the reciprocal of the payback period (often expressed as a percentage); in certain circumstances it approximates to the DCF method, the internal rate of return.

Multiple payback - the time taken to recover the initial outlay not once but several times.

4.6   Activity

A project requires an initial investment of £550,000 and will bring the following cash receipts.

Year	1	2	3	4	5	6
Receipts (£'000)	100	200	200	100	75	25

You are required to calculate the project's payback period.

4.7   Activity solution

The payback period could be found by inspection or by tabulating cumulative cash flows.

Year	0	1	2	3	4	5	6
Cumulative cash flows (£'000)	(550)	(450)	(250)	(50)	50	125	150

After 3 years £50,000 is still 'outstanding'; the inflow over the fourth year is £100,000. **If** cash inflows accrue evenly over the year, the payback period is **3½ years**.

5   RETURN ON CAPITAL EMPLOYED (ROCE)

5.1   Definition

The return on capital employed (ROCE) which may also be called the accounting rate of return (ARR) expresses the profits from a project as a percentage of capital cost. However, what profits are used and what figure for capital cost may vary. The most common approach produces the following definition.

$$\text{ROCE} = \frac{\text{Average annual (post depreciation) profits}}{\text{Initial capital costs}} \times 100$$

In the absence of any instructions to the contrary, this is the method that should be used (profits before interest and tax, but after depreciation). Other methods discovered by a recent survey were:

- using average book value of the assets over their life;
- using first year's profits;
- using total profits over the whole of the project's life.

Example

A project involves the immediate purchase of an item of plant costing £110,000. It would generate annual cash flows of £24,400 for five years, starting in year 1. The plant purchased would have a scrap value of £10,000 in five years, when the project terminates. Depreciation is on a straight line basis.

You are required to calculate the ROCE.

Solution

Annual cash flows are taken to be profit before depreciation.

Average annual depreciation	=	(£110,000 – £10,000) ÷ 5
	=	£20,000
Average annual profit	=	£24,400 – £20,000
	=	£4,400

$$\text{ROCE} = \frac{\text{Average annual profit}}{\text{Initial capital cost}} \times 100$$

$$= \frac{£4,400}{£110,000} \times 100 = \quad 4\%$$

5.2   Using average book values of investments

This variation on the calculation of an ROCE produces a figure which is, under certain circumstances, closer to the conventional financial accounting view of return on capital employed. However, students have been known to suffer amazing mental aberrations when calculating a simple average in these circumstances.

Example

Using the figures in the previous example produce revised calculations based on the average book value of the investment.

Solution

Average annual profits (as before) = £4,400

Average book value of assets = $\dfrac{\text{Initial capital cost } + \text{* Final scrap value}}{2}$

  = $\dfrac{£110,000 \; + \; £10,000}{2} = £60,000$

ROCE = $\dfrac{£4,400}{£60,000} \times 100 = 7\frac{1}{3}\%$

* Note that the scrap value **increases** the average book value.

5.3   Merits of accounting rate of return for investment appraisal

(a) **Simplicity**

As with the payback period, it is easily understood and easily calculated.

(b) **Link with other accounting measures**

Return on capital employed, calculated annually to assess a business or sector of a business (and therefore the investment decisions made by that business), is widely used and its use for investment appraisal is consistent with that.   The ROCE is expressed in percentage terms with which managers and accountants are familiar.   However, neither this nor the preceding point necessarily justify the use of ROCE.

5.4   Criticisms of ROCE

There are a number of specific criticisms of the ROCE:

(a) It fails to take account of either the project life or the timing of cash flows (and time value of money) within that life.

(b) It will vary with specific accounting policies, and the extent to which project costs are capitalised.   Profit measurement is thus 'subjective', and ROCE figures for identical projects would vary from business to business.

(c) It might ignore working capital requirements.

(d) Like all rate of return measures, it is not a measurement of absolute gain in wealth for the business owners.

(e) There is no definite investment signal.   The decision to invest or not remains subjective in view of the lack of an objectively set target ROCE.

Conclusion   To summarise, it is concluded that the return on capital employed does not provide a reliable basis for project evaluation.

5.5   Activity

A project requires an initial investment of £800,000 and then earns net cash inflows of:

Year	1	2	3	4	5	6	7
Cash inflows (£'000)	100	200	400	400	300	200	150

In addition, at the end of the seven-year project the assets initially purchased will be sold for £100,000.

You are required

(a)   to calculate the project's payback period;

(b)   to determine its return on capital employed.

5.6   Activity solution

(a)   **Payback period**

Cumulative cash flows are tabulated below.

Year	0	1	2	3	4	5	6	7
Cumulative (£'000)	(800)	(700)	(500)	(100)	300	600	800	950

The payback period appears during the fourth year in which £400,000 arises. Since £100,000 still has to be paid off at the start of the fourth year, the payback period is **3¼ years**.

(b)   **Return on capital employed**

This uses **profits** rather than cash flows.

Average annual inflows	=	£1,750,000 ÷ 7	=	£250,000
Average annual depreciation	=	(£800,000 – £100,000) ÷ 7	=	£100,000

(A net £700,000 is being written off as depreciation over 7 years.)

Average annual profit	=	£250,000 – £100,000	=	£150,000

$$\text{ROCE} = \frac{\text{Average annual profit}}{\text{Initial investment}} \times 100 = \frac{£150,000}{£800,000} \times 100$$

$$= \mathbf{18.75\%}$$

(Note: if ROCE had been based on the average book value of assets, £150,000 would have been divided by the average of initial capital cost, £800,000, and final scrap value, £100,000 ie, £450,000, to give an accounting rate of return of 33⅓%.*)*

6   SELF TEST QUESTIONS

6.1   Define an investment. (1.1)

6.2   What is revenue investment? (1.1)

6.3   What is the modern approach to working capital funding? (1.4)

6.4   Define 'corporate appraisal'. (2.2)

6.5   Despite its limitations, why is the payback period a popular means of investment appraisal? (4.3)

6.6   What variations of the payback period method exist? (4.5)

6.7   What are the limitations of the use of the return on capital employed? (5.4)

7   EXAMINATION TYPE QUESTION

7.1   Paradis plc

Stadler is an ambitious young executive who has recently been appointed to the position of financial director of Paradis plc, a small listed company. Stadler regards this appointment as a temporary one, enabling him to gain experience before moving to a larger organisation. His intention is to leave Paradis plc in three years time, with its share price standing high. As a consequence, he is particularly concerned that the reported profits of Paradis plc should be as high as possible in this third and final year with the company.

Paradis plc has recently raised £350,000 from a rights issue, and the directors are considering three ways of using these funds. Three projects (A, B and C) are being considered, each involving the immediate purchase of equipment costing £350,000. One project only can be undertaken and the equipment for each project will have a useful life equal to that of the project, with no scrap value. Stadler favours project C because it is expected to show the highest accounting profit in the third year. However, he does not wish to reveal his real reasons for favouring project C and so, in his report to the chairman, he recommends project C because it shows the highest internal rate of return. The following summary is taken from his report:

Years				Net cash flows (£'000)						Internal rate of return
Project	0	1	2	3	4	5	6	7	8	%
A	(350)	100	110	104	112	138	160	180	-	27.5
B	(350)	40	100	210	260	160	-	-	-	26.4
C	(350)	200	150	240	40	-	-	-	-	33.0

The chairman of the company is accustomed to projects being appraised in terms of payback and accounting rate of return, and he is consequently suspicious of the use of the internal rate of return as a method of project selection. Accordingly, the chairman has asked for an independent report on the choice of project. The company's cost of capital is 20% and a policy of straight-line depreciation is used to write off the cost of equipment in the financial statements.

You are required:

(a)   to calculate the payback period for each project;   **(5 marks)**

(b)   to calculate the accounting rate of return for each project.   **(5 marks)**
                                                                        (Total: 10 marks)

Note: ignore taxation.

8 **ANSWER TO EXAMINATION TYPE QUESTION**

8.1 **Paradis plc**

Note: this question requires standard calculations.

(a) **Payback period for each project**
(Time taken to repay original outlay of £350,000.)

	£'000
Project A:	
Cash in first 3 years	314
Balance required	36
Initial investment	350
Cash in 4th year	112

Payback = 3 years + $\dfrac{36}{112}$ years = 3.32 years

(assuming cash flows accrue evenly - otherwise 4 years)

Project B:	
Cash in first 3 years	350,000
Payback	3 years

Project C:	
Cash in first 2 years	£350,000
Payback	2 years

(b) **Accounting rate of return for each project**

	Project A £'000	Project B £'000	Project C £'000
Total cash flow	904	770	630
Less: Total depreciation (no scrap value)	350	350	350
Total accounting profit	554	420	280
Project life (years)	7	5	4
Average profit per year (£'000)	79.14	84	70[1]
Initial capital employed	350	350	350[2]
Accounting rate of return (1) ÷ (2)	22.6%	24%	20%
(Alternatively, ROCE could be computed as average profit ÷ average capital employed, giving)	45.2%	48%	40%

27 APPENDIX

This appendix contains a revision of net present value and internal rate of return calculations as covered in Paper 3. You must be confident in these areas before you progress to Chapter 28.

1 NET PRESENT VALUE

1.1 Introduction

There are two basic discounted cash flow (DCF) methods:

- net present value (NPV)
- internal rate of return (IRR).

The first is theoretically more sound (as will be shown later), but the second is more popular (almost three times as common in a recent survey). Both have the advantage over the traditional methods in that they recognise the 'time value of money'.

1.2 The time value of money

A simple method of comparing two investment projects would be to compare the amount of cash generated from each – presumably, the project which generates the greater net cash inflow (taking into account all revenues and expenses) is to be preferred. However, such a simple method would fail to take into account the **time value of money**, the effect of which may be stated as the general rule below:

> 'There is a time preference for receiving the same sum of money sooner rather than later. Conversely, there is a time preference for paying the same sum of money later rather than sooner.'

1.3 Reasons for time preference

The reasons for time preference are threefold:

(a)   **Consumption preference** – money received now can be spent on consumption.
(b)   **Risk preference** – risk disappears once money is received.
(c)   **Investment preference** – money received can be invested in the business, or invested externally.

If consideration is given to these factors it can be seen that inflation affects time preference but is not its only determinant. Higher inflation for instance, will produce greater consumption preference and thus greater time preference, all else being equal. It is best to ignore inflation initially when considering DCF techniques.

The discounting analysis is based on (c), and in particular the ability to invest or borrow and receive or pay interest. The reason for this approach is that even where funds are not actually used and borrowed in this way, interest rates do provide the market measure of time preference.

The analysis, therefore, proceeds in terms of the way interest payments and receipts behave.

1.4   Compound interest

In previous studies it would have been noted that the discounting process that is fundamental to DCF calculations is analogous to compound interest in reverse. A short compound interest calculation is included here as revision.

Simple interest arises when interest accruing on an investment is paid to the investor as it becomes due, and is **not** added to the capital balance on which subsequent interest will be calculated.

Compound interest arises when the accrued interest is added to the capital outstanding and it is this revised balance on which interest is subsequently earned.

Example

Barlow places £2,000 on deposit in a bank earning 5% compound interest per annum.

You are required:

(a)   to find the amount that would have accumulated:

      (i)   after one year;
      (ii)   after two years; and
      (iii)   after three years.

(b)   to find the amount that would have to be deposited if an amount of £2,500 has to be accumulated:

      (i)   after one year;
      (ii)   after two years; and
      (iii)   after three years.

Solution

(a)   **Terminal values**

Although compound interest calculations can be produced using common sense, some may prefer to use a formula:

$$S = P(1 + r)^n$$

where
$$S = \text{Final amount accumulated (terminal value)}$$
$$P = \text{Principal (initial amount deposited)}$$
$$r = \text{interest rate per annum (as a decimal)}$$
$$n = \text{number of years principal is left on deposit}$$

(i)   After 1 year, S $=$ £2,000 × (1.05) $=$ £2,100

(ii)   After 2 years, S $=$ £2,000 × 1.05 × 1.05

                  $=$ £2,000 × 1.05^2 $=$ £2,205

(iii)   After 3 years, S $=$ £2,000 × 1.05^3 $=$ £2,315.25

(b)   **Present values**

In this case the final amount, S, is known and the principal, P, is to be found. Again the formula could be used, reROCEanging it to become:

$$\text{Principal, P} = \frac{S}{(1+r)^n}$$

(i)   If £2,380.95 is required in 1 year's time, a principal, P, has to be invested such that:

$$P \times 1.05 = £2,500$$

$$P = £2,500 \times \frac{1}{1.05} = £2,380.95$$

(If £2,381 is invested for a year at 5% interest, 5% of £2,380.95 or £119.05 is earned making the total amount £2,500 as required.)

(ii)   If £2,500 is required in 2 years time:

$$P \times 1.05^2 = £2,500$$

$$P = £2,500 \times \frac{1}{1.05^2} = £2,267.57$$

(It can be checked that £2,267.57 will accumulate to £2,500 after 2 years.)

(iii) If £2,500 is required in 3 years time:

$$P = £2,500 \times \frac{1}{1.05^3} = £2,159.59$$

This second group of calculations is the mechanics behind discounted cash flow calculations, the calculation of a present value. For example in (b) (i) one would be equally happy with receiving £2,500 in one year's time or £2,380.95 now. Although the immediate receipt is less than £2,500, if invested for a year at 5% it would amount to £2,500 hence the indifference between the two sums. £2,380.95 is called the **present value** (at 5%) of a sum of £2,500 payable or receivable in one year's time.

1.5   Discounting

Having said that people have a time preference for money and would prefer to receive money sooner rather than later, it is inappropriate to give the same value to similar sums receivable at different times over the life of a project. This is what traditional methods of investment appraisal do as illustrated in the context of the payback period. Because of investors' rates of time preference for money, a more suitable method of investment appraisal reduces the value of later cash flows (discounts them) to find that sum with which one would be equally happy now as a given receipt due in several years' time. This calculation (of a present value) is what was illustrated with the compound interest calculations.

1.6   Formula

The present value (PV) of a single sum, S receivable in n years' time, given an interest rate (a discount rate) r is given by:

$$PV = S \times \frac{1}{(1+r)^n}$$

Illustrations

Find the present values of:

(a)   £1,000 receivable in 1 year's time given a discount rate of 10%;

(b)   £4,000 receivable in 2 years time given a discount rate of 5%; and

(c)   £10,000 receivable in 5 years time given a discount rate of 8%.

In each case the process of reducing the cash flows to find that sum with which one would be equally happy now follows a procedure similar to compound interest backwards.

(a)   PV   = $£1,000 \times \dfrac{1}{1.10}$ =   £909.09

(One would be equally happy with £909.09 now as £1,000 in one year's time. With £909.09 available now to invest for one year at 10%, £90.91 interest is earned and the whole sum accumulates to £1,000 in one year's time.)

(b)   PV   = $£4,000 \times \dfrac{1}{(1.05)^2}$ =   £3,628.12

(Check for yourself that £3,628.12 will accumulate to £4,000 in two years if interest is earned at 5% pa.)

(c)   PV   = $£10,000 \times \dfrac{1}{(1.08)^5}$ =   £6,806

1.7   Annuities

It may be the case that certain types of cash flow (since cash flows rather than accounting profits are discounted) are expected to occur in equal amounts at regular periods over the life of a project. Calculating the present value of annuities can be made more simple by use of a second formula.

Illustration

Find the present value of £500 payable for each of three years given a discount rate of 10% if each sum is due to be paid annually in ROCEears.

The PV can be found from three separate calculations of the present value of a single sum.

$$PV = \left[£500 \times \frac{1}{(1.10)}\right] + \left[£500 \times \frac{1}{(1.10)^2}\right] + \left[£500 \times \frac{1}{(1.10)^3}\right]$$

Although this can be evaluated

=   £455   +   £413   +   £376   =   £1,244

it might be worth looking again at the expression for the present value and restating it as:

$$PV = £500 \times \left[\frac{1}{(1.10)} + \frac{1}{(1.10)^2} + \frac{1}{(1.10)^3}\right]$$

This can be evaluated

=   £500 × 2.48685   =   £1,243

(The difference is attributable to rounding.)

The last expression for the present value might be recognised as a geometric progression and a formula can be produced (which could be proved although there is no need to do so) for the present value of an annuity:

$$PV = A \times \frac{1}{r}\left(1 - \frac{1}{(1+r)^n}\right)$$

where now A is the annual cash flow receivable in **ROCEears**.

In this case

$$PV = £500 \times \frac{1}{0.10}\left(1 - \frac{1}{(1.10)^3}\right)$$

$$= £500 \times \frac{1}{0.10}(1 - 0.7513148)$$

$$= £500 \times 2.48685 \quad = \quad £1,243$$

(Tables exist for the value of this formula given different figures for r and n; for the next activity note that tables will not be used.)

1.8   Activity

Lindsay Ltd wishes to make a capital investment of £1.5m but is unsure whether to invest in one of two machines each costing that amount. The net cash inflows from the two projects are shown below.

Time	1	2	3
Denis plc Machine (£'000)	900	600	500
Thomson plc Machine (£'000)	700	700	700

You are required to find the present value of the two patterns of cash flows at the company's required rate of return of 10% and thus decide which of the two identically priced machines (if any) should be acquired. (Assume all cash flows occur annually in ROCEears on the anniversary of the initial investment.)

1.9   Activity solution

Cash inflows from Denis machine:

$$PV = \frac{£900,000}{1.10} + \frac{£600,000}{1.10^2} + \frac{£500,000}{1.10^3}$$

$$= £818,182 + £495,868 + £375,657 = £1,689,707$$

Cash inflows from Thomson machine:

$$PV = \frac{£700,000}{1.10} + \frac{£700,000}{1.10^2} + \frac{£700,000}{1.10^3}$$

$$= £700,000 \times \frac{1}{0.10} \times \left(1 - \frac{1}{(1.10)^3}\right)$$

$$= £700,000 \times 2.48685 = £1,740,796$$

Despite the earlier receipts from the Denis machine, the extra £100,000 in total receipts gives the Thomson machine the advantage.

Since the present value of the inflows exceeds the (present value of) the initial cost, the Thomson machine project is worthwhile. (It has a net present value of £1,740,796 – £1,500,000 = £240,796.)

Simple projects such as these two can be analysed by calculations taking a single line; but slightly more complex projects merit a tabular layout as follows.

Denis machine

Time		Cash flow £'000	10% Discount Factor	Present Value £'000
0	Capital cost	(1,500)	1	(1,500)
1	Inflow	900	$\frac{1}{1.10}$	818
2	Inflow	600	$\frac{1}{1.10^2}$	496
3	Inflow	500	$\frac{1}{1.10^3}$	376
	Net present value (£'000)			190

Thomson machine

Time		Cash flow £'000	10% Discount Factor	Present Value £'000
0	Capital cost	(1,500)	1	(1,500)
1 - 3	Inflow	700	2.48685	1,741
	Net present value (£'000)			241

The Thomson machine project has the higher NPV and would be preferred.

Note:

- A nROCEative column has been included which here is not of great use, but in larger projects makes workings much clearer.

- PV's have been rounded to the nearest £'000; it is not worth stating them to the nearest penny and, when using tables, round to the nearest three significant figures (perhaps to the nearest £'000 or £m if that is not too different from 3 significant figures) although only the first 2 significant figures are really accurate.

- Again brackets are used for outflows.

- The first column has been headed 'Time' rather than year, since the calendar year in which expenditure falls is not as important (yet) as whether it falls one or two years, say after the initial outlay - which is usually taken to occur at time 0. The stated assumption of cash flows at annual intervals is common in DCF calculations.

- For larger calculations with many cash flow estimates changing from year to year another layout will be recommended.

1.10   Present value factor tables

To make investment appraisal calculations simpler, tables are produced (and are available for use in exams) of discount factors. A copy of the tables issued in the exam appears at the front of this Examination Text. These provide values of:

Individual discount factors, $Vn.r = \dfrac{1}{(1+r)^n}$ (or $(1+r)^{-n}$)

Cumulative discount factors for annuities, $A\overline{n}|r = \dfrac{1}{r}\left(1 - \dfrac{1}{(1+r)^n}\right) = \dfrac{1-(1+r)^{-n}}{r}$

The two NPV calculations for Lindsay, using the tables might look as follows.

Denis machine

NPV (£'000)   = $-1{,}500 + [900 \times 0.909] + [600 \times 0.826] + [500 \times 0.751]$

              =   189

Thomson machine

NPV (£'000)   = $-1{,}500 + [700 \times 2.487]$

              =   241

1.11 Perpetuities

Sometimes it is necessary to calculate the present values of annuities which are expected to continue for an indefinitely long period of time, 'perpetuities'. The cumulative present value factor tables only go up to a finite number of years and so a formula is required. The present value of £A receivable for n years given a discount rate r is:

$$A \times \frac{1}{r}\left(1 - \frac{1}{(1+r)^n}\right)$$

What happens to this formula as n becomes large? As n tends to infinity, $(1+r)^n$ also tends to infinity and $\dfrac{1}{(1+r)^n}$ tends to zero. The cumulative discount factor tends to $\dfrac{1}{r}(1-0)$ or $\dfrac{1}{r}$.

> **Conclusion**   The present value of an annuity, A receivable in ROCEears in perpetuity given a discount rate r is given by
>
> $$\text{PV perpetuity} \quad = \quad \frac{A}{r} \left(= \frac{\text{Annual cash flow}}{\text{discount rate (as a decimal)}} \right)$$

Example

The present value of £5,000 receivable annually in ROCEears at a discount rate of 8% is:

    = $\dfrac{£5{,}000}{0.08}$ =   **£62,500**

2 INTERNAL RATE OF RETURN (IRR)

2.1 Definition

For so-called conventional projects, that is those where a single cash outflow is followed by subsequent cash inflows, it is often useful to compute the internal rate of return (IRR) of the project.

> **Definition**   The internal rate of return is that discount rate which gives a net present value of zero.

It is sometimes known as the yield, or DCF yield, or internal yield, but these terms are confusing and their use is not recommended.

In general, it is necessary to compute the IRR by trial and error, that is to compute NPVs at various discount rates until the discount rate is found which gives an NPV of zero.

The IRR can be thought of as the maximum rate of interest that can be paid on the finance for a project without making a loss.

Example

Find the IRR of the Denis machine that Lindsay decided not to acquire.

Solution

The net present value at 10% was £190,000.

The aim is to find the discount rate that gives an NPV of zero. Since the project has a positive NPV at 10%, the later cash flows haven't been reduced, discounted enough, and a higher discount rate must be chosen; try 15%.

$$\text{NPV at 15\% (£'000)} = -1,500 + \frac{900}{1.15} + \frac{600}{(1.15)^2} + \frac{500}{(1.15)^3} = 65$$

This is clearly closer to the IRR than 10%, but not that close. However, rather than continue to try ever increasing discount rates an approximate short cut can be taken. If the two discount rates and NPV's are plotted on a graph, the following is seen.

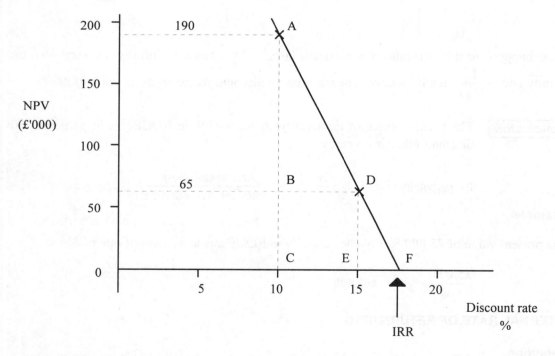

From the graph the IRR appears to be about 17½%. An estimate of the IRR could be found logically:

*   NPV has fallen from 190 to 65 (by 125) as the discount rate has increased by 5% (from 10% to 15%) - this is a fall of 25 per %age point increase.

*   To find the IRR the NPV needs to fall another 65.

*   To achieve this, the discount rate must be increased by $65 \times \dfrac{5\%}{125} = 2.6\%$ to 17.6%.

A formula could be produced (based on similar triangles)

$$\frac{AC}{CF} = \frac{AB}{BD} \quad \text{or} \quad \frac{190}{IRR - 10\%} = \frac{190 - 65}{5\%}$$

ReROCEanging this one gets:

$$190 \times 5\% \quad = \quad (IRR - 10\%)(190 - 65)$$

$$\text{or} \quad IRR \quad \approx \quad 10\% + \left(\frac{190}{190 - 65}\right) \times 5\% \quad = \quad 17.6\%$$

2.2   Formula

Although, for projects such as this with uneven cash flows, one of the above approaches is perfectly satisfactory (even estimating the IRR from a graph would do), it may be quicker for exam purposes to remember the form of the expression used to find the IRR.

$$IRR \approx A + \frac{N_A}{N_A - N_B}(B - A)$$

where
A = lower discount rate (10%)
B = higher discount rate (15%)
N_A = NPV at rate A (190)
N_B = NPV at rate B (65)

Note:

- The formula applies whether the discount rates chosen both give positive NPV's, both give negative NPV's, or give one of each.

- If negative NPV's appear, be careful with signs.

- The formula is only approximate since it assumes that the relationship between NPV and discount rate is linear; as the graph below shows, it is not; it is not worth quoting an IRR found in this way to more than one decimal place (and even that might be too much).

- The closer the two rates (A and B) are to the true IRR the more accurate will be the result. (It is sometimes suggested that the IRR can only be found if one NPV is positive and one negative; this is not so and may lead to inaccuracy or wasting time as attempts are made to produce these types of result.)

Graph of NPV v discount rate

(showing non-linearity)

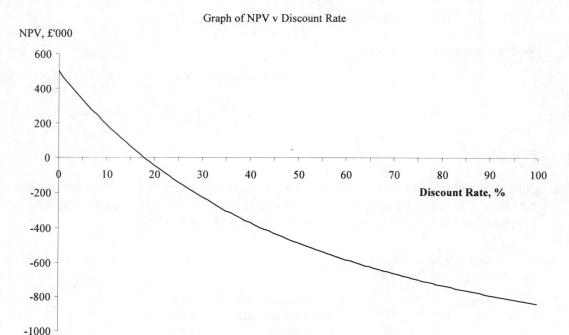

Graph of NPV v Discount Rate

2.3   Activity

The Thomson machine required an outlay of £1.5m to produce three inflows of £0.7m. At 10% the NPV of this project was £241,000. Find the IRR using the method above and taking 20% as the next discount rate.

2.4   Activity solution

NPV at 20% (£'000) $\quad = \quad -1,500 + \dfrac{700}{1.20} + \dfrac{700}{(1.20)^2} + \dfrac{700}{(1.20)^3} = -25.$

In using 20% a discount rate has been found that is slightly higher than the IRR. The IRR can be estimated using:

$$\text{IRR} \quad \approx \quad A + \left(\frac{N_A}{N_A - N_B} \right)(B - A)$$

$$\approx \quad 10 + \left(\frac{241}{241 - (-25)} \right)(20 - 10)$$

$$\approx \quad 10 + \left(\frac{241}{241 + 25} \right)10 \quad = \quad \mathbf{19\%}$$

(Note a cumulative discount factor of 2.106 could have been used to find the NPV at 20% but would have given the same IRR.)

2.5 Even annual cash flows

A simpler approach can be used to find the IRR of simple projects in which the annual cash inflows are equal (as with the previous example). The IRR can be found via a cumulative discount factor as the following exercise with the Thomson machine project shows.

NPV calculation

		Cash flow £'000	(c)% Discount Factor	Present Value £'000
Time				
0	Investment	(1,500)	1	(1,500)
1 - 3	Inflow	700	(b)	(a)
	Net present value (£'000)			NIL

The aim is to find the discount rate that produces an NPV of nil; therefore the PV of inflows (a) must equal the PV of outflows, £1,500,000. If the PV of inflows (a) is to be £1,500,000 and the size of each inflow is £700,000, the discount factor required must be 1,500,000 ÷ 700,000 = 2.143. The discount rate (c) for which this is the 3 year factor can be found by looking along the 3 year row of the cumulative discount factors shown in the annuity table. The figure of 2.140 appears under the 19% column suggesting an IRR of 19% is the closest. The necessary procedure for exam purposes can be summarised as follows.

Step 1 Find the cumulative discount factor, $A_{\overline{n}|r}$ $\dfrac{\text{Initial investment}}{\text{Annual inflow}}$

Step 2 Find the life of the project, n.

Step 3 Look along the n year row of the cumulative discount factors till the closest value to $A_{\overline{n}|r}$ is found.

Step 4 The column in which this figure appears is the IRR.

2.6 Perpetuities

Just as it is possible to calculate the PV of a perpetuity so it is a simple matter to find the IRR of a project with equal annual inflows that are expected to be received for an indefinitely long period.

Formula

The IRR of a perpetuity $= \dfrac{\text{Annual inflow}}{\text{Initial investment}} \times 100$

This can be seen by looking at the formula for the PV of a perpetuity and considering the definition of internal rate of return.

Illustration

Find the IRR of an investment that costs £20,000 and generates £1,600 for an indefinitely long period.

$$\text{IRR} = \frac{\text{Annual inflow}}{\text{Initial investment}} \times 100 = \frac{£1,600}{£20,000} \times 100 = \textbf{8\%}$$

28 INVESTMENT APPRAISAL USING DCF METHODS

INTRODUCTION & LEARNING OBJECTIVES

The most important methods of capital investment appraisal use DCF techniques to recognise the time value of money. There are two methods: NPV and IRR. This chapter should convince you that NPV is theoretically superior to IRR so, when the two methods give conflicting advice, follow the NPV criterion. The chapter also examines replacement theory.

When you have studied this chapter you should be able to do the following:

- Calculate, interpret and compare net present values and internal rates of return.

- Recommend optimal replacement strategies for capital assets that wear out.

---

1 NPV v IRR

1.1 Different types of investment decision

Two different basic DCF methods have been seen, NPV and IRR. When used to analyse a project, the decision is easily made:

- if a project has a positive NPV it should be accepted;
- if a project has an IRR greater than the required rate of return, accept it.

Since the two basic DCF methods are based on the same underlying principle, the time value of money, one would expect them to give identical investment decisions. This is not always so.

Three types of investment decision can be identified.

- Single investment decision.
- Mutually exclusive investments.
- Projects with multiple yields.

The two DCF methods may not always give the same conclusion. The three types of decision are considered in turn.

1.2 Single investment decision

When deciding whether or not to accept a single capital project if neither of the other conditions apply, no ambiguity arises. A project will be accepted if it has a positive NPV at the required rate of return; if it has a positive NPV then it will have an IRR that is greater than the required rate of return. The previous graph of NPV v Discount Rate should illustrate the point.

1.3 Mutually exclusive investments

Organisations may often face decisions in which only one of two or more investments can be undertaken; these are called mutually exclusive investment decisions. In these circumstances NPV and IRR may give conflicting recommendations.

Example

Barlow Ltd is considering two short-term investment opportunities which they have called project A and project B which have the following cash flows.

Time	0	1
Project A (£'000)	(200)	240
Project B (£'000)	(100)	125

Barlow has a cost of capital of 10%. Find the NPV's and IRR's of the two projects.

Solution

		NPV £'000	IRR %
Project A:	240 ÷ 1.10 − 200	18.18	20
Project B:	125 ÷ 1.10 − 100	13.64	25

The IRR's could be found either by trial and error or by using a formula. It would be easier to notice that project A, over 1 year, earns £40,000 on an investment of £200,000 (a 20% return) whilst project B earns £25,000 on £100,000 (25%).

It is worth noticing that A has the higher NPV whilst B has the higher IRR - a conflict.

Graphical explanation

If the NPV's of the two projects were calculated for a range of discount rates and two graphs of NPV against rate plotted on the same axes it would look as shown below. (This is worth trying yourself.)

NPV v Discount rate for mutually exclusive projects

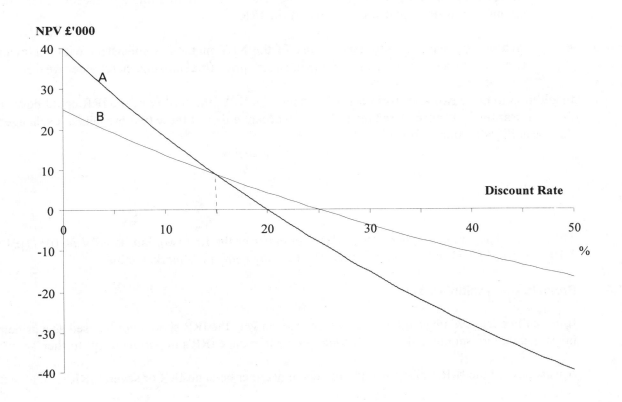

As in the previous section (when describing IRR) each graph slopes downwards (NPV decreases as r increases for a 'conventional' project) and shows a slight curve. Line A starts at (£240,000 – £200,000) £40,000; line B starts at (£125,000 – £100,000) £25,000. The lines cut the horizontal axis at their IRR's of 20% and 25% and intersect at (what seems to be) 15%. Project B has the higher IRR, whereas at the cost of capital of 10% (in fact at any rate below 15%) project A has the higher NPV.

1.4   Mutually exclusive projects - rationale and resolution

Although NPV and IRR are based on the same principle of the time value of money they are calculated in very different ways and there is no reason why they should give the same ranking for mutually exclusive projects. However if firm reasons for the different ranking are required one would cite:

- **Absolute and relative measures** - the NPV is an absolute measure but the IRR is a relative measure of a project's viability.

- **Reinvestment assumption** - the two methods are sometimes said to be based on different assumptions about the rate at which funds generated by the projects are reinvested - NPV assumes reinvestment at a firm's cost of capital, IRR assumes reinvestment at the IRR.

When deciding between the two projects it must be realised that it is only their nature that causes us to choose between them, not shortage of funds. These might represent two alternative uses of the same building which can't be carried out together. Going for B or, more particularly A, does not restrict our ability to accept other profitable projects that become available. In view of this the decision should be:

Accept the project with the larger NPV

The reasons for this are:

- **Better reinvestment assumption** - if the relevance of reinvestment is accepted, the NPV's assumption is more realistic than that of the IRR.

- **Achieving corporate objectives** - use of the NPV method is consistent with achieving a firm's corporate objective of maximising share price (maximising shareholder wealth).

In addition to these two reasons in favour of using the NPV, the futility of the IRR could be seen if the firm, Barlow Ltd, surrendered their chance to accept either of these two projects in exchange for the possibility of a third project:

	Time	Cash flow £
Project C:	0	(10)
	1	14

This project has a much higher IRR (40%) than either of the first two, but its NPV at 10% ([£14 ÷ 1.10] – £10) of £2.73 will not have much effect on any company's market value.

1.5   Projects with multiple yields

If mutually exclusive investments provide one reason why the IRR should not be used as a principal investment appraisal method, multiple yields serve to reduce IRR's importance still further.

A weakness of the IRR method is that projects may either have no IRR or several IRR's.

1.6 Activity

Consider the following projects with cash flows over a three year period.

Time	Project A £	Project B £	Project C £
0	(5,000)	(10,000)	(100,000)
1	2,000	23,000	360,000
2	2,000	(13,200)	(431,000)
3	2,000	(1,000)	171,600

You are required to calculate the NPV of these projects over the range 0 - 40% at 5% intervals and plot the results on three separate graphs. (Hint: it may be safer to use a formula rather than tables.)

1.7 Activity solution

The NPV at 0% is found by adding up the (undiscounted) cash flows.

Rate	0	5	10	15	20	25	30	35	40
NPV_A	1,000	447	(26)	(434)	(787)	(1,096)	(1,368)	(1,608)	(1,822)
NPV_B	(1,200)	(932)	(751)	(639)	(579)	(560)	(574)	(612)	(671)
NPV_C	600	162	0	(25)	0	19	0	(76)	(219)

The three graphs are shown below.

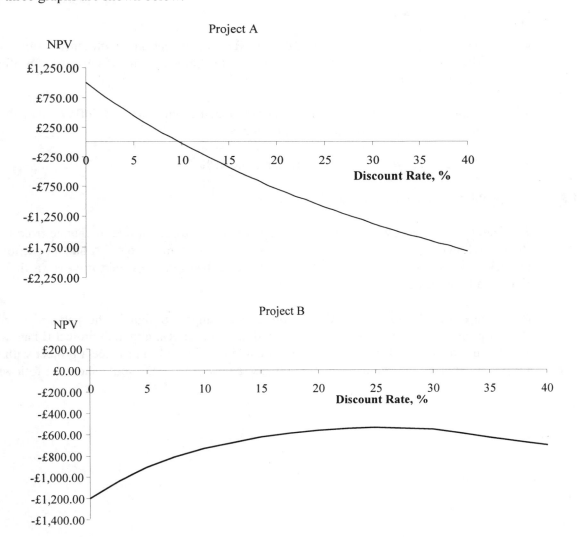

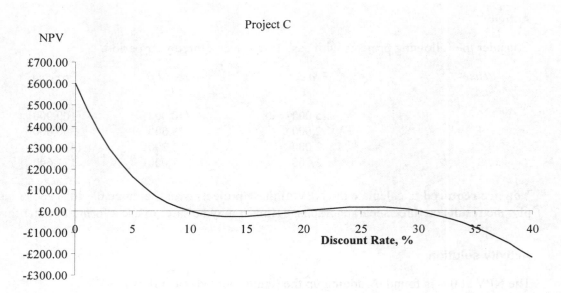

Project C

Comment

- Project A is a 'conventional' project, with one outflow followed by several net inflows and shows the expected pattern of NPV decreasing as discount rate increases.

- Project A has one IRR at 10%.

- Project B has no IRR.

- Project B's cash flows could be described as unconventional with outflows **of a significant size** appearing at the beginning and end of the 'project' (which is always unprofitable but is least unprofitable at 25%).

- Project C's cash flows alternate between being outflows and inflows and the graph of NPV v discount rate alternately falls and rises.

- Project C has three IRR's at 10%, 20% and 30%.

1.8 The problem of non-conventional cash flows

The feature of projects which causes the graph of NPV v discount rate to change from the standard shape as shown by project A is more than one 'change in sign'. Project A had an outflow followed by inflows (one change in sign), whereas project B had outflows then inflows (a first change in sign), but then further outflows (two changes in sign).

Rule: there **may** be as many IRR's as there are changes in sign in the patterns of cash flows. Clearly project C has three changes in sign and has three IRR's; although project B has two changes in sign but no IRR's. Project B's cash flows could be adjusted to produce a project with two IRR's simply by ignoring the last outflow. In that case a new project, D, would show the following.

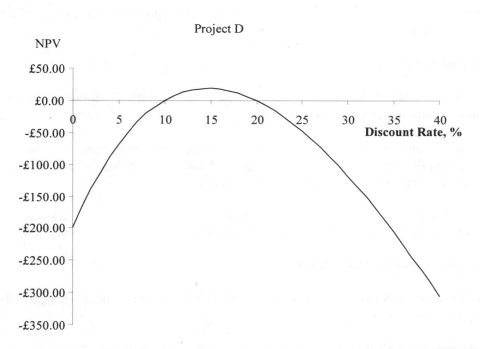

Project D

This type of cash flow pattern might occur with projects such as mining or oil exploration. An initial investment is followed by receipts from sales for a few years but, at the end of the project, the sizeable cost of reparations have a major effect on the project. The authors Lorie and Savage discussed this type of project at length.

Clearly it is difficult to use the IRR method in these circumstances. Attempts can be made to modify the cash flows in such a way as to be able to find a single IRR without invalidating the analysis. However, multiple yields merely provide further evidence that the NPV method is superior to IRR. Despite having several IRR's projects will have only one NPV at the required rate of return which will be either positive or negative (or zero).

2   CASH FLOWS

2.1   Costs to ignore

Before looking at those cash flows that should be included in any DCF analysis, it is worth emphasising those items that should be excluded.

Depreciation - this is not a cash flow and any depreciation charges should be excluded from DCF calculations. If profit figures after depreciation have been provided, the profit needs to be increased by adding back fixed costs.

Apportioned fixed costs - the cost of producing an item may include an apportionment of factory-wide fixed costs using some standard basis for absorption. These should be excluded; fixed costs may appear in a DCF calculation, but only if it is known that they will increase as a result of accepting a project.

Book values of assets - these fall into the same category as depreciation, they are not cash flows and must be ignored.

Interest payments - in most cases it can be assumed that the cost of interest has been taken into account by the discounting process. Interest payments should be ignored since to do otherwise would be 'double counting'.

Dividend payments - whilst these will be particularly important in later papers, at this stage they are irrelevant and should be ignored.

Sunk costs - any sums that have already been spent or committed and cannot be influenced by the investment decision should be ignored.

2.2   Relevant cash flows

The cash flows that should be included are those which are **specifically incurred as a result of the acceptance or non-acceptance of the project**.

They are incremental cash flows associated with a project; they could require a use of opportunity cost considerations.   When deciding what figure should be included in any DCF calculation it sometimes helps to tabulate for a particular element of cost.

Cash flow if project accepted	−	Cash flow if project rejected	=	Relevant cash flow

2.3   Absolute and incremental cash flows

When deciding between two projects, only one of which can be accepted (ie, **mutually exclusive projects**), two approaches are possible:

(a)   discount the cash flows of each project separately and compare NPVs; or

(b)   find the **differential** (or **incremental**) cash flow year by year ie, the **difference** between the cash flows of the two projects.   Then use the discounted value of those differential cash flows to establish a preference.

Either approach will lead to the same conclusion.

Example

Two projects, A and B, are under consideration.   Either A or B, but not both, may be accepted.   The relevant discount rate is 10%.

You are required to recommend A or B by:

(a)   discounting each cash flow separately; and
(b)   discounting relative (incremental or differential) cash flows.

The cash flows are as follows:

Time	Project A £	Project B £
0	(1,500)	(2,500)
1	500	500
2	600	800
3	700	1,100
4	500	1,000
5	Nil	500

Solution

(a)   **Discounting each cash flow separately**

Time	PV factor at 10%	Project A Cash flow £	PV £	Project B Cash flow £	PV £
0	1.000	(1,500)	(1,500)	(2,500)	(2,500)
1	0.909	500	455	500	455
2	0.826	600	496	800	661
3	0.751	700	526	1,100	826
4	0.683	500	341	1,000	683
5	0.621	Nil	Nil	500	310
NPV			£318		£435

Project B is preferred because its NPV exceeds that of A by £(435 – 318)   =   £117

(b)   **Discounting relative cash flows**

Time	Project A	Project B	Incremental cash flow B – A	PV factor at 10%	PV of incremental cash flow
0	(1,500)	(2,500)	(1,000)	1.000	(1,000)
1	500	500	Nil	0.909	Nil
2	600	800	200	0.826	165
3	700	1,100	400	0.751	300
4	500	1,000	500	0.683	341
5	Nil	500	500	0.621	311
NPV of incremental cash flow					£117

In other words, the present value of the cash flows of project B are £117 greater than those of project A. B is preferred. Note the result is exactly the same in (a) and (b). This gives a useful short cut to computation when comparing two projects **as long as it is known in advance that one of the projects must be undertaken**. However, where this is not the case, care should be taken with the 'differential' approach or the technique may result in acceptance of a project with a negative NPV (the other project having a larger negative NPV). There must be a tacit third option from A and B, namely to do neither.

2.4   A worked problem

The following example is typical of the type of problem relating to incremental cash flows:

Smith Ltd has decided to increase its productive capacity to meet an anticipated increase in demand for its products.   The extent of this increase in capacity has still to be determined, and a management meeting has been called to decide which of the following two mutually exclusive proposals – A and B – should be undertaken.

The following information is available:

		Proposal A £	Proposal B £
Capital expenditure:			
	Buildings	50,000	100,000
	Plant	200,000	300,000
	Installation	10,000	15,000
Net income:			
	Annual pre-depreciation profits (note (i))	70,000	95,000
Other relevant income/expenditure:			
	Sales promotion (note (ii))	-	15,000
	Plant scrap value	10,000	15,000
	Buildings disposable value (note (iii))	30,000	60,000
Working capital required over the project life		50,000	65,000

Notes:

(i)   The investment life is ten years.

(ii)   An exceptional amount of expenditure on sales promotion of £15,000 will have to be spent in year two of proposal B. This has not been taken into account in calculating pre-depreciation profits.

(iii) It is the intention to dispose of the buildings in ten years' time.

Using an 8% discount rate, you are required to evaluate the two alternatives.

Solution

Since the decision has been made to increase capacity (ie, 'to do nothing' is not an alternative), the easiest approach is to discount the **incremental** cash flows.

The tabular approach introduced earlier is still appropriate particularly as the project lasts for 10 years (other forms of presentation will appear later).

Time		A £'000	B £'000	B – A £'000	8% **Factor**	PV £'000
0	Capital expenditure	(260)	(415)	(155)	1	(155)
0	Working capital	(50)	(65)	(15)	1	(15)
2	Promotion	-	(15)	(15)	0.857	(13)
1 - 10	Net income	70	95	25	6.710	168
10	Scrap proceeds	40	75	35	0.463	16
10	Working capital	50	65	15	0.463	7
	Net present value (£'000)					8

The present value of proposal B exceeds that of proposal A by £8,000 at 8% and therefore proposal B is preferred.

Assumptions

(a)   The disposal value of buildings is realistic and that all other figures have been realistically appraised.

(b)   Expenditure on working capital is incurred at the beginning of the project life and recovered at the end.

(c)   Adequate funds are available for either proposal.

(d)   All cash flows occur annually in arrears on the anniversary of the initial investment.

3   REPLACEMENT THEORY

3.1   The nature of replacement problems

The replacement problem is concerned with the decision to replace existing operating assets. The two questions to be evaluated are:

(a)   when should the existing equipment be replaced;

(b)   what should be the replacement policy thereafter (ie, the future replacement cycle)?

This may be represented diagrammatically:

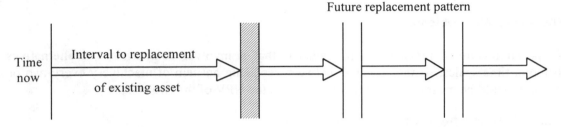

It is difficult to determine the replacement policy of the existing asset in isolation, because that decision will be dependent on the cost of the future replacement pattern, a fact that will be demonstrated in the sections which follow.

3.2   Relevance of replacement decisions

Within the UK, it is estimated that 50% to 60% of total investment incorporates replacement. Yet the evidence also suggests that replacement appraisal is somewhat haphazard. In particular:

(a)   there is a failure to take account of the time-scale problems;

(b)   techniques such as payback and accounting rate of return are used, which are unsuitable for replacement decisions;

(c)   taxation and investment incentives are ignored;

(d)   inflation is ignored.

This section is concerned with developing a systematic approach to replacement analysis.

3.3   Factors in replacement decisions

The factors to be considered include:

(a)   **Capital cost of new equipment** – the higher cost of equipment will have to be balanced against known or possible technical improvements.

(b) **Operating costs** – operating costs will be expected to increase as the machinery deteriorates over time. This is referred to as **operating inferiority**, and is the result of:

    (i) increased repair and maintenance costs;

    (ii) loss of production due to 'down-time' resulting from increased repair and maintenance time;

    (iii) lower quality and quantity of output.

(c) **Resale value** – the extent to which old equipment can be traded in for new.

(d) **Taxation and investment incentives.**

(e) **Inflation** – both the general price level change, and relative movements in the prices of input and outputs.

3.4   The time-scale problems

A special feature of replacement problems is that it involves comparisons of alternatives with different time-scales. If the choice is between replacing an item of machinery every two or three years, it would be meaningless simply to compare the NPV of the two costs.

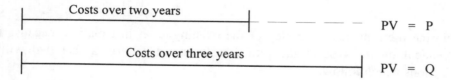

Almost certainly $P < Q$. However, this does not take account of the cost of providing an asset for the third year. A method of calculating an equivalent cost over a common time period is required.

There are three methods available in order to take account of this:

(a) **Lowest common multiple (LCM)**

The LCM of the various replacement cycles is computed (in this case the LCM of two and three is six) and the PV of costs over this period is computed ie, the cost of 3×2 year cycles is compared with those of 2×3 year cycles.

The method rapidly becomes unwieldy – for a machine which can be replaced every five or seven years the LCM is thirty-five years.

(b) **Finite time horizon**

To avoid the problem of very long periods to be considered under the LCM method it is possible to consider costs only over a finite period – say ten years. Thus the PV of costs incurred over this finite period are compared – the costs arising after this time are ignored on the basis that they will be discounted heavily anyway and thus their PV will be negligible.

The problem with this method is that strictly 'like' is not being compared with 'like'. For example, in the case of a machine which could be replaced every five or seven years then at the end of a ten year period the five year cycle would end up with a five year old machine, and the seven year cycle would end with a three year old machine.

(c)   **Equivalent annual cost (EAC)**

The neatest solution is to compute the PV of costs over one cycle and then turn it into an EAC by the use of an annuity factor. Thus, the costs associated with any particular cycle can be considered as equivalent to having to pay this EAC every year throughout the cycle and throughout subsequent cycles. This will be made clearer by use of the following example.

3.5   Worked example

A decision has to be made on replacement policy for vans. A van costs £12,000 and the following additional information applies:

Interval between replacement (years)	Trade in allowance £
1	9,000
2	7,500
3	7,000

Age at year end	Maintenance cost paid at year end £
Year of replacement	Nil
1	2,000
2	3,000

Calculate the optimal replacement policy at a cost of capital of 15%. There are no maintenance costs in the year of replacement. Ignore taxation and inflation.

3.6   Solution

The solution will be calculated using the equivalent annual cost (EAC) technique discussed in the last section.

It is assumed that a brand new van is owned at the beginning of the cycle, and therefore must be owned at the end of the cycle.

The costs incurred over a single cycle are computed and the EAC is found as follows.

(i)   Replace every year

NPV of a single cycle $= \quad -£12,000 + \dfrac{£9,000}{1.15} = £(4,174)$

1 year 'annuity' factor $= \quad 0.870$

Equivalent annual cost $= \quad \dfrac{\text{NPV}}{\text{annuity factor}} = \dfrac{£(4,174)}{0.870} = £(4,798)$

(ii)   Replace every two years

NPV of a single cycle $= \quad -£12,000 - \dfrac{£2,000}{1.15} + \dfrac{£7,500}{1.15^2} = £(8,068)$

2 year 'annuity' factor $= \quad 1.626$

Equivalent annual cost $= \quad \dfrac{£(8,068)}{1.626} = £(4,962)$

(iii)   Replace every three years

NPV of a single cycle $=$ $-£12,000 - \dfrac{£2,000}{1.15} - \dfrac{£3,000}{1.15^2} + \dfrac{£7,000}{1.15^3} = £(11,405)$

3 year 'annuity' factor   =   2.283

Equivalent annual cost   = $\frac{£(11,405)}{2.283} = £(4,996)$

The optimal replacement period is every year (as in the previous two instances).

Note: the equivalent annual cost is that sum that could be paid annually in arrears to finance the three replacement cycles. It is equivalent to the budget accounts that various public services encourage customers to open to spread the cost of those services more evenly. The present value of annual sums equal to the EAC's is the same as the PV of the various receipts and payments needed to buy and maintain a van.

3.7   Activity

A company with a cost of capital of 12% wishes to determine the optimum replacement policy for its computers. Each computer costs £5,000 and can either be traded in at the end of the first year for £3,000 (no maintenance cost paid) or traded in at the end of the second year for £2,000 (£500 maintenance paid after one year). Calculate the equivalent annual cost of each policy and recommend which should be implemented.

3.8   Activity solution

(i)   Replace every year

NPV of 1 cycle   = $-£5,000 + \frac{£3,000}{1.12} = £(2,321)$

EAC   = $\frac{£(2,321)}{0.893} = £(2,599)$

(ii)   Replace every other year

NPV of 1 cycle   = $-£5,000 - \frac{£500}{1.12} + \frac{£2,000}{1.12^2} = £(3,852)$

EAC   = $\frac{£(3,852)}{1.690} = £(2,279)$

Replacing every two years is the cheaper option.

4   SELF TEST QUESTIONS

4.1   Why might NPV and IRR give conflicting conclusions and how should this be resolved? (1.4)

4.2   Under what circumstances may a project have more than one IRR? (1.8)

4.3   What costs should be ignored in any DCF calculation? (2.1)

4.4   If using an incremental approach to decide between two alternative investment opportunities, what tacit third option must not exist? (2.3)

4.5   What three approaches could be used to tackle a replacement problem when deciding whether to replace every year, every two years or every three years? (3.4)

5 EXAMINATION TYPE QUESTIONS

5.1 Khan Ltd

Khan Ltd is an importer of novelty products. The directors are considering whether to introduce a new product, expected to have a very short economic life. Two alternative methods of promoting the new product are available, details of which are as follows:

Alternative 1 would involve heavy advertising and the employment of a large number of agents. The directors expect that an immediate cash outflow of £100,000 would be required (the cost of advertising) which would produce a net cash inflow after one year of £255,000. Agents' commission amounting to £157,500 would have to be paid at the end of two years.

Alternative 2 would involve a lower outlay on advertising (£50,000, payable immediately) and no use of agents. It would produce a net cash inflow of zero after one year and £42,000 at the end of each of the subsequent two years.

Mr Court, a director of Khan Ltd, comments 'I generally favour the payback method for choosing between investment alternatives such as these. However, I am worried that the advertising expenditure under the second alternative will reduce our reported profit next year by an amount not compensated by any net revenues from sale of the product in that year. For that reason I do not think we should even consider the second alternative'.

The cost of capital of Khan Ltd is 20% per annum. The directors do not expect capital or any other resource to be in short supply during the next three years.

You are required:

(a)   to calculate the net present values and estimate the internal rates of return of the two methods of promoting the new product;   **(10 marks)**

(b)   to advise the directors of Khan Ltd which, if either, method of promotion they should adopt, explaining the reasons for your advice and noting any additional information you think would be helpful in making the decision; and   **(8 marks)**

(c)   to comment on the views expressed by Mr Court.   **(7 marks)**
(Total: 25 marks)

5.2 Atlas plc

Atlas plc supports the concept of terotechnology or life cycle costing for new investment decisions covering its engineering activities. The financial side of this philosophy is now well established and its principles extended to all other areas of decision making.

The company is to replace a number of its machines and the Production Manager is torn between the Exe machine, a more expensive machine with a life of 12 years, and the Wye machine with an estimated life of 6 years. If the Wye machine is chosen it is likely that it would be replaced at the end of 6 years by another Wye machine. The pattern of maintenance and running costs differs between the two types of machine and relevant data are shown below.

		Exe £		Wye £
Purchase price		19,000		13,000
Trade-in value		3,000		3,000
Annual repair costs		2,000		2,600
Overhaul costs	(at year 8)	4,000	(at year 4)	2,000

	Estimated financing costs averaged over machine life	10% pa	10% pa

You are required:

(a)   to recommend, with supporting figures, which machine to purchase, stating any assumptions made;   **(10 marks)**

(b)   to describe an appropriate method of comparing replacement proposals with unequal lives.
                                                                                              (4 marks)
                                                                                 (Total: 14 marks)

6   ANSWERS TO EXAMINATION TYPE QUESTIONS

6.1   Khan Ltd

(a)   NPV calculations and IRR estimation

Note: two substantial reversals of cash flow are involved in Project 1 and it is therefore sensible to check for multiple solutions to the IRR using trial and error.

Alternative 1

			At 20%
Time	*Cash flow* £	*Discount factor*	*Present value* £
0	(100,000)	1.000	(100,000)
1	255,000	0.833	212,415
2	(157,500)	0.694	(109,305)
	£(2,500)	NPV	£3,110

Alternative 2

			At 20%
Time	*Cash flow* £	*Discount factor*	*Present value* £
0	(50,000)	1.000	(50,000)
1	-	0.833	-
2	42,000	0.694	29,148
3	42,000	0.579	24,318
	£34,000		£3,466

Alternative 1

		At 20%		*5%*	
Time	*Cash flow in/out* £	*Discount factor*	*PV of cash flow* £	*Discount factor*	*PV of cash flow* £
0	(100,000)	1.000	(100,000)	1.00	(100,000)
1	255,000	0.833	212,415	1/1.05	242,857*
2	(157,500)	0.694	(109,305)	$1/(1.05)^2$	(142,857)*
	£(2,500)	NPV	£3,110	NPV	£0

Time	Cash flow in/out £	At 30% Discount factor	PV of cash flow £	50% Discount factor	PV of cash flow £
0	(100,000)	1.00	(100,000)	1.00	(100,000)
1	255,000	1/1.3	196,154	1/1.5	170,000
2	(157,500)	$1/(1.3)^2$	(93,195)	$1/(1.5)^2$	(70,000)
	£(2,500)	NPV	£2,959	NPV	£0

Note: discount factors have not been used at 5% as these lead to a rounding error. You should still be able to draw similar conclusions even if discount tables were employed.

Graph of NPV v cost of capital

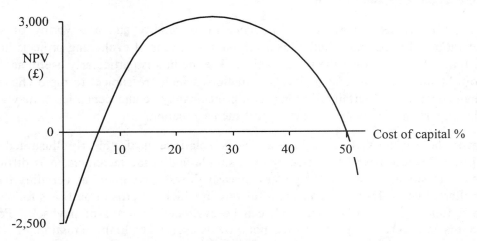

It can be seen from the table and the graph that there are two internal rates of return, 5% and 50%. At any cost of capital between these two limits, this alternative has a positive value.

Alternative 2

Time	Cash flow £	PV at 20% £	At 25% Discount factor	Present value £
0	(50,000)	(50,000)	1.00	(50,000)
1	-	-	0.80	-
2	42,000	29,148	0.64	26,880
3	42,000	24,318	0.51	21,420
	£34,000	£3,466		£(1,700)

∴ IRR is between 20% and 25%. Interpolating between 20% and 25%:

$$IRR = 20\% + \left(\frac{3,466}{1,700 + 3,466} \times 5\% \right)$$

$$\simeq 23.3\%$$

Summary of results

	Alternative 1	Alternative 2
NPV at 20%	£3,110	£3,466
IRR (approx.)	5%, 50%	23.3%

(b)   **Advice to the directors of Khan Ltd**

The two projects, although relating to the same product, have totally different cash flow patterns. It is difficult to see why this should be so. In particular, why does heavy promotion result in no sales in years 2 and 3? Further information would be helpful.

The choice between the two projects should be made on the basis of the net present value. A comparison of internal rates of return is not a valid basis for a decision. This is because the internal rate of return measures only the relative, not absolute, scale of cash flows.

In business decisions it is the absolute size of the surplus, indicated by the net present value, which is important. This is consistent with shareholder wealth maximisation.

(c)   **Comments on Mr Court's views**

The views expressed by Mr Court do have some validity and are worthy of serious consideration. The payback method is a very simple means of evaluating projects in terms of the time taken to recover the initial outlay. The method is particularly useful as a quick way of obtaining a view of a project in situations which are subject to rapid change and where the degree of uncertainty in long-term projects may be unacceptable. It may well be that the importing of novelty products is just such a situation.

However, the weakness of payback, as a serious technique, is also clearly illustrated by the examples. Because payback is essentially a simple and crude technique, it is difficult to employ it in situations where the pattern of cash flows is complex, as certainly happens under alternative 1. There is no meaningful way in which patterns of outflows followed by receipts, followed by further outflows, can be evaluated in terms of payback. For this reason it is considered the payback does not provide useful data in this situation.

The second point made by Mr Court concerns the effect of the projects on reported profits. Though this is unrelated to his other point about the payback and does indicate some muddled thinking, nevertheless it is a point that management should consider. It is a major weakness of net present value that it provides only a single measure of a project. No account is taken of the pattern of cash flows and their effect on reported profits over the life of the project. Yet such data is of major concern to a company, both because of the effect on shareholders, on the company's ability to raise finance in the market, and the company's ability to finance its operations.

(Tutorial note: the analysis based on net present values relies upon the model of investor behaviour known as the dividend valuation model. The core of this model is that share prices are totally determined by anticipated future dividends. Furthermore, it assumes that the objective of the company should be to maximise the wealth of the equity investors, reflected in the value of their shares. Under this model it is logical to select projects which have the maximum NPV.

In an efficient capital market share prices should rise to reflect the NPV of the project. However, in practice, investors do not have access to full information about the company's expectations, nor would they necessarily believe them if they were given such access. The empirical evidence is that short term share prices are most heavily influenced by the current level of dividends. However, reported profits are obviously a factor of considerable importance, both in their own right and because they directly influence the level of dividends. If the company were to accept projects which had an adverse short-term impact on profits or dividends, it is likely that this would have more effect on share prices than any estimated long-term surplus. Therefore, in making its selection of projects the company should have a view, not only to their net present value, but also to their effect on the pattern of profits and the company's ability to pay dividends.   This is particularly true if the managers of the firm feel they are being judged on short term profitability which is typically the case in traditional budgeting systems.*)*

In addition, there is the company's continuing need to finance its operations.   Again, it may well be that projects which are attractive in terms of net present value give rise to financing requirements which the company cannot meet.   Furthermore, the company's ability to raise external finance will be hampered by any adverse pattern of reported profits.

Finally there is the uncertainty inherent in each of the two projects.   No data is available. However, introducing a new product into a market which is very much subject to fashion and crazes must involve a high degree of uncertainty.   The evaluation should be extended to consider the probability distribution of both the cost and revenue items, and their correlation to the returns from other activities of the business.

It is concluded that while Mr Court's views are expressed in naive terms, they nevertheless contain substantial elements of truth which should properly be considered in the evaluation.

6.2   Atlas plc

(a)   Discount over life of machine
Exe - 12 years.

Item	Year	Cash £	DF	PV £
Purchase	0	19,000	1.000	19,000
Overhaul	8	4,000	0.467	1,868
Trade-in	12	(3,000)	0.319	(957)
Annual repair	1-12	2,000	6.814	13,628
				33,539

Divide by annuity factor (12 years, 10%) to obtain annualised equivalent.

Annualised equivalent = £33,539/6.814
                      = £4,922

Wye - 6 years

Item	Year	Cash £	DF	PV £
Purchase	0	13,000	1.000	13,000
Overhaul	4	2,000	0.683	1,366
Trade-in	6	(3,000)	0.564	(1,692)
Annual repair	1 - 6	2,600	4.355	11,323
				23,997

Annualised equivalent = £23,997/4.355 = £5,510

The company should purchase the Exe machine as it has the lowest annualised equivalent cost.

Assumptions.

(1)   Cash flows occur at the year end.
(2)   The cashflow estimates for each machine have the same level of accuracy.
(3)   Inflation has been ignored
(4)   Both machines have the same level of reliability and both perform to at least the standards required for the job.

(b)   The method used in part (a) to compare two machines with unequal lives is to use the annualised equivalent method.

The steps are:

(a)   Determine the net present value taking into account all the relevant cashflows over the lifetime of the machines.

(b)   Divide each net present value by the annuity factor based on the cost of capital and the expected lifetime of the machine. This gives the annualised equivalent.

(c)   Select the machine with the lowest annualised cost.

(c)   Life cycle costing (also known as Terotechnology) is applying a combination of management, engineering, financial and other practices to physical assets in pursuit of economic life cycle costs. It is concerned with determining the most economical approach taking into account the total cost over the life time of the asset being considered. The costs should include not only the acquisition costs but also the operating costs over the full period and the disposal cost.

Examples of life cycle costing:

(a)   Replacement: deciding when to replace an existing asset.

Deciding between a number of alternative possibilities when replacing an asset taking into account different initial costs, different lifetimes, different levels of reliability.

(b)   Purchase of an asset from a choice of possibilities (a variation of (a) eg, buying a car).

(c)   Product design: increase manufacturing costs to improve reliability and quality and hence be able to sell at a higher price. There may be changes which are more difficult to quantify eg, benefits and disadvantages of moving upmarket.

29 PROJECT APPRAISAL ALLOWING FOR INFLATION AND TAXATION

INTRODUCTION & LEARNING OBJECTIVES

In this chapter we extend the analysis of projects to include the effects of inflation and taxation.

When you have studied this chapter you should be able to do the following:

- Understand the difference between real cash flows and money cash flows

- Be able to discount cash flows that are affected by inflation by either discounting the money cash flows at the money cost of capital, or real cash flows at the real cost of capital

- Adjust cash flows for the effect of taxation

---

1 INFLATION AND UNCERTAINTY

1.1 Definition of inflation

For the purpose of this subject, inflation may be defined as **a general increase in prices**, or **a general decline in the real value of money**.

Inflation generally alters the cashflows in projects. In general, the effects are the following.

(a) Revenues increase;
(b) Costs increase;
(c) Interest and debt liabilities may well increase.

In a period of increasing inflation lenders will require an increasing return. Interest rates typically comprise two components, a **real** underlying interest rate, and an allowance for inflation.

1.2 Example

An investor lends £100 now, for repayment in one year of the principal, plus £15.50 interest. During the intervening year a rate of inflation of 5% is expected.

Analyse the interest charge between real interest and the allowance for inflation.

Solution

The investor has £100 now. In order to maintain the purchasing power of the money £100 + 5% will be needed in one year ie, £105.

To the investor:

£105 purchases the same quantity of goods in one year's time as £100 now.

£115.5 therefore purchases the equivalent of $\frac{£115.5}{£105} \times £100$, or £110 now.

The investor has therefore experienced a 10% return in **real** terms (ie, in terms of the quantity of product that can be purchased).

Put another way, the real interest is

£115.5 − £105 = £10.5

Expressed as a percentage this is

$$\frac{£10.5}{£105} \times 100 = 10\%$$

Thus:

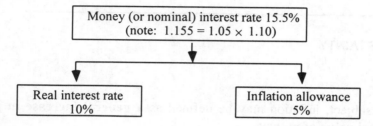

From this example you should note two key concepts.

(a)   Money interest rates and cashflows include the effect of inflation.

       Real interest rates and cashflows exclude the effect of inflation.

(b)   Analysis can take place in either money or real terms, as long as the two are not muddled.

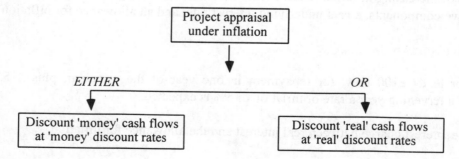

It is further worthy of note that you may obtain real rates of return using:

$$(1 + r) \quad = \quad \frac{(1 + m)}{(1 + i)};$$

where r, m, and i are the real, money, and inflation rates, respectively. In the last example:

$$(1 + r) \quad = \quad \frac{(1 + 0.155)}{(1 + 0.05)} \quad = \quad 1.1, \quad \text{giving the real rate of return as 10\%.}$$

1.3   Activity

Consider the level of interest rates current at the time that you are reading this. How much of the money interest rate is the real interest rate and how much the effects of inflation?

1.4   Activity solution

For example, when this paragraph was written, the gross yield on long gilts was 8.18% (on 2½ % Consols) while inflation was 1.90% pa.

m = money rate of interest = 8.18%
i = inflation rate = 1.90%

∴ real rate of interest, r, is given by

$$1 + r = \frac{1+m}{1+i} = \frac{1.0818}{1.0190} = 1.0616$$

The real rate of interest is 6.16% pa.

1.5   Example

A project has the following cashflows before allowing for inflation:

Year	Cashflow £
0	(750)
1	330
2	242
3	532

These are not, therefore, the flows expected if all figures grow in line with inflation.

The discount rate has been calculated to include an allowance for inflation at 15.5%. The rate of inflation is expected to remain constant at 5%.

You are required to evaluate the project in terms of

(a)   real cashflows and discount rates;
(b)   money cashflows and discount rates.

Solution

(a)   **Real discount rates and cashflows**

Discount rate as per the question of 15.5% includes investor's/lender's inflation expectation of 5%.

Hence 'real' discount rate, r, is given by

$$1 + r = \frac{1+m}{1+i}$$

where m =   money interest rate
            i =   rate of inflation

Substituting

$$1 + r = \frac{1 + 0.155}{1 + 0.05} = 1.10$$

and   r is once again 0.10 or 10%

Discounting the cashflows as per the question:

Year	Cashflow £	PV factor @ 10%	Present value £
0	(750)	1.000	(750)
1	330	0.909	300
2	242	0.826	200
3	532	0.751	400
Net present value			150

(b)   Money discount rates and cashflows

The discount rate as per the question of 15.5% is the money discount rate. Cashflows, however, need to be increased by 5% compound each year from year 0, to allow for inflation.

Year (i)	Real cash flow (ii) £	Inflation factor (iii)	Money* cash flow (iv) = (ii) × (iii) £	Discount factor @ 15.5%	Present value
0	(750)	1	(750)	1.000	(750)
1	330	1 + 0.05	346	0.866	300
2	242	$(1 + 0.05)^2$	267	0.750	200
3	532	$(1 + 0.05)^3$	616	0.649	400
Net present value					150

Conclusion It is concluded that, provided a constant rate of inflation applies to all factors, either approach yields identical conclusions (allowing for rounding). When appraising a project, either discount actual (money) cashflows using actual (money) discount rates, or real cashflows using real discount rates.

1.6   Varying impact of inflation on costs and revenues

In practice, inflation does not affect all costs to the same extent. Some may increase at above and some below the 'average' rate of inflation. Clearly, in relation to a given project, such variations are important and must be taken into account. This is much more easily dealt with by using money cashflows and discount rates.

Example

A company is considering a cost-saving project. This involves purchasing a machine costing £7,000, which will result in annual savings on wage costs of £1,000, and on material costs of £400.

The following forecasts are made of the rates of inflation each year for the next five years.

Wage costs	10%
Material costs	5%
General prices	6%

The cost of capital of the company, in money terms, is 15%.

Evaluate the project, assuming that the machine has a life of five years and no scrap value.

Solution

The first stage is to calculate money cash savings each year.

Year	Labour cash savings			Material cash savings			Total savings
	£		£	£		£	£
1	$1,000 \times 1.1$	=	1,100	400×1.05	=	420	1,520
2	$1,000 \times (1.1)^2$	=	1,210	$400 \times (1.05)^2$	=	441	1,651
3	$1,000 \times (1.1)^3$	=	1,331	$400 \times (1.05)^3$	=	463	1,794
4	$1,000 \times (1.1)^4$	=	1,464	$400 \times (1.05)^4$	=	486	1,950
5	$1,000 \times (1.1)^5$	=	1,610	$400 \times (1.05)^5$	=	510	2,120

Net present value evaluation:

Year	Cashflow	PV factor @ 15%	PV of cashflow
	£		£
0	(7,000)	1.000	(7,000)
1	1,520	0.870	1,322
2	1,651	0.756	1,248
3	1,794	0.658	1,180
4	1,950	0.572	1,115
5	2,120	0.497	1,054

Net present value (1,081)

Therefore the project is not worthwhile.

Note: the general rate of inflation has not been used in, and is irrelevant to, this calculation.

2 TAXATION

2.1 The effect of taxation

Taxation has two major effects.

Firstly, project cashflows will give rise to taxation which itself has an impact on project appraisal. There will be natural differences between the cashflows earned and the level of profits on which the payment of taxation is based, particularly as regards capital expenditure, but in general cash receipts will give rise to tax payable and **vice versa**.

Secondly, the relief on interest payments will reduce the effective rate of interest which a firm pays on its borrowings, and hence the opportunity cost of capital.

2.2   Net-of-tax cashflows from projects

The effects of taxation are complex, and are influenced by a number of factors including the following.

(a)   The taxable profits and tax rate;
(b)   The company's accounting period; and tax payment dates;
(c)   Amounts paid as Advance Corporation Tax (ACT);
(d)   Capital allowances;
(e)   Losses available for set-off.

Unless information is given to the contrary, the following assumptions should be adopted in the examination.

(a)   Taxable profits are the net project cashflows, and the current tax rate applies;

(b)   Tax cashflows occur with a one year delay on the underlying project cashflows on which they are based ie, the pay date is 12 months after the cashflows arise;

(c)   Ignore Advance Corporation Tax;

(d)   Where a tax loss arises from the project, there are sufficient taxable profits elsewhere in the organisation to allow the loss to reduce any relevant (subsequent) tax payment (and thus may be treated as a cash inflow);

(e)   The first capital allowance claim is immediate, with the first benefit one year later. The company is also assumed to have sufficient taxable profits to obtain full benefit from capital allowances, and there are balancing adjustments on the disposal of all assets.

Whenever tax is relevant to an appraisal, careful reading of the question and stating of any assumptions is essential.

Example

KL Ltd is considering manufacturing a new product. This requires machinery costing £20,000, with a life of four years and a terminal value of £5,000. Profits before depreciation from the project will be £8,000 pa. However, there will be cashflows which will differ from profits by the build-up of working capital during the first year of operations and its run-down during the fourth year, amounting to £2,000.

Tax allowances on the machine are 25% pa reducing balance. At the end of the project's life a balancing charge or allowance will arise equal to the difference between the scrap proceeds and the tax written down value.

Tax is payable one year after the end of the accounting year in which it is based, at a rate of 35%. The start of the project is also the start of the accounting year.

The cost of capital is 15%.

Should the project be accepted?

Solution

Project appraisal

Year	Profit	Working capital	Machine	Tax	Net cash flow	PV factor at 15%	Present value
	£	£	£	£	£		£
0	-	-	(20,000)	-	(20,000)	1.000	(20,000)
1	8,000	(2,000)	-	1,750	7,750	0.870	6,743
2	8,000	–	-	(1,488)	6,512	0.756	4,923
3	8,000	–	-	(1,815)	6,185	0.658	4,070
4	8,000	2,000	5,000	(2,062)	12,938	0.572	7,401
5	-	-	-	(2,335)	(2,335)	0.497	(1,160)

Net present value   1,977

It is therefore concluded that the project is worthwhile.

Working

Year	Profit	Capital allowances and balancing allowance	Tax payable on	Tax at 35%
	£	£	£	£
0	-	5,000	(5,000)	-
1	8,000	3,750	4,250	(1,750)
2	8,000	2,813	5,187	1,488
3	8,000	2,109	5,891	1,815
4	8,000	1,328 **	6,672	2,062
5	-	-	-	2,335

** Balancing allowance = (20,000 – (5,000 + 3,750 + 2,813 + 2,109)) – 5,000 = £1,328

Note: the examination convention is that of making the first capital allowance claim **at** year 0, with first benefit thereby at year 1.

3   SELF TEST QUESTIONS

3.1   What is the general impact of inflation on evaluation of a capital project? (1.2)

3.2   Distinguish between real cashflows and money cashflows. (1.2)

3.3   What are the two major effects of taxation on a capital project? (2.1)

4   EXAMINATION TYPE QUESTION

4.1   AB plc

AB plc is considering a new product with a three-year life. The product can be made with existing machinery, which has spare capacity, or by a labour-saving specialised new machine which would have zero disposal value at the end of three years.

The following estimates have been made at current prices:

Sales volume	1 million units per annum
Selling price	£15 per unit
Labour cost (without m/c)	£6 per unit
Material cost	£2 per unit
Variable overheads	£2 per unit

Additional fixed overheads for the new product are estimated to be £3 million per year.

The new machine would cost £5 million now and would halve the labour cost per unit.

Because of competition, selling price increases will be limited to 2% per annum although labour cost is expected to rise at 12% per annum and all other costs at 8% per annum.

The company's money cost of capital is 15% and, apart from the cost of the new machine, all other cash flows can be assumed to arise at year ends.

You are required:

(a)   to calculate the NPV of the new product assuming that manufacture uses existing machinery;   **(7 marks)**

(b)   to calculate the NPV assuming that the new machine is purchased;   **(7 marks)**

(c)   to recommend what action should be taken, and to comment on your recommendation;   **(5 marks)**

(d)   to explain what changes, if any, there would be in your analysis if the existing machinery was already fully utilised on other production.   **(3 marks)**
                                                                      (Total: 22 marks)

5   ANSWER TO EXAMINATION TYPE QUESTION

5.1   AB plc

(Tutorial note: with a product with a three-year life and inflation rates that don't link conveniently to the money cost of capital, the approach to this question is to produce a table showing the cash flows at time 0, 1, 2 and 3. You may wish to state an assumption about the point when cashflows are first subject to inflation. It is worth limiting your calculations to the nearest £'000 to save time. Plan ahead, since many of the calculations for (a) are also needed for (b).)

(a)   **NPV With Existing Machine**

Time	0	1	2	3
	£m	£m	£m	£m
Revenue	-	15.30	15.606	15.918
Labour cost	-	(6.72)	(7.526)	(8.430)
Materials and overheads	-	(7.56)	(8.165)	(8.818)
Net cash flow	-	1.02	(0.085)	(1.330)
15% discount factors	-	0.870	0.756	0.658
Present value	-	0.887	(0.064)	(0.875)

NPV = (£52,000)

(b)   **NPV With New Machine**

Time	0	1	2	3
	£m	£m	£m	£m
Net cash flow from (a)	-	1.02	(0.085)	(1.330)
Labour saving	-	3.36	3.763	4.215
Machine	(5.0)	-	-	-
Net cash flow	(5.0)	4.38	3.678	2.885
15% discount factors	1.0	0.870	0.756	0.658
Present value	(5.0)	3.811	2.781	1.898

NPV = £3,490,000

(c)   **Recommendation and comment**

(Tutorial note: there are one or two general comments to make that would apply to all investment appraisal calculations but for the rest you need to think practically about the problem.*)*

With a positive NPV of £3.49m, the firm should buy the new machine to develop the products.

- Reliability of estimates - Using the new machine appears a very safe project but it would be worth checking on how accurate each estimate is felt to be.

- Hidden costs of new machine - The suppliers of the new machine have made substantial claims, it is worth obtaining guarantees of its performance and considering whether other costs such as maintenance and higher running costs will be incurred.

- Installation costs - No mention has been made of these including delivery, lost production and possibly extra factory space.

- Alternative machinery - Do these exist? If the product is risky, a cheaper machine providing lower savings might prove to be a preferable option.

- Effect on other costs - Is there any possible saving of variable overheads of the labour saving and what is the effect on materials cost of using the new machine?

- True labour savings - Although labour cost per unit will fall, will the firm be able to lay off staff and thereby save costs; will there be any redundancy costs?

(d)   **Existing Machinery Fully Utilised**

The decision has been made to use the new machine therefore this additional complication **does not affect the decision**.

The analysis in (a) would have to be adjusted to take into account the **opportunity cost of lost production** (lost contribution) if the existing machine was used for this new product.

30 PROJECT APPRAISAL UNDER RISK

INTRODUCTION & LEARNING OBJECTIVES

When you have studied this chapter you should be able to do the following:

- Be able to apply sensitivity analysis to help identify risk.
- Be able to calculate expected values.
- Make decisions using decision trees and expected values.
- Use simulation to allow for uncertainty in projects.

---

1 NATURE OF RISK

1.1 The problem

(a) all decisions are based on forecasts
(b) all forecasts are subject to varying degrees of uncertainty
(c) how can uncertainty be reflected in a financial evaluation?

Some authorities draw a distinction between risk and uncertainty:

Definition **Risk** - probabilities are attached to possible outcomes, giving an expected outcome that can be calculated mathematically.

Definition **Uncertainty** - the future outcome cannot be predicted mathematically from available data.

Thus, risk is quantifiable, whilst uncertainty is not.

Although there is a clear distinction between these two problems, in practice the words risk and uncertainty are used interchangeably.

The risk situation is best handled by probability distributions. The vast bulk of the literature is concerned with this problem.

2 SENSITIVITY ANALYSIS

2.1 Introduction

The major problem with any capital investment decision is that the figure reached in any calculation (a positive or negative NPV) is only as reliable as the estimates used to produce that figure. One only has to look at the revisions made to estimates of large capital sums in major investment programmes such as the Channel Tunnel between Folkestone and Calais or road or rail investment to see how unreliable some of these estimates can be. Estimating the long term benefits presents even greater problems.

One way of providing useful supplementary information for an investment decision is to consider a range of figures for various estimates and establish whether these give positive or negative NPV's. With the increased use of spreadsheet packages, this exercise is easy to perform, sometimes being referred to as posing 'What if?' questions; however, it is important to be able to determine what variations in estimates are reasonable and what are unlikely. This analysis is usually applied to one estimate at a time although it can be applied to each estimate simultaneously.

A more concise form of analysis takes each estimate in turn and assesses the percentage change required to change an investment decision. It is customary to apply it to single estimates although, if any relationship between variables is known, it can be applied to groups of figures. It is this form of sensitivity analysis that is considered here.

2.2   Illustration

Bacher Ltd is considering investing £500,000 in equipment to produce a new type of ball. Sales of the product are expected to continue for three years at the end of which the equipment will have a scrap value of £80,000. Sales revenue of £600,000 per annum will be generated at a variable cost of £350,000. Annual fixed costs will increase by £40,000.

You are required:

(a)   to determine whether, on the basis of the estimates given, the project should be undertaken assuming that all cash flows occur at annual intervals and that Bacher Ltd has a cost of capital of 15%; and

(b)   to find the percentage changes required in the following estimates for the investment decision to change:

(i)   initial investment;
(ii)   scrap value;
(iii)   selling price;
(iv)   sales volume;
(v)   cost of capital.

Solution

Although part (a) could be completed most efficiently by finding net annual inflows (£600,000 − £350,000 − £40,000) of £210,000, part (b) would be most effectively negotiated if the separate present values were found.

(a)   **NPV calculation**

Time		Cash flow £'000	15% Discount factor	Present value £'000
0	Equipment	(500)	1	(500)
1 - 3	Revenue	600		1,370
1 - 3	Variable costs	(350)	2.283	(799)
1 - 3	Fixed costs	(40)		(91)
3	Scrap value	80	0.658	53

Net present value (£'000)   33

The project should, on the basis of these estimates, be accepted.

(b)   **Sensitivity analysis**

    (i)   Initial investment

For the decision to change, the NPV must fall by £33,000. For this to occur the cost of the equipment must rise by £33,000. This is a rise of:

$$\frac{33}{500} \times 100 \quad = \quad \textbf{6.6\%}$$

    (ii)   Scrap value

If the NPV is to fall by £33,000, the present value of scrap proceeds must fall by £33,000. The PV of scrap proceeds is currently £53,000; it must fall by:

$$\frac{33}{53} \times 100 \quad = \quad 62.26\%, \text{ say } \textbf{62\%}$$

(This would bring the scrap proceeds down by 62.26% to £30,192; the PV of the scrap proceeds would be £19,866 ie, just over £33,000 less than in (a). There are some slight differences from rounding due to the use of 3 decimal place discount factors.)

    Conclusion   To find the percentage change required in an estimate to change an investment decision, find:

$$\frac{\text{NPV of project}}{\text{PV of those figures that vary with estimate concerned}}$$

    (iii)   Sales price

If sales price varies, sales revenue will vary (assuming no effect on demand). If the NPV of the project is to fall by £33,000, the selling price must fall by:

$$\frac{33}{1,370} \times 100 \quad = \quad 2.4\%$$

    (iv)   Sales volume

If sales volume falls revenue and variable costs fall (contribution falls); if the NPV is to fall by £33,000, volume must fall by:

$$\frac{33}{(1,370-799)} \times 100 \quad = \quad 5.8\%$$

    (v)   Cost of capital

If NPV is to fall, cost of capital must rise; the figure to which the cost of capital has to rise, that gives an NPV of zero, is the project's IRR. To find the IRR, which is probably not much above 15%, the NPV at 17% can be found using the summarised cash flows.

$$\text{NPV (£'000)} \quad = \quad -500 + [210 \times 2.210] + [80 \times 0.624]$$
$$= \quad 14$$

The IRR is a little more than 17%, possibly 18%, but the formula (based on similar triangles) can be used.

$$\text{IRR} \approx A + \left(\frac{N_A}{N_A - N_B}\right)(B - A) \approx 15 + \left(\frac{33}{33 - 14}\right) \times (17 - 15)$$

$$\approx 18.47\%, \text{ say } \mathbf{18\frac{1}{2}\%}$$

The cost of capital would have to increase from 15% to 18½% before the investment decision changes.

2.3   Activity

Using the data in the previous example about Bacher's new equipment, estimate the percentage changes in unit variable cost and annual fixed cost needed to change the investment decision.

2.4   Activity solution

(a)   **Change in unit variable cost**

The project's NPV must fall by £33,000 therefore the PV of the variable costs must rise by £33,000. Since the PV of variable costs is £799,000, a rise of £33,000 is an increase of:

$$\frac{33}{799} \times 100 \quad = \quad \mathbf{4.1\%}$$

(b)   **Change in annual fixed costs**

The percentage increase in annual fixed costs required

$$= \quad \frac{\text{NPV of project}}{\text{PV of annual fixed costs}} \times 100$$

$$= \quad \frac{33}{91} \times 100 \quad = \quad \mathbf{36\%}$$

2.5   Strengths and weaknesses of sensitivity analysis

Strengths

(a)   No complicated theory to understand.

(b)   Information will be presented to management in a form which facilitates subjective judgement to decide the likelihood of the various possible outcomes considered.

(c)   Identifies areas which are crucial to the success of the project; if it is proceeded with, those areas can be carefully monitored.

(d)   Indicates just how critical are some of the forecasts which are considered to be uncertain.

Weaknesses

(a)   It assumes that changes to variables can be made independently eg, material prices will change independently of other variables. This is unlikely. If material prices went up the firm would probably increase selling price at the same time and there would be little effect on NPV. A technique called simulation (see later) allows us to change more than one variable at a time.

(b)   It only identifies how far a variable needs to change, it does not look at the probability of such a change. In the above analysis sales volume appears to be the most crucial variable, but if the firm were facing volatile raw material markets a 65% change in raw material prices would be far more likely than a 29% change in sales volume.

(c)   It is not an optimising technique. It provides information on the basis of which decisions can be made. It does not point to the correct decision directly.

3   EXPECTED VALUES AND PROBABILITY DISTRIBUTIONS

3.1   Revision of expected values

When considering an investment decision it may be possible to make several predictions about alternative future outcomes and to assign probabilities to them.

For example, cash flows from a new restaurant venture may depend on whether a competitor decides to open up the same area. We make the following estimates:

Competitor opens up	Probability	Project NPV £
Yes	0.3	(10,000)
No	0.7	20,000

The expected net present value of this venture is $(0.3 \times -10,000) + (0.7 \times 20,000) = £11,000$

The simple decision rule using expected values is to say:

Accept projects with a positive expected NPV. When choosing between projects accept those projects with the highest expected NPVs.

The *expected value* is, however, simply the *arithmetic mean* of a probability distribution. It does not necessarily represent what the outcome will be, nor does it represent the *most likely* result (that is £20,000).

What it really represents is the average pay-off per occasion if the project were repeated many times (ie, a 'long-run' average).

There are two main problems with using expected values in this way:

(a)   The project will only be carried out once. It could result in a sizeable loss and there may be no second chance to win our money back.

(b)   The probabilities used are simply subjective estimates of our belief, on a scale from 0 to 1. There is probably little data on which to base these estimates.

These problems must be faced, and are discussed in detail in the following sections. However, it is first necessary to revise the use of expected values and decision trees in a project appraisal situation.

3.2   Decision matrix example

Hofgarten Newsagents stocks a weekly magazine which advertises local second-hand goods. Marie, the owner, can buy the magazines for 15p each and sell them at the retail price of 25p. At the end of each week unsold magazines are obsolete and have no value.

Like most newsagents, Marie sits down and estimates a probability distribution for weekly demand, which looks like this:

Weekly demand in units	Probability
10	0.20
15	0.55
20	0.25
	———
	1.00
	———

If Marie is to order a fixed quantity of magazines per week how many should that be? Assume no seasonal variations in demand.

3.3   Solution

The first step is to set up a decision matrix of possible courses of action (numbers ordered) and possible demand levels, as follows:

Probability	Outcome (No. demanded)	Strategy (No. bought) 10	15	20
0.20	10			
0.55	15			
0.25	20			

The 'payoff' from each combination of action and outcome is then computed.

No sale   →   loss of 15p per magazine.

Sale   →   profit of 25p – 15p = 10p per magazine.

Payoffs in pence are shown for each combination of action and outcome.

Probability	Outcome (No. demanded)	Payoff (No. bought) 10 P	15 P	20 P
0.20	10	100 (W(i))	25 (W(ii))	(50)
0.55	15	100	150	75
0.25	20	100	150	200

WORKINGS

(i)   If 10 magazines are bought, then 10 are sold no matter how many are demanded and the payoffs is always $10 \times 10p = 100p$.

(ii)   If 15 magazines are bought and 10 are demanded, then 10 are sold at a profit of $10 \times 10p = 100p$, and 5 are scrapped at a loss of $5 \times 15p = 75p$, making a net profit of 25p.

(iii)   The other contributions are similarly calculated.

Probabilities are then applied to compute the expected value resulting from each possible course of action.

In the same matrix, probability × payoff can be inserted in each cell and totalled to give the expected payoff.

Probability	Outcome	Payoff (No. bought)		
	(No. demanded)	10	15	20
		P	P	P
0.20	10	20	5.00	(10.00)
0.55	15	55	82.50	41.25
0.25	20	25	37.50	50.00
1.00	EV	100	125.00	81.25

The expected values are listed on the bottom line, in pence. From this it can be seen that the strategy which gives the highest expected payoff is to *stock 15 magazines each week.*

What does this expected value mean? It means that if the strategy is followed for many weeks, then on average the profit will be 125p per week. What actually happens is that eight weeks out of ten the payoff is likely to be 150p and two weeks out of ten it drops to 25p. This strategy produces the highest long-run profit for the firm.

The expected value technique is ideally suited to this sort of problem which is repetitive and involves only small outlays of money.

4   DECISION TREES EXAMPLE

4.1   Introduction

Decision trees represent combinations of actions and outcomes in diagrammatic form. They are particularly useful if a succession of decisions has to be made.

The symbols used are as follows:

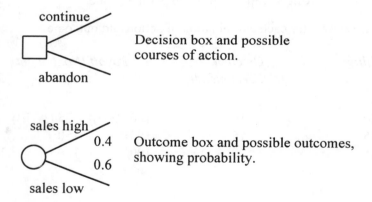

Putting the symbols together produces a tree, as follows:

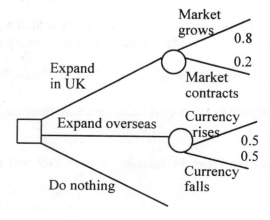

4.2   Example

Equitone plc is considering spending £400,000 on a two year research and development project in the development of a new product, code named Belladonna. It is estimated that there is a 50% chance of development success by the end of this two year period. Development success indicates that the product could be marketed from the end of year two, and it is estimated that it would have a six year life span. It is not known how the market would react to Belladonna, but the following estimates of present value of contributions are made:

Sales	Probability	PV of contribution £'000
High	0.2	1,600
Medium	0.5	800
Low	0.3	400

Development failure by the end of year 2 would not necessarily indicate the end of the project. It would be possible to invest a further £200,000 at that stage to finance a further two years of development. The probability that this would succeed is estimated at 0.3. If the later development succeeded, it might still be worthwhile introducing the product onto the market late, giving it a life span of four years, and estimated present values of contribution as follows:

Sales	Probability	PV of contribution £'000
High	0.1	1,200
Medium	0.5	600
Low	0.4	300

You are required to draw a decision tree to represent the above problem. Using the expected value technique, determine whether it is worthwhile starting the R and D project.

4.3   Solution

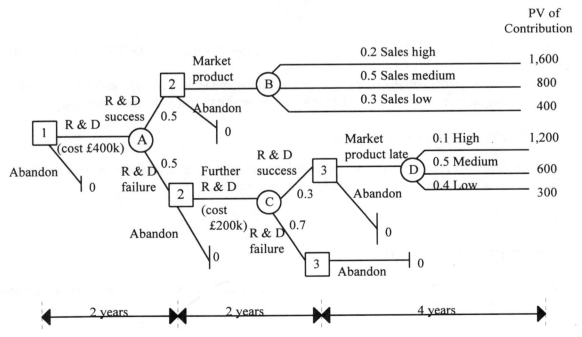

The solution using expected values is found by the 'roll-back' technique: start at the right hand side and roll back towards the left.

(a)   EV at outcome point B = (0.2 × 1,600) + (0.5 × 800) + (0.3 × 400) = £840k.

(b)   If initial R&D is a success, decision 2 should be to market (EV £840k) rather than abandon (EV £0).

(c)   EV at outcome point D = $(0.1 \times 1{,}200) + (0.5 \times 600) + (0.4 \times 300) = £540k$.

(d)   If substituting R&D is a success, decision 3 should be to market (EV £540k) rather than abandon.

(e)   EV at outcome point C is therefore $(0.3 \times 540) + (0.7 \times 0) = £162k$.

(f)   But this is the expected contribution before counting the cost of the second phase of research (£200k). The net expected value of proceeding to the second phase of research is therefore £-38k.

(g)   If initial R&D is a failure, decision 2 is therefore to abandon rather than incur further losses of £38k.

(h)   The summarised tree now looks like this:

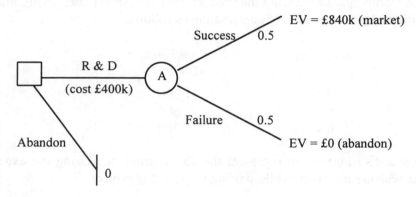

The EV at outcome point A   = $(0.5 \times 840) + (0.5 \times 0)$
                              =   £420k

(i)   The expected NPV of proceeding with the project is therefore £420k – £400k = £20k.

(j)   The sequence of decisions which should be made is (a) implement the ten-year R&D programme. If it succeeds then market the product. If it fails, then abandon.

4.4   Advantages and limitations of expected value

It is common for many examination questions to involve a discussion of the advantages and limitations of using the simple expected value decision rule.

These are now presented in summary form:

Advantages of expected values

(a)   Recognises that there are several possible outcomes and is, therefore, more sophisticated than single value forecasts.

(b)   Enables the probability of the different outcomes to be quantified.

(c)   Leads directly to a simple optimising decision rule.

(d)   Calculations are relatively simple.

Limitations of expected values

(a)   By asking for a series of forecasts the whole forecasting procedure is complicated. Inaccurate forecasting is already a major weakness in project evaluation. The probabilities used are also usually very subjective.

(b)   The expected value is merely a weighted average of the probability distribution, indicating the average pay-off if the project is repeated many times.

(c)   The expected value gives no indication of the dispersion of possible outcomes about the expected value. The more widely spread out the possible results are, the more risky the investment is usually seen to be. The expected value ignores this aspect of the probability distribution.

(d)   In ignoring risk, the expected value technique also ignores the investor's attitude to risk. Some investors are more likely to take risks than others.

Conclusions on expected values

The simple expected value decision rule is appropriate if three conditions are met or approximated to:

(a)   There is a reasonable basis for making the forecasts and estimating the probability of different outcomes.

(b)   The decision is relatively small in relation to the business. Risk is then small in magnitude.

(c)   The decision is of a category of decisions that is often repeated. A technique which maximises average pay-off is then valid.

5   SIMULATION AND INVESTMENT APPRAISAL

5.1   Introduction and design

Sensitivity analysis considered the effect of changing one variable at a time. Monte Carlo simulation allows us to consider the effect of all possible combinations of variables. Simulation involves the construction of a mathematical model to recreate, for example, a potential investment project. The model can include all random events that might affect the success or failure of such a project, like a competitor appearing, changes in consumer taste, changes in inflation or exchange rates etc. It is then possible to form a distribution of the possible cashflows from the project from which the probability of different outcomes can be calculated. This should result in better decisions than those based on the calculation of a single net present value or internal rate of return figure, because there are bound to be factors affecting the outcome which are beyond the company's control and will affect the cashflows used in the calculation.

The approach breaks down into three stages, and is greatly helped by the use of a computer.

Stage 1 - Specify major variables

Variables will differ between investment projects but typical examples are:

Market details

(a)   Market size;
(b)   selling price;
(c)   market growth rate;
(d)   market share.

Investment costs

(a)   Investment required;
(b)   residual value of investment.

Operating costs

(a)   Variable costs;
(b)   fixed costs;
(c)   taxation;
(d)   useful life of plant.

Stage 2 - Specify the relationships between variables to calculate a NPV

Sales revenue = market size × market share × selling price.

Net cashflow = sales revenue – (variable costs + fixed costs + taxation) etc.

Stage 3 - Simulate the environment

To conduct the simulation we need to attach a probability distribution to each variable. For example, the cost accountant may provide the following estimates of variable cost.

Variable cost per unit £	4.00	4.50	5.00
Probability	0.3	0.5	0.2

Random numbers are then assigned to represent the above probability distribution.

Variable cost per unit £	4.00	4.50	5.00
Probability	0.3	0.5	0.2
Random number range	00-29	30-79	80-99

If two digit random numbers are then generated the probability of occurrence of each range will reflect the underlying probability distribution.

Probability distributions and random number ranges are assigned to each variable. Care must be taken at this stage to allow for dependence between variables. For example, selling price and market share could clearly be related and it could be necessary to specify a probability distribution of market shares for each selling price.

Finally to simulate the project we need to:

(a)   draw a random number for each variable (note that most computers can generate random numbers);

(b)   select the value of each variable corresponding with the selected random number and compute an NPV;

(c)   repeat the process many times until we have a probability distribution of returns.

Results of simulation

The results of a simulation exercise will be a probability distribution of NPVs.

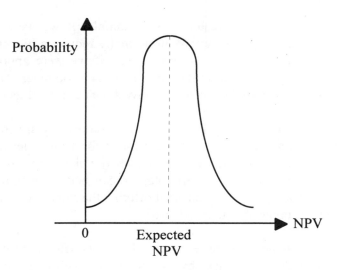

Instead of choosing between expected values, decision-makers can now take the dispersion of outcomes and the expected return into account.

5.2 Merits of simulation

The major advantages of simulation are that:

(a)   It includes all possible outcomes in the decision making process.

(b)   It is a relatively easily understood technique.

(c)   It has a wide variety of applications (stock control, component replacement, corporate models etc.)

However, it does have some significant drawbacks:

(a)   Models can become extremely complex, particularly where dependent probabilities are involved, and thus the time and costs involved in their construction can be more than is gained from the improved decisions.

(b)   Probability distributions may be difficult to formulate.

5.3 Reducing the risk of projects

Techniques for reducing the risk of projects include:

(a)   setting a minimum payback period;

(b)   increasing the discount rate subjectively in order to give the project a high 'hurdle' rate;

(c)   making prudent estimates of cash flows to assess the worst possible situation;

(d)   assessing both best and worst possible situations to obtain a range of NPVs; and

(e)   using sensitivity analysis to measure the 'margin of safety' on input data.

The analysis of risk and uncertainty concentrates in some way on altering future returns to allow for uncertainty of outcome (eg, using probability distributions of returns). An alternative approach is to allow for uncertainty by increasing our required rate of return on risky projects.

This latter approach is commonly taken by investors. For example, if we were comparing a Building Society investment with one in equities we would normally require a higher return from equities to compensate us for their extra risk. In a similar way if we were appraising equity investments in a food retailing company against a similar investment in a computer electronics firm we would usually demand higher returns from the electronics investment to reflect its higher risk.

Clearly use of a Risk Adjusted Discount Rate can be employed in almost any situation involving risk. The practical problem is how much return should we demand for a given level of risk. To solve this problem we can turn to the Stock Exchange – a place where risk and return combinations (securities) are bought and sold every day. If, for example, we can better the return earned by investors on the stock market by investing in a physical asset offering the same level of risk, we can increase investor wealth and the investment should be adopted.

Unfortunately the required approach is not as simple as this. Investors seldom hold securities in isolation. They usually attempt to reduce their risks by 'not putting all their eggs into one basket' and therefore hold portfolios of securities. Before we can deduce a risk-adjusted discount rate from stock exchange returns we need to identify the risks taken by investors in their diversified investment portfolios.

6   SELF TEST QUESTIONS

6.1   What is the difference between risk and uncertainty? (1.1)

6.2   How do you calculate the sensititivity of a project to changes in the cost of capital? (2.2)

6.3   How do you use a payoff matrix to help reduce risk? (3.3)

7   EXAMINATION TYPE QUESTIONS

7.1   Mentor Products plc

Mentor Products plc are considering the purchase of a new computer controlled packing machine to replace the two machines which are currently used to pack products X. The new machine would result in reduced labour costs because of the more automated nature of the process and, in addition, would permit production levels to be increased by creating greater capacity at the packing stage. With an anticipated rise in the demand for product X, it has been estimated that the new machine will lead to increased profits in each of the next three years. Due to uncertainty in demand however, the annual cash flows (including savings) resulting from purchase of the new machine cannot be fixed with certainty and have therefore been estimated probabilistically as follows:

Annual cash flows (£'000)

Year 1	Prob.	Year 2	Prob.	Year 3	Prob.
10	0.3	10	0.1	10	0.3
15	0.4	20	0.2	20	0.5
		30	0.4		
20	0.3	40	0.3	30	0.2

Because of the overall uncertainty in the sales of product X, it has been decided that only three years cash flows will be considered in deciding whether to purchase the new machine. After allowing for the scrap value of the existing machines, the net cost of the new machine will be £42,000.

The effects of taxation should be ignored.

You are required:

(a)   Ignoring the time value of money, identify which combinations of annual cash flows will lead to an overall negative net cash flow, and determine the total probability of this occurring.

(5 marks)

(b)   On the basis of the average cash flow for each year, calculate the net present value of the new machine given that the company's cost of capital is 15%.

Relevant discount factors are as follows:

Year	Discount factor
1	0.870
2	0.756
3	0.658

(5 marks)

(c)   Analyse the risk inherent in this situation by simulating the net present value calculation. You should use the random numbers given at the end of the question to simulate five sets of cash flows. On the basis of your simulation results, what is the expected net present value and what is the probability of the new machine yielding a negative net present value?

	Set 1	Set 2	Set 3	Set 4	Set 5
Year 1	4	7	6	5	0
Year 2	2	4	8	0	1
Year 3	7	9	4	0	3

(10 marks)

(Total: 20 marks)

7.2   Butcher Ltd

Butcher Ltd is considering whether to set up a division in order to manufacture a new product, the Azam. The following statement has been prepared, showing the projected profitability per unit of the new product:

	£	£
Selling price		22.00
Less: Direct labour (2 hours @ £2.50 per hour)	5.00	
Material (3 kg @ £1.50 per kg)	4.50	
Overheads	11.50	
		21.00
Net profit per unit		1.00

A feasibility study, recently undertaken at a cost of £50,000, suggests that a selling price of £22 per Azam should be set. At this price, it is expected that 10,000 Azams would be sold each year. Demand for Azams is expected to cease after five years. Direct labour and material costs would be incurred only for the duration of the product life.

Overheads per unit have been calculated as follows:

	£
Variable overheads	2.50
Rent (see note (1) - £8,000 ÷ 10,000 units)	0.80
Manager's salary (see note (2) - £7,000 ÷ 10,000 units)	0.70
Depreciation (see note (3) - £50,000 ÷ 10,000 units)	5.00
Head office costs (see note (4) - 2 hours @ £1.25 per hour	2.50
	11.50

Notes:

(1)   Azams would be manufactured in a factory rented specially for the purpose. Annual rental would be £8,000 payable only for as long as the factory was occupied.

(2)   A manager would be employed to supervise production of Azams, at a salary of £7,000 pa. The manager is at present employed by Butcher Ltd, but is due to retire in the near future on an annual pension of £2,000, payable by the company. If he continued to be employed, his pension would not be paid during the period of his employment. His subsequent pension rights would not be affected.

(3)   Manufacture of the Azam would require a specialised machine costing £250,000. The machine would be capable of producing Azams for an indefinite period, although due to its specialised nature, it would not have any resale or scrap value when the production of Azams ceased. It is the policy of Butcher Ltd to provide depreciation on all fixed assets using the straight line method. The annual charge of £50,000 for the new machine is based on a life of five years, equal to the period during which Azams are expected to be produced.

(4)   Butcher Ltd allocates its head office fixed costs to all products at the rate of £1.25 per direct labour hour. Total head office fixed costs would not be affected by the introduction of the Azam to the company's range of products.

The cost of capital of Butcher Ltd is estimated at 5% pa in real terms, and you may assume that all costs and prices given above will remain constant in real terms. All cash flows would arise at the end of each year, with the exception of the cost of the machine which would be payable immediately. The directors of Butcher Ltd are very confident about the accuracy of all the estimates given above, with the exception of those relating to product life, annual sales volume and material cost per Azam.

You are required:

(a)   to prepare net present valuation calculations, based on the estimates provided, to show whether Butcher Ltd should proceed with manufacture of the Azam.

(b)   to prepare a statement showing how sensitive the net present value of manufacturing Azams is to errors of estimation in each of the three factors: product life, annual sales volume and material cost per Azam.

Ignore taxation.

8   ANSWERS TO EXAMINATION TYPE QUESTIONS

8.1   Mentor Products plc

(a)   The combinations leading to a negative net cash flow are listed in the following table (£'000s)

Year				Probability			Net cash flow
0	1	2	3				
-42	10	10	10	$0.3 \times 0.1 \times 0.3$	=	0.009	-12
-42	10	10	20	$0.3 \times 0.1 \times 0.5$	=	0.015	-2
-42	10	20	10	$0.3 \times 0.2 \times 0.3$	=	0.018	-2
-42	15	10	10	$0.4 \times 0.1 \times 0.3$	=	0.012	-7
-42	20	10	10	$0.3 \times 0.1 \times 0.3$	=	0.009	-2
				Total		0.063	

The total probability of a negative cash flow is <u>0.063</u>

Tutorial note: the probabilities are obtained using the multiplication law:

$P(A \text{ and } B \text{ and } C) = P(A) \times P(B) \times P(C)$

(b)   Calculation of average (expected) cash flows (£'000s)

	Year 1			Year 2			Year 3	
CF	Prob	CF × Prob	CF	Prob	CF × Prob	CF	Prob	CF × Prob
10	0.3	3	10	0.1	1	10	0.3	3
15	0.4	6	20	0.2	4	20	0.5	10
20	0.3	6	30	0.4	12	30	0.2	6
			40	0.3	12			
Expected cash flows		15			29			19

Discounting the expected CF to obtain present values (£'000s):

Year	Expected cash flow	Discount factor	Present value
0	-42	1.000	-42
1	15	0.870	13.050
2	29	0.756	21.924
3	19	0.658	12.502
			5.476

The expected net present value is £5,476

(c)   Allocate the digits 0 to 9 to the cash flows each year such that the number of digits is proportional to the probability (£'000s)

	Year 1			Year 2			Year 3	
CF	Prob	digits	CF	Prob	digits	CF	Prob	digits
10	0.3	0-2	10	0.1	0	10	0.3	0-2
15	0.4	3-6	20	0.2	1-2	20	0.5	3-7
20	0.3	7-9	30	0.4	3-6	30	0.2	8-9
			40	0.3	7-9			

Select digits from the table of random numbers and record the corresponding cash flows (£'000s)

Set	Year 0 CF	Year 1 D factor = 0.870 RN	CF	DCF	Year 2 D factor = 0.756 RN	CF	DCF	Year 3 D factor = 0.658 RN	CF	DCF	NPV
1	-42	4	15	13.05	2	20	15.12	7	20	13.16	-0.67
2	-42	7	20	17.40	4	30	22.68	9	30	19.74	17.82
3	-42	6	15	13.05	8	40	30.24	4	20	13.16	14.45
4	-42	5	15	13.05	0	10	7.56	0	10	6.58	-14.81
5	-42	6	10	8.70	1	20	15.12	3	20	13.16	-5.02
											11.77

The average net present value is 11.77/5 (£'000s) = £2,354

Three out of five outcomes are negative. The probability of a negative value is therefore 3/5 = 0.6. However, probabilities are based on the relative frequency in a large number of trials. In practice, many hundreds of simulations would need to be carried out.

In comparing this result with part (a), it should also be remembered that the cash flows in part (a) are higher because they have not been discounted, leading to a lower probability of a negative net cash flow.

8.6   Solution

(a)   **Step 1 - calculate the NPV of the project based upon the above forecasts**

Cash flows resulting from manufacture and sale of Azams

Time (years)		0	1 - 5
	Ref to notes	£'000	£'000
Machine	(a)	(250)	-
Factory rental		-	(8)
Manager's salary (net)	(b)	-	(5)
Variable production costs	(c)	-	(120)
Total outflows		(250)	(133)
Sales		-	220
Net inflows/(outflows)		(250)	87
Discount factor @ 5%		1.00	4.329
Present value		(250)	376.623

Net present value   £126,623

On the basis of the estimates given, manufacture of the Azam is worthwhile.

Notes:

(a)   Machine depreciation is irrelevant, being a non-cash item.

(b)   Only the extra salary payable to the manager is relevant: £2,000 would be payable regardless of the decision on the Azam.

(c)   The only relevant costs per unit are:

	£
Direct labour	5.00
Material	4.50
Variable overheads	2.50
	12.00

Head office costs are not affected in total by the introduction of the Azam and are, therefore, irrelevant. The other items included in overheads per unit have been dealt with separately.

(b)   **Step 2 - determine how far each of the specified variables could change (independently) before a zero NPV was obtained**

Sensitivity to forecast errors

Item	Upper/lower limit for project acceptability	Maximum percentage error not affecting decisions
Product life	3.2 years (approx)	36%
Annual sales volume	7,075 units	29%
Material cost per Azam	£7,425	65%

The table shows that the manufacture of Azams would still be worthwhile if product life fell to about 3.2 years, or if annual sales fell to 7,074 units, or if material costs increased to £7.43 per Azam.   These figures represent percentage errors of 36%, 29% and 65% respectively on the original estimates. If the actual figures were within these percentages of the original estimates, the decision to go ahead would still be valid.   These are large percentages and the net present value is, therefore, remarkably insensitive to errors of estimation in the three factors.

WORKINGS

(W1)   **Product life**

Annual cash flow	=	£87,000
Initial outlay	=	£250,000

For positive NPV at 5% cost of capital:

PV of annual cash flow	$\geq$	250,000
87,000 × PV factor for product life	$\geq$	250,000
$\therefore$ PV factor for product life	$\geq$	$\dfrac{250,000}{87,000}$
	=	2.874
PV factor for 3 years @ 5%	=	2.723
PV factor for 4 years @ 5%	=	3.546

$\therefore$ Project NPV is positive if life is greater than $3 + \dfrac{2.874 - 2.723}{3.546 - 2.723}$ years

$$= \quad 3.2 \text{ years (approx)}$$

(W2)   **Annual sales volume**

Contribution per unit = £10 (sales revenue £22 − variable cost £12)

The fall in annual contribution which gives a drop in NPV to break-even point (ie, a drop of £126,623) is:

$$\frac{£126,623}{a\,\overline{5|}\,0.05} = \frac{£126,623}{4.329}$$

$$= \quad £29,250$$

This is caused by a fall in annual demand of $\dfrac{£29,250}{£10}$ units $=$ 2,925 units

ie, a fall of 29%

(W3)   **Material price**

The material price given is £4.50. If the annual drop in contribution was caused by an increase in unit price, this would be $\frac{£29,250}{10,000} = £2.925$ per unit.

If this unit price increase was entirely caused by an increase in material price, the percentage increase would be $\frac{2.925}{4.50} \times 100\% = 65\%$.

31 CAPITAL RATIONING

INTRODUCTION & LEARNING OBJECTIVES

When you have studied this chapter you should be able to do the following:

- Understand when to apply capital rationing.
- Optimise project values with single period capital rationing.
- Optimise project values with multi-period capital rationing.

1 CAPITAL RATIONING

1.1 Introduction

Capital rationing is a situation that needs to be appreciated when looking at capital budgeting. Capital rationing arises when an organisation has a restriction on the amount of funds available to initiate all worthwhile projects (ie, projects that have a positive net present value).

There are two causes of capital rationing.

(a) **External capital rationing** – Although, theoretically, finance is always available at a price, in practice most lending institutions decide that there is a point beyond which they will not lend, at any price. This may provide an absolute limit to the funds available.

(b) **Internal capital rationing** – Particularly following a period of economic depression, many managements may be more concerned with survival than growth. In order to minimise risk, they adopt conservative growth and financing policies. Also, they want to maintain stable dividends rather than use cash for expansion.

The cause does not affect the analysis.

1.2 Single and multi-period capital rationing

Two types of capital rationing may be distinguished.

(a) **Single period** – shortage of funds now, but funds are expected to be freely available in all later periods.

(b) **Multi-period** – where the period of funds shortage is expected to extend over a number of years, or even indefinitely.

1.3   Divisible and indivisible projects

Projects may also be divided into two categories.

(a)   **Divisible** – either the whole project, or any fraction of the project, may be undertaken. If a fraction only is undertaken, then both initial investment and cash inflows are reduced **pro rata**.

(b)   **Indivisible** – either the project must be undertaken in its entirety, or not at all.

For example, quoted shares represent a divisible investment – varying numbers of shares may be purchased, with resultant prorating of investment returns.

On the other hand, decisions about introducing new product ranges are indivisible – either new products are introduced or they are not.

In reality, almost all projects are indivisible. However, the assumption of divisibility enables the easier use of mathematical tools. Its implications are reconsidered later.

1.4   Optimising policy in single period capital rationing with divisible projects

The object is to select projects so as to maximise their total net present value using the business cost of capital. This is achieved by ranking projects according to their 'net present value per £1 of initial investment' (or cost-benefit ratio), then selecting from amongst them until all available funds are utilised.

1.5   Profitability index (or cost-benefit ratio)

The profitability index (PI) is regarded by some authorities as a means of comparing NPVs of different projects.

By comparing NPV with initial cash outflows, a measure of returns relative to size is obtained. This is comparable with the IRR approach. It suffers from the same criticisms as the latter in that it measures relative, not absolute, returns. In the capital rationing situation, however, this is what is required, since a selection of projects with the highest PIs will result in the maximum net present value for limited funds available.

1.6   Example

C Ltd, with a cost of capital of 10%, has £40,000 available for investment in Year 0.

Four divisible projects are available.

Project	Outlay	Receipts (cash flows)			
	Year 0	Year 1	Year 2	Year 3	Year 4
	£	£	£	£	£
1	100,000	40,000	100,000	80,000	60,000
2	30,000	40,000	40,000	40,000	40,000
3	20,000	40,000	30,000	40,000	50,000
4	40,000	20,000	30,000	30,000	30,000

You are required to calculate the optimal investment policy.

1.7   Solution

Project	Net present value at 10%	Profitability indices – net present value per £1 of outlay at 10%	Ranking
	£	£	
1	120,255	1.203	III
2	96,894	3.230	II
3	105,479	5.274	I
4	46,079	1.152	IV

Note: when reviewing your own workings to pre-worked NPV figures in this or any other text, allow for possible small differences due to rounding of present value factors.

Summary for optimal plan for C Ltd:

Project	Fraction of project accepted	Outlay at time 0	Net present value
		£	£
3	1.00	20,000	105,479
2	2/3	20,000	64,596*
		————	
Capital used and available		40,000	
		————	
Net present value obtained			170,075
			————

* Two-thirds of £96,894.

Technical note: you might think that the IRR approach, as a measure of relative profitability, could be used to rank projects in a capital rationing situation. In fact this approach does not always give the correct ranking, but it may be used in the examination if profitability indices cannot be calculated from the information given.

1.8   Optimising policy in single period capital rationing with indivisible projects

The object remains to select projects so as to maximise their total net present value at the cost of capital. This can only be achieved by selecting from amongst the available projects on a trial and error basis. **Because of the problem of indivisibility this may leave some funds unutilised.**

1.9   Example

PQ Ltd has £50,000 available to invest. Its cost of capital is 10%. The following indivisible projects are available:

Project	Initial outlay	Return pa to perpetuity
	£	£
1	20,000	1,500
2	10,000	1,500
3	15,000	3,000
4	30,000	5,400
5	25,000	4,800

1.10   Solution

The first stage is to calculate the NPV of the projects.

Project	Initial outlay £	PV of cash flows ** £	NPV £
1	20,000	15,000	(5,000)
2	10,000	15,000	5,000
3	15,000	30,000	15,000
4	30,000	54,000	24,000
5	25,000	48,000	23,000

$$** \text{ PV of perpetuity} = \frac{\text{Annual receipt}}{\text{Discount rate as a proportion}}$$

The approach is then one of considering all possible combinations of projects under the investment limit of £50,000. Try this yourself.

The optimum selection of projects is:

Projects	Initial outlay £	NPV £
2	10,000	5,000
3	15,000	15,000
5	25,000	23,000
	50,000	43,000
Unused funds	Nil	
Funds available	50,000	

Note: this may be compared to the ranking, if these were divisible projects:

Project	Cost/benefit ratio			Ranking	Fraction of project accepted	NPV £
1	−5/20	=	−0.25	V	-	
2	5/10	=	0.50	IV	-	
3	15/15	=	1.00	I	1.00	15,000
4	24/30	=	0.80	III	1/3	8,000
5	23/25	=	0.92	II	1.00	23,000
						46,000

The projects selected do not coincide with this ranking because of the fact that they are not divisible. Given this constraint, and that for finance, no solution will give a higher NPV than £43,000.

1.11   Investment of surplus funds

In addition to specific investment opportunities, there may be a general opportunity to invest surplus funds on the market. Assuming equal risk levels, the rate of interest earned cannot, in the long run, be higher than the cost of the capital of the company, otherwise the cost of capital would be found to increase.

The rate of interest payable on surplus funds is therefore likely to be below the cost of capital. In a single period capital rationing situation, there is rarely any advantage in investing surplus funds at below the cost of capital (ie, in projects with negative NPVs). However, if a project with a negative NPV has a cash inflow at year 0, rather than an outflow, investment could be worthwhile as it might free up funding for investment in other profitable projects which would otherwise be rejected under the capital rationing constraints.

2 THE MULTI-PERIOD CAPITAL RATIONING PROBLEM

2.1 Introduction

This has already been defined as the situation where the cash shortage extends into a number of future periods. The problem is too complex to be suitable for a trial-and-error approach.

However, it may be defined so as to be suitable for a linear programming approach. For linear programming to be suitable, the following must apply.

(a)   The proportions undertaken of each of the projects available are the variables.

(b)   Projects are assumed to be divisible.

(c)   There are only two projects being considered (more than two projects requires the simplex technique which is not examinable in paper 8).

(d)   NPVs are linearly related to the proportion of each project accepted.

(e)   Cash limits year by year form the constraints.

(f)   The objective is to maximise the NPV of cash flows at the cost of capital.

You should also note that the linear programming problems examined assume that projects cannot be deferred, and have cash outflows extending over several periods. Multi-period rationing problems in the examination will generally be suitable for solution using linear programming.

To demonstrate the technique, an artificially simple example with only two projects will be examined.

2.2 The basic problem - example

A company is proposing to invest in two projects. The projects are divisible ie, they can be accepted in whole or in part. If accepted in part, both cash outflows and subsequent cash receipts are reduced **pro rata**.

The two projects and associated cash flows are:

Year	Project A Cash flow £	Project B Cash flow £
0	(10,000)	(20,000)
1	(20,000)	(10,000)
2	(30,000)	-
3	100,000	60,000

The company's cost of capital is 10%. All cash flows occur at exactly 12 month intervals, starting in year 0.

The funds available are restricted as follows.

Year 0	–	£20,000
Year 1	–	£25,000
Year 2	–	£20,000

Funds not utilised in one year will not be available in subsequent years. Projects cannot be deferred.

You are required to find the company's optimum investment policy.

2.3   Solution

It is first necessary to calculate the net present value of each project at 10%.

Year	10% discount factor	Project A Cash flow £	Project A Present value £	Project B Cash flow £	Project B Present value £
0	1.000	(10,000)	(10,000)	(20,000)	(20,000)
1	0.909	(20,000)	(18,180)	(10,000)	(9,090)
2	0.826	(30,000)	(24,780)	-	-
3	0.751	100,000	75,100	60,000	45,060
NPV			22,140		15,970

Let a be proportion of project A accepted.
Let b be proportion of project B accepted.

The constraints are:

Year 0	$10{,}000a$ + $20{,}000b$	$\leq$	20,000	or	a + $2b$	$\leq$	2
Year 1	$20{,}000a$ + $10{,}000b$	$\leq$	25,000	or	$4a$ + $2b$	$\leq$	5
Year 2	$30{,}000a$	$\leq$	20,000	or	$3a$	$\leq$	2

General non-negativity constraints: $0 \leq a \leq 1$
                                         $0 \leq b \leq 1$

The objective is: to maximise $22{,}140a + 15{,}970b$ (NPV from investment.)

The problem may be viewed graphically.

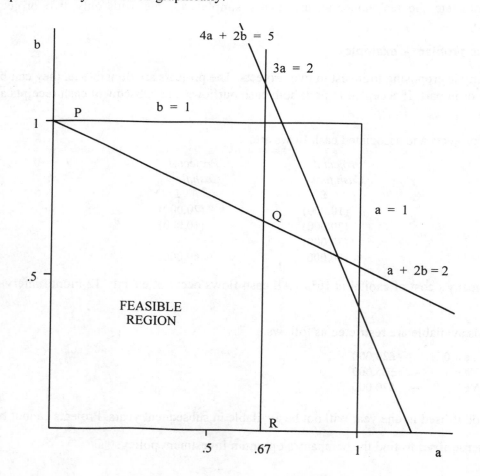

The feasible region has three corners as well as zero: P, Q and R. Proportions accepted and resulting NPVs are as follows:

Corner	Value of b	a	Interpretation	NPV £
P	1	Nil	Accept B entirely and A not at all	15,970
Q	2/3	2/3	Accept 2/3 of each project	25,400
R	Nil	2/3	Accept 2/3 project A only	14,760

Clearly the optimum solution is to invest in 2/3 of each project – ie, the solution suggested at point Q.

WORKINGS

At Q two equations are satisfied:

$$a + 2b = 2 \qquad \text{----------- (1)}$$

$$3a = 2 \qquad \text{----------- (2)}$$

(2) becomes $\qquad a = 2/3$

Substitute in (1) $\qquad 2b = 1\ 1/3 \qquad \text{----------- (3)}$

$$b = 2/3$$

Note that this solution leaves funds unused in year 1. This poses the question of whether it would be worthwhile to hold funds available from year 1 to year 2, even if they have to be invested below 10% – even say at Nil%.

2.4   Availability of investment opportunities below the cost of capital

Suppose £1,000 of the funds spare in year 1 can be held at a zero rate of interest until year 2.

Does this alter the optimal investment policy?

The investment of £1,000 is itself a mini-project whose NPV is computed as follows:

Year	Cash flow £	Discount factor	PV £
1	(1,000)	0.909	(909)
2	1,000	0.826	826
			(83)

As expected the NPV of this project is negative.

However the effect of undertaking this short term investment is to tighten the cash constraint in year 1 (to £24,000) and relax it in year 2 (to £21,000).

Thus the problem becomes:

Constraints: Year 0 (unchanged) $a + 2b \leq 2$
                Year 1 $20a + 10b \leq 24$
                Year 2 $30a \leq 21$
                Non-negativity $0 \leq a \leq 1$
                                           $0 \leq b \leq 1$

Objective:

To maximise $22{,}140a + 15{,}970b - 83$

Solving the equations at corner Q as before

$a = 7/10$
$b = 13/20$

Thus, the NPV $= (22{,}140 \times 7/10) + (15{,}970 \times 13/20) - 83$

$= £25{,}800$

This represents a gain of £400 over the previous optimum solution, and hence it is worthwhile to accept the opportunity (provided possible) to retain the £1,000 despite having a rate of return (nil) below 10%.

3   EXTENSION TO MORE COMPLEX MULTI-PERIOD PROBLEMS

3.1   Introduction

The example above has enabled the problems to be handled computationally. However, the technique is only relevant in reality where there are a number of projects.

You are not likely to be asked to solve such problems numerically, but it will be helpful if you can formulate the objective and constraint equations (ie, the linear programming model).

3.2   Example

A company has four divisible projects available. The cash outlays are as follows:

Project	Outlay Year 0 £'000	Outlay Year 1 £'000	Net present value at 10% £'000
1	20	-	10
2	40	20	30
3	50	80	60
4	30	30	15

Capital rationing is expected to extend over the next two years, with £100,000 available now and £80,000 next year before accepting any of the projects.

3.3   Solution

Let x_1 be the proportion of project (1) accepted

x_2 be the proportion of project (2) accepted

x_3 be the proportion of project (3) accepted

x_4 be the proportion of project (4) accepted

Hence x_1 can take any value between 0 and 1 ie,

$$0 \leq x_1 \leq 1, \text{ and so on.}$$

Objective:

To maximise net present value $= 10x_1 + 30x_2 + 60x_3 + 15x_4$

Constraints:

Year	Funds available	Funds utilised
0	$100 \geq$	$20x_1 + 40x_2 + 50x_3 + 30x_4$
1	$80 \geq$	$20x_2 + 80x_3 + 30x_4$

Logic (non-negativity) constraints:

$$0 \leq x_1 \leq 1, \qquad 0 \leq x_2 \leq 1, \qquad \text{etc.}$$

The optimum solution can now be found by one of the standard techniques for manipulating linear programming problems eg, the Simplex method.

4   CONCLUSIONS

Although the approach to single period capital rationing is straightforward, multi-period situations are much more complex: they require more data, and the methods of analysis become more complex.

It may well be, however, that the multi-period capital rationing situation is the rule rather than the exception; if such is the case, the programming techniques introduced in this section may become very important analytical tools.

5   SELF TEST QUESTIONS

5.1   When does capital rationing arise? (1.1)

5.2   What is meant by an indivisible investment project? (1.3)

5.3   Which quantitative method is used in solving multi-period capital rationing problems? (2.1)

6   EXAMINATION TYPE QUESTION

6.1   Flourine Ltd

Flourine Ltd is choosing which investment to undertake during the coming year. The following table has been prepared, summarising the main features of available projects.

	Cash outlays		Cash receipts	
	Time 0	Time 1	Time 1	Time 2
Project	£'000	£'000	£'000	£'000
Sodium	20	50	20	80
Magnesium	40	35	40	55
Aluminium	50	35	10	115
Silicon	40	15	10	75
Phosphorus	30	40	20	80

There will be no cash flows on any of the projects after time 2. All projects are regarded as being of equal risk. Flourine uses only equity sources of finance at an estimated cost of 20% per annum.

The cash flows given above represent estimated results for maximum possible investment in each project; lower levels of investment may be undertaken, in which case all cash flows will be reduced in proportion.

You are required:

(a)   To prepare calculations to identify the optimal set of investments assuming that capital available is limited to £100,000 at time 0, and £200,000 at time 1; assume for the purpose of this requirement only that the Aluminium project and the Silicon project are mutually exclusive. (Hint: firstly check in which years capital rationing occurs); and   **(10 marks)**

(b)   To explain what calculation you would undertake to identify the optimal set of investments assuming that capital available is limited to £100,000 at time 0 and to £40,000 at time 1; give reasons for your choice of method but do not give calculations.   **(10 marks)**

(Total: 20 marks)

Ignore taxation.

7   ANSWER TO EXAMINATION TYPE QUESTION

7.1   Flourine Ltd

(a)   **Optimal investment for Flourine Ltd**

Step 1   Determine in which years capital is rationed.

Project	Cash flows with Aluminium		Cash flows with Silicon	
	Time 0	Time 1	Time 0	Time 1
	£000	£000	£000	£000
Sodium	(20)	(30)	(20)	(30)
Magnesium	(40)	(5)	(40)	(5)
Aluminium	(50)	(25)		
Silicon			(40)	(5)
Phosphorus	(30)	(20)	(30)	(20)
Total	(140)	(70)	(130)	(50)
Capital available	100	200	100	200

It is therefore concluded that effective capital rationing exists only at time 0 ie, a single period of capital rationing situation.

Step 2   Use profitability index to select best mix of projects.

Profitability index

Project	Cash flows			PV of cash flows @ 20%				Profitability index
	0	1	2	0	1	2	NPV	
	£000	£000	£000	£000	£000	£000	£000	£000
Sodium	(20)	(30)	80	(20)	(24.90)	55.20	10.3	0.515
Magnesium	(40)	5	55	(40)	4.15	37.95	2.1	0.0525
Aluminium	(50)	(25)	115	(50)	(20.75)	79.35	8.6	0.17
Silicon	(40)	(5)	75	(40)	(4.15)	51.75	7.6	0.19
Phosphorus	(30)	(20)	80	(30)	(16.60)	55.20	8.6	0.2867

In time 0 with only £100,000 available projects would be introduced in order of profitability as shown.

Aluminium without Silicon

Project	Proportion accepted	Funds used at Time 0	Total NPV
	%	£000	£000
Sodium	100	20	10.3
Phosphorus	100	30	8.6
Aluminium	100	50	8.6
Magnesium	Nil	Nil	Nil
Funds utilised and available		100	27.5

Silicon without Aluminium

Project	Proportion accepted	Funds used at Time 0	Total NPV
	%	£000	£000
Sodium	100	20	10.3
Phosphorus	100	30	8.6
Aluminium	100	40	7.6
Magnesium	25	10	0.5
Funds utilised and available		100	27.0

Conclusion   Aluminium without Silicon is to be preferred as it yields a higher NPV.

Note: Aluminium is selected in preference to Silicon even though it has a lower profitability index.

This is because the choice is effectively between investing £50,000 in Aluminium with an NPV of £8,600 (PI = 0.17) or a package containing a £40,000 investment in Silicon and a £10,000 investment in Magnesium with a combined NPV of £8,100. This package has a profitability index of only 0.162 and is therefore rejected.

(b)   **Linear progamming solution for Flourine Ltd**

In the situation described, linear programming provides a mathematical technique for calculating the optimum solution, since the requirements of a linear programming problem are met.

These are as follows.

(i)   A single objective – to maximise NPV at the cost of capital
(ii)   A series of constraints – projects and funds available

(iii)   A linear relationship between factors

(iv)   Completely divisible inputs and outputs

(v)   All external factors are static

(vi)   The results of decisions are known with certainty.

The problem may now be formulated. Aluminium and Silicon are no longer mutually exclusive (see part a).

Data

	Proportion accepted	Max cash outlay Time 0	Max cash outlay Time 1	Max cash receipt Time 1	Net cash outlay Time 1
	Positive fraction less than one	£'000	£'000	£'000	£'000
Sodium	x_1	20	50	20	30
Magnesium	x_2	40	35	40	(5)
Aluminium	x_3	50	35	10	25
Silicon	x_4	40	15	10	5
Phosphorus	x_5	30	40	20	20

Let S be surplus funds not used on projects invested at time 0 at a rate of interest 'i', $S \geq 0$.

Cash constraints then become (£000):

Time 0: $100 \geq 20x_1 + 40x_2 + 50x_3 + 40x_4 + 30x_5 + S$

Time 1: $40 \geq 30x_1 - 5x_2 + 25x_3 + 5x_4 + 20x_5 - S(1 + i)$

The objective is to maximise the NPV of the total investment ie, maximise

$$10.3x_1 + 2.1x_2 + 8.6x_3 + 7.6x_4 + 8.6x_5 + \frac{S(1+i)}{1.2} - S$$

This problem can now be solved by using a technique such as the Simplex method.

Note:

The value $\frac{S(1+i)}{1.2} - S$ is the PV of investing S at an interest of i in time 0. Unless i is greater than 20% it will be a negative value.

32 LEASING DECISIONS

INTRODUCTION & LEARNING OBJECTIVES

This chapter examines the question of whether a company should lease assets or buy them outright. In the earlier chapter on sources of finance we considered leasing and hire purchase as possible sources of medium term finance. In this chapter we calculate the costs of such finance so that the financial manager can compare them with the cost of say a bank loan in coming to the financing decision.

When you have studied this chapter you should be able to do the following:

- Understand the different types of leases.

- Calculate the cost inherent in a decision to lease.

- Decide whether an asset should be leased or bought.

1 HIRING AND HIRE PURCHASE

1.1 Hire purchase

Hire purchase (HP) is a method of obtaining assets by paying for them over a period of time rather than in a lump sum. The buyer agrees to pay a number of weekly or monthly instalments (the hire charge based on the cash price plus additional financing charges). The final instalment includes a nominal sum, say £1, which is the actual purchase consideration for the article. The buyer does not therefore own the asset until the hire purchase agreement has been completed, and the seller has the security of being able to repossess the asset if the buyer does not pay the required instalments.

The cost of hire purchase is often considerable. Interest is calculated on the whole of the purchase price, but it is of course only at the outset of the agreement that this amount is owed, each instalment serving to reduce the outstanding amount. The **effective** rate of interest is thus often in excess of 25% pa. However, many people use hire purchase to obtain finance when no other source is available.

1.2 Activity

The cash price of a machine is £6,000. If it is bought on hire purchase, the terms are an initial deposit of £2,000, followed by 24 monthly payments of £205. What is the total interest cost?

1.3   Activity solution

Step 1   Calculate the total hire purchase cost.

	£
Deposit	2,000
Monthly instalments 24 × £205	4,920
Total cost	6,920

Step 2   The total interest paid is the difference between the hire purchase cost and the cash price.

Total interest = £6,920 – £6,000 = £920.

1.4   Hiring of capital assets

It is possible to obtain the use of certain types of durable goods eg, plant and machinery, by hiring them instead of purchasing them. By so doing, hirers do not have to pay in advance for the service the goods will render during their effective life. They are relieved of the burden, and of many of the risks, of financing them.

Where goods are available either for purchase or hire, intending users must decide which they prefer. If they have not, or cannot obtain the necessary finance to buy, they may be compelled to hire. However, if they can afford to buy, the decision may depend on whether their need is purely temporary (and if so, whether it would be cheaper to hire than to buy and re-sell), and whether they are prepared to take the risk of a fall in prices and deprive themselves of the chance of buying cheaper later on. There is also the question of maintenance and repairs, which the supplier may be better able to provide than the hirer.

1.5   Contract hire

A further form of hiring and renting assets, is contract hire, which is particularly applicable to private cars and small commercial vehicles. Motor dealers offer comprehensive hiring systems which cover the supply, servicing, replacement and licensing of such vehicles. Many finance companies offer a vehicle-hiring system without the facility of servicing, etc.

1.6   Instalment credit

Instalment credit relates to the payment for goods by instalments and is thus similar to hire purchase, except that the ownership of the goods passes to the buyer immediately on delivery ie, there is no hire element. Therefore, the seller cannot recover the goods in the event of default by the buyer unless the loan is specifically secured on the asset.

An instalment credit agreement can be spread over five years and, unlike a bank overdraft, there is no possibility of early enforced repayment. Although instalment credit is relatively expensive, it is widely used as it provides a second line of credit behind the bank overdraft which can then be used to meet any unexpected problem that arises. For taxation purposes, it is considered that the whole of the expenditure on plant and equipment has been incurred when the first instalment has been paid.

2   LEASING

2.1   Introduction

Leasing has grown over recent years to be a particularly important source of finance. Leasing is now common for vehicles, office and production equipment etc.

There are many different types of lease arrangement. In particular, lease-purchases are the modern equivalent of HP.

2.2   Definition of leasing

Leasing is a means of financing the use of capital equipment, the underlying principle being that use is more important that ownership. It is a medium-term financial arrangement, usually from one to ten years, by which the firm has a legal obligation to make payments over the predetermined length of time. Leasing should be distinguished from short-term hire, contract hire and rental, which are all means of filling a temporary need. In the case of leasing, the firm intending to use the equipment selects its own supplier and then approaches the finance house which purchases the equipment and leases it to the user. Leasing differs from hire-purchase, in so far as there is no initial deposit, other than the first instalment of rent, and it is not, in itself, a means of acquiring ownership.

2.3   Operating leases and finance leases

It is important to realise that there are fundamentally two types of lease agreement, as follows.

(a)   Operating leases;
(b)   Capital or finance leases.

This section is concerned primarily with capital leases. The differences between the two types can be summarised as follows:

> A capital or finance lease is defined in SSAP 21 as a lease that transfers substantially all the risks and rewards of ownership of an asset to the lessee. It should be presumed that such a transfer of risks and rewards occurs if at the inception of a lease the present value of the minimum lease payments, including any initial payment, amounts to substantially all (normally 90% or more) of the fair value of the leased asset.

The following criteria distinguish finance leases from operating leases.

	Finance lease	*Operating lease*
1	One lease exists for the whole useful life of the asset.	The lease period is less than the useful life of the asset. The lessor relies on subsequent leasing or eventual sale of the asset to cover his capital outlay and show a profit.
2	The lessor does not usually deal directly in this type of asset.	The lessor may very well carry on a trade in this type of asset.
3	The lessor does not retain the risks or rewards of ownership.	The lessor is normally responsible for repairs and maintenance.
4	The lease agreement cannot be cancelled. The lessee has a liability for all payments.	The lease can sometimes be cancelled at short notice.
5	The substance of the transaction is the purchase of the asset by the lessee financed by a loan from the lessor ie, it is effectively a source of medium- to long-term debt finance.	The substance of the transaction is the short-term rental of an asset.

2.4   The leasing agreement

A leasing agreement is usually divided into two periods - primary and secondary. The primary period is usually between one and seven years (although ten year primary periods, or even longer, may be possible) and it is in this period that the lessor would expect to recover the value of the equipment. The lessee is bound to pay the rental throughout the primary period.

During the secondary period, which will also usually be between one and seven years, rentals are nominal only and the agreement can be terminated at any time without further payment. When the agreement is terminated, the lessee may ask the leasing company to sell the equipment to a third party. The agreement will usually allow the lessee to receive most of the proceeds of sale (75% to 95%).

The lessee is responsible for maintenance, insurance and operating costs in both periods and will normally take over the benefits of any guarantee or warranties.

3   LEASE OR BUY DECISIONS

3.1   Introduction

Leasing is a method by which an asset can be used within a business without the outright purchase of the asset. Essentially, leasing is a form of finance. In this section we are concerned with the questions asked from a decision making perspective – should an asset be leased or bought?

3.2   The lease or buy decision

The decision is more a financing decision rather than an investment decision. The first decision is whether the asset is worth acquiring. If so, the second decision is whether to lease or buy.

Clearly the two decisions may not be independent. For example, an asset may not be a worthwhile acquisition if purchased but the leasing alternative could be sufficiently cheap to make the use of the asset attractive.

Therefore we have to take care to ensure we evaluate all possibilities. Consider the following example.

3.3   Example

A firm is considering acquiring a new machine to neutralise the toxic waste produced by its refining plant. The machine would cost £6.4 million and would have an economic life of five years. The machine will reduce operating costs of the firm by £2.1 million pa. Capital allowances of 25% pa on a declining balance basis are available for the investment. Taxation of 35% is payable on operating cash flows one year in arrears. It is considered that a discount rate of 20% would reflect the risk of the project's operating cash flows.

The firm intends to finance the new plant by means of a five-year fixed interest loan at 18% pa, principal repayable in five years' time. As an alternative a leasing company has proposed a finance lease over five years at £1.5 million per year payable in advance. Scrap value of the machine under each financing alternative will be zero.

You are required to advise the firm whether the project should be undertaken and if so which financing method to adopt if:

(a)   the firm will be in a taxpaying position throughout the project's life; and

(b)   the firm will be in a non-taxpaying position throughout the project's life.

3.4   Solution

(a)   **Firm in a taxpaying position**

Step 1   As a first step we must analyse the operating cash flows of the project which are unaffected by the method of financing ie, ignoring all cash and tax flows relating to the method of finance.

£ million

Year	Operating cash flow	Tax 35%	Net cash flow	PV factor @ 20%	PV
1	2.1		2.1	0.833	1.749
2	2.1	(0.735)	1.365	0.694	0.947
3	2.1	(0.735)	1.365	0.579	0.790
4	2.1	(0.735)	1.365	0.482	0.658
5	2.1	(0.735)	1.365	0.402	0.549
6	0	(0.735)	(0.735)	0.335	(0.246)
					4.447

Present value of the project's operating cash inflows = £4.447m

Step 2   We must now examine the financing aspects of the investment. This has been a controversial area over the years and text books still contain much variation as to the prescribed method of analysis. However, currently the generally accepted approach is to treat the leasing option as being equivalent in financial risk terms to the firm borrowing sufficient funds to enable it to purchase the machine outright. If the shareholders view the adoption of a lease as equivalent in financial risk terms to taking on a loan at 18% pa (pre-tax) then the decision as to which is the preferred alternative is to find the one with the lower cost (since they are regarded as being equivalent risk).

Step 3   To find the cheaper option we must first calculate the after-tax cost of the loan.

Year	1	2	3	4	5	6
	£m	£m	£m	£m	£m	£m
Interest	(1.152)	(1.152)	(1.152)	(1.152)	(1.152)	
Tax relief @ 35%		0.403	0.403	0.403	0.403	0.403
Principal					(6.400)	
Net cash flow	(1.152)	(0.749)	(0.749)	(0.749)	(7.149)	0.403

To find the after-tax cost of the loan we must find the discount rate that equates these cash flows with the amount of funds advanced, i.e. £6.4m. This is simply an IRR calculation.

Trial and error would reveal this to be approximately 12%:

Year	1	2	3	4	5	6
	£m	£m	£m	£m	£m	£m
Net cash flow	(1.152)	(0.749)	(0.749)	(0.749)	(7.149)	0.403
PV factor @ 12%	0.893	0.797	0.712	0.636	0.567	0.507
Present value	(1.029)	(0.597)	(0.533)	(0.476)	(4.053)	0.204

= (£6.484m)

The effective after-tax cost of the loan is approximately 12%.

Step 4   To determine the cheaper option discount the leasing and the borrowing and buying cash flows at this discount rate.

Year	0	1	2	3	4	5
	£m	£m	£m	£m	£m	£m
Lease:						
Lease payment	(1.5)	(1.5)	(1.5)	(1.5)	(1.5)	
Tax relief		0.525	0.525	0.525	0.525	0.525
Net cash flow	(1.5)	(0.975)	(0.975)	(0.975)	(0.975)	0.525
PV factor @ 12%	1.000	0.893	0.797	0.712	0.636	0.567
PV	(1.5)	(0.871)	(0.777)	(0.694)	(0.620)	0.298

NPV = (£4.164m)

Borrow and buy:

Purchase price	(6.4)					
Tax saving from capital allowance **		0.56	0.42	0.315	0.236	0.177	0.532
PV factor @ 12%	1.000	0.893	0.797	0.712	0.636	0.567	0.507
PV	(6.4)	0.500	0.335	0.224	0.150	0.100	0.270

NPV = (£4.821m)

** including balancing allowance

Year of claim	Capital allowance calculation Opening value £m	Allowance £m	Closing value £m	Tax saving (Allowance × 0.35) £m
0	6.400	1.600	4.800	0.560
1	4.800	1.200	3.600	0.420
2	3.600	0.900	2.700	0.315
3	2.700	0.675	2.025	0.236
4	2.025	0.506	1.519	0.177
5	1.519	1.519 **	0	0.532

** including balancing allowance

Note: all tax savings are lagged by one year. Timing of capital allowances can vary depending upon the date of purchase. Assume that time 0 is the last day of the year preceding the operation of the project, and therefore the tax relief (on capital allowances and/or leasing payments) commences twelve months later (the typical assumption by examiners).

Conclusion: leasing is the cheaper alternative.

To determine the overall NPV of the investment we must subtract the cost of the cheaper financing alternative from the present value of the operating cash flows of the project.

Overall NPV of the project = PV of operating cash flows – PV of the cheaper financing alternative

    = £4.447 m – £4.164m
    = £0.28m

Conclusion: the new machine should be acquired using the leasing contract. If the firm chose to borrow and buy, the investment would entail a loss of £4.447m – £4.821m = £0.37m.

(b)   **Analysis in a no-tax situation**

Step 1   Calculate the value of the operating benefits of the project

As there would be no tax consequences the present value would equal:

$a_{\overline{5}|0.20}$ × £2.1m = 2.991 × £2.1m = £6.281m

Step 2   Evaluate the cheaper financing alternative

As there is no tax relief on the loan its cost would be 18% pa.

The lease proposal would cost:

(£1.5m) + $a_{\overline{4}|0.18}$ × (1.5m) = (£1.5m) + 2.690 × (1.5m) = (£5.535m)

Whereas purchasing would cost £6.4m as the benefit of capital allowances would not be available.

Conclusion: the cheaper financing option is to lease. The overall benefit of the project would then be:

£6.281m – £5.535m = £0.746m

Note: that leasing has become relatively more attractive due to the loss of the substantial tax relief from the capital allowances.

The above example gives a thorough demonstration of the lease versus buy decision. In examination situations you might be required to perform only part of this analysis. For example, questions commonly state that the decision to acquire the asset has already been made and the analysis is simply to decide which form of finance is the cheaper.

4   SELF TEST QUESTIONS

4.1   What are the differences between operating and finance leases? (2.3)

4.2   What is the essential point of the lease v buy decision? (3.2)

5   EXAMINATION TYPE QUESTION

5.1   Ceder Ltd

Ceder Ltd has details of two machines which could fulfil the company's future production plans. Only one of these machines will be purchased.

The 'standard' model costs £50,000, and the 'de-luxe' £88,000, payable immediately. Both machines would require the input of £10,000 working capital throughout their working lives, and both machines have no expected scrap value at the end of their expected working lives of four years for the standard machine and six years for the de-luxe machine.

The forecast pre-tax operating net cash flows associated with the two machines are:

	Years hence					
	1	*2*	*3*	*4*	*5*	*6*
	£	£	£	£	£	£
Standard	20,500	22,860	24,210	23,410		
De-luxe	32,030	26,110	25,380	25,940	38,560	35,100

The de-luxe machine has only recently been introduced to the market and has not been fully tested in operating conditions. Because of the higher risk involved, the appropriate discount rate for the de-luxe machine is believed to be 14% per year, 2% higher than the discount rate for the standard machine.

The company is proposing to finance the purchase of either machine with a term loan at a fixed interest rate of 11% per year.

Taxation at 35% is payable on operating cash flows one year in arrears, and capital allowances are available at 25% per year on a reducing balance basis.

You are required:

(a)   to calculate for both the standard and the de-luxe machine:

(i)   payback period;
(ii)   net present value.

Recommend, with reasons, which of the two machines Ceder Ltd should purchase.

(Relevant calculations must be shown.)   **(13 marks)**

(b)   If Ceder Ltd were offered the opportunity to lease the standard model machine over a four year period at a rental of £15,000 per year, not including maintenance costs, evaluate whether the company should lease or purchase the machine.   **(7 marks)**

(Total: 20 marks)

6   ANSWER TO EXAMINATION TYPE QUESTION

6.1   Ceder Ltd

(a)

Calculation of tax liability

	Year 1	Year 2	Year 3	Year 4	Year 5	Year 6
	£	£	£	£	£	£
Standard						
Operating cash flows	20,500	22,860	24,210	23,410		
Capital allowance	12,500	9,375	7,031	21,094*		
	8,000	13,485	17,179	2,316		
Taxation (35%)	2,800	4,720	6,013	811		
De-luxe						
Operating cash flows	32,030	26,110	25,380	25,940	38,560	35,100
Capital allowance	22,000	16,500	12,375	9,281	6,961	20,883*
	10,030	9,610	13,005	16,659	31,599	14,217
Taxation (35%)	3,511	3,363	4,552	5,831	11,060	4,976

* Including balancing allowance

Forecast after-tax cash flows

	Year 0	Year 1	Year 2	Year 3	Year 4	Year 5
	£	£	£	£	£	£
Standard						
Fixed assets	(50,000)					
Working capital	(10,000)				10,000**	
Operating cash flows		20,500	22,860	24,210	23,410	
Taxation			(2,800)	(4,720)	(6,013)	(811)
	(60,000)	20,500	20,060	19,490	27,397	(811)
Discount factor (12%)		0.893	0.797	0.712	0.636	0.567
Present values	(60,000)	18,307	15,988	13,877	17,424	(460)

Payback period is approximately three years
Net present value is £5,136

	Year 0 £	Year 1 £	Year 2 £	Year 3 £	Year 4 £	Year 5 £	Year 6 £	Year 7 £
Standard								
Fixed assets	(88,000)							
Working capital	(10,000)						10,000**	
Operating cash flows		32,030	26,110	25,380	25,940	38,560	35,100	
Taxation			(3,511)	(3,363)	(4,552)	(5,831)	(11,060)	(4,976)
	(98,000)	32,030	22,599	22,017	21,388	32,729	34,040	(4,976)
Discount factor (14%)		0.877	0.769	0.675	0.592	0.519	0.456	0.400
Present values	(98,000)	28,090	17,379	14,861	12,662	16,986	15,522	(1,990)

Payback period is approximately four years
Net present value is £5,510

** Assumes working capital is released immediately. In reality some time-lag will exist.

Normally the project with the highest NPV would be selected. However, as the projects have unequal lives, it can be argued that although the de-luxe has a higher NPV, this is only achieved by operating for two more years. If the machines are to fulfil a continuing production requirement the time factor needs to be considered.

The annual equivalent cost approach is not appropriate as both machines have different level of risk. In this situation the most useful approach is to assume infinite reinvestment in each machine and calculate their NPVs to infinity.

$$\text{NPV} \infty = \frac{\text{NPV of the investment} \div \text{Present value}}{\text{Discount rate}}$$
of an annuity of appropriate years and discount rate

Standard

$$\text{NPV} \infty = \frac{5,136 \div 3.037\#}{0.12} = £14,092$$

De luxe

$$\text{NPV} \infty = \frac{5,510 \div 3.889\#}{0.14} = £10,120$$

\#   The present values of annuities are taken for four and six years as these are the useful lives of the projects.

As the standard machine has the higher NPV ∞, it is recommended that this machine should be purchased.

An alternative approach to the problem of different lives might be to assume a reinvestment rate for the shorter investment and to use this rate to equalise the lives of the investments.

(b)   Lease payments are usually made at the start of the year.

	Year 0 £	Year 1 £	Year 2 £	Year 3 £	Year 4 £	Year 5 £
Lease						
Cost of machine saved	50,000					
Capital allowance lost			(4,375)	(3,281)	(2,461)	(7,383)
Lease payments	(15,000)	(15,000)	(15,000)	(15,000)		
Tax relief on lease		5,250	5,250	5,250	5,250	
Net cash flow of lease	35,000	(9,750)	(14,125)	(13,031)	2,789	(7,383)
Discount factor (7.15%) ↑		0.933	0.871	0.813	0.759	0.708
	35,000	(9,097)	(12,303)	(10,594)	2,117	(5,227)

Cash flows

Net present value is (£104).

> As the net present value is negative, it appears that the purchase of the machine is the recommended alternative.

> ↑   The choice of discount rates in lease versus buy analysis is contentious. The approach used here is to regard the lease as an alternative to purchasing the machine using debt finance. The discount rate is, therefore, the amount that the company would have to pay on a secured loan on the machine, the loan being repayable on the terms that are implicit in the lease rental schedule. This discount rate is the after-tax cost of the equivalent loan, 11% (1-0.35) = 7.15%.

This discount rate is only likely to be valid if leases and loans are regarded by investors as being equivalent, and all cash flows are equally risky.

Student Questionnaire

Because we believe in listening to our customers, this questionnaire has been designed to discover exactly what you think about us and our materials. We want to know how we can continue improving our customer support and how to make our top class books even better - how do you use our books, what do you like about them and what else would you like to see us do to make them better?

1 Where did you hear about AT Foulks Lynch ACCA Textbooks?

☐ Colleague or friend   ☐ Employer recommendation   ☐ Lecturer recommendation

☐ AT Foulks Lynch mailshot   ☐ Conference   ☐ ACCA literature

☐ Students Newsletter   ☐ Pass Magazine   ☐ Internet

☐ Other ....

2 Overall, do you think the AT Foulks Lynch ACCA Textbooks are:

☐ Excellent   ☐ Good   ☐ Average   ☐ Poor   ☐ No opinion

3 Please evaluate AT Foulks Lynch service using the following criteria:

	Excellent	Good	Average	Poor	No opinion
Professional	☐	☐	☐	☐	☐
Polite	☐	☐	☐	☐	☐
Informed	☐	☐	☐	☐	☐
Helpful	☐	☐	☐	☐	☐

4 How did you obtain this book?

☐ From a bookshop   ☐ From your college   ☐ From us by mail order

☐ From us by telephone   ☐ Internet   ☐ Other ....

5 How long did it take to receive your materials? .... days.

☐ Very fast   ☐ Fast   ☐ Satisfactory   ☐ Slow   ☐ No opinion

6 How do you rate the value of these features of the Managerial Finance Textbook?

		Excellent	Good	Average	Poor	No opinion
1	Syllabus referenced to chapters	☐	☐	☐	☐	☐
2	Teaching Guide referenced to chapters	☐	☐	☐	☐	☐
3	Step by step approach and solutions	☐	☐	☐	☐	☐
4	Activities throughout the chapters	☐	☐	☐	☐	☐
5	Self test questions	☐	☐	☐	☐	☐
6	Examination type questions	☐	☐	☐	☐	☐
7	Index	☐	☐	☐	☐	☐

Continued/...

7 Have you purchased any other AT Foulks Lynch ACCA titles?

If so, please specify title(s) and your rating of each below:

Title	Excellent	Good	Average	Poor	No opinion
....	☐	☐	☐	☐	☐
....	☐	☐	☐	☐	☐
....	☐	☐	☐	☐	☐
....	☐	☐	☐	☐	☐

8 Have you used publications other than AT Foulks Lynch ACCA titles?

If so, please specify title(s) and your rating of each below:

Title and Publisher	Excellent	Good	Average	Poor	No opinion
....	☐	☐	☐	☐	☐
....	☐	☐	☐	☐	☐
....	☐	☐	☐	☐	☐
....	☐	☐	☐	☐	☐

9 Will you buy the AT Foulks Lynch ACCA Textbooks again?

☐ Yes   ☐ No   ☐ Not sure

Why? ....

10 Please write here any additional comments you might have on any of the above areas or tell us what you would like us to do to make the books even better:

....

....

....

....

11 Your details: these are for the internal use of the ACCA and AT Foulks Lynch Ltd only and will not be supplied to any outside organisations.

Name
....

Address
....

....

Telephone
....

Do you have your own e-mail address?   ☐ Yes   ☐ No

Do you have access to the World Wide Web?   ☐ Yes   ☐ No

Do you have access to a CD Rom Drive?   ☐ Yes   ☐ No

Please send to:

Quality Feedback Department
FREEPOST 2254
AT Foulks Lynch Ltd, 4 The Griffin Centre, Staines Road, Feltham, Middlesex, TW14 0BR.

Thank you for your time.

ACCA
AT FOULKS LYNCH

HOTLINES
Telephone: 0181 844 0667
Enquiries: 0181 831 9990
Fax: 0181 831 9991

AT FOULKS LYNCH LTD
Number 4, The Griffin Centre
Staines Road, Feltham
Middlesex TW14 0HS

Examination Date:
☐ December 98
☐ June 99

	98 Edition Textbooks	2/98 Edition Revision Series	2/98 Edition Lynchpins	Distance Learning (Include helpline & marking except for overseas Open Learning)	Open Learning (Include helpline & marking except for overseas Open Learning)
Module A - Foundation Stage					
1 Accounting Framework	£17.95 [UK] [IAS]	£10.95 [UK] [IAS]	£5.95 ☐	£85 ☐	£89 ☐
2 Legal Framework	£17.95 ☐	£10.95 ☐	£5.95 ☐	£85 ☐	£89 ☐
Module B					
3 Management Information	£17.95 ☐	£10.95 ☐	£5.95 ☐	£85 ☐	£89 ☐
4 Organisational Framework	£17.95 ☐	£10.95 ☐	£5.95 ☐	£85 ☐	£89 ☐
Module C - Certificate Stage					
5 Information Analysis	£17.95 ☐	£10.95 ☐	£5.95 ☐	£85 ☐	£89 ☐
6 Audit Framework	£17.95 [UK] [IAS]	£10.95 [UK] [IAS]	£5.95 ☐	£85 ☐	£89 ☐
Module D					
7 Tax Framework FA(2)97 Dec 98	£17.95 ☐	£10.95 ☐	£5.95 ☐	£85 ☐	£89 ☐
7 Tax Framework FA98 Jun 99	£17.95 ☐	£10.95 ☐	£5.95 ☐	£85 ☐	£89 ☐
8 Managerial Finance	£17.95 ☐	£10.95 ☐	£5.95 ☐	£85 ☐	£89 ☐
Module E - Professional Stage					
9 ICDM	£18.95 ☐	£10.95 ☐	£5.95 ☐	£85 ☐	£89 ☐
10 Accounting & Audit Practice	£22.95 [UK] [IAS]	£10.95 [UK] [IAS]	£5.95 ☐	£85 ☐	£89 ☐
11 Tax Planning FA(2)97 Dec 98	£18.95 ☐	£10.95 ☐	£5.95 ☐	£85 ☐	£89 ☐
11 Tax Planning FA98 Jun 99	£18.95 ☐	£10.95 ☐	£5.95 ☐	£85 ☐	£89 ☐
Module F					
12 Management & Strategy	£18.95 ☐	£10.95 ☐	£5.95 ☐	£85 ☐	£89 ☐
13 Financial Rep Environment	£20.95 [UK] [IAS]	£10.95 [UK] [IAS]	£5.95 ☐	£85 ☐	£89 ☐
14 Financial Strategy	£19.95 ☐	£10.95 ☐	£5.95 ☐	£85 ☐	£89 ☐
P & P + Delivery UK Mainland	£2.00/book	£1.00/book	£1.00/book	£5.00/subject	£5.00/subject
NI, ROI & EU Countries	£5.00/book	£3.00/book	£3.00/book	£15.00/subject	£15.00/subject
Rest of world standard air service	£10.00/book	£8.00/book	£8.00/book	£25.00/subject	£25.00/subject
Rest of world courier service†	£22.00/book	£20.00/book	£14.00/book	£47.00/subject	£47.00/subject

SINGLE ITEM SUPPLEMENT: If you only order 1 item, INCREASE postage costs by £2.50 for UK, NI & EU Countries or by £10.00 for Rest of World Services

TOTAL					
Sub Total £					
Post & Packing £					
Total £					

Telephone number essential for this service   **Payments in Sterling in London**   **Order Total £** ____

DELIVERY DETAILS
☐ Mr ☐ Miss ☐ Mrs ☐ Ms Other _____

Initials _____ Surname _____

Address _____

Postcode _____

Telephone _____ Deliver to home ☐

Company name _____

Address _____

Postcode _____

Telephone _____ Fax _____

Monthly report to go to employer ☐   Deliver to work ☐

PAYMENT OPTIONS
1. I enclose Cheque/PO/Bankers Draft for £_____
   Please make cheques payable to AT Foulks Lynch Ltd.

2. Charge Access/Visa A/c No: Expiry Date |__|__|__|

|__|__|__|__|__|__|__|__|__|__|__|__|__|__|

Signature _____ Date _____

DECLARATION
I agree to pay as indicated on this form and understand that
AT Foulks Lynch Terms and Conditions apply (available on
request). I understand that AT Foulks Lynch Ltd are not liable
for non-delivery if the rest of world standard air service is used.

Signature _____ Date _____

Please allow:		
UK mainland	- 5-10 workdays	
NI, ROI & EU Countries	- 1-3 weeks	
Rest of world standard air service	- up to 6 weeks	
Rest of world courier service	- 10 workdays	

Notes: All delivery times subject to stock availability. Signature required on receipt (except rest of world standard air service). Please give both addresses for Distance Learning students where possible.

Form effective from June 98 (ACCATXJ8).   *All details correct at time of printing.*   **Source: ACCATXJ8**